THE NEW INTERNATIONAL COMMENTARY
ON THE
OLD TESTAMENT

General Editors

R. K. HARRISON
(1968–1993)

ROBERT L. HUBBARD, JR.
(1994–)

The Book of
GENESIS
Chapters 1–17

by

VICTOR P. HAMILTON

WILLIAM B. EERDMANS PUBLISHING COMPANY
GRAND RAPIDS, MICHIGAN

Publisher's Note

This commentary was planned and written as a single volume, but its length dictated the need to publish it in two volumes. The reader should note that the Introduction in the present volume covers the entire book of Genesis; thus the second volume comprises only commentary on Genesis 18–50.

For the reader's convenience, each volume has its own table of contents, abbreviation list, and indexes.

2140 Oak Industrial Drive N.E., Grand Rapids, Michigan 49505

Printed in the United States of America

17 16 15 14 13 12 17 16 15 14 13 12

Library of Congress Cataloging-in-Publication Data

Hamilton, Victor P.
The book of Genesis: chapters 1–17 / by Victor P. Hamilton.
p. cm. —(New international commentary on the Old Testament)
Includes index.
ISBN 978-0-8028-2521-6
1. Bible. O.T. Genesis I–XVII—Commentaries. I. Title. II. Series.
BS1235.3.H32 1990
222′.1107—dc20 90-36511
CIP

www.eerdmans.com

To

Heather
Paul
Dawn
David

CONTENTS

AUTHOR'S PREFACE

I would like to express my appreciation to Professor Emeritus R. K. Harrison of Wycliffe College, University of Toronto, for his invitation to write the Genesis commentary for the NICOT series and for his counsel in preparing the manuscript. Although apprehensive at first about starting such a monumental project, I accepted the challenge after nudging and encouragement from my seminary mentor and now the President of Asbury College, Dr. Dennis Kinlaw. One reason for my hesitancy was the numerous commentaries on Genesis already available that deserve the label *opus magnum.* I had in mind, from an earlier period, the work of Gunkel and Skinner, and from a more recent time, the work of von Rad and Westermann. As one colleague put it to me, rather laconically, "How much more juice can be squeezed from the lemon?" I would like to acknowledge my deep sense of gratitude to this vast array of Genesis commentators. But once I launched into the project, it occurred to me very quickly that the last and definitive word on Genesis has not yet been said, and probably never will be said.

It is a privilege for me to acknowledge and thank the Faculty Research and Development Committee of the College for granting me two work leaves, thus freeing me from teaching commitments and committee responsibilities, and allowing uninterrupted time for focused research and writing on this commentary.

I am also indebted to Mr. Gary Lee, my editor at Eerdmans. He has read my manuscript most carefully and patiently, and I thank him for suggestions on ways to improve its quality.

Mrs. Cheryl Smith, now of Rochester, New York, typed the opening chapters of my commentary into the computer, and for that I thank her. But the bulk of the commentary has been put on the word processor by my wife Shirley. In addition to her responsibilities as mother, wife, and homemaker, she accepted this major task and did it in a professional way. I also thank her for the encouragement and stimulation she has provided throughout the years of producing this commentary.

Lastly, I offer my thanks to God for his sustaining grace, grace for research, grace for reflection, and grace for writing.

VICTOR P. HAMILTON

Publisher's Note:

This commentary was planned and written as a single volume, but its length dictated the need to publish it in two volumes. The reader should note that the Introduction in the present volume covers the entire book of Genesis; thus the second volume comprises only commentary on Genesis 18–50.

For the reader's convenience, each volume has its own table of contents, abbreviation list, and indexes.

PRINCIPAL ABBREVIATIONS

AASOR	*Annual of the American Schools of Oriental Research*
AB	Anchor Bible
AJSL	*American Journal of Semitic Languages and Literatures*
Akk.	Akkadian
AnBib	Analecta Biblica
ANEP	J. B. Pritchard, ed., *The Ancient Near East in Pictures.* 2nd ed. Princeton: Princeton University, 1969
ANET	J. B. Pritchard, ed., *Ancient Near Eastern Texts Relating to the Old Testament.* 3rd ed. Princeton: Princeton University, 1969
AnOr	Analecta Orientalia
ANQ	*Andover Newton Quarterly*
AOAT	Alter Orient und Altes Testament
AOS	American Oriental Series
Arab.	Arabic
Aram.	Aramaic
ARM	Archives royales de Mari
ASTI	*Annual of the Swedish Theological Institute*
ATR	*Anglican Theological Review*
AusBR	*Australian Biblical Review*
AUSS	*Andrews University Seminary Studies*
AV	Authorized (King James) Version
BA	*Biblical Archaeologist*
BAR	*Biblical Archaeology Review*
BASOR	*Bulletin of the American Schools of Oriental Research*
BDB	F. Brown, S. R. Driver, C. Briggs, *Hebrew and English Lexicon of the Old Testament.* Repr. Oxford: Clarendon, 1959
BeO	*Bibbia e Oriente*
BETS	*Bulletin of the Evangelical Theological Society*

BHK	R. Kittel, ed., *Biblia Hebraica.* 3rd ed. Stuttgart: Württembergische Bibelanstalt, 1937
BHS	K. Elliger and W. Rudolph, eds., *Biblia Hebraica Stuttgartensia.* Stuttgart: Deutsche Bibelstiftung, 1967–1977
Bib	*Biblica*
BibOr	Biblica et Orientalia
BiTod	*Bible Today*
BJRL	*Bulletin of the John Rylands University Library of Manchester*
BKAT	Biblischer Kommentar: Altes Testament
BN	*Biblische Notizen*
BR	*Biblical Research*
BRev	*Bible Review*
BSac	*Bibliotheca Sacra*
BSOAS	*Bulletin of the School of Oriental and African Studies*
BT	*The Bible Translator*
BTB	*Biblical Theology Bulletin*
BWANT	Beiträge zur Wissenschaft vom Alten und Neuen Testament
BZ	*Biblische Zeitschrift*
BZAW	Beihefte zur *Zeitschrift für die alttestamentliche Wissenschaft*
CAD	I. J. Gelb, et al., eds., *The Assyrian Dictionary of the Oriental Institute of the University of Chicago.* Chicago: Oriental Institute, 1956–
CBQ	*Catholic Biblical Quarterly*
CBQMS	Catholic Biblical Quarterly Monograph Series
CHAL	W. Holladay, *A Concise Hebrew and Aramaic Lexicon of the Old Testament.* Grand Rapids: Eerdmans, 1971
CNFI	*Christian News From Israel*
ConBOT	Coniectanea biblica, Old Testament
CT	*Christianity Today*
CTA	A. Herdner, *Corpus des tablettes en cunéiformes alphabétiques.* 2 vols. Paris: Imprimerie Nationale, 1963
CTJ	*Calvin Theological Journal*
CTM	*Concordia Theological Monthly*
CTQ	*Concordia Theological Quarterly*
CurTM	*Currents in Theology and Mission*
DD	*Dor le Dor*
Egyp.	Egyptian
EncJud	C. Roth and G. Wigoder, eds., *Encyclopaedia Judaica.* 16 vols. Jerusalem: Keter, 1971–1972
ETL	*Ephemerides Theologicae Lovanienses*

EvQ	*Evangelical Quarterly*
ExpTim	*Expository Times*
fem.	feminine
Fest.	Festschrift
FOTL	Forms of the Old Testament Literature
GKC	*Gesenius' Hebrew Grammar.* Ed. E. Kautzsch. Tr. A. E. Cowley. 2nd ed. Oxford: Clarendon, 1910
GTJ	*Grace Theological Journal*
HBT	*Horizons in Biblical Theology*
HeyJ	*Heythrop Journal*
HKAT	Handkommentar zum Alten Testament
HS	*Hebrew Studies*
HSS	Harvard Semitic Studies
HSM	Harvard Semitic Monographs
HTR	*Harvard Theological Review*
HUCA	*Hebrew Union College Annual*
ICC	International Critical Commentary
IDB(S)	G. A. Buttrick, et al., eds., *The Interpreter's Dictionary of the Bible.* 4 vols. Nashville: Abingdon, 1962. *Supplementary Volume.* Ed. K. Crim, et al., 1976
IEJ	*Israel Exploration Journal*
IJT	*Indian Journal of Theology*
Int	*Interpretation*
ISBE	G. W. Bromiley, et al., eds., *The International Standard Bible Encyclopedia,* 4 vols. Rev. ed. Grand Rapids: Eerdmans, 1979–1988
ITQ	*Irish Theological Quarterly*
JAAR	*Journal of the American Academy of Religion*
JANES	*Journal of the Ancient Near Eastern Society of Columbia University*
JAOS	*Journal of the American Oriental Society*
JASA	*Journal of the American Scientific Affiliation*
JB	Jerusalem Bible
JBL	*Journal of Biblical Literature*
JBLMS	Journal of Biblical Literature Monograph Series
JBR	*Journal of Bible and Religion*
JCS	*Journal of Cuneiform Studies*
JEA	*Journal of Egyptian Archaeology*
JES	*Journal of Ecumenical Studies*
JETS	*Journal of the Evangelical Theological Society*

JJS	*Journal of Jewish Studies*
JNES	*Journal of Near Eastern Studies*
JNWSL	*Journal of Northwest Semitic Languages*
JPOS	*Journal of the Palestine Oriental Society*
JPT	*Journal of Psychology and Theology*
JQR	*Jewish Quarterly Review*
JRT	*Journal of Religious Thought*
JSNT	*Journal for the Study of the New Testament*
JSOT	*Journal for the Study of the Old Testament*
JSOTSup	Journal for the Study of the Old Testament—Supplement Series
JSS	*Journal of Semitic Studies*
JTS	*Journal of Theological Studies*
KB	L. Koehler and W. Baumgartner, *Lexicon in veteris testamenti libros*. Leiden: Brill, 1958
KD	*Kerygma und Dogma*
Lat.	Latin
Leš	*Lešonénu*
LTQ	*Lexington Theological Quarterly*
LXX	Septuagint
masc.	masculine
mg.	margin
ms(s).	manuscript(s)
MT	Masoretic Text
NAB	The New American Bible
NCBC	New Century Bible Commentary
NEB	New English Bible
NICNT	New International Commentary on the New Testament
NICOT	New International Commentary on the Old Testament
NIGTC	New International Greek Testament Commentary
NIV	New International Version
NJPS	New Jewish Publication Society Version
NKJV	New King James Version
NovT	*Novum Testamentum*
NT	New Testament
NTS	*New Testament Studies*
OBT	Overtures to Biblical Theology
Or	*Orientalia*
OT	Old Testament
OTL	Old Testament Library
OTS	*Oudtestamentische Studiëen*

PEQ	*Palestine Exploration Quarterly*
Pesh.	Peshitta
PIBA	*Proceedings of the Irish Biblical Association*
pl.	plural
PRU	C. F. A. Schaeffer, et al., eds., *Palais royal d'Ugarit.* Paris: Imprimerie Nationale, 1955–
PTR	*Princeton Theological Review*
PTMS	Pittsburgh Theological Monograph Series
RA	*Revue d'assyriologie et d'archéologie orientale*
RB	*Revue biblique*
RefR	*Reformed Review*
REJ	*Revue des études juives*
RestQ	*Restoration Quarterly*
RevExp	*Review and Expositor*
RevQ	*Revue de Qumran*
RSV	Revised Standard Version
SAOC	Studies in Ancient Oriental Civilization
SBLASP	Society of Biblical Literature Abstracts and Seminar Papers
SBLDS	Society of Biblical Literature Dissertation Series
SBLMS	Society of Biblical Literature Monograph Series
SBT	Studies in Biblical Theology
ScEs	*Science et Esprit*
SEÅ	*Svensk Exegetisk Årsbok*
sg.	singular
SJT	*Scottish Journal of Theology*
SNTSMS	Society for New Testament Studies Monograph Series
SOTSMS	Society for Old Testament Studies Monograph Series
SP	Samaritan Pentateuch
SR	*Studies in Religion/Sciences Religieuses*
ST	*Studia Theologica*
StBTh	*Studia Biblica et Theologica*
Sum.	Sumerian
Symm.	Symmachus (ancient Greek version)
Targ.	Targum
T.B.	Babylonian Talmud
TD	*Theology Digest*
TDNT	G. Kittel and G. Friedrich, eds., *Theological Dictionary of the New Testament.* 10 vols. Tr. G. W. Bromiley. Grand Rapids: Eerdmans, 1964–1976
TDOT	G. Botterweck and H. Ringgren, eds., *Theological Dictionary of*

the Old Testament. Vols. I–. Tr. D. Green, et al. Grand Rapids: Eerdmans, 1974–

TGUOS — *Transactions of the Glasgow University Oriental Society*

THAT — E. Jenni and C. Westermann, eds., *Theologisches Handwörterbuch zum Alten Testament.* 2 vols. Munich: Kaiser, 1971–1976

TJ — *Trinity Journal*

TNTC — Tyndale New Testament Commentaries

TOTC — Tyndale Old Testament Commentaries

TS — *Theological Studies*

TUSR — *Trinity University Studies in Religion*

TWOT — R. L. Harris, et al., eds., *Theological Wordbook of the Old Testament.* 2 vols. Chicago: Moody, 1980

TynBul — *Tyndale Bulletin*

TZ — *Theologisches Zeitschrift*

UF — *Ugarit-Forschungen*

Ugar. — Ugaritic

USQR — *Union Seminary Quarterly Review*

UT — Cyrus H. Gordon, *Ugaritic Textbook.* AnOr 38. Rome: Pontifical Biblical Institute, 1965

Vulg. — Vulgate

VT — *Vetus Testamentum*

VTSup — Vetus Testamentum, Supplements

WC — Westminster Commentaries

WMANT — Wissenschaftliche Monographien zum Alten und Neuen Testament

WTJ — *Westminster Theological Journal*

ZA — *Zeitschrift für Assyriologie*

ZAW — *Zeitschrift für die alttestamentliche Wissenschaft*

ZDMG — *Zeitschrift der deutschen morgenländischen Gesellschaft*

ZPEB — M. Tenney, et al., eds., *Zondervan Pictorial Encyclopedia of the Bible.* 5 vols. Grand Rapids: Zondervan, 1975

ZTK — *Zeitschrift für Theologie und Kirche*

INTRODUCTION

I. TITLE

The title "Genesis" comes to us by way of the Latin Vulgate *(Incipit Liber Bresith id est Genesis),* which in turn borrowed, or transliterated, from the Greek LXX, *Génesis.* This word is best reproduced in English by "origin."

In postbiblical Hebrew usage the title is *berē'šîṯ,* which is, in fact, simply the first word of 1:1 ("In [the] beginning"). This follows the custom of naming the books of the Pentateuch on the basis of either their first word, their first two words, or an expression near the beginning of the first verse. Thus the titles for the rest of the Torah books are as follows: Exodus—*we'ēlleh šemôṯ* ("and these [are] the names of"); Leviticus—*wayyiqrā'* ("and he called"); Numbers—*bemiḏbar* ("in the wilderness of"); Deuteronomy—*'ēlleh haddeḇārîm* ("these [are] the words").[1] This custom is followed only sporadically in the Hebrew Bible once one moves beyond its first five books (e.g., "Song of Songs," *šîr haššîrîm,* and "Lamentations," *'êḵâ*).[2]

Some Hebrew manuscripts from the Middle Ages used titles like "First Book," "Book of the Creation of the World," and "Book of the Righteous." Rabbi Isaac Abrabanel (1427–1508) writes at the end of his commentary on Genesis: "*B'reshith* is called 'The Book of Creation' *(Sepher ha-B'riah)* or 'The Book of Formation' *(Sepher ha-Yetsirah).*" Nahmanides likewise writes in his introduction: "*B'reshith,* which is the Book of *Yetsirah,* teaches that the world is new." Midrash Habiur raises the question: "Why is

1. Modern Hebrew usage sometimes abbreviates titles (*šemôṯ* for Exodus, *deḇārîm* for Deuteronomy), or slightly changes the title (*bammiḏbar,* "in *the* wilderness," for Numbers).

2. "Lamentations" derives from LXX *thrēnoi* and Vulg. *threni,* which is a translation of *qînôṯ,* the title given to this OT book by the Babylonian Talmud (*Baba Batra* 14b, 15a) and other early Jewish writings (Jerusalem Talmud, *šabbat* 16:15c, which uses the expression *megillaṯ qînôṯ*).

B'reshith called 'The Book of *Yashar*' (the righteous)?" It then answers, "Because it contains the history of Abraham, Isaac, and Jacob, who were called the Righteous, as it is written, 'Let me die the death of the righteous' (Num. 23:10)."

Genesis is obviously a book concerned with origins—the origin of earth's creation, of humankind, of institutions by which civilization is perpetuated, of one special family chosen by God as his own and designated as the medium of world blessing. Transcending all of these emphases on beginnings is God. There is no *génesis theoú* (theogony) in Scripture's introductory book, nor any theobiography. He is one without *rē'šîṯ* (beginning) and *'aḥarîṯ* (end).

II. STRUCTURE

Few books of Scripture reveal the lines of demarcation between their individual units as clearly as does Genesis. This is due to the presence of the formula *'ēlleh ṯôl^eḏôṯ,* used ten times throughout Genesis. At some points it appears preferable to translate the formula "this is the story (or history) of *X*." At other points "these are the descendants (or generations) of *X*" seems better. The choice between these two at any given occurrence depends mostly on the nature of the material following the formula. If the formula is followed by a genealogy then the preference is for the latter. If it is followed by narrative then the preference is for the former. The ten are (and we translate "generations" only for continuity):

1. 2:4a: "these are the generations of the heavens and the earth"
2. 5:1a: "these are the generations of Adam"
3. 6:9a: "these are the generations of Noah"
4. 10:1a: "these are the generations of the sons of Noah"
5. 11:10a: "these are the generations of Shem"
6. 11:27a: "these are the generations of Terah"
7. 25:12a: "these are the generations of Ishmael"
8. 25:19a: "these are the generations of Isaac"
9. 36:1a, 9a: "these are the generations of Esau"
10. 37:2a: "these are the generations of Jacob"

Closer examination of these occurrences reveals that in five of them the formula is followed by narrative: #1 (creation), #3 (the flood), #6 (Abraham story), #8 (Jacob story), #10 (Joseph story). In these five the introductory note should read "this is the story of *X*." Yet most of the modern versions of Scripture are not consistent. For example, one finds for 11:27a "these are Terah's descendants" (JB) or "this is the table of the descendants of Terah" (NEB), principally because of the presence of genealogical notes in 11:27b–32. Additionally NEB renders 25:19a as "This is the table of the descendants of Abraham's son Isaac."

The remaining five all appear as headings for genealogies: #2 ("the descendants of *Adam*"), #4 ("the descendants of *the sons of Noah*"), #5 ("the descendants of *Shem*"), #7 ("the descendants of *Ishmael*"), #9 ("the descendants of *Esau*"). Furthermore, these five genealogies in Genesis fall into one of two types. One type is the vertical genealogy, which traces one line of descent. This is found in 5:1ff. (#2), the ten-generation genealogy of Adam to Noah; and in 11:10ff. (#5), the ten-generation genealogy of Shem to Abraham. Both of these genealogies conclude with a reference to an individual who fathered three children:

Noah: Shem, Ham, Japheth
Terah: Abram, Nahor, Haran

The second type of genealogy in Genesis is a horizontal or segmented type in which the genealogy is not traced through one son (the oldest), but through various children. This type is found in 10:1 (#4), descendants of Shem/Ham/Japheth; in 25:12 (#7), the twelve descendants of Ishmael; and lastly in 36:1, 9 (#9), Esau's family tree.[1] These last three genealogies protrude little into the narrative sections of Genesis. At points they seem almost tangential.

The first of these ten occurrences of the formula is clearly the most interesting. It is the only one of the ten in which a personal name does not appear. Instead, one finds "the *tôl*ᵉ*ḏôṯ* of the heavens and the earth." And it is precisely here that a major problem of interpretation emerges. Does the first of these structure-providing formulae conclude what has just been recounted, or does it introduce what follows? If it is retrogressive, then 2:4a must be read with 1:1–2:3. If it is prospective, then 2:4a must be read with

1. See B. S. Childs, *Introduction to the Old Testament as Scripture* (Philadelphia: Fortress, 1979), p. 145. See also S. Tengström (*Die Toledotformel und die literarische Struktur der priesterlichen Erweiterungsschicht im Pentateuch* [Lund: Gleerup, 1981]) for the phrases "narrative genealogy" (i.e., Gen. 5) and "genealogical tables" or "tribal tree" (i.e., Gen. 10). Tengström's novel suggestion that the seven attestations of the formula that remain in Genesis, after one subtracts the four that introduce genealogical tables (10:1; 25:12; 36:1, 9), are meant to parallel the seven days of creation in P (the Priestly source) is farfetched. How could the ancient writer have made the distinction between the two categories into which Tengström fits the eleven usages of the formula in Genesis?

2:4bff. Furthermore, this develops into the larger problem of whether all the instances of the *tôlᵉḏôṯ* formula should be read as titles, introducing what follows, or as conclusions, summarizing what has preceded.

First, let us examine 2:4a. The majority of modern versions of the Bible handle 2:4a as a subscript to 1:1–2:3 (see, e.g., RSV, JB, NEB, NAB, Speiser). This division is reflected also in the typesettings of two of the recent editions of the Hebrew Bible, *BHK* and *BHS.* So understood, "generations" of 2:4a relates to the numerical pattern of the seven days of 1:1–2:3.

It is equally arguable that 2:4a is an introduction to what follows. This is our preference, for the following reasons. First, an almost insurmountable problem is created if one tacks on 2:4a to 1:1–2:3, and yet wishes to hold on to Priestly (1:1–2:3) and Yahwistic (2:4bff.) creation stories. Almost all commentators agree (exceptions will be noted below) that the phrase in question functions everywhere else in Genesis as a superscript. Here, however, would be the one time where it is a subscript. Von Rad, sensitive to this point, argues in a strained fashion that the Priestly interpolator placed the formula uncharacteristically at the conclusion of the pericope for two reasons. One reason was his penchant for order and system—thus the presence of this rubric to accentuate that neat structure. The second reason was that the beginning of the chapter was canonically fixed and hence untouchable.[2]

It seems jarring, however, to designate seven days of creation as "generations." In all the other instances where *tôlᵉḏôṯ* appears, it designates the descendants of *X* by generation, or introduces a narrative about the descendants of *X.* If one links 2:4a to what has gone before, then one must be prepared to attach an awkward and unique meaning or nuance to *tôlᵉḏôṯ* in 2:4a.

A second reason for reading the formula in 2:4a as a superscript is that the ancient versions (see, e.g., LXX) lend no supporting evidence for the dissection of 2:4. If anywhere, the break comes at 2:3, not at 2:4a. Note that the Masorah supports the unity of 2:4. Overall the Masorah divides Genesis into ninety-one *pārāšîyôṯ* ("sections, pericopes"), forty-three of which are *pᵉṯûḥôṯ,* indicated by a *p* ("open sections"), and forty-eight of which are *sᵉṯûmôṯ,* indicated by an *s* ("closed sections").[3] Observe that 2:4a begins one of these *pᵉṯuḥôṯ.*

2. See G. von Rad, *Genesis,* OTL, rev. ed., tr. J. H. Marks (Philadelphia: Westminster, 1972), p. 63.

3. On *pārāšîyôṯ, sᵉḏārîm, pᵉṯuḥôṯ,* and *sᵉṯumôṯ,* see A. Dotan, "Masorah," *EncJud,* 16:1406–7.

Third, since the formula is always followed by "the genitive of the progenitor, never of the progeny," the phrase can only refer to that which is generated by the heavens and the earth, and not to the generation of the heavens and the earth themselves.[4] So understood, the formula can only be read as a superscription to what follows. Thus 2:5ff. designates man and woman as the offspring of the heavens and earth, much as Seth is of Adam and Abram is of Terah.

There may be a deliberate reason for this type of styling. In the opening chapter of Genesis the male and female whom God created bore the divine image and likeness. Possibly these unique endowments might have been understood as providing qualification for Adam and Eve as the *tôl^e^d̠ôṯ ʾĕ lōhîm*. The OT at large does not shy away from labeling certain individuals (kings especially) as "sons of God," but the phrase is conspicuously absent from Gen. 1–2. The only "sons of God" in Genesis are those in bondage to unrestrained lust (6:1–4). We would suggest that 2:4ff. forms a polarity with 1:1–2:3, and is *k^e^negd̠ô* ("as a complement") to 1:1–2:3 as is Eve to Adam. The one without the other is incomplete, and one is not more truthful, or more important, or more indispensable than the other. Just as 1:1–2:3 focus on humanity's divine origins and endowments, so 2:4ff. focus on humanity's mundane origins. For this reason 1:1–2:3 draws our attention to a primal couple created with authority ("you shall," 1:29), while 2:4ff. draws our attention to a primal couple created under authority ("you shall not," 2:17).

Thus, for the above reasons we prefer to understand 2:4a as a superscript to what follows, and as an introduction to the first of ten units in the book of Genesis, all of which are preceded by an introductory unit (1:1–2:3). We now turn our attention to the remaining nine instances of the formula.

It is widely accepted that all of the *tôl^e^d̠ôṯ* formulae, with the possible exception of 2:4a, function in Genesis as titles that introduce a new unit. A number of writers also identify them as colophons. A colophon may be defined as an inscription usually placed at the end of a book or manuscript and usually containing facts relative to its production (e.g., the author's name).

4. The quotation is from J. Skinner, *A Critical and Exegetical Commentary on the Book of Genesis,* ICC (Edinburgh: T. & T. Clark, 1910), p. 41. See also B. Childs, *Introduction,* p. 145; and F. M. Cross, *Canaanite Myth and Hebrew Epic* (Cambridge: Harvard University, 1973), pp. 301–5, and esp. p. 302 for his discussion at length of 2:4a.

In ancient Near Eastern literature the existence of colophons is well documented. Leading the way in terms of bulk is cuneiform literature from Mesopotamia. We are indebted here to the work of H. Hunger, who has collected 563 text colophons from literature composed over two millennia.[5] He defines the colophon as "a notice appended to a text by a scribe at the end of a tablet, including literary contents, statements about the tablet and the persons connected with its production." In his introduction, Hunger compiles the types of information given in colophons—bibliographical information (e.g., catchline, title of work, tablet number, number of lines), personal data (e.g., the names of scribe, owner, or commissioner of the tablet), purpose of writing, wishes, curses, prayers, date. Of the 563 colophons collected by Hunger, nos. 1–39 are from the Old Babylonian period; nos. 40–72 are from the Middle Babylonian/Assyrian period; and nos. 75–563 are from the Late Babylonian/Assyrian period. In other words, 491 of the entries are from the period after 1000 B.C. Two key facts emerge from Hunger's study. One, the author's name is absent in the Akkadian colophons; and two, the colophon always comes at the end of the text.

The usage of colophons is also found in Canaan, as is well demonstrated from Ugarit. Thus *UT,* 62, has a title, "Pertaining to Baal," the main body of the text, and then ends with this colophon: "The scribe is Elimelech, the Šbn-ite. The narrator is Atn-prln, chief of the priests (and) chief of the herdsmen, the Ṭʿ-ite. (Dated in the reign of) Niqmad, king of Ugarit, Master of Yrgb, Lord of Ṭmrn."[6] The lengthy and significant Epic of Aqhat ends with this colophon: "The scribe is Elimelech, the Ṭʿ-ite."[7] *UT,* 51, ends with the colophon: "[ ] the Ṭʿ-ite; Niqmad, king of Ugarit,"[8] which is a line on the edge of the tablet giving the name of the scribe (who belonged to the tribe of Thaʿ), and the name of the king (Niqmad II) during whose reign the tablet was written. In many of the tablets from Ugarit, however, both the

5. H. Hunger, *Babylonische und assyrische Kolophone* (Kevelaer: Verlag Butzon and Berker/Neukirchen-Vluyn, 1968). See also the study by E. Leichty, "The Colophon," in *Studies Presented to A. Leo Oppenheim,* ed. R. D. Briggs and J. A. Brinkman (Chicago: Oriental Institute, 1964), pp. 147–54. On the colophons appearing on each of the three tablets of the Old Babylonian version of Atrahasis, see W. G. Lambert and A. R. Millard, *Atra-ḫasīs: The Babylonian Story of the Flood* (Oxford: Clarendon, 1969), pp. 31–32. These colophons include: date of writing (month/day/name of king [Ammi-ṣaduqa]), title, number of lines, and name of scribe ("written by Ku-Aya, the junior scribe").

6. See C. H. Gordon, *Ugarit and Minoan Crete* (New York: Norton, 1966), p. 87.

7. Ibid., p. 120.

8. Ibid., p. 74.

beginning and end of the inscription are lost or too faint to be read. Thus most of the titles or colophons have not been preserved. In contrast with cuneiform literature, hieroglyphic texts from Egypt show less evidence of the use of colophons.[9]

Turning to the Hebrew Bible, one does not need to look far for the presence of colophons.[10] Leaving aside the instances of the formula under discussion, one might appeal to passages like Gen. 10:20, 31–32 ("these are the sons/families of Ham/Shem/Noah"); 22:23 ("these eight Milcah bore to Nahor, brother of Abraham"); 25:4b ("all these were the children of Keturah"); 25:16 ("these are the sons of Ishmael"); 25:36b ("these are the sons of Jacob"); 36:5 ("these are the sons of Esau"); 49:28a ("all these are the twelve tribes of Israel"). For examples beyond Genesis cf. Exod. 6:15b, 24b, 25b; 19:6b; 38:21;[11] and Deut. 28:69 (Eng. 29:1).

What these OT references have in common is that they are nominal sentences introduced with the demonstrative "these"; they function as a summary statement; they round off a genealogy (except for Exod. 38:21 and Deut. 28:69 [Eng. 29:1]—which summarize speeches or activities). If one looks for a colophon in the OT that is introductory rather than summarizing, then perhaps the closest we can come is Deut. 4:45–49 ("this is the law which Moses set before the people . . ."). This extended colophon either encapsulates Deut. 1–4, or, more likely in our opinion, like a title it introduces Deut. 5ff.

There is nothing comparable to the colophons we cited from Ugaritic literature (i.e., an addendum at the text's end) except in the LXX ending of Esther: "In the fourth year of the reign of Ptolemy and Cleopatra, Dositheus, who claimed to be a priest and a Levite, and Ptolemy his son, brought the above letter of Purim, which they claimed was authentic and had been translated by Lysimachus the son of Ptolemy, a member of the Jerusalem community."[12]

9. See J. Černý, *Paper and Books in Ancient Egypt* (London: H. K. Lewis, 1952), pp. 24ff.

10. See H. M. L. Gevaryahu, "Biblical colophons: a source for the 'biography' of authors, texts, and books," in *Congress Volume: Edinburgh, 1974,* VTSup 28 (Leiden: Brill, 1975), pp. 42–59.

11. See F. I. Andersen, *The Sentence in Biblical Hebrew* (The Hague/Paris: Mouton, 1974), p. 54 (§ 3.7.5.2).

12. Translation of C. A. Moore, *Esther,* AB (Garden City, NY: Doubleday, 1971), pp. 112–13. Earlier treatments of this addition are found in E. Bickerman, "The Colophon of the Greek Book of Esther," *JBL* 63 (1944) 339–62; R. Marcus, "Dositheus, Priest and Levite," *JBL* 64 (1945) 269–71.

Now let us return to the formula "these are the *tôlᵉḏôṯ* of *X*" in Genesis. If we can agree that these ten instances in Genesis are further illustrations of biblical colophons, then we must next decide whether they are introductory (the majority view) or summarizing (the minority view). We have observed in the brief discussion above that colophons in texts from the cuneiform world are always at the end of texts. The same is true of the "these are . . ." or the "this is . . ." colophons scattered throughout the Pentateuch.

Nevertheless, we have argued above for reading 2:4a as introductory to 2:4bff. It leads in to what follows, rather than summarizing 1:1–2:3. Similarly it seems to make sense to read the second instance of the formula as a title (5:1a) introducing what follows (5:1bff.), and so on.

In 1936 P. J. Wiseman made the first concerted attempt to challenge the consensus.[13] He has been followed by his son D. J. Wiseman and by R. K. Harrison.[14] Their main argument for reading the colophons as conclusions, apart from the examples in nonbiblical literature, is as follows. In several instances at least, most of the information in the biblical text about the person named in the formula appears *before* the name itself. For example, the name of Adam appears in 5:1, yet everything about Adam precedes 5:1 apart from his death notice. In 37:2 the name Jacob appears, yet the Jacob material precedes 37:2. What follows 37:2 is mostly narrative about Joseph. Thus it would seem that the formula points to the conclusion rather than to the commencement of a unit.

This proposal suggests the discovery in Genesis of eleven literary units or tablets, to which the Joseph narrative has been appended:

Tablet 1: 1:1–2:4: The history/origin of the cosmos
Tablet 2: 2:5–5:2: This history/origin of Adam/mankind
Tablet 3: 5:3–6:9a: The history/origin of Noah
Tablet 4: 6:9b–10:1: The history/origin of Noah's sons
Tablet 5: 10:2–11:10a: The history/origin of Shem
Tablet 6: 11:10b–27a: The history/origin of Terah
Tablet 7: 11:27b–25:12: The history/origin of Ishmael
Tablet 8: 25:13–19a: The history/origin of Isaac
Tablet 9: 25:19b–36:1: The history/origin of Esau (and Jacob)

13. P. J. Wiseman, *New Discoveries in Babylonia about Genesis* (London: Marshall, 1936). The book has recently been reissued under the title *Ancient Records and the Structure of Genesis* (Nashville: Nelson, 1985), with a foreword by the author's son, D. J. Wiseman, the famous Assyriologist, and a preface by R. K. Harrison.

14. See R. K. Harrison, *Introduction to the Old Testament* (Grand Rapids: Eerdmans, 1969), pp. 543–47; idem, "Genesis," *ISBE,* 2:436–37.

Tablet 10: 36:2–9: The history/origin of Esau
Tablet 11: 36:10–37:2a: The history/origin of Jacob's family

Now, of course, this suggestion relates not only to the issue of the structure of Genesis, but also bears on the question of the authorship and composition of Genesis. We shall discuss this second matter in a subsequent section of this introduction.

The proposal of Wiseman and Harrison has several problems. For one thing, in the five instances where the formula precedes a genealogy (5:1; 10:1; 11:10; 25:12; 36:1), it is difficult not to include the colophon with what follows. DeWitt has admitted this point, though he wishes to retain the basic outlines of the Wiseman-Harrison approach.[15] His proposal is to read "these are the generations of" as a colophon at the bottom of a tablet to identify its contents, with the further observation that the colophon denotes both the history on the face of the tablet and the genealogy probably inscribed on the back of the tablet. DeWitt ends with ten tablets rather than the eleven of Wiseman and Harrison, and his idea forces some significant reconstruction on the text in the text's emergence from tablet order to canonical order (e.g., see his tablets 9 and 10).

A second problem rising from the Wiseman-Harrison reconstruction is that it suggests that Ishmael was primarily responsible for preserving the history of Abraham (11:27b–25:12, tablet 7), that Isaac was responsible for preserving Ishmael's history (25:13–19a, tablet 8), that Esau preserved Jacob's history (25:19b–36:1, tablet 9), and that Jacob preserved Esau's history (36:10–37:2, tablet 11).[16] To say the least, this explanation is highly unlikely.

A third problem is this view's interpretation of the Hebrew word *tôl^eḏôṯ*. The noun comes from the verb *yālaḏ* ("to father, give birth to, bear"), and must refer to that which is born, or produced, that is, the historical result. In the genitive, "these are the *tôl^eḏôṯ* of," we have the starting point, the origin. In the noun *tôl^eḏôṯ* we have the conclusion or the result.[17] The cosmos's *tôl^eḏôṯ* has for its center Adam and Eve, as opposed to other parts of creation. Noah's *tôl^eḏôṯ* has for its center Shem, as opposed to other sons. Shem's *tôl^eḏôṯ* has for its center Terah, as opposed to other descendants. Terah's *tôl^eḏôṯ* has for its center Abram, as opposed to two other sons. Isaac's

15. D. S. DeWitt, "The Generations of Genesis," *EvQ* 48 (1976) 196–211.

16. See D. Kidner, *Genesis,* TOTC (Downers Grove, IL: Inter-Varsity, 1979), p. 24.

17. See M. H. Woudstra, "The *Toledot* of the Book of Genesis and Their Redemptive-Historical Significance," *CTJ* 5 (1970) 187.

tôl^{e}ḏôṯ has Jacob for its center, as opposed to another son. Jacob's *tôl^{e}ḏôṯ* has Joseph for its center, as opposed to other brothers. Each of the *tôl^{e}ḏôṯ,* then, focuses on one personality and weeds out lesser individuals. In this way the book of Genesis displays evidence of both literary and theological unity. Obviously, these narratives are not biographies. If they were, we should have a "generation" of Abraham and of Joseph. Rather, the *tôl^{e}ḏôṯ* structure of Genesis suggests a movement from a starting point to a finishing point, from a cause to an effect, from a progenitor to a progeny who is the key individual at that point in either implementing or perpetuating God's plan and will in his heavens and earth.

Leaving aside the *tôl^{e}ḏôṯ* formula, one notices other indicators of structural design in Genesis. For example, there is a clear geographical design within Genesis. Chapters 1–11 are set in Babylonia; chs. 12–36 are set in Palestine; chs. 37–50 are set in Egypt.[18] In other words, each part of the Mediterranean world is highlighted in some part of Genesis.[19] The crucial center section of Genesis (chs. 12–36) is bracketed geographically by two sections of the Near Eastern world with whose history that of Israel would be constantly interlocked. The impact created by these broad geographical contours is that Genesis is a book about world history. This is true not only in the very opening chapters that deal with the whence of the cosmos and humankind, but in all the narratives that follow. The ultimate reason for the election of Abraham is that the nations of the earth (such as those falling within the geographical boundaries of chs. 1–11 and 37–50) might find the knowledge of God and his blessing.

Another point is uncovered as one scans Genesis for structural design. It is hardly accidental that four-fifths of Genesis (chs. 12–50) describes the history of only four generations (Abraham to Joseph), while one-fifth of Genesis (chs. 1–11) describes the history of twenty generations (Adam to Abraham). Why is Genesis preoccupied maximally with the four generations, but only minimally with the first twenty generations?[20] As an extension of

18. The same kind of tripartite geographical focus emerges from Exodus: (1) 1:1–12:36, in Egypt; (2) 12:37–18:27, to Sinai; (3) 19:1–40:38, at Sinai.

19. See W. W. Hallo, "Biblical History in Its Near Eastern Setting: The Contextual Approach," in *Scripture in Context: Essays on the Comparative Method,* ed. Carl D. Evans, et al., PTMS 34 (Pittsburgh: Pickwick, 1980), p. 15; idem, "Genesis and Ancient Near Eastern Literature," in *The Torah: A Modern Commentary. Genesis,* ed. W. G. Plaut (New York: Union of American Hebrew Congregations, 1974), 1:xxix.

20. The same disproportion appears in the Pentateuch at large. Genesis, covering the time span from the creation of the world to Joseph, occupies approximately 25 percent

this point, why does the Creation story, certainly an indispensable part of Genesis and all of Scripture for that matter, receive only two chapters, while the Abraham story is allotted thirteen chapters and part of two others? Why is the account of the "Fall" limited to one chapter, while the Joseph narrative occupies the last third of Genesis?

The clear-cut division between chs. 11 and 12 has provided sufficient evidence for dividing Genesis into two main bodies. The first is chs. 1–11, designated as primeval history. The second is chs. 12–50, designated as patriarchal history. In chs. 1–11 we read of individuals who had land, but are either losing it or being expelled from it. In chs. 12–50 the emphasis is on individuals who do not have land, but are on the way toward it. One group is losing; another group is expecting.[21]

In chs. 1–11 one finds, via the narratives contained therein, either an increasing alienation from God (von Rad), or examples of the variety and scope of humanity's alienation from God with no particular crescendo of evil or sin intended (Westermann). After the series of sorry examples presented in chs. 1–11, we are meant to read chs. 12ff. (patriarchal history) as the solution to this problem. Will there be more Adams and more tower builders? Or is there a way out of this dilemma? The obedient model of Abraham contrasts to all the sorry models who have gone before him.[22] He is one not intent on making his name great. Rather, he is one upon whom greatness is bestowed. A covenant with humankind (Gen. 8–9) is now augmented by a covenant with a family. Genesis is moving us progressively from generation (chs. 1–2), to degeneration (chs. 3–11), to regeneration (chs. 12–50).

III. COMPOSITION

Discussion about Genesis' composition has run in cycles—in two uneven cycles at least—for the last two millennia. For almost eighteen hundred years (the first cycle) hardly anyone questioned the unity of Genesis, whether the writers were the rabbinical scholars of Judaism or the ecclesiastical scholars

---

of the total text of the Pentateuch. Exodus–Deuteronomy, covering only the time span of Moses' 120 years, occupies 75 percent of the total text of the Pentateuch. See R. P. Knierim, "The Composition of the Pentateuch," in SBLASP, 1985, p. 395.

21. See W. Brueggemann, *The Land,* OBT 1 (Philadelphia: Fortress, 1977), p. 15.

22. See G. Coats, "The God of Death: Power and Obedience in the Primeval History," *Int* 29 (1975) 234.

of Christendom. Thus a Maimonides within Judaism, an Augustine within Catholicism, and a Calvin within Protestantism shared no disagreement on the point of Genesis' origin and composition. For all of them Genesis was a unified work, and more specifically, the work of Moses. It is now fashionable to label such an approach as "traditional" or "precritical." The latter term especially is an opprobrious one, for it suggests that modern scholars consider such writers of only slight usefulness in the interpretation of the biblical text, essentially limited to showing how such commentators of old fill in the gaps in one's treatment of the history of Genesis' interpretation. Thus their contribution to the whole is primarily archaic. Hence, unfortunately, the valid insights they have to offer are often ignored in the light of supposedly more germane and judicious studies. To be sure, such precritical scholars did not have at their disposal some of the historical apparatus available to the modern scholar. Even if they had had access to such modern aids, it remains to be seen whether an Ibn Ezra would zealously have embraced the Yahwist, or a Luther, preoccupied with the exclusive sacerdotalism of the Catholic Church, would have expatiated at length in his writings on Genesis' Priestly traditions. "Calvin on the Elohist" would not seem to fall within the interests of Geneva's famous theologian.

The second cycle of interpretations is approximately two centuries old. So dominant is it today that it has replaced the older precritical approach as the traditional one. To challenge it is to wade into the waters of heterodoxy, to risk the charge of hopeless obfuscation, or at worst, to be labeled "fundamentalist."

This second approach finds its birth in the writings of the eighteenth-century French physician Jean Astruc, although even he has antecedents.[1] (Note that at this period in "Christian" Europe the NT maintained a sacrosanctity that removed it effectively from the biblicist's telescope. The OT, however, was open game.) Among Astruc's several observations on the biblical narratives was the puzzling distribution of different names for deity scattered throughout Genesis and the first few chapters of Exodus. His conclusion was that Moses was the redactor (not the author) of Gen. 1–Exod. 2, and that Moses collated two primary, parallel sources (one of which referred to the deity as "Yahweh," and the other referred to the deity as "Elohim"), plus ten other fragments. All of these were written before Moses' time. Astruc was no demolitionist who wished to dissociate himself from the

1. Astruc's book was published in Brussels (and secretly in Paris) anonymously in 1753 under the meandering title *Conjectures sur les mémoires originaux, dont il parait que Moyse s'est servi pour composer le livre de Genèse.*

mainstream Christianity of his day. On the contrary, he was distinctly orthodox, and his views actually represent a measured response to the free-thinkers of his day on the question of the Mosaic authorship of the Pentateuch.

At first, Astruc's view met with ridicule. It might have faded into oblivion had it not been for the work of the German historian and biblical scholar J. G. Eichhorn, who was born one year before Astruc's book was published (1752). Eichhorn aired Astruc's views in a major publication, normally labeled as the first critical introduction to the OT.[2] He resurrected Astruc's views and even extended them by establishing other criteria for multiple sources in Genesis (and the Pentateuch), such as phraseology and literary style. Much of Eichhorn's mind-set was influenced by his conviction that legitimate historical study of the Bible could be carried out only when the Bible had been liberated from the stranglehold of church dogma. Once ecclesiastical strictures are erased, Scripture study can become, *sui generis,* a bona fide scientific enterprise.

Through the remainder of the 18th century and well into the 19th century the views expressed by Astruc and Eichhorn were augmented and revised by other scholars following in their train. It is not the purpose of this commentary to trace step-by-step all the developments in the theories of Genesis' composition. The reader is directed to any of a number of excellent treatments of that subject.[3]

The emerging consensus looked as follows. Genesis was the net result of the compilation of three distinct literary sources: (1) a Yahwistic or Jahwistic (J) source; (2) an Elohistic (E) source; (3) behind these two a Priestly (P) source, which was first tagged as the *Grundschrift,* the common pool or the primary source, for J and E.

Toward the latter part of the 19th century and into the 20th, the views of Julius Wellhausen (1844–1918) dominated OT scholarship. Even to this day he remains one of the legitimate *Erzväter* (founding fathers) of biblical studies. He is to modern biblical scholarship what Abraham is to the Jew, the father of the faithful. More lucidily and compellingly than any other, he gave

2. J. G. Eichhorn, *Einleitung in das Alte Testament,* 3 vols. (Leipzig: Weidmann, 1780–1783).

3. See E. G. Kraeling, *The Old Testament since the Reformation* (London: Lutterworth, 1955); H. J. Kraus, *Geschichte der historisch-kritischen Erforschung des Alten Testaments von der Reformation bis zur Gegenwart* (Neukirchen: Erziehungsverein, 1956); R. E. Clements, *One Hundred Years of Old Testament Interpretation* (Philadelphia: Westminster, 1975); D. A. Knight and G. M. Tucker, eds., *The Hebrew Bible and Its Modern Interpreters* (Philadelphia: Fortress, 1985).

what many have considered the definitive formulation of the documentary hypothesis.[4]

In brief, this approach identifies four major literary strands behind the present canonical shape of the Pentateuch. In chronological order these are:

1. The *Yahwist* (J) (850 B.C. — Wellhausen; 960–930 B.C. — post-Wellhausen scholars), written anonymously in Judah during the reign of Solomon. This source traces Israel's history from its patriarchal beginnings to its preparation for entry into Canaan; narratives from prepatriarchal times were added at some point. It may have functioned as the national epic for the Davidic/Solomonic kingdom. "J" is the symbol for this document, primarily because of its almost exclusive use of "Yahweh."[5]
2. The *Elohist* (E) (850 B.C.), also written anonymously in northern Israel, shortly after the collapse of the united monarchy. It covers substantially the same period of Israel's history as J, but it starts with the patriarchs and not with creation. Because it prefers the name "Elohim" for God, it is styled the Elohist.[6]
3. *Deuteronomy* (D), written at least by the Josianic reform (ca. 620 B.C.), but perhaps as old as E, and originally from northern Israel, as was E. It is confined obviously, as far as the Pentateuch is concerned, to Deuteronomy.
4. The *Priestly Writer* (P) (550–450 B.C.), heavily concerned with chronological, liturgical, and genealogical matters. Wellhausen's major innovation here was to shift the Priestly code from the earliest document to the latest document, written sometime after the Babylonian exile. Unlike J and E, P is not concerned with presenting history as such, but with establishing the basis of Israel's sacral institutions through their connection with history. Thus, the Creation story provides the reason for the Sabbath's instititution (Gen. 1), and the covenant with Abraham (Gen. 17) establishes the reason for circumcision. Today debate on P focuses on two issues: (1) Is it post-D (JEDP) or is it pre-D (JEPD)? (2) Is P a source or a redaction? These issues will be examined further below.

4. Wellhausen's publications relating to Genesis and the Pentateuch are *Die Composition des Hexateuchs* (Berlin: Reimer, 1889), and *Geschichte Israels* (Berlin: Reimer, 1878), which was reissued as *Prolegomena zur Geschichte Israels* (Berlin: Reimer, 1882), and translated as *Prolegomena to the History of Ancient Israel* (repr. Cleveland/New York: World, 1965).

5. "J" is from the German spelling Jahweh/Jahwist.

6. As "J" may represent both "J/Yahweh" and "Judah," E may represent both "Elohim" and "Ephraim."

An analogy for this hypothesis might be an electrical cord. The wiring on the outside, visible to the eye, gives the impression of unity, one substance. Once the outer casing is removed, however, one detects immediately several different wires, indicated by color, inside the casing.

There are a number of reasons for positing the existence of a multi-traditional Pentateuch. In descending order of significance, they are: (1) The different names for God. This is apparent, for example, in the Creation story, which uses "Elohim" consistently in 1:1–2:3 and "Yahweh Elohim" in 2:4–3:24, and in the Flood account (Gen. 6–9), which uses both "Elohim" and "Yahweh."

(2) The presence of duplications, a story told twice (or thrice), but in such a way that the two accounts are irreconcilable. Thus there are two Creation accounts (1:1–2:4a and 2:4bff.), two Flood accounts (meshed in chs. 6–9), two accounts of God's covenant with Abraham (chs. 15 and 17), two accounts of Hagar's banishment (chs. 16 and 21), two accounts of Jacob's name change to Israel (chs. 32 and 35), two accounts of Joseph's sale to merchants bound for Egypt (37:25-27, 28b and 37:28a, 36), three accounts of wife abduction (chs. 12, 20, and 26), and so forth.

(3) The presence of anachronisms, which must be dated much later than the patriarchal or the Mosaic period. One thinks, for example, of references to Abraham's Ur as "Ur of the Chaldeans"—the "Chaldeans" do not appear in Mesopotamia until long after the patriarchal period; or of the mention of "Philistines" and domesticated "camels" in the Genesis narratives. The list of Edomite kings in Gen. 36 is interesting, especially in the light of the fact that the Edomites did not settle in Transjordan before the 13th century B.C.

(4) The detection in Genesis of distinctive literary styles or religious ideology within a section or unit. For instance, P's style is reckoned to be more formal and repetitious, while J's is more simple. Or again, J, with his anthropomorphic tendencies when talking about God, presents the contact between God and the patriarchs as direct, while E tends to dilute this contact by introducing dreams and angels as intermediate factors.

Since D is confined to Deuteronomy, the book of Genesis will be a compilation of only three of the four sources listed above—JEP. Their suggested appearance throughout Genesis is as follows:

1:1–31 (P)
2:1–4a (P)
4b–25 (J)
3:1–24 (J)
4:1–26 (J)
5:1–28 (P)
29 (J)
30–32 (P)
6:1–8 (J)
9–22 (P)
7:1–5 (J)
6 (P)
7–10 (J)
11 (P)
12 (J)
13–16a (P)
16b (J)
17a (P)
17b (J)
18–21 (P)
22–23 (J)
24 (P)
8:1–2a (P)
2b–3a (J)
3b–5 (P)
6–12 (J)
13a (P)
13b (J)
14–19 (P)
20–22 (J)
9:1–17 (P)
18–27 (J)
28–29 (P)
10:1–7 (P)
8–19 (J)
20 (P)
21 (J)
22–23 (P)
24–30 (J)
31–32 (P)
11:1–9 (J)
10–27 (P)
28–30 (J)
31–32 (P)
12:1–4a (J)
4b–5 (P)
6–20 (J)
13:1–5 (J)
6 (P)
7–11a (J)
11b–12a (P)
12b–18 (J)
14:1–24 (X)
15:1–2a (J)
2b–3a (E?)
3b–4 (J)
5 (?)
6–12 (J)
13–16 (?)
17–21 (J)
16:1a (P)
1b–2 (J)
3 (P)
4–14 (J)
15–16 (P)
17:1–27 (P)
18:1–33 (J)
19:1–28 (J)
29 (P)
30–38 (J)
20:1–18 (E)
21:1a (J)
1b (P)
2a (J)
2b–5 (P)
6–32 (E)
33 (J)
34 (E)
22:1–19 (E)
20–24 (J)
23:1–20 (P)
24:1–67 (J)
25:1–6 (J)
7–11a (P)
12–17 (P)
18 (J)
19–20 (P)
21–26a (J)
26b (P)
27–34 (J)
26:1–33 (J)
34–35 (P)
27:1–45 (J)
46 (P)
28:1–9 (P)
10 (J)
11–12 (E)
13–16 (J)
17–18 (E)
19 (J)
20–21a (E)
21b (J)
22 (E)
29:1–14 (J)
15–23 (E)
24 (P)
25–28a (E)
28b–29 (P)
30 (E)
31–35 (J)
30:1–2 (E)
3–5 (J)
6 (E)
7–16 (J)
17–20a (E)
20b (J)
21–23 (E)
24–43 (J)
31:1–18a (J and E)
18b (P)
19–54 (J and E)
32:1–3 (E)
4–33 (J)
33:1–17 (J)
18a (P)
18b–20 (E)
34:1–31 (J)
35:1–8 (E)
9–13 (P)
14 (J)
15 (P)
16–20 (E)
21–22a (J)
22b–29 (P)
36:1–43 (P)
37:1–2a (P)
2b–20 (J)
21–24 (E)
25–27 (J)
28a (E)
28b (J)
28c–36 (E)
38:1–30 (J)
39:1–23 (J)
40:1–23 (E)
41:1–45 (E)
46a (P)
46b–57 (E)
42:1–26 (E)
27–28 (J)
29–38 (E)
43:1–34 (J)
44:1–34 (J)
45:1–28 (J and E)
46:1 (J)
2–5 (E)
6–27 (P)
28–34 (J)
47:1–5a (J)
5b–6a (P)
6b (J)
7–12 (P)
13–27a (J)
27b–28 (P)
29–31 (J)
48:1–2 (E)
3–7 (P)
8–22 (E and J)
49:1–27 (X)
28–33 (P)
50:1–11 (J)
12–13 (P)
14 (J)
15–26 (E)[7]

7. I am following the divisions suggested by E. A. Speiser, *Genesis,* AB, 2nd ed. (repr. Garden City, NY: Doubleday, 1978). His division of the biblical material into different sources is fairly standard. Others might dissent here or there.

At least in 11:27–50:26, the J source predominates. Within this large patriarchal section of J, 730 verses are to be attributed to J, 336 verses to E, and 153 verses to P.[8] E is surprisingly represented nowhere in the primeval history. E's first connected narrative contribution to Genesis appears not until ch. 20. E's presence is more apparent in the Jacob and Joseph cycle than it is in the Abraham cycle. This is what one might expect in a northern document, since Jacob is more frequently associated with northern sites, while Abraham is as often associated with southern sites. As a narrative source, P is present only sparingly, in four passages to be exact (1:1–2:4a; 6:1–9:29; 17:1–27; 23:1–20). P's major contribution is found in the genealogies and in the framework he provides to the narratives of J and E with his inclusion of numbers, dates, and years.[9]

These, then, are the three strands from which, according to the theory, the final text of Genesis was woven. They will not, of course, be as readily identifiable by the layperson as they are by the biblical scholar. Thus, some modern versions (e.g., JB) publish in their footnotes notations at to where and when a particular unit is to be identified as Elohist, Yahwist, or Priestly. One Bible edition is, in fact, known as "the Rainbow Bible." It colorcodes the three sources in Genesis–Numbers, one color background for J, one for E, one for P. To some this project will be helpful. To others it will be dismissed as nothing more than an exercise in coloring.

Wellhausen took his source analysis of Genesis a step further than merely isolating the various traditions in the redacted text. He argued that none of these traditions could give any authentic information about the patriarchs or Moses. They were only reliable for the period in which they were composed (viz., the middle of the 9th century B.C. and later). In other words, none of the three literary strands in Genesis had any preliterary history.

While firmly endorsing Wellhausen's view of the literary sources, later scholars sought to affirm through the use of other and newer scholarly disciplines (form criticism, tradition criticism) that the sources themselves had a long prehistory, that in fact J and E probably existed in oral tradition long before they became a written tradition.

8. The tabulations are those of N. Gottwald, *The Hebrew Bible—A Socio-Literary Introduction* (Philadelphia: Fortress, 1985), p. 150. Gottwald includes Gen. 14 and 49:1–27, which we marked with the undesignated X, with J.

9. S. E. McEvenue (*The Narrative Style of the Priestly Writer,* AnBib 50 [Rome: Biblical Institute, 1971]) attempts (with a good degree of success) to rescue P from the charge of being monotonous and pedantic. He explores the possibility of comparing P with children's literature in his discussion of matters like panel structure, repetitious patterns, and symmetrical structure.

The major work in this field was done by Hermann Gunkel (1862–1932), particularly in his commentary on Genesis, first published in 1901, the introduction of which was translated into English and published under the title *The Legends of Genesis.*[10] Gunkel's main dissatisfaction with Wellhausen was the latter's attempt to write the history of Israel purely in chronological terms and exclusively from the perspective of historical criticism. Appealing to the literature of other cultures, Gunkel argued for the oral prehistory of the literary sources in Genesis, and presented his case for classifying this material into the appropriate categories of oral forms (narratives, hymns, laws, etc.) and literary genres (of which the most prominent in Gen. 12–50 is saga).

Gunkel also felt that many, if not all, of the individual narratives within Genesis had at this earlier stage a function (tied to an original *Sitz im Leben* or life setting) different from the function the narrative assumed when it was incorporated into the written traditions. For example, the offering of Isaac (22:1–19, E), which functions in the literary strands as a story in which Abraham's faith in God is tested, had an altogether different relevance in the preliterary setting. There the story was told to explain why the Hebrews offered animals and not human beings to their God. The "Fall" scene of Gen. 3 (J), now the ultimate test of the primal couple, originally explained why snakes do not have an upright posture.

In attempting to excavate the original, preliterary form of JEP, Gunkel believed, contra Wellhausen, that he could make a case for the great antiquity of the sagas, legends, and traditions of Genesis. Of course, for Gunkel great antiquity and facticity had nothing to do with each other. This is one reason why the conservative movement in OT scholarship has never been enamored of Gunkel, and even less of his Genesis study (where historical concerns are paramount) than with his work on Psalms (where historical concerns are meager). Accordingly, this branch of scholarship has chosen instead to go the route of archeology to substantiate historicity (a view that is coming under more and more trenchant attack), when in point of fact *Formgeschichte* (form criticism) may yield greater dividends.

Gunkel's observations were carried one step further by Martin Noth.[11] He attempted to show how these short narrative units, deciphered by

10. H. Gunkel, *Genesis,* HKAT 1/1, 6th ed. (Göttingen: Vandenhoeck & Ruprecht, 1963); idem, *The Legends of Genesis,* tr. W. H. Carruth (New York: Schocken, 1964).

11. M. Noth, *Überlieferungsgeschichte des Pentateuch* (Stuttgart: Kohlhammer, 1948), part of which was translated by B. W. Anderson as *A History of Pentateuchal Traditions* (Englewood Cliffs, NJ: Prentice-Hall, 1972).

Gunkel in their oral stage, were amalgamated with each other and in the process created much larger narrative complexes. Noth identified five component themes in the Pentateuch which like a magnet drew together these smaller traditions. Only the first of these five themes is found in Genesis, and that is the patriarchal theme that God promised to Abraham, and after him to Isaac and Jacob, a great land and prosperity.[12] These themes, which later formed an oral or written *Grundlage* (foundation) for J and E, arose among various tribal clans (which later made up "Israel") in cultic celebrations. Later these five themes were filled out with other narratives and then connected so as to give an appearance of chronological sequence. At this later point the primeval history (Gen. 1–11) was prefixed to the story of the patriarchs. Noth would say that Abraham, Isaac, and Jacob are historical figures but that little if anything about them in Genesis is historical. The reason for this skepticism is that, according to Noth, the stories about the patriarchs originated in different places and among various clans, and the connecting of these stories is, at best, artificial.[13]

Putting together, then, the perspective of Wellhausen-Gunkel-Noth, one arrives at the scholarly consensus that Genesis (and Exodus–Numbers as well) evidences the following stages of composition:

1. The oral formation of small narratives, 1800–1200 B.C. (Gunkel)
2. The assembling of these smaller narratives into larger complexes around history-like themes, as part of a liturgical affirmation of faith in community acts of worship, 1200–1000 B.C.[14] (Noth)
3. The writing of the J source, 950 B.C.

12. The remaining four themes are: (2) the Exodus theme, depicting Israel's escape from Egyptian bondage; (3) the conquest theme, depicting God's gift of land to Israel; (4) the wilderness theme, depicting God's sustaining of Israel in very inimical circumstances in a barren wasteland; (5) the Sinai theme, God's revelation of himself to Israel at the sacred mountain (and, as noted by von Rad, the one theme absent from the credo-like confessions one finds in Deut. 6:20–24; 26:5b–9; Josh. 24:2b–13).

13. Noth's skeptical attitude toward the patriarchs extends to his treatment of Moses. He eliminates Moses from all of the above-mentioned themes (see n. 12 above), except possibly the wilderness theme. Moses' involvement, say, with the Exodus events or the Sinai theophanies is only an insertion, but historically he had nothing to do with them. In fact, the only certain valid information Noth felt we have about Moses is that he was buried in "the valley opposite Beth-peor" (Deut. 34:6)!

14. The dates I have provided are not meant to draw a hard-and-fast line between oral activities and scribal activities as if they were only sequential. Probably the two were at some points concurrent, with oral tradition being perpetuated even after some of the original inscripturation.

4. The writing of the E source, 850 B.C.
5. The redaction of JE
6. The writing of the P source, 550 B.C. or later
7. The redaction of JEP, either by P himself or by an independent editor, ca. 400 B.C. (nos. 3–7, Wellhausen)

Especially since the 1960s mounting criticism has appeared against the above consensus. This criticism ranges from minor adjustments, to major overhauling, to the suggested scrapping of the documentary hypothesis as a viable explanation of the origin of the Pentateuch in general, and of Genesis in particular.

The category of minor adjustments includes those who argue that there never was a Priestly narrative independent of JE. Rather, P was an exilic tradent who systematized JE and gave to it its genealogical parameters. This position would argue for a JED theory of the Pentateuch. Or more particularly as far as Genesis is concerned, Genesis represents a collection of JE epic traditions whose present order and collocation we owe to this exilic or postexilic tradent. The most vocal proponent of this position, at least in the English-speaking world, is F. M. Cross.[15] This is not a new position; indeed, A. Klostermann gave it its original stimulus in the 19th century.[16] This approach is not a refutation of the documentary hypothesis but an alternative formulation of the same. As such, it bears closest resemblance to that view of earlier generations which has been labeled as the "supplementary hypothesis." This position assumed the existence of one basic document or body of tradition (an Elohistic source at that) to which a later editor added supplementary material. This position was advanced by H. Ewald, F. Bleek, and Franz Delitzsch.[17]

More radical surgery on the documentary hypothesis is advocated by a number of current scholars. The most controversial contribution from that flank is the work of John Van Seters, much of which owes its original impetus to the stimulus of Van Seters's mentor at the University of Toronto, F. W. Winnett.[18]

15. F. M. Cross, *Canaanite Myth and Hebrew Epic* (Cambridge: Harvard University, 1973). See esp. his section entitled "Exile and Apocalyptic," pp. 293–325. For the same perspective on P see the work of Sven Tengström, *Die Toledotformel und die literarische Struktur der priesterlichen Erweiterungsschicht im Pentateuch.*

16. A. Klostermann, *Der Pentateuch* (Leipzig: A. Deichert, 1893).

17. See H. Ewald, *Die Komposition der Genesis Kritisch untersucht* (Göttingen: Vandenhoeck & Reprecht, 1823); F. Bleek, *Einleitung in das AT* (Berlin: G. Reimer, 1878); F. Delitzsch, *Neuer Commentar über Genesis* (Leipzig: Dörfling und Franke, 1887).

18. J. Van Seters, *Abraham in History and Tradition* (New Haven/London: Yale University, 1975); F. W. Winnett, "Re-examining the Foundations," *JBL* 84

Since Van Seters's study is confined to the Abraham traditions in Genesis, it has limitations for a study of the composition of Genesis. It remains to be seen whether Van Seters will follow with a sequel, "Jacob in History and Tradition" or even "Joseph in History and Tradition," since both these units of Genesis are also considered compilations of JEP.

Van Seters's purpose is twofold. The first section of his book (approximately one-third of the whole) directly attacks the position that claims any kind of historicity for Abraham. He is particularly disturbed (and properly so) by the indiscriminate use of second-millennium B.C. literature for the purpose of establishing a historically credible Bronze Age Abraham. It is his contention that Neo-Babylonian parallels are much closer to the patriarchal narratives than parallels adduced from Mari and Nuzi especially.

The second, more constructive part of his book attempts to trace the development of Abraham "in tradition." This is the section that concerns us here, and it occupies almost two-thirds of the text. In his first section Van Seters opposed the views of W. F. Albright, C. H. Gordon, E. A. Speiser, R. de Vaux, and H. Cazelles, all of whom as historians treated the Genesis text and the patriarchal narratives conservatively; in this second section Van Seters opposes with equal passion the views of Gunkel, von Rad, and Noth, all of whom gave a large place to oral tradition in the formation of these narratives. He fails to discern or attribute any formative role for oral tradition.

He suggests, on the contrary, an exclusively literary development for the Abraham tradition which is spread over five stages: (1) a pre-Yahwistic first stage; (2) a pre-Yahwistic second stage (= E?); (3) Yahwist; (4) Priestly; (5) post-Priestly. Thus Van Seters rejects Wellhausen's JEDP and Cross's JE < P, and erects his own J_1EJ_2P Post-P. Everything in Gen. 12–26 is assigned to one of these five segments.

Van Seters rejects Albright's attempt to substantiate a historical, second-millennium B.C. Abraham based on archeological studies and parallels. Similarly he rejects the attempts of Noth and Gunkel to recover data about the patriarch(s) by unraveling the preliterary stages which were the antecedents for the literary narratives. There were no preliterary stages! Van Seters dates the Abraham traditions to the Neo-Babylonian period (6th century B.C.). For him there is no historical Abraham, but only a kerygmatic Abraham.

(1965) 1–19. Winnett's position on the patriarchal narratives is that it is wrong to put J in Judah and E in Israel, for the E stories are effective and comprehensible only when placed in close proximity to the J stories. More than likely, argues Winnett, there was only a J story of Abraham, which was then corrected by having E stories appended to it.

Van Seters has not yet succeeded in toppling the traditional formulation of the documentary hypothesis. But he is not alone in espousing a late date for the Yahwist. In this position he is joined by H. H. Schmid.[19] Most of Schmid's study focuses on J material in Exodus (the call of Moses, the plagues, the sea crossing, and the Sinai theophany), and hence is of less interest to us than Van Seters's study. He does have one section devoted to "The Promise to the Patriarchs," but he feels this material was not primary for the Yahwist. He does suggest that Gen. 15 has very close ties with, and is indebted to, Isa. 7, which is a royal victory oracle. Similarly he catalogues Gen. 15:6 ("And Abram believed Yahweh") as a concept springing from verses in Deuteronomy that talk of Israel's faith or lack thereof.

Schmid's thesis is that the texts of the Yahwist presuppose the preexilic prophets and/or Deuteronomic theology. This thesis is demonstrated for Schmid, for example, by the presence in J of lengthy, expanded monologues as opposed to short prophetic speeches. He appeals primarily to Exod. 3–4 (J), a long speech punctuated only by Moses' objections. Or again, the stubbornness of Pharaoh throughout the plagues draws from Deuteronomy's emphasis on Israel's stubborn refusal to hear Yahweh's voice. Schmid's conclusion is that J represents a tradition process rather than the work of an author, and was assembled between the decline of the monarchy and the beginning of exile. Accordingly he reshuffles the documentary hypothesis and produces EDJP. For some reason it never occurs to Schmid that the common themes between J and Deuteronomy may be explained otherwise. Why might not Deuteronomy have drawn from J? Might not Deuteronomy have antecedents as well as successors? If the covenant institution is as late in Israel's history as Schmid's Yahwist, then what is one to do with the early, preexilic prophets (Amos, Hosea) whose writings not only presuppose but are consumed with this topic?

Returning to the study of Van Seters, we draw attention to the limitations of his work for making conclusions and generalizations about the presence and date of J in Genesis–Exodus. It would be interesting, for example, to see what Van Seters would do with J in the Jacob narratives. Since the eighth-century B.C. Hosea makes substantive use of the Jacob traditions, would Van Seters date J materials in this part of Genesis to the 8th century or earlier, and if so, what then becomes of his sixth-century Yahwist? Or would he include these materials in one of the two stages before the Yahwist proper, that is, J or E? Van Seters nowhere indicates the length of

19. H. H. Schmid, *Der sogenannte Jahwist: Beobachtungen und Fragen zur Pentateuchforschung* (Zurich: Theologischer Verlag, 1976).

time between these two strata and the Yahwist. For him all the other stages are dwarfed by the third one, the Yahwist. Recall the title of his book: *Abraham in History and Tradition* (singular), not "Abraham in History and Traditions" (plural).

Another major problem confronts Van Seters. He would have us believe that at some point in the middle of the 1st millennium B.C. some writer or writers created and then projected an Abraham tradition back into the pre-Mosaic, preliterary period of Israel's life, for some purpose not explained by Van Seters. Nor does Van Seters explain the alacrity with which such a composition, composed only recently, assumed such a significant place in the mainstream of Israel's religious traditions. Furthermore, we might ask if the literature of JE, given its emphasis on growth and grandeur, could have been written in the exilic period, which was a time of decided decline. Certainly that is a possibility, but is it the most likely and rational possibility? If the J source, especially in Genesis, is informed by the idea of a great nation which is to expand and conquer other nations, could this idea have crystallized in a time of national decline and disgrace? Perhaps Van Seters would see the Yahwist as some kind of Churchill, motivating and inspiring his people from the verge of defeat on to victory. Or would Van Seters have the Yahwist say to his Judean peers, "the reports of our demise are greatly exaggerated"?

To Van Seters the most impressive confirmation of his literary analysis comes from his examination of the three stories in Genesis about Abraham and Isaac each passing off his wife as sister (12:10–20; 20:1–17; 26:1–11). Van Seters assigns the first of these stories (12:10–20) to the pre-Yahwistic stage (J_1). The second (20:1–17) he assigns to the second pre-Yahwistic stage, or Elohist (E). The third (26:1–11) he assigns to the Yahwist (J). He suggests that the first was oral in origin. The second story was written as an evaluative comment on the first one. Finally, the third of these stories was written by the Yahwist in immediate literary dependence on the first two accounts. This analysis has two obvious implications for the composition of Genesis, as popularly understood. First, it obviates the need for redactors. We no longer need anybody to tie together JE, and later to tie together JEP and JEDP. Second, if the account in ch. 26 (J) is dependent on the account in ch. 20 (E), then the Yahwist must come after the Elohist, a great reversal for consensus source analysis.

This reconstruction hardly stands up to further scrutiny. For instance, if the author of the second account penned his story in order to insert some orthodoxy into the first account, then why did he not simply rework the first account instead of composing an alternative account? Why leave the embarrassing account in at all? Or again, if account three is dependent on account two, then why does account three not use account two's solution to the problem, and why then does the author change the story so obviously?

Van Seters is much taken by the fact that outside J (and E?) Abraham and the promises made to him are of little significance in the biblical narrative until the time of Jeremiah and Ezekiel. We grant the correctness of his observation, but not of his conclusion—that is, the Abraham traditions and the promises scattered throughout the narratives came into existence with no perceivable antecedents at the time of these prophets. Why may not the exilic prophets be drawing upon earlier traditions rather than upon concurrent traditions? The proliferation of patriarchal motifs in exilic prophetic literature may point to a revitalization and recapturing of these themes in such a bleak time as exile. With its back to the wall, and with all its other supports knocked out beneath it, Israel can only maintain its faith by reappropriation of that one divine moment of God's dealing with and creation of his people.

We have not said everything that could be said about Van Seters's tome, both positive and negative,[20] but enough has been discussed to convey our impression that Van Seters has not succeeded in replacing the Wellhausen consensus with a Van Seters challenge. This leads us to examine the views of those who suggest that the time has come not to revise the Wellhausen scheme but to abandon it.

Rolf Rendtorff has made a prominent contribution.[21] He exhibits no restraint in his criticism of JEDP as a viable explanation of the Pentateuch's

20. Some positive points: his boldness in breaking new ground and challenging cherished positions; his insistence on the priority of internal sources over external sources in determining the character and chronological context of the patriarchal traditions. Some negative points: his too facile attribution of the name "Abraham" to the 1st millennium B.C. exclusively, when in point of fact the name (or its equivalents) is much more plausible in the previous millennium; his false contrast between sedentary and nomadic life; his handling of the Arabian proper names in Genesis and their counterparts in extant cuneiform literature. The little that has been published of the enormous discoveries at Ebla does not add confidence to Van Seters's reconstruction.

21. R. Rendtorff, *Das überlieferungsgeschichtliche Problem des Pentateuch,* BZAW 147 (Berlin/New York: de Gruyter, 1977); idem, *The Old Testament: An Introduction,* tr. John Bowden (Philadelphia: Fortress, 1986), pp. 132–39 (for Genesis), pp. 157–64 (for the Pentateuch as a whole). See also Rendtorff's article "The 'Yahwist' as Theologian? The Dilemma of Pentateuchal Criticism," *JSOT* 3/3 (1977) 2–10, with responses by R. N. Whybray (pp. 11–14), J. Van Seters (pp. 15–19), N. Wagner (pp. 20–27), G. Coats (pp. 28–32), H. H. Schmid (pp. 33–42), and R. E. Clements (pp. 46–56), and a rejoinder by Rendtorff (pp. 43–45). See also R. North, "Can Geography Save J from Rendtorff?" *Bib* 63 (1982) 47–55.

fabric: "The positing of 'sources' in the sense of the documentary hypothesis can no longer make any contribution to understanding the development of the Pentateuch."[22] Coming as it does from a scholar fully trained in and comfortable with the literary-critical school, rather than from apologetics, this statement is nothing short of revolutionary.

In lieu of J, E, D, and P, Rendtorff proposes the independent existence of six larger units: (1) primeval history; (2) patriarchal history; (3) the Exodus story; (4) the Sinai experience; (5) the sojourn in the wilderness; and (6) settlement in the land. In his first book at least, Rendtorff's preoccupation is with the second of these traditions (patriarchal history) as he attempts to buttress his position. His basic reason for advancing the existence of the above traditions is essentially an argument from silence. He reasons, for example, that because primeval history demonstrates minimal (if any!) connection with patriarchal history,[23] or more importantly, because the section on patriarchal history and the Exodus story are independent of each other, the case for autonomy is heightened. How might one justifiably speak, say, of the presence of J in these three sections of the Pentateuch, when each of them betrays far more self-containment than literary relationship?

Our interest here is on Genesis and Rendtorff's understanding of the composition of Genesis. For him Gen. 1–11 is a potpourri of sagas (chs. 2, 4, 6–8), myths (3:1–24; 6:1–4), narrative-like material in theological outlines (1:1–2:3; 9:1–17), and genealogies (chs. 5, 10; 11:10–32). These disparate materials were edited and shaped by the appropriate distribution of "these are the *tôl*^{e}*ḏôṯ* of." About the origin of all this material we cannot be clear.

The patriarchal narratives represent a cluster of originally independent materials (an Abraham cycle, an Isaac cycle, a Jacob/Joseph cycle). Each of these cycles is composed of independent individual sagas and larger narrative complexes as well (esp. in the Jacob cycle). At some point these patriarchal narratives were pulled together and united by the theme of divine promise. It is important for Rendtorff's thesis to argue that the promise motif in Genesis is not a part of the original narratives. Rather, the promise theme is a redactional element. He so argues on the basis that, in his estimation, the promises in the Genesis narratives are only loosely connected with those narratives and additionally are confined almost exclusively to divine speeches or citations of these addresses. They were inserted to give unity and continuity to the various cycles and to the collection of these cycles. Given

22. Rendtorff, *Problem,* p. 148.

23. Thus, 12:1–3, far from being a continuation of chs. 1–11, marks a new beginning.

the fact of the heavy emphasis of descendants and land in these promises, Rendtorff suggests that this editing took place at a time when the existence of the people and their possession of land was questionable, that is, during the Exile. As for the entire Pentateuch, Rendtorff suggests that these large, independent units were all joined together at least in a first collection by a Deuteronomic redactor after the Exile, which was then followed by a Priestly stratum of revision. Of the two schools the Deuteronomistic circles played a larger and more crucial role in the redaction of the Pentateuch.

How shall we assess Rendtorff? In some ways he does not repudiate the documentary hypothesis as much as he presents it in a new disguise. In essence he too ends up with a multilayered Genesis, and he will need to demonstrate that his composite Genesis stands up under scrutiny better than does Wellhausen's composite Genesis. In our judgment he rightly takes to task those who would speak not of the theology of Genesis or of the Pentateuch, but of the theologies of Genesis and of the Pentateuch. He is impatient, and rightly so, with those who would claim to decipher the Yahwist's theology in Genesis, or the Elohist's.[24] But then he sanctifies a kindred fragmentation of Genesis by proposing to write a theology of the primeval history or of the Abraham cycle. Clearly Rendtorff has no interest in a holistic interpretation of Genesis' theology, perhaps because he believes it demonstrates none. It is possible to replace Wellhausen's three sources (JEP) with Rendtorff's four blocks of tradition (primeval history, Abraham cycle, Jacob cycle, Joseph novella), but the changes are more cosmetic than substantive.

Many of Rendtorff's views rest upon his heavily used argument from silence. He discovers, for example, nothing in the subsequent blocks of tradition in the Pentateuch which reflects knowledge and conscious use of the promise speeches in the patriarchal unit. Since Exodus and Numbers do not refer to the patriarchs and the promises made to them (except for later sources, i.e., P), he concludes that the connection of the patriarchs and the Exodus tradition is only redactional.

This position sidesteps a number of pre-Priestly references in the Pentateuch which clearly unite the two. Certainly verses like Gen. 15:13–16; 46:3–4; and 50:24–25 anticipate the major motifs of Exodus–Numbers (exodus—sojourn—conquest). In the other direction, Rendtorff overlooks the significance of the four references to the patriarchs in Exod. 3:6, 15, 16; 4:5. To be sure, none of these passages replays the promise theme, but in each

24. The best example of which is H. Wolff and W. Brueggemann, *The Vitality of Old Testament Traditions* (Atlanta: John Knox, 1975).

of them one finds the phrase "the God of your/their father(s)" in the mouth of God. Whenever this phrase occurs in Genesis as an address by or to deity, it is always used in connection with the promises of God to the patriarchs (Gen. 26:24; 28:13; 32:9; 46:3).[25]

The argument from silence betrays another weakness. Let us look at two other blocks of pentateuchal traditions. Because the exodus theme is not found in the wilderness theme, shall we conclude that the unity between the Exodus and the wilderness sojourn is only apparent?[26] Clearly, no. Yet that is precisely what Rendtorff has done in juxtaposing Genesis and Exodus. It is not exodus themes in the wilderness unity that unites the two sections, but rather the presence of Moses. Similarly, what unites Genesis and the Exodus tradition is not a resurfacing of the promises per se, but rather a reading of Exodus that sees the Exodus tradition as a fulfillment of those promises.

One may also argue whether the promises to the fathers are as tangential to the Genesis narratives as Rendtorff would claim. Granted, some of the promises may be secondary, but it seems to be going too far to confine all the patriarchal promises to the Priestly redactors. Stripped of the promises, many of these narratives become pointless. Think, for example, how much of the Abraham narrative is rooted in the tension created by the absence of an heir and the presence of a sterile spouse. Abraham moves from perplexity and annoyance to final triumph and possession. All of these dynamics are surrendered if one extrapolates the divine promises from the stories. And in that case the talents of the Priestly redactors contrast boldly with the blandness of the original storytellers.

Before we move further in this survey, it may be profitable to ask whether anything analogous to JEDP as an explanation of a composition's history may be documented from literature of the ancient Near East. That is, do we have any evidence that an epic went through various stages of composition that involved revision (through addition or deletion) and conflation? Now, even a lack of evidence does not in itself invalidate the theory of an evolutionary Genesis. The absence of parallels may no more challenge a position than the presence of parallels confirms automatically a position. Conservative biblical scholarship in particular has been quite vocal in its assertion that one of the most serious flaws in the documentary hypothesis is the inability of its adherents to provide evidence from ancient literature of a similar phenomenon.

While the evidence is not copious, we would draw attention to J. H.

25. See J. Van Seters, response to Rendtorff, *JSOT* 3/3 (1977) 18.
26. See G. Coats, response to Rendtorff, *JSOT* 3/3 (1977) 30–31.

Tigay's studies of the Samaritan Pentateuch (SP) and the Gilgamesh Epic.[27] On the first of these, Tigay maintains, using portions from Exodus, that the Samaritan Exodus represents a conflate text of the "Masoretic" Exodus and the "Masoretic" Deuteronomy. A comparison of the three suggested to Tigay that the SP often reconciles conflicting accounts in Exodus (MT) and Deuteronomy (MT), and in the process often was forced either to drop a phrase or to add a detail here and there, and even to rearrange some of the inherited material. In other words, some kind of finished or canonical SP represents a reworking and redacting of earlier traditions. In the SP one can uncover four strata: (1) a Masoretic Exodus; (2) a Masoretic Deuteronomy; (3) a proto-Samaritan layer (from Qumran); (4) the Samaritan Pentateuch.

Of course, one is dealing here with four extant, objective documents. We have access to the Masoretic Exodus and Deuteronomy, the proto-Samaritan Exodus manuscript from Qumran, and the SP. To put the issue in reverse, having only the last of these documents, would it have been possible to reconstruct the first three on the basis of the SP? Tigay has not necessarily provided empirical evidence for the documentary hypothesis; rather, he has provided substantiation for a universally accepted axiom: that ancient writers freely compiled from other works. Whether it is the use of Samuel–Kings in Chronicles, or the use of Mark or Q by the other Synoptics, scholars agree that this practice was widespread.

As for the Gilgamesh Epic, Tigay documents the well-known evolution of the Epic from separate Sumerian sources, to a more integrated form by the Old Babylonian period, and to a final form in the Neo-Assyrian period. At the beginning of the 2nd millennium B.C. there were five independent Sumerian Gilgamesh Epics. From some of these five versions (only one of which survived after the Sumerian period) a single Babylonian epic was compiled. This version also passed through stages of development until it reached its "canonical" form in the time of Ashurbanipal. This last stage, that is, the standard Babylonian version, represents the quintessential stage of an epic that had a chequered literary history spanning almost two thousand years.

Scholars who study the cuneiform literature of Mesopotamia have a luxury not available to biblical scholars—the availability of copies of literary texts spanning two-and-a-half to three millennia. Thus the ability to trace the development of text over centuries becomes much easier. The biblical scholar

27. On the former, see J. H. Tigay, "An Empirical Basis for the Documentary Hypothesis," *JBL* 94 (1975) 329–42; on the latter, see idem, *The Evolution of the Gilgamesh Epic* (Philadelphia: University of Pennsylvania, 1982).

must remain content with a relatively static number of texts, most of which are far removed from the autographs. One may, therefore, trace the development of something like the Gilgamesh Epic with much more confidence than the development of Genesis. A multiedited Gilgamesh Epic is empirically verifiable. A multiedited Genesis remains, at best, a hypothesis. The recovery of several editions of Genesis or the discovery of the antecedent documents is the only sure way of putting the issue to rest once and for all.

The most recent challenges to the mainstream view that stresses heterogeneity in Genesis are coming from a school or a discipline that may be described as rhetorical criticism. Leading the way here is Isaac M. Kikawada.[28] Kikawada is not hostile to JEDP. In the very first sentence of the book he coauthored with Arthur Quinn they pay profound gratitude to this approach: "No thesis has had a more liberating effect on biblical scholarship during the past hundred years than the documentary hypothesis of the Pentateuch."[29] Yet in the last chapter they state, "We offer a persuasive refutation of the documentary analysis of Genesis 1–11. . . . One thing, if anything, we are certain of: the documentary hypothesis at present is woefully overextended."[30]

To reach that conclusion, the authors demonstrate that the rhetorical features of Gen. 1–11 are so distinctly woven into one tapestry as to constitute an unassailable case for the unity of the section, and most likely composition by a single hand. In particular they find chiasmus in these biblical accounts. For example, Gen. 1–11 demonstrates a five-part structure (Creation [1:1–2:3]; First Threat [2:4–3:24]; Second Threat [4:1–26]; Final Threat [5:1–9:29]; Resolution [10:1–11:32]) that mirrors very closely a five-part structure in the Atrahasis Epic. In addition, this five-part structure of Gen. 1–11 also parallels the chiastic, five-part structure of Genesis as a whole (Creation, Adam, Cain, Flood, Dispersion//Primeval History, Abraham, Isaac, Jacob, Joseph). In fact, Gen. 1–11 or Gen. 1–50 also provides parallels with a chiastic, three-part Pentateuch (Genesis is a foretelling of the Exodus; Exodus–Numbers is the Exodus story; Deuteronomy is a retelling of the Exodus).[31] It is refreshing to note that on more than one occasion Kikawada

28. I. M. Kikawada, "The Shape of Genesis 11:1–9," in *Rhetorical Criticism: Essays in Honor of James Muilenburg,* ed. J. J. Jackson and M. Kessler, PTMS 1 (Pittsburgh: Pickwick, 1974), pp. 18–32; I. M. Kikawada and A. Quinn, *Before Abraham Was: The Unity of Genesis 1–11* (Nashville: Abingdon, 1985).

29. Kikawada and Quinn, *Before Abraham Was,* p. 9.

30. Ibid., p. 125.

31. Is it coincidence that Kikawada and Quinn divide their own book into five chapters, chiastically arranged? The central chapter of the book is the third, and

and Quinn pay their respects to the late Umberto Cassuto and his literary analysis of the opening chapters of Genesis. For all too long Cassuto's views on Genesis have been lampooned and harpooned as uncritical and apologetic, and therefore of little interest to the serious, "critical" scholar. Kikawada and Quinn will have nothing to do with such patronizing.

Kikawada is, of course, primarily concerned with Gen. 1–11, and only minimally with the rest of Genesis, and even less with the remainder of the Pentateuch. And nowhere does he expressly posit a date for the composition of Gen. 1–11. Yet he does suggest that the structure of Gen. 1–11 is shared with the older Atrahasis Epic, a point not without some possible implications for the antiquity of Gen. 1–11. Furthermore, the replication of the structure of Gen. 1–11 in the later history of the Davidic monarchy (Adam and Eve parallel David and Bathsheba; Cain and Abel parallel Amnon and Absalom; Noah and the Flood parallel the rebellion of Absalom; the tower of Babel parallels Solomon and his temple) is not accidental. Kikawada happily disagrees with those who would use these parallels to argue that the events of court history were used to shape the sequence of primeval history in Genesis.[32] If, however, Kikawada is correct in his contention that the sequence of Gen. 1–11 is derived from a common, and early, Near Eastern tradition, then the likelihood is increased that primeval history provided a base on which the later events of court history were patterned. The author of Gen. 1–11 is not a court theologian celebrating the monarchy. Rather, the author of Samuel–Kings is a court theologian celebrating primeval history.

In sum, let us reemphasize that Kikawada's primary concern is to provide empirical evidence that Gen. 1–11 is anything but a patchwork. In this endeavor he succeeds admirably in our judgment. A frontal assault has been made on the cherished position that Gen. 1–11 is a composite of J and P materials. Thus the detection of two Creation stories or two Flood stories based on different names for deity and inconsistencies loses its appeal. The case for homogeneity is much greater than the case for heterogeneity.

A recent study on Genesis by Gary Rendsburg also marshals convinc-

---

it carries the book's title. It is flanked by chapters two ("Many Noahs, Many Floods") and four ("One Noah, One Flood"). Chapters 1 and 5 also parallel each other ("Before the Patriarchs Were: Genesis 1–11 as a Paradigm of Biblical Diversity" and "After Abraham Was: Genesis 1–11 as a Paradigm of Biblical Unity"). There is even a brief Prologue balanced by an equally brief Epilogue.

32. Cf. W. A. Brueggemann, "David and His Theologian," *CBQ* 30 (1968) 156–81. Brueggemann's article is filled with stimulating and fresh insights; unfortunately, in my opinion, he draws an invalid conclusion from his discoveries.

ing arguments against understanding Genesis as a conflate of J, E, and P.[33] Employing a form of rhetorical criticism, Rendsburg makes a strong case for a purposeful literary structure in the primeval history, the Abraham cycle, the Jacob cycle, and the Joseph cycle. So uniform is each of these units that Rendsburg is prepared to posit one compiler or collator for each of them. He even opens the door to the possibility that these four compilers may be one and the same person, thus suggesting a single editor or author for all of Genesis. This is only a possibility, and an unprovable possibility at that. The Kikawada-Quinn study mentioned above moves us more in that direction, however, than does Rendsburg's. It does what the Rendsburg theory does not do, in that it proposes an integrating structure for Genesis. Rendsburg is content to propose an integrating structure for each of the four cycles only.

As for a possible date when these collations may have been penned, Rendsburg suggests the time of David-Solomon. He does so primarily on the basis of historical allusions in Genesis.[34] For example, the relationship between Jacob and Esau is a reflection of Israelite-Edomite relationships during the time of David (Esauites/Edomites serve Jacobites/Israelites). At the same time Rendsburg hastens to add that much in Genesis antedates the 10th century B.C., a point illustrated by (1) the absence of Yahwistic names in Genesis (which were very popular during the early monarchy); (2) the unique divine names in Genesis; (3) the presence in Genesis of customs that are outlawed by later pentateuchal law; and (4) if one accepts the Genesis stories as illustrative of epic literature, let it be remembered that Near Eastern epic literature (Ugaritic, Egyptian, and Babylonian) was in its apogee in the 2nd millennium. Homeric epic would be the only sure Mediterranean epic literature from the early part of the 1st millennium.

Rendsburg is at his best when he deals with the JEP approach to Genesis. He suggests, in the light of his study, that the documentary hypothesis is "untenable" and should be "discarded."[35] Let us take two illustrations from his study of the Abraham Cycle to show his method of analysis. First, according to traditional source criticism, Gen. 12:1–9 is mostly from J and Gen. 22:1–19 is from E (the first uses "Yahweh" for deity and the second uses "Elohim"). Thus these two accounts about Abra(ha)m were written one hundred years apart from each other, and in different parts of Canaan: 12:1–9

33. G. A. Rendsburg, *The Redaction of Genesis* (Winona Lake, IN: Eisenbrauns, 1986).

34. Following the study of B. Mazar, "The Historical Background of the Book of Genesis," *JNES* 28 (1969) 73–83.

35. Rendsburg, *Redaction of Genesis,* pp. 104–5.

in the south, 22:1–19 in the north. Now it is undeniable, as Cassuto first pointed out, that 12:1–9 and 22:1–19 are connected with each other. Rendsburg lists sixteen parallels or correspondences between the two sections.[36] Three explanations are possible. (1) We have a catena of delightful serendipities. That is, J and E quite inadvertently a century apart from each other wrote accounts about two different events in the life of the same person that literally dovetailed perfectly with each other. (2) Some redactor reworked his sources in such a way that he produced literary symmetry out of a jigsaw puzzle. (3) Whoever wrote 12:1–9 was also responsible for 22:1–19. Rendsburg thinks the third explanation is best.

Second, source criticism suggests, on the one hand, that everything in Gen. 12–16 (with the possible exception of ch. 14) is from J. In these chapters the patriarch is styled only as "Abram." On the other hand, the material in Gen. 17–22 is a composite of J, E, and P. It is the Priestly tradition (ch. 17) that informs us that "Abram" became "Abraham." Yet when one moves into chs. 18 and 19 (a J narrative about the Sodom-Gomorrah incident) one finds the Priestly name "Abraham," not the Yahwistic name "Abram." How might J have used "Abraham" when that name is Priestly and thus several hundred years later than J? It is most unlikely that a final editor made the necessary stylistic changes. Any redactor who was not bothered by "inconsistencies" in the Creation or Flood traditions he received, or in the interchange of the names "Jacob" and "Israel," would not feel compelled to smooth out the Abram-Abraham shift.

One final contribution to the question of Genesis' origin is the work of the Swedish scholar Sven Tengström.[37] He joins with his Scandinavian colleagues in expressing his disenchantment with source criticism and even with form and tradition criticism. At the same time, he parts company with his Scandinavian peers when he plays down any significant role for oral tradition in the development of the Hexateuch (i.e., Genesis–Joshua).

In brief, his main thesis is as follows. In broad terms the Hexateuch is a literary unit composed at or near Shechem by someone best described as an author rather than a compiler, and at some point prior to the rise of the monarchy in Israel. This earliest text, which he labels as the *Urerzahlung* (original story) or the *Gründerzahlung* (foundational story), is described as

36. Ibid., pp. 32–33.

37. S. Tengström, *Die Hexateucherzählung: Eine literaturgeschichtliche Studie,* ConBOT 7 (Lund: Gleerup, 1976). It is interesting that three major monographs (Van Seters's, Rendtorff's, and Tengström's) were published in 1975–76, each challenging the Wellhausen consensus from radically different perspectives.

"a thoroughly composite epic work."[38] The basic theme that runs like a cable through this *Gründerzahlung* is the tradition of the promises to the patriarchs and their subsequent fulfillment, especially in Joshua with the acquisition of the promised land. Several centuries later, according to Tengström, the Deuteronomists built on to the original *Erzahlung* with additions like the book of Deuteronomy. Finally, P represents a later reworking of the expanded text that he inherited from the Deuteronomistic school.

The linchpin in Tengström's thesis is the role of Shechem. To this subject he devotes the middle two chapters of his book. If parts of the Hexateuch were composed during the heyday of the united monarchy (David-Solomon), then why is Jerusalem scarcely mentioned, and why, by constrast, is Shechem so prominent from Gen. 12:6 to Josh. 24:1? Of course, Tengström is well aware of Gen. 14 and its Salem-Jerusalem orientation, but he feels no problem about dismissing Gen. 14 from the original epic as a *Fremdkörper* (foreign body).

Tengström is at least opening the door to several possibilities normally not welcomed in pentateuchal studies. His emphasis on a single author rather than a series of authors or compilers for the earliest text of the Hexateuch is one. Another is his repeated call to deal with the text that we have, and the text we have as a whole, rather than parts of it. The sum is greater than its parts. Third is his opposition to the consensus that would date Israel's first writing to the time of the united monarchy (apart from some archaic poetry). Fourth is his rejection of attempts to date the Yahwist late in Israel's history, and the replacement of this late source with an eleventh-century B.C. epical *Gründerzahlung*. Fifth is his emphasis on the theological unity of the Hexateuch, which is an extension of the literary unity of the Hexateuch.[39]

Tengström's handling of sections of Scripture is not without problems. We have already alluded to his out-of-hand deletion of Gen. 14 because it does not "fit" his central thesis. It seems a poor hermeneutical process to line up one's thesis, then dismiss from that structure anything that is not supportive of that thesis. Also, Tengström prefers as original the tribal order of the sons of Jacob in the birth narratives (chs. 29–30) over the order of the sons in the Blessing of Jacob (ch. 49), primarily because chs. 29–30, which

38. On "epic" see C. Conroy, "Hebrew Epic: Historical Notes and Critical Reflections," *Bib* 61 (1980) 1–30.

39. One of the more sympathetic treatments of Tengström is found in E. E. Carpenter, "Recent Pentateuchal Studies," *Asbury Theological Journal* 41 (1986) 19–35, esp. pp. 23–29.

he believes organizes the tribes geographically around Shechem, is more palatable to his thesis. His suggestion that 11:27–13:18 (minus the intrusive 12:10–20) marks the beginning of the *Gründerzahlung* is wholly arbitrary. This suggestion, if correct, cuts the Gordian knot between the call of Abraham and the primeval history (chs. 1–11), and discounts any connection between the two. It effectively removes the patriarchs from fulfilling any function of divine redress to the spread of sin delineated in chs. 3–11. The patriarchs then become a *creatio ex nihilo*. The above criticisms notwithstanding, we believe that Tengström has raised many valid points about the date, provenance, and structure of much of the hexateuchal materials.

Using the computer, Y. T. Radday and H. Shore have recently subjected the language of Genesis to a thorough word-level linguistic analysis.[40] In essence, their work is an attempt to throw light on the authorship of Genesis by means of computer investigation. Throughout their study one question is constantly raised: to what degree may one calculate the probability that any one section of Genesis attributed, say, to J, was written by the same person to whom an E or P section is ascribed? The authors analyzed the 20,504 words in Genesis, for each of which nine pieces of information (mostly grammatical) were recorded. Two of these nine bits of data involved identifying to which of the three sources (J, E, P) documentarians ascribed this particular word, and the placement of a siglum beside each word indicating whether the word occurs in the narrator's description (N), in direct human speech (H), or in direct divine speech (D).

For convenience Genesis was divided into three major divisions: (a) the Prologue (chs. 1–11); (b) the Main Body (chs. 12–36); (c) the Epilogue (chs. 37–50), with (a) representing 19 percent of the whole; (b) representing 52 percent of the whole; and (c) representing 31 percent of the whole. The distribution, in percentages, of N, H, and D throughout the three sections of Genesis was as follows:

	1–11	12–36	37–50
N:	74%	56%	53%
H:	5%	34%	47%
D:	21%	10%	0%

The authors conclude on the basis of their studies that the only real difference in Genesis is between N and H-D (i.e., between narrative speech and direct speech). They strongly oppose the existence of J over against E.

40. Y. T. Radday and H. Shore, *Genesis: An Authorship Study in Computer-Assisted Statistical Analysis,* AnBib 103 (Rome: Biblical Institute, 1985).

In fact, for them J = E. Only P is granted some minimal possibility of autonomy, but more likely this is due to subject matter rather than to different authorship. Two letters written by the same person, one a legal brief to be read in court and the other a personal letter to his fiancée, would evidence a radically different style. In the following sentence Radday and Shore present their final position: "with all due respect to the illustrious Documentarians past and present, there is massive evidence that the pre-Biblical triplicity of Genesis, which their line of thought postulates to have been worked over by a late and gifted editor into a trinity, is actually a unity."[41]

Radday's and Shore's work has not proved the Mosaic authorship of Genesis, although they would have eliminated that possibility had their studies come down in favor of Genesis' heterogeneity rather than homogeneity. Even the invalidation of Genesis as J + E + P does not establish the unity of Genesis per se. In fact, using Radday's and Shore's own findings, Shemaryahu Talmon, in a stimulating response essay in the same volume, proposes a novel theory of Genesis' composition. Using the internal consistency in language behavior of H and D, and their mutual difference from the language behavior of N, he suggests that N made use of preexisting materials which he incorporated into his composition by quoting verbatim D(ivine) and H(uman) speeches from these *Vorlagen*.[42]

It will be interesting to see whether any subsequent computer studies of the Torah confirm or challenge Radday's and Shore's analysis of the Hebrew text of Genesis. More than likely, others using computers in biblical studies will challenge the propriety of the type of information that Radday and Shore have fed the computer or the method they have pursued. Questions are already beginning to arise from this quarter.[43]

Until the rise of source criticism in the 18th century, the unity of Genesis was taken for granted, with an occasional disclaimer to be heard only here or there. A concomitant of this position was the teaching of the Mosaic authorship of Genesis (and of the rest of the Pentateuch). It is accurate to say that those in the 20th century who have advocated that position are in the minority. To argue for the Mosaic authorship of Genesis was akin to arguing for the flatness of the earth. Among Jewish scholars, Benno Jacob, Umberto

41. Ibid., p. 190. Conservative scholars will no doubt applaud this conclusion, but it needs to be balanced by Radday's earlier computer analysis of Isaiah, *The Unity of Iṣaiah in the Light of Statistical Linguistics* (Hildesheim: Gerstenberg, 1973), which supports "two Isaiahs."

42. Talmon, in Radday and Shore, *Genesis,* pp. 232–33.

43. For example, E. Talstra, "Genesis Bit by Bit," *Bib* 67 (1986) 557–64.

Cassuto, and M. H. Segal have been most vocal in their defense of the unity of Genesis' authorship and composition.[44] While not dealing per se with Genesis, Cyrus H. Gordon's evaluations of the documentary hypothesis are also worthy of note.[45] In our judgment Cassuto has mounted the most convincing case against JEDP, and yet most of his conclusions have been ignored by the establishment of biblical scholarship, primarily because in their opinion his conclusions are rooted in polemics and apologetics, rather than in undistilled scholarship.

Turning to the Christian tradition, one notes that it is the evangelical wing of Protestantism that continues to provide the majority of voices who support the unitary (and Mosaic) character of Genesis. From an earlier day one might cite the works of W. H. Green, James Orr, and O. T. Allis, and later J. S. Wright and E. J. Young.[46]

In more recent times the dominant contributions have come from K. A. Kitchen and R. K. Harrison.[47] Kitchen's work in particular has been aimed more at the demolition of the documentary hypothesis than at the substantiation of a Bronze Age, unitary Genesis. Perhaps he believes that in refuting the former, he automatically establishes the latter.

Kitchen's main argument with JEDP is that such a theory of literature formation is anomalous in the ancient Near East. His most programmatic statement is as follows: "Now, nowhere in the Ancient Orient is there

44. B. Jacob, *Das erste Buch der Tora—Genesis* (Berlin: Schocken, 1934; abridged English translation, *The First Book of the Bible: Genesis* [New York: Ktav, 1974]); U. Cassuto, *A Commentary on the Book of Genesis,* 2 vols., tr. I. Abrahams (Jerusalem: Magnes, 1961–64). Cassuto addressed critically the larger issue of the documentary hypothesis in *The Documentary Hypothesis and the Composition of the Pentateuch,* tr. I. Abrahams (Jerusalem: Magnes, 1961); see also M. H. Segal, *The Pentateuch: Its Composition and Authorship and Other Studies* (Jerusalem: Magnes, 1967).

45. C. H. Gordon, "Higher Critics and the Forbidden Fruit," in *A Christianity Today Reader* (New York: Meredith, 1966), pp. 67–73.

46. W. H. Green, *The Higher Criticism of the Pentateuch* (New York: Charles Scribner's Sons, 1896); J. Orr, *The Problem of the Old Testament* (New York: Charles Scribner's Sons, 1906); O. T. Allis, *The Five Books of Moses* (Philadelphia: Presbyterian Publishing Co., 1943); J. S. Wright, *How Moses Compiled Genesis* (Grand Rapids: Eerdmans, 1946); E. J. Young, *An Introduction to the Old Testament* (Grand Rapids: Eerdmans, 1952), pp. 109–53.

47. K. A. Kitchen, *Ancient Orient and Old Testament* (Chicago: Inter-Varsity, 1966), esp. pp. 112–46; idem, *The Bible in Its World* (Downers Grove, IL: Inter-Varsity, 1978); idem, "The Old Testament in its Context 1," *TSF Bulletin* 59 (1971) 2–10; R. K. Harrison, *Introduction to the Old Testament* (Grand Rapids: Eerdmans, 1969), pp. 542–65; "Genesis," *ISBE,* 2:431–43.

anything which is definitely known to parallel the elaborate history of fragmentary composition and conflation of Hebrew literature . . . as the documentary hypothesis would postulate."[48] This statement, at first very impressive, is marginally inaccurate and probably, in the long run, irrelevant. True, no one has yet advanced the equivalent of a JEDP theory for the origin of any notable hieroglyphic or cuneiform document, but we have drawn attention above to Tigay's study of both the Gilgamesh Epic and the SP that shows the growth of a composition over a period of time and the weaving of different accounts into one fabric. Furthermore, the absence or presence of a parallel is not the acid test for establishing legitimacy. Perhaps the Hebrews were unique in producing such a composition. After all, what other ancient society produced the equivalent of a Bible or a Torah corpus? At the same time that Kitchen discounts any parallels to a composite Genesis, he eagerly (and correctly) accepts parallels from Near Eastern literature in order to establish historicity for the patriarchs. Unlike most who write in this area, he is able, because of his training in Egyptology, to bring in many parallels from the hieroglyphic world.

As far as Genesis itself is concerned, Kitchen's position is that quite possibly Genesis was "composed as we have it about the time of the Exodus. . . . Proclaimed to the tribes before the exodus or en route to Sinai. . . . The most fitting author would be the man mandated to lead them towards that destiny, namely Moses."[49]

In the previous section on "Structure" we have already referred to the view of R. K. Harrison. He suggests that Gen. 1–36 originally had an independent existence as eleven, distinct cuneiform tablets, each with its own identifying colophon. It would have been "a comparatively easy matter for a talented person such as Moses to compile the canonical book by arranging the tablets in a rough chronological order, adding the material relating to Joseph, and transcribing the entire corpus on a leather or papyrus roll."[50]

Let it be admitted that Kitchen's written-in-Egypt Genesis and Harrison's tablet-Genesis are only possibilities, and are therefore neither more nor less hypothetical than Wellhausen's JEP Genesis or Rendtorff's *Überlieferungen* Genesis. In a book that is patently anonymous, and where all original texts have long since disappeared, it is most likely that a project to determine Genesis' authorship and mode of composition is doomed from the start.

48. Kitchen, *Ancient Orient and Old Testament,* p. 115.
49. Kitchen, *TSF Bulletin* 59 (1971) 9.
50. Harrison, "Genesis," *ISBE,* 2:437.

More than likely several more decades of research into this issue and the appearance of four or five more monographs will not succeed in resolving the issue. What it will do is add four or five more options to the pile we already have. Theories about Genesis' origin grow like the old pagan pantheons. New ideas are added; old ideas are never discarded. For some this all boils down to an exercise in futility. For others this is the genius of scholarship, the endless (literally!) pursuit of empirical truth, "always searching, but never coming to a [consensus] knowledge of the truth" (2 Tim. 3:7).

We do not believe that an evangelical view of Scripture is necessarily wedded to the Mosaic authorship of Genesis, as if one cannot have the first without having the second. "Composite" is not a synonym for "errant." Nor is it incumbent that one read Genesis as a "seamless garment" in order for that view of Scripture to be sustained. Even those who do so believe would be prepared to admit that Genesis gives clear evidence of a post-Mosaic touching up and contemporization (as in the frequent phrase, "until this day").

Still, it is not without significance that recent studies have tended to support the essential unity of Genesis. Leading the way are insights gleaned from discourse grammar (Andersen), rhetorical criticism (Kikawada and Quinn; Rendsburg), and literary/aesthetic criticism (Alter and Sternberg).[51]

IV. THEOLOGY

Many biblical scholars would dispute the attempt even to discuss a theology of Genesis. Such an exercise, they would claim, promises far more than it can ever produce. In its place they would promote the theologies of Genesis,

51. F. I. Andersen, *The Sentence in Biblical Hebrew* (The Hague/Paris: Mouton, 1974); R. Alter, *The Art of Biblical Narrative* (New York: Basic Books, 1981); M. Sternberg, *The Poetics of Biblical Narrative* (Bloomington: Indiana University, 1985). One quote from Alter and one from Sternberg will suffice: "The biblical writers and redactors . . . had certain notions of unity rather different from our own, and that the fullness of statement they aspired to achieve as writers in fact led them at times to violate what a later age and culture would be disposed to think of as canons of unity and logical coherence. The biblical text may not be the whole cloth imagined by pre-modern Judeo-Christian tradition, but the confused textual patchwork that scholarship has often found to displace such earlier views may prove upon further scrutiny to be purposeful pattern" (Alter, p. 133). "Traditional speculations about documents and sources and twice-told tales have now piled up so high on the altar of genesis as to obscure the one remarkable fact in sight, which bears on poetics. Granting the profusion of variants that went into the making of the Bible, the fact remains that the finished discourse never introduces them *as* variants but rather strings them together into continuous action" (Sternberg, p. 127).

say, the theology of the Yahwist or of the Elohist (Wolff and Brueggemann), or the theology of the Abraham cycle and of the Jacob cycle (Rendtorff). Where an attempt is made to discern some overarching theme or motif in Genesis that transcends literary sources or blocks of tradition, an impasse is still encountered in the attempt to dovetail primeval history (chs. 1–11) with patriarchal history (chs. 12–50).

Let us begin by concentrating on patriarchal history, since it constitutes approximately four-fifths of Genesis. Almost everybody who has written on the subject agrees that the theme of divine promise unites the patriarchal cycles. This is not to say that some form of promise from deity appears in every chapter, or that every single narrative is informed principally by the promise theme. In fact, in numerous narratives in Genesis the dynamics are created by the presence of a subsidiary theme. The above consensus does claim, however, that the connecting bridge over which one passes most frequently from narrative to narrative within Gen. 12–50 is the theme of divine promise.

One might cite with approval von Rad's statement on the final text of Genesis: "The whole has nevertheless a scaffolding supporting it and connecting it, the so-called promise to the patriarchs. At least it can be said that this whole variegated mosaic of studies is given cohesion of subject-matter . . . by means of the constantly recurring divine promise."[1] Brevard Childs makes the same point with his statement that the promises in Genesis provide "the constant element in the midst of all the changing situations of this very chequered history."[2]

It is, of course, a highly disputed question whether these many promises scattered throughout Gen. 12–50 are original in the narratives where they are found, or whether they are secondary and later additions. We now have five recent studies on this subject (by Hoftijzer, Westermann, Rendtorff, Lohfink, and Emerton), and although they approach the issue from different angles, all agree that the majority of these promise speeches are accretions. Having made that determination, they must then decide which promise (or form of the promise) is primary and which is secondary, at what particular points in the historical spectrum these promises were inserted, and what was the rationale, the stimulation for the insertion of such promises at such a time.

1. G. von Rad, *Old Testament Theology,* tr. D. M. G. Stalker, 2 vols. (New York: Harper & Row, 1962–65), 1:167.

2. B. S. Childs, *Introduction to the Old Testament as Scripture* (Philadelphia: Westminster, 1979), p. 151.

J. Hoftijzer is most skeptical about the originality of promises in the patriarchal narratives.[3] He suggests that they are all secondary, except for the promises of Gen. 15, and were inserted shortly before the Exile in order to bolster the confidence of a people soon to be without land, perhaps without descendants, under the judgment of God, and with a very uncertain future. Classifying as he does the bulk of the promises into an "El Shaddai" group (corresponding to P in the Pentateuch), Hoftijzer refuses to entertain the possibility that these kinds of themes could have arisen during the days of the early monarchy, or even earlier.

C. Westermann handles the issue a bit differently.[4] He discerns seven originally independent promises in the Genesis narratives: (1) a son; (2) a new territory; (3) aid; (4) the land; (5) increase; (6) blessing; (7) covenant. Only the first three are rooted in the patriarchal period; the remaining four belong to later stages of the tradition and are the products of subsequent theological reflection. It is no accident that Westermann lists first the promise of a son, for in his judgment this is the primary form of the promise tradition.

R. Rendtorff's major thesis is that the evidence for stages in the development of the promises is to be seen in the way they are formulated.[5] He focuses on two of the promises in Genesis, that of land and that of mediated blessing. Note the following different indirect objects of "give" associated with the land: (1) "I am giving it *to you*" (13:17; 15:7); (2) "I will give it *to you and to your seed*" (13:15; 26:3; 28:13; 35:13); (3) "I will give it *to your seed*" (12:7; 15:18; 24:7). Looking at the second of these promises (mediated blessing), Rendtorff observes the following: (a) "*all families of the earth* shall be blessed [Niphal] in *you*" (12:3 [*in him,* 18:18]); (b) "*all families of the earth* shall be blessed [Niphal] in *you and your seed*" (28:14); (c) "all peoples of the earth shall be blessed [Hithpael] in *your seed*" (22:18; 26:4). For Rendtorff the change in object indicates the stages of development of the promises. First, they were made to Abraham himself. Then "seed" was added to make the promises applicable to post-Abrahamites. Lastly, "seed" replaced the patriarch altogether in the final stage of development. A weakness in this analysis is Rendtorff's penchant for drawing overly fine distinctions based on the placement of a verb or varying objects of a verb. Flexibility and improvisation are categories of literary style that Rendtorff will not entertain.

3. J. Hoftijzer, *Die Verheissungen an die drei Erzvater* (Leiden: Brill, 1956).

4. C. Westermann, *The Promises to the Fathers: Studies on the Patriarchal Narratives,* tr. D. Green (Philadelphia: Fortress, 1980).

5. R. Rendtorff, *Das überlieferungsgeschichtliche Problem des Pentateuch,* BZAW 147 (Berlin/New York: de Gruyter, 1977).

N. Lohfink's study is mostly an investigation of Gen. 15, and particularly the meaning of "covenant" in v. 18.[6] Lohfink agrees strongly with R. Clements that the land promise dwarfs all other promises in Gen. 15. For Clements the "land" is, originally at least, the region around Hebron, possibly to be associated with a local Canaanite cult. For Lohfink, however, Gen. 15 is pre-J in origin, and in its most ancient form the land promise was an incubation narrative which was localized at a Canaanite sanctuary (Shechem?).

J. Emerton votes in favor of those who read the promises as clearly secondary.[7] He is sympathetic with the interpretation that the promises (unconditional as they are) are an unfortunate attempt to evade the challenges of the prophets. The prophets' "you must change your ways or else" is set in collision with "God will, God will." So read, the promises in Genesis come fairly close to playing the same theme as the false prophets. They state that God keeps his promises unconditionally in spite of the prophets' fulminations to the contrary. Emerton also suggests that some explosion of religious zeal (such as Josiah's reform) fostered much of these emphases.

Most of the above views share an insistence that (a) few, if any, of the promises are original with the narratives with which they are presently connected; (b) the entire emphasis on promises in Genesis is the result of a long stage of development through revision and accretion; and (c) the bulk of the promises were added sometime during the late monarchy in order to rejuvenate wilted spirits, and to take the sting out of the threat of exile.

We remain unconvinced that the promissory speeches in Genesis are secondary and late, and in the overview above we have offered some brief responses to these positions. For example, almost anybody who has addressed critically Abraham's offering of Isaac (Gen. 22) agrees that vv. 15–18 are secondary. These four verses are introduced with "Yahweh's angel called to Abraham from heaven a second time," and then comes a series of promises, which this time are rooted in Abraham's obedience (". . . because you have obeyed me"). The sudden shift in the story from "God" (vv. 1–14 [but note "Yahweh" in vv. 11, 14]) to "the angel of Yahweh" indicates a source change, and the awkward phrase "a second time" is a clear editorial phrase

6. N. Lohfink, *Die Landverheissung als Eid* (Stuttgart: Katholisches Bibelwerk, 1967). Lohfink's study may be compared with R. Clements, *Abraham and David: Genesis xv and Its Meaning for Israelite Tradition,* SBT 2/5 (Naperville: Allenson, 1967).

7. J. A. Emerton, "The origin of the promises to the Patriarchs in the older sources of the book of Genesis," *VT* 32 (1982) 14–32.

which functions as a lead-in for the promises. In other words, the story of Isaac's offering originally concluded with v. 14.

The originality of vv. 15–18, however, may be defended on both contextual and structural grounds.[8] The story loses much of its impact if it is truncated by the deletion of vv. 15–18. Lost would be the emphasis that Abraham's act of obedience had a positive result. Because he did not withhold one descendant, he will be given many descendants. The real danger to the promises of God was not the death of Isaac but the disobedience of Abraham. A dead Isaac and an obedient Abraham present a better hope than a living Isaac and a disobedient Abraham. Structurally, the promises of Gen. 22:15–18 balance the promises of 12:2–3.

Even granting the legitimacy, in whole or in part, of the redactional interpretation of the promises, one cannot write a theology of Genesis without consideration of the promises. The attempt to excise the promises from their canonical context and reassign them to a new context, admittedly at best a speculative exercise, almost eliminates the possibility of theologizing on Genesis. It is our position that an articulation of the theology of Genesis is possible only when one has before him a holistic text. Theology must be based on the text as we have it, not on what it might once have been.

Westermann, we saw, discerned seven kinds of promises in Genesis. D. Clines isolates three major promises in the Pentateuch (descendants, relationship, land), and then follows these with later allusions to these promises.[9] His totals are as follows:

1. promise of descendants: Genesis, 19 times
2. promise of relationship: Genesis, 10 times; Exodus, 8 times; Leviticus, 1 time
3. promise of land: Genesis, 13 times; Exodus, 5 times
4. allusions to the promise: Genesis, 17 times; Exodus, 11 times; Leviticus, 11 times; Numbers, 37 times; Deuteronomy, 50 times[10]

Both the life of Abraham and of Jacob are bracketed by divine speeches of promise. God's first word to Abraham is a series of "I will's" (12:1–3), in

8. For the contextual grounds, see J. Van Seters, *Abraham in History and Tradition,* pp. 30–31, 238–39. For the structural grounds, see G. Rendsburg, *Redaction of Genesis,* pp. 33–34.

9. D. J. A. Clines, *The Theme of the Pentateuch,* JSOTSup 10 (Sheffield: JSOT, 1978), pp. 32–43.

10. The proliferation of references throughout Exodus–Deuteronomy to the patriarchal promises argues heavily for the unity of the Pentateuch, at least in its final shape. One must rethink the alleged wide disparity between the patriarchal blocks of tradition in the Pentateuch and the remaining blocks of tradition in the Pentateuch.

which the movement is from imperative (v. 1) to indicative, future tense (vv. 2–3). God's last word to Abraham also begins with an imperative (22:1), and ends with an indicative, future tense (22:15–18). In between these two speeches of promise (12:1–3; 22:15–18) the odyssey of Abraham is detailed.

The same is true of the Jacob story. God's first word to Jacob is a word of promise (28:13–15), as is God's last speech to Jacob (46:3–4). The initial divine speech to Jacob is of special interest when contrasted with the first revelation to Abraham. Abraham receives his revelation outside the land of promise but on the way to the land of promise (Haran). Jacob receives his revelation while he is on his way to Haran (28:10), away from the land of promise.

God's revelation to Abraham comes at the very beginning of the scriptural account of Abraham. Jacob, however, has a number of experiences with his brother and father before God enters the picture. Only after an encounter with Esau and Isaac is there an encounter with God. The interesting point here is that not one word is spoken by God about Jacob's previous behavior with Esau (exploitation) or with Isaac (duplicity). It is ignored. Instead, Jacob becomes the recipient of an unsolicited series of divine promises. He is promised land, descendants, spiritual influence, and the presence of God. If election were based on merit and not on grace, Jacob would never have qualified!

To summarize thus far, Gen. 12–36 (Abraham-Isaac-Jacob) focuses on three individuals (a father, a son, and a grandson) who represent the first three generations of a family whom God has chosen to bless, who have been promised land and descendants who may occupy that land, who have been chosen by God as the means of bringing blessing to the nonchosen. The point is frequently made throughout these chapters of Genesis that the selection of these patriarchs is not based on their behavior. They are not chosen because they are good. They are chosen on the basis of God's sovereign will. Even when they are guilty of highly unethical behavior, God remains true to his promise.

It is clear to the reader of Genesis that the patriarchs are not above engaging in highly questionable behavior. On two occasions Abraham encourages his wife to lie about her identity and places her in a very vulnerable position—in fact, makes her an adulteress (12:10–20). At his wife's suggestion Abraham cohabits with another woman (ch. 16). Isaac imitates his father's duplicity when he too finds himself an alien on foreign soil (ch. 26). Jacob exploits his brother (25:29–34), deceives his father (ch. 27), and even after his spiritual transformation and renaming still lies to Esau (33:12–18). Judah fathers twins by his daughter-in-law, who is disguised as a harlot (ch.

38). And Joseph brings false charges against his brothers ("you are spies") and acts clandestinely to make them look like thieves.

The interesting point in all of these instances of aberrant behavior is that God never clearly rebukes any of the patriarchs. He sends no voice of conscience after them, no Nathan with his condemning "you are the man." The closest element to a divine rebuke is found in Yahweh's word to Abraham about Sarah—"Why did Sarah laugh?" (18:13, followed by the accusation and denial, v. 15). So there is a "Why did Sarah laugh?" but no "Why did Abraham lie?" or "Why did Jacob deceive?" or "Why did Joseph frame?" It is true that Jacob did suffer a number of personal setbacks and tragedies and was himself the victim of deceit on several occasions, and the narration of these misfortunes has led some commentators (Cassuto, Sarna) to see nemesis at work in Jacob's life. Jacob, the source of misery for so many others, is now on the receiving end of retributive justice. But even if this interpretation is valid, the Jacob cycle still does not have any clear-cut divine condemnation of his unethical behavior. Again, if Jacob is called to account, indirectly, for his actions, why are his father and grandfather not treated to similar acts of retributive justice for their actions? Abraham and Isaac seem no better or worse than Jacob.

Now in a number of places in Genesis individuals are held accountable for their sins. Primeval history is loaded with illustrations. Adam and Eve are banished from the garden for their decision to sidestep the divine prohibition. Cain is made a wanderer and refugee for killing Abel. The human life span is radically reduced because of the union of the "sons of God" and the "daughters of men." Noah's ungodly peers drown in the waters of the Flood. The language of the tower builders is confused, thus forcing stoppage of the building program, and the builders are scattered. Gen. 3–11 is quite clear in its message that one cannot sin with impunity or immunity.

Similarly, there are instances in Gen. 12ff. where God judges an individual for a deviant course of action. The sin of Abram (12:10–20) is ignored by the biblical account, but Pharaoh's inadvertent sin in taking Sarai is met with plagues (12:17). The four mighty kings from the East are humiliated and defeated by Abram and his modest force of 318 men (ch. 14). It may be compared with Gideon's nocturnal raiding party of 300 (Judg. 7:8). Sodom and Gomorrah are destroyed because of their depravity (ch. 19). Yahweh closed the wombs of the women in Abimelech's house because Sarah was taken by Abimelech from Abraham (20:18). Only a prevenient revelation from God restrained Laban from punishing Jacob (31:24, 29); otherwise, Laban would have had to contend with Jacob's God.

Of course, all these incidents—except for Gen. 19—are describing a sin of one outside the chosen family (an Egyptian, a Philistine) against a member of the chosen family. Even their sins of ignorance are judged. It may be that narratives like these illustrate one part of the fulfillment of the divine promise within the patriarch's lifetime. One of God's promises to Abram in 12:3 was "and I will curse him who curses you."[11] To curse an Abrahamite includes, among other things, taking his wife. Such action provokes a divine response.[12]

All readers of Genesis have noticed the often dubious, even immoral, antics of the three patriarchs. By itself, this immorality is not unique, for Scripture is loaded with similar incidents in the lives of others of its characters. Witness a Saul, a David, a Solomon, one of the kings, or Israel as a whole (often portrayed as a harlot). In each of those instances, however, the culpable one pays a high price for disregarding God's law.

But the patriarchs escape prosecution. In fact, after the Tower of Babel story in Gen. 11, one does not encounter any story before Exod. 32 in which the followers of God experience the voice of judgment (except for Er and Onan, the sons of Judah, Gen. 38). The golden calf incident is the first event that provokes a negative divine response. Even there, the people are spared total annihilation not because they repent but because God repents. Moses challenges God, and not his people, to repent, and part of Moses' appeal is to God's unilateral promises to the patriarchs (Exod. 32:13).

If Gen. 12–50 is punctuated with stories highlighting unconscionable behavior in the lives of the major actors, so is Exod. 1–31. Why, for instance, does God give his people manna in the desert when they murmur and complain (Exod. 16)? God answers prayer; does he answer grumbling too? Why, then, when they grumble about food a second time (Num. 11), does God send them food, but "while the meat was still between their teeth . . . he struck them with a severe plague" (Num. 11:33)? Both Exod. 16 and Num. 11 describe the same kind of sin, but in Exod. 16 there are no consequences, while in Num. 11 there are grave consequences. Would Exod. 16 and Num. 11 lead us to the conclusion that the God of Israel is inconsistent and

11. In Genesis the curse of God is directed at any who would hurt the bearers of the promise. By contrast, in Deuteronomy or Leviticus the curse is directed at the the bearers of the covenant promises. Genesis says "I will curse him who curses you." Deuteronomy says "I will curse you if. . . ."

12. It is instructive to compare these kinds of stories with Samson's prayer for punitive vindication to redress the humiliation he suffered at the hands of the Philistines (Judg. 16:28). Does God restore Samson's strength because of Samson's prayer, or because the Philistines have "cursed" one of God's own, and will now in turn be cursed? On the root *nqm* in this verse, see G. Mendenhall, *The Tenth Generation* (Baltimore: Johns Hopkins University, 1973), pp. 92–93.

unpredictable? Of course, the difference between Exod. 16 and Num. 11 is that Exod. 16 is about a pre-Sinaitic, pre-covenant sin, and Num. 11 is about a post-Sinaitic, post-covenant sin. The signing and acceptance of a covenant of God makes all the difference in the world. The greater the privileges, the greater the responsiblities. This principle may be illustrated in the different penalties attached to fornication (Exod. 22:16–17), a premarital sexual sin, and adultery (Deut. 22:22), a postmarital sexual sin. In the latter the penalty is death; in the former the penalty is a fine on the man, and marriage with the virgin he seduced if her father approves.

In the light of the divine silence, earlier commentators on Genesis have tried to sidestep the moral, ethical issues or even justify the patriarchs, when those patriarchs were involved in scandalous behavior. Many of the church fathers avoided the problem, primarily by opting for an allegorical reading over against a literal reading of the biblical text. Early Jewish exegesis similarly sidestepped the issue by embellishing the Genesis stories with folklore and legend. Thus, Abraham did not betray Sarah, but rather concealed her in a box.[13] The Reformers, such as Luther and Calvin, argued that the patriarchs were given, albeit temporarily, a special dispensation to break the moral law.[14] For the last four centuries attempts have been made either to exonerate the patriarchs or to dismiss them as curmudgeons of a primitive morality.

Either of these approaches misses the focus of Gen. 12–50. Genesis is not interested in parading Abraham, Isaac, and Jacob as examples of morality. Therefore, it does not moralize on them. What Gen. 12–50 is doing is bringing together the promises of God to the patriarchs and the faithfulness of God in keeping those promises. Even if the bearers of those promises represent the greatest threat to the promises, the individual lives of the promise bearers cannot abort those promises. Whenever they find themselves in a delicate situation (in Egypt, in prison, with another not one's spouse, running from one's brother, in famine), God saves his elected own from destruction. God will no more scrap this chosen family, their moral inadequacies notwithstanding, as an object of his blessing and as the light and salt of the earth's nations, than he would scrap the new covenant equivalent of this family, that is, the church (Gk. *ekklēsía,* "the called").

So then, Gen. 12–50 is to be read as an illustration of God's faithfulness to his promises. These same chapters may not be read as justifying sinful

13. The example is taken from B. S. Childs, *Old Testament Theology in a Canonical Context* (Philadelphia: Fortress, 1985), p. 213.

14. See R. Bainton, "The Immoralities of the Patriarchs according to the Exegesis of the Late Middle Ages and the Reformers," *HTR* 23 (1930) 39–49.

behavior in God's children, as if that is one of their major theological contributions. "To be human is to be sinful (even after redemption)" is a dictum neither of Gen. 12–50 nor of the rest of Scripture. Rather, it borders on a gnostic fallacy that would equate our created humanity with sinfulness.

One may argue that Abram lied about the identity of Sarai in Egypt in order to prevent God's promises from being frustrated. That is, he did a wrong thing for a good reason.[15] How could God make of Abram a great nation if Abram is dead? (Would the same be true of the incident in 20:1ff.?) If that is the motivation for Abram's lie, Gen. 12 (or 20) nowhere hints at it. It is the famine more than Egypt that really threatens Abram's existence. One might also argue that Abram cohabits with Hagar (ch. 16) for the same reason. His first ruse was designed to prevent a dead Abram. His second move, at his wife's suggestion, was designed to overcome a "dead" Sarah. Actually, the only clearly designated threat to these promises is the possibility of a dead Isaac. Abraham fathers Isaac decades after God promised him a special son. Years of waiting and dashed hopes are capped by the birth of a son who is given the infectious name "he laughs" (who is the "he" in "he laughs"?). At some subsequent point the life of this son of promise is placed in jeopardy when God instructs the father to sacrifice that son as a burnt offering. How will the family of promise continue when the second link in that chain is removed?

The story of Isaac is considerably abbreviated in Genesis in comparison to that of Abraham and Jacob. We should not conclude from this lack of attention that Isaac is the ordinary son of an extraordinary father or the ordinary father of an extraordinary son. But Isaac does almost get lost in the shuffle between the first and third generation. It is to his credit, however, that his intercessory prayer solves the problem of Rebekah's sterility (25:21), and the result is a double blessing: twins. While the boys are still in the womb, the divine announcement is made that the older of the twins and the nation he generates will serve the younger and the nation he generates. As with the Abraham narrative, everything here is declaratory, promissory, and eschatological. The selection of Jacob over Esau is a pre-birth announcement. If God had made this declaration, say, near the end of Jacob's life, then the assumption would be that God chose Jacob on the basis of performance rather than on the basis of grace.

Sometime after the birth of the twins and their growing into adulthood, another famine threatens Isaac's family with extinction. The problems presented earlier by a barren wife are now resurrected by a barren land.

15. Much as the ten Boom family of Amsterdam did during World War II when they hid Jews from the Nazis, or when Brother Andrew, a modern missionary, smuggles Bibles into Russia.

Isaac's instinct is to flee to Egypt as his father had done. He is thwarted from doing so by an epiphanic visitation.[16] First Isaac spoke to Yahweh (25:21). Now Yahweh speaks to Isaac (26:2–5). As with Yahweh's first speech to Abram, the progression is from imperative ("do not go down"; "live"; "stay") to future indicatives. The promises include (1) the divine presence; (2) blessing; (3) descendants; (4) land; and (5) oath confirmation.

The interesting added point is that Yahweh makes these promises to Isaac only "because Abraham obeyed me and kept . . . my laws" (26:5). The father's "so Abram left" (12:4) is matched by the son's "so Isaac stayed" (26:6). The direct beneficiary of Abraham's faithful obedience is Isaac. Isaac receives the promises not because of his own behavior, although it is model thus far, but because of his father's behavior. Both Abraham's faith and his obedience pave the way for God's promises to move toward realization. Even Yahweh's promise to be "with Isaac" (26:3, 23) finds immediate fulfillment in the Gerarites' response, "we saw clearly that Yahweh was with you" (26:28). However, the promise of God's presence and blessing with him prevents neither grief (26:35) nor embarrassment and confusion (27:1ff.) for Isaac.

The chapters of Genesis given over to Isaac abound with illustrations of Jacob's bizarre behavior that produced great friction among his relatives. His relationships with his brother Esau, his father Isaac, and his father-in-law Laban appear at times to be strained to the breaking point. Jacob moves from grasping Esau's heel (25:26), to grasping Esau's birthright (25:33), to grasping Esau's blessing (27:1ff.), to grasping for Esau's mercy (33:1ff.). He also infuriates Laban when he leaves Laban's house furtively with Laban's daughters (31:1ff.). Sandwiched between these strife-producing scenarios are encounters with God (28:10–22; 32:22–31). In the first Jacob receives the old promises (28:13–15); in the second he receives the new name (32:28). In the first God's promises are prospective; in the second God's promises are concurrent ("then he blessed him there," v. 29b).

G. Coats has rightfully drawn attention to the proliferation of episodes throughout Genesis in which the constant theme is (1) intimacy (2) which is ruptured by strife, (3) which in turn may or may not be resolved by reconciliation.[17] One may start with the intimacy of Gen. 1–2 which is shattered by the strife created by the narrative of ch. 3. This pattern continues throughout the biblical text right into the Joseph narrative, where one reads about a family torn

16. See S. Terrien, *The Elusive Presence: Toward a New Biblical Theology* (New York: Harper & Row, 1978), pp. 63–105.

17. G. Coats, "Strife and Reconciliation: Themes of a Biblical Theology in the Book of Genesis," *HBT* 2 (1980) 15–37.

by dissension, with reconciliation coming at the end (ch. 50). In all of these narratives the theme of intimacy-strife-reconciliation is fundamental, and in many of them the promise theme is marginal, if present at all. So argues Coats.

This pattern is particularly obvious in the Jacob narratives, which is the section of Gen. 12–36 most fully explored by Coats in his article. There is brother against brother, father and brother against mother and brother, brother against father, wife against wife, son-in-law against father-in-law, and vice versa. Jacob is constantly getting into or out of trouble. In many ways it reads like a modern soap opera, with recurring motifs like exploitation, deception, deep resentment and anger, sleeping with somebody other than one's wife, polygamy, the beautiful woman, jealousy, manipulation, clandestine activity, theft, lies, rape, and violence.

It is of no little interest, however, that in the four theophanies involving Jacob (28:10–22; 32:22–31; 35:9–13; 46:2–4), God does not speak one word about any of Jacob's unethical actions. On the contrary, each theophany contains some kind of promise.

The same emphasis appears in post-Torah reflections on patriarchal history. Whether one looks at the Psalter (e.g., Pss. 105, 106), the prophets (e.g., Mal. 1:2–3),[18] or the historical books (e.g., Josh. 24), the point is repeatedly made that the patriarchs are the chosen of God and the recipients of a covenant promised to Abraham and later confirmed to Isaac and Jacob. Childs remarks, "It is astonishing to see the extent to which the ethical difficulties of the Genesis story are completely disregarded. The narrative is read to illustrate something entirely different, namely the faithfulness of God."[19] Unholy acts do not sidetrack the holy, decretive will of God. This is what Childs calls repeatedly "the theocentric interpretation" of Gen. 12–36 by the rest of the OT canon. Incidentally, the NT assumes the same approach to the patriarchal narratives as do the Prophets and the Writings. A glance at passages like Acts 7, Rom. 9, Heb. 11, or Jas. 2 shows that they also do not comment on the moral turpitudes of the patriarchs. The emphasis is either on the divine choice of these individuals or else on the faith and faithfulness of the patriarchs. The same goes for most of the remaining characters of the OT. Witness in Heb. 11 the use of Moses, Gideon, Samson, and David as parade examples of faith, their serious character flaws in other areas notwithstanding. To label such individuals paradigms of

18. Hos. 12:2–4 does use the story of Jacob's wrestling with an "angel" to underscore the forthcoming judgment of God against Judah, and in the process is outspokenly critical of Jacob's behavior, one of the very few times a patriarch is so condemned by a prophet.

19. Childs, *Old Testament Theology,* p. 215.

faith does not mean endorsement of their behavior in other areas of their lives. And note that no NT writer felt constrained to draw attention to what was patently illicit in the lives of his models, as if it was not self-evident, and no NT writer exonerated the sinful with "by faith Abram lied about his sister" or "by faith Jacob deceived his father."

The Joseph story (Gen. 37–50) has no divine speeches, so one will not find any catalogue of promises addressed to Joseph or his siblings as there were to Abraham, Isaac, or Jacob. The occurrence of yet another famine, however, does present a threat to the physical survival of Abraham's descendants. Whereas Abraham was able to flee to Egypt to escape the famine in Canaan of his day, and Isaac was prepared to head for Egypt to escape the ravages of a later famine in Canaan, in Joseph's time Egypt does not offer a refuge, for it too is a victim of famine. Thus the solution is not as simple as a change in scenery; more than geographical relocation is needed.

Joseph heads for Egypt not of his own volition, as did his great-grandfather, but against his will. Jealous of the preferential treatment that he received from his father, and irritated by the braggart's sharing of his dreams, Joseph's brothers sold him to some Arabian caravaneers heading to Egypt. On the surface this event is tragic, inhumane, and indicative of the deep hate Jacob's other children have for Joseph. Little do we know at this point that out of this debacle Joseph will emerge as the means of the survival both of his family and of Egypt. This kind of idea or theme is the basic connection of the Joseph story with the promise theme of Gen. 12–36. Because Joseph is where he is (in Egypt), and because Joseph is who he is (a man with authority and filled with wisdom and insight, diligent, and devoid of a vindictive spirit), God's promise to raise up many descendants of Abraham will not be crushed. The Joseph story does not guarantee that God's promise of land will be fulfilled, for Genesis ends with Joseph "in a coffin in Egypt." Like Joseph (50:24–25), however, Jacob is convinced that one day the reality of that promise will be fulfilled (48:21–22). Joseph's certainty is based on only one line of evidence—"God promised it on oath to Abraham, Isaac, and Jacob."

Judah, and not Joseph, is the actual son through whom the covenant promises are to be perpetuated. Much of Gen. 37–50 presents a striking contrast between these two brothers. All that Joseph is, Judah is not. If Joseph represents the means of preservation of God's promises, then Judah represents the means of endangering those promises. The line of chosen son should have been Abraham-Isaac-Jacob-Judah-Er. Er's death threatens the continuation of that line, and only a shrewd move by his daughter-in-law prevents the break in succession, and as a result Er's place is taken by Perez.

One last item needs to be discussed: the relationship theologically of primeval history (Gen. 1–11) to the remaining sections of Genesis.[20] Clines discusses three suggested themes for Gen. 1–11, the first two originally forwarded by von Rad and Westermann.[21] These three are: (1) a Sin-Speech-Mitigation-Punishment theme: (2) a Spread-of-Sin, Spread-of-Grace theme; (3) a Creation-Uncreation-Re-creation theme. Clines opts for a combination of the last two, for they incorporate all the materials of Gen. 1–11, the narratives and the genealogies. The first of these focuses only on the narratives, but ignores the Creation story and the genealogies.

Unlike chs. 12–50, which focus on one family, chs. 1–11 center on mankind. The Hebrew word *'āḏām* occurs 562 times in the OT, and 45 of these are found in Genesis. All of these except one (16:12) are confined to chs. 1–11. These chapters identify some individuals by name (Adam, Eve, Cain, Abel, Noah), and such persons become the focus of major narratives. Others are but names inserted in a genealogy. Thus, after reading Gen. 1–11, one knows more about Cain than about Mehujael. Still, other individuals are known by ambiguous titles like "sons of God" and "daughters of men." Lastly, a third group is known by their relationship to some prominent person (the men of Noah's day) or to some prominent project (building a tower). These individuals and groups comprise families. They are the families of the earth, and they are spread over twenty generations. The primeval history pays little attention to geography, apart from repeated but vague references to "the east." We can trace Abraham's movements from Ur to Haran to Shechem to Beer-sheba to Egypt and back, but tracing the movements of an Adam or a Cain is not so easy.

The first two chapters of Genesis introduce the paradisiacal world and the family that inhabits the world. Paradise is a place of blessing, one unsullied by sin. The God-hating snake is absent, a phenomenon that is true again only in the last two chapters of Revelation, for the world of Gen. 3 to Rev. 20 is a combat zone between God and the snake. Mankind is not yet fruitful and multiplying, but man is blessed by God. His relationship with

20. The studies of Gen. 1–11 are legion, but I would recommend J. J. Scullion, "New Thinking on Creation and Sin in Genesis i–xi," *AusBR* 22 (1974) 1–10; R. A. Oden, Jr., "Divine Aspirations in Atrahasis and in Genesis 1–11," *ZAW* 93 (1981) 197–216; E. Combs, "The Political Teachings of Genesis I–XI," *Studia Biblica, 1978* (Sheffield: JSOT, 1979), 1:105–10; G. V. Smith, "Structure and Purpose in Genesis 1–11," *JETS* 20 (1977) 307–19; N. Weeks, "The Hermeneutical Problem of Genesis 1–11," *Themelios* 4 (1978) 12–19; G. Coats, "The God of Death: Power and Obedience in the Primeval History," *Int* 29 (1975) 227–39; P. D. Miller, *Genesis 1–11: Studies in Structure and Theme,* JSOTSup 8 (Sheffield: University of Sheffield, 1978); D. J. A. Clines, "Themes in Genesis 1–11," *CBQ* 38 (1976) 483–507; idem, *Theme of the Pentateuch,* pp. 61–79.

21. Clines, *Theme of the Pentateuch,* pp. 61ff.

God, with himself, with his spouse, with the soil, and with the animals is in order. Blessing means the absence of friction, everything working in harmony as God designed it.

Chapters 3ff. introduce the theme of God's judgment, which is the withdrawal of his blessing. The primal family, as well as their offspring, overstep their boundaries, and this trespass turns God's blessing into judgment. Chs. 3–11 are laced with narratives whose common theme is "I have not learned in whatsoever state I am to be content." In other words, they are not content simply to exercise the power over nature that God gave them at creation. That is not sufficient power. Their power must be extended to include things like power to be morally autonomous, power over somebody else's life, power over the determination of one's future.

Inevitably this desire for power produces divine judgment, which results in alienation from God. Adam, Eve, and Cain are driven from God's presence. Human life span is lowered. Degenerates are drowned. Tower builders are scattered.

To be sure, throughout these narratives the voice of grace and promise is not muted. Adam and Eve are clothed. A seed of Eve is promised who will crush the snake. Cain is divinely protected. God announces a covenant never to flood the earth again. We suggest that all of these redemptive acts of God move toward the major divine action against sin and evil. This action comes about by the juxtaposition of chs. 1–11, which concern the families of the earth, and ch. 12, which focuses on the chosen family. The families of the earth will never be reconciled to God simply by clothing, or by a sign on the forehead, or by the absence of a deluge, as comforting as they may be.

The election of Abraham is not designed to isolate this family from the other families of the earth. On the contrary, this family is to become the vehicle by which all families of the earth may be reconciled to God. In Abraham and in his descendants "all the nations of the earth are to be blessed." Thus the selection of Abraham's family is a means to an end in God's overall plan for his world. How will this blessing come about? Gen. 12:1ff. makes it clear that reconciliation with God is possible only when there is reconciliation with Abraham, or at least the absence of strife. One cannot be reconciled with God and be at odds with Abraham. "I will bless/curse those who bless/curse you," is the promise of ch. 12 and elsewhere. Abraham and his descendants are nothing less than a mediator and a catalyst of God's promised blessing. Chs. 12–50 perhaps should not be read as "Paradise Regained," but they may be read as "Reconciliation Regained" or "Hope Regained." Chs. 12–50 do not recapture chs. 1–2, but they do resolve the dilemma of chs. 3–11, which is the problem of escalating trespass for which a lasting solution is needed.

V. PROBLEMS IN INTERPRETATION

A. THE "DAYS" OF GENESIS 1

As far as the opening chapter of Genesis is concerned, the battle lines are drawn between the interpretation of the Creation story and scientific knowledge about the origin of the earth and mankind. The revised form of Tertullian's question—"What has Jerusalem to do with Athens?"—is "What has Gen. 1 to do with science?" and the answer to that ranges from "much indeed" to "nothing at all." At one end are those who find a high degree of compatibility between science's latest discoveries and assertions and a very literal interpretation of Gen. 1. At the other extreme are those who are convinced that any attempt to forge a marriage between the Creation story and, say, paleontology or the laws of thermodynamics partakes of the reductionistic spirit of a technological age.

The literal understanding of "day" in Gen. 1 teaches that God created and then populated his world in a 144-hour period (6 24-hour days).[1] It does not, of course, document whether God worked the entire 24-hour period or just a portion thereof. It needs to be affirmed that in the Hebrew Bible the normal understanding of *yôm* is a day of the week. There are, to be sure, places where it may refer to an unmeasured period of time or to an era such as in the prophets' phrase "in that day," or to an unusually long period of time, even up to a millennium (Ps. 90:4). The burden of proof, however, is on those who do not attribute to *yôm* in Gen. 1 its normal and most common interpretation, especially when *yôm* is always described as being composed of an evening and a morning.

Two caveats are in order. First, the literal understanding of "day" is not necessarily a more spiritual and biblical interpretation, and therefore is not inherently preferable. Second, a conservative reading of Gen. 1 does not always produce a conservative conclusion. For instance, James Barr agrees with the most ardent creationist that the days of Gen. 1 are meant as literal 24-hour days.[2] For Barr the crucial hermeneutical decision is not what the modern interpreter believes about "day," but what whoever wrote Gen. 1 believed about "day." And whoever wrote Gen. 1 believed he was talking about literal days. Now, over the last few centuries science has shown that it is absurd and preposterous to think that the universe was created in one week.

1. See, e.g., H. Morris, *The Remarkable Birth of Planet Earth* (Minneapolis: Bethany House, 1972).

2. J. Barr, *Fundamentalism* (Philadelphia: Westminster, 1978), pp. 40ff.

What conclusion should one draw from this scientific finding? According to Barr, it shows clearly that Gen. 1 can only be interpreted as myth and legend. For Barr, this is the reason why so many conservative commentators shy away from a literal interpretation of Gen. 1 and replace it with a figurative interpretation. The inexorable end of a literalist reading of Gen. 1 is the admission into inerrant Scripture of the categories of myth and legend, that is, a mix that is mutually exclusive. It never occurs to Barr that there may be other reasons why a nonliteral interpretation may be advanced than to keep biblical inerrancy from being refuted. This point will be developed further below.

A variation of the literal understanding of "day" is to read it as designating epochs, and Ps. 90:4, so well known because of the hymn "O God Our Help in Ages Past," is pushed into service at this point for substantiation. Thus thousands of years of history may be subsumed in any one of Gen. 1's uses of "day." The immediate advantage to this interpretation is that it is more reconcilable with science, or so it appears. Gen. 1 does not describe an instantaneous creation but one that happened in stages, possibly over aeons.

Let us apply this interpretation to the sixth day of creation, which deals with the creation of humanity. Every so often anthropologists announce the discovery, usually in Africa, of the remains of a human-like being that pushes the origins of mankind back millions of years. Yet the characters of the early chapters of Genesis are anything but Neanderthal. They engage in shepherding, farming, city building, music, working with metals, and ship building. These skills developed relatively late and are normally connected with the hominids of the Neolithic Revolution (i.e., 10,000–8000 B.C.). Reading the sixth day as the sixth epoch of creation opens the door to the possibility of some kind of pre-Adamic *homo sapiens.*

It is highly debatable whether the interpretation of Genesis' days as metaphorical for geological ages can be sustained. For one thing, it allows the concerns of establishing concord with science (ever changing in its conclusions) to override an understanding of a Hebrew word based on its contextual usage. Furthermore, one would have to take extreme liberty with the phrase, "there was evening, and there was morning—the *x* day." Lastly, how would one possibly take in stride scientifically a major stage in the creation process that has an epoch which brings about vegetation precede an epoch which brings about the sun and stars?

The third approach to "day" in Gen. 1 is the literary interpretation. This approach leaves open the possibility for taking "day" literally or nonliterally. It begins by placing the Gen. 1 Creation story in its historical context. This is a word from God addressed to a group of people who are surrounded by nations whose cosmology is informed by polytheism and the mythology that flows out of that polytheism. Much in Gen. 1 is patently anti-pagan.[3] The contest is not between a religious view (Israel's) and a secular view (non-Israel's). There were no Charles Darwins in the ancient world who operated from nontheistic presuppositions. The authors of compositions like the Gilgamesh Epic or the Atrahasis Epic, whoever they were, were hardly secular, humanistic, or agnostic. In these myths of origin the emphasis falls on procreation rather than on creation, and on the genealogy of deities (theogony) rather than of nature (cosmogony). Gen. 1 is written, at least partially, to present an alternative to that worldview. The writer's concerns, then, were theological and historical—what happened, and why, and so what.

The clear progression of thought in Gen. 1 may be described as tripartite. First is the threefold problem identified in v. 2: (1) darkness, (2) watery abyss; (3) a formless earth. Second, days 1–3 are days of preparation which address these problems. Darkness is separated from light (day 1); waters above are separated from waters below (day 2); dry land and vegetation appear (day 3). Third, days 4–6 are days of population (luminaries [day 4], birds and aquatic life [day 5], land animals and humanity [day 6]).[4] The relationship in content between days 1–3 and 4–6 is reflected in 2:1, "the heavens and the earth were completed [days 1–3] in all their vast array [days 4–6]" (NIV; cf. RSV "and all the host of them"). The parallel between the first three days and the last three was noted at least as early as the church father Augustine (*City of God* 11.6), and many writers have since drawn attention to it. The point of this deliberate and delightful symmetry in Gen. 1 is that form is as important as content. In the Creation account of Gen. 1 eight creative acts are spread over six days. It is not necessary to resort here to numerology, as does Hyers (i.e., 7 is the numerological meaning of wholeness and completeness), to explain the six-plus-one days.

A literary reading of Gen. 1 still permits the retention of "day" as a solar day of 24 hours. But it understands "day" not as a chronological account of how many hours God invested in his creating project, but as an analogy

3. See G. Hasel, "The Polemic Nature of the Genesis Cosmology," *EvQ* 46 (1974) 78–80.

4. See C. Hyers, *The Meaning of Creation: Genesis and Modern Science* (Atlanta: John Knox, 1984), pp. 67–71; idem, "The Narrative Form of Genesis 1: Cosmogonic, Yes; Scientific, No," *JASA* 36 (1984) 208–15, esp. p. 211.

of God's creative activity.[5] God reveals himself to his people in a medium with which they can identify and which they can comprehend. The Creation account portrays a God who speaks, who evaluates, who deliberates, who forms, who animates, who regulates. The intended audience of Gen. 1 will fully identify with that model. The Creation account also portrays a God who created on six days and rested on the seventh. The audience, accustomed to their own workweek, will identify with that model too.

B. GENESIS AS MYTH

The word *myth* is found only in the later books of the NT. Writing to Timothy, Paul urges him not to pay attention to myths (1 Tim. 1:4). Later Paul predicts that the time is coming when people will find myths more attractive than the truth (2 Tim. 4:4). Paul instructs Titus to reprove those who are absorbed with Jewish myths, an aberration which detracts from sound faith (Titus 1:14). Peter declares to the recipients of his epistle that the basis of certainty behind his message is that he was "an eyewitness of his majesty," and not cleverly devised myths (2 Pet. 1:16).

In these four NT passages one encounters myth in its best-known definition. What is mythical is not true. What is true is not mythical. If one is told that the flood of Noah's day is a myth, or that the resurrection of Jesus Christ is a myth, the hearer will assume that what is meant is that these two events are really fictitious narratives, invented stories. The speaker of the above statements may qualify his position by saying that Noah's flood or Jesus' resurrection is true theologically but not true historically. In that sense he believes these stories are myths. They are ahistorical. The attaching of theological or kerygmatic value keeps these stories from being dismissed. Thus a teacher of Bible can vehemently dissociate himself in a Friday afternoon lecture class from belief in the virginal conception of Jesus of Nazareth, and yet have no problem in reciting the Apostles' Creed ("born of the virgin Mary") at his church on Sunday morning. He perceives no inconsistency in his Friday afternoon denial and his Sunday morning affirmation.

The reason why the stories of Gen. 1–11 in particular are often labeled as myth is that they reflect a prescientific or nonscientific worldview. Anything that is treated as the work of a supernatural being, but which a scientific worldview would interpret as the operation of impersonal laws and

5. See C. E. Hummel, "Interpreting Genesis One," *JASA* 38 (1986) 175–85, esp. pp. 181–83.

forces, is by this position understood as myth. Myth is not only a figurative expression of truth, but a false expression of truth as well. In this definition myth becomes, essentially, any story about God or gods or any kind of supernatural powers.

Bultmann has given the classic definition of this approach to myth: "Mythology is the use of imagery to express the otherworldly in terms of this world and the divine in terms of human life, the other side in terms of this side."[6] In order for modern people to appropriate and understand these portions of Scripture, they must be demythologized. Bultmann's interest is in demythologizing the text, not in dekerygmatizing it (which is what a thoroughgoing "liberal" would do). Whether he actually avoids dekerygmatizing is open to debate. Can one grasp the theological contribution of a biblical event if his basic hermeneutical presupposition is: whether the story is historical is inconsequential; what is important is its teachings?

The above definition of myth has at least three problems. First, it is so broad in its definition that it reduces any kind of theistic statement to a mythical statement. Second, it suggests that such stories about God(s) reflect a naive concept of truth which science has dismantled. A good case can be made for the fact that in the ancient world science did not follow religion, but religion flowed out of science.[7] Third, such a definition of myth does not grow out of a study of mythology but from the opposition of myth to science. Bultmann did not arrive at the above definition of myth by probing the myths of oriental and classical literature. He has given us a rationalistic, philosophical definition of myth rather than a phenomenological one.

Many scholars would be quite content to interpret the Creation story or the Fall as neither history nor myth. It is not history, according to them, in the sense that Gen. 1–2 or Gen. 3 describes past events that actually happened. But neither are they myths, at least in the historical-philosophical definition of myth.

The truth is that scholars disagree about the definition of the word. One recent writer has isolated nine definitions of myth and another documents twelve aspects of myth.[8] This proliferation of definitions of myth is

6. R. Bultmann, *Kerygma and Myth,* tr. R. H. Fuller, ed. H. W. Bartsch (New York: Harper & Row, 1961), p. 10 n. 2.

7. See C. H. Gordon, "Ancient Middle East Religions," *The New Encyclopaedia Britannica,* 15th ed. (1986), 24:64.

8. The former is G. B. Caird, *The Language and Imagery of the Bible* (Philadelphia: Westminster, 1980), pp. 219–24. The latter is J. W. Rogerson, *Myth in Old Testament Interpretation,* BZAW 134 (Berlin/New York: de Gruyter, 1974), pp. 174–78.

the reason why one scholar would look at Gen. 1–11 and say it is free of myth, while another scholar would look at Gen. 1–11 and pronounce it entirely mythical. One has to understand what any given writer means when he uses the word.

Rejecting both a broad definition (myth is a prescientific worldview) and narrow definition (myth is a story about gods) of myth, Brevard Childs has suggested the following: "Myth is a form by which the existing structure of reality is understood and maintained. It concerns itself with showing how an action of a deity, conceived of as occurring in the primeval age, determines a phase of contemporary world order. Existing world order is maintained through the actualization of the myth in the cult."[9] This he calls a phenomenological definition of myth.

Childs then proceeds to examine six OT passages, three of which are from Genesis (1:1–2; 3:1–5; 6:1–4). He suggests that the OT handled mythic material in three ways. First, a myth could be divorced from its original context and used (a) to illustrate a new reality (Isa. 11:6–9) or (b) as an extended figure of speech (Isa. 14:12–21). Second, myths might be historicized as legend or saga (Exod. 4:24–26). Third, mythical fragments were broken away from their original setting in such fashion as to fit meaningfully into a Yahwistic theological framework (Gen. 1:1–2; 3:1–5; 6:1–4). In essence, the author of Gen. 1–11 demythologized his material, and this assimilation was done only with varying degrees of success, thus leaving some tension in the biblical record. Presumably Childs is not using "demythologize" as Bultmann used it. Perhaps by "demythologize" he means to excise from a myth those elements that do not fit within the parameters of OT faith. For Childs, myth, phenomenologically understood, is conspicuously absent from Gen. 1–11.

Myth is spawned by a worldview in which the difference between God and nature is nonexistent. In *Enuma elish,* for example, both gods and the world came from the same womb. This lack of distinction obliterates any difference between the worship of nature and the worship of the gods of

9. B. S. Childs, *Myth and Reality in the Old Testament,* SBT 1/27 (London: SCM, 1960), pp. 29–30. Childs provides only one illustration of myth being actualized in cult from Mesopotamia *(Enuma elish)* and none at all from Egypt. The connection of myth and ritual has always played a prominent role in the Scandinavian school of OT interpretation, as can be observed in the essay by B. Otzen, "The Use of Myth in Genesis," in B. Otzen, H. Gottlieb, and K. Jeppesen, *Myths in the Old Testament* (London: SCM, 1980). Defining myth as "a vehicle for an explanation of existence," Otzen accepts that Gen. 1–11 is a step removed from pure myth in its present form, but nevertheless bears strong testimony to underlying cultic myths.

nature.[10] The mythmaker, unlike the Hebrew, could make no distinction between lifting his eyes unto the hills for help and lifting his eyes to the Lord of those hills for help. For the mythmaker, the relationship between the hills and god is not figurative but ontological. The hills are god, and god is the hills. In clearly demarcating the two, Israel, in the words of James Barr, broke "the correspondence pattern of mythology."[11] Nature is not deified; God is not naturalized.

Thus even though Gen. 1–11 seems to imply a "three-story" universe, a snake that converses with human beings, and supernatural beings mating with women, it is irresponsible and incorrect to speak of these stories as myths on those bases. The worldview of Gen. 1–11, with its articulation of God, nature, and ethical choices, transcends the worldview of the mythopoeic mind. To say all this, of course, says nothing about the truthfulness or falsehood of these stories. It claims only that they are nonmythic.[12]

C. THE PATRIARCHS AND HISTORY

Wellhausen stated his own convictions about the historical Abraham with these words: "Here [in Genesis] no historical knowledge about the patriarchs is to be gotten, but only the period in which the stories about them arose among the Israelite people. This later period was simply to be projected back into hoary antiquity and reflected there like a glorified mirage."[13] He did not state that "there are no historical patriarchs" but rather that "there is no historical knowledge about the patriarchs." For Wellhausen the historical Abraham is irretrievably lost, and it is a waste of time to search for him. This position became the standard evaluation of Abraham's historicity, especially among European OT scholars.

This particular issue is a problem for the following reasons. First, there are no references to Abraham, Isaac, or Jacob in any other inscriptions

10. See Y. Kaufmann, *The Religion of Israel,* tr. and ed. M. Greenberg (New York: Schocken, repr. 1972), pp. 21–40.

11. J. Barr, "The meaning of 'mythology' in relation to the Old Testament," *VT* 9 (1959) 7.

12. I have profited greatly from two essays of John Oswalt, "The Myth of the Dragon and Old Testament Faith," *EvQ* 49 (1979) 163–72; idem, "A Myth Is a Myth Is a Myth: Toward a Working Definition," in *A Spectrum of Thought: Essays in Honor of Dennis F. Kinlaw,* ed. M. L. Peterson (Wilmore, KY: Francis Asbury, 1982), pp. 135–45.

13. J. Wellhausen, *Prolegomena to the History of Israel,* p. 318.

that are contemporary with any writing of the OT. Names like those of the patriarchs do appear in cuneiform literature, but nobody suggests that any of these are the patriarchs themselves. Thus our knowledge of Abraham and his family is limited to the OT. Of course, this limitation in itself does not cast a cloud of doubt over Abraham's existence.

Further, even if one accepts the Mosaic authorship of Genesis, the earliest records about the patriarchs are separated from the patriarchs by perhaps four centuries. (That interlude is at least doubled if one accepts the first writing down of patriarchal traditions sometime in the 10th century B.C.) For Wellhausen this interlude meant that Abraham *qua* Abraham was unknowable and unrecoverable, for how could any tradition survive with any degree of accuracy for centuries before it was reduced to writing? The issue is compounded by the fact that no single event in any of the patriarchal cycles can be associated with a high degree of certainty with any other event knowable from ancient Near East history. The most frequently used bit of evidence is the possible association of Abraham's family migration from Ur to Har(r)an to Canaan with what is known as the Amorite Hypothesis. This theory refers to the move westward of the Amurru ("westerners") from Mesopotamia through Syria and Palestine and on into Egypt, something documented in cuneiform texts from the last portion of the 3rd millennium and later. Of course, Genesis nowhere connects the two. If one confines himself to the biblical record, he would not come away with the impression that the move of Terah's family was part of a much larger movement of peoples.

Wellhausen's view of the patriarchal period was by and large maintained by later scholars. Individuals like von Rad and Noth granted the likely existence of patriarchal traditions sometime in the 2nd millennium B.C., but refused to speak with any degree of historical confidence about the period. All that we know is how later communities envisioned that period.

Reaction to this minimalist view of the patriarchal period came mostly from American scholars. Two archeologists, Nelson Glueck and W. F. Albright, led the way in attempting to rebut this negative evaluation. Glueck worked in Transjordan and in the Negeb; in Genesis Abraham is connected with the latter and Jacob is connected with the former.

On the basis of his work in Transjordan in the 1930s Glueck concluded that there was a hiatus in settled life in that region between 1900 B.C. and 1300 B.C.[14] He attributed this cessation of occupied settlements in Transjordan to the invasion of the four kings from the east, described in Gen.

14. N. Glueck, *The Other Side of the Jordan* (New Haven: AASOR, 1940).

14. This absence of settlement over 500–600 years in Transjordan means that Jacob must be placed prior to 1900 B.C. In the 1950s Glueck began his explorations of the Negeb, and again to him the evidence there suggested the establishment of many settlements in that region in the 21st century which were destroyed in the 19th century.[15] Abraham traveled throughout the Negeb area, then, sometime during that period. By dovetailing these two claims Glueck dated Abraham to the period known archeologically as Middle Bronze I (commonly abbreviated MBI; 2100–1900 B.C.).

Albright accepted Glueck's conclusions concerning Transjordan and the Negeb, and beyond that provided evidence that many of the Canaanite towns with which the patriarchs were associated (Shechem, Bethel, Hebron, Gerar) demonstrated human occupation during MBI. The proliferation of towns throughout the MBI period led Albright to the conclusion that Abraham was a donkey caravaneer who conducted his business by shuttling among most of these settlements.

Thus Glueck and Albright felt they had provided indubitable archeological evidence for a historical Abraham of the MBI period, and for the historicity of many of the events in Genesis involving Abraham, especially that described in Gen. 14. Hence, a marked cleavage emerged between the more skeptical German school and the more positive American school in terms of a factual basis, or the lack thereof, for genuine knowledge of the patriarchs.

Other scholars buttressed the conclusions of Albright and Glueck by appealing to inscriptions from the cuneiform world, especially those texts that talked of family customs.[16] Since so much of Genesis is about family history, where is a more logical place to look for parallels to some of the items in Genesis than in that part of the world from which Abraham came and to which Jacob returned?

Tablets from Mari (1800 B.C.) provided the first parallels. Their contribution was twofold. First, they revealed place names and personal names (a) equivalents of which are found in the early chapters of Genesis (e.g., Naḫuru [Nahor], Ḫarranu [Haran]), and (b) most of these names were restricted to the Bronze Age. The second contribution from Mari concerned customs from there demonstrating the importance of keeping family land intact in perpetuity, a concern also in the patriarchal narratives.

15. Idem, *Rivers in the Desert: A History of the Negev* (New York: Norton, 1959).

16. The most convenient discussion of these customs, and the question of their links with Genesis material, is M. J. Selman, "Comparative Customs and the Patriarchal Age," in *Essays on the Patriarchal Narratives,* ed. A. R. Millard and D. J. Wiseman (Winona Lake, IN: Eisenbrauns, 1983), pp. 91–139.

Much more appeal has been made to the texts from Nuzi (15th century B.C.); the major contributors here have been E. A. Speiser and and C. H. Gordon. Among the suggested parallels we may cite the following:

1. A marriage to a niece (11:29)
2. A husband obtains the status of a brother by adopting his wife (12:1–20; 21:1–34; 26:1–35)
3. A childless couple might adopt someone, even a servant, to take care of them; in the end this person would inherit their property. Any naturally born son, however, replaces the adoptee (15:2–3)
4. A barren wife must provide her husband with a surrogate, normally the wife's slave girl (16:1–2; 30:1–13)
5. The status of the slave girl and her offspring is protected against the jealousy or whims of either wife or husband (21:9–14)
6. A brother may adopt his sister in order to give her in marriage to someone else, providing she agrees (24:1–67)
7. A birthright might be sold to another (25:29–34)
8. A patriarchal blessing carries the weight of law and is not to be subjected to revision (27:35–37; 48:8–22)
9. A couple might adopt a son-in-law as their own son (30:1–2)
10. Possession of the household gods was seen as legal title to an inheritance (31:34)

Now neither Speiser nor Gordon used any of these parallels to prove the existence of the patriarchs or the accuracy of Genesis. But Speiser did feel that these parallels were sufficient to lend probability to the idea of a MBII (1900–1550 B.C.) Abraham. That the Nuzi texts came after this period presented no problem, for to Speiser these texts represented customs that had been in vogue long before the 15th century B.C. Gordon, however, felt that the Nuzi and the Ras Shamra texts were contemporaneous with the patriarchal period, and thus he dated Abraham to the Amarna period (early 14th century).

Four fruits of archeology, then, were introduced to establish the existence of the patriarchs as historical: (1) excavation in Transjordan, (2) excavation in the Negeb, (3) excavation in Cisjordanian settlements, and (4) inscriptions mostly from Nuzi, but also from Mari, Cappadocia, and Anatolia. While the question of patriarchal historicity remains unsettled because the interpretation of this archeological evidence is still uncertain, published discoveries at Ebla may strengthen the case for a MBI Abraham, if not for an Early Bronze (EB) Abraham (i.e., 2650–2350 B.C.).[17]

17. See D. N. Freedman, "The Real Story of the Ebla Tablets: Ebla and the Cities of the Plain," *BA* 41 (1978) 143–63.

A reading of the section on the patriarchal period in John Bright's *A History of Israel* reveals his total acceptance of the conclusions of this Albright-Glueck-Speiser-Gordon approach. Subsequent editions of the *History* have brought about only cosmetic changes in the treatment of this section.[18] By contrast, Noth's *History of Israel* essentially ignores the patriarchal period. This difference reflects the distance between these two schools of interpretation. Not only are they worlds apart in their conclusions, but they are equally differentiated by the methodology used to arrive at those conclusions. For the American school the discipline has been archeology. For the European school the discipline has been historical-critical methods of research. The first focused primarily on external sources; the second primarily on internal sources.

In the last several decades a major assault against the Albrightian consensus has been launched. The most formidable contributions have come from John Van Seters and T. L. Thompson.[19]

Van Seters makes two major points, the first demolitional and the second reconstructive, and thus the division of his book into two sections—Abraham (1) in History and (2) in Tradition (see above for a discussion of the "Tradition" section). In his first section Van Seters makes his case for the fact that it is impossible, both on external and internal grounds, to date the Abraham story to any time during the 2nd millennium B.C. This case flies directly in the face of what we said above about Albright, et al.

Thompson is as militant in denying any second-millennium B.C. context for the Abraham story, sometimes agreeing with Van Seters, sometimes disputing with him. Some have suggested that what Van Seters and Thompson have done is turn the clock back to Wellhausen. We are not convinced that what has emerged is an anti-Albright, pro-Wellhausen position. If we understand correctly the difference between Wellhausen/Noth and Van Seters/Thompson, the former taught that the patriarchal traditions are historically unrecoverable, while the latter teach that the patriarchal traditions are historically unrecoverable because there never were any patriarchs! In terms of positive historical discoveries, the subtitle of Thompson's work *(The Quest for the Historical Abraham)* may well have been "The Quest for

18. Even in the 3rd edition (1981) Bright dismisses the challenges of Thompson and Van Seters to his earlier treatment of the patriarchal age in two brief paragraphs, expressing his doubts about the challenges and reaffirming his acceptance of the historicity of the patriarchs and the patriarchal traditions (pp. 73–74).

19. See Van Seters, *Abraham in History and Tradition;* T. L. Thompson, *The Historicity of the Patriarchal Narratives: The Quest for the Historical Abraham,* BZAW 133 (Berlin/New York: de Gruyter, 1974).

the Historical Adam," in that the project is doomed to failure from the start. Thompson, against Van Seters, accepts the time of the early monarchy as the period in which these traditions were produced, though the endeavor was still a thoroughly imaginary one.

Van Seters's main objection (contra Speiser, Gordon, et al.) is that hardly any of the social customs in the patriarchal narratives point exclusively to an early second-millennium B.C. background. He offers some criticisms and then presents an alternative. His criticisms are that either (a) too much was read into the Nuzi texts to make them compatible with the Genesis stories, or (b) too much was read into the Genesis stories to make them parallel to their Nuzi counterparts. In other words, the parallels are contrived, forced, and necessitate either trimming or augmentation in the stories and customs under consideration. Van Seters's alternative is to suggest that there are much better parallels in middle and late first-millennium B.C. cuneiform texts (i.e., Neo-Assyrian, Neo-Babylonian literature). This is the foundation stone in his edifice in later arguing for a seventh/sixth-century B.C. Abraham tradition.

Thompson does not share Van Seters's enthusiasm for first-millennium B.C. parallels any more than Van Seters shares Speiser's enthusiasm for second-millennium B.C. parallels. He feels that Van Seters's Neo-Assyrian and Neo-Babylonian parallels carry no more weight than Speiser's Nuzi parallels. This is one of the differences between the two authors. Van Seters subordinates archeological studies to literary-critical studies of the Genesis text, while for Thompson archeological studies almost get lost in his consumption with literary-critical studies. Still, it is of interest that of Thompson's twelve chapters, the longest chapter is ch. 10, "Nuzi and the Patriarchal Narratives" (pp. 196–297), one-third of the book. The first nine chapters are all variations on one area of debate, the Amorite problem, in which archeological concerns are paramount.

We believe that the most helpful and convincing part of Section 1 of Van Seters's book is his demonstration that many of the second-millennium B.C. parallels, especially those from Nuzi, introduced to support a historical, Middle Bronze Age Abraham, are forced, superficial, and too selective. Throughout the remainder of Section 1, however, he repeatedly makes broad assertions, given his penchant for any supports for a first-millennium context, that just do not stand up under further scrutiny. For example, he discredits any relationship between Ur and Haran (mentioned in Gen. 11–12) in the 2nd millennium, but believes the two cities might be properly united in the time of the Neo-Babylonian king Nabonidus (555–539 B.C.). Yet what will he do with the recently published text from Ebla that speaks of "Haran in the territory of Ur"? Even in a third-millennium B.C. text the two sites are connected. Again, Van Seters claims that the Arabian names in Genesis must be from the 1st millennium, for none of them appears in extant documents from Mesopotamia earlier than the reign of Shalmaneser III (8th century B.C.). This is greatly overextending the argument from silence. The reason no Arabian names appear in pre-eighth-century Mesopotamian texts is that prior to this time the powers of the Tigris-Euphrates area had little contact with Palestine.

Yet again, Van Seters suggests that very little in the patriarchal stories reflects the nomadic life of the 2nd millennium B.C., and assuming Abraham was a nomad, the promise of land inheritance would be irrelevant to a person with such a life-style. In addition, the mention of "tents" is, for Van Seters, a sure sign of the mid-first millennium B.C. All three of these statements are open to objection. First, it is not certain or provable that Abraham should even be called a nomad, at least in the sense of one who roamed very great distances with flocks. Second, most civilizations of the 2nd millennium, especially at Mari, are dimorphic societies, showing characteristics of both nomadic and sedentary groups. Third, there are actually more references to tents in the 2nd millennium than in the 1st, which is the exact opposite of Van Seters's claim.[20]

Van Seters makes much of the fact that several sites, featured prominently as places visited by Abraham and others, show no evidence of occupation before the Iron Age. In particular he (and Thompson) highlight Beer-sheba and Shechem.[21] Of course, nowhere do the narratives imply that Beer-sheba was a town in Abraham's day. Genesis does witness to a well being there (21:19, 30; 26:32), and to Abraham's worship there (21:33), as well as Jacob's (46:1). These references do not necessarily imply a permanent settlement. The only place where it is clearly called a "town" is in an editorial passage ("and to this day the name of the town has been called Beer-sheba," 26:33). In sum, we would suggest that Van Seters has made an excellent case for holding back on "parallelomania" vis-à-vis Mari and Nuzi. He has, however, not made a convincing case for dating the Abraham traditions to the 1st millennium B.C.

Turning our attention to Thompson, we believe his to be a much more

20. See D. J. Wiseman, "Abraham Reassessed," in *Essays on the Patriarchal Narratives,* pp. 143–45. Note also the twentieth-century B.C. Egyptian Sinuhe, who lives in tents and raids his enemy's tent (*ANET,* pp. 18–22).

21. Cf. Y. Aharoni, "Nothing Early and Nothing Late: Re-writing Israel's Conquest," *BA* 39 (1976) 55–76.

penetrating study than Van Seters's. While he places more emphasis on challenging a cherished position than does Van Seters, he does not devote as much attention to constructing an alternative as does Van Seters. As we mentioned earlier, the first two-thirds of his book deal in one way or another with a refutation of the idea that the historicity of the patriarchs is established by linking them with Mesopotamian Amorite movements near the end of the 3rd millennium B.C.[22] In the eight chapters (2–9) that he devotes to the subject he has pointed out some real flaws in the Amorite Hypothesis. For example, we find persuasive his case that the Amu of Egyptian texts do not provide evidence for the Amorites (?) in Palestine. These people are indigenous inhabitants of Egypt's western borders. Thompson also convincingly challenges archeological evidence of a break between EBIV and MBI in Palestine-Syria, which is a pillar of the Amorite migration theory. If the evidence for a break between these two periods is unfounded, then it is unlikely that a large group of outsiders entered Palestine during MBI. To say all this, however, does not send Gen. 12ff. crashing to the ground historically. N. Sarna has correctly observed, "If Abraham's migration can no longer be explained as part of a larger Amorite migration from east to west, it should be noted that what has fallen by the wayside is a scholarly hypothesis, not the Biblical text. Genesis itself presents the movement from Haran to Canaan as an individual, unique act undertaken in response to a divine call, an event, not an incident, that inaugurated a new and decisive stage in God's plan of history. The factuality or otherwise of this Biblical evaluation lies beyond the scope of scholarly research."[23] In other words, events of salvation history can be neither proved nor disproved.

How then does Thompson understand the place of these patriarchal narratives in Israel? He believes that they were created *ex nihilo* by early Israelite communities in which an illusory past was imaginatively formed for the purpose of giving encouragement in the present and hope for the future. In other words, according to Thompson, it is the faith of the religious community that creates Abraham. This perspective is the direct opposite of the biblical writers' view that it is Abraham who stimulates the faith of the religious community.[24] How shall we account for the fact that the events of

22. J. T. Luke ("Abraham and the Iron Age: Reflections on the New Patriarchal Studies," *JSOT* 4 [1977] 39) notes that Thompson takes a nihilistic attitude toward the Amorite Hypothesis but, unfortunately, not a correct one. Because of earlier overstatements about this hypothesis, it is not necessary to scrap the entire idea as fallacious.

23. N. Sarna in a letter to the editor in *BAR* 4/1 (1978) 2.

24. See J. Goldingay, "The Patriarchs in Scripture and History," in *Essays on the Patriarchal Narratives,* pp. 29–30.

both the Exodus under Moses and the conquest under Joshua are grounded in the patriarchal events of Genesis? If the latter are fictional, then the grounds of faith are no more for the former—unless we have fictional events that are rooted in additional fictional events. We are not saying that the patriarchal traditions have to be true to be of value. Of course they do not. If they are not true, what is surrendered is the canonical witness of Genesis that biblical history at the covenant level begins not with an exodus from Egypt to which a patriarchal tradition has beeen appended, but with a patriarchal tradition out of which an exodus and conquest themes develop. We must also consider what is lost for the biblical message of redemption, the NT included, if the patriarchs are nonexistent. According to the biblical revelation Abraham is the first link in that program and Jesus Christ, the son of Abraham, climaxes God's provision for the redemption of humanity.

D. THE RELIGION OF THE PATRIARCHS

For the lay reader of Scripture it may seem odd even to have to discuss this issue. Is not the religion of the patriarchs self-evident, and therefore not in need of elaboration? Did not Abraham worship the same God as Moses? Did not John, Peter, and Paul worship the same God as Moses? Therefore, may not the modern believer, Jewish or Christian, claim that his God is Abraham's God?

The answer to all these questions is obviously yes. Yet the critical reader of Scripture might remind us that centuries passed between the time in which the patriarchs practiced their religion and the time in which these practices were actually committed to writing. Thus one might ask, "Do we know the religion per se of the patriarchs?" or only J's, E's, and P's version of that religion? Is it possible that in the canonical structuring of the Torah, an otherwise complicated picture has been simplified?

Several things separate patriarchal religion from Mosaic religion. For one thing, Abraham in particular is rooted directly, via his family, in a pagan, polytheistic milieu. It is one thing for Abraham to leave his world geographically. But how shall he leave it theologically? Nothing in Abraham's background prepares him for that revolutionary transition. If Samuel did not recognize the voice of God and confused it with Eli's, what means did Abraham possess in Ur or Haran for recognizing the voice of God when it called him? Is it possible that Abraham's shift from a polytheistic faith to a monotheistic one was not an abrupt, overnight shift? If that is the case, one might expect to discover vestigial remains of that original faith throughout Gen. 12–50.

One final point. The religion of the patriarchs is an ante-Mosaic faith (which does not mean an anti-Mosaic faith). Thus the patriarchal religion is pre-covenant, pre-tabernacle, and pre-priestly. The implication of this point is that there are no representatives between the patriarchs and the God of the patriarchs, such as Moses or the priests or the prophets were for Israel. Accordingly revelation will be direct.

The scholarly investigation of the origins of the religion of the patriarchs has been pursued along two lines. The first we may call the traditio-historical approach; its best-known proponent is A. Alt.[25] The second line of investigation is what we shall call the comparative religion approach; its leading proponent is F. M. Cross.[26]

Alt discerned the following stages in the development of patriarchal religion:

1. The three patriarchs of Genesis actually represent three tribes or three groups of tribes, each of whom worshiped a different god: (a) the god of Abraham; (b) the god of Isaac (called "the Fear of Isaac" in 31:42, 53); (c) the god of Jacob (called "the Mighty One of Jacob" in 49:24).
2. It is this situation which is reflected in the popular phrase in Genesis, "the god of my/your/his father."
3. When these tribal groups arrived in Canaan they encountered an indigenous religion, one characteristic of which was the association of an El god with each holy place. This is the ultimate source of Genesis' El Roi, "the God who sees," 16:13; El Olam, "the eternal God," 21:33; El Elohe Israel, 33:20; El Bethel, 31:13; El Shaddai, 17:1; El Elyon, "God Most High," 14:19, 22.[27]
4. At some point these local numina were amalgamated with the above gods of the fathers.
5. Genealogies were created of the founding fathers of these cults in order to give them the semblance of a three-generation family.
6. During the Mosaic period Yahwism was introduced, and Yahweh was identified with these gods of the fathers or El deities. Decisive for Alt that Yahwism was not a part of patriarchal religion is the testimony of Exod. 6:3, "by my name Yahweh I did not make myself known to Abraham, Isaac, and Jacob."

25. A. Alt, *Essays on Old Testament History and Religion,* tr. R. A. Wilson (Garden City, NY: Doubleday, 1968), pp. 3-86.

26. F. M. Cross, "Yahweh and the God of the Patriarchs," *HTR* 55 (1962) 225–59; idem, *Canaanite Myth and Hebrew Epic* (Cambridge: Harvard University, 1973).

27. I am omitting the marks for vowel lengths as well as for *aleph* and *ayin.*

7. J's and E's picture of patriarchal religion is not as authentic as P's.[28]

Cross goes in a different direction. He rejects Alt's idea that the various El gods mentioned in Genesis are local numina, and suggests instead that these El names refer to the cosmic Canaanite deity El, father of the gods about whom we read in the Ugaritic texts. It is this head god of Canaan that the patriarchs worshiped. He also rejects Alt's suggestion of the amalgamation of anonymous patriarchal deities and these Elim (the plural of El). A phrase like "the God of Abraham" does not mean, as Alt maintained, "the (unknown) god whom Abraham worshiped," but designates the special relationship Abraham had with God (i.e., El Shaddai). And, argues Cross, since the El cult was especially popular in the 2nd millennium B.C., the antiquity of the picture of patriarchal religion in Genesis is substantiated. As for the origin of Yahwism, Cross suggests that Yahweh was originally a cultic name of El, but eventually a differentiation between Yahweh and El led to Yahweh's displacement of El.[29]

M. Haran has presented some telling arguments against the Canaanite origin of Genesis' Elim.[30] While many of these Elim are associated with specific localities (e.g., El Olam with Beer-sheba, 21:33; or El Beth-El with Bethel, 31:13), several of them are not. The most obvious name lacking a locale is El Shaddai (17:1; 28:3; 35:11; 48:3). Remarks Haran, "The primarily Hebrew character of *'El Shaddai* is perhaps the most outstanding feature of the Patriarchal traditions."[31]

Another evidence pointing against Canaanite origins is the lack of Baal names anywhere in Genesis, for Baal is as prominent and powerful, if

28. For brief evaluations of Alt's and Cross's views see G. J. Wenham, "The Religion of the Patriarchs," in *Essays on the Patriarchal Narratives,* pp. 161–95, esp. 172–73 (Alt) and 176–79 (Cross).

29. R. de Vaux ("The Religion of the Patriarchs," in *The Early History of Israel,* tr. D. Smith [Philadelphia: Westminster, 1978], pp. 267–87) takes a moderating position between Alt and Cross. For de Vaux patriarchal religion is a combination of the religion of the god of the father and the Canaanite religion of El. The first is a religion of a nomadic people. The second is a religion of a settled people. De Vaux goes further than Cross, however, in asserting that patriarchal religion took over only the name El and the concept of El's supremacy. In every other instance patriarchal religion shows a radical demythologization of the Canaanite El. Following his earlier dating of the Genesis traditions, Van Seters dates the El epithets to the exilic period and ties in the religion of the patriarchal stories with this late period ("The Religion of the Patriarchs in Genesis," *Bib* 61 [1980] 220–33). Thus he rejects Alt-Cross-de Vaux completely.

30. M. Haran, "The Religion of the Patriarchs," *ASTI* 4 (1965) 34–35.

31. Ibid., p. 34.

not more so, than El in the Canaanite pantheon. An "Isra*el*" or Ishma*el*" or "Beth*el*" is acceptable, but not an "Israbaal," or an "Ishmabaal," or a "Bethbaal." To quote Haran again, the simplest explanation for this phenomenon is that "the *'Elîm* appellations were accepted in Israel as names for Yahweh . . . precisely because they constituted an Hebraic, pre-Mosaic heritage, which was not the case with Baal."[32]

One last item calls for discussion, and that is the issue of whether the patriarchs knew God as Yahweh. At first reading Exod. 6:2–3 would seem to rule that out: "I appeared to Abraham, to Isaac, and to Jacob as El Shaddai, but by my name the LORD [Heb. Yahweh] I did not make myself known to them" (NIV). Of course, these verses in Exod. 6 are attributed to P. Several references attributed to P, however (17:1; 21:1), indicate that Yahweh was known to the patriarchs by that name, to say nothing of the copious references in J. Thus either P and J boldly disagree with each other concerning the knowledge of Yahweh in the pre-Mosaic period, or else Exod. 6:2–3 requires a different interpretation. Although often dismissed as apologetic, the old suggestion that Exod. 6:2–3 teaches a deeper revelation of Yahweh to the post-Mosaic age than to the pre-Mosaic age is by no means unsatisfactory.

To be sure, the understanding of God possessed by God's people, individuals or groups, advanced with the passing of time. Abraham saw through a glass dimly. He was both a product of his times and one who transcended his times. It is unlikely he ever worked out, or could have worked out, a theological disquisition on monotheism. But he had a relationship with his God that was dynamic, trusting, maturing, and tested.

Certainly one of the main characteristics of patriarchal religion is its emphasis on a covenant by which the God of the patriarchs enters into a personal relationship with the patriarchs. Abraham is not a seeker after God, at least not at first. Rather, God is a seeker after Abraham. It is God who appears to Abraham and calls him to follow obediently. He is a God who makes both promises and demands, and usually in that order. Thus, in Gen. 12–50, God is associated more with individuals than with places, concerned more with the formation of holy lives than with the sanctification of cultic sites. This emphasis sets apart patriarchal religion from Canaanite religion in which deities are attached to holy places. To be sure, the ancestors of Israel visited the environs of such holy sites (e.g., Bethel, Gen. 28:17, "the gate of heaven"), but such sites were resting points, not places of settlement. For the

32. Ibid., p. 49 n. 1.

mobile God of the fathers is not himself bound to any place. There is no "is not this Jerusalem which I have chosen?" in Gen. 12–50, or any predecessor of Jerusalem. Abraham, Isaac, and Jacob are challenged to live lives of wandering and adventure, but it is not aimless wandering. What makes the wandering significant is the patriarchs' realization that "their family life is in the hand of the mobile God, who leads them into the future, toward the realization of the divine promises."[33]

That the patriarchs prayed (18:23-33; 25:21; 28:20-22), built altars (12:7, 8; 13:18; 26:25; 33:20; 35:3, 7), offered sacrifices (22:13; 31:54), and practiced circumcision (17:9-14, 23-27) does not make patriarchal religion something unique. These were practices that Israel's ancestors either brought with them from Mesopotamia or observed while in Canaan or in Egypt. It is even quite possible that the patriarchs brought with them from Mesopotamia their knowledge of their deity El, and that such perceptions were reinforced by exposure to the cults of the Elim scattered throughout Canaan. What sets patriarchal religion apart from Bronze Age counterparts is not its outward ritual, but rather its conception of God as one who elects, one who promises, one who is mobile, and one who brings into a close relationship with himself those he has called.[34]

VI. CANONICITY

By "canonicity" we mean the acceptance by religious communities (Jewish, Christian) of certain authoritative documents in the shaping of their faith, practice, and doctrine. The reason for this acceptance was the widespread conviction that such literature was divinely inspired, and not just inspirational. Many religious compositions might fall into the second category without falling into the first category, but no composition could fall into the first category without falling into the second category simultaneously. So understood, canonicity needs to be distinguished from canonization.

No Christian or Jewish source ever raised questions over the legitimacy of Genesis' presence in the biblical canon. In only a few of these sources is Genesis mentioned by name. Normally it is subsumed under the umbrella word *Torah.* For example, Ben Sira's grandson (ca. 130 B.C.), in his preface

33. B. W. Anderson, *Understanding the Old Testament,* 4th ed. (Englewood Cliffs, NJ: Prentice-Hall, 1986), p. 45.

34. W. S. LaSor, D. A. Hubbard, and F. W. Bush, *Old Testament Survey* (Grand Rapids: Eerdmans, 1982), p. 111.

to the Greek translation, speaks of "the law and the prophets and other books of our fathers."

Philo of Alexandria (ca. 30 B.C.–A.D. 50) in his writings has approximately 2000 citations from the Torah, but only 50 citations from the remainder of the OT.[1] Josephus (ca. A.D. 37–107) speaks of "the twenty-two" books of the Bible.[2] He begins to expand on this with, "Of these, five are the books of Moses, comprising the laws and the traditional history from the birth of man down to the death of the lawgiver."

Only scraps of Genesis have been discovered at Qumran. But obviously the best-known material related to Genesis from there is the Genesis Apocryphon (1QapGen), testifying to Genesis' popularity in the Qumran community in the 1st century B.C. Of this composition J. Fitzmyer states, "Though it depends on the biblical text of Genesis and displays at times traits of targumic and midrashic composition, it is in reality a free reworking of the Genesis stories, a re-telling of the tales of the patriarchs."[3]

The NT distinguishes the Law and the Prophets (John 1:45) or Moses and the Prophets (Luke 24:27). In both cases the NT gives to the Law a Christocentric emphasis (John 1:45, "the one Moses wrote about in the Law"; Luke 24:27, "and beginning with Moses . . . he explained to them what was said in all the Scriptures concerning himself"). According to one source, there are 238 quotations from or allusions to Genesis in the NT.[4] Every chapter of Genesis is represented in this listing except 10, 20, 31, 34, 36, 43, and 44.

At the end of the 2nd and beginning of the 3rd century A.D., the famous church father Origen made the following statement: "There are twenty-two canonical books according to the Hebrew tradition . . . that which is entitled with us Genesis, but with the Hebrews, from the beginning of the book, Bresith, that is 'In the beginning.' "[5]

The most famous talmudic statement about the books of the Bible is found in T.B. *Baba Batra* 14b–15a: "Our Rabbis taught: The order of the Prophets is Joshua, Judges. . . . Who wrote the Scriptures?—Moses wrote his own book and the portion of Balaam and Job." Of interest here is that *Baba Batra* does not even list the order of the books of the Torah, for

1. See S. Z. Leiman, *The Canonization of Hebrew Scripture: The Talmudic and Midrashic Evidence* (Hamden, CT: Archon Books, 1976), p. 31.

2. Josephus *CAp* 1.37–43.

3. See J. Fitzmyer, *The Genesis Apocryphon of Qumran Cave I: A Commentary,* 2nd ed., BibOr 18A (Rome: Biblical Institute, 1977), p. 10.

4. "Index of Quotations," in *The New Testament Greek and English,* 2nd ed., ed. K. Aland, et al. (New York: American Bible Society, 1968), p. 897.

5. Found in Eusebius *Ecclesiastical History* 4.26.

Genesis–Deuteronomy were so universally recognized both in importance and sequence that their inclusion was unnecessary.

In spite of its strategic contents and placement in the Hebrew Bible, Genesis never did enjoy the wide use in the literature of postbiblical Judaism as did other books of the Torah. That honor goes to Leviticus, the concerns of which occupy nearly one-half of talmudic literature. In the Qumran community Genesis does not appear to have had nearly as much influence as Deuteronomy had.

VII. THE HEBREW TEXT

The translation in this commentary is based on the text in *BHK* and *BHS*. Both of these are based on the text of the Leningrad Public Library Ms. B 19, written in A.D. 1008. Unfortunately we do not have major finds from Qumran on Genesis (the Aramaic 1QapGen excepted), as we do with Deuteronomy or Isaiah, and thus we are unable to compare much of *BHK*'s and *BHS*'s Hebrew text, based as it is on manuscripts from the Middle Ages, with a Hebrew text written a millennium earlier.

Most of the Hebrew of Genesis reads quite smoothly. Gen. 49, one of the specimens of archaic poetry in the OT, is an exception to this rule, and its Hebrew will test the mettle of even the best Hebraist. There are very few foreign (i.e., non-Hebrew) words in the text of Genesis. If one would expect the intrusion of these non-Hebrew words anywhere in the Bible, surely it would be in the Joseph story, which is set in Egypt. In his study of Egyptian loanwords in the Hebrew Bible, T. O. Lambdin identifies about 40 Egyptian words in the Bible.[1] But only 5 of these occur in the Joseph story, and none of them is unique to Gen. 37–50.

R. Polzin has attempted to discern in Genesis and elsewhere a distinctive Hebrew syntax and morphology that reflect Late Biblical Hebrew.[2] The focus is on ascertaining linguistic evidence for P. If certain forms in P sections of Genesis are demonstrably similar to the Hebrew of Chronicles, then an exilic and postexilic date for at least one stratum of Genesis will be substantiated. Other studies have shown that many of the supposedly unique linguistic features of P in Genesis (and the remainder of Exodus–Leviticus) and Chronicles are scattered throughout the entire OT (often in J and E sections of the

1. T. O. Lambdin, "Egyptian Loanwords in Hebrew," *JAOS* 73 (1953) 145–55.

2. R. Polzin, *Late Biblical Hebrew: Toward an Historical Typology of Biblical Hebrew Prose,* HSM 12 (Missoula, MT: Scholars, 1976).

Pentateuch as well).[3] Accordingly, one must be extremely cautious about dating the Hebrew of Genesis late on the basis of linguistic analysis.

The MT and LXX have only minor differences in Genesis.[4] Here are some of the differences and the probable reasons for them. (1) Some of the differences are due to contextual harmonization. For example, the MT of 2:2 reads: "God completed his work on the *seventh* day." The LXX (with SP) reads: "on the *sixth* day." The translators wondered how God could finish his work on the seventh day when he did not work on that day at all. (2) Sometimes the LXX apparently confused two letters in the archaic Hebrew script that looked similar. Chief among these are *daleth (d)* and *resh (r)*. This accounts for the difference between "*another* ram" (MT) and "*one* ram" (LXX) in 22:13. Another illustration of the same confusion is found in 3:17: "cursed is the ground *because of you*" (MT) and "cursed is the ground *in your labors*" (LXX), plus 8:21: "I will not curse the ground any more *because of* man" (MT) and "I will not curse the ground anymore *because of the works of men*" (LXX). (3) At several points the LXX replaced a rare word with a common word. One example of this is 15:11, where speaking of the birds the MT says, "And Abram drove them away [*nāšaḇ*]." The LXX reads (the impossible), "And Abram sat down with them [*yāšaḇ*]"! The same is true of MT's enigmatic "Shiloh" (49:10), which LXX read "which are for him." A third illustration is found in 26:20. In the MT the well is called "Esek" (with a *sin*) by Isaac because Gerar's herdsmen disputed *(ʿāśaq)* with him. The LXX reads the well as "Eshek," for there the herdsmen "oppressed" *(ʿāšaq)* him. This LXX translation involves the confusion of the graphemes *sin* and *shin.* (4) On occasion the LXX adds a phrase lacking in the MT, and its presence in the LXX makes sense. After hearing of Reuben's adultery with Bilhah, the MT says, "Israel heard of it." LXX adds, understandably, "and it was evil in his eyes." (5) The most serious difference between the MT and LXX is the chronological system in chs. 5, 8, 11. The LXX partially agrees with the SP.[5]

3. See G. Rendsburg, "Late Biblical Hebrew and the Date of 'P'," *JANES* 12 (1980) 65–80; A. Hurvitz, *A Linguistic Study of the Relationship Between the Priestly Source and the Book of Ezekiel* (Paris: Gabalda, 1980), esp. pp. 163–70.

4. On the LXX of Genesis see J. W. Wevers, ed., *Genesis,* Septuaginta: V.T. graecum auct. Acad. Scientarium Gottingensis editum, 1 (Göttingen: Vandenhoeck & Ruprecht, 1974); idem, *Text History of the Greek Genesis* (Göttingen: Vandenhoeck & Ruprecht, 1974). One will find Wevers's observations on the particular features of the Greek of Genesis in *Genesis,* pp. 62–65.

5. See R. W. Klein, "Archaic Chronologies and the Textual History of the OT," *HTR* 67 (1974) 255–63 (although Klein does not take a position as to whether the LXX reflects a different Hebrew *Vorlage*).

VIII. BIBLIOGRAPHY

Aalders, G. Ch. *Genesis.* 2 vols. Tr. J. Vriend. Bible Student's Commentary. Grand Rapids: Zondervan, 1981.

Aberbach, M. and B. Grossfeld, *Targum Onkelos to Genesis.* New York: Ktav, 1982.

Ackroyd, P. R. "The Teraphim." *ExpTim* 62 (1950/51) 378–80.

Ahroni, R. "Why Did Esau Spurn the Birthright? A Study in Biblical Interpretation." *Judaism* 29 (1980) 323–31.

Aitken, K. T. "The Wooing of Rebekah: A Study in the Development of a Tradition." *JSOT* 30 (1984) 3–23.

Albright, W. F. "From the Patriarchs to Moses." *BA* 36 (1973) 19–26.

Alexander, T. D. "Genesis 22 and the Covenant of Circumcision." *JSOT* 25 (1983) 17–22.

Allegro, J. "A Possible Mesopotamian Background to the Joseph Blessing of Gen XLIX." *ZAW* 64 (1952) 249–51.

Allen, C. G. "Who was Rebekah?" In *Beyond Androcentrism: New Essays on Women and Religion.* Ed. Rita M. Gross. Missoula, MT: Scholars, 1977. Pp. 183–216.

_____, "On Me Be the Curse, My Son." In *Encounter with the Text: Form and History in the Hebrew Bible.* Ed. M. J. Buss. Philadelphia: Fortress, 1979. Pp. 159–72.

Alonso-Schökel, L. "Sapiential and Covenant Themes in Genesis 2–3." In *Studies in Ancient Israelite Wisdom.* Ed. J. Crenshaw. New York: Ktav, 1976. Pp. 468–80.

Alter, R. "A Literary Approach to the Bible." *Commentary* 60/6 (1975) 70–77.

_____. "Joseph and His Brothers." *Commentary* 70/5 (1980) 59–69.

_____. *The Art of Biblical Narrative.* New York: Basic Books, 1981.

_____. "How Convention Helps Us Read: The Case of the Bible's Annunciation Type-Scene." *Proof* 3 (1983) 115–30.

Anbar, M. "Genesis 15: A Conflation of Two Deuteronomic Narratives." *JBL* 101 (1982) 39–55.

Andersen, F. I. "Note on Genesis 30:8." *JBL* 88 (1969) 200.

_____. *The Hebrew Verbless Clause in the Pentateuch.* JBLMS 14. Nashville: Abingdon, 1970.

_____. *The Sentence in Biblical Hebrew.* Janua Linguarum, Series Practica 231. The Hague/Paris: Mouton, 1974.

Anderson, B. W. "An exposition of Genesis XXXII." *AusBR* 17 (1969) 21–26.

_____. "A Stylistic Study of the Priestly Creation Story." In *Canon and Authority: Essays in Old Testament Religion and Authority.* Ed. G. Coats and B. Long. Philadelphia: Fortress, 1977. Pp. 148–62.

_____. "Babel: Unity and Diversity in God's Creation." *CurTM* 5 (1978) 69–81.
_____. "From Analysis to Synthesis: The Interpretation of Genesis 1–11." *JBL* 97 (1978) 23–39.
_____. ed. *Creation in the Old Testament.* Issues in Religion and Theology 6. Philadelphia: Fortress, 1984.
Andreasen, N.-E. A. "Genesis 14 in its Near Eastern Context." In *Scripture in Context: Essays on the Comparative Method.* Ed. Carl D. Evans, et al. PTMS 34. Pittsburgh: Pickwick, 1980. Pp. 59–77.
Archer, G. "Old Testament History and Recent Archaeology—From Abraham to Moses." *BSac* 127 (1970) 3–25.
Armstrong, J. F. "A Critical Note on Genesis VI 16a." *VT* 10 (1960) 328–33.
Astour, M. C. "Sabtah and Sabteca: Ethiopian Pharaoh Names in Genesis 10." *JBL* 84 (1965) 422–25.
_____. "Political and Cosmic Symbolism in Genesis 14 and Its Babylonian Sources." In *Biblical Motifs: Origins and Transformations.* Ed. A. Altmann. Cambridge: Harvard University, 1966. Pp. 65–112.
_____. "Tamar the Hierodule: An Essay in the Method of Vestigial Motifs." *JBL* 85 (1966) 185–96.
Bailey, J. "Initiation and the Primal Woman in Gilgamesh and Genesis 2–3." *JBL* 89 (1970) 137–50.
_____. *The Pentateuch.* Nashville: Abingdon, 1981.
Baker, J. "The Myth of Man's 'Fall'—A Reappraisal." *ExpTim* 92 (1980/81) 235–37.
Barnard, A. N. "Was Noah a Righteous Man? Studies in Texts: Genesis 6,8." *Theology* 74 (1971) 311–14.
Barnouin, M. "Recherches numériques sur la généalogie de Gen. V." *RB* 77 (1970) 347–65.
Barr, J. "The Image of God in the Book of Genesis—A Study of Terminology." *BJRL* 51 (1968) 11–26.
_____. "Man and Nature—The Ecological Controversy and the Old Testament." *BJRL* 55 (1972) 9–32.
_____. "*erizō* and *ereidō* in the Septuagint: a note principally on Gen xlix,6." *JSS* 19 (1974) 198–215.
Barthes, R. "The Struggle with the Angel: Textual Analysis of Genesis 32:23–33." In *Structural Analysis and Biblical Exegesis: Interpretational Essays.* Tr. A. M. Johnson. PTMS 3. Pittsburgh: Pickwick, 1974. Pp. 21–33.
Bartlett, J. R. "The Edomite King-list of Genesis XXXVI 31–39 and I Chron I 43–50." *JTS* 16 (1965) 301–14.
Basset, F. W. "Noah's Nakedness and the Curse of Canaan, A Case of Incest?" *VT* 21 (1971) 232–37.
Baumgarten, A. L. "Myth and Midrash: Genesis 9:20–29." In *Christianity,*

Judaism and Other Greco-Roman Cults: Studies for Morton Smith at Sixty. 4 vols. Ed. J. Neusner. *Part III: Judaism Before 70.* Leiden: Brill, 1975. Pp. 55–71.

Beattie, D. R. G. "What is Genesis 2–3 About?" *ExpTim* 92 (1980/81) 8–10.

Beeston, A. F. L. "What Did Anah See?" *VT* 24 (1974) 109–10.

Berg, S. B. *The Book of Esther: Motifs, Themes and Structure.* SBLDS. Missoula, MT: Scholars, 1979. Pp. 123–42.

Bergmeier, R. "Zur Septuagintaubersetzung von Gen 3,16." *ZAW* 79 (1967) 77–79.

Bird, P. A. " 'Male and Female He Created Them': Gen. 1:27b in the Context of the Priestly Account of Creation." *HTR* 74 (1981) 129–59.

Blass, T. "The Tenacity of Impressions and Jacob's Rebuke of Simeon and Levi." *JPT* 7 (1982) 55–61.

Blenkinsopp, J. "The Oracle of Judah and the Messianic Entry." *JBL* 80 (1961) 55–64.

_____. *Gibeon and Israel: The Role of Gibeon and the Gibeonites in the Political and Religious History of Early Israel.* SOTSMS 2. Cambridge: Cambridge University, 1972.

_____. "The Structure of P." *CBQ* 38 (1976) 275–92.

_____. "Abraham and the Righteous of Sodom." *JJS* 33 (1982) 119–32.

Blocher, H. *In the Beginning: The Opening Chapters of Genesis.* Tr. David G. Preston. Downers Grove, IL: Inter-Varsity, 1984.

Blythin, I. "A Note on Genesis 1,2." *VT* 12 (1962) 120–21.

Bonhoeffer, D. *Creation and Fall.* Tr. J. C. Fletcher. London: SCM, 1959.

Booij, T. "Hagar's Words in Genesis xvi 13b." *VT* 30 (1980) 1–7.

Boomershine, T. E. "Structure and Narrative Rhetoric in Genesis 2–3." In SBLASP, 1978. 1:31–49.

Brock, S. "Genesis 22: Where was Sarah?" *ExpTim* 96 (1984) 14–17.

Brodie, L. T. "Jacob's Travail (Jer 30:1–13) and Jacob's Struggle (Gen 32:22–32): A Test Case for Measuring the Influence of the Book of Jeremiah on the Present Text of Genesis." *JSOT* 19 (1981) 31–60.

Brueggemann, W. "David and His Theologian." *CBQ* 30 (1968) 156–81.

_____. "Of the Same Flesh and Bone (GN 2,23a)." *CBQ* 32 (1970) 532–42.

_____. "Kingship and Chaos. (A Study in Tenth Century Theology)." *CBQ* 33 (1971) 317–32.

_____. "From Dust to Kingship." *ZAW* 84 (1972) 1–18.

_____. *Genesis.* Interpretation. Atlanta: John Knox, 1982.

_____. " 'Impossibility' and Epistemology in the Faith Tradition of Abraham and Sarah." *ZAW* 94 (1982) 615–34.

_____. "Genesis L 15–21: a theological exploration." In *Congress Volume: Salamanca, 1983.* Ed. J. A. Emerton. VTSup 36. Leiden: Brill, 1985. Pp. 40–53.

Brueggemann, W. and H. W. Wolff, *The Vitality of Old Testament Traditions.* Atlanta: John Knox, 1975.
Bryan, D. T. "A Reevaluation of Gen 4 and 5 in the Light of Recent Studies in Genealogical Fluidity," *ZAW* 99 (1987) 180–88.
Buchanan, G. W. "The Old Testament Meaning of the Knowledge of Good and Evil." *JBL* 75 (1956) 114–20.
Burrows, M. "The Complaint of Laban's Daughters." *JAOS* 57 (1937) 259–76.
Calvin, J. *Commentaries on the First Book of Moses Called Genesis.* 2 vols. Tr. John King. Repr. Grand Rapids: Eerdmans, 1948.
Campbell, E. F. and J. F. Ross, "The Excavation at Shechem and the Biblical Tradition." *BA* 26 (1963) 2–27.
Caquot, A. "L'alliance avec Abram (Genèse 15)." *Semitics* 12 (1962) 321–49.
Carlson, G. J. "The Two Creation Accounts in Schematic Contrast." *BiTod* 66 (1973) 1192–94.
Carmichael, C. M. "Some Sayings in Genesis 49." *JBL* 88 (1969) 435–44.
_____. *Women, Law, and the Genesis Traditions.* Edinburgh: University, 1979.
_____. "Forbidden Mixtures." *VT* 32 (1982) 394–415.
_____. *Law and Narrative in the Bible.* Ithaca: Cornell University, 1985.
Cassuto, U. *The Documentary Hypothesis and the Composition of the Pentateuch.* Tr. I. Abrahams. Jerusalem: Magnes, 1961.
_____. *A Commentary on the Book of Genesis.* Vol. I: *From Adam to Noah.* Vol. II: *From Noah to Abraham.* Tr. I. Abrahams. Jerusalem: Magnes, 1961–64.
_____. "The Episode of the Sons of God and the Daughters of Men (Genesis 6:1–4)." In *Biblical and Oriental Studies.* 2 vols. Tr. I. Abrahams. Jerusalem: Magnes, 1973. 1:17–28.
_____. "The Story of Tamar and Judah." In *Biblical and Oriental Studies.* 2 vols. Tr. I. Abrahams. Jerusalem: Magnes, 1973. 1:29–40.
Castellino, G. R. "Genesis IV 7." *VT* 10 (1960) 442–45.
Cazelles, H. "Connexions et structure de Gen XV." *RB* 69 (1962) 321–49.
Charny, I. W. "And Abraham Went to Slay Isaac: A Parable of Killer, Victim, and Bystander in the Family of Man." *JES* 10 (1973) 304–18.
Childs, B. S. "Eden, Garden of." *IDB.* 2:22–23.
_____. "Eve." *IDB.* 2:181–82.
_____. "Tree of Knowledge, Tree of Life." *IDB.* 4:695–97.
_____. *Myth and Reality in the Old Testament.* SBT 1/27. London: SCM, 1962.
_____. "A Study of the Formula, 'Until This Day.' " *JBL* 82 (1963) 279–82.
_____. "The Etiological Tale Re-examined." *VT* 24 (1974) 387–97.
_____. *Introduction to the Old Testament as Scripture.* Philadelphia: Fortress, 1979. Pp. 136–60.

Christensen, D. "Janus Parallelism in Genesis 6:3," *HS* 27 (1986) 20–24.
Clark, W. M. "The Animal Series in the Primeval History." *VT* 18 (1968) 433–49.
_____. "A Legal Background to the Yahwist's Use of 'Good and Evil' in Genesis 2–3." *JBL* 88 (1969) 266–78.
_____. "The Flood and the Structure of the Pre-patriarchal History." *ZAW* 83 (1971) 184–211.
_____. "The Righteousness of Noah." *VT* 21 (1971) 261–80.
Clarke, E. "Jacob's Dream at Bethel as Interpreted in the Targums and the New Testament." *SR* 4 (1974/75) 367–77.
Clements, R. *Abraham and David: Genesis XV and Its Meaning for Israelite Tradition.* SBT 2/5. London: SCM, 1967.
_____. *In Spirit and in Truth.* Atlanta: John Knox, 1985. Pp. 27–37.
Clines, D. J. A. "The Image of God in Man." *TynBul* 19 (1968) 53–103.
_____. "Noah's Flood: I: The Theology of the Flood Narrative." *Faith and Thought* 100 (1972–73) 128–42.
_____. "The Tree of Knowledge and the Law of Yahweh." *VT* 24 (1974) 8–14.
_____. "Themes in Genesis 1–11." *CBQ* 38 (1976) 483–507.
_____. "The Significance of the 'Sons of God' Episode (Genesis 6:1–4) in the Context of the 'Primeval History' (Genesis 1–11)." *JSOT* 13 (1979) 33–46.
_____. *The Theme of the Pentateuch.* JSOTSup 10. Sheffield: JSOT, 1978.
Coats, G. W. "Widow's Rights: A Crux in the Structure of Gen 38." *CBQ* 34 (1972) 461–66.
_____. "Abraham's Sacrifice of Faith: A Form-Critical Study of Genesis 22." *Int* 27 (1973) 389–400.
_____. "The Joseph Story and Wisdom: a Reappraisal." *CBQ* 35 (1973) 285–97.
_____. "Redactional Unity in Genesis 37–50." *JBL* 93 (1974) 15–21.
_____. *From Canaan to Egypt: Structural and Theological Context for the Joseph Story.* CBQMS 4. Washington: Catholic Biblical Association, 1975.
_____. "Power and Obedience in the Primeval History." *Int* 29 (1975) 227–39.
_____. "Strife without Reconciliation—A Narrative Theme in the Jacob Traditions." In *Werden und Wirken des Alten Testaments.* Fest. C. Westermann. Ed. R. Albertz, et al. Göttingen: Vandenhoeck & Ruprecht, 1979. Pp. 82–106.
_____. "Strife and Reconciliation: Themes of a Biblical Theology in the Book of Genesis." *HBT* 2 (1980) 15–37.
_____. "The Curse in God's Blessing: Genesis 12:1–4a in the Structure and Theology of the Yahwist." In *Die Botschaft und die Boten.* Fest. H. W.

Wolff. Ed. Jörg Jeremias and L. Perlitt. Neukirchen-Vluyn: Neukirchener, 1981. Pp. 31–41.
_____. *Genesis with an Introduction to Narrative Literature*. FOTL 1. Grand Rapids: Eerdmans, 1983.
_____. "A Threat to the Host." In *Saga, Legend, Tale, Novella, Fable: Narrative Forms in Old Testament Literature*. Ed. G. W. Coats. JSOTSup 35. Sheffield: JSOT, 1985. Pp. 71–81.
_____. "Lot: A Foil in the Abraham Saga." In *Understanding the Word: Essays in Honour of Bernhard W. Anderson*. Ed. James T. Butler, et al. JSOTSup 37. Sheffield: JSOT, 1985. Pp. 113–32.
Cohen, H. H. *The Drunkenness of Noah*. Alabama: University of Alabama, 1974.
Cohen, M. "*m^{e}kērōtēhem* (Genèse xlix 5)." *VT* 31 (1981) 472–82.
Cohn, R. L. "Narrative Structure and Canonical Perspective in Genesis." *JSOT* 25 (1983) 3–16.
Coote, R. "The Meaning of the Name Israel." *HTR* 65 (1972) 137–46.
Coppens, J. "La Bénédiction de Jacob." In *Volume du Congres: Strasbourg 1956*. VTSup 4. Leiden: Brill, 1957. Pp. 100–102.
Cornelius, I. "Genesis XXVI and Mari." *JNWSL* 12 (1984) 53–61.
Couffignal, R. "Le Songe de Jacob: Approaches nouvelles de Gn 28,10–22." *Bib* 58 (1977) 342–60.
Crenshaw, J. L. "Method in Determining Wisdom Influence upon 'Historical' Literature." *JBL* 88 (1969) 129–42.
_____. "Popular Questioning of the Justice of God in Ancient Israel." *ZAW* 82 (1970) 390–95.
_____. "Journey into Oblivion: A Structural Analysis of Gen 22:1–19." *Soundings* 58 (1975) 243–56.
Croatto, J. S. "'abrek 'Intendant' dans Gen XLI,41, 43." *VT* 16 (1966) 113–15.
Cross, F. M. *Canaanite Myth and Hebrew Epic*. Cambridge: Harvard University, 1973.
Cross, F. M. and D. N. Freedman, *Studies in Ancient Yahwistic Poetry*. SBLDS 21. Missoula, MT: Scholars, 1975. Pp. 69–93.
Culley, R. C. "Structural Analysis: Is It Done with Mirrors?" *Int* 28 (1974) 165–81.
_____. *Studies in the Structure of Hebrew Narrative*. Philadelphia: Fortress, 1976.
_____. "Action Sequence in Gen 2–3." In SBLASP, 1978. 1:51–60.
Dahood, M. J. "A New Translation of Gen 49:6a." *Bib* 36 (1955) 229.
_____. "Is *'Eben Yiśrā'ēl* a Divine Title? (Gn 49,24)." *Bib* 40 (1959) 1002–7.
_____. "*MKRTYHM* in Genesis 49,5." *CBQ* 23 (1961) 54–56.
_____. "The Name *yišmāʿ'ēl* in Genesis 20,11." *Bib* 49 (1968) 87–88.
_____. "Nomen-Omen in Gen 16,11." *Bib* 61 (1980) 69.

_____. "Eblaite *ì–du* and Hebrew *'ēd*, 'Rain Cloud,'" *CBQ* 43 (1981) 534–38.

Daube, D. "How Esau Sold his Birthright." *Cambridge Law Journal* 8 (1942–44) 70–75.

_____. *Studies in Biblical Law.* Repr. New York: Ktav, 1969.

_____. "The Night of Death." *HTR* 61 (1968) 629–32.

Daube, D. and R. Yaron, "Jacob's Reception by Laban." *JSS* 1 (1956) 60–62.

David, M. "ZABAL (GEN XXX 26)." *VT* 1 (1951) 59–60.

Davies, E. W. "Inheritance Rights and the Hebrew Levirate Marriage." *VT* 31 (1981) 138–44, 257–68.

Davies, J. D. *Beginning Now: A Christian Exploration of the First Three Chapters of Genesis.* Philadelphia: Fortress, 1971.

Davies, P. R. and B. D. Chilton, "The Aqedah: A Revised Tradition History." *CBQ* 40 (1978) 514–46.

Delitzsch, F. *A New Commentary on Genesis.* Tr. S. Taylor. 2 vols. Repr. Minneapolis: Klock & Klock, 1978.

Deurloo, K. A. "*tšuqh,* 'dependency', Gen 4, 7," *ZAW* 99 (1987) 405–6.

Dever, W. G. and W. M. Clark, "The Patriarchal Traditions." In *Israelite and Judaean History.* OTL. Ed. J. H. Hayes and J. M. Miller. Philadelphia: Westminster, 1977. Pp. 70–148.

DeWitt, D. S. "The Generations of Genesis." *EvQ* 48 (1976) 196–211.

_____. "The Historical Background of Genesis 11:1–9: Babel or Ur?" *JETS* 22 (1979) 15–26.

Diamond, J. A. "The Deception of Jacob: A New Perspective on an Ancient Solution to a Problem." *VT* 34 (1984) 211–13.

Donner, H. *Die literarische Gestalt der alttestestamentlichen Josephgeschichte.* Heidelberg: Winter, 1976.

Doré, J. "La rencontre Abraham-Melchisédech et le problème de l'unité littéraire de Genèse 14." In *De la Tôrah au Messie.* Fest. H. Cazelles. Ed. M. Carrez, et al. Paris: Desclée, 1981.

Doukhan, J. B. *The Genesis Creation Story.* Berrien Springs, MI: Andrews University, 1978.

Draffkorn, A. "*ILĀNI/ELOHIM.*" *JBL* 76 (1957) 216–24.

Driver, G. R. "Gen XXXVI 24: Mules or Fishes." *VT* 25 (1975) 109–10.

Driver, S. R. *The Book of Genesis.* WC. 15th ed. London: Methuen, 1948.

Eichrodt, W. "In the Beginning." In *Israel's Prophetic Heritage: Essays in Honor of James Muilenburg.* Ed. B. W. Anderson and W. Harrelson. New York: Harper, 1962. Pp. 1–10.

Elliger, K. "Der Jakobskampf am Jabbok. Gen 32:23ff als hermeneutisches Problem." *ZTK* 48 (1951) 1–31.

Ellington, J. "Man and Adam in Genesis 1–5." *BT* 30 (1979) 201–5.

Ellis, P. F. *The Yahwist: The Bible's First Theologian.* Notre Dame: Fides, 1968.

Emerton, J. A. "Some Difficult Words in Genesis 49." In *Words and Meanings: Essays Presented to David Winton Thomas.* Ed. P. R. Ackroyd and B. Lindars. Cambridge: Cambridge University, 1968. Pp. 81–93.
_____. "The Riddle of Genesis XIV." *VT* 21 (1971) 403–39.
_____. "Some False Clues in the Study of Genesis XIV." *VT* 21 (1971) 24–27.
_____. "Some Problems in Genesis XXXVIII." *VT* 25 (1975) 338–61.
_____. "An Examination of a Recent Structural Interpretation of Genesis XXXVIII." *VT* 26 (1976) 79–98.
Engnell, I. " 'Knowledge' and 'Life' in the Creation Story." In *Wisdom in Israel and in the Ancient Near East.* VTSup 3. Fest. H. H. Rowley. Ed. M. Noth and D. W. Thomas. Leiden: Brill, 1955. Pp. 103–19.
Enslin, M. S. "Cain and Prometheus." *JBL* 86 (1967) 88–90.
Eslinger, L. "A Contextual Identification of the *bene ha'elohim* and *benoth ha'adam* in Genesis 6:1–4." *JSOT* 13 (1979) 65–73.
Exum, C. and J. W. Whedbee, "Isaac, Samson, and Saul: Reflections on the Comic and Tragic Visions." *Semeia* 32 (1985) 5–21.
Fensham, F. C. "The Son of a Handmaid in Northwest-Semitic." *VT* 19 (1969) 312–21.
_____. "Gen XXXIV and Mari." *JNWSL* 4 (1975) 15–38.
Finkelstein, J. J. "An Old Babylonian Herding Contract and Genesis 31:38." *JAOS* 88 (1968) 30–36.
Fishbane, M. "Composition and Structure in the Jacob Cycle (Gen. 25:19–35:22)." *JSS* 26 (1975) 15–38. Repr. in *Text and Texture: Close Readings of Selected Biblical Texts.* New York: Schocken, 1979. Pp. 40–62.
Fisher, E. "Gilgamesh and Genesis: The Flood Story in Context." *CBQ* 32 (1970) 392–403.
Fisher, L. R. "Abraham and His Priest-King." *JBL* 81 (1962) 264–70.
_____. "An Ugaritic Ritual and Gen. 1:1–5." In *Ugaritica* 6 (Paris: Geuthner, 1969) 197–205.
_____. "Creation at Ugarit and in the Old Testament." *VT* 15 (1965) 313–24.
Fitzmyer, J. A. *The Genesis Apocryphon of Qumran Cave 1: A Commentary.* 2nd ed. BibOr 18A. Rome: Biblical Institute, 1971.
Foh, S. T. "What is the Woman's Desire?" *WTJ* 37 (1975) 376–83.
Fokkelman, J. P. *Narrative Art in Genesis: Specimens of Stylistic and Structural Analysis.* Amsterdam: Van Gorcum, 1975.
Fox, E. *In The Beginning: A New English Rendition of the Book of Genesis.* New York: Schocken, 1983.
Fox, M. V. "The Sign of Covenant: Circumcision in the Light of Priestly *'ot* Etiologies." *RB* 81 (1974) 557–96.
Frankena, R. "Some Remarks on the Semitic Background of Chapters XXIX–XXXI of the Book of Genesis." *OTS* 17 (1972) 53–64.

Franxman, T. W. *Genesis and the "Jewish Antiquities" of Flavius Josephus.* BibOr 35. Rome: Biblical Institute, 1979.
Freedman, D. "A New Approach to the Nuzi Sistership Contract." *JANES* 2 (1970) 77–85.
Freedman, D. N. "The Original Name of Jacob." *IEJ* 13 (1963) 125–26.
Fretheim, T. E. "The Jacob Traditions: Theology and Hermeneutic." *Int* 26 (1972) 419–36.
Frymer-Kensky, T. "What the Babylonian Flood Stories Can and Cannot Teach Us About the Genesis Flood." *BAR* 4/4 (1974) 32–41.
_____. "The Atrahasis Epic and Its Significance for Our Understanding of Genesis 1–9." *BA* 40 (1977) 147–55.
Gabriel, J. "Die Kainitengenealogie: Gen 4:17–24." *Bib* 40 (1959) 409–27.
Gammie, J. G. "Loci of Melchizedek Tradition of Genesis 14,18–20." *JBL* 90 (1971) 385–396.
_____. "Theological Interpretation by Way of Literary and Tradition Analysis: Genesis 25–36." In *Encounter with the Text: Form and History in the Hebrew Bible.* Ed. M. J. Buss. Philadelphia: Fortress, 1979. Pp. 117–34.
Garcia-Treto, F. "Genesis 31 and Gilead." *TUSR* 9 (1967/68) 13–17.
_____. "Genesis 31,44 and 'Gilead.' " *ZAW* 79 (1967) 13–17.
_____. "Jacob's 'Oath-Covenant' in Genesis 28." *TUSR* 10 (1975) 1–10.
Gehrke, R. "The Biblical View of the Sexual Polarity." *CTM* 41 (1970) 195–205.
Geller, S. A. "The Struggle at the Jabbok: The Uses of Enigma in Biblical Narrative." *JANES* 14 (1982) 37–60.
Gevirtz, S. *Patterns in the Early Poetry of Israel.* SAOC 32. Chicago: University of Chicago, 1963.
_____. "Abram's 318." *IEJ* 19 (1968) 110–13.
_____. "Of Patriarchs and Puns: Joseph at the Fountain, Jacob at the Ford." *HUCA* 46 (1975) 33–54.
_____. "The Issachar Oracle in the Testament of Jacob." In *Spr Nlswn Glyq.* Ed. B. Mazar. Jerusalem: Jewish Institute of Religion, 1975. Pp. 104–12.
_____. "Adumbrations of Dan in Jacob's Blessing on Judah." *ZAW* 83 (1981) 21–37.
Gilbert, M. "Only One Flesh." *TD* 26 (1978) 206–9.
Ginsberg, H. L. "Abram's 'Damascene' Steward." *BASOR* 200 (1970) 31–32.
Gispen, W. H. "Genesis 2:10–14." In *Studia Biblica et Semitica.* Fest. T. C. Vriezen. Wageningen: Veenman, 1966. Pp. 115–24.
Goldin, J. "The Youngest Son, or Where does Genesis 38 Belong." *JBL* 96 (1977) 27–44.
Good, E. M. "The 'Blessing' on Judah, Gen 49:8–12." *JBL* 82 (1963) 427–32.

_____. *Irony in the Old Testament.* Philadelphia: Westminster, 1965.
Gordon, C. H. "Parallèles nouziens aux lois et coutumes de l'Ancien Testament." *RB* 44 (1935) 35–41.
_____. "The Story of Jacob and Laban in the Light of the Nuzi Tablets." *BASOR* 66 (1937) 25–27.
_____. "Abraham and the Merchants of Ura." *JNES* 17 (1958) 28–31.
_____. "Abraham of Ur." In *Hebrew and Semitic Studies.* Fest. G. R. Driver. Ed. W. D. McHardy. Oxford: Clarendon, 1963. Pp. 77–84.
_____. "Hebrew Origins in the Light of Recent Discovery." In *Biblical and Other Studies.* Ed. A. Altmann. Cambridge: Harvard University, 1963. Pp. 3–14.
_____. *The Ancient Near East.* 3rd ed. New York: Norton, 1965.
_____. "Where Is Abraham's Ur?" *BAR* 3 (1977) 20–21, 52.
_____. "The Seventh Day." *UF* 11 (1979) 299–301.
_____. "Ebla and Genesis 11." In *A Spectrum of Thought.* Fest. D. F. Kinlaw. Ed. Michael L. Peterson. Wilmore, KY: Francis Asbury, 1982. Pp. 125–34.
Gordon, R. "Targum Onkelos to Genesis 49:4 and a Common Semitic Idiom." *JQR* 66 (1975–76) 224–26.
Grayson, A. K. and J. Van Seters, "The Childless Wife in Assyria and the Stories of Genesis." *Or* 44 (1975) 485–86.
Greenberg, M. "Another Look at Rachel's Theft of the Teraphim." *JBL* 81 (1962) 239–48.
Greengus, S. "Sisterhood Adoption at Nuzi and the 'Wife–Sister' in Genesis." *HUCA* 46 (1975) 5–31.
Griffiths, J. G. "The Celestial Ladder and the Gate of Heaven ('Genesis 28:12,17')." *ExpTim* 76 (1964/65) 229.
Gross, W. "Jakob, der Mann des Segens. Zu Traditionsgeschichte und Theologie der priesterschriftlichen Jakobsüberlieferungen." *Bib* 49 (1968) 321–44.
Gros Louis, K. R. R., ed. *Literary Interpretations of Biblical Narratives.* 2 vols. Nashville: Abingdon, 1982. 2:37–133.
Gruber, M. I. "Was Cain Angry or Depressed?" *BAR* 6 (Nov.–Dec. 1980) 35–36.
_____. "The Tragedy of Cain and Abel: A Case of Depression." *JQR* 69 (1978) 89–97.
Gunkel, H. *Genesis.* HKAT 1/1. 6th ed. Göttingen: Vandenhoeck & Ruprecht, 1963.
_____. *The Legends of Genesis.* Tr. W. H. Carruth. Repr. New York: Schocken, 1966.
Habel, N. C. "The Gospel Promise to Abraham." *CTM* 40 (1969) 346–55.
_____. *Literary Criticism of the Old Testament.* Philadelphia: Fortress, 1971.
Hallo, W. W. "Antediluvian Cities." *JCS* 23 (1970–71) 57–67.

_____. "Genesis and Ancient Near Eastern Literature." In *The Torah: A Modern Commentary.* Vol. I: *Genesis.* Ed. W. G. Plaut. New York: Union of American Hebrew Congregations, 1974. Pp. XXIX–XXXIV.
Hartmann, T. C. "Some Thoughts on the Sumerian King List and Genesis 5 and 11b." *JBL* 91 (1972) 25–32.
Harrison, R. K. "Genesis." *ISBE.* 2:431–42.
Hasel, G. F. "Recent Translations of Gen 1,1." *BT* 22 (1971) 154–68.
_____. "The Significance of the Cosmology in Genesis 1 in Relation to Ancient Near Eastern Parallels." *AUSS* 10 (1972) 1–20.
_____. "The Polemic Nature of the Genesis Cosmology." *EvQ* 46 (1974) 81–102.
_____. "The Meaning of 'Let Us' in Gn 1:26." *AUSS* 13 (1975) 58–66.
_____. "The Genealogies of Gen 5 and 11 and Their Alleged Babylonian Background." *AUSS* 16 (1978) 361–74.
_____. "The Meaning of the Animal Rite in Gen. 15." *JSOT* 19 (1981) 61–78.
Hauge, M. R. "The Struggles of the Blessed in Estrangement." *ST* 29 (1975) 1–30, 113–46.
Hauser, A. J. "Linguistic and Thematic Links Between Genesis 4:1–16 and Genesis 2–3." *JETS* 23 (1980) 297–305.
_____. "Genesis 2–3: The Theme of Intimacy and Alienation." In *Art and Meaning: Rhetoric in Biblical Literature.* Ed. D. J. A. Clines, et al. JSOTSup 19. Sheffield: JSOT, 1982. Pp. 20–36.
Helyer, L. R. "The Separation of Abram and Lot: Its Significance in the Patriarchal Narratives." *JSOT* 26 (1983) 77–88.
Hendel, R. S. "Of Demigods and the Deluge: Toward an Interpretation of Genesis 6:1–4," *JBL* 106 (1987) 13–26.
Hermant, D. "Analyse littéraire du premier récit de la création." *VT* 15 (1965) 437–51.
Hermisson, H.-J. "Jakobs Kampf am Jabbok (Gen 32:23–33)." *ZTK* 71 (1974) 239–61.
Higgins, J. M. "The Myth of Eve: The Temptress." *JAAR* 44 (1976) 639–47.
Hoffmeier, J. K. "Some Thoughts on Genesis 1–2 and Egyptian Cosmology." *JANES* 15 (1983) 39–49.
Hoftijzer, J. *Die Verheissungen an die drei Erzväter.* Leiden: Brill, 1956.
_____. "Some Remarks to the Tale of Noah's Drunkenness." *OTS* 12 (1958) 22–27.
Hopkins, D. C. "Between Promise and Fulfillment: von Rad and the 'Sacrifice of Abraham' [Gn 22]." *BZ* 24 (1980) 180–93.
Horwitz, W. J. "Were There Twelve Horite Tribes?" *CBQ* 35 (1973) 69–71.
Houtman, C. "What Did Jacob See in His Dream at Bethel? Some Remarks on Genesis xxviii 10–22." *VT* 27 (1977) 337–51.
_____. "Jacob at Mahanaim. Some Remarks on Genesis xxxii 2–3." *VT* 28 (1978) 37–44.

Humbert, P. "Trois Notes sur Genèse 1." In *Interpretationes ad Vetus Testamentum pertinentes Sigmundo Mowinckel.* Ed. N. A. Dahl and A. S. Kapelrud. Oslo: Forlaget Land og Kirche, 1955. Pp. 85–96.

Humphreys, W. L. "Joseph Story." *IDBSup.* Pp. 491–92.

_____. "Novella." In *Saga, Legend, Tale, Novella, Fable: Narrative Forms in Old Testament Literature.* Ed. G. W. Coats. JSOTSup 35. Sheffield: JSOT, 1985. Pp. 82–96.

Hunt, I. *The World of the Patriarchs.* Englewood Cliffs, NJ: Prentice-Hall, 1967.

Hvidberg, F. "The Canaanite Background of Gen I–III." *VT* 10 (1960) 285–94.

Hyers, C. *The Meaning of Creation.* Atlanta: John Knox, 1984.

Irvin, D. *Mytharion: The Comparison of Tales from the Old Testament and the Ancient Near East.* AOAT 32. Neukirchen-Vluyn: Neukirchener, 1978.

Jackson, B. S. *Theft in Early Jewish Law.* Oxford: Clarendon, 1972.

Jacob, B. *The First Book of the Bible: Genesis.* Repr. New York: Ktav, 1974.

Jacobsen, T. "The Eridu Genesis." *JBL* 100 (1981) 513–29.

Jenks, A. W. *The Elohist and North Israelite Traditions.* SBLMS 22. Missoula, MT: Scholars, 1977.

Jobling, D. "A Structural Analysis of Genesis 2:4b–3:24." In SBLASP, 1978. 1:61–69.

Johnson, B. "Who Reckoned Righteousness to Whom?" *SEÅ* 51/2 (1986/7) 108–15.

Johnson, M. D. *The Purpose of the Biblical Genealogies.* SNTSMS 8. Cambridge: Cambridge University, 1969.

Joines, K. R. *Serpent Symbolism in the Old Testament.* Haddonfield, NJ: Haddonfield House, 1974.

_____. "The Serpent in Genesis 3." *ZAW* 87 (1975) 1–11.

Kaiser, O. "Traditionsgeschichtliche Untersuchung von Genesis 15." *ZAW* 70 (1958) 107–26.

_____. "Stammesgeschichtliche Hintergründe der Josephgeschichte." *VT* 10 (1960) 1–15.

Kapelrud, A. "The Mythological Features in Genesis 1 and the Author's Intention." *VT* 24 (1974) 178–86.

Kardimon, S. "Adoption as a Remedy for Infertility in the Period of the Patriarchs." *JSS* 3 (1958) 123–26.

Keel, O. "Das Vergraben der 'fremden Goetter' in Gen XXXV 4b." *VT* 23 (1973) 305–36.

Keil, C. F. and F. Delitzsch. *Commentary on the Old Testament.* 10 vols. Vol. 1: *The Pentateuch.* Tr. James Martin. Repr. 3 vols. in 1. Grand Rapids: Eerdmans, 1973.

Kessler, M. "The 'Shield' of Abraham." *VT* 14 (1964) 494–97.
_____. "Genesis 34—An Interpretation." *RefR* 19 (1965) 3–8.
Kevers, P. "Étude littéraire de Genèse XXXIV." *RB* 87 (1980) 38–86.
Kidner, D. *Genesis.* TOTC. Downers Grove, IL: Inter-Varsity, 1967.
Kikawada, I. M. "Two Notes on Eve." *JBL* 91 (1972) 33–37.
_____. "The Shape of Genesis 11:1–9." In *Rhetorical Criticism: Essays in Honor of James Muilenburg.* Ed. J. J. Jackson and M. Kessler. PTMS 1. Pittsburgh: Pickwick, 1974. Pp. 18–32.
Kikawada, I. and A. Quinn, *Before Abraham Was: The Unity of Genesis 1–11.* Nashville: Abingdon, 1985.
Kilian, R. *Die vorpriesterlichen Abrahamüberlieferungen, literarkritisch und traditionsgeschichtlich untersucht.* Bonn: Hanstein, 1966.
_____. *Isaaks Opferung. Zur Überlieferungsgeschichte von Gen 22.* Stuttgart: Katholisches Bibelwerk, 1970.
Kingsbury, E. C. "He Set Ephraim Before Manasseh." *HUCA* 38 (1967) 129–36.
Kirkland, J. R. "The Incident at Salem: A Reexamination of Gen 14:18–23." *StBTh* 7 (1977) 3–23.
Kitchen, K. A. "The Old Testament in its Context: 1: From the Origins to the Eve of the Exodus." *TSF Bulletin* 59 (1971) 2–10.
_____. "Joseph." *ISBE.* 2:1126–30.
Kline, M. "Divine Kingship and Genesis 6:1–4." *WTJ* 24 (1962) 197–204.
Kline, M. "Abram's Amen." *WTJ* 31 (1968) 1–11.
_____. *By Oath Consigned: A Reinterpretation of the Covenant Signs of Circumcision and Baptism.* Grand Rapids: Eerdmans, 1968.
_____. "Oracular Origin of the State." In *Biblical and Near Eastern Studies.* Fest. W. S. LaSor. Ed. G. Tuttle. Grand Rapids: Eerdmans, 1978. Pp. 132–41.
Knauf, A. "Alter und Herkunft der edomitischen Königsliste Gen 36, 31–39." *ZAW* 97 (1985) 245–53.
Kodel, J. "Jacob Wrestles With Esau (Gen 32:23–32)." *BTB* 10 (1980) 65–70.
Kraeling, E. "The Significance and Origin of Gen. 6:1–4." *JNES* 6 (1947) 193–208.
Kraft, R. A. "A Note on the Oracle of Rebecca (Gen XXV 23)." *JTS* 13 (1962) 318–20.
Kramer, S. N. "The 'Babel of Tongues': A Sumerian Version." *JAOS* 88 (1968) 108–11.
Kugel, J. *The Idea of Biblical Poetry.* New Haven: Yale University, 1981.
Kuyper, L. J. "To Know Good and Evil (Gen 3,22a)." *Int* 1 (1947) 490–92.
Lack, R. "Le sacrifice d'Isaac—Analyse structurale de la couche élohiste dans Gen 22." *Bib* 56 (1975) 1–12.
Lambert, W. G. "A New Look at the Babylonian Background of Genesis." *JTS* 16 (1965) 287–300.

_____. "Trees, Snakes and Gods in Ancient Syria and Anatolia." *BSOAS* 48 (1985) 435–51.

Lambert, W. G. and A. R. Millard. *Atra-ḫasīs: The Babylonian Story of the Flood.* Oxford: Clarendon, 1969.

Landes, G. M. "Creation Tradition in Proverbs 8:22–31 and Genesis 1." In *A Light unto My Path.* Fest. J. M. Myers. Ed. H. N. Bream, et al. Philadelphia: Temple University, 1974. Pp. 279–93.

Lane, W. R. "The Initiation of Creation." *VT* 13 (1963) 63–73.

Larson, G. "Chronological Parallels Between the Creation and the Flood." *VT* 27 (1977) 490–92.

LaSor, W. S. "Notes on Genesis 1:1–2:3." *Gordon Review* 2 (1956) 26–32.

Laurin, R. B. "The Tower of Babel Revisited." In *Biblical and Near Eastern Studies.* Fest. W. S. LaSor. Ed. G. Tuttle. Grand Rapids: Eerdmans, 1978. Pp. 142–45.

Leach, E. R. *Genesis as Myth and Other Essays.* London: Cape, 1969.

Lehmann, M. R. "Abraham's Purchase of Machpelah and Hittite Law." *BASOR* 129 (1953) 15–18.

Lehming, S. "Zur Überlieferungsgeschichte von Gen 34." *ZAW* 70 (1958) 228–50.

_____. "Zur Erzählung von der Geburt der Jacobssöhne." *VT* 13 (1963) 74–81.

Lemaire, A. "Les benê Jacob. Essai d'une interprétation historique d'une tradition patriarchale." *Bib* 85 (1978) 321–37.

Leupold, H. C. *Exposition of Genesis.* 2 vols. Grand Rapids: Baker, 1950.

Levin, S. "The More Savory Offering: A Key to the Problem of Gen. 4:3–5." *JBL* 98 (1979) 85.

Lewis, J. "Gen 32:23–33, Seeing a Hidden God." In SBLASP, 1972. 1:449–57.

Limburg, J. "What Does It Mean—Have Dominion Over the Earth?" *Dialog* 10 (1971) 221–26.

_____. *Old Stories for a New Time.* Atlanta: John Knox, 1983.

Lindblom, J. "The Political Background of the Shiloh Oracle." *Congress Volume: Copenhagen, 1953.* VTSup 1. Leiden: Brill, 1953. Pp. 78–87.

Loewenstamm, S. E. "Zur Traditionsgeschichte des Bundes zwischen den Stücken." *VT* 18 (1968) 500–506.

_____. "The Divine Grants of Land to the Patriarchs." *JAOS* 91 (1971) 509–10.

_____. "*'ānôkī 'aḥaṭṭenāh.*" *ZAW* 90 (1978) 410.

Lohfink, N. "Gen 2–3 as 'Historical Etiology.'" *TD* 13 (1965) 11–17.

_____. *Die Landverheissung als Eid. Eine Studie zu Gen 15.* Stuttgart: Katholisches Bibelwerk, 1967.

_____. "Textkritisches zu Gn 17, 5.13.16.17." *Bib* 48 (1967) 439–42.

Long, B. O. *The Problem of Etiological Narrative in the Old Testament.* BZAW 109. Berlin: de Gruyter, 1968.

Longacre, R. "The Discourse Structure of the Flood Narrative." In SBLASP, 1976. Pp. 235–62.

Loretz, O. "Hebraïsch *ḥwṭ* 'bezahlen, erstatten' in Gen 31,39." *ZAW* 87 (1975) 207–8.

_____. "Repointing und Redivision in Genesis 16,11." *UF* 8 (1976) 452–53.

Lowenthal, E. I. *The Joseph Narrative in Genesis.* New York: Ktav, 1973.

Lundbom, J. R. "Abraham and David in the Theology of the Yahwist." In *The Word of the Lord Shall Go Forth.* Fest. D. N. Freedman. Ed. Carol L. Meyers and M. O'Connor. Winona Lake, IN: Eisenbrauns, 1983. Pp. 203–9.

Luther, M. *Lectures on Genesis.* 8 vols. Ed. J. Pelikan. St. Louis: Concordia, 1958–1966.

Luyster, R. "Wind and Water: Cosmogonic Symbolism in the Old Testament." *ZAW* 93 (1981) 1–10.

Maag, V. "Jakob—Esau—Edom." *TZ* 13 (1957) 418–29.

Maars, R. "The Sons of God (Genesis 6:1–4)." *RestQ* 23 (1980) 218–24.

Mabee, C. "Jacob and Laban. The structure of judicial proceedings (Genesis XXXI 25–42)." *VT* 30 (1980) 192–207.

McAlpine, T. H. "The Word Against the Nations." *StBTh* 5 (1975) 3–14.

McCarthy, D. J. "Three Covenants in Genesis." *CBQ* 26 (1964) 179–89.

_____. " 'Creation Motifs' in Ancient Hebrew Poetry." *CBQ* 39 (1967) 393–406.

McEvenue, S. E. *The Narrative Style of the Priestly Writer.* AnBib 50. Rome: Biblical Institute, 1971.

_____. "A Comparison of Narrative Styles in the Hagar Stories." *Semeia* 3 (1975) 64–80.

_____. "The Elohist at Work." *ZAW* 96 (1984) 315–32.

McGuire, E. "The Joseph Story. A Tale of Son and Father." In *Images of Man and God: Old Testament Short Stories in Literary Focus.* Ed. B. O. Long. Sheffield: Almond, 1981. Pp. 9–25.

McKane, W. *Studies in the Patriarchal Narratives.* Edinburgh: Handsel, 1979.

McKenzie, B. A. "Jacob's Blessing on Pharaoh: An Interpretation of Gen 46:31–47:26." *WTJ* 45 (1983) 386–99.

McKenzie, J. L. "The Literary Characteristics of Genesis 2–3." *TS* 15 (1954) 541–72.

_____. "Jacob at Peniel: Gn 32,24–32." *CBQ* 25 (1963) 71–76.

Mckenzie, S. "You Have Prevailed." *RestQ* 23 (1980) 225–31.

Malamat, A. "King Lists of the Old Babylonian Period and Biblical Genealogies." *JAOS* 88 (1968) 163–73.

Malull, M. "More on *paḥad yiṣḥaq* (Genesis XXXI 42, 53) and the Oath by the Thigh." *VT* 35 (1985) 192–200.
Margulis, B. "Gen XLIX 10/Deut XXXIII 2–3." *VT* 19 (1969) 202–10.
Martin, R. A. "The Earliest Messianic Interpretation of Genesis 3:15." *JBL* 84 (1965) 425–27.
Maxwell-Mahon, W. D. " 'Jacob's Ladder': A Structural Analysis of Scripture." *Semitics* 7 (1980) 118–30.
May, H. G. "The Evolution of the Joseph Story." *AJSL* 47 (1930/31) 83–93.
Mazar, B. "The Historical Background of the Book of Genesis." *JNES* 28 (1969) 73–83.
Mazor, Y. "Genesis 22: The Ideological Rhetoric and the Psychological Composition." *Bib* 67 (1986) 81–88.
Meinhold, A. "Die Gattung der Josephgeschichte und des Esterbuches: Diasporanovelle I." *ZAW* 87 (1975) 306–24.
Melchin, K. R. "Literary Sources in the Joseph Story." *ScEs* 31 (1979) 93–101.
Melugin, R. F. "Muilenburg, Form Criticism, and Theological Exegesis." In *Encounter with the Text: Form and History in the Hebrew Bible.* Ed. M. J. Buss. Philadelphia: Fortress, 1979. Pp. 91–100.
Mendenhall, G. E. "The Shady Side of Wisdom: The Date and Purpose of Genesis 3." In *A Light unto My Path.* Fest. J. M. Myers. Ed. H. N. Bream, et al. Philadelphia: Temple University, 1974. Pp. 319–34.
Merode, M. de, " 'A Helper Fit for Him': Gen. 2:18–24." *TD* 27 (1979) 117–19.
Merwe, B. J. van der, "Joseph as Successor of Jacob." In *Studia Biblica et Semitica.* Fest. T. C. Vriezen. Wageningen: Veenman, 1966. Pp. 221–32.
Mettinger, T. N. D. "Abbild oder Urbild? 'Imago Dei' in traditionsgeschichtlicher Sicht." *ZAW* 86 (1974) 403–24.
Michaud, R. *L'historie de Joseph, le Makirite (Genèse 37–50).* Paris: Editions du Cerf, 1976.
Millard, A. R. "The Celestial Ladder and the Gate of Heaven (Genesis 28:12, 17)." *ExpTim* 78 (1966/67) 86–87.
_____. "A New Babylonian 'Genesis' Story." *TynBul* 18 (1967) 3–18.
_____. "The Meaning of the Name Judah." *ZAW* 86 (1974) 216–18.
Millard, A. R. and D. J. Wiseman, eds. *Essays on the Patriarchal Narratives.* Winona Lake, IN: Eisenbrauns, 1983.
Miller, J. M. "In the 'Image' and 'Likeness' of God." *JBL* 91 (1972) 289–304.
_____. "The Descendants of Cain: Notes on Genesis 4." *ZAW* 86 (1974) 164–74.
Miller, P. D. "*yeled* in the Song of Lamech." *JBL* 85 (1966) 477–78.
_____. *Genesis 1–11: Studies in Structure and Theme.* JSOTSup 8. Sheffield: University of Sheffield, 1978.

_____. "Syntax and Theology in Gen XII 3a." *VT* 34 (1984) 472–75.
Miller, W. T. *Mysterious Encounters at Mamre and Jabbok.* Chico, CA: Scholars, 1984.
Miscall, P. D. "The Jacob and Joseph Stories as Analogies." *JSOT* 6 (1978) 28–40.
_____. "Literary Unity in Old Testament Narrative." *Semeia* 15 (1979) 27–35.
_____. *The Workings of Old Testament Narrative.* Philadelphia: Fortress, 1983.
Mitchell, J. J. "Abram's Understanding of the Lord's Covenant." *WTJ* 32 (1969) 24–48.
Moran, W. L. "Genesis 49,10 and Its Use in Ez 21,32." *Bib* 39 (1958) 405–25.
Morrison, M. A. "The Jacob and Laban Narrative in Light of Near Eastern Sources." *BA* 46 (1983) 155–64.
Muffs, Y. "Abraham the Noble Warrior: Patriarchal Politics and Laws of War in Ancient Israel." *JJS* 33 (1982) 81–107.
Muilenburg, J. "The Birth of Benjamin." *JBL* 75 (1956) 194–201.
_____. "Abraham and the Nations: Blessing and World History." *Int* 19 (1965) 387–98.
Naidoff, B. "A Man to Work the Soil: A New Interpretation of Genesis 2–3." *JSOT* 5 (1978) 2–14.
Neff, R. W. "The Birth and Election of Isaac in the Priestly Tradition." *BibRes* 15 (1970) 5–18.
_____. "The Annunciation in the Birth Narrative of Ishmael." *BibRes* 17 (1972) 51–60.
Neiman, D. "The Date and Circumstances of the Cursing of Canaan." In *Biblical Motifs: Origins and Transformations.* Ed. A. Altmann. Cambridge: Harvard University, 1966. Pp. 113–34.
_____. "The Supercaelian Sea." *JNES* 29 (1969) 243–49.
Neusner, J. *Genesis Rabbah: The Judaic Commentary to the Book of Genesis.* 3 vols. Atlanta: Scholars, 1985.
Nichol, G. C. "Reuben's Reversal." *JTS* 31 (1980) 536–39.
Niditch, S. "The Wrong Woman Righted: An Analysis of Genesis 38." *HTR* 72 (1979) 143–49.
_____. "The 'Sodomite' Theme in Judges 19–20: Family, Community, and Social Disintegration." *CBQ* 44 (1982) 365–78.
Nielsen, E. "Creation and the Fall of Man: A Cross-Disciplinary Investigation." *HUCA* 43 (1972) 1–22.
Noth, M. *A History of Pentateuchal Traditions.* Tr. B. W. Anderson. Englewood Cliffs, NJ: Prentice-Hall, 1972.
Obed, B. "The Table of Nations (Genesis 10)—A Socio-Cultural Approach." *ZAW* 98 (1986) 14–31.

O'Callaghan, M. "The Structure and Meaning of Genesis 38: Judah and Tamar." *PIBA* 5 (1981) 72–88.

O'Connor, M. *Hebrew Verse Structure.* Winona Lake, IN: Eisenbrauns, 1980.

Oden, R. A. "Divine Aspirations in Atrahasis and in Genesis 1–11." *ZAW* 93 (1981) 197–216.

_____. "Jacob as Father, Husband, and Nephew; Kinship Studies in the Patriarchal Narratives." *JBL* 102 (1983) 189–205.

Oeming, M. "Ist Genesis 15^{16} ein Beleg für die Anrechnung des Glaubens zur Gerechtigkeit?" *ZAW* 95 (1983) 182–97.

Olson, W. S. "Has Science Dated the Biblical Flood?" *Zygon* 2 (1967) 274–78.

Oppenheim, A. L. *The Interpretation of Dreams in the Ancient Near East.* Philadelphia: 1956.

Orlinsky, H. M. "The Plain Meaning of Ruah in Gen 1–2." *JQR* 48 (1957) 174–82.

Otto, E. "Jakob in Bethel. Ein Beitrag zur Geschichte der Jakobüberlieferung." *ZAW* 88 (1976) 165–90.

Pasinya, L. M. "Le cadre littéraire de Genèse 1." *Bib* 57 (1976) 225–41.

Paul, S. M. "Unrecognized Biblical Legal Idioms in the Light of Comparative Akkadian Expressions." *RB* 86 (1979) 237–39.

Payne, D. F. *Genesis One Reconsidered.* London: Tyndale, 1964.

Peck, W. J. "Murder, Timing, and the Ram in the Sacrifice of Isaac." *ATR* 58 (1976) 23–43.

Pedersen, J. "The Fall of Man." In *Interpretationes ad Vetus Testamentum pertinentes Sigmundo Mowinckel.* Ed. N. A. Dahl and A. S. Kapelrud. Oslo: Forlaget Land og Kirche, 1955. Pp. 162–72.

Peter, M. "Die historische Wahrheit in Genesis 14." In *De la Tôrah au Messie.* Fest. H. Cazelles. Ed. M. Carrez, et al. Paris: Desclée, 1981.

Petersen, D. L. "A Thrice-Told Tale: Genre, Theme, and Motif." *BibRes* 18 (1973) 30–43.

_____. "The Yahwist on the Flood." *VT* 26 (1976) 438–46.

_____. "Covenant and Ritual: A Traditio-Historical Perspective." *BibRes* 22 (1977) 7–18.

_____. "Genesis 6:1–4, Yahweh and the Organization of the Cosmos." *JSOT* 13 (1979) 47–64.

Petschow, H. "Die neubabylonische Zwiegesprächsurkunde und Genesis 23." *JCS* 19 (1965) 103–20.

Phillips, A. "Nebalah." *VT* 25 (1975) 237–41.

_____. "Uncovering the father's skirt." *VT* 30 (1980) 40–41.

Piper, J. "The Image of God: An Approach from Biblical and Systematic Theology." *StBTh* 1 (1971) 15–32.

Pitt-Rivers, J. *The Fate of Shechem or the Politics of Sex: Essays in the*

Anthropology of the Mediterranean. Cambridge: Cambridge University, 1977.

Polzin, R. "The Ancestress of Israel in Danger." *Semeia* 3 (1975) 81–98.

Porten, B. and U. Rappaport, "Poetic Structure in Genesis IX,7." *VT* 21 (1971) 363–69.

Pratt, R. L. "Pictures, Windows, and Mirrors in Old Testament Exegesis." *WTJ* 45 (1983) 156–67.

Premsager, P. "Theology of Promise in the Patriarchal Narratives." *IJT* 23 (1974) 112–22.

Rad, G. von, "Faith Reckoned as Righteousness." In *The Problem of the Hexateuch and Other Essays.* Tr. E. W. Trueman Dicken. New York: McGraw-Hill, 1966. Pp. 125–30.

_____. "The Joseph Narrative and Ancient Wisdom." In *The Problem of the Hexateuch and Other Essays.* Tr. E. W. Trueman Dicken. New York: McGraw-Hill, 1966. Pp. 292–300.

_____. *Das Opfer des Abraham.* Munich: Kaiser, 1971.

_____. *Genesis.* Tr. J. H. Marks. OTL. Rev. ed. Philadelphia: Westminster, 1972.

Radday, Y. and H. Shore, *Genesis: An Authorship Study.* AnBib 103. Rome: Biblical Institute, 1985.

Ramsey, G. W. "Is Name-Giving an Act of Domination in Genesis 2:23 and Elsewhere?" *CBQ* 50 (1988) 24–35.

Redford, D. B. "The 'Land of the Hebrews' in Gen XL 15." *VT* 15 (1965) 529–32.

_____. *A Study of the Biblical Story of Joseph (Genesis 37–50).* Leiden: Brill, 1970.

Reicke, B. "The Knowledge Hidden in the Tree of Paradise." *JSS* 1 (1956) 193–201.

Rendsburg, G. "Janus Parallelism in Gen 49:26." *JBL* 99 (1980) 291–93.

_____. "Notes on Genesis XXXV." *VT* 34 (1984) 361–66.

_____. *The Redaction of Genesis.* Winona Lake, IN: Eisenbrauns, 1986.

Rendtorff, R. "Genesis 8,21 und die Urgeschichte des Jahwisten." *KD* 7 (1961) 69–78.

_____. *Das überlieferungsgeschichtliche Problem des Pentateuch.* BZAW 147 (Berlin/New York: de Gruyter, 1977).

_____. "Jakob in Bethel. Beobachtungen zum Aufbau und zur Quellenfrage in Gen 28:10–22." *ZAW* 94 (1982) 511–23.

Reventlow, H. G. *Opfere deinen Sohn. Eine Auslegung von Genesis 22.* Neukirchen-Vluyn: Neukirchener, 1968.

Reviv, H. "Early Elements and Late Terminology in the Description of non-Israelite Cities in the Bible." *IEJ* 22 (1977) 189–96.

Rice, G. "Cosmological Ideas and Religious Truth in Genesis One." *JRT* 23 (1966) 15–30.

Richard, E. "The Polemical Character of the Joseph Episode in Acts 7." *JBL* 98 (1979) 255–67.
Richardson, A. *Genesis.* Torch Bible Commentaries. London: SCM, 1953.
Richter, W. "Das Gelübde als theologische Rahmung der Jakobsüberlieferungen." *BZ* 11 (1967) 21–52.
Riemann, P. "Am I My Brother's Keeper?" *Int* 24 (1970) 482–91.
Robertson, D. A. *Linguistic Evidence in Dating Early Hebrew Poetry.* SBLDS 3. Missoula, MT: Scholars, 1972.
Robertson, O. P. "Genesis 15:6: New Covenant Expositions of an Old Testament Text." *WTJ* 42 (1979/80) 259–89.
Robinson, I. "*běpetaḥ ʿênayim* in Genesis 38:14." *JBL* 96 (1977) 569.
Rodd, C. S. "Shall Not the Judge of All the Earth Do What Is Just?" *ExpTim* 83 (1972) 137–39.
Rogers, C. L. "The Covenant With Abraham." *BSac* 127 (1970) 241–56.
Ross, A. P. "The Curse of Canaan." *BSac* 137 (1980) 223–40.
_____. "The Table of Nations in Genesis 10—Its Structure." *BSac* 137 (1980) 340–53.
_____. "Jacob's Vision: The Founding of Bethel." *BSac* 142 (1985) 224–37.
_____. "Jacob at the Jabbok, Israel at Peniel." *BSac* 142 (1985) 338–54.
Roth, W. M. W. "The Wooing of Rebekah. A Tradition-Critical Study of Genesis 24." *CBQ* 34 (1972) 177–87.
_____. "Structural Interpretations of 'Jacob at the Jabbok' (Genesis 32:22–32)." *BibRes* 22 (1977) 51–62.
Rudolph, W. "Die Josefsgeschichte." In P. Volz and W. Rudolph, *Der Elohist als Erzähler—Ein Irrweg der Pentateuchkritik?* BZAW 63. Giessen: Töpelmann, 1933. Pp. 143–84.
Ruger, H. P. "On Some Versions of Genesis 3,15, Ancient and Modern." *BT* 27 (1976) 105–10.
Ruppert, L. "Die Sündenfallerzählung (Gn 3) in vorjahwistischer Tradition und Interpretation." *BZ* 15 (1971) 185–202.
_____. *Die Josepherzählung der Genesis: Ein Beitrag zur Theologie der Pentateuchquellen.* Munich: Kösel, 1965.
_____. "Die Aporie der gegenwärtigen Pentateuchdiskussion und die Joseferzählung der Genesis." *BZ* 29 (1985) 31–48.
Ruprecht, E. "Vorgegebene Tradition und theologische Gestaltung in Genesis 12:1–3." *VT* 29 (1979) 171–88.
Sabottka, "Noch einmal Gen 49,10." *Bib* 51 (1970) 225–29.
Salkin, J. K. "Dinah, The Torah's Forgotten Woman." *Judaism* 35 (1986) 284–89.
Salo, V. "Joseph, Sohn der Färse." *BZ* 12 (1968) 94–95.
Sarna, N. *Understanding Genesis.* Repr. New York: Schocken, 1978.
_____. "The Anticipatory Use of Information as a Literary Feature of the Genesis Narratives." In *The Creation of Sacred Literature: Composi-*

tion and Redaction of the Biblical Text. Ed. R. E. Friedman. Berkeley: University of California, 1981. Pp. 76–82.

_____. "Genesis Chapter 23: The Cave of Machpelah." *HS* 23 (1982) 17–21.

Sasson, J. "Word Play in Gen 6:8–9." *CBQ* 37 (1975) 165–66.

_____. "A Genealogical 'Convention' in Biblical Chronography?" *ZAW* 90 (1978) 171–85.

_____. "The 'Tower of Babel' as a Clue to the Redactional Structuring of Primeval History [Gen. 1–11:9]." In *The Bible World: Essays in Honor of Cyrus H. Gordon.* Ed. Gary Rendsburg, et al. New York: Ktav, 1980. Pp. 211–19.

_____. "*welō' yitbōšāšû* (Gen 2,25) and Its Implications." *Bib* 66 (1985) 418–21.

Savage, M. "Literary Criticism and Biblical Studies: A Rhetorical Analysis of the Joseph Narrative." In *Scripture in Context: Essays on the Comparative Method.* Ed. Carl D. Evans, et al. PTMS 34. Pittsburgh: Pickwick, 1980. Pp. 79–100.

Sawyer, J. F. A. "The Meaning of *beṣelem 'ĕlōhîm* ('In the Image of God') in Genesis I–XI." JTS 25 (1974) 418–26.

Schaeffer, F. *Genesis in Space and Time.* Downers Grove, IL: Inter-Varsity, 1972.

Schatz, W. *Genesis 14. Eine Untersuchung.* Bern: Lang, 1972.

Schmidt, L. *"De Deo": Studien zur Literarkritik und Theologie des Buches Jona, des Gesprächs zwischen Abraham und Jahwe in Gen 18:22ff. und von Hi 1.* BZAW 143. Berlin: de Gruyter, 1976.

Schmitt, G. "Zu Gen 26:1–14." *ZAW* 85 (1973) 143–56.

Schmitt, H.-C. *Die nichtpriesterliche Josephsgeschichte. Ein Beitrag zur neuesten Pentateuchkritik.* BZAW 154. Berlin: de Gruyter, 1980.

_____. "Die Hintergründe der 'neuesten Pentateuchkritik' und der literarische Befund der Josefsgeschichte Gen 37–50." *ZAW* 97 (1985) 161–79.

Schneider, N. "Patriarchennamen in zeitgenössischen Keilschrifturkunden." *Bib* 33 (1952) 518–19.

Scullion, J. J. "New Thinking on Creation and Sin in Genesis i–xi." *AusBR* 22 (1974) 1–10.

Seebass, H. *Geschichtliche Zeit und theonome Tradition in der Joseph-Erzählung.* Gütersloh: Gerd Mohn, 1978.

Selman, M. J. "The Social Environment of the Patriarchs." *TynBul* 27 (1976) 114–36.

Seybold, K. "Der Turmbau zu Babel. Zur Entstehung von Genesis XI 1–9." *VT* 26 (1976) 453–79.

Shanks, H. "How the Bible Begins." *Judaism* 81 (1972) 51–58.

_____. "Have Sodom and Gomorrah Been Found?" *BAR* 6/5 (1980) 26–36.

Shea, W. H. "Adam in Ancient Mesopotamian Traditions." *AUSS* 15 (1977) 27–41.

Simons, J. "The 'Table of Nations' (Gen 10): Its General Structure and Meaning." *OTS* 10 (1954) 155–84.

Skinner, J. *A Critical and Exegetical Commentary on the Book of Genesis.* ICC. 2nd ed. Edinburgh: T. & T. Clark, 1930.

Smith, G. V. "Structure and Purpose in Genesis 1–11." *JETS* 20 (1977) 307–19.

Smith, P. J. "A Semotactical Approach to the Meaning of the Term *rûaḥ 'ĕlōhîm* in Genesis 1:2." *JNWSL* 8 (1980) 99–104.

Smith, R. H. "Abram and Melchizedek (Gen 14:18–20)." *ZAW* 77 (1965) 129–53.

Smyth, K. "The Prophecy Concerning Juda: Gen 49:8–12." *CBQ* 7 (1945) 290–305.

Snijders, L. A. "Genesis XV. The Covenant with Abram." *OTS* 12 (1958) 261–79.

Soggin, J. A. "Die Geburt Benjamins, Genesis 35:16–20 (21)." *VT* 11 (1961) 432–40.

_____. *Old Testament and Oriental Studies.* BibOr 29. Rome: Biblical Institute, 1975.

Speiser, E. A. *Oriental and Biblical Studies.* Ed. J. J. Finkelstein and M. Greenberg. Philadelphia: University of Pennsylvania, 1967.

_____. *Genesis.* AB. 2nd ed. Garden City, NY: Doubleday, 1978.

Steinberg, N. "Gender Roles in the Rebekah Cycle." *USQR* 39 (1984) 175–88.

Stern, H. S. "The Knowledge of Good and Evil." *VT* 8 (1958) 405–18.

Sternberg, M. *The Poetics of Biblical Narrative.* Bloomington, IN: Indiana University, 1985.

Stigers, H. G. *A Commentary on Genesis.* Grand Rapids: Zondervan, 1976.

Stitzinger, M. F. "Genesis 1–3 and the Male/Female Role Relationship." *GTJ* 2 (1981) 23–44.

Stoebe, H. J. "Gut and Böse in der jahwistischen Quelle des Pentateuch." *ZAW* 65 (1953) 188–204.

Strus, A. *Nomen-Omen. La Stylistique sonore des noms propres dans le Pentateuque.* AnBib 80. Rome: Pontifical Biblical Institute, 1978.

Stuart, D. *Studies in Early Hebrew Meter.* HSM 13. Missoula, MT: Scholars, 1976.

Swindell, A. C. "Abraham and Isaac: An Essay in Biblical Interpretation." *ExpTim* 87 (1975) 50–53.

Thomas, W. H. Griffith. *Genesis: A Devotional Commentary.* Repr. Grand Rapids: Eerdmans, 1958.

Thompson, J. A. "Samaritan Evidence for 'All of them in the land of Shinar' (Gen 10,10)." *JBL* 90 (1971) 99–102.

Thompson, P. "The Yahwist Creation Story." *VT* 21 (1971) 197–208.
Thompson, T. L. *The Historicity of the Patriarchal Narratives: The Quest for the Historical Abraham.* BZAW 133. Berlin/New York: de Gruyter, 1974.
_____. "Conflict of Themes in the Jacob Narratives." *Semeia* 15 (1979) 5–26.
Thompson, T. L. and D. Thompson. "Some Legal Problems in the Book of Ruth." *VT* 18 (1968) 79–99.
Treves, M. "Shiloh (Genesis 49:10)." *JBL* 85 (1966) 353–56.
Trible, P. "Eve and Adam: Genesis 2–3 Reread." *ANQ* 14 (1972) 251–58.
_____. *God and the Rhetoric of Sexuality.* OBT 2. Philadelphia: Fortress, 1978.
_____. "The Other Woman: A Literary and Theological Study of the Hagar Narratives." In *Understanding the Word: Essays in Honour of Bernhard W. Anderson.* Ed. James T. Butler, et al. Sheffield: JSOT, 1985. Pp. 221–46.
Trudiger, L. P. " 'Not Yet Made' 'Newly Made,' A Note on Gen. 2:5." *EvQ* 47 (1975) 67–69.
Tsevat, M. "Hagar and the Birth of Ishmael." In *The Meaning of the Book of Job and Other Biblical Studies.* New York: Ktav, 1980. Pp. 53–76.
_____. "Two Old Testament Stories and their Hittite Analogues." *JAOS* 103 (1983) 321–26.
Tsmura, D. T. "*Nabalkutu, tu-a-bi[ú]* and *tōhû wābōhû,*" *UF* 19 (1987) 309–15.
Tucker, G. M. "The Legal Background of Genesis 23." *JBL* 85 (1966) 77–84.
_____. *Form Criticism of the Old Testament.* Philadelphia: Fortress, 1971.
_____. "The Creation and the Fall: A Reconsideration." *LTQ* 13 (1978) 113–24.
Tur-Sinai, N. H. "The Riddle of Genesis VI.1–4." *ExpTim* 71 (1959) 348–50.
Van Gemeren, W. A. "The Sons of God in Genesis 6:1–4 (An Example of Evangelical Demythologization?)." *WTJ* 43 (1981) 320–48.
Van Seters, J. "The Problem of Childlessness in Near Eastern Law and the Patriarchs of Israel." *JBL* 87 (1968) 401–8.
_____. "Jacob's Marriages and Ancient Near Eastern Customs: A Reexamination." *HTR* 62 (1969) 377–95.
_____. *Abraham in History and Tradition.* New Haven: Yale University, 1975.
Vaux, R. de, *The Early History of Israel.* Tr. David Smith. Philadelphia: Westminster, 1978.
Vawter, B. "The Canaanite Background of Genesis 49." *CBQ* 17 (1955) 1–18.
_____. *A Path Through Genesis.* Garden City, NY: Doubleday, 1956.
_____. *On Genesis: A New Reading.* Garden City, NY: Doubleday, 1977.

Vergote, J. *Joseph en Égypte: Génèse ch. 37–50 à la lumière des études égyptologiques récentes.* Louvain: Publications Universitaires, 1959.

Vogt, E. "Benjamin geboren 'eine Meile' von Ephrata." *Bib* 56 (1975) 30–36.

Wacholder, B. Z. "How long did Abraham stay in Egypt?" *HUCA* 35 (1964) 43–56.

Wallace, H. N. *The Eden Narrative.* HSM 32. Atlanta: Scholars, 1985.

Walsh, J. A. "The Dream of Joseph, a Jungian Interpretation." *JPT* 11 (1983) 20–27.

Walsh, J. T. "Genesis 2:4b–3:24: A Synchronic Approach." *JBL* 96 (1977) 161–77.

Waltke, B. "The Creation Account in Genesis 1:1–3." *BSac* 132 (1975) 25–36, 136–44, 216–28, 327–42.

_____. "Cain and His Offering." *WTJ* 48 (1986) 363–72.

Walton, J. "The Antediluvian Section of the Sumerian King List and Genesis 5." *BA* 44 (1981) 207–8.

Ward, W. A. "Egyptian Titles in Genesis 39–50." *BSac* 114 (1957) 40–59.

_____. "The Egyptian Office of Joseph." *JSS* 5 (1960) 144–50.

Watson, P. "The Tree of Life." *RestQ* 23 (1980) 232–38.

Watson, W. G. E. "Hebrew 'to be happy'—an Idiom Identified." *VT* 31 (1981) 92–95.

_____. *Classical Hebrew Poetry.* JSOTSup 26. Sheffield: JSOT, 1984.

Weeks, N. "Man, Nuzi, and the Patriarchs: A Retrospect." *Abr-Nahraim* 16 (1975–76) 73–82.

_____. "The Hermeneutical Problem of Genesis 1–11." *Themelios* 4 (1978) 12–19.

Weimar, P. "Aufbau und Struktur der priesterschriftlichen Jakobgeschichte." *ZAW* 86 (1974) 174–203.

Weinfeld, M. "God the Creator in Gen. 1 and in the Prophecy of Second Isaiah." *Tarbiz* 37 (1967–68) 233–37. [Heb.]

_____. "Sabbath, Temple, and the Enthronement of the Lord: The Problem of the Sitz im Leben of Genesis 1:1–2:3." In *Mélanges bibliques et orientaux en l'honneur de M. Henri Cazelles.* Ed. A. Caquot and M. Delcor. AOAT 212. Kevelaer: Butzon und Bercker, 1981. Pp. 501–12.

Weir, C. J. "The Alleged Hurrian Wife-Sister Motif in Genesis." *TGUOS* 22 (1967/68) 14–25.

Wenham, G. J. "The Coherence of the Flood Narrative." *VT* 28 (1978) 336–48.

_____. "The Symbolism of the Animal Rite in Genesis 15: A Response to G. F. Hasel, *JSOT* 19 (1981) 61–78." *JSOT* 22 (1982) 134–37.

Westerbrook, R. "Purchase of the Cave of Machpelah." *Israel Law Review* 6 (1971) 29–38.

Westermann, C. *The Genesis Accounts of Creation.* Tr. Norman E. Wagner. Philadelphia: Fortress, 1968.

_____. *Beginning and End in the Bible.* Tr. Keith Crim. Philadelphia: Fortress, 1972.

_____. *Creation.* Tr. J. J. Scullion. Philadelphia: Fortress, 1974.

_____. "Genesis 17 und die Bedeutung von *bĕrît,*" *TLZ* 101 (1976) 161–70.

_____. *The Promises to the Fathers: Studies on the Patriarchal Narratives.* Tr. David E. Green. Philadelphia: Fortress, 1980.

_____. *Genesis.* 3 vols. Tr. John J. Scullion. Minneapolis: Augsburg, 1984–1986.

Wevers, J. *Genesis.* Septuaginta: Vetus Testamentum Graecum. Göttingen: Vandenhoeck & Ruprecht, 1974.

White, H. C. "French Structuralism and OT Narrative Analysis: Roland Barthes." *Semeia* 3 (1975) 99–127.

_____. "The Initiation Legend of Ishmael." *ZAW* 87 (1975) 267–305.

_____. "The Initiation Legend of Isaac." *ZAW* 91 (1979) 1–30.

_____. "The Joseph Story: A Narrative Which 'Consumes' Its Context." *Semeia* 31 (1985) 49–69.

Whybray, R. N. "The Joseph Story and Pentateuchal Criticism." *VT* 18 (1968) 522–28.

Wickham, L. R. "The Sons of God and the Daughters of Men: Gen VI 2 in Early Christian Exegesis." *OTS* 19 (1974) 135–47.

Wiesel, E. *Messengers of God: Biblical Portraits and Legends.* Tr. Marion Wiesel. New York: Random House, 1976.

Wifall, W. "The Breath of His Nostrils: Gen. 2:7b." *CBQ* 36 (1974) 237–40.

_____. "Gen. 3:15—A Protevangelium?" *CBQ* 36 (1974) 361–65.

_____. "Gen. 6:1–4—A Royal Davidic Myth?" *BTB* 5 (1975) 294–301.

_____. "God's Accession Year According to P." *Bib* 62 (1981) 527–34.

Williams, A. J. "The Relationship of Genesis 3:20 to the Serpent." *ZAW* 89 (1977) 357–74.

Williams, J. G. "The Comedy of Jacob: A Literary Study." *JAAR* 46 (1978) 208, and Supplement B, pp. 241–66.

_____. "The Beautiful and the Barren: Conventions in Biblical Type-Scenes." *JSOT* 17 (1980) 107–19.

_____. "Genesis 3." *Int* 35 (1981) 274–79.

Wilson, R. R. *Genealogy and History in the Biblical World.* New Haven: Yale University, 1977.

Wilson, S. G. "The Image of God." *ExpTim* 85 (1974) 356–61.

Wiseman, D. J. "Genesis 10: Some Archaeological Considerations." *925th Ordinary General Meeting of the Victoria Institute.* December 6, 1954. Pp. 14–24.

_____. "Abraham in History and Tradition." *BSac* 134 (1977) 123–30, 228–37.

_____. "They Lived in Tents." In *Biblical and Near Eastern Studies.* Fest. W. S. LaSor. Ed. G. Tuttle. Grand Rapids: Eerdmans, 1978. Pp. 195–200.

Wiseman, P. J. *Ancient Records and the Structure of Genesis.* Repr. Nashville: Abingdon, 1985.

Woudstra, M. H. "The *Toledot* of the Book of Genesis and their Redemptive-Historical Significance." *CTJ* 5 (1970) 184–89.

_____. "Recent Translations of Genesis 3:15." *CTJ* 6 (1971) 194–203.

Wright, G. E. "The Nature of Man: An Exposition of Gen. 3." In *The Rule of God: Essays in Biblical Theology.* Garden City, NY: Doubleday, 1960. Pp. 21–43.

Wright, G. R. H. "The Positioning of Genesis 38." *ZAW* 94 (1982) 523–29.

Wyatt, N. "Interpreting the Creation and Fall Story in Genesis 2–3." *ZAW* 93 (1981) 10–21.

Xella, P. "L'épisode de Dnil et Kothar et Gen 18:1–16." *VT* 28 (1978) 483–86.

Yamauchi, E. "Archaeological Evidence for the Philistines." *WTJ* 35 (1972/73) 315–23.

Yaron, R. "The Rejected Bridegroom." *Or* 33 (1964) 23–29.

Young, D. W. "A Ghost Word in the Testament of Jacob (Gen 49:5)?" *JBL* 100 (1981) 335–42.

Young, E. J. "The Relationship of the First Verse of Genesis One to Verse Two and Three." *WTJ* 21 (1958–59) 133–46.

_____. "The Interpretation of Genesis 1,2." *WTJ* 23 (1960/61) 151–78.

_____. "The Days of Genesis." *WTJ* 25 (1962/63) 1–24.

_____. *Studies in Genesis One.* Philadelphia: Presbyterian & Reformed, 1976.

Zachman, L. "Beobachtungen zur Theologie in Gen 5." *ZAW* 88 (1976) 272–74.

Zakovitch, Y. "Assimilation in Biblical Narratives." In *Empirical Models for Biblical Criticism.* Ed. Jeffrey H. Tigay. Philadelphia: University of Pennsylvania, 1985. Pp. 185–92.

Zimmerli, W. "Abraham und Melchisedek." In *Das ferne und nahe Wort.* Fest. L. Rost. Ed. F. Maass. BZAW 105. Berlin: Töpelmann, 1967. Pp. 255–64.

Zobel, H.-J. *Stammesspruch und Geschichte.* Berlin: Töpelmann, 1965.

TEXT AND COMMENTARY

I. PRIMEVAL HISTORY (1:1–11:32)

A. THE CREATION OF THE WORLD (1:1–2:3)

1. IN THE BEGINNING (1:1–2)

1 *In the beginning*[1] *God created the universe.*[2]

2 *And the earth—it was a desert and a wasteland; darkness was on the face of the deep; and the Spirit of God was hovering over the surface of the waters.*

1 Among the most well-known passages of Scripture is its very first verse, traditionally translated as above. Nevertheless, no small controversy among biblical scholars has swirled around both the translation and the meaning of the verse.

The issues are at least twofold. First, should v. 1 be translated as an independent clause, which is the approach taken in this commentary? Or is the verse to be understood as a dependent clause, "When God began to create . . . ," and thus subordinated to some following main clause? Second, what is the relation of v. 1 to v. 2, and for that matter, what is its relation, chronologically, exegetically, and theologically, to the remainder of the chapter?

First, the proper translation of the verse. A number of options are available here: (1) The first word, *b^{e}rē’šîṯ,* is in the absolute state (i.e., it functions independently of any other word) and all of v. 1 is an independent clause and a complete sentence. (2) The first word is an indeterminate noun,

1. For the problems surrounding the vocalization of *rō’š, ri’šôn,* and *rē’šîṯ,* see C. H. Gordon, "Extensions of Barth's Law of Vocalic Sequence," *Or* 51 (1982) 395.

2. Lit., "the heavens and the earth," which is to be taken as an illustration of hendiadys (an idea expressed by two nouns connected by "and"), or of merism (a means of expressing totality through two contrasting parts).

used as a relative temporal designation: "Initially (or first, to start with) God created. . . ." (3) The first word is in the construct state (i.e., it functions in close connection with another word, usually a noun) and the verse is a temporal clause subordinated to v. 2: "When God began to create . . . the earth was without form and void." (4) The first word is in the construct state and the verse is a temporal clause subordinated to v. 3, with v. 2 taken as a parenthesis: "When God began to create the heavens and the earth—the earth being without form and void—God said. . . ."

How shall we decide among these possibilities? A knowledge of the Hebrew language will not be sufficient in itself to settle the matter, for all four positions have been advocated by competent Hebraists, both ancient and modern. A survey of the extensive literature on the subject reveals that interpretations (1) and (4) have by far the widest support.

The main lines of argument in support of taking v. 1 as a dependent clause which prepares for the main clause in v. 3 are as follows. (a) The vowels in the word *b^{e}rē'šîṯ* indicate the word to be construct, not absolute, and the phrase must thus translate as "In the beginning of," not "In the beginning," for which one would expect *bārē'šîṯ.* (b) In the "second" Creation account (2:4bff.) the temporal construction is employed—"when the Lord God made the cosmos"—and is a structural parallel to 1:1. (c) The word *rē'šîṯ* occurs some fifty times in the OT, and all of these, except possibly Isa. 46:10, are in the construct state.[3] Is it likely that Gen. 1:1 contains an exception? (d) Taking the first verse as a dependent clause provides further substantiation for the Babylonian background of this "Priestly" account of creation. That is, in the Babylonian Epic of Creation—the *Enuma elish*—the first nine lines parallel the first two verses of Genesis.[4] Thus:

(1) *protasis*	(2) *parenthetical clauses*	(3) *apodosis*
Gen. 1:1	1:2	1:3
Enuma elish, lines 1-2	lines 3-8	line 9

Specifically then, Gen. 1:1—"When God began to create the heavens and the earth"—is the equivalent of the first two lines of *Enuma elish:* "When above, the heaven had not been named (and) below, the earth had not been called by name."

3. See P. Humbert, "Trois Notes sur Genèse 1," in *Interpretationes ad Vetus Testamentum pertinentes Sigmundo Mowinckel septuagenario missae,* ed. N. A. Dahl and A. S. Kapelrud (Oslo: Forlaget Land og Kirche, 1955), pp. 85–96, esp. pp. 85–88; idem, "Encore le premier mot de la Bible," *ZAW* 76 (1964) 121–31.

4. Among others, see E. A. Speiser, *Genesis,* p. 12; H. M. Orlinsky, "The New Jewish Version of the Torah," *JBL* 82 (1963) 252–53.

Several of the more recent translations of the Bible have accepted this rendering: NEB, NAB, NJPS, RSV, and AB, but only in a footnote. Others, however, have retained the traditional translation; among them, NASB, NKJV, NIV, and JB.

The issue between these two options—"In the beginning when" and "In the beginning"—is not esoteric quibbling or an exercise in micrometry. The larger concern is this: Does Gen. 1:1 teach an absolute beginning of creation as a direct act of God? Or does it affirm the existence of matter before creation of the heavens and the earth? To put the question differently, does Gen. 1:1 suggest that in the beginning there was one—God; or does it suggest that in the beginning there were two—God and preexistent chaos? The latter approach separates itself from the former in that it dictates the existence of chaos prior to creation. But the concept of the creation of chaos would be a contradiction in terms.

In order to avoid this conclusion, several scholars (e.g., Westermann) have opted for the traditional translation, not on the basis of objective linguistic grounds—for they believe the Hebrew word itself to be ambiguous in form—but on the grounds of the wider context of the chapter. It is claimed, for instance, that the Creation story of Gen. 1 is a deliberate repudiation and demythologizing of a pagan cosmogony such as is found in *Enuma elish.*

If that be the case, is it possible to believe that the author would leave unchanged and unmolested, and thus endorse, one of the distinguishing concepts of the mythical worldview, viz., the creation of the world from preexistent matter which is outside the creator's divine activity? Would such a vestigial motif be left undisturbed? Thus, speaking of v. 1, Brevard Childs says, "This verse can be interpreted grammatically in two different ways.... While there is a choice grammatically the theology of P excludes the latter possibility [viz., that 1:1 is a dependent, temporal clause subordinated to v. 3] ... we have seen the effort of the Priestly writer to emphasize the absolute transcendence of God over his material."[5]

But one does not argue for the translation of 1:1 simply on the grounds of a biblical writer's creation theology. While this is a legitimate criterion, if

5. B. S. Childs, *Myth and Reality in the Old Testament,* SBT 1/27 (London: SCM, 1960), p. 32. Von Rad takes essentially the same avenue: "Syntactically perhaps both translations are possible, but not theologically. . . . God, in the freedom of his will, creatively established for 'heaven and earth,' i.e., for absolutely everything, a beginning of its subsequent existence" (*Genesis,* p. 48). This attempt to translate the verse on the basis of the deciphered theology of the biblical writer by the biblical commentator is not without its detractors. See W. R. Lane, "The Initiation of Creation," *VT* 13 (1963) 64–65.

it is the only criterion the case for seeing absolute creation is seriously weakened. In our opinion valid lexical, grammatical, syntactical, comparative, and stylistic arguments have been advanced to substantiate the translation *In the beginning.*[6]

They may be presented briefly as follows. Lexically, P. Humbert's two studies are quite correct in their observation that *rēʾšîṯ* is almost always used in the OT in the construct state, the one departure being Isa. 46:9–10—"I am God . . . declaring the end *[ʾaḥarîṯ]* from the beginning *[mērēʾšîṯ].*" It cannot be denied that the prophet, in quoting God, is thinking in terms of God's absolute disposition over beginning and end, with beginning and end indicating not "a specific period of time within history, but rather historical time as such."[7] Now if one grants that, apart from the possibility of Gen. 1:1, Isa. 46:10 is the only bona fide illustration of this word in the absolute state, then this one example is sufficient to demonstrate that *rēʾšîṯ* may be used to express a temporal meaning by use of the absolute state construction.

The same word used here in Gen. 1:1, *bᵉrēʾšîṯ* (preposition plus noun), appears four other times in the OT (Jer. 26:1; 27:1; 28:1; 49:34, "in the beginning of the reign of *X*").[8] Each time the noun is followed by another noun. Only in Gen. 1:1 is the noun followed by a verb in a finite form (specifically, a perfect form). This construction is not frequent, but it is known in most of the Semitic languages.[9] Here contrast needs to be made with Gen. 2:4b, literally, "in the day of Yahweh God's making earth and heavens." Everybody agrees that this is a relative sentence, "when Yahweh God made

6. Of the many studies, we may mention here: E. J. Young, "The Relation of the First Verse of Genesis One to Verses Two and Three," in *Studies in Genesis One* (Philadelphia: Presbyterian & Reformed, 1976), pp. 1–14; W. Eichrodt, "In the Beginning," in *Israel's Prophetic Heritage: Essays in Honor of James Muilenburg,* ed. B. W. Anderson and W. Harrelson (New York: Harper and Brothers, 1962), pp. 1–10; G. F. Hasel, "Recent Translations of Genesis 1:1. A Critical Look," *BT* 22 (1971) 154–68; H. Shanks, "How the Bible Begins," *Judaism* 21 (1972) 51–58; B. K. Waltke, "The Creation Account in Genesis 1:1–3. Pt. III: The Initial Chaos Theory and the Precreation Chaos Theory," *BSac* 132 (1975) 222–28.

7. Eichrodt, "In the Beginning," in *Israel's Prophetic Heritage,* p. 6.

8. W. Wifall ("God's Accession Year According to P," *Bib* 62 [1981] 527–34) traces the source of the language and formula in Gen. 1:1 to the Deuteronomistic historian's account of the reigns of the kings of Judah and Israel, royal chronicles that served as a model for the Priestly writer in his description of the reign of earth's king. Creation, however, has replaced reigning.

9. See GKC, § 130d. Interestingly, GKC cites Hos. 1:2, a close morphological parallel to Gen. 1:1, but does not cite Gen. 1:1 itself in this paragraph. See C. H. Gordon, *UT,* pp. 56, 125.

earth and heavens." But the noun in this verse is followed not by a verb in a finite form, as in 1:1, but by a verb in a nonfinite form (specifically, an infinitive construct). Is it not plausible to suggest a different nuance in the two verses by virtue of their different verbal forms?

The absence of the article is not a fatal argument against construing the word as absolute. For one thing, if as we have argued Isa. 46:10 shows *rē'šîṯ* used in an absolute sense, it also provides us with an illustration of this word used both absolutely and indeterminately, and thus an exact parallel to Gen. 1:1. Second, all the ancient versions translate the word as an absolute and the whole verse as an independent clause.[10] Third, the Masoretes understood the word to be absolute, for they accented the word with the disjunctive accent called a *ṭip̱ḥâ,* which is normal for words in the absolute state, rather than with a conjunctive accent, which is normal for words in the construct state.[11]

Syntactically, the argument in support of the traditional translation, or the translation that subordinates the first verse to the following, revolves around the interpretation of the verse's relationship to vv. 2 and 3. Related to this matter is the comparative cosmogonic literature, that is, the alleged parallel in syntax between Gen. 1:1–3, 2:4bff. and lines 1–9 of *Enuma elish.* It is more accurate to say that there is a syntactical similarity between *Enuma elish* 1–9 and Gen. 2:4bff., but not between *Enuma elish* 1–9 and Gen. 1:1–3. If there is any parallel between Gen. 1:1–3 and *Enuma elish* 1–9 it is this: Gen. 1:2 parallels *Enuma elish* 1–8, and Gen. 1:3 parallels *Enuma elish* 9. Obviously Gen. 1:1 is unique. Gunkel was quite correct when he said, "The cosmogonies of other people contain no word which would come close to the first word of the Bible."[12]

On stylistic grounds the traditional translation conforms to the pattern of sentence lengths throughout the chapter. The rule is not long sentences

10. For example, compare LXX *En archḗ epoíēsen ho theós tón ouranón kaí tḗn gḗn* and Vulg. *In principio creavit Deus coelum et terram.*

11. Note, however, that the uses of *bᵉrē'šîṯ* in Jeremiah are clearly in construct, yet they are also given a disjunctive accent, not a conjunctive one. See B. Waltke, *BSac* 132 (1975) 224. A. Sperber (*A Historical Grammar of Biblical Hebrew* [Leiden: Brill, 1966], pp. 463–64) also notes the appearance of the disjunctive *ṭip̱ḥā'* on words in a construct case, and concludes: "There exists no interrelation between accentuation and interpretation" (p. 465). At the same time Sperber makes the important observation (p. 627, § 100, and p. 637) that vocalization with a *shewa* may have a determinate meaning. Thus all agree that Gen. 38:25 has Tamar saying: "By *the* man [*lᵉ'îš*] to whom these belong." On p. 637 Sperber places *bᵉrē'šîṯ* in this category.

12. Quoted in Hasel, *BT* 22 (1971) 163; and in Waltke, *BSac* 132 (1975) 225. See H. Gunkel, *Genesis.*

combining subordinate and principal clauses, but rather a whole series of brief, terse sentences in paratactic style. Thus H. Shanks can say, "Why adapt a translation that has been aptly described as a *verzweifelt geschmacklose* [hopelessly tasteless] construction, one which destroys a sublime opening to the world's greatest book?"[13]

Finally, we may say a word about the interpretation that takes the first verse of the Bible with adverbial force, "initially, first," *zuerst* as opposed to *im Anfang.*[14] Though this translation is possible, such a nuance would be expressed more directly in Hebrew by the phrase *bārî' šōnâ* (Gen. 13:4; Num. 10:13–14; etc.), rather than by *b^erē'šîṯ.*

2 *And the earth—it was a desert and a wasteland.* As we move beyond v. 1 and into v. 2, we do not, unfortunately, leave behind all problems of translation and interpretation. As will shortly become evident, v. 2 bristles with points of debate as much as does v. 1.

The first issue is the understanding of the two words *tōhû wāḇōhû.* It is unusual, but not unheard of, to have two juxtaposed words in Hebrew that rhyme. Rhyming could indicate, along with other factors, that the verse is poetry rather than prose.[15] It is less likely that the phrase is to be understood as farrago, that is, an expression made up of meaningless words but whose meaning may be determined from context.[16] No sure Semitic cognate for *bōhû* has yet been discovered, but *tōhû* may be safely equated with Ugar. *thw,* "desert."[17]

Both these words are nouns, and thus we have translated them *a desert and a wasteland.* The rendering "without form and void" (e.g., AV, RSV) might give the impression that the words are adjectives. But what do they imply and how does one arrive at a proper translation? On the one hand, the second word—*bōhû*—appears only three times in the OT and always in conjunction with *tōhû* (here; Isa. 34:11, "the line of confusion [*tōhû*] and the

13. H. Shanks, "How the Bible Begins," *Judaism* 21 (1972) 58.

14. See W. R. Lane, *VT* 12 (1963) 68; R. K. Harrison, "Genesis," *ISBE,* 2:438.

15. See J. M. Sasson, "Wordplay in the Old Testament," *IDBS,* p. 969. Compare our expressions "hodge-podge," "helter-skelter," "shilly-shally," and "willy-nilly," all of which have rhyme.

16. This last passage from Jeremiah is not without significance, for it is used ironically by the prophet in portraying the reverse of the creation, God in judgment against his people undoing his creation. See M. Fishbane, "Jeremiah IV 23–26 and Job III 3–13: A Recovered Use of the Creation Pattern," *VT* 21 (1971) 151–53.

17. D. T. Tsumura ("*Nabalkutu, tu-a-bi[ú]* and *tōhû wābōhû,*" *UF* 19 [1987] 309–15) is inclined to see *tōhû waḇōhû* reflected in Ugar. *tu-a-bi[ú],* with the latter meaning "to be out of order, be unproductive."

plummet of chaos [*bōhû*]"; and Jer. 4:23, "the earth, and lo it was waste [*tōhû*] and void [*bōhû*]").[18]

On the other hand, *tōhû* appears twenty times in the OT and unlike *bōhû* may stand on its own. Eleven of these occurrences are in Isaiah (24:10; 29:21; 34:11; 40:17, 23; 41:29; 44:9; 45:18, 19; 49:4; 59:4). In Deut. 32:10 the word is used in parallel with "desert" *(miḏbār)* and "wilderness" *(yᵉšîmōn)*. The word also designates "desert" in Job 6:18, here a place of virtual death for any straying travelers. It is used to describe a deserted city in Isa. 24:10. The same concept of vastness and emptiness is illustrated by Job 26:7, "He stretches the north over the void [*tōhû*], suspends the earth on nothing [*bᵉlîmâ*]."

Figuratively, the word describes that which is without substance or reality, something that is groundless, be that conversation (Isa. 29:21), the religious idols of the nations ("wind [*rûaḥ*] and emptiness are their images") (Isa. 41:29); also the makers of these idols (Isa. 44:9); and apparent futility in labor, as expressed by the suffering servant (Isa. 49:4, parallel with *heḇel*).

For our purposes Isa. 45:18–19 is most interesting: "Yahweh . . . did not create it [the earth] a chaos . . . I did not say . . . 'Look for me in chaos.' " As we shall see shortly, an issue is raised in the interpretation of Gen. 1:2 on the basis of whether Isa. 45:18 reads "Yahweh did not create the earth a chaos" or "Yahweh did not create the earth to be a chaos." In sum, we observe that the nuance of *tōhû* is brought out most clearly by words with which it appears in parallel: desert, wilderness, wind, nothing, vanity. None of these obviously appeals to one's sense of the pleasurable and the aesthetic. At the same time we shall need to discuss below whether the use of these two nouns in Gen. 1:2 designates a creation once pristine but now perverted, or whether 1:2 teaches a creation from a primordial chaos, or whether the expression is a generalization of which vv. 3ff. are a particularization. We reserve comment until we discuss the syntax of the entire verse.

darkness was on the face of the deep. Although Gen. 1 states that God created light (v. 3), it does not say that he created darkness. May we assume from this that darkness, unlike light, is not a part of God's creation, but is independent of it?[19] Is day superior to night? Can one place spiritual meanings on physical phenomena? Other creation traditions within the OT do place darkness within the sphere of God's creative acts. Compare Isa. 45:7, "I form light and I create darkness."[20]

18. See J. S. Kselman, "The Recovery of Poetic Fragments from the Pentateuchal Priestly Source," *JBL* 97 (1978) 163–64.

19. As does Childs, *Myth and Reality,* p. 34.

20. See J. L. McKenzie's comment on Isa. 45:7: "In Israelite thought nothing, not even evil and darkness, could be removed from the dominion of Yahweh. Gen.

Beginning with the discovery and publication of *Enuma elish* in the late 1800s, much attention has been given to the relationship between one deity in this epic, Tiamat, and the Hebrew word for *deep, t^ehôm.* In Babylonian lore, Tiamat is the belligerent and monstrous ocean goddess. As one who leads battle against the supreme god Anu, she is the personification of evil. Before she is able to win this battle, however, another deity—Marduk—defeats and kills her, then slits her corpse lengthwise "like a shellfish."[21] From these two parts of her body Marduk forms heaven and earth.

Lending credence to the possible relationship between *t^ehôm* and Tiamat was the fact that the Hebrew word is feminine, and in all of its thirty-five occurrences it appears without the article except in Isa. 63:13 and Ps. 106:9. This fact suggests that *t^ehôm* may indeed be a proper name.

Further support for *t^ehôm* as a Hebraized form of Tiamat is found (a) in its association with verbs that can be applied only to human beings or animals; thus Gen. 49:25, "the deep that lies [couches or crouches] below," and Hab. 3:10, "the deep gave forth its voice";[22] (b) in several uses of *t^ehôm,* apart from Gen. 1:2, that occur in a paragraph dealing with Yahweh's obliteration of superhuman monsters. The best example is Isa. 51:9–11, where a list of Yahweh's conquests includes Rahab, the dragon, the sea, and the waters of the great "deep."

Even if the etymological equivalence of *t^ehôm* and Tiamat be granted, this still does not demonstrate that the biblical Creation story has a Babylonian background. For one thing, many ancients believed in a primeval watery mass out of which the orders of creation emerged, whether these ancients were the Egyptians with their concept of the god of the primeval waters—Nu—who is the source of all things, or the Greek philosopher

---

i 3–5 makes darkness the result of a work of division, not of creation in the sense in which the word is used elsewhere in Gen. i" (*Second Isaiah,* AB [Garden City, NY: Doubleday, 1968], p. 77). If darkness is assumed in Scripture to be a threatening situation, what is one to do with a verse like Ps. 18:12 (Eng. 11), which states that God dwells in darkness, and darkness is his covering? Possibly darkness has both a benign and sinister nuance in the Bible. It is sinister in the sense of being the opposite of light, that out of which light evolves. But there is also a darkness that is protective, a darkness that conceals the location of a thief and acts as a veil for God, lest human eye behold him.

21. *ANET,* p. 67.

22. Note that the pronominal suffix on "voice" is 3rd masc. sing. ("his voice," not "her voice"), indicating that *t^ehôm* was also understood as masculine. Also, the verb here is 3rd masc. sing. perfect. In fact, *t^ehôm* is masc. in form. The fem. is indicated when an adjective (*t^ehôm rabbâ,* Gen. 7:11) or a participle (*t^ehôm rōḇeṣeṯ,* Gen. 49:25) follows, and in the pl. form *(t^ehōmōṯ, t^ehōmôṯ, t^ehômōṯ).*

Thales.[23] Second, the *deep* of Gen. 1 is so far removed in function from the Tiamat of *Enuma elish* that any possible relationship is blurred beyond recognition. The *deep* of Gen. 1 is not personified, and in no way is it viewed as some turbulent, antagonistic force.

Strong negative arguments may be sounded regarding the linguistic relationship between Heb. *t^{e}hôm* and Babylonian Tiamat.[24] Much more likely is the correspondence between Heb. *t^{e}hôm* and Ugar. *thm* (dual, *thmtm,* plural *thmt*), "deep, depth(s)," or even earlier Eblaite *ti-'a-matum,* "ocean abyss."[25]

and the Spirit of God was hovering over the surface of the waters. The main issues in this phrase are the translation of the couplet *w^{e}rûaḥ 'ĕlōhîm* ("the Spirit of God, the spirit of God, a wind from God, an awesome gale") and the translation of the verb *m^{e}raḥepeṯ.*

As for *w^{e}rûaḥ 'ĕlōhîm,* the translation "an awesome gale" may be disposed of most easily. This suggestion takes *rûaḥ* as "wind" (a valid translation for the word in many biblical passages) and *'ĕlōhîm* not as a name for deity but as a way of expressing the superlative in Hebrew—hence "a powerful, awesome, tempestuous, raging wind." To sustain this picture of intensity and a storm-like atmosphere the following participle, *m^{e}raḥepeṯ,* is rendered something like "was sweeping" or "was stirring."[26]

Several factors militate against this translation. First, none of the other eighteen occurrences of this phrase in the OT means anything like "mighty wind." The next appearance of this phrase is Exod. 31:3, where

23. See W. G. Lambert, "A New Look at the Babylonian Background of Genesis," *JTS* 16 (1965) 293.

24. See R. L. Harris, *"thm," TWOT,* 2:966.

25. See G. Pettinato, "The Royal Archives of Tell-Mardikh-Ebla," *BA* 39 (1976) 50. M. J. Dahood (*Psalms,* AB, 3 vols. [Garden City, NY: Doubleday, 1965–1973], 2:231) wonders why scholars who know well the Ugaritic evidence continue to maintain an "incontestable connection" between Babylonian Tiamat and *t^{e}hôm,* both mythologically and philologically.

26. A modern commentator taking this approach is G. von Rad, *Genesis,* p. 49. His suggestion is "a terrible storm." Cf. also B. Vawter, *On Genesis: A New Reading,* pp. 40–41. Referring to his own translation, "the mighty wind," he says: "In this probably correct assessment of the expression, we have a final stroke added to the picture of initial disorder, with the world-to-be as yet inundated by the dark primordial waters and whipped into a vortex by a driving wind." Similarly, the evangelical scholar R. K. Harrison opts for "an awesome gale" ("Genesis," *ISBE,* 2:438). This approach assumes that the three parts of v. 2 all describe in substantially the same way the primordial chaos, instead of limiting such description to v. 2a-b, but not v. 2c. See further P. J. Smith, "A Semotactical Approach to the Meaning of the Term *rûaḥ 'ĕlōhîm* in Genesis 1:2," *JNWSL* 81 (1980) 99–104.

Bezalel is filled with the *rûaḥ ʾĕlōhîm* in order to be equipped to build the tabernacle. Obviously a "tempestuous wind" did not come upon Bezalel. This key phrase unites, via an intertextual allusion, world building and tabernacle building, the creation of a world and the creation of a shrine.[27] It is most unlikely, therefore, that the phrase be read negatively in Gen. 1 and positively in Exod. 31.

Second, it is true that there are some plausible examples in the Hebrew Bible of *ʾĕlōhîm* used as a superlative, that is, as an attributive adjective rather than a noun.[28] But even these examples are ambiguous. Thus, in Gen. 23:6, is Abraham addressed as "a prince of God" or as "a mighty prince"? In 30:8 does Rachel wrestle with "wrestlings of God" or with "mighty wrestlings"? Is Nineveh "a great city of God" or "an exceedingly great city" (Jon. 3:3)? But even if the translation were transparent in these three references, this would not allow one to apply the same force to *ʾĕlōhîm* in Gen. 1:2c, for two reasons. First, how could the reader of the original or the translator be expected to differentiate the *ʾĕlōhîm* of v. 2c from all other occurrences of *ʾĕlōhîm* in the first chapter? Second, taking *ʾĕlōhîm* as superlative, and as a further descriptive part of the chaos of formlessness and darkness, places *ʾĕlōhîm* in v. 2c in opposition to the *ʾĕlōhîm* who in v. 1 creates the heaven and the earth, and who in v. 3 speaks.[29]

As our third objection to this translation, we note that if the author had intended to say "a mighty wind" he could have used unambiguous expressions such as *rûaḥ gᵉḏôlâ* (1 K. 19:11; Job 1:19; Jon. 1:4, "a great wind") or *rûaḥ ṣᵉʿārâ* (Ps. 107:25; 148:8, "a stormy wind").

The preferable translation, then, is either "S/spirit" or "wind" of God. In modern times H. M. Orlinsky has made the most cogent presentation of the arguments for "wind."[30] For Orlinsky the translation "S/spirit" is an inauthentic "christianizing" of the Hebrew text, a tradition that is traceable

27. See M. Fishbane, *Text and Texture: Close Readings of Selected Biblical Texts* (New York: Schocken, 1979), p. 12.

28. See D. W. Thomas, "A Consideration of Some Unusual Ways of Expressing the Superlative in Hebrew," *VT* 3 (1953) 209–24. Thomas's own conclusion is expressed on p. 218: "In the Old Testament it is, I believe, difficult, if not impossible, to point to any unambiguous example of the use of the divine name as an intensifying epithet and nothing more." The first scholar to suggest that *ʾĕlōhîm* is a superlative was J. M. P. Smith, "The Syntax and Meaning of Genesis 1:1–3," *AJSL* 44 (1928) 111–12; idem, "The Use of Divine Names as Superlatives," *AJSL* 45 (1929) 212–13.

29. See B. Childs, *Myth and Reality,* p. 36.

30. H. M. Orlinsky, "The Plain Meaning of *Rûaḥ* in Gen. 1.2," *JQR* 48 (1957/58) 174–82; idem, "The New Jewish Version of the Torah," *JBL* 82 (1963) 254–57.

to the philosophical interpretation of *rûaḥ* by Philo, the famous Jewish philosopher from Alexandria in the first half of the 1st century A.D. In Orlinsky's judgment *rûaḥ,* which appears almost 400 times in the OT, does not translate as "spirit" in Genesis until 41:8, "in the morning his [Pharaoh's] spirit was troubled." By contrast, earlier uses of *rûaḥ* in Genesis clearly demand "wind" or "breath." Thus, 3:8, "they heard the sound of the Lord God walking in the garden in the cool of the day [*lᵉrûaḥ hayyôm*]," that is, in the windy or breezy time of the day. Similarly in 8:1, "God caused a wind [*rûaḥ*] to blow over the earth, and the waters subsided." "Breath" seems most natural for *rûaḥ* in 6:17; 7:15, 22, "the breath of life."

Some support for the translation "wind" is found in the Jewish targums, which are translations of the Hebrew Bible into Aramaic. So Targum Onqelos reads *wᵉrûḥāʾ min-qoḏam-yᵉyā mᵉnaššᵉḇāʾ ʿal-ʾappê mayyāʾ*, "and a wind from before the Lord was blowing over the face of the waters." The other famous targums, Targum Jonathan and the Jerusalem Targum, both retain the verb "blowing" but, interestingly, qualify its subject as a "*rûḥāʾ* of mercy from before the Lord."

The translations of the LXX and Vulg. do not clearly support either translation. The LXX *kaí pneúma theoú epephéreto epánō toú hýdatos* is exactly reproduced by the Vulg. *spiritus Dei ferebatur. . . .* Orlinsky translates the LXX "and the wind of God was sweeping over the water." Note, however, that both *epephéreto* and *ferebatur* are passives; thus a literal translation would be "was brought" or "was carried."[31] The passive form of the verbs reduces the necessity of rendering *pneúma/spiritus* as "wind."

Probably the weakest part of Orlinsky's argument is his contention that the translation "wind" provides another link between Gen. 1 and *Enuma elish.* In this myth Anu creates the four compass winds primarily as part of his arsenal to eliminate the antagonist Tiamat and then carry away her remains to a remote place. One would be hard-pressed to see any valid relationship between the *rûaḥ* of Gen. 1 and these storms or winds, called *abubu* and *imhullu,* which are Marduk's weapons.[32]

Further support for Orlinsky's arguments comes from R. Luyster's contention that the key to the phrase "the *rûaḥ* of God" is the entire clause: "the *rûaḥ* of God was hovering over the face of the waters."[33] God's ability

31. See E. J. Young, *Studies in Genesis One,* p. 41.

32. Ibid., p. 40. Also, W. F. Albright, "Contributions to Biblical Archaeology and Philology," *JBL* 43 (1924) 368.

33. R. Luyster, "Wind and Water: Cosmogonic Symbolism in the Old Testament," *ZAW* 93 (1981) 1–10.

to contain and rule over the cosmic waters is a sure indication of his power; for example, "you rule the raging of the sea" (Ps. 89:10 [Eng. 9]). Moreover, God's wind or breath (as opposed to spirit) is a most potent manifestation of his presence. These two facts suggest that in Gen. 1:2 the antipode to the surging waters is God's breath or wind, but not his spirit.

The arguments of both Orlinsky and Luyster seem inconsistent. First, one may safely say that the basic concept in *rûaḥ* is "breath." Normally the context will indicate whether by "breath" is meant "wind" or "spirit." What Luyster has not noticed is that in those passages he quotes about the wind as the most potent manifestation of God's presence, the wind is destructive. Thus, Exod. 15:10, "you did blow with your wind, the sea covered them" (cf. also Isa. 11:15; 40:7; Hos. 13:15).

In those texts in which one has a legitimate choice between "breath" and "spirit" (cf. Gen. 6:3; Job 27:3; 33:4; 34:14; Ps. 104:30; Ezek. 37:14), the emphasis is one of energizing, giving life and vitality, creating and not uncreating.[34] If the emphasis that Gen. 1:2 wishes to make is that the *rûaḥ* is a destructive force, then we must opt for "wind." If the emphasis that Gen. 1:2 wishes to make is that the *rûaḥ* is a beneficent force, then we must opt for "S/spirit." It seems clear that the latter option is the preferable one. Even Luyster takes the participle *meraḥep̱eṯ* to mean "to hover" as a leader, a guide, a protector. Of course, the Hebrew alphabet, unlike modern alphabets, does not distinguish between upper case and lower case. Accordingly, there is no way to tell from the Hebrew whether one should read "spirit" or "Spirit." To translate "Spirit" runs the risk of superimposing trinitarian concepts on Gen. 1 that are not necessarily present.

We turn our attention now to the force of the participle *meraḥep̱eṯ,* which is variously translated "was moving" (RSV), "moved" (AV), "was hovering" (NIV), "hovered" (JB), "swept" (NEB), "sweeping" (Speiser), "brooding" (Gunkel), "rushing" (Peters),[35] "swirled" (Fishbane). Obviously translations like "swept," "sweeping," "rushing," "swirled" are dictated by the choice of "wind" for *rûaḥ*.

The verb is used infrequently in the OT. The Qal stem is used in Jer. 23:9: "my heart is broken within me [*šāḇar*]; all my bones shake [*rāḥap̱*]." The only other use is in Deut. 32:11 (in the Piel stem as in Gen. 1:2): "like an eagle that stirs up [*ʿûr*] its nest, that hovers [*rāḥap̱*] over its young."

34. This important observation was made by W. H. McClellan, "The Meaning of *ruaḥ Elohim* in Genesis 1,2," *Bib* 15 (1934) 523.

35. J. P. Peters, "The Wind of God," *JBL* 30 (1911) 44–54; idem, *JBL* 33 (1914) 81–86.

Scholars have traditionally supposed that this verse concerns how a bird teaches its young to fly, specifically how the parent provokes the young to flight. The parent bird drives the young eagle from the perch by intimidation, by rushing at the young while vigorously flapping its wings.

But this interpretation may be called into question by the possibility that *ʿûr* in Deut. 32:11 does not mean "to stir up," but rather "to watch over, to protect," as in Ugar. *ǵyr.*[36] This parallel would indicate the likelihood of a similar meaning for *rāḥap̱,* at least in the Deuteronomy passage. In Gen. 1:2 is the *rûaḥ* "sweeping" over the waters or "watching over" the waters? If the latter, then "spirit" would be decidedly more accurate. Yes, there is a formlessness there, a forboding darkness, but all is kept in check and under control by the spirit of God.

Interestingly, in the Ugaritic texts this verb is always associated with eagles. For Ugar. *rḥp* C. H. Gordon suggests the meaning "soar."[37] It has been found thus far only in the Epic of Aqhat: "Over him [Aqhat] eagles will soar, there will hover a [flight of b]irds" (3 Aqhat, obverse, line 20); "over him eagle[s] soar, there hovers a flight of bird[s. Among] the eagles soars ʿAnat" (3 Aqhat, obverse, lines 31–32); "Eagles so[ar] over the house of her father, there hovers a flight of birds" (1 Aqhat, line 32). Thus from the Ugaritic passages and from the Deuteronomy passage it appears that *rāḥap̱* describes the actions of birds, not winds.[38]

Finally, we must discuss the syntax of the entire verse. This verse has three circumstantial clauses with three different subjects and three different kinds of predication: a perfect verb (v. 2a), a nominal clause (v. 2b), and a participle (v. 2c). But do the contents of v. 2 describe something that came to be after God created an originally perfect universe? Or does v. 2 expand on and clarify the shape of the earth when God first created it? Or does v. 2 describe the situation before God begins his actual creation as introduced in v. 3?

The first of these suggestions is popularly known as the gap theory. In essence, this reconstruction suggests that v. 1 describes the original creation, which was flawless. Then something catastrophic happened (Satan's fall from heaven?), throwing God's perfect earth into turmoil and judgment so that it *became* (not "was") without form and void. Subsequently

36. See H. N. Richardson, "A Ugaritic Letter of a King to His Mother," *JBL* 66 (1947) 322; M. J. Dahood, *Psalms,* 1:56.

37. *UT,* p. 484, no. 2327.

38. See T. Friedman, "*Werûaḥ ʾĕ lōhîm meraḥep̱eṯ ʿal-penê hammāyim* (Gen. 1:2)," *Beth Mikra* 25 (1980) 309–12 (Hebrew).

God started a second creation, so that v. 3 describes not creation but re-creation.[39] The length of this gap between the first and second creation is impossible to determine.

For this analysis two points are essential. The first is that v. 2 be understood as describing something sequential to v. 1. This is accomplished by understanding the verb "was" in v. 2 as having an active rather than a stative force, and by reading the verb as a pluperfect: "the earth had become. . . ." The second necessary ingredient is that the phrase "a desert and a wasteland" be interpreted as a result of divine judgment, for it describes the exact opposite of a beneficent creation. Special appeal is made to Isa. 45:18—"he did not create it a chaos [*tōhû*]" as opposed to the translation "he did not create it to be a chaos."

Now, at times the verb "to be" in the perfect tense can have an obvious active force. Certainly 3:22 says, "Behold, the man has become [*hāyâ*] like one of us." But for two reasons it cannot have this force in 1:2. First, if the writer had intended v. 2 to be read as a sequence to v. 1, he would never have used the construction he did: *waw* consecutive plus subject plus verb (in the perfect). Instead it would be: *waw* conversive attached to the verb (in the imperfect) plus subject. Thus, one would expect *wattᵉhî hā'āreṣ* rather than what we do have: *wᵉhā'āreṣ hāyᵉṯâ.*

Second, in other circumstantial clauses the verb *hāyâ* in the perfect tense normally carries its stative sense (3:1, "the serpent was wiser"; 29:16, "and Rachel was pretty; 34:5, "his sons had been [or were] in the field"; Exod. 1:5, "and Joseph was in Egypt"; Jon. 3:3, "now Nineveh was an exceedingly great city"). The burden of proof, then, is upon those who insist that here we have an instance of *hāyâ* in a circumstantial clause with the meaning "became."

We have already voiced our reasons for not interpreting *tōhû wāḇōhû* as a kind of early Sheol or Hades against which God's wrath has been loosed. Instead, we see here a reference to the situation prior to specific creation, a situation of formlessness but over which God's spirit superintends.[40]

Syntactically, two possibilities remain in understanding v. 2. First, it

39. The so-called gap theory has been given a wide hearing principally through the very popular Scofield Bible (particularly, *The New Scofield Reference Bible* [New York: Oxford University, 1907], p. 1 n. 5, p. 752 n. 2). See also A. C. Custance, *Without Form and Void* (Brockville, Ontario: Custance, 1970).

40. See G. M. Landes, "Creation Traditions in Proverbs 8:22–31 and Genesis 1," in *A Light unto My Path: Old Testament Studies in Honor of Jacob M. Myers,* ed. H. N. Bream, et al. (Philadelphia: Temple University, 1974), p. 286.

may describe a condition concurrent with that described in v. 3, "the earth being without form and void, God said. . . . " This is the approach of Orlinsky, Speiser, and others. The most serious objection to this view is that contemporaneous circumstance is adequately handled by a verbless clause.[41] We would expect *wᵉhā'āreṣ tōhû wāḇōhû.* Hence, we opt for the second possibility, that on syntactical grounds v. 2 be understood as distinct from and prior to v. 3.

In sum, the position taken here is that v. 1 is an opening statement functioning both as a superscription and as a summary. As such, it is the functional equivalent to the colophon "these are the generations of," which is the introductory sentence to each of the remaining major divisions of Genesis.

Verse 2 then describes the situation prior to the detailed creation that is spelled out in vv. 3ff.[42] It has long been observed that the creation days fall into the pattern of a movement from generalization to particularization. Days 1, 2, and 3 parallel days 4, 5, and 6. Thus day 1, the creation of light, goes with day 4, the creation of particular kinds of lights.[43] We suggest that this same movement occurs in v. 2 (generalization) and vv. 3–31 (particularization).

41. See F. I. Andersen, *The Sentence in Biblical Hebrew* (The Hague/Paris: Mouton, 1974), p. 85: "It is more likely that Gen. 1:2a means the earth *had become* (or *had come to be*) . . . as a circumstance prior to the first fiat recorded in Gen. 13, than that it means *the earth was* . . . as a circumstance accompanying the first fiat." This statement does not contradict our earlier contention about the translation of *hāyâ* in circumstantial clauses. Andersen is simply saying that the activity in v. 2 is prior to that in v. 3. He is not saying, if I understand him correctly, that the activity in v. 2 is also sequential to v. 1. On stylistic grounds B. W. Anderson argues that v. 3 cannot be the apodosis of a temporal clause whose protasis begins with v. 1 ("A Stylistic Study of the Priestly Creation Story," in *Canon and Authority: Essays in Old Testament Religion and Theology,* ed. G. W. Coats and B. O. Long [Philadelphia: Fortress, 1977], p. 153). This would be further evidence against interpreting v. 2 as a parenthetical clause that is to be conjoined with v. 3.

42. Among those embracing this position see B. Waltke, "The Creation Account in Genesis 1:1–3," *BSac* 132 (1975) 225–28.

43. "From form to fullness" or "preparation and accomplishment" is D. Kidner's choice of words (*Genesis,* TOTC [Downers Grove, IL: Inter-Varsity, 1967], p. 46).

2. THE FIRST DAY (1:3–5)

3 *And God said, "Let there be light," and there was light.*

4 *And God saw how*[1] *beautiful the light was. God separated between*[2] *the light and the darkness.*

5 *God named the light "day"; the darkness he named "night."*[3] *And there was evening and morning—a first day.*[4]

1. Here I take *kî* as an emphatic rather than simply a subordinate conjunction "that." Cf. W. F. Albright, "The Refrain 'and God saw *KI TOB*' in Genesis," in *Mélanges bibliques rédigés en l'honneur de André Robert* (Paris: Bloud & Gay, 1957), pp. 22–26. J. L. Kugel ("The Adverbial Use of *kî ṭôb,*" *JBL* 99 [1980] 433–35) circumvents the ambiguous "[it was] good" by taking the phrase adverbially, "and God was very pleased with the light." He does not consider whether *kî* may be understood as an emphatic. Kugel, however, is unable to see that the referential point for "good" is the immediately concluded action. See further J. G. Janzen, "Kugel's Adverbial *kî ṭôb:* An Assessment," *JBL* 102 (1983) 99–106.

2. The Hebrew language calls for the repetition of the preposition *bên* in phrases that mean "between *x* and *y*." Here the text reads literally "*between* light *and between* darkness." The OT uses this construction 10 times in conjunction with the Hiphil of the verb *bāḏal,* as here. The reproduction of the preposition in English produces only redundancy.

3. This translation preserves the chiastic arrangement of this part of the verse: verb—indirect object/indirect object—verb, again suggesting the possibility of a poetic substratum here, although *wayyiqrā' . . . qārā'* is standard for Hebrew prose. See J. Kselman, "Recovery of Poetic Fragments," *JBL* 97 (1978) 164; A. R. Ceresko, "The Chiastic Word Pattern in Hebrew," *CBQ* 38 (1976) 309.

4. Or, "day one." The Hebrew uses the cardinal form of the numeral, *'eḥāḏ,* rather than the ordinal *rî'šôn.* Yet *'eḥāḏ* can mean not "one" but "first," e.g., Gen. 8:5, "on the first day of the month" *(be'eḥāḏ laḥōḏeš);* and 2:11, "the name of the first is Pishon" *(šēm hā'eḥāḏ pîšôn).* Cf. GKC, § 134p, for instances of the cardinals used instead of the ordinals. C. H. Gordon has suggested that if *'eḥāḏ* is a name of God, then perhaps the first day of the week may be named after him (just as many Christians refer to Sunday as "the Lord's Day"). The phrase then in Gen. 1:5 would be "Day of [the] One" (C. H. Gordon, "His Name is 'One,' " *JNES* 29 [1970] 198–99; idem, "The Seventh Day," *UF* 11 [1979] 299–300). An Ugaritic text has been published (no. 611) which records a rite in which the king and queen present offerings to *Ušḫr* the serpent-god, and then partake themselves of the offerings. The composition concludes with this calendrical formula (line 14): *ym aḥd,* "Day: One." L. Fisher ("An Ugaritic Ritual and Genesis 1:1–5," *Ugaritica* [Paris: Geuthner, 1969], 6:197–205) took this formula as evidence that Gen. 1 reflects a liturgical background. But the simple appearance of the phrase in an Ugaritic cultic text is rather shallow evidence for assuming the same origin for Gen. 1. Cf. also S. Loewenstamm, "Ugarit and the Bible II," *Bib* 59 (1978) 112–13.

3 This first day of six days of divine activity produces the creation of light. This is quite natural, for the existence of light is the sine qua non for the creation of anything else. All creation takes place in the light.

These three verses contain the words of both God and the narrator. Actually there are only two narrated words of God on this first day: *yᵉhî 'ôr, "Let there be light."* Everything else (introduction of the deity, a description of the created object, a statement of evaluation, information on subsequent activities of God, a chronological note) is from the narrator. Yet it is the words of God, however brief, that are paramount. The narrator's contributions function as something of an appendage. God is the soloist; the narrator is the accompanist.

Verse 3 also introduces the reader to the frequently used phrase of Gen. 1—*and God said* (vv. 3, 6, 9, 14, 20, 24, 26). It is the Vulg. translation of v. 3, *fiat lux,* "Let there be light," that has given birth to the phrase "creation by *fiat.*" The emphasis is on creation by speech as command.

All Creation stories, biblical and nonbiblical, describe creation in one of four ways: (1) through action of some deity or deities; (2) through conflict with antagonistic forces; (3) through birth and self-reproduction; (4) through speech. Obviously the second and third are not found in Gen. 1 and 2, but both chapters do reflect the use of the first and fourth.

Worth pursuing is the interpretation that claims that there is a basic distinction between the mode of creation in 1:1–2:3 and that of 2:4–31. The contrast is between creation by word and creation by action, God said versus God formed/planted/took a rib. (By the way, this difference is one of the criteria that source critics use to drive a wedge between these two chapters; they label 1:1–2:4a as "Priestly" and therefore late, and 2:4bff. as "Yahwistic" and therefore earlier, maybe 9th/8th century B.C.)

A closer examination of the two chapters shows that such a distinction is not maintained in the text itself. One observes that the only item in Gen. 1 that is created by *fiat,* strictly speaking, is light: "And God said, 'Let there be light,' and there was light." Everything else is created, or emerges, in Gen. 1 by *fiat* plus some subsequent activity that is divinely instigated. Thus, there is no " 'let there be a vault,' and there was a vault," nor any " 'let there be lights/animals/man,' and there were [was] lights/animals/man." So, after the "Let there be" of day 2 (v. 6a) comes "And God *made* the vault."

4 This verse logically follows v. 3, for *x* can be separated from *y* only on the assumption that both *x* and *y* are already in existence. *separated* means here not to pull apart, but to assign each part to its respective sphere and slot.

God's work in Gen. 1 is often a work of separation. The verb is used five times in this chapter (vv. 4, 6, 7, 14, 18), once with light and darkness, twice with the celestial vault, and twice with the luminaries. A. Kapelrud has suggested that this verb appears as often as it does in Gen. 1—and nowhere else in Genesis—for a deliberate reason. Beginning with the idea that this story was composed for the sake of exiled Judeans who were in jeopardy of compromising their faith, Kapelrud makes the point that the proliferation of "separate" in Gen. 1 functions as a subtle exhortation to the exiles to separate themselves from every possibility of contamination with pagans.[5]

This suggestion strikes us as more fanciful and imaginative than exegetical. If anything, these opening chapters of Genesis provide a contrast between a separation that is wholesome and a separation that is malignant. In creation there is separation toward order: light from darkness, waters above from waters below, day from night, woman from man. In sin and trespass there is a separation toward disorder: man and woman from God; man from woman; man from the soil; man from a garden.

The major difference between this work of separation and the other two in Gen. 1 is that here the pronouncement of God's benedictional statement—*God saw how beautiful the light was*—precedes the separation. In vv. 6–8 and 14–19 this sentence of evaluation follows the separation. Thus it is the light itself that is *beautiful* (or good, Heb. *ṭôḇ*), not the creation per se of time into units of light and darkness.

Still, it is important, as was indicated above, that we place in proper perspective what happens on the first day in comparison with following days. God's first creation is time (vv. 3–5). His second creation is space (vv. 6–10).[6] Can it be without significance that this Creation story commences in the context of time and concludes (2:1–3) with a return to that category, a day of rest? A civilization whose concept of time is essentially cyclical will for obvious reasons not sanctify the category of time. Its exclusive obsession will be with the sanctification of space. The Genesis concept of the sanctification of time (compare the root *qdš* in Gen. 2:3) receives more prominence than does the concept of the sanctification of space; in fact, not until Exod. 3:5, which is incidentally the next occurrence of the root *qdš* ("sanctify"), does one encounter the concept of the sanctification of space—"for the *ground* on which you are standing is *holy* ground."

5. A. Kapelrud, "The Mythological Features in Genesis 1 and the Author's Intention," *VT* 24 (1974) 185.

6. See C. Westermann, *Creation,* tr. John J. Scullion (Philadelphia: Fortress, 1974), p. 43.

It will perhaps strike the reader of this story as unusual that its author affirms the existence of light (and a *day* for that matter) without the existence of the sun, which is still three "days" away. The creation of light anticipates the creation of sunlight. Eventually the task of separating the light from the darkness will be assigned to the heavenly luminaries (v. 18). It is unnecessary to explain such a claim as reflecting scientific ignorance. What the author states is that God caused the light to shine from a source other than the sun for the first three "days."[7]

5 The fact that *evening* is placed before *morning* throughout this chapter is not a foolproof indication that the OT reckons a day from sunset to sunset. There is some evidence that strongly suggests that the day was considered to begin in the morning at sunrise. For example, this view is supported by the fact that when the OT refers to a second day the time reference is the morning (Gen. 19:33–34; Judg. 6:38; 21:4). Similarly, the phrase "day and night" is much more frequent than "night and day."[8] Thus it seems likely that this refrain in Genesis refers not to the computation of a day but rather to the "vacant time till the morning, the end of a day and the beginning of the next work."[9]

3. THE SECOND DAY (1:6–8)

6 *And God said, "Let there be a vault in the middle of the waters, and let it be a separator*[1] *between waters and waters."*

7. The Bible begins and ends by describing an untarnished world that is filled with light, but no sun (cf. Rev. 22:5). Should not the one who is himself called "light" (1 John 1:5) have at his disposal many sources by which he dispatches light into his creation? Just as Gen. 1 says there can be a day and light without sun, so Matt. 2 says there can be a son without a father. Calvin comments, "Therefore the Lord, by the very order of creation, bears witness that he holds in his hands the light, which he is able to impart to us without the sun and moon" (*Commentaries on the First Book of Moses Called Genesis,* tr. John King, 2 vols. [Grand Rapids: Eerdmans, repr. 1948], 1:76).

8. A verse such as Lev. 23:32, dealing with Day of Atonement observance, calls for the keeping of the sacred day on "the evening of the ninth day of the month, from this evening to the next evening." This verse does not indicate a sunset-to-sunset reckoning, but rather the fact that certain sacred festivals are to be held also on the night of the preceding day.

9. R. de Vaux, *Ancient Israel,* 2 vols., tr. J. McHugh (New York: McGraw-Hill, repr. 1965), 1:181. See also U. Cassuto, *A Commentary on the Book of Genesis,* 2 vols., tr. I. Abrahams (Jerusalem: Magnes, 1961–1964), 1:28–30.

1. The translation attempts to bring out the force of the Hiphil participle of *bāḏal* used here.

7 *So, God made the vault and he separated between the waters beneath the vault and the waters above the vault. And it was so.*
8 *God called the vault "sky." And there was evening and morning—a second day.*

6 The word we have translated as *vault* is Heb. *rāqîaʿ*, which appears as "firmament" in the AV (from Vulg. *firmamentum*). The basic meaning of the noun is determined by a consideration of the verb *rāqaʿ*. Here the basic idea is "to spread out," and specifically the spreading out of the earth at creation (cf. Ps. 136:6; Isa. 42:5; 44:24) or the spreading out of the sky (cf. Job 37:18). In Isa. 40:19 the meaning is to overlay or plate (with gold). A *rāqîaʿ*, then, is something that is created by being spread out either by stretching (e.g., a tent) or by hammering (e.g., a metal; cf. Deut. 28:23, in which the sky in a time of drought is likened to bronze; cf. also the use of *rāqaʿ* in Exod. 39:3, where the meaning is clearly "to hammer out").

The function of this vault is to separate *between waters and waters.* It will be observed that the prepositions before "waters" in v. 6 are *bên . . . l^e* (or *lā*), while the prepositions before "waters" in v. 7 are *bên . . . bên.* The first combination appears only thirty times in the OT, while the latter combination appears some 126 times. Gen. 1:6 is the only example of *bên . . . l^e* in Genesis. The next occurrence of this combination is not until Lev. 20:25.

The combination *bên . . . l^e* appears to be used consistently to draw a distinction between *x* and *y*,[2] and when this distinction refers to unspecified classes such as man:wife; father:daughter; clean:unclean. For example, to express that there was a war between Israel and the Philistines (i.e., specific people) the expression *bên . . . bên* would be used. But in expressions like "knowing the difference between good and evil" (i.e., nonspecifics), the combination is usually *bên . . . l^e*. Thus in Gen. 1:6–7, perhaps v. 6 refers to waters in general. But once the division is made (v. 7), two specific sets of water emerge, those above and those beneath the vault.[3]

7 Syntactically the subject of *separated* could be either God (he separated) or the vault (it separated). Without being dogmatic, we prefer the former on the basis of the parallel in v. 4, where God is clearly the subject of

2. Especially those times when *x* and *y* are the same words, as here and in Deut. 17:8 (between blood and blood, legal right and legal right, assault and assault); Ezek. 18:8 (between man and man); Ezek. 34:17, 22 (between sheep and sheep); Ezek. 41:18 (between cherub and cherub). An exception is Gen. 32:17 (Eng. 16).

3. See J. Barr, "Some Notes on *ben* 'between' in Classical Hebrew," *JSS* 23 (1978) 1–22, esp. p. 11.

the same verb. Also, the expressed subject of the verb in the first clause functions as the subject of the verb in the next principal clause unless there is an obvious indication of a subject change, either through a new subject or through a change in the second verbal form, or both. In favor of attaching the verb with vault as subject is the fact that later in the narrative the work of separation is assigned to the created items themselves, and not to the creator (vv. 14, 18).

Many commentators have shifted MT *wayᵉhî-ḵēn, And it was so,* from the end of this verse to the end of v. 6, following the LXX at this point. Consistently in Gen. 1 this expression follows God's opening declarative statement (vv. 9, 11, 15, 24). Here the *And it was so* follows the *Tatbericht* (the report of action) instead of the *Wortbericht* (the report of speech). There is a similar placement of the phrase on the sixth day (see v. 30 below).

8 One may compare the creation of the *sky* as delineated in these verses with the parallel in *Enuma elish* to see some of the wide discrepancy in mentality between the biblical story and the pagan account. The appropriate lines in *Enuma elish* read:

> Then the lord [Marduk] paused to view her dead body [Tiamat],
> That he might divide the monster and do artful works.
> He split her like a shellfish into two parts;
> Half of her he set up and ceiled it as sky,
> Pulled down the bar and posted guards.
> He bade them to allow not her waters to escape.[4]

In this myth, sky is made not only from preexisting material but specifically from one-half of the cadaver of an evil goddess. Then Marduk must provide locks and guards to deter Tiamat from unleashing her threatening waters on the earth. Heaven as antagonist operates under restraint.

In Canaanite mythology much attention is given to this celestial sea and to Baal, whose primary function is rainmaker. Assuming a central role here are the windows of heaven. By contrast such sluice gates are mentioned only infrequently in Scripture, Gen. 7:11 being the one passage that explicitly mentions the means by which these waters above were released. Preponderantly the OT describes the process of rainfall much as we do, that is, as a concomitant of lightning, clouds, and thunder (Gen. 9:14; Judg. 5:4; 1 K. 18:45; Isa. 5:6; and even poetic passages such as Job 26:8 and Ps. 77:18 [Eng. 17]).[5]

4. Translation of E. A. Speiser in *ANET,* p. 67.
5. See D. Neiman, "The Supercaelian Sea," *JNES* 29 (1969) 243–49.

Only in connection with this second day is the phrase "and God saw how beautiful it was" absent in the MT. LXX has the phrase, probably artificially and for the sake of consistency. It is unlikely that the LXX represents an earliest form of the Hebrew text. The omission of the phrase in v. 8 may indicate that the author viewed the creation of the vault as only a preliminary stage to the emergence of dry land in v. 10, and thus he reserved the phrase until its most appropriate time. The "waters above" are now edged out of the Creation story and dropped from further concern by the author.

4. THE THIRD DAY (1:9–13)

9 *And God said, "Let the waters beneath the sky be gathered into one collection*[1] *and let the dry land appear." And it was so.*
10 *God named the dry land "earth"; the collection of waters he named "seas." God saw how beautiful it was.*
11 *And God said, "Let the earth be green with verdure: seed-bearing plants, and every kind*[2] *of fruit trees—whose seed is enclosed in it—producing fruit on earth." And it was so.*
12 *The earth brought forth verdure: every kind of seed-bearing plants, every kind of fruit trees—whose seed is enclosed in it. God saw how beautiful it was.*
13 *And there was evening and morning—a third day.*

9–10 Perhaps the use of two jussives in v. 9 suggests that the two developments (the concentration of the subcelestial waters and the emergence of dry

1. The MT reads *māqôm 'eḥāḏ,* "one place." On the basis of several factors—the word *miqwēh,* "collection, assembly," in the following verse; the LXX rendering of *māqôm* in v. 9 by *synagōgḗ,* "assembly"; the reading *miqwēh* in v. 11 in 4QGen—the suggestion has been made to emend the text here from *māqōm* to *miqwēh* (see, e.g., *BHK, BHS*). The consonantal text is able to stand in v. 11, however, once it is recognized that the *-m* on *mqwm* is an enclitic and serves as a glide between *-e* and the glottal stop of *'eḥāḏ*. See D. N. Freedman, "Notes on Genesis," *ZAW* 64 (1952) 190–91; M. J. Dahood, "Northwest Semitic Notes on Genesis," *Bib* 55 (1974) 77; F. C. Fensham, "Ugaritic and the Translation of the Old Testament," *BT* 18 (1967) 72.

2. Traditionally translated "(each) according to its kind." Here the MT reads *l*^{e}*mînô,* but in the following verse (twice) and in v. 25 it reads *l*^{e}*mînēhû.* The former appears 4 times in the OT (here and Lev. 11:15, 22, which uses both forms; Deut. 14:14), and the latter 12 times. According to D. N. Freedman (*ZAW* 64 [1952] 190), *l*^{e}*mînô* is anomalous and goes back to a form *l*^{e}*mînāw,* from *l*^{e}*mînāhû,* the *-a-* here representing an old accusative ending.

land) be understood as concomitant events. If the author had intended the relationship between the two events to be simultaneous, sequential, or cause and effect, one would expect a different construction in the phrase *and let the dry land appear.* Thus it seems best to read the *waw* on this second jussive simply as *and* instead of supplying something like "and [at the same time] . . . ," or "and [subsequently] . . . ," or "so that. . . ."

Verse 10 is structured exactly like v. 5. They share both the verbal pattern *wayyiqrā' . . . qārā',* and the chiastic structure *abc::bac* (verb, indirect object, object::indirect object, verb, object).

The narration of the Creation story now advances from the category of time to that of space. This is the last time, in the creation context, that God will name anything. He continues to create, but he ceases to name. That responsibility will be delegated to man, once he arrives on the scene (2:19, 20, 23; 3:20; 4:17, 25, 26; 5:3, 29).

Just as there is a shift of emphasis in 1:1 from "heavens and earth" to simply "earth" in v. 2, so on this third day of creation there is a shift away from *waters/seas* and *dry land/earth* (vv. 9–10) to *dry land/earth* alone in vv. 11–12. Also, although the waters are mentioned before the dry land in v. 9, the dry land is named first in v. 10. The geocentric emphasis of the Creation story thus begins to emerge.[3]

11–13 These verses move from the creation of the bare earth to the ornamentation of that earth. Unlike the first and second days, which feature one act of creation, this day has two acts of creation: earth and vegetation. For this reason creations involving divine separation are now augmented by a creation involving a divine covering. He who will later cover Adam and Eve in the garden with garments of skin first covers his earth with lush vegetation. Shortly he will dot his sky with luminaries.

Actually Gen. 1 describes eight creative acts by God over a six-day period. The pattern into which these creative acts fall provides even further evidence of the author's intention to describe the creation schematically:

Day one: one work: light
Day two: one work: vault
Day three: two works: earth and vegetation (indicated by the double use of the evaluation, vv. 10, 12)

Day four: one work: luminaries
Day five: one work: birds, fish
Day six: two works: land animals and man (indicated by the double use of the evaluation formula, vv. 25, 31)

3. The OT has at least three poetic allusions to God's creation of the earth that involve a separation from water: Job 38:4–11; Ps. 104:5–9; Prov. 8:27–29. As one might expect, a bit of poetic license is used in these verses that is not found in the more prosaic account of Genesis.

It is a moot point whether vv. 11 and 12 refer to three different types of plant growth or to two. The Hebrew allows either possibility. But for two reasons this translation assumes, though not dogmatically, that *deše', verdure,* is an all-inclusive word that is then defined by two representatives, *'ēśeḇ,* plant(s), and *'ēṣ,* tree(s). For one thing, a distinction is made only between plants and trees. The former bear their seeds externally and the latter bear theirs internally, inside the fruit. More tellingly, vv. 29–30 inform us that God gave two of these three items to man for consumption: *'ēśeḇ* and *'ēṣ.* Then again, vv. 11–12 may simply describe the appearance of three types of plant growth, of which only two are edible by man.

God's creative design is that both the plants and the trees will reproduce themselves by bearing seed "each according to its kind" (AV, RSV). Here the concept of both the supernatural and the natural have their place.[4] What exists exists because of the creative word of God. This spoken word is the ultimate background to all terrestrial phenomena. Yet this same word grants the means of self-perpetuation to various species and orders of creation. Here then is both point and process, with neither eclipsing the other. It is probably too restrictive to insist that the Hebrew word *mîn,* "kind(s)," be limited to "species." Heb. *mîn* is broad enough to allow "species" as well as "genus, family, order."[5]

With the conclusion of the third day yet another color is added to God's cosmos. To the basic white and black of day and night has been added the blue of sky and sea. Now the canvas is adorned with green. The golden-yellow sun and the reddish human being will complete this rainbow of colors.

5. THE FOURTH DAY (1:14–19)

14 *And God said, "Let there be luminaries*[1] *in the vault of the sky to separate between day and night; let them be indicators of seasons, days, and years,*[2]

4. See D. Kidner, *Genesis,* p. 48.

5. See W. C. Kaiser, *TWOT,* 1:503–4, versus the stricter interpretation of J. B. Payne, "The Concept of 'Kinds' in Scripture," *JASA* 10 (1958) 17–19.

1. The translation "luminaries" is evoked by the Hebrew word used here, *mā'ôr,* lit., "place of light," which is thus distinguished from the word *'ôr,* translated as "light" in vv. 3, 4, 5, 18. Other possibilities would be "light bearers" or "lamps."

2. Speiser (*Genesis,* p. LXVII) sees in v. 14b no less than four distinct uses of the particle w^e: (1) introductory; (2) connective in hendiadys; (3) explicative; (4) plain connective. Most questionable is his detection of hendiadys here, but he is supported by H. C. Brichto, *The Problem of "Curse" in the Hebrew Bible,* JBLMS 13 (Philadelphia: Society of Biblical Literature, 1968), p. 99 n. 46.

15 *luminaries in the vault of the sky to shine upon the earth." And it was so.*
16 *God made the two great luminaries, the greater luminary as ruler of the day and the lesser luminary as ruler of the night—also the stars.*
17 *God placed them in the vault of the sky to shine upon the earth,*
18 *to rule over the day and the night, and to separate between the light and the darkness. God saw how beautiful it was.*
19 *And there was evening and morning—a fourth day.*

14–15 There is progression here from light in general or unspecified (day 1) to specific sources of light (day 4). These sources of light, however, are described first of all only by an all-inclusive term—*luminaries.* Unlike the previous three days, where a statement about the raison d'être of the created item is either omitted or only briefly noted, here a threefold function is assigned to these celestial light bearers: to separate between day and night, to serve as signs of the passage of time, and to illuminate the earth. So important is the delineation of these functions that they are repeated in vv. 17–18, in reverse order, perhaps as an attention-getting device.

Few commentators deny that this whole chapter has a strong anti-mythical thrust. Perhaps in no other section—except the sixth day—does this polemic appear so bluntly as it does here. It is sufficient to recall the proliferation of astral deities in most Mediterranean religions: the sun, the moon, and the stars are divine. As such they are autonomous bodies. Around each of them focus various kinds of religious cults and devotees. In the light of this emphasis Gen. 1:14ff. is saying that these luminaries are not eternal; they are created, not to be served but to serve.[3] That is the mandate under which they function.

16–18 The author's polemical concerns continue in these verses as indicated, first of all, by his choice of terminology. He uses the unusual expression *the greater luminary* instead of the normal word for sun—*šemeš*—of which he undoubtedly was aware. In the same way he opts for *the lesser luminary* instead of the familiar *yārēaḥ,* "moon." The reason for this choice of terms may be due to the fact that these words—which are very similar in other Semitic languages—are the names of divinities.[4] Thus this

3. Von Rad (*Genesis,* p. 55) sees in this section an attitude of the biblical writer toward the heavenly lights that he labels as "prosaic and degrading." Similarly Westermann, *Creation,* p. 44: "The utter creatureliness of the heavenly bodies has never before been expressed in such revolutionary terms."

4. For example, in the Ugaritic texts *Špš* and *Yrḫ*. Echoes of these traditions may be reflected in the biblical names of Canaanite cities: Beth-shemesh, "House (or

text is a deliberate attempt to reject out of hand any apotheosizing of the luminaries, by ignoring the concrete terms and using a word that speaks of their function.

Second, the antimythical thrust of this section is indicated by the order in which the luminaries are listed: sun, moon, stars. This order contrasts with the order in *Enuma elish,* in which priority is given to the stars, following which Marduk organizes the calendar and fixes the polestar. Only then do the moon and sun (in that order) come into play:

> He bade the moon come forth;
> entrusted night (to him);
> assigned to him adornment of the night
> to measure time.[5]

In fact, *Enuma elish* does not record the creation of these lights, for they are "great gods." They are simply placed in their cosmic positions as constellations (stars) or instructed by Marduk (moon and sun). It is significant that in Gen. 1 the reference to the stars, which are so prominent in pagan cosmogonies, is touched on so briefly and quite anticlimactically. Given the MT's word order in v. 16, one may safely describe the creation of the stars as almost an afterthought or a parenthetical addition.[6]

---

shrine) of the sun," and Jericho, which is related to the word for moon in the Semitic languages (e.g., Heb. *yeraḥ,* Ugar. *yrḫ*).

5. Translation of T. Jacobsen, *The Treasures of Darkness: A History of Mesopotamian Religion* (New Haven: Yale University, 1976), p. 179.

6. See E. J. Young, *Studies in Genesis One,* p. 94; G. Hasel, "The Polemic Nature of the Genesis Cosmology," *EvQ* 46 (1974) 89; idem, "The Significance of the Cosmology in Genesis 1 in Relation to Ancient Near Eastern Parallels," *AUSS* 10 (1972) 11–14. It should be noted that Tablet V of *Enuma elish* provides fairly advanced information about these luminaries, and such details are not found in the biblical account. Thus, the epic says that 3 constellations of stars were established for each month to fix the days of the year. The moon exists not only to "adorn the night" but to fix the monthly cycle and maintain a relationship with the sun. C. H. Gordon remarks that "details of this sort reflect the sophistication and scientific superiority of the Babylonians as against the Hebrews who were satisfied with less astronomical data" (*The Ancient Near East,* 3rd ed. [New York: Norton, 1965], p. 44).

6. THE FIFTH DAY (1:20–23)

20 *And God said, "Let the waters teem with swarming living creatures*[1]
and let birds fly above the earth, beneath the vault of the sky."[2]
21 *God created the large marine creatures and every kind of creeping living creature with which the waters teem, and every kind of winged bird. God saw how beautiful it was.*
22 *God blessed them, saying, "Be fertile, multiply, and fill the sea's waters, and let the birds multiply on the earth."*
23 *And there was evening and morning—a fifth day.*

20–21 Just as days one and four correspond, so days two and five are related. Day two brought into existence the necessary environment and habitat—the sky to separate the waters. Now on day five those creatures are created who inhabit the sky and the waters—birds and aquatic beings.

Those creatures who live in water are divided into two categories: (1) extremely large and mostly water-related mammals or reptiles (crocodile, whale, large snakes; hence RSV "the great sea monsters"); and (2) smaller fish and other more diminutive aquatic creatures, who either glide through the water or creep along its bed.

Much discussion has focused on the identity of the enormous marine creatures (Heb. *tannînim,* v. 21), which particularly in three OT texts are juxtaposed with the name of dragonesque creatures who have met, or will meet, defeat at God's hands. Ps. 74:13–14 relates that God has "broken the heads of the dragons on the waters," thus including "dragons" as one of the powers subjugated by God (others are the sea and Leviathan). Vv. 15–17 continue the allusion to the creation event. Isa. 27:1 announces the eschatological day on which Yahweh will both punish Leviathan "and slay the dragon that is in the sea." Isa. 51:9 also refers to the past when God cut Rahab to pieces, pierced the dragon, and dried up the sea and the waters of the great deep *(tᵉhôm rabbâ).* Of the nine other OT references to *tannîn,* most indicate simply some land or sea creature (serpent: Exod. 7:9, 10, 12; Deut. 32:33; Ps. 91:13; perhaps "crocodile" in Ezek. 29:3 and 32:2).[3] Still, there are these

1. The occurrence of this same expression—*nep̄eš ḥayyâ*—to describe man in 2:7 should provide sufficient evidence against seeing any uniqueness in man because of a "soul" (as *nep̄eš* is often translated; see, e.g., AV). It is unwise to translate as "living being, creature" (animals) in 1:20 and "living soul" (man) in 2:7.

2. LXX adds "And it was so," which reflects the LXX's tendency to systematize and make the text uniform. Here it supplies "and it was so" to parallel the phrase used in the preceding days (vv. 6, 11, 15).

3. A very interesting text here is Ps. 148, a hymn which calls upon all created

three verses in which the *tannîn* appear as an antagonist to God. Is this another literary parallel, asked the scholars, to *Enuma elish* in which Marduk created the earth by first conquering and slaying the monster Tiamat and then cutting her corpse in half?

Even more interest was drawn to the subject with the discovery of *tnn* in Ugaritic texts. Ugar. *tnn* is another name for Yamm (Sea), who is consistently pictured as an enemy of Baal. Thus in one text (ʿnt III:34–39) Baal's sister-wife Anat says:

> What enemies risen 'gainst Baal?
> What foe 'gainst the Rider of Clouds?
> Crushed I not El's Belov'd Yamm?
> Destroyed I not El's Flood Rabbim?
> Did I not, pray, muzzle the Dragon [*tnn*]?
> I did crush the crooked serpent [*ltn,* viz., Leviathan],
> Shalyat the seven-headed.[4]

Unlike *Enuma elish,* the Canaanite Baal versus Yamm (Sea) and Mot (Death) cycle has nothing to do with world origins. Instead the concern here is with the annual cycles in nature and whether there will be dearth or fertility in the land.

Genesis 1 does not even hint of a battle. The *tannînim* are simply large creatures of the water and are created by God. Perhaps the reappearance in v. 21 of the verb *create,* not used since v. 1, underlines this point. This is a verb whose only subject in the OT is God, and whose accusative is always the product and never the material.[5] Even some of the later texts that use battle imagery place such battles not at creation per se but rather "in days of old" (Isa. 51:9).

The Bible obviously does not hesitate to use the language of myth. The references in Ps. 74, Isa. 27, and Isa. 51 defy any other explanation. Curiously, Genesis does *not* use the language of myth in its narration of the Creation story. Gen. 1 could not be written with a more antimythical basis.[6]

---

things—of which one is the *tannîn,* v. 7—to praise Yahweh. Vv. 1–6 list elements in the sky that are to praise Yahweh. Vv. 8–14 focus on terrestrial elements that are to praise him. Only one verse—v. 7—invokes aquatic elements to doxology.

4. Translation of H. L. Ginsberg, *ANET,* p. 137. Such seven-headed beasts figure also in the vision received by John on Patmos (see Rev. 13:1). For an ancient representation of such a beast, see *ANEP,* no. 691.

5. See J. Skinner, *Genesis,* p. 15; G. Hasel, *EvQ* 46 (1974) 85–87.

6. Of course, the appropriation of literary figures from a polytheistic milieu in no way indicates that these are the basic beliefs and understandings of the biblical

22–23 For the first time in the Creation narrative God speaks to somebody. Soliloquy gives way to monologue, indicated by the introduction of the second person imperative mood. But God's blessing precedes his commands. He gives a blessing and then issues an order. The recipient of God's first blessing in the Bible is not man—that must wait until v. 28—but fish and fowl. Quite evidently, the essence of God's blessing is the capacity to be fertile, to reproduce oneself. Everything thus far in the created order has received God's inspection. To that is now added God's blessing.

7. THE SIXTH DAY (1:24–31)

24 *And God said, "Let the earth bring forth every kind of living creature: cattle, reptiles, and every kind of wild animal."*[1] *And it was so.*

25 *God made every kind of wild animal, every kind of cattle, every kind of land reptile. God saw how beautiful it was.*

26 *And God said, "Let us make man in our image, as our likeness. Let them exercise dominion over fish of the sea, over birds of the sky, over the cattle, over all the earth, and over every reptile that crawls on the earth."*

27 *God created man in his image. In the image of God he created him; male and female he created them.*

28 *God blessed them, saying to them: "Be abundantly fruitful,*[2] *fill the earth, and subdue it. Exercise dominion over fish of the sea, over birds of the sky, and over every living thing that moves on the earth."*

---

writer. Both the psalmist and the prophet utilize battle imagery to say that God deals with evil by redemption. Here is where disorder is defeated. See J. N. Oswalt, "The Myth of the Dragon and Old Testament Faith," *EvQ* 49 (1977) 163–72.

1. The *-ô* on *ḥay*^{e}*ṯô-'ereṣ* looks strange in the light of the parallel phrase in v. 25, *ḥayyaṯ hā'āreṣ*. This *-ô* is usually explained as a *waw compaginis* and is said to reflect the remains of early case endings, here an archaic nominative ending *-u*. Thus behind the MT stands an original Canaanite *ḥayyatu 'arṣi*. See GKC, § 90o; Dahood, *Psalms,* 2:250. There are two other possible explanations of the *waw*. D. Robertson ("The morphemes *-y[-ī]* and *-w[-ō]* in Biblical Hebrew," *VT* 19 [1969] 211–23, esp. pp. 221–23) points to 12 instances of this particular *waw* in the OT, in 7 of which the *waw* is added to *ḥyt:* Gen. 1:24; Ps. 50:10; 79:2; 104:11, 20; Isa. 56:9; Zeph. 2:14. He suggests that the *-o* relates not to the function of the word to which it is affixed but to its form, in particular its bound (construct) state. The other explanation parses the *-o* as the prospective pronominal suffix anticipating *'ereṣ,* as in Prov. 13:4, *naḇšô ʿāṣēl,* "the soul of the sluggard." See G. Rendsburg, "Late Biblical Hebrew and the Date of 'P'," *JANES* 12 (1980) 67 n. 10.

2. Perhaps it is better to take these two verbs here, and in v. 22, as illustrative of hendiadys in conjunctive sentences. Thus "be fruitful, multiply" means "be abundantly fruitful."

29 *God also said, "Indeed, I have given to you as food every seed-bearing plant on the face of the earth and every tree whose fruit bears seed.*
30 *To every wild animal of the earth, to every bird of the sky, to every living creature that crawls, (I give) every green plant as food." And it was so.*
31 *God looked over everything he made, and indeed it was very beautiful. And there was evening and morning—the sixth day.*

24–25 The development in creation is now from aquatic and aerial animals (fifth day) to terrestrial animals (sixth day). The corresponding day to day six (i.e., third day) saw the emergence of the dry land. Now the creatures who inhabit the dry land appear.

Three categories of land creatures are described in these two verses. By *cattle* is meant primarily large quadrupeds which are domesticated. *reptiles* (lit., "creeping [or crawling] thing") designate the legless creatures such as lizards and snakes. The third category, *every kind of wild animal,* is simply the Hebrew word for "living thing."

For some unknown reason the land animals are not the direct recipient of a divine blessing as are the aquatic creatures (v. 22). Perhaps the announcement of the divine blessing is reserved for the three most critical junctures in the narrative: the introductory statement (v. 1); the creation of organic life (v. 20); and the creation of human life (v. 26).

Like the plants, all living creatures—terrestrial, celestial, and aquatic—are created according to kind. They are created to be self-propagating. The Creator makes creators.

The order in which the land animals appear is different in the two verses. Thus, v. 24: cattle, reptiles, wild animals; v. 25: wild animals, cattle, reptiles. (This three-part division of the mammal world is condensed in v. 28 into one expression: "every living thing that moves on the earth.") It is unlikely that the sequence of one of the two verses is earlier or more correct than the other. More than likely the summary heading in v. 24—*nep̱eš ḥayyâ*—provides a reason in this verse for not starting with *ḥayᵉṯô 'ereṣ.*

26 This verse bristles with issues that have been the subjects of innumerable articles and monographs. The first area of debate is over the striking use of the first person plural pronouns: *us . . . our.* Needless to say, earlier Christian commentators were prone to see here a reference to the Trinity. But even if one grants that Moses was in some way responsible for Gen. 1, it is going too far to call Israel's hero a trinitarian monotheist! Christian readers of the OT may indeed see a trinitarian context in Gen. 1.

The question remains whether that was the author's intention and understanding. The theological battle of Moses' day was not trinitarianism versus unitarianism. The battle centered around the belief in one God who is himself uncreated, merciful, and sovereign versus the belief in multiple gods and demons who are capricious, unpredictable, and often immoral.

In order to understand the *us* of v. 26 historically and grammatically, scholars have suggested at least six possibilities for interpretation.[3] (1) A mythological interpretation understands the *us* to refer to other gods. Thus this text is a remnant of the earliest form of the story that somehow escaped the editor who removed from his borrowed tale any pagan elements that would be offensive and unacceptable to monotheists.[4]

(2) In the biblical adaptation of the story the pantheon concept was replaced with the heavenly court concept. Thus, it is not to other gods, but to the angelic host, the "sons of God," that God speaks.[5]

(3) God speaks to something he has recently created and the most likely addressee would be the earth. Thus man owes his origin to both God and the ground.[6]

(4) Some grammarians have opted here for what they call a plural of majesty, for the word *God* is itself plural—*'ĕlōhîm.* Comparison has been made to the "us" in Gen. 11:7 and Isa. 6:8.[7]

(5) Other grammarians have interpreted the *us* to be a plural of

3. See D. J. A. Clines, "The Image of God in Man," *TynBul* 19 (1968) 62–69; G. Hasel, "The Meaning of 'Let Us' in Gn 1:26," *AUSS* 13 (1975) 58–66.

4. H. Gunkel, *Genesis,* p. 111.

5. Among the scholars who have written on the subject, this approach is probably the most widely held. M. Weinfeld ("God the Creator in Gen. 1 and in the Prophecy of Second Isaiah," *Tarbiz* 37 [1968] 105–32 [Hebrew]) so understands the pronoun and then assumes a rejection of this concept in Isa. 40:13–14 and 44:24. According to the prophet, God acted alone at creation and consulted nobody. For this reason and others, Weinfeld dates Gen. 1 prior to "Second" Isaiah. For him Gen. 1 is more primitive and mythical. If one follows the "council" understanding of "us," it is not absolutely necessary to assume that the writer would convey the idea that the angels are man's co-creators. We know that in this primeval context both cherubim (3:24) and sons of God (6:2) are present. May the writer simply want to say that these newly created creatures of earth are in some fashion like *all* the inhabitants of heaven? See P. D. Miller, *Genesis 1–11: Studies in Structure and Theme,* JSOTSup 8 (Sheffield: University of Sheffield, 1978), pp. 13–14.

6. W. Caspari, "Imago Divina," in *Festschrift Reinhold Seeberg,* I, ed. W. Koepp (Leipzig, 1929), p. 207.

7. P. Joüon (*Grammaire de l'Hébreu biblique* [Rome: Pontifical Biblical Institute, 1947], §§ 136 d-e) observes the existence of the plural of majesty with nouns in Biblical Hebrew, but never with verbs or pronouns.

deliberation. God speaks to himself.[8] This would be comparable to an individual who might say to himself: "Let's see, should I walk to work tomorrow or take the bus?" Biblical uses of this plural of deliberation have been claimed and challenged for Cant. 1:9–11, "I . . . we," and 2 Sam. 24:4, "us . . . me."

(6) The best suggestion approaches the trinitarian understanding but employs less direct terminology. Thus Hasel calls the *us* of v. 26 a "plural of fullness," and Clines is close to that with his phrase "duality within the Godhead."[9] According to Clines, God here speaks to the Spirit, mentioned back in v. 2, who now becomes God's partner in creation. It is one thing to say that the author of Gen. 1 was not schooled in the intricacies of Christian dogma. It is another thing to say he was theologically too primitive or naive to handle such ideas as plurality within unity. What we often so blithely dismiss as "foreign to the thought of the OT" may be nothing of the sort. True, the concept may not be etched on every page of Scripture, but hints and clues are dropped enticingly here and there, and such hints await their full understanding "at the correct time" (Gal. 4:4).

The shift from the consistent use of the verb in the jussive (e.g., "Let there be") to a cohortative ("Let us make") is enough to prepare the reader for something momentous on this sixth day. That momentous element is the creation of man *in our image, as our likeness.* This brings us to the second major issue in this verse: what meaning is conveyed by these two nouns, which occur in parallelism only in this verse, and what is their relationship to each other?

The basic phrase "the image of God" is found only four times in the OT: Gen. 1:26, 27 (twice); 9:6. Related to these passages is 5:3—Adam fathered a son "after his image." The Hebrew word for "image" is *ṣelem,* which the LXX normally renders by *eikṓn* (icon).

Several times *ṣelem* describes an idolatrous image that is to be destroyed (Num. 33:52; 2 K. 11:18 par. 2 Chr. 23:17; Ezek. 7:20; 16:17; 23:14; Amos 5:26). But two texts in the Psalms seem to require a less concrete meaning for *ṣelem.* Thus in Ps. 39:7 (Eng. 6) *ṣelem* parallels *heḇel,* "vanity": surely man "moves like a phantom *[ṣelem];* the riches he piles up are no more

8. According to Dale Patrick, here we have "internal dialogue . . . a glimpse into the thinking of the actor behind the act" (*The Rendering of God in the Old Testament,* OBT 10 [Philadelphia: Fortress, 1981], pp. 15–16). C. Westermann (*Genesis,* tr. J. J. Scullion, 3 vols. [Minneapolis: Augsburg, 1984–1986], 1:145) is one recent commentator who defends this theory.

9. G. Hasel, *AUSS* 13 (1975) 65; D. J. A. Clines, *TynBul* 19 (1968) 68.

than vapour *[hebel]"* (NEB). In 73:20 *ṣelem* parallels "dream" *(ḥ^a^lôm):* "like a dream [*ḥ^a^lôm*] when a man rouses himself, O Lord, like images [*ṣelem*] in sleep which are dismissed on waking" (NEB). If *ṣelem* in these two texts is the same word used in Genesis and in the passages cited above,[10] then it may be used for purposes other than describing the physical imitation of something. Here *image* would be something conveying the idea of emptiness, unreality, unsubstantiality.

The only other occurrences of *ṣelem* in the OT are in 1 Sam. 6:5 (twice), 11. Here the Israelite priests instruct the Philistines, before they return the ark to the Israelites, to make "images" or "models" of the tumors and the mice that the Lord had sent upon them. Outside Genesis, then, this is the only passage where *ṣelem* designates the representation of something else, without also suggesting that such representation was taboo or illicit.[11]

What, then, does Gen. 1 signify by designating man as one made *in the image of God?* We have had occasion to mention above several ways in which Gen. 1 narrates the Creation story in a way radically different from the creation accounts of neighboring cultures. Perhaps such polemicizing continues here.

It is well known that in both Egyptian and Mesopotamian society the king, or some high-ranking official, might be called "the image of God." Such a designation, however, was not applied to the canal digger or to the mason who worked on a ziggurat. Gen. 1 may be using royal language to describe simply "man." In God's eyes all of mankind is royal. All of humanity is related to God, not just the king. Specifically, the Bible democratizes the royalistic and exclusivistic concepts of the nations that surrounded Israel.

We now need to ask the significance of the second phrase, *as our likeness.*[12] The prevailing opinion is that *likeness* is less important than *image,* hence its omission in the verse that follows. Man is created in the image of God, but to avoid the possibility that man be viewed as an exact image of God, the word *likeness* is appended. The physical nuance of the

10. J. Barr ("The Image of God in the Book of Genesis: A Study in Terminology," *BJRL* 51 [1968] 21) sees in the two instances of *ṣelem* in the Psalter not a word meaning "image" but a homonym meaning "darkness, obscurity." In any case the word is not connected with idols or idolatry in the Psalms. Still, the pejorative overtones are not missing.

11. Barr (ibid., pp. 22–23) suggests that of all the Hebrew words associated in one way or another with the language of idolatry, the least offensive and the one with the least negative history is *ṣelem,* and thus the reason for its selection is Gen. 1. This view takes for granted, of course, that Gen. 1 is essentially a postexilic composition.

12. See my brief study of this word in *TWOT,* 1:191–92.

concrete term "image" is toned down by the more abstract term "likeness." Some support for this interpretation is found in the extensive use of *d^{e}mûṯ* ("likeness") in Ezek. 1–10. Here the prophet never says that he saw God, but only the likeness of God or the likeness of something associated with God. Ezekiel's own description of the theophany is decidedly reserved (see 1:5, 10, 13, 16, 22, 26, 28; 8:2; 10:21, 22). Thus Gen. 1:26 would be an instance of the writer leading with a major word—*image*—and following it with a minor word—*likeness*—just as he started with the major verb "create" and followed it with "make."

Another approach reverses this understanding and suggests that *likeness* actually specifies and strengthens *image.*[13] This interpretation intensifies rather than diminishes the creature's reflection of the Creator. It suggests that something about God may be known by studying his image, man. Of course, theologies whose distinguishing feature is the large and impenetrable gulf between an infinite God and a finite man will be unlikely to accept such a possibility. Such theologies stress the sinfulness of man (excluding any other emphases) to the degree that it is impossible to work from man to God as part of an educating process.[14]

Some debate has emerged over the use of the preposition *b^{e}* attached to *ṣelem* ("image") and *k^{e}* attached to *d^{e}mûṯ* ("likeness"), translated above as *in* and *as* respectively. In Gen. 1–9 twelve prepositional terms express a relationship of similarity between two entities. Six of these are with the preposition *b^{e}* and another six with *k^{e}.*[15] Eight of these twelve instances involve either the noun *image* or the noun *likeness.* Thus *b^{e}* is prefixed to "image" in 1:26, 27 (twice); 9:6; and to "likeness" in 5:1, 3. *k^{e}* is prefixed to "image" in 5:3 and to "likeness" in 1:26.

One might think that the choice of preposition is not significant, and that we have here simply a stylistic variant. Thus, compare Gen. 1:26, "Let us make man . . . as [*k^{e}*] our likeness" with Gen. 5:1, "In [*b^{e}*] the likeness of God . . . he made him." But Clines has argued at length for taking the *b^{e}* in *b^{e}ṣelem* of 1:26 as a *beth essentiae.* So, the passage would read, "Let us make man *as/in the capacity of/to be* our image."[16] The existence of the *beth*

13. So Clines, *TynBul* 19 (1968) 91: "*d^{e}mûṯ* specifies what kind of an image it is: it is a 'likeness'-image, not simply an image; representational, not simply representative."

14. See R. L. Koteskey, *Psychology from a Christian Perspective* (Nashville: Abingdon, 1980).

15. See J. F. A. Sawyer, "The Meaning of *b^{e}ṣelem 'ĕlōhîm* ('In the Image of God') in Genesis I–XI," *JTS* 25 (1974) 421.

16. See Clines, *TynBul* 19 (1968) 75–80.

essentiae is well established in biblical Hebrew, Exod. 6:3 being the classic illustration, "I appeared *as* [*b*e] El Shaddai."

There are two arguments against this interpretation. First, in the Pentateuch the closest parallel to Gen. 1:26 in which something earthly is modeled after something nonearthly is Exod. 25:40, "And see that you make them *according to* [*b*e] the pattern of them which you were shown in the mountain." This parallel clearly bears the standard use of *b*e, "in, according to, after." Second, when the *b*e is the *beth essentiae* it normally indicates a property of the subject of the verb, not the object of the verb.[17] Certainly 1:26 intends that *ṣelem,* "image," is a property of *'āḏām,* "man," which is the direct object of *bārā',* "create."

It is clear that v. 26 is not interested in defining what is the image of God in man. The verse simply states the fact, which is repeated in the following verse.[18] Nevertheless, innumerable definitions have been suggested: conscience, the soul, original righteousness, reason, the capacity for fellowship with God through prayer, posture, etc. Most of these definitions are based on subjective inferences rather than objective exegesis. Any approach that focuses on one aspect of man—be that physical, spiritual, or intellectual—to the neglect of the rest of man's constituent features seems doomed to failure. Gen. 1:26 is simply saying that to be human is to bear the image of God. This understanding emphasizes man as a unity. No part of man, no function of man is subordinated to some other, higher part or activity.

Verse 26 has begun by stating man's relationship to the Creator. It now progresses to spelling out man's relationship to the rest of the created order. He is to *exercise dominion (rāḏâ)* over all other living creatures. This verb appears twenty-two times in the Qal stem. The majority of these deal either with human relationships (Lev. 25:43, 46, 53—a master over a hired servant; 1 K. 5:30 [Eng. 16]; 9:23—an administrator over his employees; 1 K. 5:4 [Eng. 4:24]; Ps. 72:8; 110:2—a king over his subjects), the rule of one nation over another (Lev. 26:17; Num. 24:19; Neh. 9:28; Ps. 68:28 [Eng. 27]; Isa. 14:2, 6; Ezek. 29:15), or a shepherd's supervision of his flock (Ezek. 34:4).

The last passage—Ezek. 34:4—shows that *rāḏâ* could be connected

17. See Barr, *BJRL* 51 (1968) 17.

18. The NEB takes v. 26b as a definitional statement of the *imago dei:* "Let us make man in our image . . . to rule the fish in the sea. . . ." Thus the image of God has to do only with man's domination of the world. See also N. Snaith, "The Image of God," *ExpTim* 86 (1974) 24. It is more likely that the relationship of 1:26b to 1:26a is consequential rather than explicative: "with the result that he will. . . ."

with force and harshness. Such is not the normal nuance of the verb, however. Thus the three passages from Lev. 25 expressly say the master is not to rule over his servants with harshness. Solomon's dominion (1 K. 5:4 [Eng. 4:24]) was a peaceful dominion. The reigning king of Ps. 72 is also the champion of the poor and the disadvantaged. What is expected of the king is responsible care over that which he rules. Thus, like "image," *exercise dominion* reflects royal language. Man is created to rule. But this rule is to be compassionate and not exploitative. Even in the garden of Eden he who would be lord of all must be servant of all.[19]

27 In this verse the direct discourse of v. 26 is replaced by narrated discourse. Thus in v. 26 we heard the voice of God, and in v. 27 we hear the voice of the narrator. The first part of the verse essentially reports the implementation of God's words recorded in the previous verse. Note, however, that the narrator reports God making man *in his image.* Perhaps the use of the third person singular pronominal suffix is deliberate and undercuts the possibility of any misunderstanding of the "our" in v. 26. May this be the writer's way of saying that when man was created in the image of *'ĕlōhîm,* he meant "God" and not "divine council"? If the narrator had meant the latter, then we would expect, "so God created man in *their* image."

Unlike God, *man* is characterized by sexual differentiation. Unlike animals, *man* is not broken down into species (i.e., "according to their kinds" or "all kinds of"), but rather is designated by sexuality: *male and female he created them.* Sexuality is applied to animal creatures, but not in the Creation story, only later in the Flood narrative (6:19).

The idea is not unknown in ancient literature that man was first created bisexual and only subsequently were the sexes differentiated. Such is clearly not the meaning here. Rather, the verse affirms that God created in his image a male *'āḏām* and a female *'āḏām.* Both share the image of God. Sexuality is not an accident of nature, nor is it simply a biological phenomenon. Instead it is a gift of God. While sexual identity and sexual function

19. Lynn White ("The Historical Roots of our Ecological Crisis," *Science* 155 [March, 1967] 1203–7) places the blame for the current raping of our environment directly on Gen. 1, which he thought to teach both arrogance toward nature and that it is God's will for man to exploit nature. Later readers of Scripture may have drawn such inferences from Gen. 1:26, but they did so by extravagances of interpretation. For some good exegetical studies in this area see, among others, J. Barr, "Man and Nature—The Ecological Controversy and the Old Testament," *BJRL* 55 (1972) 9–32; J. Limburg, "What Does It Mean to 'Have Dominion over the Earth'?" *Dialog* 10 (1971) 221–23; C. E. Armerding, "Biblical Perspectives on the Ecology Crisis," *JASA* 25 (March, 1973) 4–9.

are foreign to God's person, they are nevertheless a part of his will for his image bearers.[20]

The placement of this phrase—*male and female he created them*—allows it to function as a bridge between the first part of v. 27 and the verses that immediately follow. As such, the phrase identifies who exactly bears the image of the divine. It also prepares the way for the blessing of fertility that follows. Here the emphasis is on the male and female as procreators, rather than their role of companions.[21]

28 God gives two assignments to the male and the female: procreation and dominion. Like the animals over whom they rule (v. 22), at the moment of their creation God gives them the power to reproduce themselves. In view of the fact that, at least in Mesopotamia and maybe in Canaan, creation motifs were often employed in fertility rites, Gen. 1 may be saying that reproduction is a blessing and gift from God, and is in no way dependent upon subsequent rites or activities.[22]

To the previously mentioned "exercise dominion" as one of God's mandates to man (v. 26, repeated in v. 28) is added the word *subdue.* Man is to subdue the earth and to dominate the creatures of sky and land and water. Man's divinely given commission to rule over all other living creatures is tempered, or better, brought into sharp relief, by the fact that such dominion does not allow him to kill these creatures or to use their flesh as food. Only much later (9:3, post-Flood) is domination extended to include consumption.

Of the two verbs *rāḏâ,* "exercise dominion," and *kāḇaš,* "subdue," the latter connotes more force. Thus it refers to subjecting someone to slavery (2 Chr. 28:10; Neh. 5:5; Jer. 34:11, 16), to physical abuse and assault (Esth. 7:8), to treading (sins) under foot (Mic. 7:19 and Zech. 9:15, where it parallels "devour"), and to militarily subjecting the population of a city (Num. 32:22, 29; Josh. 18:1). All these references suggest violence or a display of force. For reasons already indicated, it appears unlikely that we need to transfer the nuance of force and dictatorship into the use of *kāḇaš* in Gen. 1:28. Probably

20. W. Brueggemann, *Genesis,* Interpretation (Atlanta: John Knox, 1982), p. 33.

21. I am unable to follow P. Bird (" 'Male and Female He Created Them': Gen. 1:27b in the Context of the Priestly Account of Creation," *HTR* 74 [1981] 129–51) in her contention that "male and female" refers only to the issues of fertility and is in no way related by the author to the concept of *imago dei.* Note also that the delegation to male and female of authority and dominion over the natural world does not include similar dominion over other human creatures or even over each other (G. Mendenhall, *The Tenth Generation* [Baltimore: Johns Hopkins, 1973], p. 211).

22. See P. Bird, *HTR* 74 (1981) 147.

what is designated here is settlement and agriculture; "subdue the land" in ch. 1 is a semantic parallel to "till and keep the land" in 2:5, 15.

We have had occasion to refer to the Mesopotamian *Enuma elish.* This story's account of man's creation provides another interesting counterpoint to the biblical story. In *Enuma elish* the earth is created from one-half of Tiamat's corpse. All the deities who had sided with Tiamat against Marduk now receive as their sentence the opprobrious duty of maintaining the earth. Such manual labor is weary and beneath their dignity. In response to their pleas, and in return for building a house for him, Marduk proceeds to create man from the blood of a fallen god, Kingu:

> Arteries I will knot
> and bring bones into being.
> I will create *Lullu,* "man" be his name
> I will form *Lullu,* man
> Let him be burdened with the toil of the gods,
> that they may freely breathe—
> They bound him (Kingu), held him before Ea
> inflicted the penalty on him,
> severed his arteries;
> and from his blood he formed mankind
> imposed toil on man, set the gods free.[23]

Man is created as an afterthought, and when he is created he is predestined to be a servant of the gods. There is nothing of the regal and the noble about him such as we find in Gen. 1. Basically he is a substitute, one who is created from the blood of a rebellious deity. The anthropologies of Gen. 1 and *Enuma elish* could not be wider apart.

29–30 What God creates he preserves. What he brings into being he provides for. Man is to have as his food the seed and fruit of plants. Animals and birds are to have the leaves. (The latter point accords with the description of the eschatological age when "the lion shall eat straw like the ox," Isa. 11:7; 65:25.) At no point is anything (human beings, animals, birds) allowed to take the life of another living being and consume it for food. The dominion assigned to the human couple over the animal world does not include the prerogative to butcher. Instead, humankind survives on a vegetarian diet. What is strange, and probably unexplainable (from a scientific position), is the fact that the animals too are not carnivores but also vegetarians. The text of Gen. 1 does not state whether human beings and animals had the

23. Translation of T. Jacobsen, *Treasures of Darkness,* pp. 180–81.

wherewithal to take the life of another living being, or whether they possessed such strength but held it in check.

31 Two features distinguish this last verse of the chapter from the preceding verses. First, "beautiful" now becomes *very beautiful.* Second, the preceding five days are all referred to indeterminately—a second day, a third day, etc. But this day is called "*the* sixth day." Both of these unique factors help to mark this sixth day as the acme of God's creation thus far. Note also that the sixth day is treated much more extensively than the earlier days.

8. THE SEVENTH DAY (2:1–3)

1 *Thus the universe and all its company was completed.*

2 *And God had completed his work which he had been doing on the seventh day, and God rested on the seventh day from all his work which he had undertaken.*

3 *God blessed the seventh day and made it holy,*[1] *for on it he rested from all the work he had creatively made.*[2]

1 Silence and stillness once again enter the atmosphere. The mood of the prologue now resurfaces in this epilogue.[3] There is no activity, no noise, no speaking. All that God has willed and designed for his canvas of the universe is now in its place.

Specific reference is made to all the *company* of the universe. This Hebrew word, *ṣāḇā'*, may refer to an army (e.g., Gen. 21:22), the stars (Deut. 4:19), or the angels (1 K. 22:19). It is applicable to an organized and disciplined body. According to Speiser, "The Hebrew term is collective; in the present context it designates the total made up of the various component parts in the planned design of creation; hence array, ranks, company."[4]

The Hebrew word for *completed* or "finished," *kālâ,* especially in the Piel stem, has two nuances, as does the English verb. To finish may mean to finish off, to destroy, to consume (as in Gen. 41:30; Josh. 24:20), or to bring

1. I take the Piel of *qāḏaš* as a factitive Piel, as in Exod. 20:8, "Remember the Sabbath day to *make it holy.*"

2. The literal translation sounds almost pleonastic: "which he created to make." The complementary infinitive in Hebrew is frequently equivalent to an adverbial modifier (GKC, § 114o).

3. See M. Fishbane, *Text and Texture* (New York: Schocken, 1979), p. 9.

4. Speiser, *Genesis,* p. 7.

to completion. The context offers no reason to apply the first nuance to Gen. 2:1–2. The point made by this verb is that the universe is no longer in a process of being created. What Gen. 1 allows for is not additional creation but procreation and self-perpetuation.

2 The rendering of v. 2 in many modern versions suggests that God performed some creative act on the seventh day and only at the completion of this activity did he rest. In fact, both LXX and SP read "sixth day" in v. 2. The reading of these ancient versions is probably a deliberate emendation rather than a reflection of a *Vorlage* to the MT. The most simple and legitimate solution is to read the verb as a pluperfect, *God had completed his work . . . on the seventh day.*[5]

God's creative activity is described twice as *his work.* The OT has two words for "labor," *m*^{e}*lā'ḵâ* and *ʿ*^{a}*ḇōḏâ.* The second word emphasizes labor that is raw and unskilled. The first—and the one used here—designates skilled labor, work that is performed by a craftsman or an artisan. Such is the measure of the finesse and professional skills of God's work.[6]

It is readily apparent that the term "Sabbath day" (Heb. *yôm haš-šabbaṯ*) is absent from this paragraph, although the writer uses the verb *šāḇaṯ.* Instead, *the seventh day (yôm hašš*^{e}*ḇîʿî)* occurs. C. H. Gordon has suggested that the writer used the colorless *seventh day* in his desire to continue to demythologize the story. Vestiges of an original connection between *šbt* and myths of holy days is reflected in the postbiblical Hebrew word "Shabbetai," which translates as "Saturn," the pagan deity.[7]

We are of the opinion that the Hebrew noun *šabbāṯ,* the completion of the week, is to be identified philologically with Akk. *šapattu,* the day of the full moon, that is, the fifteenth day of a lunar month. There is no evidence that the *šapattu* was a day of rest. It is described as the "day of the quieting of the heart (of the deity)," probably by rituals for appeasement. The

5. U. Cassuto (*Genesis,* 1:61–62) traces the verb *kālâ* in Genesis and Exodus, where it has a distinctive reference to action that is already terminated. See also Westermann, *Genesis,* 1:169–70. A. Heidel (*The Babylonian Genesis: The Story of Creation,* 2nd ed. [Chicago: University of Chicago, 1951)], p. 127) takes the verb to be declarative: "God declared his work finished." This interpretation would provide a nice parallel to the root *qdš* in the following verse if it too be understood as a declarative: "God declared it holy." Cf. n. 1 above. See also N.-E. A. Andreasen, *The Old Testament Sabbath,* SBLDS 7 (Missoula, MT: Scholars, 1972), pp. 63–64; R. Gordis, *Koheleth—The Man and His World,* 3rd ed. (New York: Schocken, 1968), p. 230.

6. See J. Milgrom, *Studies in Levitical Terminology,* I (Berkeley: University of California, 1970), pp. 76–80 and nn. 292–97 for references.

7. See C. H. Gordon, "The Seventh Day," *UF* 11 (1979) 299–301.

deliberate omission of "sabbath" in Gen. 2 may be due to a desire to avoid any possibility of uniting the seventh day with the pagan festival.[8]

In both *Enuma elish* and the Atrahasis Epic the gods rest after the creation of man.[9] With man to do the menial work of the day-to-day maintenance of the earth, the gods are now free for less demanding administrative tasks in the world. In appreciation for release from this manual work, the gods promise to build Babylon and its temple for Marduk. The gods' surrogate is now man, who is "charged with the service of the gods that they might be at ease."[10] It is not difficult to see how different the Mesopotamian concept of rest for the divine is from the biblical concept. Thus, not only the omission of "Sabbath" but also the particular use of divine resting demonstrate the uniqueness of the biblical story of creation.

3 In addition to blessing those who are made in his image (1:28), God also *blessed the seventh day.* Indeed, it is correct to say that the Creation account moves to its conclusion on the seventh day, not the sixth day. It is not an appendage. All the preceding days God called either "beautiful" or "very beautiful." This day alone he sanctified. Nothing in the creation context that is connected with space is called *holy.*[11] As is well known, the Hebrew verb *qāḏaš* means "to set apart." By virtue of being sanctified, one day of rest is set apart from six days of activity. It is divine designation alone that marks the seventh day as holy. Humanity does not confer sanctity on this day by abstention from work. In the words of Westermann, "The sanctification of the Sabbath institutes an order for humankind according to which time is divided into time and holy time. . . . By sanctifying the seventh day God instituted a polarity between the everyday and the solemn, between days of work and days of rest, which was to be determinative for human existence."[12]

8. See N. Sarna, *Understanding Genesis* (New York: Schocken, repr. 1978), pp. 18–21. Sarna comments on p. 21, "The day derives its special character solely from God, and is to be completely divorced from, and independent of, any connection with the phases of the moon . . . its sanctity is a reality irrespective of human activity."

9. See W. G. Lambert, "A New Look at the Babylonian Background of Genesis," *JTS* 16 (1965) 297–98.

10. *ANET,* p. 68.

11. A. J. Heschel, *The Sabbath,* rev. ed. (Cleveland/New York: World, 1952), pp. 9–10.

12. Westermann, *Genesis,* 1:171.

THE NEW TESTAMENT APPROPRIATION

a. Gen. 1:1–5 and John 1:1–5

All writers agree that John draws upon the opening verses of Genesis for his own prologue, although no quotations per se appear in the prologue. Quite obviously, the *en archē* in John 1:1 is based on *b^erē'šîṯ* in Gen. 1:1. Unlike Genesis, however, John's "In (the) beginning" refers not to the beginning of creation but to the undeterminable period prior to creation. As such, the phrase is "a designation, more qualitative than temporal, of the sphere of God."[1]

The relationships between Gen. 1 and John 1 go beyond the introductory formula. Peder Borgen has argued that John's prologue is essentially a targumic exposition of Gen. 1:1–5.[2] Specifically Borgen argues that John 1:1–5 is the basic exposition of Gen. 1:1–5, while John 1:6ff. is an elaboration of pivotal terms and phrases in vv. 1–5, but in reverse order: (a) vv. 1–2, the word, God; (b) v. 3, "all things came through him"; (c) vv. 4–5, the light; (c′) vv. 7–9, the light; (b′) vv. 10–13, "the world was made through him"; (a′) vv. 14–18, the word, God.[3]

While his case for the chiastic structure of John's prologue may be open to challenge, Borgen's observations about the Genesis background to John 1:1–5 seem quite legitimate. The evangelist informs us in v. 3 about the role of the Word in creation. The Word is both the *agent* in creation—"through him"—and the indispensable element in creation—"without him was not anything made." Thus John begins with the place of Jesus Christ in creation. In vv. 4–5 John shifts from the fact and the form of creation to the content of creation. John chooses to speak about only one of the created phenomena—light. While Gen. 1 speaks of light as something natural, John uses light to designate something eternal. "That which had especially come to be in God's creative word was the gift of eternal life."[4]

1. See R. Brown, *The Gospel According to John,* 2 vols., AB (Garden City, NY: Doubleday, 1966–1970), 1:4.

2. P. Borgen, "Observations on the Targumic Character of the Prologue of John," *NTS* 16 (1970) 288–95; idem, "Logos was the True Light: Contributions to the Interpretation of the Prologue of John," *NovT* 14 (1972) 115–30.

3. Borgen's proposal has been challenged on the grounds that he ignores other key terms and phrases in the prologue which, if taken into consideration, would force an alteration in his analysis of the prologue's structure. See R. A. Culpepper, "The Pivot of John's Prologue," *NTS* 27 (1980) 5. For another criticism of Borgen see C. T. R. Haywood, "The Holy Name of the God of Moses and the Prologue of St. John's Gospel," *NTS* 25 (1978) 27 n. 2.

4. See R. Brown, *Gospel According to John,* 1:27.

b. Gen. 1 and Col. 1:15–20

Paul here piles up title after title in his delineation of the nature and position of Christ: image, firstborn, head, the beginning. Like John, he identifies Jesus as the necessary agency in creation (v. 16). But he adds two new factors. One is a statement about the purpose of creation ("for him," v. 16), and the other is a remark about the perpetuation of creation ("in him all things hold together," v. 17).

In the midst of describing the ministry of Jesus vis-à-vis creation, Paul applies to him, among other titles, the designation "the beginning." A number of years ago C. F. Burney suggested that in Col. 1:16–18 Paul presents an elaborate midrashic exposition on the first word of Gen. 1:1, *b^erē'šîṯ,* in which the apostle connects "beginning" in Gen. 1:1 and Prov. 8:22 with Christ. Indeed, for Paul, these two OT references to "beginning" refer to Christ.[5] Christ fulfills every meaning which may be extracted from *rē'šîṯ.*

As suggestive as such an insight may be, it is still important to keep in mind that Paul's argument is circumstantially determined. It is not faithful to the context to attribute such phrases to a Hellenistic milieu of which Paul was a part. Rather, Paul, directing a frontal attack against incipient Gnostic elements at Colossae, affirms the absolute primacy and priority of Christ over everything, especially creation and cosmology.[6] The world is not evil—it is Christ's. A remarkably parallel message emerges in Heb. 1:2–3.

c. Gen. 1:26 and NT Terminology

Many NT passages allude to Gen. 1:26, but none quotes it exactly. For purposes of organization we may note that NT references to "image" and "likeness" terminology fall into one of three categories:

(1) Christ as the image of God: 2 Cor. 4:4 speaks of "the glory of Christ who is the image of God." Similarly, Col. 1:15 refers to Christ as "the image of the invisible God." Here the *imago dei* concept is interpreted christologically. God's glory is seen in his image, who is Christ, not man. The relationship between original and image is one of substantial identity, not

5. See C. F. Burney, "Christ as the APXH of Creation," *JTS* 27 (1926) 160–77. For support by a more recent writer see W. D. Davies, *Paul and Rabbinic Judaism,* 3rd ed. (Philadelphia: Fortress, 1970), pp. 150–52. Not all commentators agree that Col. 1:15–20, and esp. vv. 16–17, contain specimens of rabbinical exegesis. See A. Van Roon, "The Relation Between Christ and the Wisdom of God according to Paul," *NovT* 16 (1974) 233.

6. See R. N. Longenecker, "Some Distinctive Early Christological Motifs," *NTS* 14 (1968) 526–45, esp. pp. 539–41.

simply formal similarity. For this reason both passages connect image with revelation.

Related to these two verses, but using different terminology, is Phil. 2:6, which speaks of Christ being "in the form of God."[7] Quite similar is Heb. 1:3, with its emphasis on Christ as "the reflection, one who bears the very stamp of the nature of God." Again, the emphasis is that Christ shares the essence of God so completely that he can be described as an exact representation of God rather than one who merely resembles God. Note that while the NT does not hesitate to describe Christ as the image *(eikṓn)* of God, it never describes him as the likeness *(homoíōsis)* of God (cf. the LXX in Gen. 1:26).

(2) Man as the image of God: 1 Cor. 11:7 says matter-of-factly that man is "the image and glory of God," and here the phrase is limited to the male. Woman is subsequently described as "the glory of man." This is the only NT text setting forth a doctrine of the "image" that stresses the sexual differentiation, and some suggest that Paul clearly intends to exclude woman from the image of God, something which Gen. 1:26–27 does not say. If Paul wanted to make that point dramatically, one suspects that he would have clinched his point by continuing, "for woman is the image and the glory of man." The fact that he carefully avoids designating woman as the *eikṓn* of the man should warn the reader against seeing too much in this verse.[8]

Close to 1 Cor. 11:7 is Jas. 3:9, a reference to the tongue with which we bless God and curse men, "who are made after the likeness of God." "Men" here means any man, redeemed or unredeemed, and thus the verse provides grounds for attributing the image of God to everybody. It is unlikely that James has in mind the possibility of believers "cursing" other believers!

(3) Man as the image of Christ: a number of scattered references allude to the believer being conformed to the image of Christ (Rom. 8:29), being changed into Christ's likeness (2 Cor. 3:18), putting on the new nature

7. The relationship between Phil. 2:6 and Gen. 1:26 has been treated suggestively by R. P. Martin, *Carmen Christi: Philippians ii.5–11 in Recent Interpretation and in the Setting of Early Christian Worship,* rev. ed. (Grand Rapids: Eerdmans, 1983), pp. 99–133.

8. See F. F. Bruce, *1 and 2 Corinthians,* NCBC (Grand Rapids: Eerdmans, repr. 1982), p. 105. See also M. D. Hooker, "Authority on her Head: An Examination of I Cor. xi.10," *NTS* 10 (1964) 411, who observes that while Paul is able to say that woman is the glory of man (as man is of God), it would be nonsensical to say that woman is created in man's image (as man is in God's).

which is renewed after the image of its Creator (Col. 3:10). Other verses speak eschatologically; for example, one day we shall bear the image of the "man of heaven" (1 Cor. 15:49). Unlike 1 Cor. 11:7 and Jas. 3:9, which say that the image is a part of all humanity, these verses are talking about a Christ-likeness in the lives of those who have professed faith in Christ. It is not adequate simply to receive Christ as savior. This act of faith must be followed by an appropriation of Christ into one's daily life so that the believer gradually becomes like Christ.

In sum, we may quote Clines: "In Christ man sees what manhood was meant to be . . . men are the image of Christ so far as they are like Christ . . . this is how man, the image of God, who is already man, already the image of God, can become fully man, fully the image of God."[9]

d. Gen. 1:27 and Matt. 19:4 par. Mark 10:6

Both Matthew and Mark record the incident in which Pharisees approach Jesus to interrogate him on the subject of divorce. Mark's account suggests that the issue was the permissibility of divorce, while Matthew's account suggests that the issue was the grounds for divorce. Since Deut. 24:1–4 permits divorce instituted by the husband, Jesus' interrogators were presumably not really troubled by the question of the legality of divorce. Rather, the issue would be the permissible grounds for divorce.

In response, Jesus does not address himself to that issue at all. Instead, he refers back to Gen. 1:27 and challenges these Pharisees to consider God's original purpose in the creation of mankind as male and female. The concern of the inquisitors is how and why to terminate a marriage. Jesus' answer emphasizes why a marriage should be initiated and perpetuated.

To Gen. 1:27 Jesus adds 2:24. Of course, both of these texts precede the Noachian and Sinaitic covenants. Perhaps then the prohibition regarding divorce applies only to Gentiles, Deut. 24:1–4 granting exemption to the Jews. To counteract this kind of spurious logic, Jesus prefaces his quotation from Gen. 1:27 and 2:24 with the important phrase "from the beginning."

9. Clines, *TynBul* 19 (1968) 103; see also S. G. Wilson, "Image of God," *ExpTim* 85 (1974) 356–61; M. B. Wynkoop, *A Theology of Love: The Dynamic of Wesleyanism* (Kansas City, MO: Beacon Hill, 1972), pp. 102–24. Cf. also J. I. Cook, "The Old Testament Concept of the Image of God," in *Grace upon Grace: Essays in Honor of Lester J. Kuyper*, ed. J. I. Cook (Grand Rapids: Eerdmans, 1975), pp. 85–94, esp. p. 92: "Once the identification between Christ and the image of God was made the concept was inevitably shifted from its original locus in the doctrine of creation to that of redemption."

This all-inclusive statement serves to remind his interlocutors that no double standard is operating here. God's precepts in Gen. 1 and 2 apply to all human beings from the beginning down to the present.[10]

e. Gen. 1:27 and Gal. 3:28

Addressing himself to the issue of unity and equality in Christ, Paul lists three categories of opposites which may not serve as discriminatory criteria for admission to or exclusion from the church of Jesus Christ: Jew/Greek (ethnic), slave/free (cultural), and male/female (sexuality).

The last one is a phrase that Paul takes from Gen. 1:27. It seems to us a severe misunderstanding and an unfortunate interpretation to play off against each other the enlightened, progressive Paul when he applies Gen. 1:27 to husband-wife relationships, and the rabbinic, regressive Paul when he applies material from Gen. 2–3 to husband-wife relationships.

Paul appropriates Gen. 1:27 in the midst of his exhortation on soteriology to the Galatians without the slightest interest in establishing or denying a chain of authority. Egalitarianism versus hierarchicalism is just not the issue.[11] The issue is the identity of the irreducible minimum for becoming and being Christian. Circumcision is not an entrance requirement, nor is the observance of special days, months, seasons, and years (Gal. 4:10). Now obviously both of these concepts either bypass the woman completely or involve her only marginally. How is a woman then to be saved? Later Jewish tradition (see T.B. *Yebam.* 113a; *Qidd.* 7a; *Sanh.* 76a) suggested marriage and childbearing. But such an idea is earlier than the rabbinic material. For example, both Targum Onqelos and Targum Jonathan on Gen. 3:16 interpret the verse to mean that because of her sin the woman finds salvation in subordinating herself to her husband via marriage. Note that Ruth (albeit a non-Israelite) enters the covenant family first by marriage, then by conver-

10. See K. J. Thomas, "Torah Citations in the Synoptics," *NTS* 24 (1977) 85–96. "Jesus was not concerned with subtle distinctions and casuistic interpretations which derive from an atomizing literalism. . . . We do not find him abrogating or relaxing any particular injunction, but rather placing them all in a comprehensive perspective" (p. 96). See also B. Vawter, "The Divorce Clauses in Mt 5,2 and 19,9," *CBQ* 16 (1954) 166. The juxtapositioning of Gen. 1:27 with 2:24 provides an illustration of Jesus appealing both to example (what God has done) in Gen. 1:27, and to precept (what God said should be done) in Gen. 2:4. See D. Daube, *The New Testament and Rabbinic Judaism* (London: Athlone, 1956), pp. 76–79.

11. See J. J. Davis, "Some Reflections on Galatians 3:28, Sexual Roles, and Biblical Hermeneutics," *JETS* 19 (1976) 201–8.

sion. The idea was paramount among the Romans as well. One of the decrees of Augustus penalized bachelorhood and rewarded marriage and childbearing.[12] D. Daube draws attention to the fact that also in a Greek context it was common to emphasize the duty to marry and propagate.[13] In rejecting this position Paul says: "(There is) not any Jew or Greek, not any slave or free, not any male *and* female," this last phrase representing a faithful reproduction of the LXX of Gen. 1:27.[14] While ordained by God, marriage is not for everybody. Most poignantly, to become a member of the community of faith, it is not necessary for a woman to join herself to a man any more than it is for a Gentile to become a Jew.[15]

f. Gen. 2:2 and Heb. 4:4

The quotation of Gen. 2:2 in Heb. 4:4 is closer to the LXX than to the MT, but it departs from the LXX too.[16] Thus in Heb. 4:4 *ho theós en* from Gen. 2:2a is inserted after "he rested," *katépausen,* whereas in Gen. 2:2b *katépausen* supplies the subject and preposition for both parts of the sentence. The point made by the author of Hebrews is that, just as God rested, others have the opportunity to share this rest which has been rescinded from the

12. J. P. V. D. Balsdon, *Roman Women: Their History and Habits* (London: Bodley Head, 1962), pp. 45ff.

13. D. Daube, *The Duty of Procreation* (Edinburgh: Edinburgh University Press, 1977), pp. 9ff.

14. Most translations (RSV, AV, NEB, etc.) render *ouk éni ársen kaí thḗly* as "neither male nor female," even though the wording in the first two contrasting pairs ("neither Jew nor Greek, neither slave nor free") is *ouk éni . . . oudé* and not *ouk éni . . . kaí* as in the third contrasting pair. More than likely too much should not be made of this difference in that *ársen kaí thḗly* in Gal. 3:28 is intended as a conscious allusion to Gen. 1:27 in the LXX. Apparently the expressions are interchangeable for Paul, for while he uses *ouk éni Ioudaios oudé Hellēn* in Gal. 3:28, he uses *ouk éni Hellēn kaí Ioudaios* in Col. 3:11. See F. F. Bruce, *The Epistle to the Galatians,* NIGTC (Grand Rapids: Eerdmans, 1982), p. 189.

15. See B. Witherington, "Rite and Rights for Women—Galatians 3:28," *NTS* 27 (1981) 593–604. It is interesting to note that in 1 Cor. 12:13, a verse close to Gal. 3:28, Paul uses two of the opposites he used in Gal. 3:28, Jew/Greek and slave/free, but he omits the pair male/female. The context here is baptism into the body of Christ via the Spirit. The first two antipodes represent areas which are secondary or cultural and thus are of no consequence in initiation into Christ's body. But entrance into Christ's body does not negate sexual differentiation. For the suggestion of an anti-Philo, anti-rabbinical thrust in 1 Cor. 12:13, see D. L. Balch, "Backgrounds of I Cor. vii: Sayings of the Lord in Q," *NTS* 18 (1972) 364.

16. See G. Howard, "Hebrews and Old Testament Quotations," *NovT* 10 (1968) 209.

disobedient Israelites. This rest will be a cessation from labor, just as God has ceased from any further work.[17]

The author of Hebrews is concerned to do more than simply draw an analogy between the generation of Israelites that failed to enter rest and his present audience whom he is challenging to enter that rest. If that was his only concern, then his remarks about and allusions to God resting on the seventh day would be otiose. Through his references to both Genesis and Joshua, in that order, the writer is subordinating "Canaan rest" (from turmoil) to "Sabbath rest" (from work). It is the latter, not the former, which he urges the Hebrew Christians to appropriate.

B. THE GARDEN OF EDEN AND ITS FIRST OCCUPANTS (2:4–25)

1. THE FORMATION OF A GARDENER (2:4–7)

4 *These are the generations of the heavens and the earth*[1] *when they were created. When Yahweh God made earth and heaven,*

5 *no shrub of the field was yet in the earth, no plant of the field sprouted, because Yahweh God had not sent rain on the earth, nor was there any man to work the soil.*

6 *But groundwater came up from the underworld*[2] *and watered all the surface of the ground.*

7 *Yahweh God crafted man, dust from the ground, and blew into his nostrils the breath of life. Thus man became a living person.*

4 Here one encounters the first of ten appearances of the formula *These are the generations of* (Heb. *ʾēlleh tôl*^{e}*ḏôṯ*) in Genesis (see also 6:9; 10:1; 11:10, 27; 25:12, 19; 36:1, 9; 37:2; cf. 5:1 for a variant of the formula ["this is the book of the generations of Adam"]). This first one differs from the others in

17. K. J. Thomas ("The Old Testament Citations in Hebrews," *NTS* 11 [1965] 307-8) sees in Heb. 4:4 a rejection of Philo's view that in six days God completed the mortal creation, but on the seventh day, a day which comprehends all time, God began the creation of divine things. See also H.W. Attridge, "'Let Us Strive to Enter That Rest': The Logic of Hebrews 4:1-11," *HTR* 73 (1980) 279-88.

1. This is the same Hebrew phrase translated as "universe" in 1:1 and 2:1. The more literal translation "heavens and earth" is retained here in order to reflect the pl. pronominal suffix *(-ām)* on "in their creation" (Heb. *b*^{e}*hibbār*^{e}*ʾām*).

2. The meaning "underworld" and not just "world, earth" for *ʾereṣ* enjoys growing assent from Hebraists. See W. Holladay, "'*Ereṣ*—'Underworld': two more suggestions," *VT* 19 (1969) 123.

that it describes the *generations of the heavens and the earth* while the others introduce either the descendants of some person or a narrative about some person (e.g., Noah, sons of Noah/Terah/Ishmael/Isaac/Esau/Jacob). While something like "offspring, descendants" would fit many of the last nine, it may seem strange to refer to the "offspring" or "children" of the universe, but that is expressly what Gen. 2:4 intends.

Many of the recent translations of Genesis (RSV, NEB, JB, NJPV, Speiser, Vawter) divide this verse into two parts. According to this analysis, the section *These are the generations of the heavens and the earth when they were created* goes with 1:1–2:3. Thus the first unit within Genesis is 1:1–2:4a. The remainder of v. 4—*When Yahweh God made earth and heaven*—is then taken as the beginning of the next unit. Source analysis ascribes 1:1–2:4a to the exilic Priestly writer(s) or school and 2:4bff. to the earlier Yahwistic source.

Those who subscribe to the bifurcation of v. 4 suggest that v. 4a serves as a subscription or a summary conclusion to the Priestly account of creation. The problem with this suggestion is that elsewhere in Genesis the phrase functions as an introduction, not a conclusion. It seems artificial to suggest that v. 4a originally stood before 1:1 and through some accident was misplaced in the text.

We take the approach that 2:3 concludes the first unit of Genesis and 2:4a begins the second unit. Two lines of evidence support this interpretation. We have already alluded to one: that is, everywhere else in Genesis the *tôl^{e}ḏôṯ* formula functions as a superscription to what follows. There is no indication that v. 4a is an exception to this norm.[3] The second piece of confirming evidence is the important observation made by John Skinner that the *tôl^{e}ḏôṯ* formula is always followed by the genitive of the progenitor, never of the progeny. Thus the phrase *the generations of the heavens and the earth* describes not the process by which the heavens and the earth are generated, but rather that which is generated by the heavens and the earth. Quite obviously this would be a most inaccurate description of the process of creation as delineated in 1:1–2:3.[4]

3. See F. M. Cross, *Canaanite Myth and Hebrew Epic* (Cambridge: Harvard University, 1973), pp. 301–5; B. W. Anderson, "A Stylistic Study of the Priestly Creation Story," in *Canon and Authority,* pp. 160–61.

4. So Skinner (*Genesis,* p. 41) concludes: "In short, neither as superscription nor as subscription can the sentence be accounted for as an integral part of the Priestly Code." Skinner's point is endorsed by Childs, who then goes on to suggest that it is simply inaccurate to say Gen. 1–2 contains two creation stories. Rather, in ch. 1 the concern is indeed legitimately creation, whereas in 2:4ff. the concern is offspring along the lines of an analogy of a son to his father (Childs, *Introduction,* pp. 145, 149).

If one takes 2:4a as a superscription to what follows, and if one is faithful to source criticism, then he will be faced with the oddity of an indubitably Priestly trademark (for anything genealogical in the Pentateuch is traced to P) introducing a non-Priestly composition. This anomaly is, of course, one of the major reasons why so many commentators have divided 2:4. To solve this impasse, source critics who take v. 4 as a unit introduce a post-P redactor (deus ex machina) who borrows the phrase from P in order to unite the two traditions, viz., 1:1–2:3 and 2:4bff. Any theory on the biblical text's early history that must rely on the readily available redactor to eliminate any possible inconsistencies may be open to question and challenge.

Proceeding to other matters in the verse, we note the sudden shift in name for deity from simply "God" to *Yahweh God.* This designation for deity is used consistently throughout the remainder of the chapter and through ch. 3 (19 times in all). But curiously enough the combination appears in the Pentateuch only once more (Exod. 9:30), though it occurs about twenty times elsewhere in the OT (mostly in Samuel, Kings, and Chronicles). There are, of course, many instances of phrases such as "Yahweh, our God," "Yahweh your God," "Yahweh, the God of heaven," "Yahweh, the God of Abraham," and so forth. The combination *Yahweh God* (Heb. *yhwh ʾĕlōhîm*) that we have in Gen. 2:4–3:24 needs to be distinguished from "Adonai Yahweh" (Heb. *ʾaḏōnāy yhwh*), which occurs in 15:2, 8. The use of *Yahweh God* in the so-called J source here seems strange when all other portions of Genesis identified as being from J use simply "Yahweh."

Scholars have put forth several theories to account for the sudden appearance of the compound name for deity in 2:4ff. (which is usually assigned to the J source), specifically for the presence of *ʾĕlōhîm* in J. An older suggestion is that the double name is the result of an amalgamation of sources. These sources would be Je, which used only *ʾĕlōhîm,* and Jj, which used only the tetragrammaton (the four Hebrew letters, *yhwh,* usually vocalized Yahweh). When these two recensions were joined, the editor harmonized them by juxtaposing *ʾĕlōhîm* to *yhwh.*

Hesitant to accept a hypothesis that is so tendentious, other scholars have proposed a more modest scheme. This theory suggests that, true to his form elsewhere, J penned this story in 2:4bff. using only the name Yahweh. Subsequently, and after the completion of 1:1–2:4a by P, a redactor—who joined P and J—merely inserted *ʾĕlōhîm* after Yahweh in order to give as firm a footing as possible to the identification of the deity of 1:1–2:4a with the deity of 2:4bff. He wanted no one to think that the creator of ch. 1 and the author of life in ch. 2 were different beings.[5]

This proposal appears as improbable as the first one. Should we really believe that the contemporaries of the post-P redactor would have been led into confusion and bewilderment by the appearance in their literature of two names for deity? In addition, if the appearance of *ʾĕlōhîm* in J is to be accounted for by the redactor, why did he suddenly break his own pattern in 3:1–5, where apparently, if this theory be true, he excised the tetragrammaton from his text—an unheard-of procedure—and replaced it with *ʾĕlōhîm?*

Now, it is no secret that in the religions of the ancient Near East compound names were used to designate one god. One thinks of Amon-Re in Egypt and Kothar(-wa-)Ḫasis at Ugarit. This phenomenon also existed in Israel, as illustrated by Yahweh-Elohim. But why should it suddenly surface in 2:4a and disappear shortly thereafter? Apart from the suggestion of redactional addition alluded to above, one may make the following suggestion by appealing to content as the determining factor rather than redactional activity. In Gen. 1 the emphasis is on creation via the majestic God who speaks and it is done. The more generic name for God—*ʾĕlōhîm*—fits this emphasis admirably. By contrast, the emphasis in 2:4ff. is more personal. The context here is not a universe but a garden. Also, the picture of man here is not of one with authority but of one under authority, a vassal in a covenant relationship. To be sure, Yahweh would be the proper designation for the deity at this point. The author proceeded, however, to append *ʾĕlōhîm* to Yahweh to conjoin the concept of a God whose sovereign control extends to both the material and the moral world.[6] At the same time, and this time only in this unit, the author abstained from using God's name "Yahweh" in 3:1b–5. It would be anomalous to have the serpent quote Yahweh *qua* Yahweh, since it is cast in the role of divine antagonist. Instead he quotes *ʾĕlōhîm.* The Bible's first conversation about God is about *ʾĕlōhîm,* not Yahweh.

5 The scene described here is that of a barren desert. There is neither shrub nor plant in the fields. Two factors account for this emptiness. God is not doing what he is accustomed to doing—sending rain. Nor is there a man to till the soil, something that he will do when he arrives on the scene. If plant life is to grow in this garden, it will be due to a joint operation. God will do his part and man will expedite his responsibilities. Rain is not sufficient. Tillage is not sufficient. God is not a tiller of the soil and man is not a sender

5. See S. R. Driver, *Genesis,* p. 37. See also Vawter, *On Genesis,* p. 66.
6. See Cassuto, *Genesis,* 1:86–87.

of rain. But the presence of one being without the other guarantees the perpetuation of desertlike conditions.

It would be premature to say that 2:5 flatly contradicts 1:11–12. The latter two verses describe the creation of vegetation on the third day, three days before man is created. In 2:5–7 the reader is informed that when God created man there were no plants or shrubs. To begin with, if this is such a blatant inconsistency, why did the redactor do nothing to smooth it out? It will do no good to say that the biblical compilers hesitated to tamper with the received texts, for the source analysis theory has already posited redactional tampering in the addition of a second name for God in the received J document. Is it logical that the editors would edit the text at one point to remove possible confusion but would leave untouched chronological inconsistencies that the reader might find puzzling and unexpected?

Indeed, one of the two words used here—*ʿēśeḇ, plant*—was also used in 1:11–12. The other word—*śîaḥ, shrub*—does not appear in ch. 1. It occurs only three more times in the OT. Young Ishmael was placed under a *śîaḥ* in the wilderness by his mother (21:15). A *śîaḥ* grows in a place where the dejected and the debilitated seek shelter and perhaps food (Job 30:4, 7). Thus the reference is to some kind of desert shrub or bush.

We suggest that the reference to shrub and plant in 2:5 is anticipatory and is explained further by 3:18, where God says to Adam: "thorns and thistles [the *śîaḥ?*] it shall bring forth to you; and you shall eat the plants [*ʿēśeḇ*] of the field."[7] The "plants" referred to in Gen. 1 must be those that grow wild, those that reproduce themselves by seed alone. The *plants* referred to in Gen. 2 must be those that grow only as a result of human cultivation through planting and artificial irrigation. Neither of these kinds of growth appears in the fields until after the creation of man and after man's transgression.

6 The picture is not one of total aridity. Though rain does not yet pour from the heavens, an *'ēḏ* does rise from the ground to water the earth's surface. The translation of this word is uncertain, as a glance at the versions will show. Is it a mist, a river, a flood, a cloud, or something else? Both LXX *(pēgḗ)* and Vulg. *(fons)* interpreted it as "spring." Unfortunately the word appears only once more in the OT, Job 36:27, "he [God] draws the waterdrops that distill rain from the flood [*'ēḏô*]."[8]

7. See H. G. Stigers, *A Commentary on Genesis* (Grand Rapids: Zondervan, 1976), p. 65.

8. This is the translation of M. Pope, *Job,* AB, rev. ed. (Garden City, NY: Doubleday, 1973), pp. 267, 273. He suggests that the ending *-ô* on *'ēḏô* may not be the pronominal suffix "his" but rather a modification of Akk. *edû.* RSV retains "mist"

Etymologically Heb. *'ēḏ* has been connected with Akk. *id,* "river," which is a loanword from Sum. *ID.*[9] Thus the phenomenon alluded to in 2:6 would be a subterranean freshwater stream. C. H. Gordon has correctly observed that the translation of *'ēḏ* in 2:6 as "river" is unlikely in that rivers descend rather than rise.[10]

Wider support has been given to the possible connection between Heb. *'ēḏ* and Akk. *edû,* "flood, waves, swell," which is a loanword from Sum. *A.DÉ.A.* Speiser notes particularly that cuneiform texts use *edû* and other aquatic terms with verbs such as *melu,* "to flow, to flood," and *bu-tuq-tum,* "to break through" to water the fields *(šaqu ša eqli),* all suggesting the irruption of subterranean waters.[11] Historical support for the idea of an underground river that overflows its bank and seeps to the surface may be found in the tradition preserved by Strabo that the Euphrates, or some branch of it, flowed underground and subsequently surfaced to form lagoons beside either the Persian Gulf or the Mediterranean Sea.[12]

Perhaps it is not mandatory that we turn to Akkadian for the etymology of *'ēḏ*. Dahood has observed that an Eblaite calendar from King Ibbi-Sipiš calls November-December *itu NI.DU* (elsewhere this month is called *itu ga-šúm,* "the month of heavy rain"). His proposal is that the Sum. *NI.DU* be read as Semitic *ì-du,* which he associates with Heb. *'ēḏ*. Thus he translates Gen. 2:6: "So he made a rain cloud come up from the nether ocean and it watered all the surface of the ground."[13]

---

as in Gen. 2:6—"he distills his mist in rain"—and chooses among other things to render a pl. verb as a singular.

9. See W. F. Albright (with S. Mowinckel), "The Babylonian Matter in the Predeuteronomic Primeval History (JE) in Gen. 1–11," *JBL* 58 (1939) 102–3 and also p. 102 n. 25.

10. C. H. Gordon, *Homer and Bible* (Ventnor, NJ: Ventnor, 1967), p. 26. Gordon goes on to suggest that what rises from the earth to water the ground is a mountain carrying its streams to the countryside below. In this connection he notes Ida, a high mountain in central Crete mentioned in the Ugaritic texts (*UT,* 51:I:35, *hdm id,* "a footstool of Ida"). It is unlikely that we have here an opaque use of mountain terminology, for the implicit suggestion throughout this chapter is of terrain that is flat and alluvial.

11. E. A. Speiser, "*'ED* in the Story of Creation," in *Oriental and Biblical Studies,* ed. J. J. Finkelstein and M. Greenberg (Philadelphia: University of Pennsylvania, 1967), pp. 19–22.

12. See G. R. Driver, "Notes on Notes," *Bib* 36 (1955) 71–73.

13. M. Dahood, "Eblaite *ì-du* and Hebrew *'ēḏ,* 'Rain Cloud,' " *CBQ* 43 (1981) 534–38. The verb in this part of the verse *(ya'ᵃleh)* may be read as either a Qal or a Hiphil, since both forms are the same with *'ālâ.* But *'ēḏ* is surely the subject of the Hiphil *hišqâ,* there being no other alternative in the verse. Note here the tenses of

This proposal shifts the all but unanimous identification of *'ēḏ* with a Sumerian origin to the possibility of a Semitic origin. Should this connection receive further substantiation, it will lend greater credence to the likelihood of a West Mediterranean origin for many of the biblical narratives. Given the limited texts that have thus far been published from Ebla, scholars are still reluctant to champion too many connections between Eblaite and Biblical Hebrew. One suspects, however, that such hesitancy will prove to be unnecessary. Ebla's contributions to our understanding of the language of the OT will no doubt continue to grow and shed light on some of the enigmatic passages in the OT.

7 Verses 4b–7 are one long sentence in Hebrew, containing a protasis (v. 4b), a series of circumstantial clauses (vv. 5–6), and an apodosis (v. 7). This apodosis informs us that God the craftsman formed man from the dust of the ground. The Hebrew uses assonance here: God formed *hā'āḏām . . . min-hā'ᵃḏāmâ.* It is hard to capture this play on sounds in English, but it is something like "God formed earthling from the earth." The verb for *crafted* is Heb. *yāṣar,* which on several occasions explicitly describes the vocation or work of a potter (2 Sam. 17:28; Isa. 29:16; Jer. 18:2, 3, 4, 11), especially when used in participial form *(yōṣēr).* "Potter," however, is a suitable translation only when the context clearly points to the fact that the work of formation being described is that of a potter. For example, the verb is used in Isa. 44:12 to describe the work of an ironsmith on metals, and hence the verb would carry a meaning like "forge." A potter, of course, works with mud or clay *(ḥōmer),* not dust *('āpār).* And for instances of *yāṣar* ("to do the work of a potter") with clay *(ḥōmer)* compare Isa. 41:25 and Jer. 18:4, 6. (Job 33:6 has Elihu saying that he was formed from clay, but "form" in this instance is *qāraṣ*. Similarly Job reminds God that he has made him [*'āśâ*] of clay [10:9].) It is taking too much liberty with Heb. *'āp̄ār* to render it "mud" or "clay" so that *yāṣar* in v. 7 may carry the force of "do the work of a potter." There are, to be sure, instances where *ḥōmer* is used in parallelism with *'āp̄ār* (Job 4:19; 10:9; 27:16; 30:19), but such parallelism argues at best for overlap in meaning rather than identity in meaning.

In contrast to 1:26ff., here we are told that mankind was made from something already in existence. The word of God (1:26ff.) is now augmented by the work of God (2:7), a work that includes both formation and animation.

---

the verb: imperfect followed by perfect with *wᵉ*. Rather than taking *ya'ᵃleh* as an imperfect to describe completed action, I take it as a frequentative imperfect which then determines the thrust of the following perfect, i.e., repeated action in the past. See GKC, § 112e.

"It is as though for the climactic performance the usual act of will was reinforced by an act of divine effort."[14]

We should note that neither the concept of the deity as craftsman nor the concept of man as coming from earthy material is unique to the Bible. For example, from ancient Egypt we have a picture of the ram-headed god Khnum sitting on his throne before a potter's wheel, on which he fashions the prince Amenhotep III (ca. 1400 B.C.) and his *ka* (an alter ego which protected and substained the individual?).[15] Referring to this particular painting, the Egyptologist John Wilson makes the interesting observation that Egypt lacked a specific account of mankind's creation. The reason for this lack, he argues, "is that there was no firm and final dividing-line between gods and men. Once a creation was started with beings, it could go on, whether the beings were gods, demi-gods, spirits, or men."[16]

Mesopotamian literature provides numerous examples of man's derivation from clay. We have already seen that in *Enuma elish* man is created from the blood of a god. In the Gilgamesh Epic (a Babylonian deluge story) the nobles of Uruk pester the gods and ask them to create one equal in strength to the oppressive Gilgamesh. The gods then ask Aruru the creator to make a counterpart to Gilgamesh:

> Thou, Aruru, didst create [the man];
> Create now his double, . . .
> When Aruru heard this,
> A double of Anu she conceived within her.
> Aruru washed her hands,
> Pinched off clay and cast it on the steppe.
> [On the step]pe she created valiant Enkidu.[17]

A sister composition to the Gilgamesh Epic is the Atrahasis Epic, another literary tradition about the creation and early history of man. As in *Enuma elish,* here too man is created to relieve the gods of heavy work. His creation is described as follows:

> Wê-ila (a god), who had personality,
> They slaughtered in their assembly.
> From his flesh and blood
> Nintu mixed clay . . . .

14. N. Sarna, *Understanding Genesis,* p. 14.

15. *ANEP,* no. 569.

16. John A. Wilson, "Egypt," in H. Frankfort, et al., *Before Philosophy: The Intellectual Adventure of Ancient Man* (Baltimore: Penguin, 1949), p. 64.

17. *ANET,* p. 74.

After she had mixed that clay
She summoned the Anunnaki, the great gods.
The Igigi, the great gods,
Spat upon the clay.
Mami opened her mouth
And addressed the great gods,
"You have commanded me a task, I have completed it;
You have slaughtered a god together with his personality.
I have removed your heavy work,
I have imposed your toil on man."[18]

Nowhere does Gen. 2 imply that *dust* is to be understood as a metaphor for frailty. Some kind of qualification would have to be added for that nuance to be apparent, as is done, for example, in Gen. 18:27. Gen. 2 simply says that *dust* was the raw material out of which man was created, as "rib" was the corresponding raw material for the woman. Dust is the womb from which man emerges and the receptacle to which one day he will return (3:19). It defines the beginning and end of his life. True, 3:19 may indicate that man of dust is not an infinite creature, but in so stating, Genesis is not demeaning man.

The dust image appears sporadically throughout the OT and into the NT. Especially interesting for possible connections with Gen. 2:7 are those passages which speak of an exaltation from dust, with the dust representing pre-royal status (1 K. 16:2), poverty (1 Sam. 2:8; Ps. 113:7), and death (Isa. 26:19; Dan. 12:2). To "be raised from the dust" means to be elevated to royal office, to rise above poverty, to find life. Here man is formed from dust to be in control of a garden. Thus, the emphasis on the dust in Gen. 2:7, far from disagreeing with ch. 1, affirms ch. 1's view of man's regality. He is raised from the dust to reign.[19]

The remainder of v. 7 supports this interpretation. *into his nostrils* the deity blows *the breath of life*. In Lam. 4:20 the people refer to King Zedekiah as "the breath of our nostrils" (though the word for "breath" there is *rûaḥ,* not *n^e^šāmâ* as here, passages like Isa. 42:5 and Job 27:3 show that *n^e^šāmâ* and *rûaḥ* are sufficiently related, both meaning "breath"). In ancient Egypt, especially in the cult of Hathor (the divine mother of the king), young princesses appear before the king with several objects in their hands to present to him. As they present these objects they say: "May the Golden One

18. W. G. Lambert and A. R. Millard, *Atra-ḫasīs: The Babylonian Story of the Flood* (Oxford: Clarendon, 1969), p. 59.

19. See W. Brueggemann, "From Dust to Kingship," *ZAW* 84 (1972) 1–18.

(Hathor) give life to thy nostrils. May the Lady of the Stars unite herself with thee."[20] In our comments on Gen. 1:26 we suggested that the application of the divine image to "man," as opposed to the king, represented perhaps both a demythologizing of royal mythology and a democratization of society in Israel. Such would seem to be the case here too. It is man, as representative of subsequent humanity, who receives the divine breath. It is not something only for the elite of society.[21]

Instead of using *rûaḥ* for "breath" (a word appearing nearly 400 times in the OT), Gen. 2:7 uses *n*e*šāmâ* (25 times in the OT). Unlike *rûaḥ,* which is applied to God, man, animals, and even false gods, *n*e*šāmâ* is applied only to Yahweh and to man. (The *n*e*šāmâ* of animals is not expressly mentioned except in the oblique reference in 7:22.)[22] Thus 2:7 may employ the less popular word for breath because it is man, and man alone, who is the recipient of the divine breath. Now divinely formed and inspired, he is *a living person.* Until God breathes into him, man is a lifeless corpse.

As we shall see below, in 1 Cor. 15:45 Paul emphatically identifies "the man" of Gen. 2:7 with Adam. He amplifies the simple LXX *egéneto ho ánthrōpos,* "the man became. . . ," into *egéneto ho prṓtos ánthrōpos Adam,* "The first man Adam became. . . ." This Pauline use of 2:7 will serve as but one example of the thirty-four uses of *'āḏām* in Gen. 1:5 and how they should be translated. In essence the problem is this: is *'āḏām* to be understood generically (mankind) or is it a proper name? And if in translation we shift from one to another, on what basis do we make the shift?

As a general rule, when *'āḏām* appears without the definite article, we may translate it as a personal name, following the rule that personal names are not normally preceded by the definite article. When it occurs with the definite article *(hā'āḏām),* we may translate it as "man."

That this neat rule does not apply to all of the instances of *'āḏām* is borne out by an examination of some of the modern English translations of the Bible. Thus AV has "Adam" eighteen times and "man" sixteen times in chs. 1–5. RSV has "Adam" eight times and "man" twenty-six times. NEB has "Adam" four times and "man" thirty times. JB has "Adam" six times and "man" twenty-eight times.[23] In addition, these modern versions disagree as

20. H. Frankfort, *Kingship and the Gods* (Chicago: University of Chicago, 1948), p. 172.

21. See W. Wifall, "The Breath of His Nostrils: Gen. 2:7b," *CBQ* 36 (1974) 237–40.

22. See H. W. Wolff, *Anthropology of the Old Testament,* tr. M. Kohl (Philadelphia: Fortress, 1974), pp. 59–60.

23. See J. Ellington, "Man and Adam in Genesis 1–5," *BT* 30 (1979) 201–5.

to the first legitimate appearance of "Adam" as a personal name: 2:19 (AV, also LXX and Vulg.); 2:20 (NIV); 3:17 (RSV); 3:21 (NEB); 4:25 (JB).

Those who embrace the theory of two sources (P [1:1–2:4a and 5:1ff.] and J [2:4b–4:26]) in these five chapters are faced with the interesting use of *'āḏām* by P first in a generic sense (1:26–27), then as a proper name (5:1). If indeed P once existed as a separate document, the shift in meaning of *'āḏām* from 1:26–27 to 5:1 would be decidedly jarring. For why would the author use the same word in back-to-back positions to convey two radically different concepts?

One can argue that this shift in meaning is prepared for by the final editor's deliberate and skillful placing of J (2:3–4:26), in which a shift in meaning from "man" to "Adam" is already manifest.[24] Or, one can suggest that 1:5 is the product of one hand in which there is a progression in the use of *'āḏām* from mankind to mankind/Adam to Adam. We have observed the progression from the general to the specific in the Creation story of Gen. 1. Perhaps the same movement is in operation in the use of *'āḏām* in these opening chapters of Scripture.

There is no doubt that "Adam" as a personal name has ancient textual support. Old Akkadian and Old Babylonian texts feature names such as *A-da-mu, A-dam-u,* and *'Á-da-mu,*[25] while the Ebla texts have produced a reference to *A-da-mu,* a provincial governor under King Igriš-Ḥolam. In Ugarit one of the titles of El is *il ab adm,* "El, the father of mankind."[26]

2. ONE GARDEN, TWO TREES (2:8–9)

8 *Yahweh God planted a garden in Eden, eastward,*[1] *and he placed there the man whom he had formed.*

9 *Out of the ground Yahweh God made every kind of tree grow, delightful in appearance, good for eating. In the middle of the garden was the tree of life and the tree of the knowledge good and evil.*[2]

---

24. See B. S. Childs, "Adam," *IDB,* 1:42; idem, *Introduction,* p. 148.

25. References in M. Pope, "Adam," *EncJud,* 2:235.

26. See M. J. Dahood, "Ebla, Ugarit, and the Bible," in G. Pettinato, *The Archives of Ebla: An Empire Inscribed in Clay* (Garden City, NY: Doubleday, 1981), p. 274.

1. Note the locative rather than the partitive use of the preposition *min.* The expression *miqqeḏem* may have either a directional meaning as here ("eastward," or lit., "in front"), or a temporal meaning ("of old"), which Vulg. mistakenly applies to 2:8 with its *in principio.*

2. The traditional translation "the tree of the knowledge of good and evil" suggests that what we have in the Hebrew for "the knowledge of good and evil" is a

8 Verses 4–7 pictured God as a potter. Now the divine image that appears is that of God as a planter, as a horticulturalist. He plants *a garden in Eden. Eden* appears thirteen times in the OT in the singular and three times in the plural to designate a place. Only three references in Genesis specifically distinguish between the *garden* and *Eden* as a place where the garden was planted (2:8, 10; 4:16). The expression in 2:8, *gan-beʿēḏen, garden in Eden,* contrasts with that in 2:15 and 3:23–24, *gan-ʿēḏen,* "garden of Eden," "Eden-garden."

Etymologically Heb. *ʿēḏen* is often connected with Sumerian-Akkadian *edinu,* "plain, flatland, wilderness, prairie," a term used as a geographical designation for the plain between the Tigris and Euphrates in southern Mesopotamia. In 3:23 LXX *paradeísou tḗs tryphḗs,* "paradise of delight," seems to relate Heb. *ʿēḏen* to the verb *ʿāḏan,* which occurs only once, and that in the Hithpael stem—"to delight oneself" (Neh. 9:25), and to the related words *ʿeḏnâ,* "pleasure" (Gen. 18:12), and *ʿaḏînâ,* "pleasure seeker" (Isa. 47:8).

There are other expressions throughout the OT for *the garden of Eden,* namely, "the garden of Yahweh" (Gen. 13:10; Isa. 51:3) and "the garden of God" (Ezek. 28:13; 31:9). The writer of Gen. 2 does not use any such phrase, perhaps to refrain from giving the impression that this garden is where God lives. He is its planter, but not its occupant.

To be sure, the concept of a primeval paradise is not unknown in ancient literature. For example, the Sumerian myth of Enki (god of waters) and Ninhursag (Mother Earth) begins by describing the land of Dilmun, east of Sumer.[3] It is a land—or island—that is pure, clean, and bright (lines 1–13), and it is also a place where there is no sickness or death and where all animals live in harmony (lines 14–30). It is a land full of sweet water and of crop-producing fields (lines 31–64). After this initial description of Dilmun, however, the narrrative proceeds to describe Enki's successive copulation

---

noun in the construct case followed by a genitive. But this is plainly not so. What we do have is an infinitive construct preceded by the definite article and followed by two accusative nouns (or adjectives?) without the article. It is true, as Gesenius has pointed out (§ 115d), that the infinitive construct functions as a verbal noun. But if that is the case here, then we have the very unusual case of the definite article *(haddaʿaṯ)* on the first word in a construct chain. The translation "the tree of the knowledge of good and evil" would be quite correct if the phrase read *ʿēṣ daʿaṯ ṭôḇ wārāʿ*. A more literal translation, then, is "the tree of the knowledge good and evil," suggesting that the whole phrase is crucial for interpretation and not just the last part, "good and evil." For the syntax cf. *haddaʿaṯ ʾōṯî* in Jer. 22:16.

3. See *ANET,* pp. 37–41. Discussion of this myth is found in T. Jacobsen, "Mesopotamia," in H. Frankfort, et al., *Before Philosophy,* pp. 170–74.

with the goddess Ninhursag, with his daughter Ninmu, with his granddaughter Ninkurra, and eventually with his great-granddaughter Uttu. Recriminations between Enki and Ninhursag follow.

No human beings are involved in this story, and the description of Dilmun is only prolegomenon. The myth is concerned primarily with the interplay of two forces in the universe, earth and water. It seems farfetched, then, to suggest that the paradise motif of Mesopotamia provided the main antecedent and inspiration for the Genesis garden of Eden.

A number of factors in Gen. 2 suggest that the author presents his material in a way that is decidedly antimythical. Thus, we read of man's creation (v. 7) before we read of the garden's creation (v. 8). We do not read that the garden is a place of blissful enjoyment. If it is such a place, the text does not pause to make that observation. Instead, man is placed in the garden "to till it and keep it" (v. 15).[4]

9 This verse focuses on one aspect of the garden—the trees. They do not appear *ex nihilo* or grow overnight from saplings to towering trees. Only two remarks (both aesthetic) are made about these trees: they are *delightful in appearance* and *good for eating.*

Singled out for special mention are two trees, *the tree of life and the tree of the knowledge good and evil.* The phrase *In the middle of* [*beṯôḵ*] *the garden* need not be taken literally to mean that these two trees were in the exact center of the garden. The reference may be simply to the placement of one element in a larger area, as in 1:6, "a vault *in the middle of* the waters"; 3:8, "the sound of Yahweh God walking *in* the garden; 9:21, "he lay uncovered *in* his tent"; 18:24, 26, "the righteous *in* the city"; 23:10, "Ephron was sitting *among* the Hittites." All of these passages use the term *beṯôḵ*.

The OT refers only twice to *the tree of the knowledge good and evil,* here and in 2:17. By contrast, *the tree of life* appears not only in the OT (Gen. 2:9; 3:22, 24; Prov. 3:18; 11:30; 13:12; 15:4—all of these Proverb passages should be understood as using the phrase "tree of life" metaphorically) but also in apocryphal literature (1 Enoch 24:4; 2 Enoch 8:3, 5, 8; 9:1; 2 Esdr. 8:52) and in the NT (Rev. 2:7; 22:2, 14, 19—all of which involve a re-creation of an Edenic existence at the eschaton).

Once again ancient Near Eastern literature provides distant parallels to the eating of plants or some edible substance and the subsequent bestowal of life. Thus in the Gilgamesh Epic Utnapishtim gives a plant to Gilgamesh

4. See B. S. Childs, "Eden, Garden of," *IDB,* 2:22–23; B. Jacobs-Hornig, "*gan,*" *TDOT,* 3:34–39, and esp. his remark on p. 38, "man's work is not related to God mythically; it grows out of the environment in which God has placed him."

which Gilgamesh calls "Man Becomes Young in Old Age." He remarks, "I myself shall eat (it) and thus return to the state of my youth."[5] But a snake swallows the plant while Gilgamesh is bathing. Similarly, the Akkadian Myth of Adapa, which shares with the Gilgamesh Epic the theme of forfeited immortality, relates Anu's offer to Adapa of the bread and food of life. Adapa rejected this offer, for he thought it was only a ruse designed not to supplement his wisdom but to kill him.[6]

Here again the Bible presents its material in a way that is quite different from that of its neighbors. The mythical idea is that life is gained through a plant, or a tree, or through bread and water. This conception is a thoroughly magical one. Read out of context and superficially, Gen. 3:22 might be interpreted to teach the same thing, i.e., trees confer life, loss of trees means death. Observe that access to the tree of life (3:22) is removed after man's disobedience, not before it. The reason for death is not due to the loss of the tree of life, but rather to the sin of this first couple in the garden.[7] The fact that v. 9 emphasizes not the tree of life but the tree's planter reinforces the idea that life is from God, not from the tree.[8]

The second tree singled out for special emphasis is *the tree of the knowledge good and evil.* As we noted above, it is not just the words *good and evil* that are crucial for the understanding of this phrase but rather *the knowledge good and evil.*

Scholars have proposed a number of theories as to the meaning of this second tree, but we shall limit our discussion to four that have gained widest acceptance.[9] One suggestion is that the knowledge is sexual.[10] As support for this theory scholars point out that the couple's first reaction after eating the forbidden fruit was that they *knew* they were naked (3:7). Before

5. *ANET,* p. 96.

6. *ANET,* p. 102.

7. See B. S. Childs, "Tree of Knowledge, Tree of Life," *IDB,* 4:697.

8. See P. Watson, "The Tree of Life," *RestQ* 23 (1980) 235.

9. C. Westermann, *Genesis,* 1:240–41, uses over half a page to provide bibliography on this one phrase alone.

10. As representatives of those embracing this position we may cite R. Gordis, "The Significance of the Paradise Myth," *AJSL* 52 (1936) 86–94; idem, "The Knowledge of Good and Evil in the Old Testament and the Qumran Scrolls," *JBL* 76 (1957) 123–38, esp. p. 130; I. Engnell, " 'Knowledge' and 'Life' in the Creation Story," in *Wisdom in Israel and in the Ancient Near East,* Fest. H. H. Rowley, ed. M. Noth and D. W. Thomas, VTSup 3 (Leiden: Brill, 1955), pp. 103–19, esp. pp. 115–16; B. Reicke, "The Knowledge Hidden in the Tree of Paradise," *JSS* 1 (1956) 193–201, esp. p. 196; J. A. Bailey, "Initiation and the Primal Woman in Gilgamesh and Genesis 2–3," *JBL* 89 (1970) 144–47.

the transgression they were naked and unashamed; after the transgression they are ashamed. A second line of support is that "to know" in the OT sometimes means "to be intimate with" (e.g., 4:1, the first mention in the Bible of sexual intercourse). Third, scholars appeal to other OT passages where "to know good and evil" may refer to the sexual urge, both before it develops (Deut. 1:39) and after it has faded (2 Sam. 19:36 [Eng. 35]). Fourth, it is pointed out that in the Gilgamesh Epic Enkidu, created to be Gilgamesh's opponent, acquired wisdom and indeed "became like a god" after a week of cohabitation with a harlot. Finally, the whole scene is in a garden, which suggests fertility.

At least two factors militate against the identification of sexual awareness. First, to be consistent, this theory must apply sexuality to God, for 3:22 does state, "the man has become like one of us, knowing good and evil." It seems strained to suggest that the reference here is to human procreation as the counterpart to divine creativity. The sexuality of the deities is, of course, a trademark of the pagan pantheons, but it is a concept conspicuously absent in the OT's delineation of the nature of God. For this reason God has no spouse, and he does not reproduce a second generation. Indeed, everything else described in Gen. 1 and 2 needs something outside itself to bring it to completion. God alone has within him the resources to be self-fulfilled.

Second, if this phrase meant sexual awareness, why would God wish to outlaw its possession, for it is this tree only that is forbidden to Adam and Eve in Gen. 2? Does not 2:24 (". . . and cleave to his wife"), which precedes the transgression, include the idea of sexual knowledge? It is also possible that the word order in 4:1 (*w^e* plus subject plus verb in the perfect form, rather than *wa* plus verb in the imperfect form plus subject, as in 4:17, 25) allows for a pluperfect—"And Adam had known"—suggesting sexual intercourse between Adam and Eve before they ate from the forbidden tree.

Another proposal is that the phrase refers to comprehensive knowledge, even omniscience. "Good and evil" is an example of the literary device called merism, which is an antonymic pair that expresses unity, wholeness, or totality.[11] According to this interpretation, when man partook of the

11. The seminal study of merism in the Bible is A. M. Honeyman, "*Merismus* in Biblical Hebrew," *JBL* 71 (1952) 11–18. A more extensive and recent work is J. Krašovec, *Der Merismus in Biblischen-hebräischen und Nordwest-semitischen* (Rome: Biblical Institute, 1977). Honeyman does not comment on the "good and evil" of Genesis, but Krašovec does interpret the phrase in Genesis as denoting knowledge that is comprehensive.

forbidden fruit he gained access to one of the deity's two unique possessions—omniscience; only immortality eluded him.[12]

The major support for this interpretation is the possibility that elsewhere in the OT the expression "good and evil" suggests everything or anything at all. So Laban's words to Jacob, "the thing comes from the Lord; we cannot speak to you bad or good," is taken to mean "we cannot say anything at all" (Gen. 24:50). Compare too 31:24, "take heed that you say not a word to Jacob, either good or bad." Perhaps the clearest passage where "good and evil" takes on such a nuance is 2 Sam. 14:17, where David is said to resemble an angel in understanding good and evil. Three verses later (v. 20) David is compared again to an angel who knows all that is on the earth.

This suggestion is untenable, however, because according to the biblical narrative man did not gain universal knowledge. Adam sees only in part and knows only in part. It is quite biblical to say God becomes man. It is nonbiblical to say that man ever becomes God. Incarnation, yes; apotheosis, no. To reject this objection by saying that the writer of Gen. 3:22 used a phrase the significance of which was lost to him seems to be forcing the facts to fit the conclusion.

A third proposal is that "the knowledge good and evil" means ethical or cultural knowledge.[13] The obvious problem with this proposal is that the text offers no clear indication that Adam's sin opened the gates for the development of culture. Also, man's original assignment to care for and till the garden can hardly be called uncivilized or primitive behavior.

Finally, we mention the view that "the knowledge good and evil" indicates moral autonomy.[14] This view appeals to many OT passages where "good and evil" is essentially a legal idiom meaning to formulate and articulate a judicial decision. To illustrate, Gen. 24:50, referred to above, says that Laban is unable to say bad or good to the servant Abraham has sent to Laban to obtain a wife for Isaac. That does not mean Laban is speechless. What it does say is that since God has led the servant to the right place and

12. See C. H. Gordon, *The Ancient Near East,* 3rd ed. (New York: Norton, 1965), p. 37; G. von Rad, *Genesis,* p. 81; R. A. Oden, Jr., "Divine Aspirations in Atrahasis and in Genesis 1–11," *ZAW* 93 (1981) 212–13.

13. Wellhausen (*Prolegomena to the History of Ancient Israel,* pp. 301–3) flirts with the possibility of comprehensive knowledge while totally rejecting ethical knowledge. In the end he opts for cultural knowledge, or as he calls it, "civilization." "As the human race goes forward in civilization, it goes backward in the fear of God" (p. 302).

14. See W. M. Clark, "A Legal Background to the Yahwist's Use of 'Good and Evil' in Genesis 2–3," *JBL* 88 (1969) 266–78.

to the right girl (24:45–49), Laban is no longer free to make his own decision on whether he should surrender his daughter to the servant. Similarly, in 31:24, 29, when Laban is told to say not a word, either good or bad, to the fleeing Jacob whom he has just overtaken, God is not outlawing any conversation between the two. Rather, God is telling Laban that he must not reprimand Jacob even though he has a legitimate grievance.

We have also already mentioned Deut. 1:39, which speaks of "your little ones . . . who this day have no knowledge of good and evil." It is hard to believe that this is a metaphorical designation for those who are too young to have experienced sexual awareness. A more natural explanation is that the reference here is to minors; "have no knowledge of good and evil" suggests that they are not legally responsible for their actions.

Solomon's prayer (1 K. 3:9) that he be able "to discern between good and evil" certainly envisions the capacity to be able to make the correct decision when confronted with alternatives. Here Solomon in fact sounds like a judge.

The Israelite king Ahab resented the prophet Micaiah, who never prophesied good for Ahab but only evil (1 K. 22:18). Again, note how good is set against its opposite evil in a context where decisions and pronouncements are made that are either favorable or unfavorable to the monarch.

It is our position that this interpretation best fits with *the knowledge good and evil* in Gen. 2–3. What is forbidden to man is the power to decide for himself what is in his best interests and what is not. This is a decision God has not delegated to the earthling. This interpretation also has the benefit of according well with 3:22, "the man has become like one of us, knowing good and evil." Man has indeed become a god whenever he makes his own self the center, the springboard, and the only frame of reference for moral guidelines. When man attempts to act autonomously he is indeed attempting to be godlike. It is quite apparent why man may have access to all the trees in the garden except this one.

3. ONE GARDEN, FOUR RIVERS (2:10–14)

10 *A river rises in Eden to irrigate the garden; outside it divides and becomes four sources.*

11 *The name of the first*[1] *is Pishon; it is the one which winds through*[2] *the whole land of Havilah, where there is gold.*

1. Again *'eḥāḏ* is used as an ordinal, as in 1:5.

2. The Hebrew verb *sāḇaḇ* may be construed as "circle on the periphery of a land," or "wind through, meander." One cannot say which is to be preferred here. Rivers more often twist and turn than encircle.

12 *The gold of that*[3] *land is choice; bdellium and lapis lazuli are there.*
13 *The name of the second river is Gihon; it is the one which winds through the whole land of Cush.*
14 *The name of the third river is Tigris; it is the one which flows*[4] *east*[5] *of Asshur. The fourth river is the Euphrates.*

These verses should be seen as an extension of v. 9, the two component parts of the garden being trees (v. 9) and rivers (vv. 10–14). The critical consensus

3. This is the first appearance of the anomalous *hw'*, the 3rd person common sing. independent pronoun. When it is used for "he" the word is pointed (spelled) *hû'*, but when it is used for "she" it is pointed *hî'*, under the label of a *Qere perpetuum* (the word is always to be read differently than it is written). Almost all grammarians take *hw'* as an incorrect form, suggesting that it arose because of some orthographic maneuvering during the transmission of the biblical text. But if that is the case, why is *hw'* found only in the Pentateuch (120 times!)? Evidence is now available that the epicene *hw'* is a genuine Hebrew form. The hill countries of Judea and Samaria had enclaves of Hurrians and Hittites. Neither of the languages spoken by these people had a gender distinction for the 3rd person sing. pronoun. Because of the interaction of the early Hebrews with these people, which the Pentateuch mentions again and again, it is only natural that the early Hebrew literature such as J should reflect a similar genderless pronominal form. The implications of this conclusion for the early dating of the writing of the Pentateuch should be obvious. See G. A. Rendsburg, "A New Look at the Pentateuchal HW'," *Bib* 63 (1982) 351–69. C. H. Gordon ("Echoes of Ebla," in *Essays on the Occasion of the Seventieth Anniversary of the Dropsie University,* ed. A. I. Katsh and L. Nemoy [Philadelphia: Dropsie University, 1979], p. 137) notes that the pronouns *swt* in Old and Middle Egyptian and *šuâti* in Old Babylonian cover "he" and "she," and that these epicene pronouns have an analogue in Heb. *hw'*. Note again that the counterparts to *hw'* are from the early stages of Egyptian and Akkadian, suggesting an early redaction of the entire Pentateuch.

Of course, biblical scholars debate the pros and cons of a Hittite or Hurrian presence in Israelite hill country at any time. For a negative conclusion to the issue see F. W. Bush, "Hurrians," *IDBS,* pp. 423–24; M. C. Astour, "Hittites," *IDBS,* pp. 412–13; and esp. R. de Vaux, *The Early History of Israel,* tr. D. Smith (Philadelphia: Westminster, 1978), pp. 134–36 (Hittites), pp. 136–37 (Hurrians). For positive evaluation of the evidence see G. Rendsburg, "A New Look," pp. 354–62; C. H. Gordon, *The Common Background of Greek and Hebrew Civilizations* (New York: Norton, 1965), pp. 29–30, 93-97; B. W. Anderson, *Understanding the Old Testament,* 4th ed. (Englewood Cliffs, NJ: Prentice-Hall, 1986), pp. 36–39.

4. The movement of the first two rivers is described as "winding through" *(sōḇēḇ).* The movement of the Tigris is described as "flowing" *(hōlēḵ).* I am not able to discern the reason for the change in verb.

5. The preposition *qiḏmaṯ* also means "before," "in front of," thus possibly pointing to a river that flows "west of Assur" (from the perspective of a writer in Canaan). But that would rule out Asshur the city, for it lay west of the Tigris.

is that these five verses are secondary[6] and that, although the reference is to real rivers, two of which are well known, still the section is based on the mythical concept of the four world rivers—Tigris, Euphrates, Nile, and Indus—which surround the entire earth.

The basic reason for suspecting this mythical background is that the traditional translation suggests that the river arose in Eden outside the garden. After passing through the garden it branches into four heads. Among other things, this interpretation would place Eden in the north, not in southern Mesopotamia, and the paragraph would then say that the Tigris and the Euphrates had a common source, which in fact they never did.

There are indeed places in the OT where the verb used in v. 10—*yāṣā'*—is used of the rise of a river at its source (e.g., Exod. 17:6; Num. 20:11; Judg. 15:19; Ezek. 47:1; Joel 4:18 [Eng. 3:18]; Zech. 14:8, which also has the preposition *min* following the verb). E. A. Speiser has shown that *yāṣā' min* in Gen. 2:10 does not mean "flow from" but rather "rise in," and what is pictured here is not a river emerging from the garden and subsequently branching into four separate rivers, but rather a river that is formed just outside the garden by the convergence of four separate branches.[7]

It should be observed that these five verses contain substantially a series of circumstantial clauses, both participial and nominal in form. W. M. W. Roth has made the interesting observation that numerical sayings in the OT have a fondness for this kind of a clause. It is apparent, for example, in the numerical proverbs of Agur (Prov. 30:18–19, 21–23, 24–28, 29–31). Here, of course, the mood is reflection and not narration. Agur is affirming what is true, not what was once true. This usage suggests that Gen. 2:10–14 describes an existing condition rather than a former situation.[8]

10 The word we have rendered *sources* is literally "heads" (NIV appropriately "headstreams"). Speiser draws attention to the use of *qᵉṣê,* "end," for the mouth of the river (Josh. 15:5; 18:19); hence *ro'šîm* refers to the upper course of a river.[9]

11–12 The *Pishon* is referred to nowhere else in the OT but does

6. See J. L. McKenzie, "The Literary Characteristics of Genesis 2–3," *TS* 15 (1954) 554.

7. E. A. Speiser, *Genesis,* pp. 19–20; idem, "The Rivers of Paradise," in *Oriental and Biblical Studies,* ed. J. J. Finkelstein and M. Greenberg (Philadelphia: University of Pennsylvania, 1967), pp. 23–34. See also R. L. Harris, "The Mist, the Canopy, and the Rivers of Eden," *BETS* 11 (1968) 179.

8. W. M. W. Roth, *Numerical Sayings in the Old Testament,* VTSup 13 (Leiden: Brill, 1965), p. 26.

9. Speiser, *Genesis,* p. 17.

appear in Sir. 24:25. It may be connected with the Hebrew root *pwš,* "scatter, press on, break loose, spring forward" (Jer. 50:11; Nah. 3:18; Hab. 1:8; Mal. 3:20 [Eng. 4:2]). Thus its meaning would be something like "Gusher." That the unknown *Pishon* and *Gihon* occur alongside the mighty Tigris and Euphrates might show that the *-ôn* ending on *Pishon* and *Gihon* is an indicator of a diminutive, and thus two considerably smaller rivers than the Tigris and the Euphrates. The *Pishon* river may be the Karun in Elam or less likely the Kerkha, both of which once flowed through separate mouths into the head of the Persian Gulf.

This river flows throughout the *land of Havilah.* In the OT *Havilah* is both a person and a place. Havilah is one of the five sons of Cush (Gen. 10:7; 1 Chr. 1:9). In the Abrahamic genealogies Havilah is the sixth generation in lineal descent from Shem and is the son of Joktan (Gen. 10:29; 1 Chr. 1:23), and Havilah's neighbors indicate a location in Arabia. Gen. 25:18 mentions a Havilah as one of the boundaries of Ishmaelite territory, "from Havilah to Shur, which is close to Egypt," that is, some point in southwestern Arabia. It is in this territory that Saul defeated the Amalekites and captured Agag their king (1 Sam. 15:7). The use of *Havilah* in Gen. 2:11 is unique in that here alone the word is preceded by the definite article, though the reason for its presence is not clear (see further below).

These other references to *Havilah* suggested to Albright that the *Pishon* and the *Gihon* are either tributaries of the Nile or two streams which unite to form the Nile. Thus he sees both Egyptian (Pishon/Gihon) and Mesopotamian (Tigris/Euphrates) influence on the biblical story.[10]

The fact that *Havilah* is preceded by the definite article in 2:11, and that 25:18 distinguishes that Havilah from any other place with the same name, would indicate the possibility that a number of places had this name. 2:11 speaks of *the* Havilah, and specifies it further by listing gold and gems connected with this site. Note that the gold is not a part of Eden. It is found only in territories outside Eden. While water, food, and monogamous marriage are a part of Eden, riches and precious metals are not.[11]

13 The second river is *Gihon,* which flows through the *land of Cush. Gihon* may be connected with the verb *gîaḥ/gûaḥ,* which means "to break loose" (Job 38:8; 40:23). There is a spring named Gihon in Jerusalem at the foot of Mt. Olivet (1 K. 1:33, 38, 45; 2 Chr. 32:30; 33:14).

The major problem here is the meaning of *Cush.* Normally in the OT

10. W. F. Albright, "The Location of the Garden of Eden," *AJSL* 39 (1922) 15–31, esp. pp. 18–21.

11. Y. T. Radday, "The Four Rivers of Paradise," *HS* 23 (1982) 30.

Cush means Ethiopia or Nubia, that is, the region of the Upper Nile.[12] Nevertheless, MT *kûš* may be a reference to the Kassites (Akk. *kaššû/kuššu*), located east of the Tigris. This possibility is reflected in the SP's rendering *Gihon* as *'Asqop,* which is the river Choaspes (modern name Kerkha), east of the Tigris.[13]

14 The series of rivers concludes with a brief mention of the *Tigris* and an even briefer mention of the *Euphrates.* The verse remarks that the Tigris *flows east of Asshur,* which may be either the Assyrian empire or the capital city of the empire. It is unlikely that the reference can be to the empire whose territory extended on both sides of the Tigris. Thus a reference to the capital city seems more likely.

We recall, however, that *Asshur* had begun to lose its importance by 1400 B.C. Would the so-called J source highlight a city in its creation epic that had long since ceased to carry any weight, or could this section have been inscribed by someone who knew the glory of the capital?[14] Westermann remarks on this point that if the ancient city of Asshur is meant, "then there must be a very ancient tradition which goes back to a time before Nineveh became the capital of the Assyrian kingdom."[15]

Of the four rivers, only the *Euphrates* is not connected with any land, and if our above identifications are correct, it is the most western of the rivers as far as Palestine is concerned. The Hebrew word for *Euphrates* is *p^erāṯ,* and may be based on Sum. *buranun,* "great river," and Akk. *purattu,* "the river." Now from the Ebla texts comes the word *ba-ra-du,* "cold river," and *ba-ra-du ma-dad,* "the great cold river," for the Euphrates. This name would be appropriate for the Euphrates, since it originates in the Armenian mountains.[16]

12. Interestingly, the LXX rendering of "Nile" in Jer. 2:18 is *Gēōn,* which is a transcription of Hebrew *gîḥôn,* but there is no other tradition to link the Nile with the Gihon.

13. If the identification of Gihon with Kerkha is correct, then the rivers of paradise are being listed in an east to west direction: Gihon, Tigris, Euphrates. Thus we would expect the Pishon to be further to the east, and the Karun in Elam fits this locale nicely. See J. H. Tigay, "Paradise," *EncJud,* 13:78.

14. See W. H. Gispen, "Genesis 2:10-14," in *Studia Biblica et Semitica,* Fest. T. C. Vriezen (Wageningen: Veenman, 1966), pp. 122–23.

15. Westermann, *Genesis,* 1:219.

16. See M. J. Dahood, "Ebla, Ugarit, and the Old Testament," *TD* 27 (1979) 128; idem, "Ebla, Ugarit, and the Bible," in G. Pettinato, *Archives of Ebla,* p. 275.

4. KEEPING BOTH THE GARDEN AND THE COMMANDMENT (2:15–17)

15 *Yahweh God then took the man and led him into the garden of Eden to dress it and keep it.*[1]

16 *Yahweh God commanded the man, saying: "You may indeed eat of any tree of the garden,*

17 *but from the tree of the knowledge good and evil you shall not eat of it, for as surely as you eat of it you shall die."*

15 There is no magic in Eden. Gardens cannot look after themselves; they are not self-perpetuating. Man is placed there *to dress it and keep it.* The word we have translated *dress* is *ʿāḇaḏ,* the normal Hebrew verb meaning "to serve." So again the note is sounded that man is placed in the garden as servant. He is there not to be served but to serve. The second verb—*keep* or "tend" (Heb. *šāmar*)—carries a slightly different nuance. The basic meaning of this root is "to exercise great care over," to the point, if necessary, of guarding. This emphasis on guarded keeping is substantiated by the fact that the poetic synonym of *šāmar* is always *nāṣar,* "to protect" (Deut. 33:9; Ps. 12:8 [Eng. 7]; 105:45; 119:34, 55–56, 145–146; 140:5 [Eng. 4]; 141:3; Prov. 2:8, 11; 4:6; 5:2; 27:18). The same root is used in the next chapter to describe the cherubs who are on guard to prevent access to the tree of life in the garden (Gen. 3:24). The garden is something to be protected more than it is something to be possessed.

The point is made clear here that physical labor is not a consequence of sin. Work enters the picture before sin does, and if man had never sinned he still would be working. Eden certainly is not a paradise in which man passes his time in idyllic and uninterrupted bliss with absolutely no demands on his daily schedule.

In a general sense v. 15 duplicates v. 8. Both verses state that God *put* man in the garden, although each verse uses a different verb (v. 8—*śîm;* v. 15—*nāḥâ* [or *nûaḥ*]). The claim is frequently made that Gen. 2–3 abounds with duplicates, intrusions, and contradictions, indicating either the existence of several Edenic stories or else the appropriation and streamlining of heterogeneous material by the J writer.[2]

1. The pronominal suffix "it" on "dress" and "keep" is feminine. "Garden" is masculine. Does this indicate that the reference is to the ground/earth (fem.) in the garden that man is to till and tend? Or is it the case that many nouns denoting place have a variable gender (GKC, § 122l)? I am inclined to prefer the former explanation, if only for the fact that nowhere else is *gān* treated as feminine.

2. For the first position see J. Dus, "Zwei Schichten in der biblischen Paradiesgeschichte," *ZAW* 71 (1959) 97–114; I. Lewy, "The Two Strata in the Eden

What may be said about the relationship of v. 15 to v. 8 other than that they say the same thing twice? Are they indeed duplicates? There is, to be sure, partial recapitulation of v. 8 in v. 15. V. 8, however, is only a general statement, telling where man was settled. This general statement is then followed by various pieces of information about the garden where man is placed. It has trees throughout and enjoys irrigation. Now follows in v. 15 a specific statement informing us why man was placed there, as the text resumes the point made back in v. 8.

16–17 In the garden God gives to Adam ample permission *(any tree)* but only a single prohibition *(but from the tree . . .)*. We will see in our discussion of ch. 3 that the serpent discreetly avoids any reference to God's generous permission but magnifies God's prohibition, which is the reversal of these two verses.

The last part of v. 17 reads literally "in the day of your eating from it dying you shall die," understanding the infinitive absolute before the verb to strengthen the verbal idea. We have already encountered the phrase *b^eyôm* (lit., "in the day") followed by the infinitive construct in 2:4—"When Yahweh God made. . . ." Here in 2:17 we have translated it as *as surely as* on the basis of its occasional use as an idiom meaning "for certain," as in 1 K. 2:37, 42, where Shimei is threatened with death "on the day you go forth and cross the brook Kidron." As the next few verses indicate, Shimei could not possibly have been executed "on the day" he exited his house. The verse is underscoring the certainty of death, not its chronology.[3] Again, Pharaoh's words to Moses, "in the day you see my face you will die" (Exod. 10:28), mean that if he values his life he ought not to seek a further conference with Pharaoh, or else Moses will be no more.

The traditional translation could be retained, however, by taking the phrase *môṯ tāmûṯ* (infinitive absolute followed by a finite form of the verb) to mean *you are doomed to die,* that is, a deferred penalty. The verse is concerned not with immediate execution but with ultimate death. The problem with this interpretation is that "doomed to die" forces on *môṯ tāmûṯ* a meaning that is not patently observable. Obviously Adam and Eve did not die when they ate of the tree. Thus, in what we consider a poor reading of the text, D. R. G. Beattie wonders why Satan is punished for telling the truth

Story," *HUCA* 27 (1956) 93–99. The second position is more widely held. For an illustrative approach cf. the section "The Unity of the Old Testament Narrative," in J. L. McKenzie, "The Literary Characteristics of Genesis 2–3," *TS* 15 (1954) 553–58.

3. See G. Vos, *Biblical Theology* (Grand Rapids: Eerdmans, 1949), pp. 48–49.

(they did become like God) and exposing God's lie (they did not die)![4] Others have suggested that God does not carry out his death penalty against Adam and Eve but rather withholds it as an indication of his grace.[5] Yet another alternative is that 2:17 means "on the day you eat of it you will become mortal."[6] This approach assumes that God created man immortal, a fact that is not explicitly stated in Genesis and seems contrary to 1 Tim. 6:16, which states that deity alone has immortality. Indeed, in no OT passage does the phrase *môṯ tāmûṯ* mean "to become mortal."

Perhaps reexamination of this phrase will shed some light on the problem. First, we need to note the distinction in sections of the OT between "he/you shall die" *(yāmûṯ/tāmûṯ),* which is the Qal form of the verb, and "he/you shall be put to death" *(yûmaṯ/tûmaṯ),* which is the Hophal form of the verb. In the former, the executioner is God; thus the sense is: "he shall die (at God's hands)." In the latter, the executioner is man, and the sense is: "he shall be put to death (by man)." Two Genesis passages illustrate this difference. In 20:7 God says to Abimelech, who is on the verge of adultery with Sarah, "restore the man's wife . . . but if you do not . . . know that you shall surely die [*môṯ tāmûṯ,* as in 2:17]." God himself will directly intervene and strike down Abimelech. In 26:11 Abimelech says to anybody tempted to take advantage of vulnerable Isaac and Rebekah: "Whoever touches this man or his wife shall be put to death [*môṯ yûmāṯ*]." That is, Abimelech himself will mete out punishment against the aggressor.[7] Clearly then, the sanction that is held out before Adam in 2:17 is one that carries a divine implementation.

Second, we need to examine the uses of *môṯ tāmûṯ* in Scripture. In addition to its appearance in 2:17 and 3:4, it appears twelve other times in the OT (Gen. 20:7; 1 Sam. 14:44; 22:16; 1 K. 2:37, 42; 2 K. 1:4, 6, 16; Jer. 26:8; Ezek. 3:18; 33:8, 14).[8] All of these passages deal with either a punish-

4. See D. R. G. Beattie, "What is Genesis 2–3 About?" *ExpTim* 92 (1980/81) 10.

5. See D. J. A. Clines, "Themes in Genesis 1–11," *CBQ* 38 (1976) 490.

6. See D. Jobling, "A Structural Analysis of Genesis 2:4b–3:24," in SBLASP, 1978, 1:64.

7. The presence of the infinitive absolute is not required for this distinction to be made. I am simply contrasting *yāmûṯ* with *yûmaṯ.* See also J. Milgrom, *Studies in Levitical Terminology* (Berkeley: University of California, 1970), 1:5–7, for illustrations of this in Exodus–Numbers. This difference is not carried through into the historical books.

8. I include here only instances of the infinitive absolute *(môṯ)* followed by the Qal 2nd masc. sing. imperfect *(tāmûṯ).* If we were to include all instances of the infinitive absolute followed by a finite verbal form of the same root the list of passages would be considerably lengthened. Still, the basic point of observation is not changed or challenged. For copious references see GKC, §§ 113l-q.

ment for sins or an untimely death that is the result of punishment. In two of these passages we observe that the threatened execution is not carried out. Thus in Jer. 26:8 a sentence of death is pronounced against Jeremiah: "You shall die!" Yet the death penalty is not exacted, for he is released on the basis of a century-old precedent set by Micah in the days of Hezekiah. In 1 Sam. 14:44 Saul says to Jonathan, who has just eaten the honey in ignorance of his father's ultimatum, "you shall surely die, Jonathan." Yet Jonathan does not die, but rather gains a reprieve.[9] Perhaps then in 1 Sam. 14:44 *môṯ tāmûṯ* means "you deserve to die."

Furthermore, note that the three passages from Ezekiel (3:18; 33:8, 14) hold out the possibility that repentance may avert death. This, then, could be another difference between *môṯ yāmûṯ* and *môṯ yûmaṯ:* the former allows for the possibility of pardon, whereas the latter does not. Of course, *môṯ yāmûṯ* by itself does not convey any idea of possible pardon or exemption from punishment. Additional information is necessary for that to be the case, as Jer. 26:8, 1 Sam. 14:44, and the three passages from Ezekiel make clear. All that *môṯ yāmûṯ* clearly conveys is the announcement of a death sentence by divine or royal decree.

5. A FIT HELPER AMONG THE ANIMALS? (2:18–20)

18 *Yahweh God said, "It is not good that the man should be alone. I will make*[1] *for him a helper suitable for him."*

19 *So Yahweh God formed from the dust of the ground every kind of wild animal of the field, every kind of bird of the sky, and he brought them to the man to see what he would call each; whatever the man called each living creature, that was to be its name.*

20 *The man gave names to all cattle, birds of the sky, and to every wild animal of the field; but by Adam*[2] *no helper suitable for him was found.*[3]

9. See J. Blenkinsopp, "Jonathan's Sacrilege. 1 Sam. 14,1–46: A Study in Literary History," *CBQ* 26 (1964) 447.

1. LXX *poiḗsōmen,* "let us make" (1st pl.), would reflect Heb. *naʿaśeh* (cf. Gen. 1:26) rather than what we have here, *ʾĕʿĕśeh* (1st sg.). See GKC, § 75l. On change of number between Hebrew verbs and their LXX counterparts, see E. Tov, *The Text-Critical Use of the Septuagint in Biblical Research* (Jerusalem: Simor Ltd, 1981), pp. 220-22.

2. *BHS* suggests *welāʾāḏām* ("and/but for the man") for MT *ûleʾāḏām,* probably to align it with the second word of the verse, *hāʾāḏām* ("the man"). *BHS* does not provide any textual support for the change. The MT *ûleʾāḏām* (i.e., without the definite article) reads the expression as a proper name, "for/by Adam."

3. There is some debate about the correct translation of the last half of the

18 Everything thus far in Genesis that has been scrutinized by God has been given a positive assessment. Every situation has come through as either good or very good. For the first time we encounter something that is *not good:* man's lack of a corresponding companion. The skies without the luminaries and birds are incomplete. The seas without the fish are incomplete. Without mankind and land animals the earth is incomplete. As a matter of fact, every phenomenon in Gen. 1–2, God excepted, is in need of something else to complete it and to enable it to function.

In this particular case we should note that it is God who makes the judgment about the unsuitability of man's aloneness. Man is not consulted for his thoughts on the matter. At no point does the man offer to God any grievance about his current circumstances.

God is not only evaluator; he is also rectifier. He is not long on analysis but short on solution. His remedy is to provide *a helper suitable for him* (i.e., for the man). The last part of v. 18 reads literally, "I will make him for him a helper as in front of him (or according to what is in front of him)." This last phrase, "as in front of him (or according to what is in front of him)" *(k^enegdô),* occurs only here and in v. 20. It suggests that what God creates for Adam will correspond to him. Thus the new creation will be neither a superior nor an inferior, but an equal.[4] The creation of this helper will form one-half of a polarity, and will be to man as the south pole is to the north pole.

This new creation which man needs is called a *helper (ʿēzer),* which is masculine in gender, though here it is a term for woman. Any suggestion

---

verse. What is the subject of *māṣāʾ* (lit., "he found"), which is a normal Qal perfect third masculine singular form? Is it Adam—"but he [Adam] did not find . . ."? What, then, would one do with *ûl^eʾāḏām,* "for Adam"? Adam did not find for Adam? May the subject be God—"but he [God] did not find . . ."? In this case one would have to read v. 20b as a circumstance prior to v. 21—"finding no helper for him, God caused a deep sleep to fall on the man." Again, the suggestion has been made (GKC, § 144d, although he does not cite this verse) that the verb, although active in form, be read as a passive expressed by an indefinite subject—"one did not find" or "there was not found." The suggestion we prefer is to revocalize the MT as a Qal passive (change MT *māṣāʾ* to *mūṣāʾ*). This rendering allows for the retention of Adam as the agent both at the beginning and at the end of the sentence. See D. N. Freedman, "Notes on Genesis," *ZAW* 64 (1952) 191; M. J. Dahood, "The Phoenician Background of Qoheleth," *Bib* 47 (1966) 278; idem, "Ebla, Ugarit, and the Old Testament," in *Congress Volume: Göttingen, 1977,* VTSup 29 (Leiden: Brill, 1978), p. 90 n. 33.

4. As a substantive *neḡeḏ* means "that which is conspicuous, in full view of, in front of." The related noun *nāḡîḏ* means "ruler" or "prince." The verb *nāḡaḏ* means "tell," "declare," "expound," "reveal," "go ahead," this last translation suggesting "achievement, pioneering, risk and deliberate thrust into the unknown" (S. Terrien, *Till the Heart Sings* [Philadelphia: Fortress, 1985], p. 11).

that this particular word denotes one who has only an associate or subordinate status to a senior member is refuted by the fact that most frequently this same word describes Yahweh's relationship to Israel. He is Israel's help(er) because he is the stronger one (see, e.g., Exod. 18:4; Deut. 33:7, 26, 29; Ps. 33:20; 115:9–11; 124:8; 146:5; etc.).[5] The LXX translation of *'ēzer* by *boēthós* offers further support for this nuance. The LXX uses *boēthós* forty-five times to translate several Hebrew words, and except for three occurrences (1 Chr. 12:18; Ezek. 12:14; Nah. 3:9) the word refers to help "from a stronger one, in no way needing help."[6] The word is used less frequently for human helpers, and even here, the helper is one appealed to because of superior military strength (Isa. 30:5) or superior size (Ps. 121:1). The verb behind *'ēzer* is *'āzar,* which means "succor," "save from danger," "deliver from death." The woman in Gen. 2 delivers or saves man from his solitude.

19 Yahweh parades before Adam members of the amimal world so that the man may confer on each its name. This is the first fulfillment of God's directive to humankind in 1:26, 28 to exercise authority over the animal, the fish, and the fowl. For to confer a name *(qārā' le)* is to speak from a position of authority and sovereignty.

Many commentators have maintained that in this verse one finds a classic illustration of a major conflict between the sequence of creation in 1:1–2:4a and that in 2:4bff. In one (1:24–25) animals precede man. In the other (2:19) animals come after man. It is possible to translate *formed* as "had formed" (so NIV). One can, however, retain the traditional translation and still avoid a contradiction. This verse does not imply that this was God's first creation of animals. Rather, it refers to the creation of a special group of animals brought before Adam for naming.[7]

20 The animals are creatures but they are not helpers. Adam must look elsewhere for his complement. Here God is creator, but not namer. In the preceding chapter it was God who conferred names on "light" (1:5), "darkness" (1:5), "the vault" (1:8), "dry land" (1:10). There "called/named" is expressed by the formula *qārā' le,* the same formula used in 2:19, 20,

5. See M. de Merode, " 'A Helper Fit for Him': Gen. 2:18–24," *TD* 27 (1979) 117–19.

6. See J. M. Higgins, "Anastasius Sinaita and the Superiority of the Woman," *JBL* 97 (1978) 253–56.

7. "Of all the species of beasts and flying creatures that had already been created and had spread over the face of the earth and the firmament of the heavens, the Lord God now formed particular specimens for the purpose of presenting them all before man in the midst of the Garden" (Cassuto, *Genesis,* 1:129).

though v. 20 adds the plural noun *šēmôṯ,* "names," as the direct object of *wayyiqrā'*. It is clear that when God confers a name on something he does so in his capacity of sovereign ruler, but *qārā' le* does not by itself suggest superiority. So it is stretching the point to suggest that in naming the animals man exercises sovereignty over them. For that to be clear, one would need a parallel to the "subdue" and "have dominion over" of ch. 1. In naming the animals, man exercises a God-given initiative. God gives to him the task of assigning labels to the only other living creatures who join him in the garden. We are told that the man obediently followed through with this assignment, but we are not told the names he conferred on each creature. In acting as name-giver, the man exhibits a quality of discernment.

6. THE CREATION OF WOMAN (2:21–25)

21 *So Yahweh God cast a deep sleep on the man so that he fell asleep, and he took one of his sides and enclosed it with flesh.*

22 *Then Yahweh God built into a woman the side that he had taken from the man and brought her to the man.*

23 *The man said: "This one, this time,*[1] *is bone of my bones and flesh of my flesh. This one shall be called 'woman,' for she was taken from man."*

24 *Therefore a man forsakes his father and mother and clings to his wife, and they become one flesh.*

25 *Both of them, the man and his wife, were naked, yet not ashamed.*

21 None of Israel's neighbors had a tradition involving a separate account of the creation of the female. In biblical thought the woman is not subsumed under her male counterpart. Gen. 1:27 simply informed us that when God created two earth creatures who would be his image bearers he created one earthling that was male and another earthling that was female. The verse said nothing about how he created them or when he created them (simultaneously or sequentially).

These verses (2:21ff.) complement 1:27. The male earthling God made first. Just as the male was "taken" from the earth (3:19, 23), so the woman is "taken" from the man. Both of these special creatures owe their existence to something that existed before them.

1. This translation takes *zō'ṯ* as the subject of the sentence and attributes demonstrative force to the article in *happa'am,* as in Gen. 29:34; 30:20. A. Berlin sees the same construction in Ps. 118:24, "this is what the Lord has done today" ("Psalms 118:24," *JBL* 96 [1977] 567–68).

Specifically, the text says that God took one of the *ṣēlāʿ* of man. Almost without exception this word has been translated as "rib" (hence even today the many puns on "Adam's rib" and "women's lib"). A better translation of *ṣēlāʿ* is *side*. The word designates a side or the shell of the ark of the covenant (Exod. 25:12, 14; 37:3, 5), the side of a building (Exod. 26:20; 36:25) or even a whole room ("side chamber, arcade, cell," Ezek. 41:5–8), or a ridge or terrace on a hill (2 Sam. 16:13). Gen. 2:21 is the only place in the OT where the modern versions render this word as "rib."[2] If we translate "side" rather than "rib," then the passage states that woman was created from an undesignated part of man's body rather than from one of his organs or from a portion of bony tissue.

But even given the preference of "side" for "rib," we should not conclude either from this verse or from 1:27 that the first human being was androgynous. This particular concept goes back at least to Aristophanes' discourse on love in Plato's *Symposium* (189–93). According to Plato there were originally three kinds of beings, who were joined back-to-back, like Siamese triplets. Each being had the faculties of two human bodies. These creatures could be either masculine, feminine, or bisexual. After an unsuccessful attempt to rebel against the gods, Zeus carved each of the three types of being, splitting them into either two men, or two women, or one man and one woman. Upon demonstrations of remorse for their rebellion, Zeus rejoined the severed halves by making possible their copulation.

A similar teaching prevails in later Jewish (Tannaitic) tradition. Thus to the question "How did male and female come into being?" the answer was given that God took a side of man and from this half made woman; only the two together restore the wholeness of God's original creation (Midrash Rabbah Gen. 8:1). But when God created Adam, he created him bisexual *('ndrwgynws)*. Parallel remarks are made by Rabbi Shemuel ben Nahman (see Midrash Rabbah Lev. 14:1).

Such teaching goes beyond the statements of Genesis, however. That Eve is formed from the side of Adam is the teaching of the text. To suggest that the primal being was an androgyne is to read into the text what is not there and to understand 1:27, "male and female created he them," as "male and female created he him (or it)."

22 The traditional translation of this verse (e.g., RSV) has the Lord God taking the rib of the man and "making" it into a woman. The Hebrew

2. More than likely the translation "rib" is traceable to an Arabic root meaning "to curve, deviate"; hence, *ṣēlāʿ* is a curved bone. See G. R. Driver, "Notes and Studies," *JTS* 47 (1946) 161–62.

word for "make" is literally "build" *(bānâ),* but the extended meaning "to make, create" is supported by the root *bny* in Ugaritic. One of the epithets of El is *bny bnwt,* "creator of created things."[3] The verb *built* by its very definition implies beauty, stability, and durability.

Working with clay, God is potter. Working with body tissue, God is builder. Eve thus becomes the first thing that is created from another living thing. Also, we need to note that it is not Eve herself but simply the raw material that is taken from the man.[4] Just as the man does not emerge until a creative divine act on the dust takes place, so woman does not emerge until a creative divine act is performed on the man's side.

23 For the first time in Scripture the words of a human being are recorded in direct discourse. The total sum of what man himself has to say in the creation narrative is an exclamatory outburst concerning his helper. She is *bone of my bones and flesh of my flesh.*

Apart from the man's statement that his helper is actually part of himself, his words may have additional meaning. If we accept the maxim that in the OT *flesh* (Heb. *bāśār*) is often a symbol for an individual's weakness and frailty, then perhaps *bone* (Heb. *ʿeṣem*) may well be its opposite—a symbol of an individual's strength.[5] The possibility that *ʿeṣem* is the antonym of *bāśār* is heightened by the fact that one of the meanings of the verb from which *ʿeṣem* is derived is "to be or make strong" (Gen. 26:16; Ps. 105:24; Dan. 8:8, 24). Thus it is the bones, not the flesh, that survive decay after death (Gen. 50:25).

Now it is true that the OT uses "flesh" by itself as a term for a close relationship, as in Gen. 37:27, "Joseph is our brother, our own flesh." Four times in the OT one finds the expression "my/your bone and flesh" (Gen. 29:14; Judg. 9:2; 2 Sam. 5:1; 19:13). This may simply be an expanded version of "flesh" and thus only an alternative way of expressing a relationship.[6]

Brueggemann argues that the phrase "my/your bone and flesh" is actually a covenant formula and that it speaks not of a common birth but of a common, reciprocal loyalty.[7] Thus when representatives of the northern

3. See J. Gray, *The Legacy of Canaan,* VTSup 5 (Leiden: Brill, 1957), pp. 58 n. 4, 189.

4. See P. Trible, *God and the Rhetoric of Sexuality,* OBT 2 (Philadelphia: Fortress, 1978), p. 101.

5. H. W. Wolff, *Anthropology of the Old Testament,* p. 26, entitles his discussion of *bāśār,* "Man in his Infirmity."

6. As argued by Wolff, ibid., p. 29.

7. See W. Brueggemann, "Of the Same Flesh and Bone (GN 2,23a)," *CBQ* 32 (1970) 532–42.

tribes visit David at Hebron and say to him, "we are your bone and flesh" (2 Sam. 5:1), this is not a statement of relationship ("we have the same roots") but a pledge of loyalty ("we will support you in all kinds of circumstances"). Taken this way, the man's *this one, this time, is bone of my bones and flesh of my flesh* becomes a covenantal statement of his commitment to her. Thus it would serve as the biblical counterpart to the modern marriage ceremony, "in weakness [i.e., flesh] and in strength [i.e., bone]." Circumstances will not alter the loyalty and commitment of the one to the other. So understood, the verse does not attribute strength to the man and weakness to the woman, as if he is the embodiment of bone and she is the embodiment of flesh. Both the man and the woman share the entire spectrum of human characteristics, from strong to weak.

In the latter part of this verse we encounter our first instance of popular etymology, a derivation that is based on assonance, "she shall be called 'woman' [*'iššâ*] because she was taken from man [*'îš*]."[8] The text does not say "she shall be called female [*n^eqēḇâ*], for she was taken out of male [*zāḵār*]." Perhaps by using two words which sound alike the narrator wished to emphasize the identity and equality of this primal couple.[9]

24 *Therefore man forsakes his father and mother.* Von Rad notes and is puzzled by the fact that in a patriarchal society it is the man who leaves his home rather than the wife who leaves hers.[10] One explanation of this verse is that it reflects an *erēbu* marriage, in which the husband leaves his family and lives with his wife's family.[11] M. M. Bravmann offers another explanation, interpreting the verse psychologically. Referring to the saying that "A son is a son till he gets him a wife, a daughter is a daughter all of her life," he suggests that the new husband has more of an emotional detachment from his home than the new wife does from her home.[12] He leaves home to a degree that she never does.

Perhaps the most crucial element in this verse is the verbs it uses:

8. The verb behind *'îš* is still much debated. A putative *'ûš,* "be strong," or *'āwaš,* "march ahead," is most frequently cited. There is equal uncertainty about the root behind *'iššâ,* with suggestions including *'ānaš,* "be weak, sick," or *'ānāš,* "be soft, be delicate" (BDB, pp. 35, 60–61).

9. N. P. Bratsiotis, "*'îš,*" *TDOT,* 1:226–27.

10. Von Rad, *Genesis,* p. 85.

11. C. H. Gordon, "*Erēbu* Marriage," in *Studies on the Civilization and Culture of Nuzu and the Hurrians. In Honor of Ernest R. Lachemann,* ed. M. Morrison and D. Owens (Winona Lake, IN: Eisenbrauns, 1981), pp. 155–61.

12. M. M. Bravmann, *Studies in Semitic Philology* (Leiden: Brill, 1977), pp. 593–95.

forsakes and *clings.* The verb *forsake* frequently describes Israel's rejection of her covenant relationship with Yahweh (Jer. 1:16; 2:13, 17, 19; 5:7; 16:11; 17:13; 19:4; 22:9; many other examples from the OT could be cited). By contrast, the verb *cling* often designates the maintenance of the covenant relationship (Deut. 4:4; 10:20; 11:22; 13:5 [Eng. 4]; 30:20). Thus, to leave father and mother and cling to one's wife means to sever one loyalty and commence another. Already Scripture has sounded the note that marriage is a covenant rather than an ad-hoc, makeshift arrangement.

Now covenantally joined with his wife, the man and his spouse *become one flesh.* Nothing is said yet about any procreating roles that this couple shall assume. The man does not leave one family to start another family. What is being pinpointed is solidarity. A man by himself is not one flesh. A woman by herself is not one flesh.

25 The climax of the creation is, interestingly, the notation that the couple *were naked* and felt no shame before each other.[13] Of course, *naked* refers primarily to physical nudity, but one may also think that no barrier of any kind drove a wedge between Adam and Eve.

With the exception of this verse, nakedness in the OT is always connected with some form of humiliation. The three major uses of nakedness are: (1) as a description of the poor (Job 24:7, 10; 31:19; Ezek. 18:16); (2) as a sign of shame or guilt (Gen. 3:7, 10, 11; Ezek. 16:22, 37, 39; Hos. 2:3; Amos 2:16; Mic. 1:8); (3) in reference to birth (Job 1:21; Eccl. 5:15). A full documentation of all passages would show that nakedness as a symbol of guilt is most frequent, and perhaps such a connection between nakedness and guilt was suggested by the abbreviated dress of slaves and prisoners of war.[14]

13. Skinner (*Genesis,* p. 70) suggests that the force of the imperfect form of the verb, *yiṯbōšāšû,* "felt no shame," is frequentative and that the use of the Hithpael stem denotes reciprocity. That would imply that the couples' reaction to each other was not based on a single moment of discovery, but refers to a state they shared from the moment of their creation. See also J. M. Sasson, "*wᵉlōʾ yitbōšāšû* (Gen 2,25) and Its Implications," *Bib* 66 (1985) 418–21, who suggests "yet, they did not shame each other."

14. "Naked" occurs with "shame" in Gen. 2:25; Isa. 20:4; 47:3; Mic. 1:11; Nah. 3:5.

THE NEW TESTAMENT APPROPRIATION

a. Gen. 2:18–23 and 1 Cor. 11:2–16; 1 Tim. 2:8–15

(1) 1 Cor. 11:2–16

In a discussion about the right and wrong ways of worship, Paul says that a man dishonors Christ by worshiping with his head covered. Similarly, he argues, a woman dishonors her husband if she worships with her head unveiled. Christ is the head of a man and a husband is the head of a wife.

As a historical precedent for this arrangement, Paul appeals to Gen. 2, from which he reminds his audience of two facts. One is that woman was made from man, not vice versa, and the other is that woman was created for man, not vice versa. Clearly what Paul expresses here is not subordination of woman to man per se, but rather the order of the creative events.[1] This is followed by the apostle's dicta regarding legislation for *both* man and woman in public worship. V. 8 is concerned to show why it is that the woman is the glory of man rather than the reverse.

Interestingly, Paul does *not* call woman "the image of man." The contrast is at the point of glory or manifestation rather than image. In a second parenthetical remark (see RSV), Paul observes that just as the primal woman owed her existence to man, subsequently man owes his existence to woman (v. 12). Perhaps this note of balance is induced by Paul's fear that his audience read too much into his earlier comments on Gen. 2.[2]

(2) 1 Tim. 2:8–15

This paragraph is the locus classicus for many exegetes in their examination of whether there should be any place for women in a ministerial or teaching

1. See R. Scroggs, "Paul and the Eschatological Woman," *JAAR* 40 (1972) 301.

2. Almost every passage dealing with the headship of the husband in any of the epistles traditionally credited to Paul is regarded as non-Pauline by most critical NT scholars. This includes 1 Tim. 2:8–15; Tit. 2:3–5; Eph. 5:22–33; Col. 3:18–19; 1 Cor. 14:33b–36. Even 1 Cor. 11:2–16 has been presented as a post-Pauline composition. See W. O. Walker, Jr., "1 Corinthians 11:2–16 and Paul's Views Regarding Women," *JBL* 94 (1975) 96–110. Thus the only indubitably Pauline statement on male-female relationships is Gal. 3:28. Such consistent textual excisions let Paul escape blame and transform him from history's all-time male chauvinist into an individual who is a thoroughgoing egalitarian, one who was centuries ahead of his time in his thoughts of liberation regarding male and female!

position. Those who answer no say that this is the plain, literal meaning. This text then becomes the determinative text for interpreting and analyzing other NT references to the role of women. Those who answer yes find, on the contrary, that this passage actually supports a public, teaching role for women.[3] Others take the passage only as an illustration of an interesting but irrelevant Christian midrash.[4]

It is not our purpose to address this particular issue. Rather, we are interested in seeing where and how 1 Tim. 2:8–15 utilizes the Creation story. The writer states in v. 12 that he permits no woman to teach or to have authority over man; she is to keep silent. Then he goes on to state (v. 13), "For Adam was formed first, then Eve." He further adds (v. 14) that it was the woman who was seduced, not Adam. Now the issue, in terms of hermeneutics, is whether Paul is dealing here with a problem (women teachers who are leading believers astray) that is of purely local import, or whether he is stating a timeless and axiomatic truth that is equally binding today.

Part of the answer to that question is to be found in how one interprets the writer's appropriation of Gen. 2–3: "he was formed first; she was deceived, not he." The writer introduces his reference to the Genesis narratives with the conjunction "for" *(gar).* This conjunction may be understood in two ways. One is to take it as an expression of causation: women are not to teach or have authority over men *because* woman was not created first and *because* she was the one deceived. Thus Eve's creation and seduction are paradigms of the nature of all women in general.[5]

The other interpretation takes *gar* as explanatory. Thus "for" means "for example, for instance," and the reference to Eve's deception functions as an illustration of how far misguided women can greatly mislead others.[6] The major problems with this view are: (1) the normal and prevalent use of *gar* is as a causal conjunction; and (2) twenty-one times in the Pastorals an

3. "In 1 Timothy 2:11–15 . . . the reasons for it [v. 12, the injunction to female silence] are spelled out in a way that defies hermeneutical ingenuity" (P. Jewett, *Man as Male and Female* [Grand Rapids: Eerdmans, 1975], p. 116).

4. D. Patte, *Early Jewish Hermeneutic in Palestine* (Missoula, MT: Scholars, 1975), pp. 315–24. A. Padgett ("Wealthy Women at Ephesus: I Timothy 2:8–15 in Social Context," *Int* 41 [1987] 19–31) argues correctly that the interpretive scheme most clearly evident in these verses is typology.

5. See D. J. Moo, "1 Timothy 2:11–15: Meaning and Significance," *TJ* 1 (1980) 68–70.

6. See P. B. Payne, "Libertarian Women in Ephesus: A Response to Douglas J. Moo's Article, '1 Timothy 2:11–15: Meaning and Significance,' " *TJ* 2 (1981) 175–77; A. H. Stouffer, "The Ordination of Women: Yes," *CT* 25 (1981) 259.

imperatival idea is followed by a clause introduced with *gar,* and in these instances the causal idea is the obvious one.[7]

In the light of the above we are inclined to agree with those who see a direct cause-and-effect relationship between Paul's understanding of the Genesis story and its definitive influence on the role of women in the church at Ephesus.

b. Gen. 2:24 and 1 Cor. 6:16; Eph. 5:31

We have already referred to Matt. 19:5 and Mark 10:7–8 in our discussion of 1:27. Jesus couples Gen. 1:27 (an action of God) with Gen. 2:24 (a teaching from God) in his response to his critics' question about the legality of divorce. Therefore in this section we will focus on the Pauline use of Gen. 2:24 in 1 Cor. 6:16 and Eph. 5:31.

(1) 1 Cor. 6:16

In the context of this verse (vv. 9–20), Paul warns against satisfying one's sexual desires in an immoral fashion. He observes that the one who joins himself to a prostitute becomes one body *(hen sṓma)* with her, and then supports this point by citing the last part of Gen. 2:24, "the two shall become one flesh [*sárka mían*]." This physical union between a man and a harlot is then contrasted with one who is united to the Lord in a spiritual union—"he . . . becomes one spirit with him" (v. 17).

What Paul is saying is that the union of a man with Christ and with a harlot are incompatible. The commitment of oneself to one of these unions makes the other union impossible. In addition, for Paul union with a harlot was more than just a temporary physical act.[8] For even here the two become one flesh.

(2) Eph. 5:31

This verse is part of a larger unit, vv. 21–33 (one of the apostle's *Haustafeln,* i.e., rules by which members of a household conduct themselves), which is devoted to teaching on marriage and particularly the relationship of the wedded partners to each other. The wife is to be subject to her husband (vv.

7. See D. J. Moo, "The Interpretation of 1 Timothy 2:11–15: A Rejoinder," *TJ* 2 (1981) 202–4.

8. See R. Batey, "The *mia sarx* Union of Christ and the Church," *NTS* 13 (1967) 278–79.

22–24), and the husband is to show nothing less than Christ-like, Calvary-like love to his wife (vv. 25–30). Paul clinches his argument (v. 31) by quoting Gen. 2:24 (LXX). But in a surprise move he suggests that "one flesh" applies ultimately and primarily to Christ and his bride, the Church (v. 32).[9]

That two can become one is, by Paul's own admission, a profound mystery. It may be an equal mystery to us how Paul can so quickly lay aside his point about marriage and draw conclusions about christology and ecclesiology. In calling the two-become-one concept a "mystery," he is presumably using "mystery" precisely as he uses it elsewhere in the book (1:9; 3:3, 4, 9; 6:19). "Mystery" does not mean something that is baffling and defies explanation. Rather, it refers to a truth whose explanation, clarification, and verification is contingent upon the coming and revelation of Christ.

Paul follows his statement, "it [viz., the two shall become one flesh] refers to Christ and the church," with "and I am saying that" *(egṓ dé légō)*. This phrase reminds one of other sayings, such as "I say, not the Lord, that . . ." (1 Cor. 7:12). An even closer parallel is the *egṓ dé légō* formula in the Sermon on the Mount, "*but I say* unto you . . . ," in which Jesus challenges a scriptural interpretation prevalent at that time by offering a different interpretation. Perhaps Paul is similarly challenging current interpretations (esp. Gnostic ones) of the one flesh idea (androgyny to distinction, and now back to androgyny). The *egṓ dé légō* formula may function not so much as polemic but as a way of indicating that in Paul's mind "one flesh" includes, but certainly goes well beyond, the idea of the physical union between a woman and a man.[10]

The important point is that for Paul Gen. 2:24 refers to the archetypal union between Christ and the Church. Moreover, the union between Christ and the Church is also the fulfillment of God's purpose for creation—the uniting of all things in Christ (Eph. 1:10). Believers are to be not only imitators of Christ (5:1–2) but also the historical continuation of his body.

9. The most exhaustive treatment of this pericope in Eph. 5 is J. P. Sampley, *'And The Two Shall Become One Flesh,'* SNTSMS 16 (Cambridge: Cambridge University, 1971). See also M. Barth, *Ephesians 4–6,* AB (Garden City, NY: Doubleday, 1974), pp. 720–38.

10. See A. T. Lincoln, "The Use of the Old Testament in Ephesians," *JSNT* 14 (1982) 33.

C. THE TEMPTATION IN THE GARDEN (3:1–24)

1. THE TEMPTER'S METHODS (3:1–7)

1 *Now the snake was the most cunning creature of the field that Yahweh God had made. He said to the woman, "Indeed! To think*[1] *that God said you are not to eat of any tree of the garden!"*

2 *The woman responded to the snake: "We may eat of the fruit of the trees in the garden;*

3 *it is only the fruit of the tree in the middle of the garden about which God said, 'You shall not eat or touch it, lest you die.' "*

4 *But the snake said to the woman: "Surely you are not going to die!*

5 *Even*[2] *God knows that as soon as you eat of it your eyes will be opened and you will be godlike, knowing good and evil."*

6 *Seeing that the tree was good for food, and a delight*[3] *to the eyes, and that the tree was desirable in acquiring wisdom, she took some of its fruit and ate; she also gave to her husband with her and he ate.*

1. The translation of Heb. *'ap̱ kî* is still open to question. If it functions here simply to introduce a question (cf. AV, RSV, NIV, etc.)—"Did God say?"—then this is the only time in the OT that *'ap̱ kî* carries interrogative force. Skinner (*Genesis,* p. 73) calls the expression "a half-interrogative, half-reflective exclamation," and he translates "Ay, and so God has said!" Von Rad (*Genesis,* p. 86 note) quotes Luther on this passage: "I cannot translate the Hebrew either in German or in Latin; the serpent uses the word *aph-ki* as though to turn up its nose and jeer and scoff at one." This interpretation seems too strong; such open contempt in the serpent's mouth would play against the subtlety that the author is attaching to the serpent's machinations. I prefer to take it as a feigned expression of surprise. So taken, Eve's words in v. 2 become a correction rather than an answer. See J. T. Walsh, "Genesis 2:4b–3:24: A Synchronic Approach," *JBL* 96 (1977) 164.

2. The first *kî* in v. 5 is concessive—"you won't die but (as) God knows. . . ." See A. Schoors, "The Particle *kî,*" *OTS* 26 (1981) 271–73.

3. The word for "delight"—*ta'ᵃwâ*—in v. 6 and the word for "aprons" in v. 7—*ḥᵃgōrōṯ*—have been cited along with others from ch. 3 as providing evidence of the late dating of the whole chapter. G. E. Mendenhall ("The Shady Side of Wisdom: The Date and Purpose of Genesis 3," in *A Light unto My Path,* Fest. Jacob M. Myers, ed. H. N. Bream, et al. [Philadelphia: Temple University, 1974], pp. 319–34) takes the approach that Gen. 3 is a *mashal,* a parable, like Job, written after 587 B.C. Part of his argument is based on the vocabulary of the chapter, which he considers archaic, and the important words of which he finds only in postexilic rather than preexilic sources. In the light of the Ebla texts, however, Mendenhall may need to reconsider his hypothesis. For now Eblaite *da-'à-wa*^{KI}, "beauty, desire," and *ù-gú-ra,* "girdle," provide an early source for Heb. *ta'ᵃwâ* and *ḥᵃgōrōṯ*. See M. J. Dahood, "Eblaite and Biblical Hebrew," *CBQ* 44 (1982) 8 n. 17, 17.

7 *Then the eyes of both of them were opened, and they were aware that they were naked; so they sewed fig leaves together and made aprons for themselves.*

1 This chapter does not refer explicitly to Satan. The tempter is simply called a *nāḥāš,* which is a common Hebrew word for a serpent (e.g., Num. 21:7–9; Deut. 8:15; Prov. 23:32; a total of 31 times in the OT). Possibly there is a connection between *nāḥāš* and *neḥōšeṯ,* "bronze." Indeed, in Num. 21:9 we read that Moses made "a bronze serpent" *(nāḥāš neḥōšeṯ).* Later religious tradition referred to this being as "Nehushtan" *(neḥuštān,* 2 K. 18:4). This connection with bronze suggests a shiny and luminous appearance, which would arrest Eve's attention.

A more directly sinister nuance may be seen in Heb. *nāḥāš* if it is to be connected with the verb *nāḥaš,* "to practice divination, observe signs" (Gen. 30:27; 44:5, 15; Lev. 19:26; Deut. 18:10). This verb appears eleven times in the OT, always in the Piel. The related noun *naḥaš* means "divination" (Num. 23:23; 24:1). Near Eastern divination formulae frequently include procedures involving a serpent.[4]

Instead of giving the name of this serpent, Gen. 3:1 provides two other pieces of information. We are told something about the serpent's character and something about its origin.

First, its character. The serpent is defined as *the most cunning (ʿārûm) creature of the field.* (Note that the acoustical similarity between *ʿārûm,* "cunning," of 3:1 and *ʿarûmîm,* "naked," of 2:25 helps to link the Creation narrative to the Fall narrative.) *ʿārûm* appears nowhere else in Genesis, but it is frequent in Proverbs, where it has the sense "prudent," "shrewd," or "clever." The person possessing this trait is commendable, and he is contrasted with the "fool" (*ʾĕwîl,* 12:16), with the "foolish" one (*kesîl,* 12:23; 13:16; 14:8), or with the "simple" (*peṯî,* 14:15, 18; 22:3; 27:12). By contrast, the two appearances of *ʿārûm* in Job (5:12; 15:5) are pejorative, and the translation "crafty" is preferable. Thus *ʿārûm* is an ambivalent term that may describe a desirable or undesirable characteristic.

Much has been made of the author's decision to describe the serpent as *ʿārûm* rather than *ḥāḵām,* the most *cunning* rather than the "wisest" of all the animals. The suggestions to explain the choice are varied. Is it due to the demythologization process at work in which the shrewd snake replaces the

4. See K. R. Joines, *Serpent Symbolism in the Old Testament* (Haddonfield, NJ: Haddonfield House, 1974), pp. 2–3, 22; G. Contenau, *La Divination chez les Assyriens et les Babyloniens* (Paris: Payot, 1940), p. 222.

wise Canaanite Baal?[5] Or do we discover here a sapiential motif?[6] Or may one explain the choice as due to the fact that *ʿārûm* is a neutral word, one that was originally without special moral connotations.[7] But why apply a word that is without moral connotations to one who is consistently evil? It appears best to take "astute, clever" as an appropriate description of the snake, one that aptly describes its use of a strategy of prudence when it engages the woman in dialogue.

Regarding the serpent's origin, we are clearly told that he was an animal made by God. This information immediately removes any possibility that the serpent is to be viewed as some kind of supernatural, divine force. There is no room here for any dualistic ideas about the origins of good and evil. Clearly Gen. 1–3 makes no room for the idea that in the beginning there were two.

This serpent addresses his first remark to the woman. Why he speaks to her rather than to him, or to both of them, is not clear. In one sense the serpent talks to both the woman and to the man, for *you* in "*you* shall not eat" (vv. 2–3), "*you* shall not touch lest *you* die" (v. 3), "*you* will not die" (v. 4), "when *you* eat of it *you* shall be" (v. 5), is in a plural form of the verb. The woman also acts as spokeswoman on behalf of her husband—"*we* may eat" (v. 2).[8] The suggestions range all the way from the castigation of the woman as the weaker, more vulnerable sex, to the other extreme that, at least in this chapter, she is the more appealing one.[9] While all the suggestions are possible, none can be proved.

But the opening thrust of the serpent's remarks is clear. As we have indicated above, his first words should not be construed as a question but as an expression of shock and surprise. He grossly exaggerates God's prohibi-

5. See F. Hvidberg, "The Canaanite Background of Gen. I–III," *VT* 19 (1960) 288–90.

6. See L. Alonso-Schökel, "Sapiential and Covenant Themes in Genesis 2–3," in *Studies in Ancient Israelite Wisdom,* ed. J. Crenshaw (New York: Ktav, 1976), p. 472.

7. See R. N. Whybray, *The Intellectual Tradition in the Old Testament,* BZAW 135 (Berlin/New York: de Gruyter, 1974), pp. 105–6.

8. J. M. Higgins ("The Myth of Eve: The Temptress," *JAAR* 44 [1976] 639–47, esp. 646–47) presents five reasons for thinking that Adam was present at this dialogue, the most telling being a literal reading of v. 6b—"and she gave also to her husband *with her*" (cf. RSV "and she also gave *some* to her husband").

9. See P. Trible, "Depatriarchalizing in Biblical Interpretation," *JAAR* 41 (1973) 40: "If the serpent is 'more subtle' than its fellow creatures the woman is more appealing than her husband . . . she is the more intelligent one, the more aggressive one, and the one with greater sensibilities."

tion, claiming that God did not allow them access to any of the orchard trees. Apart from this claim being unadulterated distortion, it is an attempt to create in the woman's mind the impression that God is spiteful, mean, obsessively jealous, and self-protective. In addition, it cleverly provides Eve with an opportunity to defend God and to clarify his position, for by this one statement of the snake God has moved from beneficent provider to cruel oppressor. The woman now becomes a partner in what Bonhoeffer has aptly called "the first conversation about God."[10]

2–3 In her response to the serpent, the woman attempts to provide a corrective. But in so doing she repeats, albeit for a different reason, the serpent's tact. That is, she exaggerates. She is correct in her rejoinder regarding accessibility to all the trees in the garden. She makes an addition, however, when she specifies the forbidden fruit to be *the fruit* of the tree in the garden's middle, and she further confuses the matter by putting words in God's mouth—*you shall not . . . touch it.* She has apparently read too much into the prohibition, for "do not eat" has been extended to mean "do not touch." These additions may be only innocent embellishments, but they pave the way for a surrejoinder by the serpent.

4–5 The serpent began with a feigned expression of surprise. Now he moves to a dogmatic assertion. Here is a direct frontal attack on God's earlier threat (2:17) as well as an immediate disclaimer about any truthfulness in Eve's concerns about death.

To buttress his case against God, the serpent appeals to God himself. First he had directed the woman's attention to God's word. Now he directs her attention to God's inner thoughts. Implicit here is the suggestion that the serpent knows God better than the woman does, for he can penetrate his mind and claim to know what God knows.

Also, far from bringing damaging repercussions—so says the snake—disobedience will bring positive blessings. Consumption of the forbidden fruit will make the woman *godlike, knowing good and evil.* Her eyes (and the man's eyes) will be opened.

The whole mixture here of misquotation, denial, and slander fed to the woman by the snake is reinforced even by the ambiguity of the passage in Hebrew. For the phrase *good and evil* may function in apposition to "God"—"you shall be as God *who* knows good and evil." More likely it is to be understood as predicative—"you shall be as God, *that is,* you shall know good and evil." Rather than providing insights about theism to Eve,

10. D. Bonhoeffer, *Creation and Fall,* tr. John C. Fletcher (London: Collins, 1959), p. 70.

the serpent intends to place before her the possibility of being more than she is and more than God intended her to be. As the narrative later makes clear, "eating the fruit is a wrong that brings an advantage, and a gain which brings a disadvantage."[11]

Should she decide to proceed and implement the serpent's suggestion she will begin her heavenward climb. Von Rad is quite correct when he says that "the serpent's insinuation is the possibility of an extension of human existence beyond the limits set for it by God at creation, an increase of life not only in the sense of pure intellectual enrichment but also familiarity with and power over, mysteries that lie beyond man."[12]

Deification is a fantasy difficult to repress and a temptation hard to reject. In the woman's case she need give in to both only by shifting her commitment from doing God's will to doing her own will. Whenever one makes his own will crucial and God's revealed will irrelevant, whenever autonomy displaces submission and obedience in a person, that finite individual attempts to rise above the limitations imposed on him by his creator.

6 The forbidden tree has three commendable virtues. It is physically appealing *(good for food),* aesthetically pleasing *(a delight to the eyes),* and sapientially transforming *(desirable in acquiring wisdom).*[13] Although the text does not inform us how the eating of the tree would make one wise, it strongly suggests that this virtue of the tree was the one that was most attractive.

Indulgence here would give to the woman something she did not, in her judgment, presently possess, and that is wisdom. The text reads literally: "When the woman saw that the tree . . . was desirable [*neḥmāḏ*] in order to become wise." Here is the essence of covetousness. It is the attitude that says I need something I do not now have in order to be happy.

The Bible's first recorded sin is limited to eight words in the Hebrew text: *wattiqqaḥ mippiryô wattōʼḵal wattittēn gam-leʼîšāh ʻimmāh wayyōʼḵal.* Despite the brevity of description, there is a distinctive sonant structure in this verse. The first four words—of which three are *waw*-consecutive imperfects—contain six instances of doubled consonants—"and she took," *wattiqqaḥ;* "of its fruit," *mippiryô;* "and she ate," *wattōʼḵal;* "and she gave," *wattittēn.* Such "extremely difficult pronunciation . . . forces a merciless concentration on each word."[14]

11. See R. Culley, "Action Sequences in Gen. 2–3," in SBLASP, 1978, 1:57.

12. See von Rad, *Genesis,* p. 89.

13. The phrases are those of P. Trible, *God and the Rhetoric of Sexuality,* p. 112.

14. See J. T. Walsh, "Genesis 2:4b–3:24: A Synchronic Approach," *JBL* 96 (1977) 166.

Contrary to popular belief, the text does not specify what fruit the man and the woman ate. The only fruit mentioned in the passage is the fig (v. 7). The time-honored tradition that identifies the fruit as an apple may have originated due to the common sound in Latin *malus,* "evil," and *malum,* "apple."

The woman does not try to tempt the man. She simply gives and he takes. He neither challenges nor raises questions. The woman allows her mind and her own judgment to be her guide; the man neither approves nor rebukes. Hers is a sin of initiative. His is a sin of acquiescence.

7 Instead of knowing good and evil, the couple now know that they are naked. This is hardly the knowledge for which they bargained. What was formerly understood to be a sign of a healthy relationship between the man and the woman (2:25) has now become something unpleasant and filled with shame. Even the word for "naked" in 2:25 *(ʿarûmîm)* is written a bit differently from the one that is used here *(ʿêrummim).*[15]

The couple's solution to this new enigma is freighted with folly. Having committed the sin themselves, and now living with its immediate consequences, i.e., the experience of shame, the loss of innocence *(they were aware that they were naked),* they attempt to alleviate the problem themselves. Rather than driving them back to God, their guilt leads them into a self-atoning, self-protecting procedure: they must cover themselves. The verb *sewed (tāpar)* occurs only three more times in the OT (Job 16:15; Eccl. 3:7; Ezek. 13:18). In Job 16:15 and Ezek. 13:18 it means "to wear" (sackcloth, arm bands, i.e., some kind of clothing that is next to the skin). Why the man and the woman chose *fig leaves* is not clear. The fig tree produces the largest leaves of any tree that grows in Palestine, and if such large-leafed trees were in the garden, then the couple would choose those that provide most coverage. The word we have translated *aprons (ḥagōrōṯ)* is, in other places, an article of woman's dress (Isa. 3:24) or the belt of a warrior (2 Sam. 18:11; 1 K. 2:5; 2 K. 3:21). It could be that the couple provided themselves with one covering, that of fig leaves which they made into an apronlike garment, or else they covered themselves first with foliage, then with skins. In either case, the man and the woman are successful in hiding their nakedness from each other, but that does not exonerate them from their sin of disobedience.

15. But there is no observable difference in meaning between the adjectives *ʿērōm* (3:7) and *ʿārōm* (2:25). See BDB, pp. 735–36.

2. GOD AND MAN MEET IN THE GARDEN (3:8–13)

8 *When they heard the rustling sound*[1] *of Yahweh God as he wandered to and fro in the garden at the cooler time of the day,*[2] *the man and his wife hid themselves from the presence of Yahweh God among the trees of the garden.*

9 *Yahweh God called to the man and said to him, "Where are you?"*

10 *He responded, "Your rustling sound I heard in the garden; but I was afraid because I was naked, so I hid myself."*

11 *He asked, "Who told you that you were naked? Have you eaten from the tree which I commanded you not to eat?"*

12 *The man replied, "The woman whom you placed by me—it was she who gave me fruit from the tree, and I ate."*

13 *Yahweh God said to the woman: "What is this you have done?" The woman replied, "The serpent tricked me, and I ate."*

8 Toward sundown the man and the woman heard Yahweh walking in the garden. The verb used here to describe the divine movement—*miṯhallēḵ*—is a type of Hithpael that suggests iterative and habitual aspects.[3] Such walks would take place in the early evening *(the cooler time of day)* rather than "in the heat of the day" (cf. 18:1).

Far from anticipating another time of fellowship with deity, the couple—who have just previously "hid" their nakedness from each other by clothing themselves—now attempt to hide even from God. Concealment is the order of the day. The narrator refrains from commenting on exactly how one can camouflage himself and thus escape detection by God. Can trees or shrubbery really come between deity and humanity?

9 The Lord addresses a question rather than a command to the

1. Lit., "voice." In poetic texts God's voice is often "thunder" (Ps. 18:14 [Eng. 13]; 46:7 [Eng. 6]; 77:17). It is improbable that the man heard a blast of thunder in the garden, however. 2 Sam. 5:24; 1 K. 14:6; 2 K. 6:32; 11:13 use *qôl* to refer to the sound of marching feet, and most likely we have that idea here.

2. Speiser (*Genesis,* p. 24) notes that the Hebrew preposition *l^e* may be used of time, but not temperature (RSV, "in the cool of the day").

3. See E. A. Speiser, "The Durative Hithpaʿel: A tan-Form," *JAOS* 75 (1955) 118–21, esp. p. 119; W. A. Ward, "Notes on Some Semitic Loan-Words and Personal Names," *Or* 32 (1963) 421 n. 5. GKC, § 54f, suggests that the Hithpael "often indicates an action less directly affecting the subject, and describes it as performed *with regard to* or *for* oneself, in one's own special interest." He cites *hiṯhallēḵ* ("to walk about for oneself") as an illustration of this use of the Hithpael, but he does not connect it with any specific verse.

secluded man, for God "must draw rather than drive him out of hiding."[4] He is the good shepherd who seeks the lost sheep. Such a context calls for a display of tenderness rather than toughness. Had God asked "Why are you hiding?" instead of "Where are you?", his question would have drawn attention to the silliness, stupidity, and futility of the couple's attempt to hide from him. "Where?" is infrequent in the mouth of deity, but compare God's question to Cain about Abel's whereabouts (4:9), and the messenger of the Lord's question to Hagar (16:8). God's question is addressed only to the man, even though both the man and his wife are in hiding. Also in the following verse, the man comments only on his behavior, "I hid myself." He does not incriminate her with "we hid ourselves." We cannot be sure why the Lord questions only the man, but possibly it is because her behavior or action is subsumed in his.

10 The man's response does not answer the question that God asks. Instead, it answers the question: "Why are you hiding?" To be driven into hiding in order to avoid meeting God is abnormal and calls for an explanation. The man, however, partially avoids the real explanation for his hiding. It was not his nakedness and his assumption that in such a state it was inappropriate to meet God that made him hide, for he has taken his fig leaves and apron with him into seclusion. Yes, he had been naked, but it is his fear of the Lord in the same garden that provoked his flight into hiding. It is not necessary for the Lord to speak for the man to panic. It is only necessary that he be present, walking in the garden. The concept of "hiding" (expressed by *ḥāḇā'*) from God is unique to vv. 8 and 10. However, the OT does hold forth the concept of something or somebody being hid from God's eyes. For example, see Gen. 4:14; Isa. 65:16; Jer. 16:17; Hos. 13:14; Ps. 38:10 (Eng. 9), all of which use the verb *sāṯar.* One also thinks of Jonah's attempt to "flee from the presence of the Lord" (Jon. 1:3), or the psalmist who reflects on the impossibility of trying to get to somewhere that God is not (Ps. 139:7–12).

11 The man's response only produces two further questions from God. The first of these questions may seem strange to the reader—*Who told you that you were naked?* Nakedness is not a condition of which one would be ignorant! Was it the serpent who told you? Was it the woman who told you? Was it your own eyes that told you? In other words, whence the man's source of guilt and shame?

4. See D. Kidner, *Genesis,* p. 70. H. Rouillard ("Les feintes questions divines dans la Bible," *VT* 34 [1984] 237–42) identifies the divine questions of Gen. 3:9 and 4:9 as a type of pretense questions which lead to accusation, as opposed to the type of questions in which the deity solicits new information (Gen. 16:8; 18:9).

Rather than pausing for an answer to that question, God follows immediately with a second question. Unlike God's earlier questions, which solicited general information, in this interrogation God becomes prosecutor. But rather than charge the man with transgression, God allows the man himself to acknowledge his crime. Thus this question urges confession rather than condemnation.

12 A simple yes would have got the matter out into the open. But the man becomes devious and defensive. He points the finger of blame both at his spouse—*she . . . gave me*—and at God—*the woman whom you placed by me.* Through rationalization the criminal becomes the victim, and it is God and the woman who emerge as the real instigators in this scenario. Adam plays up their contribution in his demise and downplays his own part. By postponing his own involvement until the last word in the verse, Adam attempts to minimize his part in this sin.

13 The woman's answer to God's question is similar to the man's. She too must exculpate herself. Neither of them exhibits any sign of contrition. Looked at more closely, however, her answer lacks some of the less attractive parts of her spouse's, although she is still, like her husband, defending herself. She does not say "the serpent whom *you* made." Nor does she say "*the man* to whom you gave me." Also, she openly admits that she was tricked or deceived.[5] The serpent, so to speak, fed her a line, presented an attractive proposition, and she bought it.

3. THE CONSEQUENCES OF TRANSGRESSION (3:14–19)

14 *Yahweh God said to the serpent: "Because you have done this, banned shall you be from all cattle and from every creature of the field.*[1] *On your belly shall you crawl, and dust shall you eat all the days of your life.*

5. The verb for "deceive" is *nāšā'*. It is used again, e.g., by Rabshakeh when he says to the people of Jerusalem, "Do not let Hezekiah deceive you, for he will not be able to deliver you out of my hand" (2 K. 18:29 [= Isa. 36:14]), and by the king of Assyria to Hezekiah: "Do not let your God deceive you" (2 K. 19:10 [= Isa. 37:10]). Jeremiah's attribution of such activity to God is electrifying (Jer. 4:10).

1. The traditional translation—"cursed are you above all cattle"—makes little sense, for it implicates all the animals in the serpent's sin, but see GKC, § 119w, for the use of *min* with separating force—"taken from." What is imposed on the serpent is alienation from the other members of the animal world; hence the translation "banned" rather than "cursed." See E. A. Speiser, "An Angelic 'Curse': Exodus 14:20," *JAOS* 80 (1960) 198–200, esp. p. 198; H. C. Brichto, *The Problem of "Curse"*

15 *Hostility will I put between you and the woman, between your offspring and her offspring; it will strike at your head, and you will strike at its heel."*
16 *To the woman he said: "I will intensify your pregnancy pains.*[2] *In pain shall you bear children. Your urge shall be for your husband, but he shall be master over you."*
17 *And to Adam*[3] *he said, "Because you listened to your wife and ate from the tree of which I had forbidden you to eat, cursed is the ground in regard to you.*[4] *In pain shall you eat*[5] *all the days of your life.*
18 *Thorns and thistles shall it bring forth*[6] *for you as you eat of the plants of the field.*
19 *By the sweat of your brow shall you get bread to eat, until you return to the ground, since from it you were taken. For dust you are, and to dust shall you return."*

---

in the Hebrew Bible, JBLMS 13 (Philadelphia: Society of Biblical Literature, 1963), pp. 83–84.

2. Lit., "your pain and your childbearing." The couplet should be understood as a hendiadys by which the two words no longer describe two discrete parts of the pair but a single unit. Dahood has suggested that behind *hērōnēḵ,* "your childbearing," a *hapax legomenon* in the OT, lies not the verb *hārâ,* "to conceive," but putative *hārar,* which in Ugaritic denotes "to desire sexually," and thus he would translate "I will multiply your pangs and your lust." See M. J. Dahood, review of C. Rabin, ed., *Studies in the Bible* (Jerusalem: Magnes, 1961), in *Bib* 43 (1962) 545–46; idem, *Ugaritic-Hebrew Philology,* BibOr 17 (Rome: Pontifical Biblical Institute, 1965), p. 57.

3. Retaining MT *ûl^{e}ʾāḏām* ("to Adam") versus the oft-proposed *w^{e}lāʾāḏām* ("to the man") (cf. *BHS*). The absence of the definite article in the MT indicates that MT read it as a personal name, since a personal name does not take the definite article.

4. I take *baʿ^{a}ḇûreḵā* not as causal, "because of you," but as relational, "in regard to you." The land is rendered recalcitrant to its tilling by the first man.

5. The verb form *tōʾḵ^{a}lennâ* may be parsed as an imperfect with suffix. In this case the translation called for is "in pain shall you eat of *it,*" with "it" referring back to *ʾ^{a}ḏāmâ,* "ground." But obviously man does not eat dirt. One may also parse it as a primitive energic form of the verb without the suffix, of which there are many examples in Ugaritic and some in Biblical Hebrew. This is the form reflected in the above translation. See D. N. Freedman, "Notes on Genesis," *ZAW* 64 (1952) 191; idem, "Archaic Forms in Early Biblical Hebrew," *ZAW* 72 (1960) 101–7, for other instances of verbs with energic *nun* in Biblical Hebrew. The same verb form appears in Ezek. 4:12.

6. MT *taṣmîaḥ,* a Hiphil, is read as a Qal in SP. Thus "thorns" and "thistles" in this version are the subject rather than the object of the verb. Once again Ugaritic offers a parallel, for in that language masc. pl. nouns are treated as collectives and construed with fem. sing. verbs. See W. F. Albright, "The Old Testament and the Canaanite Language and Literature," *CBQ* 7 (1945) 22–23, who cites Nah. 1:5b, 9b with minor emendations in the text.

14 The order of the narration of the sin and the sinner is the reverse of the order in which each comes under God's judgment. The sin of the man (vv. 9–11), the sin of the woman (v. 12), and the sin of the serpent (v. 13) are in a chiastic arrangement with the judgment on the serpent (vv. 14–15), the judgment on the woman (v. 16), and the judgment on the man (vv. 17–19).[7]

To each of the trespassers God speaks a word which involves both a life function and a relationship.[8] Thus, the snake is cursed in his mode of locomotion, and his relationship with the woman and her seed is to be one of hostility. The woman shall experience pain at the point of childbearing, and in relationship to her husband. The man will confront disappointments as a worker through his estrangement from the soil.

But one element distinguishes God's decree to the serpent from his decree to the human couple. It—but not they—is *banned.*[9] This ban involves a unique form of locomotion for the snake—he is to crawl on his belly. This posture will make him eat dust. Such a penalty matches the serpent's sin.[10] He who tempted Eve to *eat* now himself will *eat* dust. He who is *ʿārûm,* "subtle," is now *ʾārûr, banned.* The most subtle of all the animals now becomes the loneliest and oddest of the animals.

Obviously, snakes do not eat dust, and no ancient writer ever thought they did. One has to take this passage symbolically, not literally. Therefore, it is fruitless to see in this particular verse an etiology of why snakes no longer walk on legs and why they lost their legs.[11] If one is prepared to see in the decree *On your belly shall you crawl* a change in the snake's mode of locomotion, then to be consistent one must also see in the decree *dust shall you eat* a change in the snake's diet. The writer clearly intends these two facts

7. See H. Van Dyke Parunak, "Oral Typesetting: Some Uses of Biblical Structure," *CBQ* 62 (1981) 164. These opening paragraphs abound with such literary features. In this same section note in v. 19 the sequence *šûḇᵉḵā ʾel-hāʾᵃḏāmâ kî . . .* and *kî . . . wᵉʾel . . . tāšûḇ* (verb-preposition-particle::particle-preposition-verb).

8. See J. Walsh, *JBL* 96 (1977) 168.

9. One should distinguish between two curse formulae in the OT. The formula used here (and in v. 17; 4:11; 9:25; 49:7; etc.) is one in which no following reason is presented as a cause of the curse. In the other formula ("cursed" followed by either the relative particle and verb, or by the participle) the pronouncement of curse is followed by the act which prompts the curse. See P. Bus, "Deutéronome XXVII 15-26: Malédictions ou exigences de l'alliance?" *VT* 17 (1967) 478–79.

10. For further illustrations of the correspondence between sin and judgment in Gen. 4–11 see P. D. Miller, *Genesis 1–11,* pp. 27–37.

11. Westermann (*Genesis,* 1:259) quotes T. Vriezen: "The presumption clearly is that in primeval time the serpent walked upright on paws." See also Skinner, *Genesis,* pp. 78–79.

to be expressions of humiliation and subjugation (as in Ps. 72:9; Isa. 49:23; Mic. 7:17).

15 This verse is one of the most famous cruxes of Scripture. Interpreters fall into two categories: those who see in the decree a messianic import and those who see nothing of the kind. The more conservative and traditional writers (e.g., Schaeffer, Leupold, Vos, Kidner, Aalders, and Stigers) opt for the first approach, but the bulk of authors in the critical camp (e.g., Skinner, von Rad, Speiser, Vawter, and Westermann) fail to see any promise of a Messiah in this verse and agree that far too much has been read into it. At best, according to this school, the story is an etiological myth that explains why there is hostility between mankind and the serpent world.

At least three difficult issues are involved in this verse: (1) the meaning of the verb that describes what the woman's seed and the serpent's seed shall do to each other; (2) the possibilities involved in the understanding of "offspring"; and (3) the identification of the "it" who is to crush the serpent's head.[12]

First, the question of the verb—"it will *šûp̱* your head and you will *šûp̱* its heel." Presumably we should translate the verb the same way both times, there being no evidence in the Hebrew text to support divergent readings (cf. AV, RSV, NAB, NEB, Speiser). It seems unwise to translate the first *šûp̱* as "crush" and the second as "strike at," as is done in NIV and JB. For this creates the impression that the blow struck at the serpent is fatal—its head is crushed—while the blow unleashed by the serpent against the woman's seed is painful but not lethal—it comes away with a bruised heel. Such a shift in translation is not only artificial, but it forces on the text a focus that is not there. The contrast is not only between *head* and *heel* but between *it* and *you.* Note the prominence given to these pronouns, which in the Hebrew text precede the verb for added emphasis: "*as for it,* it shall. . . ," and "*as for you,* you shall. . . ."

The precedent for translating *šûp̱* in two different ways is the Vulg. rendering. While the LXX chose to translate both times with *tēréō,* "to watch, guard," the Vulg. used *conterero,* "to crush, grind, bruise," the first time, but shifted to *insidior,* "to lie in wait, to lie in ambush, to watch," in the next phrase. This change has led a number of writers to suggest that the second *šûp̱*—what the serpent will do to the woman's seed—is a by-form of *šā'ap̱* I, "to gasp, pant after, long for."[13]

12. See M. Woudstra, "Recent Translations of Genesis 3:15," *CTJ* 6 (1971) 194–203.

13. Skinner (*Genesis,* pp. 80–81) presents some convincing arguments

Another suggestion is to look to Akk. *šâpu,* "to tread with the feet," as the etymological origin of Heb. *šûp*. Hence the obvious translation would be "crush." The problem here is that while "crush with the foot" is an appropriate designation of what a man would do to a snake, it is an inappropriate description of what a snake would do to a person's heel.[14]

The verb in question occurs only two more times in the OT: Job 9:17 and Ps. 139:11. Translations such as AV, RSV, and JB opt for "cover" in Ps. 139:11, with a footnote in JB that "cover" is the reading in Symmachus and Jerome, but the Hebrew is "crush." These same versions read "crush" in Job 9:17. Dahood appeals to Arab. *šāfa,* "he watches, looks," however, and translates both passages with "observe."[15]

In order to maintain the duplication of the Hebrew verb, whatever English equivalent one decides on must be used twice. We have already suggested a reason why "crush" would not be appropriate. *strike at* covers adequately the reciprocal moves of the woman's seed and the serpent's seed against each other rather than something like: "He shall lie in wait for your head" and "you shall lie in wait for his heel."

We turn now to a discussion of *offspring* or "seed." This divinely ordained hostility is one that takes place between the serpent's seed and the seed of the woman. In the vast majority of cases where *zeraʿ* (lit., "seed") refers to an individual child, it refers to an immediate offspring rather than a distant descendant. For example, Seth is Eve's "other seed" (4:25); Abram laments that he is still without seed (15:3); Lot's daughters want to bear their father's seed (19:32, 34); Ishmael is Abraham's seed (21:13); Onan refuses the chance to father a child for his sister-in-law Tamar (38:8–9); Samuel is Hannah's seed (1 Sam. 1:11; 2:20); Solomon is David's seed (2 Sam. 7:12).[16] This observation alone should caution us about seeing too quickly a clear-cut reference here to some remote individual.

---

against this possibility. *šā'ap* may sometimes be a by-form of *šûp,* but it is unlikely that *šûp* is a by-form of *šā'ap*. Skinner allows for this possibility only in Job 9:17.

14. W. Wifall ("Gen. 3:15—A Protevangelium?" *CBQ* 36 [1974] 364) agrees with the Akkadian source and points out that in older English "to foot" was a transitive verb with double meaning, "to tread upon" and "to seize." So he translates: "he shall tread upon your head and you shall seize his heel." G. R. Driver ("Some Hebrew Verbs, Nouns, and Pronouns," *JTS* 30 [1929] 375–77) appeals to Syriac to support the translation "he shall graze your head and you shall graze his heel," but more than grazing is implied.

15. Dahood, *Psalms,* 3:291.

16. The NT's application of 2 Sam. 7:12 to Jesus, and not only to Solomon (see Heb. 1:5), supplies one instance where *zeraʿ* points to a distant descendant. For Jesus as the "seed of David" see Rom. 1:3; 2 Tim. 2:8.

Similarly, one should not force an interpretation on *her offspring* that the expression cannot bear. The LXX translates Heb. *zarʿāh* (lit., "her seed") as *spérmatos autḗs* (lit., "her seed"), and the Vulg. as *semen illius* (also lit., "her seed"), but to read the LXX as "her sperm" and the Vulg. as "her semen" (an oxymoron if there ever was one!) in order to see a hint here of the virgin birth of this seed (the absence of a sperm-supplying father) is farfetched indeed.[17] If for no other reason, Gen. 4:25 would invalidate that proposal, for here Eve says that God has given her "another seed," and certainly Seth was not born of a virgin!

Nevertheless, in a number of passages Heb. *zeraʿ* is a collective referring to distant offspring or a large group of descendants (Gen. 9:9; 12:7; 13:16; 15:5, 13, 18; 16:10; 17:7–10, 12; 21:12; 22:17–18). Although most modern translations use a plural for these references—"descendants"—the Hebrew itself never uses the plural. A translation like "posterity, offspring" captures the collective sense of *zeraʿ* more accurately. It would be difficult to prove that the word is flexible enough to denote both a group of descendants and an individual who is representative of that group.[18] At least one is hard-pressed to find examples of this flexibility in the OT itself, except for Gen. 3:15—if one follows the *zarʿāh* with "he," and this leads us to the third issue in this verse.

The question is: How should we translate the anticipatory *hûʾ* in "*it* will strike at your head"—"he" or "they" or "it"? The ancient versions offer various alternatives. Few are inclined to follow Vulg. *ipsa,* "she" (!). LXX has *autós,* "he," even though the antecedent is *spérmatos,* which is neuter in Greek. One might have expected *autó* instead of *autós.* The LXX seems to have had a messianic understanding of the verse, for, as has been pointed out, the independent personal pronoun *hûʾ* occurs more than one hundred times, but this is the only one that the LXX translates literally with *autós,* although the Greek idiom would require the neuter.[19] Nevertheless, one must decide whether the LXX should be allowed to carry so much weight here and whether it offers the correct understanding of the original intention of Gen. 3:15.

We may want to be cautious about calling this verse a messianic prophecy. At the same time we should be hesitant to surrender the time-

17. F. Schaeffer, *Genesis in Space and Time* (Downers Grove, IL: Inter-Varsity, 1972), p. 103.

18. As argued by W. C. Kaiser, *"zāraʿ," TWOT,* 1:253.

19. See R. A. Martin, "The Earliest Messianic Interpretation of Genesis 3:15," *JBL* 84 (1965) 425–27; W. C. Kaiser, *Toward an Old Testament Theology* (Grand Rapids: Zondervan, 1978), pp. 36–37.

honored expression for this verse—*the protevangelium,* "the first good news." The verse is good news whether we understand *zeraʿ* singularly or collectively. The following words of God to the woman and the man include expressions both of divine grace and of divine judgment. Yes, there will be pain for Eve, but she is promised children. Sterility will not be one of her problems. Yes, there will be frustration for Adam because of intractable soil, but he will eat and not starve to death.

One may surmise, therefore, that God's speech to the serpent contains both judgment and promise. Indeed, the serpent is banned and he becomes a crawler. He is under judgment. The promise is that some unspecified member(s) of the human race will one day lash out against this serpent's seed. More than a change in the serpent's position is involved here—it is now a question of his existence.

Would this individual, or these individuals, be among the kings of Israel and Judah who are the "offspring" of their father (2 Sam. 7:12; Ps. 89:5 [Eng. 4]), who "crush" their enemies (Ps. 89:24 [Eng. 23]) "under their feet" (2 Sam. 22:39), so that these enemies "lick the dust" (Ps. 72:9)? Later revelations will state that it is Jesus who reigns until he puts all his enemies under his feet (1 Cor. 15:25).[20]

16 The previous verse sounded a positive note about the seed of the woman who would strike at the serpent's seed. The coming of this seed, however, will not be without pain and discomfort. For the woman who is destined to conceive (v. 15) will give birth in agony.[21] At the point in her life when a woman experiences her highest sense of self-fulfillment (according to OT emphases), she will have some physical anguish. Note, however, that the woman is not cursed with infertility, which would have been the result had God pronounced the same curse on the woman as he did on the serpent. Childlessness is not her lot.

Quite clearly this verse, and the ones immediately following, teach

20. Wifall ("Gen. 3:15—A Protoevangelium?" *CBQ* 36 [1974] 361–65) allows for a messianic interpretation of Gen. 3:15, but only if the verse is seen in the context of Israel's royal ideology. For him the verse is anything but a direct prediction. I am most comfortable with LaSor's use of the verse as an illustration of *sensus plenior:* "I do find the fullness of meaning [viz., of Gen. 3:15] in some as-yet-unspecified member of the human race who would destroy the satanic serpent, thus playing a key role in God's redemptive plan. In that sense, the passage is indeed the first enunciation of the good news" (W. S. LaSor, "Prophecy, Inspiration, and *Sensus Plenior,*" *TynBul* 29 [1978] 56–57).

21. Note the poetical feature of a plethora of words (5 of 16) in this verse ending in *-k: ʿiṣṣᵉḇônēḵ wᵉhērōnēḵ . . . ʾîšēḵ tᵉšûqāṯēḵ . . . bāḵ.*

that sin has its consequences. It is less clear whether God describes or prescribes these consequences. In other words, are these negative consequences engineered directly by God, or is God simply informing the woman the way it is to be from this moment on? Perhaps this question is inappropriate, for it may assume ways of thinking that are alien to the ancient Hebrew mind. That is, it is difficult to conceive of an ancient Israelite who did not attribute all phenomena in life to God.

The point that is apparent is that sin and disobedience do not go unchecked and unchallenged. Is it not surprising in a chapter of the Bible so widely accepted as mythical that we find the classical outline of salvation history rather than myths?[22] God acts and speaks; man rebels; God punishes; God protects and reconciles.

In God's second word to the woman one does hope that God is speaking descriptively and not prescriptively. For this consequence deals with a marriage relationship that will go askew: the woman shall desire her husband but he shall lord it over her.

The Hebrew word for *urge* or "desire," *t*e*šûqâ,* occurs only here and in Gen. 4:7 and Cant. 7:11 (Eng. 10). In the Canticles reference it has a decidedly romantic and positive nuance, describing a feeling of mutual attraction between two lovers: "I am my beloved's, and his desire is for me." In Gen. 4:7 it describes sin's "desire" for man. This desire man is to repulse and dominate. Interestingly, in all three instances the LXX has *hē apostrophḗ,* "return," apparently reading *t*e*šûḇâ* for *t*e*šûqâ.* Perhaps the LXX failed to understand the Hebrew word correctly.[23]

Given the pairing of *t*e*šûqāṯô* and *timšōl* in 4:7, one suspects that the pairing of *t*e*šûqāṯēḵ* and *yimšāl* should carry the same force, whatever that is. Here is a case where the clear meaning of 4:7 illuminates a less clear meaning of 3:16. What 4:7 describes is sin's attempt to control and dominate Cain. Because his offering has been rejected by God he is seething with anger. In such an emotional state he is easy prey for sin which crouches lionlike and

22. See L. Alonso-Schökel, "Sapiential and Covenant Themes in Genesis 2–3," in *Studies in Ancient Israelite Wisdom,* ed. J. Crenshaw (New York: Ktav, 1976), p. 474.

23. See R. Bergmeier, "Zur Septuagintaubersetzung von Gen. 3:16," *ZAW* 79 (1967) 77–79. Actually *apostrophḗ* occurs here and in Gen. 4:7, while *epistrophḗ* occurs in Cant. 7:10. G. W. H. Lampe (*A Patristic Greek Lexicon* [Oxford: Clarendon, 1961/1968]) lists for *epistrophḗ*: (1) conversion (religious); (2) reform amendment; (3) correction; (4) conversion of inferior being to the attraction of a superior being (p. 536). For *apostrophḗ* Lampe (p. 214) lists: (1) turning away; (2) deterrent; (3) gift, contribution.

waits to jump on him. Cain is to fight back, turn the tables, and dominate sin and its desire.

Applied to 3:16, the desire of the woman for her husband is akin to the desire of sin that lies poised ready to leap at Cain. It means a desire to break the relationship of equality and turn it into a relationship of servitude and domination.[24] The sinful husband will try to be a tyrant over his wife.[25] Far from being a reign of co-equals over the remainder of God's creation, the relationship now becomes a fierce dispute, with each party trying to rule the other. The two who once reigned as one attempt to rule each other.

17–19 The opening chapters of Genesis heavily emphasize "the east." Yahweh God planted a garden in the east (2:8). The Tigris flows east of Assyria (2:13). He drove man eastward of Eden (3:24). Cain dwelt in the land of Nod, east of Eden (4:16). The Shemites dwelt from Mesha to Sephar, the hill country of the east (10:30). Men migrated from the east to the land of Shinar (11:2). This geographical emphasis, plus other factors, has suggested to scholars that Gen. 1–11 is set against the background of Mesopotamia.[26] If so, the word from God to man about the struggle for food seems strange, for most of Mesopotamia was fertile, especially the more southern areas.[27] A Canaanite background seems more appropriate for this curse. Then again, the emergence of agricultural hardship may be both deliberate and ironic. In a land normally characterized by plenty there will be scarcity.

The man's sin was that he *ate* (3:6, 12). Again, God's word of judgment matches the sin. In response to the man's trespass of eating, God speaks no less than five times of eating in his word to the man (vv. 17 [3 times], 18, 19). Thus the penalty on the man parallels the penalty on the serpent. To both God says a word about their eating.

Similarly, God's word to the man parallels his word to the woman, for in the experiences of both there will be *pain* (Heb. *ʿiṣṣāḇôn*). For her the

24. See S. T. Foh, "What Is the Woman's Desire?" *WTJ* 37 (1975) 376–83.

25. P. P. Saydon ("The Conative Imperfect in Hebrew," *VT* 12 [1962] 124–26) applies a conative meaning (i.e., one that expresses not fact, but attempt or endeavor) to Gen. 3:15, "he will attack you in the head, and you will try to attack him in the heel." There may be a similar conative imperfect here—"and he shall try to rule over you." This meaning removes indicative force from *yimšāl*.

26. See W. W. Hallo, "Biblical History in Its Near Eastern Setting: The Contextual Approach," in *Scripture in Context: Essays on the Comparative Method,* ed. C. Evans, et al., PTMS 4 (Pittsburgh: Pickwick, 1980), pp. 1–26. He divides Genesis geographically as follows: chs. 1–11, Mesopotamia; chs. 12–36, Syria-Palestine; and chs. 37–50, Egypt (p. 15).

27. See J. L. McKenzie, "The Literary Characteristics of Genesis 2–3," *TS* 15 (1954) 566.

pain will be connected with childbearing, and for him the pain will be connected with food. *ʿiṣṣāḇôn* and the verb *ʿāṣaḇ* obviously refer to physical pain, but they also embrace the concept of anguish, as is obvious in verses like Gen. 6:6 (God's anguish); 45:5 (the distress of Joseph's brothers); 1 Sam. 19:3 (Eng. 2) (David in grief). In fact, BDB, p. 780, lists only Eccl. 10:9 as an illustration of *ʿāṣaḇ* meaning physical pain.

To be sure, God's word to the man, unlike his word to the woman, is free from any sexual motif. This difference hardly indicates that the judgment on the man was not present in the preliterary story of the sin.[28] Both divine messages are directed to a point of highest fulfillment in the life of the female and the male. For the female that is, among other areas, her capacity of mother and wife.[29] For the male that is, among other areas, his capacity of breadwinner and family provider.

By the sweat of your brow shall you get bread. The lot of man is to be one of toil, working often with a recalcitrant soil (*Thorns and thistles,* v. 18). This is to be a permanent situation, as v. 19 indicates *(until you return to the ground).* Relief from this situation comes only when man dies.

The question involved in the interpretation of v. 19b is whether it teaches that natural death (i.e., mortality) too is a punishment for sin. The majority of commentators understand this verse to say that death is a respite, an eventual freedom and release from the subsidiary existence which is to be man's lot in this life.[30]

Leaving aside for the moment Paul's observation that death came into the world through sin (Rom. 5:12), one may raise two possible objections to this understanding. First, the theme of the larger context for v. 19b (i.e., vv. 14–19) is the ruinous consequences of sin. The context should assist in the shaping of our interpretation. Is it not logical to see everything in this unit as contributing to the elucidation of that theme? To this we would respond by agreeing that vv. 17–19 do indeed deal with the consequences of sin. For the man that consequence is work that is toilsome. The further qualification is made in v. 19b-c that such circumstances shall be with the man for his whole

28. As argued by McKenzie, ibid.

29. Westermann, *Genesis,* 1:263: "just where the woman finds her fulfillment in life, her honor and joy, namely in her relationship to her husband and as mother of her children, there too she finds that it is not pure bliss, but pain, burden, humiliation and subordination."

30. "Death . . . is not viewed as part of man's punishment. . . . Death is simply the termination of man's life of toil" (Vawter, *On Genesis,* p. 85); see also von Rad, *Genesis,* p. 95; Skinner, *Genesis,* p. 84; Westermann, *Creation,* p. 103; idem, *Genesis,* 1:266.

life. He will never be free of fatigue and toil. There is no evidence in the text that any repentance by the man can lift or remove these circumstances. They will be part and parcel of his life until he returns to the ground.[31]

Second, Walsh maintains that many translations miss the force of the Hebrew construction here. For example, RSV "you are dust and to dust you shall return" is possible only by ignoring the initial *kî* (here translated *For;* cf. also NEB). Other translations read more literally: "For (because) dust you are, and to dust you shall return" (JB, Speiser, NAB, NIV). These last two lines, as translated, do not appear to make sense: "because dust you are, *and* to dust you shall return." Walsh therefore suggests that the "and" in the second clause be understood as a *waw apodosis,* which then makes this clause the major conclusion rather than a supplement. In effect, v. 19b "thus forms the climactic decree of the monologue of judgement."[32] Two comments may be made on Walsh's suggestion. First, if Walsh faults the RSV and NEB for not translating the opening *kî,* his own translation may be faulted for not translating the *waw* on *weʾel.* A prepositional phrase followed by a regular Qal imperfect, as we have here, does not appear to fall within the type of coordinate clause introduced by a *waw apodosis.* Second, if one faults the sentence "For dust you are, and to dust you shall return" as lacking any meaning, then how does "since dust you are, to dust you shall return" improve the sense?

We note also the absence of *môṯ* ("die") anywhere in vv. 17–19. The penalty for Adam's disobedience and Cain's fratricide is not death but expulsion and wandering, i.e., removal from the safety of the garden and exposure to a life of severity and uncertainty.

4. A NEW NAME AND A NEW COVERING (3:20–21)

20 *The man called his wife's name "Eve," for she was to be the mother of all living.*

21 *Yahweh God made for Adam and his wife coats of skin and clothed them.*

20 This verse has at least three problems. (1) In what sense was Eve "the mother of all living"? (2) How may "Eve" be connected etymologically with "life"? (3) Is this verse misplaced, and if not, how does it fit in its immediate context?

31. For *šûḇ* as "return [at death] to" see W. L. Holladay, *The Root Šûbh in the Old Testament* (Leiden: Brill, 1958), pp. 74, 96.

32. Walsh, *JBL* 96 (1977) 168 n. 20. The *waw apodosis* is discussed in GKC, § 143d, but this verse is not cited.

(1) The text says Eve *was (hāyᵉṯâ)* the mother of all living. But she has yet to give birth to a second generation! Might we not have expected the imperfect *tihyeh,* "she will be"? One may explain the perfect form in two ways: as a prophetic perfect or as a precative (optative) perfect. Sometimes Hebrew uses a perfect to express future action. Such usage is called a prophetic perfect, for the use of the perfect reinforces the certainty of the distant fact. It is as good as done (e.g., 17:16).[1] Scholars debate whether Biblical Hebrew has a precative perfect, though Ugaritic has one.[2] Is it Adam's prayer that his wife will become a mother? The prophetic perfect is more likely here, if only to express a fact which was imminent in the imagination of the narrator.

(2) This issue concerns the etymology of *Eve.* Undoubtedly v. 20 connects *Eve (ḥawwâ)* with *living* or "life" *(ḥāy).* But the word *ḥawwâ* assumes that the Hebrew verb "to live" is *ḥawwâ,* when in fact it is *ḥāyâ,* that is, medial *y* rather than medial *w.*

If one abandons the equation between "Eve" and "to live," one has many other choices for an etymology of *ḥawwâ.* Thus KB list no fewer than nine possible etymologies, but they decline to make a choice.[3] Whether one of these etymologies should be pursued for further significance is unlikely. If indeed "Eve" is to be connected with the Aramaic word for "serpent" or with the "Hivites," such connections will probably tell us little about the meaning of "Eve" in 3:20.

The connection between "Eve" and "life" must not be jettisoned prematurely and dismissed as just another example of popular etymology. Indeed, her name may reflect a primitive form of the Hebrew verb "to live" with medial *w* instead of *y.* The evidence here is the Ugaritic verb "to live": *ḥwy/ḥyy.*[4] What is clear from the Ras Shamra texts is that the verb there appears with the medial *y* only in the Qal stem. By contrast, in the Piel stem

1. See GKC, § 106n; J. W. Watts, *A Survey of Syntax in the Hebrew Old Testament* (Grand Rapids: Eerdmans, 1964), pp. 39–40; R. J. Williams, *Hebrew Syntax: An Outline,* 2nd ed. (Toronto: University of Toronto, 1976), § 165.

2. The perfect used optatively in Ugaritic may be illustrated by *UT,* 51:IV:41–42: *tḥmk il ḥkm hkmt/k ʿm ʿlm ḥyt ḥẓt,* "Your decree, O El, is extremely wise, for ever may you live [*ḥyt*] and prosper [*ḥẓt*]." Cf. *UT,* p. 115, § 13.28.

3. See KB, pp. 280–81. The updating of this lexicon (*Hebräisches und Aramäisches Lexicon zum Alten Testament,* 3rd ed. [Leiden: Brill, 1967], 1:284 adds little that is new and is content to say "etym. inc." See also A. Kapelrud, *"chavvāh," TDOT,* 4:257–60.

4. On the one hand, G. R. Driver, *Canaanite Myths and Legends* (Edinburgh: T. & T. Clark, 1956), p. 139, lists the root as *ḥwy* with a by-form *ḥyy.* On the other hand, C. H. Gordon in *UT,* p. 396, no. 856, lists the root as *ḥyy* with a by-form *ḥwy.*

the verb appears only with medial *w*.[5] Furthermore, the Piel stem has a factitive meaning—"to give life, preserve." The same is true in Phoenician. Thus it is quite possible that Heb. *ḥawwâ* reflects this feature and as a *qaṭṭal* type noun means "life-giver."[6]

(3) Finally, what about the whole verse and its positioning here? The man has already called her "woman" (2:23); why a double naming? Also, everything preceding and following this verse is negative; what is this intrusive positive note doing here? Again, would this verse be more appropriate after, say, 4:1, the birth of Cain?

In an attempt to be faithful to the context, F. Zimmermann sees the verse as a judgment and condemnation by Adam on Eve. To reach that conclusion he connects "Eve" with Arab. *ḥavvah,* "be empty, fail," and so "Eve" means "emptiness, hunger, deprivation, ruin" (thus KB's 9 possibilities for the etymological background of Eve become 10!). Eve has brought Adam from Eden to emptiness.[7] Traveling a different route, Phyllis Trible condemns Adam for this act of name giving. Adam ironically calls Eve "life" and then robs her of life and reduces her to the status of an animal by calling her a name.[8] A. J. Williams sees irony in this verse too, but irony of a different type. As he understands it, even having to bear children is part of the divine penalty, but it is also a blessing, for it is the only way the human race can survive outside the garden.[9]

Both von Rad and Westermann emphasize that the verse is appropriately placed and functions in the first place as a promise from God. In spite of man's sin and disobedience, God's original command to man to multiply

5. See D. Marcus, "The Verb 'To Live' In Ugaritic," *JSS* 17 (1972) 76–82.

6. See I. Kikawada, "Two Notes on Eve," *JBL* 91 (1972) 34 n. 9.

7. F. Zimmermann, "Folk etymology of Biblical names," in *Volume du Congrès: Geneva, 1965,* VTSup 15 (Leiden: Brill, 1966), pp. 316–18.

8. P. Trible, *God and the Rhetoric of Sexuality,* p. 133; cf. idem, "Eve and Adam: Genesis 2–3 Reread," *ANQ* 13 (1973) 254, 258, where she contrasts the name-calling formula used in 2:23 with that used in 2:19, 20; 3:20; 4:17, 25, 26. See also Vawter, *On Genesis,* p. 86: "it has been placed as immediately as possible after the lines that proclaimed woman's condition as one of subjection to her husband, and namegiving is . . . the prerogative of one in dominance." For an opposing interpretation see G. W. Ramsey, "Is Name-Giving an Act of Domination in Genesis 2:23 and Elsewhere?" *CBQ* 50 (1988) 24–35.

9. A. J. Williams, "The Relationship of Genesis 3:20 to the Serpent," *ZAW* 89 (1977) 357–74. Then what does Williams do with the command to humanity in ch. 1 to be fruitful, unless he sees a disagreement between J, for whom fertility is a divine penalty, and P, for whom fertility is a divine mandate?

and be fruitful is not withdrawn.[10] In the second place Adam's naming is an act of faith on his part. Though threatened by death Adam does not believe that he and his wife are to be the first and last beings of the human race. Motherhood will emerge.[11]

Such an interpretation nicely balances the emphasis in the following verse. Just as Adam renames his spouse, so God reclothes the couple themselves. *'iššâ* gives way to *ḥawwâ,* and rudimentary clothing gives way to divinely provided leather tunics. Both actions speak of a future for the individual(s) beyond the miserable present.

21 This verse should not be read as an awkward doublet of v. 7. It serves as a contrast with v. 7, the covering of fig leaves versus the covering with tunics of animal skins. The first is an attempt to cover oneself, the second is accepting a covering from another. The first is manmade and the second is God made. Adam and Eve are in need of a salvation that comes from without. God needs to do for them what they are unable to do for themselves.

It is important for understanding the drift of this chapter that we note that the clothing precedes the expulsion from the garden. God's act of grace comes before his act of judgment. The couple are not expelled nude from the garden. They are not sent beyond the garden totally vulnerable. In the same way Cain is marked before he is exiled (4:15), and God announces the post-Flood covenant even before the Flood commences (6:18).

It is probably reading too much into this verse to see in the *coats of skin* a hint of the use of animals and blood in the sacrificial system of the OT cultus.[12] The word we have translated *coats* is the one that is used to describe the garment Jacob made for Joseph (e.g., 37:3). It is true that the word *skin* here refers to animal skins, and we do have in Genesis itself the idea of animal skins as coverings. See 27:16, where Rebekah "put on" (same verb as here) the hands and neck of Jacob "the skins of the kids" so that Jacob would feel like and smell like Esau to Isaac. But *keṯōneṯ* is more than simply a covering. It is an actual robelike garment worn next to one's skin. Both men (2 Sam. 15:32) and women (2 Sam. 13:18, 19; Cant. 5:3) could wear it (cf. Gen. 3:21). A *keṯōneṯ* was also one of the garments worn by the priests, and it was made from linen (Exod. 28:39; 39:27).

10. C. Westermann, *Creation,* p. 104.
11. Von Rad, *Genesis,* p. 96.
12. F. Schaeffer, *Genesis in Space and Time,* pp. 105–6.

5. EXPULSION FROM THE GARDEN (3:22–24)

22 *Yahweh God said, "See! The man has become like one of us in knowing*[1] *good and evil. Now, lest he put forth his hand and take also of the tree of life, and eat, and live forever . . ."*[2]

23 *So Yahweh God expelled him from the garden of Eden to till the ground from which he was taken.*

24 *Having driven out the man, he stationed east of the garden of Eden the cherubim and the fiery whirling sword*[3] *to guard the way to the tree of life.*

22 This verse is a deliberation. God dialogues with himself and observes that man has become *like one of us in knowing good and evil.* In one sense, but in only one sense, what the serpent said was true. Man has become like God. But one suspects that these words in the serpent's mouth convey one thing and the same words in God's mouth say another. The serpent held out to the couple the prospect that being like God would bring with it unlimited privileges, unheard-of acquisitions and gifts.

Alas, rather than experiencing bliss, they encounter misery. Rather than sitting on a throne, they are expelled from the garden. Rather than new prerogatives, they experience only a reversal. The couple not only fail to gain something they do not presently have; the irony is that they lose what they currently possess: unsullied fellowship with God. They found nothing and lost everything.

In our earlier discussion of 1:26 we have already commented on the use of *us* in reference to God. There we advanced the reasons why it is unlikely that the plural pronoun suggests God's speaking to the heavenly council, be that council composed of gods or of angels.[4] In addition to that

1. For *l* followed by an infinitive construct in a sentence in which a comparison is made and which defines the character of this comparison, see 2 Sam. 14:17 *(lišmōaʿ)* and 14:25 *(lᵉhallēl).* See J. Hoftijzer, "David and the Tekoite Woman," *VT* 20 (1970) 440 n. 4.

2. The sentence does not run on as a continuous whole. The RSV and other translations correctly read the verse as such and punctuate with a final dash. It is better to see the verse as an instance of anacoluthon. In effect, then, the sentence becomes not a statement as such but rather a divine deliberation, a kind of internal dialogue, of which Gen. 3–11 has at least 6 illustrations: here, 6:3, 7; 8:21–22; 11:6–7. See D. Patrick, *The Rendering of God in the Old Testament,* OBT 10 (Philadelphia: Fortress, 1981), pp. 19–20.

3. Lit., "the flame of the sword turning this way and that" (see BDB, pp. 246, 529).

4. Indeed, in some Ugaritic texts the 1st person pl. is characteristic of address

discussion, we need to note that in both the OT and the NT, as well as in nonbiblical texts, it was not unusual in referring to one person to oscillate between a singular and a plural. An individual could be addressed as "he" or "they," or a person could refer to himself as "I" or "we" (cf. Mark 5:1ff., esp. v. 9—"*My* name is Legion; for *we* are many").[5]

It is not clear whether the last half of the verse prohibits man from starting to eat or from continuing to eat. Taken by itself the wording of v. 22 could suggest that man has not yet eaten of the tree of life. How else is one to explain the use of *also* (Heb. *gam*) in the verse? And where *gam* was used earlier in the narrative (3:6), it implied new and additional activity—"she gave also to him."[6] Yet nowhere in the previous dialogue did God forbid access to the tree of life. Thus the divine prohibition in this verse has nothing to do with God's jealous protection and hoarding of divine prerogatives. God should not be diminished into something less than human!

23–24 God was concerned that the man might "put forth" *(šālaḥ)* his hand; so God *expelled* or put him out *(šālaḥ)* of the garden. The same Hebrew verb designates what man might do and what God did do (although the stem used in v. 22 is Qal and that used in v. 23 is Piel). Another repeated verb in vv. 22 and 23 is "take"—"lest he . . . take [*lāqaḥ* in the Qal] also of the tree of life" and "the ground from which he was taken [*lāqaḥ* in the Pual]."

The Qal and Piel of *šālaḥ* often do not seem to be distinguished. Thus Noah "sends out" *(šālaḥ* in the Piel) various birds from the ark (8:7, 8, 12), but he hardly expelled or banished the birds from the ark. In these Gen. 8 references the Piel of *šalaḥ* means simply "to send (forth)." But since here *šālaḥ* parallels *gāraš,* "to drive out, expel," we are obligated to translate it more strongly than simply "send," hence our choice of *expelled.* The verb *gāraš* in the Qal may mean "to drive out" (Exod. 34:11) or "to divorce" (Lev.

---

in the heavenly council. Cf. Asherah's speech to the assembly of El: *nmlk,* "let us make (him) king" (*UT,* 49:I:20, 26), and El's decree to the assembly: *mlkn 'al'iy[n] bʿl ṯpṭn w'in dʿlnh,* "our king is 'Al'iyan Baal; our judge without peer" (*UT,* 51:IV: 43–44; ʿnt V:40–41). To see such texts as the background for the "us" of Gen. 1:26; 3:22; and 11:7 means that an unabashed evidence of the polytheistic background of Gen. 1–11 has been left unedited. This is surprising when it seems that the writer did not hesitate to demythologize other forms of milder pagan vestiges. Why would he leave this blatant one untouched?

5. See A. R. Johnson, *The One and the Many in the Israelite Conception of God,* 2nd ed. (Cardiff: University of Wales, 1961), pp. 27–28.

6. G. Vos (*Biblical Theology,* p. 38) suggests that "the tree was associated with the higher, the unchangeable, the eternal life to be secured by obedience throughout the probation."

21:7, 14; 22:13). In the Piel, as here, *gāraš* is often used to refer to the driving out of the nations before Israel as she moves toward her occupation of the land of promise (Exod. 23:28–30; 33:2; Num. 22:11; Deut. 33:27; Judg. 2:3; 6:9; etc.).

The juxtaposition of these two verbs reinforces the idea that man does not leave the garden of his own will. Nor is he gently escorted to the garden's edge. In fact, he is thrown out! Sin separates from God. Intimacy with God is replaced with alienation from God. The intensity of the situation is highlighted in this prose text by the use of repetition and synonymous parallelism *(šālaḥ/gāraš),* devices one normally associates with poetry.

The expulsion of man from the garden is not an ad hoc arrangement. Something is done which cannot be undone, at least not immediately. God stations *the cherubim and the fiery whirling sword* east of the garden of Eden to prevent reentry to the garden, as if reentry into the garden is only through an opening on its east side, much as the entrance into the tabernacle/temple complex was by a gate on the eastern side. In such a capacity the cherubim function much like the later Levites who are posted as guards around the tabernacle, and who are to strike down any person who encroaches upon the forbidden sancta (Num. 1:51, 53).

Only here in the OT do the cherubim engage in police activity. All OT references to the cherubim suggest, directly or indirectly, that the cherubim are symbols of God's presence. They guard the garden of Eden, but they do not guard God. They are his means of locomotion (2 Sam. 22:11; Ps. 18:11 [Eng. 10]). In a stationary position he sits enthroned upon them (1 Sam. 4:4; 2 Sam. 6:2; 2 K. 19:15; Isa. 37:16; Ps. 80:2 [Eng. 1]; 99:1). The reference here is to the two cherubim facing one another on the two ends of the covering above the ark in the tabernacle and temple. They also represent the presence of God with his captured peoples in Babylon (Ezek. 1). Etymologically Heb. *kᵉrûḇîm* is likely to be associated with Akk. *kāribu/kurību,* from *karābu,* "to pray, to bless." No evidence suggests that the Israelites thought that cherubim had intercessory functions.

So then, man leaves the garden, and the opening behind him is barred. Paradise has been lost and forfeited. Christian theologians traditionally refer to this event as "the Fall." As an extension of this event there emerges the doctrine of "original sin." Given the OT's emphasis on corporate personality, the sins of the fathers being visited unto subsequent generations, it is perhaps surprising that the OT says virtually nothing about Adam or Eve after Gen. 5. For example, the prophets do not hesitate to draw on the catastrophe at Sodom and Gomorrah to illustrate the consequences of disobedience, but they never use the story of the expulsion from Eden to draw a similar analogy.

As a matter of fact, one must wait until Rom. 5 and 1 Cor. 15 for an extensive discussion of Adam.

Not all commentators agree that Gen. 3 describes a "fall." Thus Westermann can say, "There is but one question which determines the course of the narrative: why is man, created by God, a man who is limited by death, suffering, toil and sin?"[7] According to Westermann, to see in the text any doctrine of the transmission of sin, or the fall from original righteousness, is to read into the text something that it does not claim.

Others have suggested that Gen. 3 describes not a fall but a rise. For example, given his predilection for the autonomy of the moral will over against heteronomy, Kant praises Adam for his willingness to make his own moral judgment rather than blindly following the dictates of another, even if that other is God. For Kant Gen. 3 is an account of the "transition from an uncultured, merely animal condition to the state of humanity, from bondage to instinct to rational control—in a word, from the tutelage of nature to the state of freedom."[8]

In response to this view we note that there is little celebration in Gen. 3. Adam and Eve do not exit the garden in a doxological frame of mind. The chapter simply does not support the concept that one finds fulfillment and bliss in liberating oneself from subordination to God's word, his permissions and his denials. Man is not suddenly metamorphosed from a puppet to a free and independent thinker. In fact, he never was an automaton. If man had lacked the ability to choose, the prohibition from God not to eat of the fruit of the tree of knowledge of good and evil would have been superfluous. One is not told to abstain from something unless he has the capacity not to abstain.

It may well be that Gen. 3 lends its imprimatur to the concept of man who has always been given the capacity to make his own independent moral choice. But it goes much further than that. It says, quite strongly, that one's choices should not be made in the interests of the self. Rather, such choices should be made within the range of God's directives. What has God said on

7. C. Westermann, *Creation,* p. 109.

8. "Conjectural Beginning of Human History," in *Kant on History,* ed. L. W. Beck (Indianapolis: Liberal Arts, 1963), p. 60. According to Kant it is essential for a moral being to have "the power of choosing for himself a way of life and not being bound without alternative to a single way, like the animals" (ibid., p. 56). The biblical scholar D. R. G. Beattie takes a similar approach in "What is Genesis 2–3 About?" *ExpTim* 92 (1980/81) 8–10: "Thank God, says the story-teller, that Adam and Eve didn't eat of the tree of life lest mankind become immortal morons." Similarly, J. Baker, "The Myth of Man's 'Fall'—A Reappraisal," *ExpTim* 92 (1980/81) 235–37: "What happens there is not a 'Fall,' but an awakening" (p. 236).

the matter? Is my choice pleasing and obedient to him? Adam always has the capacity to choose. But he lacks complete control over the consequences of that choice. Freedom is not something Adam gains. It is something he forfeits. A truly liberated Adam now becomes an Adam in bondage. He has willed to be his own god, which is, of course, a sin on which he has no monopoly.

THE NEW TESTAMENT APPROPRIATION

a. Gen. 3 and Rom. 5:12–21

We will confine ourselves in this section to two portions of the NT where the biblical writer makes an unmistakable connection between Adam and Christ. Other NT texts have possible connections to Gen. 3. For example, Rom. 1, and the sequence of events described there, may be strikingly parallel to the events in Gen. 1–3, and perhaps Paul is picturing man's wickedness in terms of the biblical narrative of Adam's fall.[1] But the relation to Genesis is certainly kept indirect, if it is there at all. Again, in the kenosis hymn of Phil. 2:6–11, Paul may be contrasting Jesus, who did not consider equality with God a thing to be held on to, with Adam, who felt that equality with God must be sought at all costs. But again, can we be certain that Gen. 3 looms in the back of the writer's mind as he pens or copies the hymn about the divine self-emptying?

First, let us focus our attention on Rom. 5:12–21; later we will look at 1 Cor. 15:21–22, 45–49. Rom. 5:12–21 has become the cornerstone for the formulation of the doctrine of original sin. Here Paul affirms that sin is in the world because of Adam's sin, and death is in the world because of sin (v. 12). In addition, many have been made sinners by the disobedience of this one man (v. 19). In that his behavior affects those who follow him, Adam is for Paul an antitype of Jesus.

We have already mentioned that the OT does not explicitly tie in the sin and death of all human beings with Adam's sin. What, then, is the source and stimulus for Paul's thinking? Were there ideas similar to Rom. 5:12–21 circulating in the 1st century, and if so, where? Some have suggested that Paul here draws on Gnostic cosmological mythology, but this suggestion represents a minority view.[2] I am unable to find any scholar who believes that Paul

1. See M. D. Hooker, "Adam in Romans i," *NTS* 6 (1960) 297–306.

2. See R. Bultmann, "Adam and Christ According to Romans 5," in *Current Issues in New Testament Interpretation,* Fest. O. A. Piper, ed. W. Klassen and G. F. Snyder (New York: Harper & Row, 1962), pp. 143–65; E. Brandenburger, *Adam und*

bypasses both Gnostic thought and rabbinical doctrine and presents the concept de novo. The majority view would be that Paul's thought in Rom. 5 is a theological reflection on parallel texts of later Judaism, thus placing Paul solidly in Jewish tradition.[3] Nevertheless, his presentation of the Adam-Christ relationship is bold and novel, and may be considered an original concept.

Before looking at vv. 12–21 themselves, we need to note how this unit fits into the larger context of the epistle. If we assume that it is not an eccentric excursus, why does this emphasis come here? A brief outline of Rom. 1–8 will help us answer that question. These eight chapters may be divided as follows: (1) introduction (1:1–17); (2) the gospel in terms of the *problem*—sin (1:18–3:20); (3) the gospel in terms of the *solution*—faith in Christ's work (3:21–4:25); (4) the gospel in terms of *results,* which include both *benefits* (ch. 5) and *obligations* (chs. 6–8).[4]

Thus, the immediate context for vv. 12–21 is a discussion of the gospel in terms of its benefits. Such benefits include (vv. 1–11): peace with God, access to grace, and hope of sharing the glory of God. All these benefits are based on and made possible by reconciliation to God through Christ's death. Vv. 12–21 are then a further expansion of the effects of Christ's death. It leads to life just as Adam's life led to death. Note how Paul links both sections (vv. 1–11 and vv. 12–21) by his use of "much more" in showing the causal nexus between the past and the present (vv. 10, 15, 17).

In vv. 1–11 Paul contrasts Christ's death with human sacrifice, and in vv. 12–21 he contrasts Christ's death with Adam's sin. The underlying emphasis in the first unit is love—God showed his love for us in that his Son died for us while we were yet sinners. In the second unit the underlying emphasis is grace.[5] The word *cháris* occurs five times here ("grace," vv. 15

Christus: Exegetische-religionsgeschichtliche Untersuchung zu Röm 5,12–21 (1 Kor. 15), WMANT 7 (Neukirchen: Neukirchener, 1962), pp. 158–80; K. Barth, *Christ and Adam: Man and Humanity in Romans 5,* tr. T. A. Smail (repr. New York: Collier, 1962).

3. An illustrative list of Jewish texts teaching the effects of Adam's (and Eve's) sin on subsequent generations would include: Sir. 25:24; 4 Ezra 3:7, 21–22; 7:116–19; Wis. 1:13; 2:23; 2 Apoc. Bar. 23:4; Syr. Bar. 48:42–44. See also A. J. M. Wedderburn, "The Theological Structure of Romans v.12," *NTS* 19 (1972/73) 352–53.

4. This overview of the structure of Rom. 1–8 I owe to Professor Robert Traina of Asbury Theological Seminary and his unpublished lectures on Romans.

5. See D. Doughty, "The Priority of Charis," *NTS* 19 (1973) 163–80. Doughty (p. 174) makes much of the contrast here between trespass and grace as a parallel to the contrast between human activity with regard to sin and passivity with regard to grace.

[2 times], 17, 20, 21), and the word *chárisma* two times ("free gift," vv. 15, 16).

Here is a clue as to why it is appropriate for Paul at this point to introduce the Adam-Christ typology. The analogy Paul is making has to do with the communal effects of Adam's sin vis-à-vis the communal effects of Christ's death. Within the syndrome of a mentality that bases righteousness on works, communal effects of any kind are a dead and irrelevant issue. It is a purely individual matter. I am judged on what I do, and what someone else has done has no bearing on that judgment.

Paul protests such thinking. Adam's moral act affected others, including their destiny and their moral status. Similarly, what Christ has done has a bearing on what other people are in the sight of God. The crucial element here is not what I as an individual have done, but what Christ has done for me. To that end Paul proceeds to make an analogy between Christ and Adam (vv. 12–14); then a contrast (vv. 15–17), then back to a comparison (vv. 18–21). Paul's whole argument throughout this section is an illustration of the old rabbinic *qal waḥomer* argument, that is, from the less to the greater. He proceeds more strictly on the basis of common sense than on logic.

The main crux in this whole section is v. 12, especially the last clause. This verse articulates four facts: sin came into the world through one man, death came because of sin, death spread to all human beings, because all have sinned.

How shall we understand and translate the last four words, *eph' hṓ pántes hḗmarton?* There are no less than six possibilities:[6] (1) to take *hṓ* as masculine and to understand its antecedent to be "death"—"in which all sinned"; (2) to take *hṓ* as masculine and to understand its antecedent to be "one man," with *eph'* meaning "in"—"in whom all sinned"; (3) to take *hṓ* as masculine, to understand its antecedent to be "one man," with *eph'* meaning "because of"—"because of whom all sinned"; (4) to understand *hṓ* as neuter and *eph' hṓ* as meaning "because," and to take the "all sinned" as referring not to individuals' sinning in their own persons but to their participation in Adam's transgression; (5) to take *hṓ* as neuter and *eph' hṓ* as meaning "because," and to take "all sinned" as referring to individuals' sinning in their own persons quite independently of Adam; (6) to take *hṓ* as neuter and *eph' hṓ* as meaning "because," and to take "all sinned" as referring to individuals' sinning in their own persons, a result of the corrupt nature inherited from Adam.

6. See C. E. B. Cranfield, "On Some Problems in the Interpretation of Romans 5,12," *SJT* 22 (1969) 330ff.

We would suggest that the most viable options are numbers (2) and its variant (4), and (6). The second and fourth possibilities are the ones that have been most frequently adopted. For example, Augustine, Luther, and Calvin favored the second. The wide acceptance of this view is indicated by the Vulg., which renders *eph' hṓ* with *in quo,* "in whom." Thus the verse would affirm the federal headship of Adam and the corporate solidarity of human guilt.

F. F. Bruce, who represents position (4), takes the view that the Vulg. *in quo* is both a mistranslation and a true interpretation of the Greek.[7] Bruce's interpretation is grammatically questionable in that he must accept the antecedent of *hṓ* to be the distant "one man," and he must force the word *eph'* to mean "in."

It seem to us that position (6) does most justice to the entire verse and to the whole unit. On the one hand, it takes seriously the Adam-Christ typology on which Paul is expatiating. The actions of Adam and Christ do affect humanity, and not merely in the sense of providing examples which may be imitated (cf. position 5).[8] Sinning or living a life of righteousness is a natural cause of what Adam and Christ respectively have done. Our lives are the fruit of their activities.

On the other hand, the verse does justice to the concept of individual guilt. Paul normally uses *hámartanein* of individual, responsible sinning, which is clearly the sense of the verb thus far in Romans (2:12; 3:23). We would suggest, then, that the first three clauses of the verse teach the mediating influence of Adam's sin on his posterity. The fourth clause, by contrast, refers to the responsible, active, individual sinning of all human beings. Both corporate guilt and individual guilt must be held in proper tension.[9]

Throughout this section Paul characterizes Adam's sin as a commandment-breaking *parábasis* ("transgression," v. 14) and *paráptōma* ("trespass,"

7. F. F. Bruce, *Romans,* TNTC (Grand Rapids: Eerdmans, 1963), p. 126. Bruce further remarks, "all have sinned, that is to say, in Adam, not subsequently, in imitation of Adam's sin. . . . It is not simply because Adam is the ancestor of mankind that all are said to have sinned in his sin. . . , it is because Adam is mankind."

8. 2 Apoc. Bar. 54:15, 19 vents this Pelagian point of view: "For if Adam sinned first and brought untimely death on all, each of those who descended from him, each individual has brought future pain upon himself. Adam is thus the cause of himself alone; each of us has become his own Adam, each for himself."

9. See E. Käsemann, *Commentary on Romans,* tr. G. W. Bromiley (Grand Rapids: Eerdmans, 1980), p. 149: "Paul's concern unites what seems to us to be a logical contradiction. . . . No one commences his own history and no one can be exonerated."

vv. 15, 16, 17, 18, 20), not *harmartía.* Adam's sin was not sin in the general sense of deviation from some divine norm but rather a violation of a clear-cut demand. It is a sin that carries with it the heaviest consequences, for it is a sin that was voluntarily and willfully perpetrated.

Verse 19 must not be misinterpreted either. It would suggest that Adam is a necessary, though not a sufficient, cause of all future sinfulness. Otherwise, this verse can only be interpreted as putting forward the idea of a fatalistic determinism on the one hand or an automatic universalism on the other. A. J. M. Wedderburn suggests that the key to a proper understanding of this verse lies in Paul's polarization of tenses.[10] The characteristics of the old age are placed in the past tense ("were made," *katestáthēsan*). The characteristics of the new age are placed in the future tense ("will be made," *katastathḗsontai*).

b. Gen. 3 and 1 Cor. 15:21–22, 45–49

1 Corinthians 15:21–22 make much the same point as Rom. 5:12–21. For a second time in his writings Paul establishes a causal link between something Christ has done and what as a result will happen to the believer. In Rom. 5 Paul has said that Christ's death, and only Christ's death, makes righteousness possible. In 1 Cor. 15 he is making the point that believers can anticipate a resurrection only because Christ himself has been resurrected.

Adam is the bringer of death. Christ is the one who brings life. "In Christ shall all be made alive" *(zōopoiōēthḗsontai),* v. 22. The larger context of the chapter would suggest that "shall be made alive" refers not to present regeneration but to a dimension of life that comes after death and after the grave.

Paul returns to his Adam-Christ typology for a second time in this chapter in vv. 45–49. He begins in v. 45 by quoting Gen. 2:7, "the first man Adam became a living being." This is not a direct quote of either MT or LXX, for Paul has freely added two words, "first" and "Adam." The second part of v. 45 is a theological expansion of the first part: "the last Adam became a life-giving spirit." This spirit is what distinguishes the two Adams, the first Adam and the last Adam, from each other. The first Adam does not give life. In fact, he brings death. There may be deliberate irony here. The first Adam names his wife *ḥawwâ* (life [?]) but he cannot give *ḥayyâ* (life).

From this original contrast Paul proceeds to make three further

10. A. J. M. Wedderburn, "The Theological Structure of Romans v.12," *NTS* 19 (1972/73) 352–53.

contrasts between Christ and Adam. The relation between the two is explained in reference to order (v. 46), origin (v. 47), and followers (v. 48). Then in v. 49 the discussion addresses only one class of people, Christ's followers. Using again the polarization of tenses (see Rom. 5:19), Paul says that as they have borne (aorist) the image of the earthly man, they shall bear (future) the image of the heavenly man.

In the interest of his apologetic, Paul has ignored Genesis material to the effect that Adam too bore the image of God. His concern is not Adam's similarity to God but the similarity of Adam's followers to Adam. Also, he has downplayed the present aspect of salvation and the idea of "already made alive" in Christ by focusing exclusively on the eschaton.[11] Such a procedure by Paul is probably evoked by his audience for whom the fullness of Christian existence was thought to be enjoyed entirely in this life.[12]

One point in v. 49 might suggest that Paul's major thrust here in the Adam-Christ typology is as much moral and ethical as it is eschatological. Many ancient texts read v. 49b, "we shall also bear [*phorésomen,* future indicative] the image of the man of heaven," as "let us also bear [*phorésōmen,* subjunctive aorist] the image of the man of heaven."[13] This reading turns a statement about future fact into an exhortation. Codex Vaticanus provides the main support for *phorésomen,* but more importantly the whole thrust of the chapter addresses itself to the future event of the resurrection.[14]

In conclusion, we would suggest that Paul drew on the Adam-Christ typology, and delineated it the way he did, because it provided him material in the debate against three misunderstandings of resurrection. First, there is a resurrection—death does not mean extermination—and Christ makes it possible. Second, this resurrection is a resurrection of the body. Death is not the liberation of the soul from its incarceration in the body. Third, the resurrection body will be a *pneumatic* (or spiritual) one, not a *psychic*

11. See J. Lambrecht, "Paul's Christological Use of Scripture in I Cor. 15:20-28," *NTS* 28 (1982) 514.

12. See A. J. M. Wedderburn, "The body of Christ and related concepts in I Corinthians," *SJT* 24 (1971) 91, and see p. 94: "It is not that they reversed the order of the two levels of existence, but that they left one out altogether and imagined that they possessed their full spiritual endowment already."

13. The primarily moral and ethical thrust of 1 Cor. 15:45–49 is maintained by R. Sider, "The Pauline Conception of the Resurrection Body in I Corinthians xv.35-54," *NTS* 21 (1975) 428–39, esp. p. 434.

14. See K. Usami, " 'How are the dead raised?' (I Cor. 15,35-38)," *Bib* 57 (1976) 488 n. 73; B. M. Metzger, *A Textual Commentary to the Greek New Testament,* 3rd ed. (New York: United Bible Societies, 1971), p. 569.

(physical) one. As Paul himself says in 1 Cor. 15:50, flesh and blood cannot inherit God's kingdom. Admittedly, it is difficult to discern exactly what Paul means by a *sṓma psychikón* and a *sṓma pneumatikón* (v. 44). While granting that the Greek word *psychikós* "almost defies translation,"[15] Orr and Walther suggest that the term refers to "the body composed of the natural elements without any supernatural or divine qualities," while *pneumatikós* refers to a body "composed of spirit, or it is under the rule or power of God's Spirit, or it is both."[16] Suggesting the translation "soulish" for *psychikós,* F. F. Bruce says, "The present body is animated entirely by 'soul' and is therefore mortal; the resurrection body is animated entirely by immortal and life-giving Spirit, and is therefore called a spiritual body."[17] Paul's second point would argue against Hellenistic concepts which denied the soul's need for a body, and his third point would oppose the excesses of rabbinical materialism that would see only minor adjustments between this life and the next.[18]

D. FRATERNAL STRIFE (4:1–26)

1. ONE OFFERING ACCEPTED, ONE OFFERING REJECTED (4:1–7)

1 *Adam was intimate with his wife Eve, and she conceived and bore Cain, saying, "I have acquired a man from Yahweh."*

2 *Subsequently she bore his brother Abel. Abel became a keeper of flocks, and Cain became a tiller of the soil.*

3 *Some time later Cain brought, from the fruit of the soil, an offering to Yahweh.*

4 *As for Abel, he too brought from the firstlings of his flock, namely,*[1] *of their fattest parts. Yahweh looked favorably on Abel and his offering.*

5 *But on Cain and his offering he did not look favorably. Cain was greatly depressed and crestfallen.*[2]

15. W. F. Orr and J. A. Walther, *I Corinthians,* AB (Garden City, NY: Doubleday, 1976), p. 343.

16. Ibid., p. 347.

17. F. F. Bruce, *1 and 2 Corinthians,* NCBC (Grand Rapids: Eerdmans, 1980), p. 152.

18. See B. S. Childs, "Adam," *IDB,* 1:44.

1. I read the *waw* on *ûmēhel*^{e}*ḇēhen* as a *waw explicativum,* i.e., the *waw* is explanatory; see GKC, § 154a n. 1(b).

2. Vv. 2–5 are actually three chiastic sentences, as is clear from this literal translation:

6 *Yahweh said to Cain, "Why*[3] *are you depressed and why are you crestfallen?*
7 *Look, isn't there acceptance if you do well, and isn't sin a lurker at the door if you don't do well? Its urge is toward you, yet you are the one to master it."*

This chapter confronts the reader with a number of problems, some of which are unanswerable. First, what is the relationship of ch. 4 to ch. 3? Did it have an originally independent history, and was it attached to ch. 3 only later and artificially? Or should ch. 4 be read as a natural and legitimate continuation of ch. 3? Along these lines, how should one account for the relative absence of Adam and Eve in this family episode, apart from the birth announcements, if the two incidents were originally dependent and consecutive? Second, what is the relationship of vv. 1–16 to vv. 17–26? Third, at the level of interpretation, why is Cain provided with an etymology, but Abel is not? Fourth, why does God not accept the offering of Cain? Fifth, how does one understand and explain the language and grammar of vv. 1 and 7?

1 We have chosen to translate the common Hebrew verb *yāḏaʿ*, "to

---

A and became Abel a keeper of flocks

A′ and Cain became a tiller of the soil

B and brought Cain from the fruit of the soil . . .

B′ and Abel brought, also he, from the firstlings . . .

C and looked favorably Yahweh on Abel and his offering

C′ and on Cain and his offering he did not look favorably

See F. I. Andersen, *The Sentence in Biblical Hebrew,* p. 122.

3. A. Jepsen discusses the difference between the two Hebrew words for "why" in "Warum? Eine lexikalische und theologische Studie," in *Das Ferne und Nahe Wort,* Fest. Leonhard Rost, ed. F. Maass, BZAW 105 (Berlin: Töpelmann, 1967), pp. 106–13. In God's speech, *maddûaʿ* often follows a double question, with an obvious no answer to both, and has the force "why then?" (Jer. 2:14, 31; 8:5, 22; etc.). "But God can also ask: *lamā,* with stronger emphasis on what is not right; but here evidencing various tones, some reproachful and some wooing" (p. 112).

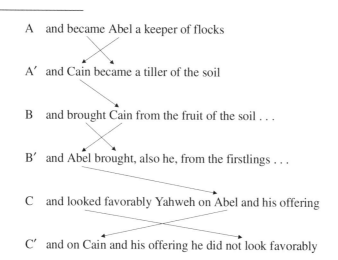

know," as *was intimate with.*[4] The same idiom appears again in this chapter in vv. 17 and 25. It is not without significance that often the sexual relationship described in the Bible is one in which the partners fully know each other.[5] One partner does not exploit the other. Rather than being an end in itself, cohabitation is a means to an end, and that end is a deeper, more intimate knowledge of each other. In other words, expressing oneself sexually is not just a glandular function.

To be sure, "know" can describe sexual relationships that are illicit, be they homosexual (19:5) or incestuous (38:26). Normally, however, the OT prefers to use either "go into" (16:2, 4; 38:16) or "lie with" (39:7) when the emphasis is not on reciprocal intimacy but on reproduction only or on lust. Yet, 4:1, 25 shows that *yāḏaʿ* also covers sexual activity in which reproduction is involved.

Upon giving birth to Cain, Eve exclaims, *I have acquired a man from Yahweh.* The verb for "acquire" is *qānâ,* which sounds much like *Cain* (Heb. *qayin*). Several scholars have suggested, correctly we believe, that this is another instance of popular etymology, based on assonance, and that *qayin* (Cain) is to be connected with Aram. *qênāyā'* or *qênā'â* and Arab. *qaynun,* meaning "smith" or "worker in metal." One of Cain's descendants, Tubal-cain, is appropriately the ancestor of metallurgists (4:22).[6]

But the meaning of *qānâ* is debated.[7] In most of its eighty-two occurrences in the OT, it seems clearly to mean "acquire, possess." But in several passages the meaning "form, produce, create," is possible (Gen. 4:1; 14:19, 22; Exod. 15:16; Deut. 32:6; Ps. 74:2; 78:54; 139:13; Prov. 8:22), though for various reasons some scholars have denied this meaning even to

4. Speiser (*Genesis,* pp. 31–32) supplies a lengthy note on why, in his judgment, "know" is inadequate here. His choice is "had experience of."

5. This deeper level of knowledge cannot be captured by an English verb, but compare the difference between French *connaitre* and *savoir* or German *erkennen* and *wissen* (although I do not believe either modern word is used to connote sexual knowledge per se).

6. W. F. Albright ("The 'Natural Force' of Moses in the Light of Ugaritic," *BASOR* 94 [1944] 34 n. 21) connects Ugar. *qny* with Arab. *qyn,* "to forge, form, decorate, repair, etc.," and with Heb. *qayin* (Gen. 4:22); see also H. L. Ginsberg, "The North-Canaanite Myth of Anath and Aqhat," *BASOR* 97 (1945) 22 n. 68. Albright and Ginsberg suggest that it is this meaning of *qānâ* that is to be found in Gen. 4:1—"I have produced a man together with Yahweh." Among modern commentators Skinner (*Genesis,* p. 102) argues most strongly for "create."

7. The foundational study of this verb in the Bible is P. Humbert, "Qânâ' en hébreu biblique," in *Festschrift Alfred Bertholet,* ed. Walter Baumgartner, et al. (Tübingen: Mohr, 1950), pp. 251–66.

these references.[8] Thus it seems best to retain here the more standard translation of *qānâ,* and render "I have acquired." Surely *qānâ* is used here more for its sound than its precise significance.[9]

Another problem concerns the word *'eṯ* that follows *qānîṯî.* This common term can be used in two ways: as the preposition "with," or as the marker of the direct object. Luther opted for the latter: "I have received a man, namely (or even), the Lord." This rendering suggests that in the birth of Cain Eve thought, mistakenly, that the divinely promised seed of 3:15 had now come in Cain. The child, whose birth is so welcomed, could be looked on as God himself.[10]

Most modern commentators prefer the former option, rendering *'eṯ* as "with the help of." The question that needs to be raised here is whether this is a legitimate translation of *'eṯ.* Does the rest of the OT support such a translation?

Cassuto reads, "I have created a man equally with the Lord." He perceives here some arrogance in Eve's statement. Yahweh created the first man. She created the second man, and thus her reproductive act is no less significant than Yahweh's productive act. Westermann follows Cassuto, but is baffled by *'eṯ* instead of the expected *k^e^*. This point is a good clue that this interpretation is specious.[11]

We have translated *'eṯ* as *from,* which, we grant, is not a normal English value for the Hebrew word. It is used in parallelism with *min,* "from," in 49:25, part of Jacob's words to Joseph: "From [*min*] the God of your father who helped you, from [*'eṯ*] Shaddai who blessed you."[12] Supporting evidence for *'eṯ* meaning "from" is now found in the Akkadian phrase *šamû 'itti,* "to buy from"[13]; this Akkadian phrase in turn may be compared with the Ugaritic clause *k yqny ǵzr b alḏyy,* "when he acquired [*yqny*] the youth from [*b*] the man of Alashia."

8. See W. A. Irwin, "Where Shall Wisdom Be Found?" *JBL* 80 (1961) 133–42; B. Vawter, "Prov. 8:22: Wisdom and Creation," *JBL* 99 (1980) 205–16, esp. pp. 208–14.

9. Vawter, *JBL* 99 (1980) 208–9.

10. I can find only one modern writer who seriously considers the *'eṯ* to be a *nota accusatavi,* and that is W. Kaiser, Jr., *Toward an Old Testament Theology* (Grand Rapids: Zondervan, 1978), p. 37.

11. See C. Westermann, *Genesis,* 1:281, 289–92. Strangely, Westermann's support of Cassuto's interpretation is not reflected in his own translation: "I have acquired a man, with Yahweh!"

12. See M. J. Dahood, "Northwest Semitic Notes on Genesis," *Bib* 55 (1974) 77.

13. For the Akkadian evidence, see R. Borger, "Gen iv 1," *VT* 9 (1959) 85–86. The phrase to which Borger refers is *It-ti-ili-a-šam-šu,* "Ich-habe-ihn-von-Gott-gekauft" ("I have bought him from God").

2 As we indicated above, it is surprising that Abel lacks an etymology, since Cain is given one by his mother in the first verse. Two etymologies are possible for *Abel* (Heb. *heḇel*). One is to connect it with Akk. *ap/blu,* "son," but why would a mother call her second child "son"? A second possibility is that it is the same as the *heḇel* made famous by Ecclesiastes, "vanity of vanities" (*hᵉḇēl hᵃḇālîm,* "the greatest vanity"). But again, would a mother name her son "vanity, vapor, nothingness"?[14] It is true that Abel does play a very small, brief role in this chapter, primarily as Cain's victim. He acts, but he never talks. Perhaps his name represents his marginal role in the narrative.

Cain carries on his father's vocation. He is *a tiller of the soil* (*ʿōḇēḏ ʾᵃḏāmâ,* lit., "a servant of the ground"), and so was his father both before his sin (*lᵉʿoḇᵉḏāh,* 2:15) and after his sin (*laʿᵃḇōḏ ʾeṯ-hāʾᵃḏāmâ,* 3:23). But the land that Adam tills in 3:23 and that which Cain tills in 4:2 is outside the garden. The trespass of ch. 3 brought with it no vocational change for Adam. The phrase "to till the soil" is confined to chs. 2–4 of Genesis. Abel, unlike his brother, is *a keeper of flocks,* a shepherd, which suggests at least the existence of domesticated animals. He is followed in that vocation by such notables as Jacob (30:36), Joseph (37:2), Moses (Exod. 3:1), and David (1 Sam. 16:11; 17:34).

Earlier commentators were fond of suggesting that in its original form this biblical story served as an illustration of the clash in ancient civilization between two conflicting life-styles, one agricultural and the other pastoral or nomadic, with the deity preferring the latter. Two problems militate against this identification of the original form of the Cain-Abel story. First, clashes in ancient times were not between agricultural and pastoral peoples, but between urban agricultural societies (with their livestock) and steppe nomads (with their livestock). Second, how could this suggestion ever fit the contours of the narrative, for in it the husbandman (Cain) is driven to nomadism, but only to end up as the founder of culture and of the first city?[15]

3–4a Here are two brothers at worship. Eden is off-limits to humanity, but God is not restricted to Eden's compound. In later texts (e.g., Leviticus) "to bring an offering to Yahweh" suggests erecting an altar and placing that offering on or before that altar. Yet "altar" is nowhere used in Gen. 4, and thus we must remain uncertain as to how the brothers "brought to Yahweh" their respective sacrifices.

14. F. Zimmermann connects "Abel" with Arab. *habala,* "to be deprived by death of a son" ("Folk etymology of Biblical names," in *Volume du Congrès: Genève, 1965,* VTSup 15 [Leiden: Brill, 1966], pp. 324–25). See also A. Guillaume, "Paronomasia in the Old Testament," *JSS* 9 (1964) 282–83, for the same suggestion.

15. See H. C. Brichto, "Cain and Abel," *IDBS,* p. 121.

Each brought an *offering (minḥâ)* appropriate to his occupation. One would expect a farmer to bring an offering from the vintage of the ground, and a shepherd to bring the sucklings of his flock. Outside of ritual codes *minḥâ* could refer to any offering of grain, but animals might also be included (here; 1 Sam. 2:17; 26:19). In Gen. 32:20 *minḥâ* also takes on the added meaning of "tribute" and describes a present made to secure or retain goodwill. As such, it is a tribute brought by subjects to their overlords, be the latter divine (Gen. 4:3–4) or human (Judg. 3:15–18). In the priestly, prescriptive texts, however, the *minḥâ* is exclusively cereal. Man's tribute to God must be from the fruit of his labors on the soil. It could consist of choice flour (Lev. 2:1–3) or choice grain (Lev. 2:14–16) to which oil and frankincense might be added. Its form would be baked loaves, or wafers, or morsels.

There seems to be no obvious distinction between the two offerings. A fruit or vegetable offering is neither superior nor inferior to an animal offering. One possible indication that Abel's offering might be more valuable than Cain's is the mention of *their fattest parts (ḥelᵉḇhēn).* In the OT sacrificial system, the fatty *(ḥēleḇ)* portions covering the animal's innards were most desirable to God. These fatty portions were forbidden for human consumption, perhaps because the fat, like the blood, belonged to God (see Exod. 29:13; Lev. 3:3–5, 9–11, 14–16; 4:8–10, 26, 31; 7:23–25; 1 Sam. 2:15–16; Ezek. 44:7, 15, both of which connect "fat" and "blood"). Noncultic sources such as Deut. 32:38; 1 Sam. 15:22; Isa. 1:11; 43:24 support this notion about the sanctity of an animal's fatty portions. Such fat was burned on the altar, and the smoke resulting from this incineration was a pleasing aroma to God (Gen. 8:21; Exod. 29:18; Lev. 1:9; etc.). Perhaps we are justified in seeing in Abel's offering a gift that is of the finest quality, as opposed to that of his brother, which is more common.

The text also states that Abel brought the firstlings *(bᵉḵōrôṯ)* of his flock. But Cain presented no *minḥaṯ bikkûrîm,* "a cereal offering of first fruits" (to use the phrase of Lev. 2:14). Later biblical codes developed the principle that just as the firstborn of human beings and of animals belong to God and were to be brought as an offering to God, so the firstfruits, including the first grains to ripen each season, were to be brought as an offering to God (Exod. 23:19; 34:26; Num. 15:17–21; 18:12–13; Deut. 26:1–11). Yet, the text does not indict Cain for not presenting the firstfruits.

4b–5 Abel's offering is accepted by God and Cain's is rejected. In ch. 3 Adam and Eve had to make a choice. Here God makes a selection. Gen. 4 does not supply a reason for or an explanation of this divine choice. The NT will indeed address itself to this issue, but the OT itself is silent. Commentators have not been reluctant to fill up this silence with a number of interesting and imaginary possibilities. Among the more popular interpretations are: (1) what grows spontaneously is a more appropriate sacrifice than what has to be cultivated (Josephus);[16] (2) Cain's fruit was not "first-fruit," and thus it was inferior to Abel's "firstlings" of his flock (Ibn Ezra, Philo);[17] (3) God does not approve of farming (Cain) because it keeps a man rooted to one spot, whereas shepherds (Abel) are peripatetic and come into contact with the world (Gunkel); (4) Cain was niggardly. The common denominator in all these suggestions is an attempt to engage in theodicy by providing a rational defense of God's conduct. Thus some inferior quality in Cain's offering must be inferred.[18]

Only a few commentators have suggested a reason for God's preference as something other than a rational one. Saul Levin thinks that God preferred Abel's sacrifice simply because it smelled better when he inhaled the soothing aroma.[19] God's decision is sensory, not rational. This explanation sounds as fanciful as the others given above.

Perhaps the silence is the message itself. As outside viewers, we are unable to detect any difference between the two brothers and their offerings. Perhaps the fault is an internal one, an attitude that is known only to God. We will see later that this is precisely the NT's interpretation of this event.

6–7 Cain is understandably upset. Still God asks him, *Why are you depressed and why are you crestfallen?* We have chosen to depart from the usual "Why are you angry?" (RSV; cf. AV) and replace it with *Why are you depressed?*[20] The second phrase *Why are you crestfallen?* (lit., "why is your face fallen?") supports our translation. To drop and hide the face is more likely a sign of depression, not anger.

Further support may be found in the two Hebrew idioms *ḥārâ 'ap̱* and *ḥārâ l*[e]. The first one (lit., "a nose burns") does indeed always indicate anger. The second one (lit., "it was burning to . . ."), which occurs here, often has the same meaning (Gen. 31:36; 34:7; Num. 16:15), but in a few places it seems to refer to despondency and grief rather than anger. When Saul heard the women singing the praises of David's military exploits, was he depressed,

16. Josephus *Ant.* 1.2.1 (53–54).

17. Philo *Sacrifices of Abel and Cain* 13.52–53; 20.72.

18. See J. Goldin, "The Youngest Son or Where Does Genesis 38 Belong," *JBL* 96 (1977) 33 n. 36.

19. S. Levin, "The More Savory Offering: A Key to the Problem of Gen 4:3–5," *JBL* 98 (1979) 85.

20. See M. I. Gruber, "The Tragedy of Cain and Abel: A Case of Depression," *JQR* 69 (1978) 89–97; idem, "Was Cain Angry or Depressed?" *BAR* 6 (Nov.–Dec. 1980) 35–36.

or angry, or both (1 Sam. 18:8)? When God spares Nineveh, is Jonah angry or despondent (Jon. 4:1)? God follows Jonah's death wish with "do you well to be so depressed (or angry)?" (4:4). When the plant is attacked by the worm, is Jonah angry or grieved (4:9)? Of course, it is easy for depression to turn into anger, and specifically anger directed at those who are the real or illusory cause of one's depression.

7 God continues to speak to Cain. It is fair to say that this is one of the hardest verses in Genesis to translate and to understand. Skinner speaks for many commentators when he says that "every attempt to extract a meaning from the verse is more or less of a *tour de force.*"[21]

Looking at the Hebrew of the verse, one detects immediately three oddities. First, what does one do with the fourth word in the verse, *śᵉʾēṯ?* In form it is an infinitive construct from *nāśāʾ,* "to lift up, raise," but there is no following word to which it bears a construct relationship. There is a *nomen regens* but no *nomen rectum!* Thus the first few words read literally, "if you do well, a lifting up of. . . (?)." To be sure, there are a few instances where an infinitive construct acts as the nominative of the subject, but these are rare.[22] Second, why is there lack of gender agreement between the subject and the predicate in *ḥaṭṭāʾṯ* (fem.) *rōḇēṣ* (masc. sing. participle), often translated "sin is crouching" (NIV; cf. RSV, NEB, AV)? Third, why are masculine pronominal suffixes used in both *tᵉšûqāṯô* (translated above *Its urge*) and *ʾattâ timšol-bô (you are the one to master it)* when the antecedent is *ḥaṭṭāʾṯ (sin),* which is feminine?

Scholars have sought to resolve these conundrums in the following ways. Some change the MT's word order, placing *ḥaṭṭāʾṯ,* "sin," after *śᵉʾēṯ,* "to lift up." The phrase *nāśāʾ ḥaṭṭāʾṯ* then refers to the forgiveness of sin: "look, if you do well, there is forgiveness for sin. . . ."[23] The main appeal of this suggestion is that it supplies a *nomen rectum* for *śᵉʾēṯ.* There is, however, no textual support for revising the word order. This suggestion may be a case of changing the text to conform to our understanding of Biblical Hebrew's syntax.

Another approach is to insert words into the passage. For example, adding *pānîm* or *pāneyḵā* after *śᵉʾēṯ* enables one to translate: "if you do well,

21. Skinner, *Genesis,* p. 107.

22. See GKC, § 114a.

23. See L. Ramaroson, "A propos de Gn 4,7," *Bib* 49 (1968) 233–37. His translation of the verse is: "Vois-tu? si tu agis bien, c'est le pardon de ton péché. Mais si tu fais le mal, le démon est à ta porte: son élan est vers toi; mais toi, tu dois le dominer" ("Do you see? if you do good, it is the pardon of your sin. But if you do evil, the demon is at your door: his desire is toward you; but you, you must dominate him").

there is a lifting of the (or your) face."[24] This line then contrasts with the earlier falling of Cain's face. If Cain refuses to capitulate to this moment of temptation, there can be a reversal of his feelings. He who now bows his head will be able to hold his head high.

A third position resorts to emending the text, both the consonants and the vocalization. Thus G. R. Driver makes the following five changes in the text.[25] Following Gunkel and some ancient versions, he emends *śeʾēṯ* to *tiśśāʾ*. He supplies *pāneyḵā* after *tiśśāʾ*. He reads *ḥaṭṭāʾṯ rōḇēṣ* as dittography for *ḥaṭṭaʾṯ tirbaṣ*.[26] He emends the Qal *timšol* into the Niphal *timmāšel*. Finally, he changes the two masculine pronominal suffixes into feminine ones. Thus Driver's translation is: "If thou doest well, dost thou not lift up (thy countenance)? But if thou doest not well, sin will be crouching at the door, and its impulse is towards thee, and thou shalt be ruled by it."[27] The fact that such a translation requires at least five changes in the MT makes it unlikely.

A fourth approach is to emend only the vocalized text. Thus Dahood changes MT *śeʾēṯ* to *šāʾattā* (assimilation from *šāʾantā*, the 2nd masc. sing. perfect of *šāʾan*, "to be at ease"). He translates: "Look, if you have behaved well you will be at ease. But if you have not, sin will be lurking at your door."[28] The root to which Dahood refers—*šʾn*—is a rare one, occurring only in Job 3:18 and Jer. 48:11. In other words, he is prepared to reject a normal form of a very popular verb and replace it with an unusual form of a very rare verb. Such a proposal seems to compound the problem rather than resolve it.

Can sense be made out of the verse without alterations of any kind? Following the lead of Andersen,[29] we suggest that the interrogative *ha*,

24. See G. R. Castellino, "Genesis iv 7," *VT* 10 (1960) 442–45. Castellino's most novel suggestion is to read the last half of the verse as a question: "Sin will be lying in wait for you, and are you sure, you shall be able to master it?" I agree that there is interrogation from God in this verse, but it does not come at the end of the statement. God is not querying Cain in this last phrase, but affirming him.

25. G. R. Driver, "Theological and Philological Problems in the Old Testament," *JTS* 47 (1946) 157–60.

26. This reading is widely accepted; see, e.g., W. Watson, "Shared Consonants in Northwest Semitic," *Bib* 50 (1969) 533.

27. This is the NEB rendering; Driver's influence is apparent throughout the NEB OT, for he was the Joint Director.

28. M. J. Dahood, "Ebla, Ugarit and the Old Testament," in *Congress Volume: Göttingen, 1977,* VTSup 29 (Leiden: Brill, 1978), p. 95; idem, "Ebla, Ugarit, and the Bible," in G. Pettinato, *The Archives of Ebla: An Empire Inscribed in Clay* (Garden City, NY: Doubleday, 1981), pp. 275–76.

29. F. I. Andersen, *The Sentence in Biblical Hebrew,* p. 114.

though appearing only once, covers both the first *'im* ("if") clause and the second one. Thus God's speech in v. 7 consists of two rhetorical questions and one statement.

Hebrew *śe'ēṯ* then takes on nominative force, meaning "acceptance" (Gen. 19:21) or "forgiveness" (50:17), two common meanings of the verb *nāśā'*. As such, *śe'ēṯ* is an abbreviation of *śe'ēṯ pānîm.* There is no real problem reconciling feminine *ḥaṭṭā'ṯ*[30] with masculine *rōḇēṣ*. Speiser has a long note to the effect that Heb. *rōḇēṣ* is to be connected with Akk. *rabiṣum,* "demon," and it is *rōḇēṣ* that supplies the proper antecedent for the two masculine suffixes.[31] Speiser goes on to say that in Mesopotamian demonology the *rabiṣum* could be either a benevolent being that lurks at the entrance of a building to protect the occupants, or just the opposite, a malevolent being that lurks at the entrance of a building to threaten the occupants. To be sure, the normal meaning of Heb. *rāḇaṣ* is "to lie down (in rest)." See, for example, the verb in this sense in connection with sheep (Gen. 29:2), with other animals in tranquility together (Isa. 11:6), and with people (Isa. 14:30; Ezek. 34:14). Gen. 49:9 is the one other clear instance, besides Gen. 4:7, that permits the translation "lie in wait for, lurk." Little attention has been given to the fact that, in Hebrew, nouns that are feminine morphologically are sometimes treated as masculine.[32] The best example of this point is the title given to the author of Ecclesiastes, certainly a male figure; he is called *qōheleṯ,* a feminine noun, and this title is always coupled with a masculine form of the verb.

Its urge is toward you. Sin's urge is aimed at Cain. The word for *urge* here, *tešûqâ,* is the same word used in the previous chapter for Eve's feelings toward Adam (3:16). Similarly, what Cain can do to sin—*you are the one to master* [*mšl*] *it*—is described with the same verb used for Adam's actions with Eve ("he shall be master over you," 3:16). This is one illustration of the number of key phrases and ideas that are repeated in these chapters. Just as Adam and Eve *knew* they were naked (3:7), Adam *knew* his wife (4:1). God's question "*where* is your brother?" (4:9) balances his earlier question, "*where* are you?" (3:9). There is a *cursing* from the earth for both Adam and Cain

30. Biblical Hebrew has a word for "sin" without the *dagesh: ḥaṭā'â* (Gen. 20:9; Exod. 32:21, 30–31; etc.), but the more common word has the *dagesh: ḥaṭṭā'ṯ.* These terms seem indistinguishable in meaning. Interestingly, the Hebrew language uses the same word for "sin sacrifice" (Lev. 4) as it does for "sin." The one word describes both the problem and the solution. The noun is built off the Piel form *ḥiṭṭē',* which is a privative Piel, "to remove sin, purify."

31. Speiser, *Genesis,* pp. 32–33.

32. See GKC, § 122r.

(3:17; 4:11). Both sinners are banished from God's presence (3:24; 4:14), to *east of Eden* (3:24; 4:16). Such parallels, and there are many more, suggest either an original unity for chs. 3 and 4 or an unusually skilled redactor who has given the two chapters the guise of unity through the creation of verbal parallels.[33] If the latter is the more cogent explanation, then those who inherited these two narratives have so changed the records as to make the original, if ever recoverable, unrecognizable. It is highly unlikely that the redactors tampered with their texts that drastically.

Cain is not to give in to this lurking sin. He is *to master* [*timšol*] *it.*[34] The sense of the Hebrew form (2nd masc. sing. imperfect) is ambiguous; it may be read as a promise ("you *shall* master it"), as a command ("you *must* master it"), or as an invitation ("you *may* master it"). Although each of these is quite possible, notice that Cain does have a choice.[35] He is not so deeply embedded in sin, either inherited or actual, that his further sin is determined and inevitable. The emphasis here is not on Cain as a constitutional sinner, one utterly depraved, but on Cain as one who has a free choice. When facing the alternatives, he is capable of making the right choice. Otherwise, God's words to him about "doing well" would be meaningless and comic. Should he so desire, Cain is able to overcome this creature who now confronts him. The text makes Cain's personal responsibility even more focused by its use of the initial emphatic pronoun: "*you,* you are to master it."

2. A JUDGE AND A CRIMINAL (4:8–16)

8 *Cain was looking for Abel his brother. When they were in the field, Cain rose up against Abel his brother and killed him.*

9 *Then Yahweh asked Cain, "Where is Abel your brother?" He responded, "I do not know. Am I my brother's guardian?"*

10 *Then he said, "What have you done! Listen! The blood of your brother is crying out to me from the soil.*

33. For links between chs. 3 and 4 cf. M. Fishbane, *Text and Texture,* pp. 26–27; A. J. Hauser, "Linguistic and Thematic Links Between Genesis 4:1–16 and Genesis 2–3," *JETS* 23 (1980) 297–305, who opts for the first of these two possibilities.

34. The pronominal suffix on *bô* might well translate as "him"—you are the one to master him—i.e., Abel, as argued by K. A. Deurloo, "*ṯšuqh,* 'dependency', Gen 4,7," *ZAW* 99 (1987) 405–6. The sudden resurfacing of Abel in the narrative, however, would be strange.

35. See W. Brueggemann, *Genesis,* pp. 58–59. A parallel to this part of the verse is found in Ps. 19:14 (Eng. 13), "restrain thy servant from presumptuous sins [*zēḏîm*]; let them not have dominion [*yimšᵉlû*] over me."

11 *Henceforth are you banned from the soil which opened its mouth to receive the blood of your brother from your hand.*
12 *Whenever you till the soil it shall not surrender its yield to you. A wandering fugitive shall you be on earth."*
13 *Cain replied to Yahweh: "My punishment is too severe to bear.*
14 *Now that you have banished me today from the soil, and I am hidden from your presence and am to be a wandering fugitive, anybody who finds me might kill me."*
15 *Yahweh said to him: "On the contrary, whoever kills Cain shall be avenged sevenfold." Yahweh put a mark on Cain lest anyone who found him should slay him.*
16 *Then Cain left Yahweh's presence and settled in Nod, eastward of Eden.*

8 It has long been observed that this verse omits what Cain actually said to his brother. The text simply reads "And Cain said unto Abel his brother. When they were in the field. . . ." On the basis of the ancient versions most modern translations insert something like: "And Cain said unto Abel his brother, 'Let us go out to the field.' "[1] The question that is now raised is whether the reading, say, of the LXX reflects the original or is itself an artificial intrusion into the text. While almost all commentators accept the addition, if only for the sake of meaning, some still try to make sense of the text as it stands. For example, A. Ehrman has suggested that *'āmar* is a polaric verb meaning both "to exalt, praise" and conversely "to despise, hold in contempt, be angry." The first meaning he supports with Isa. 3:10a and the second with Esth. 1:18; 7:5. Thus he reads Gen. 4:8 as "And Cain despised Abel his brother. . . ."[2]

Another view is that we have here an archaic use of *'āmar,* "to say," in the sense of *dābar,* "to speak": hence "And Cain spoke with Abel his brother."[3] But this interpretation is unlikely, for in Biblical Hebrew *'āmar* and *dābar* are never interchangeable.

A third suggestion, and the one embodied in our translation, is that

1. LXX *diélthōmen eis tó pedíon;* Vulg. *egrediamur foras.*

2. A. Ehrman, "What Did Cain Say to Abel?" *JQR* 53 (1962) 164–67.

3. E. Levine ("The Syriac Version of Genesis IV 1-16," *VT* 26 [1976] 71 n. 5) quotes S. E. Loewenstamm and J. Blau, *Thesaurus of the Language of the Bible* (Jerusalem: Biblical Concordance Press, 1957), p. xxx: "Sometimes a difficult passage is susceptible of explanation as it stands, and can only lose by emendation. It should not be supposed that the copyists omitted words which are so clear and so apparently necessary to the proper understanding of the text; it seems more probable that we have here an archaic use of *wy'mr* in the sense of *wydbr* 'and he spoke,' which needs no amplification."

the original meaning of Heb. *'āmar* was "to see" or "be on the lookout," as evidenced by Akkadian and Ugaritic. The shift in meaning came through the factitive sense "to show," hence "to speak."[4] In ch. 3 God strode through the garden looking for Adam; here Cain walks through the field looking for Abel.

Upon finding him, Cain kills *(hāraḡ)* Abel. This is the common verb meaning "to murder intentionally" and is to be distinguished from the one mentioned in the sixth commandment (*rāṣaḥ,* Exod. 20:13), which also encompasses manslaughter. Cain's reaction to the rejection of his offering is much more severe than either of his parents' reactions when confronted by God after their trespass. They resort to making excuses and self-exoneration, but at least they do not indulge in violence. Unable to restrain his resentment and bitterness, Cain vents his wrath on the only possible scapegoat, Abel.

It is going too far to say that "Abel is killed because of God,"[5] unless one would extend that idea to all of the OT and say "Israel is persecuted because of God." After all, God accepted it and rejected the other nations as his covenant vassal. The reason Abel is murdered is because of an unchecked envy and jealousy on Cain's part. Rather than accept God's decision, he rejects the one God has accepted. But this reaction only exacerbates Cain's dilemma. He has eliminated Abel, but what will he do with God?

9 Following the crime comes the divine investigation, as in Gen. 3. God's question is quite legitimate: *Where is Abel your brother?* The first part of Cain's response is a lie: *I do not know.* The second part of that response is a rejection of God's question as an inappropriate one: *Am I my brother's guardian?* The word we have translated *guardian* ("keeper" in most versions) is a participle, *šōmēr,* and Daube has suggested that this is a legal term for a person entrusted with the custody and care of an object.[6] So then, Cain's rejoinder may impute legal responsibility to Cain.

A study of the verb *šāmar* in the OT suggests to some that the answer

4. See W. F. Albright, "Northwest-Semitic Names in a List of Egyptian Slaves," *JAOS* 74 (1954) 229 n. 47; F. Ründgren, "Hebräisch *bäṣär* 'Golderz' und *'amar* 'sagen' Zwei Etymologien," *Or* 32 (1963) 178–83. M. J. Dahood, "Hebrew-Ugaritic Lexicography I," *Bib* 44 (1963) 295–96, all of whom cite OT passages where *'āmar* has the force of "see, look out for." Add to these Exod. 2:14, "are you looking to kill me?" and 1 Sam. 13:19, "because the Philistines saw to it lest the Hebrews make either sword or spear." See also the discussion of *'āmar* by S. Wagner in *TDOT,* 1:328–45, although there is no discussion of Gen. 4:6.

5. See G. von Rad, *Biblical Interpretation in Preaching,* tr. John E. Steely (Nashville: Abingdon, 1977), p. 20.

6. See D. Daube, *Studies in Biblical Law* (Cambridge: Cambridge University, 1947), pp. 13–15.

to Cain's question is no.[7] Nobody is ever charged with the responsibility of being "his brother's keeper." Nothing in Scripture tells us to "keep" our brother. This verb often appears in the OT to describe God's relationship to Israel. He is its keeper and as such he never slumbers or sleeps (Ps. 121:4–8, where 5 times God is called the one who "keeps" Israel). Moses' prayer for the people of Israel is that the Lord bless them and keep them (Num. 6:24). To *keep* means not only to preserve and sustain but to control, regulate, exercise authority over. For this reason today we say that zoos and prisons have keepers, that is, certain individuals who have authority over the occupants. Cain is called to be his brother's lover, claims Riemann, not his brother's keeper. We are not convinced, however, that *šāmar* must carry the nuance of "have authority over" in this verse. It may be that Cain is but disclaiming responsibility for knowing Abel's whereabouts. Thus, he is a liar, evasive and indifferent, when questioned by Yahweh.

10–12 God now shifts his role from interrogator to that of prosecutor: *What have you done!,* a question we punctuate with an exclamation point rather than a question mark, for God is making an accusation, not seeking information. His spilled blood cries from the ground and is heard by God, a concept reflected perhaps by Heb. 11:4 and its reference to "Abel being dead, yet speaks." We have taken Heb. *qôl* as an interjection—*Listen!*—instead of the noun "voice," though there is biblical precedent for attributing a voice to blood (Job 16:18, "O earth cover not my blood, and let its cry find no resting place").[8]

The word used here for *crying, ṣāʿaq,* frequently describes the cry of the oppressed, be they the afflicted in Sodom and Gomorrah (Gen. 18:13), the overworked and exhausted Israelites in Egypt (Exod. 3:7), or the afflicted stranger, widow, or orphan (Exod. 22:21–24). *ṣāʿaq* is associated with the groans of an innocent victim who is brutalized and harassed.

Note that the *blood* itself does not endanger Cain. The blood is not an autonomous, apotropaic force that is targeted at Cain. The shed blood simply cries out to God and leaves the matter with him. Presumably it is for vindication that Abel's blood cries out. For Cain is now bloodguilty; he is liable for punishment for shedding blood.[9] Implicit in this concept of blood-

7. See P. Riemann, "Am I My Brother's Keeper?" *Int* 24 (1970) 482–91; also M. Augsburger, *Faith for a Secular World* (Waco: Word, 1968), pp. 57–59.

8. See GKC, § 146b; cf. M. J. Dahood, "Hebrew-Ugaritic Lexicography IX," *Bib* 52 (1971) 341 n. 2. The pronominal suffix on "cry," *-î,* in Job 16:18 is not 1st person sing. ("my cry"), nor must the suffix be emended to *-ô.*

9. "There is no commutation of the death penalty [for unlawful homicide]. The notion that deliberate homicide cannot be commuted is the foundation stone of

guilt is the idea that acts generate consequences. A person cannot take another's life with impunity. Cain's sin will find him out too.

The reader may be surprised that God does not kill Cain for his flagrant crime. Instead, Cain is *banned from the soil,* which obviously means not that he is barred from contact with the soil but from enjoyment of its productivity.[10] V. 12 explains precisely how this ban will take effect. Far from being sedentary and having the time to harvest crops, Cain will be a *wanderering fugitive* (*nāʿ wānāḏ,* lit., "a wanderer and a fugitive"). We prefer to treat these two Hebrew words as a hendiadys, hence *a wandering fugitive.* Both of these nouns are aptly chosen to describe Cain's punishment, for they each describe the swaying motion of something like reeds or trees (Judg. 9:9; 1 K. 14:15).[11] The first of these words, *nāʿ,* is a participle of *nûaʿ,* which means "shake, reel, stagger, wander." It may refer to relatively small-scale movements, such as the visible movement of Hannah's lips as she prayed (1 Sam. 1:13), or the wandering path of a blind man (Lam. 4:14). Or it may encompass movements on a larger scale, such as the wanderings of homeless vagabonds (Lam. 4:15), or those who travel far and wide in search of water in periods of drought (Amos 4:8). The verb also is used to describe, in a moment of panic or awe, the shaking of the earth (Isa. 24:20), of people encamped at Sinai's base (Exod. 20:18), of the heart (Isa. 7:2), or the doorposts of the temple (Isa. 6:4).

The second word, *nāḏ,* is a participle of *nûḏ,* which means "wander, move to and fro, flee" (see, e.g., Jer. 4:1; 49:30; 50:3). The two verbs are used beside each other again only in Isa. 24:20a: "The earth staggers [*nûaʿ*] like a drunken man, it sways [*nûḏ*] like a hut," a parallelism that clearly indicates the aimlessness of the movement conveyed by these two verbs.

This, then, is Cain's fate. In some ways it is a fate worse than death. It is to lose all sense of belonging and identification with a community. It is to become rootless and detached. Perhaps we, the readers, should at this point view Cain not so much as a villain but as a tragic character.[12] Cain, once a farmer, is now ousted from civilization and is to become a vagabond. Rootlessness is the punishment and the wilderness is the refuge of the sinner.

---

criminal law in the Bible: human life is invaluable, hence incommutable" (J. Milgrom, "Bloodguilt," *EncJud,* 4:1118); see also M. Greenberg, "Bloodguilt," *IDB,* 1:449–50.

10. The word for "yield," *kōaḥ,* lit., "strength," usually means (physical) strength, but it can also designate the produce of the soil.

11. See P. P. Saydon, "Assonance in Hebrew as a means of expressing emphasis," *Bib* 36 (1955) 291–92.

12. See C. H. Gordon, *The Common Background of Greek and Hebrew Civilizations* (New York: Norton, 1965), pp. 15–16.

One need only recall that in biblical typology the representatives of such wanderers are Ishmael and Esau.[13]

13–14 Unlike Adam, who offers no protest against his expulsion from the garden, Cain presents before the Lord his grievance when his sentence is announced. In his opinion, this judgment is too harsh, although the text does not explicitly record why he felt God was overreacting and going beyond even the *lex talionis* concept.

In effect Cain suggests that his *punishment* is fourfold.[14] There will be only a meager return from the soil. He will be hidden from God's face. He is forced into a life of nomadism. Finally, he will be open game for anybody who meets him. This last statement is ironic! He who killed *(hāraḡ)* his own brother now frets lest someone kill *(hāraḡ)* him.

This statement suggests that at this point there are people in the world besides Adam, Eve, and Cain. The existence of others is also indicated later by the reference to Cain's wife (v. 17). Who are these people and where do they come from? Critical scholars see in these details support for the contention that the Cain-Abel story is originally independent of the Adam-Eve narrative, and that the Cain-Abel story surfaced in a period when there was a sizable population. Only later was it added to the Adam-Eve sagas, with the inconsistencies brought about by merger left intact. Or we may suggest that Cain, Abel, and Seth are the only children of Adam and Eve specifically mentioned and named. Cain's wife would be his sister, and those who might kill Cain—assuming a family proliferation that spreads over centuries—would be Cain's siblings. If that is the case, and it is the one we prefer, then the situation is even more freighted with irony. He who turned on one of his relatives now must watch out for any of his relatives. The "avenger of blood," the one who seeks retributive justice against the criminal, may be a family member.

15–16 We now encounter a drastic turnabout in the narrative. Cain, who has been receiving words of judgment, now receives a word of divine promise and an act of divine protection. God's word of judgment (vv. 11–12) and his word of promise (v. 15) are separated from each other by Cain's

13. See S. Talmon, "The Desert Motif," in *Biblical Motifs: Origins and Transformations,* ed. A. Altmann (Cambridge: Harvard University, 1966), pp. 36–37.

14. The word for "punishment" *(ʿāwōn)* can denote both evil and its inherent punishment. Here it is the consequence that is stressed. The Hebrew language has a number of instances where in the semantic process one term expresses both an act and its consequences. See J. Milgrom, *Cult and Conscience* (Leiden: Brill, 1976), p. 4, nn. 9–11, for examples from the "sin/evil" family; and R. Gordis, "Commentary on the Text of Lamentations II," *JQR* 58 (1967) 25, for other examples.

protest (vv. 13–14). This separation raises the question of whether God's action described in v. 15 is a continuation of God's speech to Cain, or whether God's hopeful word is a response and an adjustment by God to Cain's concerns. There certainly is biblical precedent for the concept of a sovereign God who, nevertheless, accommodates himself to the prayers and concern of his children (witness Abraham in Sodom and Gomorrah, Gen. 18; and Moses at the golden calf incident, Exod. 32).

To that end God says *whoever kills Cain shall be avenged sevenfold.* Here is an instance of one infrequent way in which the Bible formulates apodictic law. The person warned is introduced simply with a participle (here *hōrēḡ,* "slays"), which either stands by itself (e.g., Exod. 21:12) or is preceded by *kol* (lit., "all," here "whoever"), with no discernible difference between the two forms.[15]

The verb for *be avenged* is *nāqam.* G. Mendenhall is of the opinion that of the eighty-eight uses of this root in the Bible the only two that have anything to do with blood vengeance are the two used here in Gen. 4 (vv. 15, 24). The original associations of the root with the blood feud do not protrude in the Bible beyond Gen. 4. Instead, it takes on the nuance of either defensive or punitive vindication.[16]

God not only says something, he does something—he puts a *mark* *('ôṯ)* on Cain. Unfortunately, we do not know exactly what this mark was or where it was placed. We do know that *'ôṯ* can function in three ways.[17] First, it can be a sign of proof or evidence of God's power (Exod. 7:3, the plagues; 4:8, 9, 17, 28, 30, signs intended to show that God has sent Moses to Egypt and that the Israelites should believe in him). Second, it can be a symbol, suggesting something else by virtue of resemblance or conventional association. Thus, Ezekiel's sun-dried brick with a relief drawing of Jerusalem under siege is a "sign" for the house of Israel (Ezek. 4:3). This function of sign is

15. See J. G. Williams, "Concerning One of the Apodictic Formulas," *VT* 14 (1964) 484–89; idem, "Addenda to 'Concerning One of the Apodictic Formulas,' " *VT* 15 (1965) 113–15. He takes Gen. 4:15 with the bracketed words: "[This is addressed to] any slayer of Cain: sevenfold shall he be avenged."

16. See G. Mendenhall, "The 'Vengeance' of Yahweh," in *The Tenth Generation* (Baltimore: Johns Hopkins University, 1973), pp. 69–104. "*NQM* is used in situations calling for the exercise of force in contexts that the normal legal institutions of society cannot handle. It refers to executive rather than judicial action, but it is always either clearly based upon some sense of legitimacy. . . . It cannot, therefore, be equated with vengeance defined as the exercise of private self-help" (pp. 76–77). See also G. A. Herion, "Vengeance," *ISBE,* 4:968–69.

17. See M. V. Fox, "The Sign of the Covenant: Circumcision in the Light of the Priestly *'ôt* Etiologies," *RB* 81 (1974) 562–69.

common with the prophets. Third, it can be a sign of cognition, awakening knowledge of something in the observer. This kind of sign includes mnemonic signs (e.g., the rainbow after the Flood, Gen. 9:12, 13, 17; the eating of unleavened bread, Exod. 13:9) and identity signs, as here. The sign identifies Cain as one who is especially protected by God. Parallels to this function of sign are Exod. 12:13 (the blood on the doors at Passover which identifies the occupants); Gen. 1:14 (the heavenly lights which identify time periods); Num. 2:2 (the banners in the Israelite camp which identify the various families); Josh. 2:12 (the sign which identifies Rahab's house).

Another Hebrew word for "sign," *taw,* also functions as a symbol of identity. In his vision Ezekiel sees God's executioners coming on the city. They are told to "put a mark" on those who truly grieve over the city's sins (Ezek. 9:4). When destruction comes those who bear the "mark" are to be spared (9:6). The Hebrew word for "mark" is *taw,* which is the last letter of the Hebrew alphabet. In the older Hebrew script it was shaped like an *X.* Some early Christian exegetes saw here an anticipation of the saving power of the cross, an interpretation which is apologetic and forced, though this Ezekiel passage does serve as a background for all the references to "marking" in the book of Revelation.

Again we hear in the narrative the voice of both law and grace. Sin cannot be ignored or justified. Cain must pay a penalty for his actions. But the God who pronounces the sentence also makes available to the criminal his protection and concern that he too not become a victim of violence. Cain is banned and blessed. He is a marked man, in a positive sense. He leaves God's presence but not God's protection. What God would later say about Mt. Sinai—"whoever touches the mountain shall be put to death" (Exod. 19:12)—he first said about Cain.

The clear assumption made throughout Gen. 4 is that God and Cain are bodily present in their setting, which is somewhere east of the garden of Eden. That Cain left God's presence is Genesis' way of stating how Cain entered his life of alienation from God. Unlike Jonah who did it voluntarily and in his own self-interests (Jon. 1:3), Cain is compelled to leave that presence. He is not sent to Nod; rather he settles in Nod, as if he happens upon it in his own meanderings. *Nod* is, of course, related to the verb *nûḏ,* which had earlier been applied to Cain (Gen. 4:14). He who had been sentenced to be a *nāḏ* settles in the land of *nôḏ.* The wanderer ends up in the land of wandering. God's sentence is, thus, immediately and correctly implemented. Nod is further defined as *eastward of Eden,* a phrase that underscores the distancing of Cain from God's presence, the reality of his lot as one condemned to live the life of an outsider.

3. THE FAMILY OF CAIN (4:17–24)

17 *Cain was intimate with his wife, and she conceived and bore Enoch.*
He was a city builder, and he named the city after the name of his son
Enoch.
18 *To Enoch was born Irad,*[1] *and Irad became the father of Mehujael;*[2]
Mehujael became the father of Methushael;[3] *Methushael became the*
father of Lamech.
19 *Lamech took two wives; the name of the first, Adah, and the name of*
the second, Zillah.
20 *Adah bore Jabal; he was the ancestor of tent dwellers and those*
having livestock.
21 *His brother's name was Jubal; he was the ancestor of all who play*
the lyre and pipe.
22 *As for Zillah, she bore Tubal-cain, the hammerer of (those) fashioning*
bronze and iron.[4] *Tubal-cain's sister was Naamah.*
23 *Lamech said to his wives:*

> *"Adah and Zillah, hear my voice,*
> *wives of Lamech, give ear to my words:*
> *I would kill a man for my wound,*
> *yea, a boy for a my bruise.*
> 24 *If sevenfold avenged is Cain,*
> *then Lamech seventy-sevenfold!"*

1. Note the use of *'eṯ* before the subject of a passive verb *(wayyiwwālēḏ laḥ^{a}nôḵ 'eṯ-ʿîrāḏ),* and compare the same phenomenon in 17:5; 21:5; 27:42; 29:27. The emphatic *'eṯ* as a *nota nominativi* appears 52 times in the OT. It is not, as argued by Polzin, a unique feature of late Biblical Hebrew. In fact, only 7 of its occurrences are in Chronicles and 4 in Nehemiah. The remainder are from sources much earlier. Cf. R. Polzin, *Late Biblical Hebrew: Toward an Historical Typology of Biblical Hebrew Prose,* HSM 12 (Missoula, MT: Scholars, 1976), pp. 32–37; and G. Rendsburg, "Late Biblical Hebrew and the Date of 'P'," *JANES* 12 (1980) 66.

2. The meaning of Mehujael is uncertain. One possibility is "God makes me live" (Skinner, *Genesis,* p. 117). Dahood revocalizes MT *m^{e}ḥûyā'ēl* to *m^{e}ḥûī'ēl,* "battened by God," the Qal passive participle of *mḥy* followed by the accusative of agency ("Eblaite and Biblical Hebrew," *CBQ* 44 [1982] 9 n. 28).

3. Methushael means "man of God" and may be compared with Akk. *mutu-ša-ili.*

4. The MT admittedly looks strange here. The pattern with the first two brothers ("Jabal/Jubal: he was the ancestor of," followed by a participle with a double object) is absent with Tubal-cain. D. N. Freedman ("Notes on Genesis," *ZAW* 64 [1952] 192) attempts to restore an original text by supplying words which scribes supposedly omitted and by taking *kol-ḥōrēš* as a doublet of *kol-lōṭēš.* See also the long footnote in J. Gabriel, "Die Kainitengenealogie, Gn 4,17–24," *Bib* 40 (1959) 411 n. 1.

17 The text says nothing about Cain's marriage. This verse simply assumes that the marriage has already taken place. Cain's wife is not named, but she must be one of the "other daughters" of Adam mentioned in 5:4.

We ended the previous section discussing Cain's fears that he would be killed for the murder of his brother, and God's reassurance that that revenge probably would not occur. Vv. 17–24 confirm that it did not occur. The sign worked—nobody touched Cain. In fact, he is blessed with progeny and a family tree:

1. Cain
2. Enoch
3. Irad
4. Mehujael
5. Methushael
6. Lamech
7. Jabal | Jubal | Tubal-cain | Naamah

It may be of more than passing interest that Cain not only has a family tree, but that this tree consists of the perfect number, seven generations. At this point there is no evidence that God is "visiting the iniquities of the fathers upon the children to the third and fourth generation" (Exod. 20:5). Cain was in no way involved in the consequences of his father's sin. Nor was Enoch in any way made to suffer because of Cain's sin.

Cain's eldest son is *Enoch,* and Cain builds a city which he names after his son.[5] Just as Cain's wife is anonymous, so is the identity and locale of Cain's city. We have only "Mrs. Cain" and "Enoch-ville." The building of

5. There may be a pun in this verse: Cain, who was the builder of a city *(bōneh ʿîr),* named it after his son *(b^{e}nô). bōneh* and *b^{e}nô* are very close in sound. As the Hebrew text now stands, it clearly indicates that Cain was the builder of the city. However, Hebrew syntax would permit, if not suggest, that the subject of "he was a city builder" and "he named the city" was Enoch. For instances of calling a city after one's own name cf. Deut. 3:14 and 2 Sam. 5:9; 12:28. To name a city after oneself or after another probably implies that the named individual assumes ownership over and responsibility for the city that bears his name. See F. S. Frick, *The City in Ancient Israel,* SBLDS 36 (Missoula, MT: Scholars, 1977), p. 41.

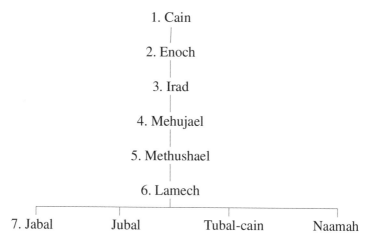

the city seems to contradict God's earlier dictum that Cain would be a fugitive. How shall we explain the shift in Cain from a nomadic life-style back to a more sedentary one?

Perhaps Cain's act is one of defiance. He has had enough of the life of the nomad. He refuses any longer to abide under God's terms. The only other reference to building a city in Gen. 1–11 is the incident at Babel: "Come, let us build ourselves a city . . ." (11:4). Here the whole city-building, tower-erecting project is one that God condemns. But nowhere in Gen. 4 does God state his displeasure with Cain's urban enterprise. Thus Cain's building of the city might represent a divine lifting of the punishment that was once mandated for Cain. He is now free to establish roots and permanence again. If this is the case, however, surely it would be stated more directly. We suggest that Cain's act of city building is an attempt to provide security for himself, a security he is not sure that God's mark guarantees. In the words of J. Ellul, Cain "wants to find alone the remedy for a situation he created, but which he cannot himself repair because it is a situation dependent on God's grace."[6]

18 Of the six generations following Cain, three (Enoch, Lamech, Lamech's children) are provided with additional information. Three others (Irad, Mehujael, Methushael) are simply listed. We are not aware of anything noteworthy they accomplished. Their only significance is that they are early descendants of Adam through Cain. Their names are in the register at least. Their important function is that they are links God provided for the population and the working of the earth.

19 For the first time in the Bible monogamous marriage breaks down. Lamech has two wives, Adah and Zillah.[7] Thus 2:24—"a man shall leave his father and mother and cleave to his wife"—becomes ". . . shall cleave to his wives." To be sure, no rebuke from God is directed at Lamech for his violation of the marital arrangement. It is simply recorded. But that is the case with most OT illustrations of polygamy. Abraham is not condemned for cohabiting with Sarah and Hagar, nor is Jacob for marrying simultaneously Leah and Rachel. In fact, however, nearly every polygamous househould in the OT suffers most unpleasant and shattering experiences precisely because of this ad hoc relationship. The domestic struggles that ensue are devastating.

20–22 Lamech and his wives produce four children. The fourth is

6. J. Ellul, *The Meaning of the City,* tr. D. Pardee (Grand Rapids: Eerdmans, 1970), p. 6. Also, F. S. Frick, *The City in Ancient Israel,* pp. 205–7.

7. For others who had "two wives" see Elkanah (1 Sam. 1:2), David (1 Sam. 27:3; 2 Sam. 2:2), and Ashhur (1 Chr. 4:5).

a daughter, *Naamah,* meaning "pleasant, graceful, gorgeous." She is only identified, and appears to be something of an appendage to the other members of the family. *Naamah* is the one child of Lamech's with no designated archetypal role. The focus is on the three sons: *Jabal, Jubal,* and *Tubal-cain.* Each of them is listed as the ancestor of some cultural accomplishment: Jabal, husbandry; Jubal, music; Tubal-cain, metallurgy.

Genesis is making the point that through the (disobedient) line of Cain many of the world's significant cultural discoveries emerged. This point may provide another illustration of the grace of God at work in this fallen line. They too have an important and wholesome contribution to make to God's world. One is reminded of the Greeks and their contributions in the areas of art and philosophy and of the Romans and their legal and political institutions. They produced what the Hebrews did not.[8]

It is often suggested that there is both an inconsistency and an anachronism with two of these three sons. *Jabal* is identified as *the ancestor of tent dwellers and those having livestock.* Was not Abel already described as a keeper of sheep? How then can Jabal be identified as the progenitor? The answer is found in the fact that the word that describes Jabal's animals *(miqneh)* is a much broader term than that used to describe Abel's flocks *(ṣō'n).* This second term refers only to smaller cattle, sheep, and goats. *miqneh* is a comprehensive term, including, for example, even camels and donkeys, and should be translated as "livestock."

Tubal-cain is identified as the *hammerer of (those) fashioning bronze and iron.* According to most reconstructions of ancient history, human advancement in civilization proceeded through four periods: Stone Age (100,000 B.C.–4000 B.C.); Chalcolithic Age (4000 B.C.–3200 B.C.); Bronze Age (3200 B.C.–1200 B.C.); Iron Age (1200 B.C.–330 B.C.). By contrast, this verse seems to suggest the simultaneous use rather than the sequential use of bronze and iron. Also some translations (RSV "forger") suggest the advanced disciplines of smelting and forging. The participle we have translated *hammerer (lōṭēš)* is from the verb *lāṭaš,* "to hammer, sharpen, whet." The reference here may be to meteoric iron and surface deposits of copper, of which there are examples from the 3rd millennium B.C. (iron magic amulets) and even from the 6th millennium B.C. (copper objects from Turkey).[9]

There is an obvious rhyme with the names *Jabal, Jubal,* and *Tubal.* They can be connected with the word *yōḇēl,* which means "ram" and then

8. See G. Vos, *Biblical Theology,* pp. 46–47.

9. See E. Yamauchi, "Civilization in Ancient Mesopotamia," *JASA* 16 (1966) 31; D. Kidner, *Genesis,* p. 77 n. 2.

"ram's horn" as a musical instrument (Exod. 19:13), and finally "the year of Jubilee" itself (Lev. 25). The basic meaning of *yāḇal* is "to bring in procession." *Jabal,* if a hypocoristicon (i.e., a name abbreviated in some way, usually by the omission of a divine element in the name) for "Jabal-el," would mean "God leads the procession." *Jubal* is a past participle, "brought in the procession." *Tubal* would be the noun "procession."[10] All of the names are festive ones. There is an excitement about each of them.

If we understand Cain's three sons to be the patriarchs of three guilds, then we need to recall that the guild is a distinctively urban phenomenon. Musicians and metalworkers would fit the urban mold nicely. But what is one to do with "tent-dwellers, and those having livestock"? It is quite possible that this group represents professional cattle-breeders and herders who lived near the city, where they were in charge of the herds of their urban patrons.[11]

23–24 The song of Lamech contrasts vividly with the mood created by the immediately preceding verses. Along with the growth in cultural advances is a growth in sin. The flowering of culture and invention does not restrain the escalation of sin. Sandwiched between two happy birth announcements (vv. 20–22, v. 25) is a particularly savage and vicious composition, Lamech's taunt song.

Most translations have Lamech claiming to have killed *(hāragtî)* a man for wounding him. The four lines of v. 23 are taken as an illustration of *parallelismus membrorum.* In other words, the second line repeats the first line, albeit with different vocabulary. For example, *Adah and Zillah* is parallel to *wives of Lamech; man* is parallel to *boy.*[12]

The problem with the latter point is that nowhere else in the OT do *'îš* ("man") and *yeleḏ* ("boy") form a word pair, as S. Gevirtz recognizes. What one would expect would be *'îš* parallel to *ben-'āḏām,* as in Num. 23:19, or *'ᵉnôš* parallel to *ben-'āḏām,* as in Ps. 8:5 (Eng. 4). The Heb. *yeleḏ* covers a wide range of ages. That *yeleḏ* encompasses people other than children is substantiated by the use of this word to describe the young

10. See R. North, "The Cain Music," *JBL* 83 (1964) 380.

11. G. Wallis, "Die Stadt in den Überlieferungen der Genesis," *ZAW* 73 (1966) 134. Note that 2 Chr. 14:14, 15, which speaks of the plundering of cities, also says, "they smote the tents of those who had cattle."

12. This is the approach of S. Gevirtz, *Patterns in the Early Poetry of Israel* (Chicago: University of Chicago, 1963), pp. 25–34. The stichometry of the verses is quite irregular; on this point see D. Stuart, *Studies in Early Hebrew Meter,* HSM 13 (Missoula, MT: Scholars, 1976), pp. 97–99; and R. Alter, *The Art of Biblical Poetry* (New York: Basic Books, 1985), pp. 5, 7–8, 9, 11–13, 17–18.

military advisors with whom Rehoboam surrounded himself (1 K. 12:8). Here *yelādîm* means "young men, young warriors." In that sense, *yeled* could be an acceptable parallel to *'îš*. We are inclined to think that this is not a word pair and that these two lines of the poem are not synonymous. Lamech, if provoked, would not hesitate to kill even a child, let alone an adult.[13] His capacity for retaliation is nondiscriminatory. Then the second line of the poem intensifies Lamech's emotions and makes the possibility for revenge even more aggravated.

The perfect form of the verb *(hāragtî)* would seem to indicate a past event. Whom has Lamech slain? Does the perfect form indicate that this song had its own independent existence, the particulars of which were either lost or deliberately set aside when the editor affixed it to the Cain story? It is possible to argue for the originality of the composition in Gen. 4 by taking the perfect form as an indicator of a conditional sense.[14] Lamech's song speaks not of something that he has already done, but of something that under duress he would not hesitate to do.

Unlike his ancestor several generations earlier who felt the desperate need of divine protection, Lamech feels he is his own security. He can handle any difficulty or any mistreatment quite adequately by himself. If Cain is avenged only sevenfold, he will be avenged seventy-sevenfold.[15] He has no scruples about taking the law into his own hands. Lamech's chief characteristics, in line with his irregular marriages, are not commendable. He is not only replete with a spirit of vindictiveness, but he is also a proud man who backs away from nobody and does not hesitate to kill anybody. Cain's mind-set now surfaces in his great-great-great grandson.

13. See P. Miller, "*Yeled* in the Story of Lamech," *JBL* 85 (1966) 477–78.

14. See J. L. Kugel, *The Idea of Biblical Poetry: Parallelism and Its History* (New Haven: Yale University, 1981), pp. 32–33. His supporting examples of this use of the perfect form are Gen. 42:38 and Judg. 9:9.

15. C. H. Gordon ("Vergil and the Near East," in *Ugaritica* 6 [Paris: Geuthner, 1969] 285–86) draws attention to the fact that the word we have translated in vv. 15 and 24 as "sevenfold"—*šiḇʿāṯayim*—is really the dual of seven, i.e., "fourteen." Following this clue, Gevirtz has observed ("The Life Spans of Joseph and Enoch and the Parallelism *šibʿātayim–šibʿîm wěšibʿāh,*" *JBL* 96 ([1977] 571) an interesting numerical parallelism in the Lamech song. The numbers 14 and 70 work out, respectively, as $1^2 + 2^2 + 3^2$ and $4^2 + 5^2 + 6^2$. Gevirtz does not suggest that such symbolic number schemes contain some profound or mystical truth. He calls such phenomena "a play of wits," "a kind of ancient brain-twister."

4. THE BIRTH OF SETH (4:25–26)

25 *Again Adam was intimate with his wife, and she bore a son whom she called Seth. "God has granted me another offspring, in place of Abel, since Cain killed him."*
26 *To Seth, in turn, was born a son. He named him Enosh. At that time*[1] *men began*[2] *to invoke Yahweh by name.*

25 Note how the Bible gives us information about Adam and Eve (chs. 2–3) and then momentarily removes them from the action (4:1–24). Before Adam reappears the exploits of the next seven generations of offspring are chronicled. Then we go back to Adam. According to the genealogy in Gen. 5, Noah is the first person to be born after the death of Adam. Thus Adam did live to see both the glories and the troubles of his children and his children's children.

There have been a lot of "twos" so far in Genesis: the two in the garden; the two forces, God and the snake, who would direct the lives of people; the voices of judgment and grace; two brothers; two wives; and so forth. Now here in ch. 4 are two births, one at the beginning and one at the end. One son goes askew and the other son fathers a good and godly line. Eve had called the newborn Cain a "man" (4:2), but she calls Seth an *offspring* (Heb. *zeraʿ*, lit., "seed"), which reminds one of the promise made to Eve in 3:15 about "her seed." The possibilities for life that are wrapped up in this seed are enormous.

Adam names the animals and his spouse, but Eve names their children, at least Cain and Seth. The father first assumes that responsibility in the next verse. The explanation Eve provided at the birth of Cain focused on herself: "I have. . . ." The explanation Eve provides at the birth of Seth focuses on God: "God has. . . ." This may indicate a spiritual maturation taking place in Eve, or simply the human role and the divine role present in all births.

26 Seth's son is *Enosh,* which is another Hebrew word for "man," often related to a Hebrew root meaning "to be weak, frail" (cf. Akk. *enēšu,* "to be weak,

1. The particle *'āz,* "then," has a variety of meanings in the OT. It can mean "after this," a time in the past which is related to another event in a temporal sequence. It may suggest "because of this," a time in the past which is related to another event in a logical sequence. It can also designate an event in the past which is not in a sequence. This is the only possible nuance of *'āz* here, the full thrust of which is captured by German *damals.*

2. Lit., "it was begun," the Hophal of *ḥālal* IV. The LXX "he [Enosh] hoped to call on the name of the Lord" is due to the fact that the translators took *hûḥal* from *yāḥal,* "to hope." The interpretations of this phrase are discussed ably by S. Sandmel, "Genesis 4:26b," *HUCA* 32 (1961) 19–29. For *hēḥēl* denoting the first occurrence of something, see P. P. Saydon, "The inceptive imperfect in Hebrew and the verb *hēḥēl* 'to begin,' " *Bib* 35 (1954) 47.

feeble"). It is not apparent, however, that *'ĕnôš* by itself carries the idea of feebleness or frailty. *'ĕnôš* does occur in contexts dealing with man's mortality (e.g., Ps. 103:15, "As for man [*'ĕnôš*], his days are like grass; he flourishes like a flower of the field") or man's hardships in life (e.g., Job 7:1, "Has not man [*'ĕnôš*] a hard service upon earth?"). But *'āḏām* occurs in similar contexts (e.g., Num. 16:29; Ps. 144:3–4), sometimes parallel to *'ĕnôš* (e.g., Ps. 73:5; Isa. 13:12), and *'ĕnôš* is also used in contexts implying strength (e.g., Ps. 56:2 [Eng. 1]; 66:12). Thus *'ĕnôš,* like *'āḏām,* seems to be a general term for "man."[3]

The last part of the verse is curious. Both Cain and Abel worshiped God. Adam and Eve talked with him in the garden, and Cain talked with him outside the garden. Yet, it is noted that only around the time of Seth's birth did men begin *to invoke Yahweh by name.* Source critics remind us that in their schemata this verse contradicts both Exod. 3:13ff. (J) and Exod. 6:3 (P), verses which attribute the worship of Yahweh *qua* Yahweh to the time of Moses. Here worship of Yahweh is connected with the antediluvians.

We suggest that a rethinking of the Exodus passages calls into serious question the alleged ignorance of Yahwism on the part of the patriarchs and earlier persons. The fine points and theological refinement about Yahweh are revealed to Moses. But even granting the jarring juxtaposition of Gen. 4:26 with Exod. 3:13 and 6:3, they may still be reconciled. That may be done by suggesting that "the worship of Yahweh was in all likelihood confined at first to a small body of seachers . . . it was this movement that found a worthy recorder in J."[4] The God of Israel is not just Israel's God, but the Lord of history who embraces all mankind.

These early chapters of Genesis have a strong emphasis on names: Adam, Eve, Cain, Seth. We observe in this last verse the twofold use of *name:*

3. See the study of *'ĕnôš* by F. Maass, *TDOT,* 1:345–48.

4. Speiser, *Genesis,* p. 37. Dahood ("Ebla, Ugarit, and the Bible," in G. Pettinato, *The Archives of Ebla* [Garden City, NY: Doubleday, 1981], pp. 276–77) notes the existence of Ya at Ebla. Applying this evidence to Gen. 4:6, he suggests the possibility that the verse preserves a north or Syrian tradition where, unlike the Exodus texts from an Egyptian tradition, the name Ya was known in the 3rd millennium B.C. See also C. H. Gordon, *The Ancient Near East,* 3rd ed. (New York: Norton, 1965), p. 38. G. Pettinato ("Ebla and the Bible," *BA* 43 [1980] 203–5) also argues for *-ya* as a theophoric element at Ebla, and appeals especially to names where *ya-* is the first element of the name and is preceded by the divine determinative, as in *ᵈyà-ra-mu.* The presence of Yah as deity in the Ebla texts is rejected by both A. Archi, "The Epigraphic Evidence from Ebla and the Old Testament," *Bib* 60 (1979) 556–60, and A. Rainey in a letter to the editor, *BAR* 3/1 (1977) 38. Both Archi and Rainey argue that *-ya* endings on personal names are simply shortened forms usually used for endearment, as in English Richard/Ricky or Donald/Donny.

he named him Enoch (Heb. *yiqrā' 'eṯ-šᵉmô 'ĕnôš,* lit., "he called his name Enoch"); *to invoke Yahweh by name* (*liqrō' bᵉšēm yhwh,* lit., "to call on the name of Yahweh"). God too has a name. But unlike all the other names, it is not something that is bequeathed to him. It is the one name in Genesis to which all other names become subservient. On that one name alone may a person call, in worship and adoration.

THE NEW TESTAMENT APPROPRIATION

a. Gen. 4 and Matt. 23:35 (par. Luke 11:51); Heb. 12:24

Each of these NT verses uses Abel's death as a foreshadowing of either Christ's sufferings (Heb. 12:24) or the persecution of believers (Matt. 23:35). Abel is coupled with Zechariah (Matt. 23:35) as the first (Gen. 4) and last (2 Chr. 24:20-22) victims of murder mentioned in the OT. (Chronicles is the last book in the Hebrew canon.) Understandably Abel is characterized as "innocent" but Zechariah is simply named.

b. Gen. 4 and 1 John 3:11-12

John admonishes his audience to love one another (cf. John 13:34; 15:12, 17). Then he provides a negative example of the behavior he is condemning. One who did not love his brother was Cain. Instead, Cain murdered his brother. (This, by the way, is the only OT story referred to in 1 John, perhaps because it provides a reference for his later allusion to a murderer—1:15.) The verb that John uses to describe Cain's murder of Abel is *spházein*, and it appears only eight more times in the NT, all in the book of Revelation (5:6, 9, 12; 6:9; etc.). It always indicates violent death and therefore may be rendered "butchered."

John adds two items not observed in Gen. 4. First, he states that Cain "was of [or 'belonged to'] the evil one." This sounds like Jesus' words "you are of your father the devil" (John 8:44). Cain was not acting totally independently. His murder of Abel was an external manifestation of the grip that Satan had on his life.[1] Second, Cain killed because his own deeds were evil. Here John may be alluding to Gen. 4:7. Cain actually did two evil deeds. The second, of course, was taking his brother's life. The first, which made possible the second, was Cain's allowing "crouching sin" to leap at him and overpower him. The problem

1. R. Brown (*The Epistles of John,* AB [Garden City, NY: Doubleday, 1982], pp. 440-44) is particularly creative in his discussion of John's use of the Cain-Abel scenario.

could have been restricted at this time, but Cain chose acquiescence rather than resistance. One evil deed thus paved the way for a second.

c. Gen. 4 and Jude 11

Jude writes his brief epistle to warn against false teachers who have infiltrated the community of believers.[2] Such opponents are characterized by him as antinomian (v. 4), immoral (v. 8), free with intemperate language (v. 10), irrational (v. 10), grumbling malcontents who worship their feelings (v. 16).

In v. 11 he compares these false teachers to three OT individuals: Cain, Balaam (Num. 22–24), and Korah (Num. 16:19–35). The first is a murderer, the second is greedy, and the third is rebellious, three of the charges Jude places against these false teachers. The three OT individuals are not listed in chronological order (where one would expect Cain, Korah, Balaam). Nor is there any indication that the order is scaled according to the seriousness of the trespasser.

In the light of the fact that elsewhere in the epistle Jude uses the present tense to describe the activities of the heretics, but here he uses three aorists, it may be that he is describing the fate of these ungodly OT individuals.[3] People who chose to live that way perished. So will these false teachers if they do not radically change their behavior.

d. Gen. 4 and Heb. 11:4

The writer of Hebrews begins his great chapter on faith with a functional definition (v. 1). Then he provides illustrations of that faith functioning in the lives of OT saints (vv. 2, 4ff.). Before going into specific illustrations of these "men of old," he has a word about faith as necessary in believing that this

2. For general background on Jude see D. J. Rowston, "The Most Neglected Book in the New Testament," *NTS* 21 (1975) 554–63. "If James is written to confront a dead orthodoxy. . . . Jude may be a tract against lively libertinism" (p. 556). James protests a distortion of the Pauline justification by grace, and Jude inveighs against a distortion of the Pauline salvation by grace.

3. See G. H. Boobyer, "The Verbs in Jude 11," *NTS* 5 (1958) 45–47. "They [the aorists in v. 12] are examples of the established use of the aorist to give more graphic expression to future events, or events intended, even initiated, but not yet reaching their consummation" (p. 47). Compare the two aorists in John 15:6, *eblḗthē* and *exēpánthē,* for the same usage ("If a man does not abide in me, he is cast forth as a branch and withers"). For the proleptic aorist see J. H. Moulton, *A Grammar of New Testament Greek, III, Syntax* (Edinburgh: T. & T. Clark, 1962), p. 74. For the related gnomic aorist, see Moulton, p. 73, and F. Blass and A. Debrunner, *A Greek Grammar of the New Testament and Other Early Christian Literature,* tr. R. W. Funk (Chicago: University of Chicago, 1961), § 333.

world is God's creation (v. 3). Thus, Adam is not directly mentioned—for his was a life of obedience rather than of faith—but the Creation story of which he is a part is mentioned.

The first in the list is Abel. Nothing is said about his righteous brother Seth. Abel's offering is distinguished from Cain's (and notice that Cain is the only person mentioned in this chapter for reasons other than a faith illustration) in that Abel presented his "by faith." No further comment is made on what was involved in Abel's faith offering.

It is his faith, not the gift per se, that is the significant element in his receiving witness from God that he is righteous (not "became righteous"). The antecedent of "through (or by) which" can grammatically be either "faith" or "sacrifice," but the former is preferred on the basis of the analogy in vv. 2–3—"faith . . . by *it*. . . ."[4] It is the attitude and not the content of the sacrifice that is the deciding factor.

Even death does not mute Abel's voice. He lives on through his example. For he is the first embodiment of how to approach God.

E. FROM ADAM TO NOAH: TEN GENERATIONS (5:1–32)

1 *This is the document concerning Adam's descendants. When God created man, in the likeness of God he made him;*

2 *male and female he created them. And when they were created he blessed them and named them "man."*

3 *Adam was 130 years old*[1] *when he fathered a son in his likeness, after his image; and he named him Seth.*

4 *Adam lived 800 years after the birth of Seth, and he fathered sons and daughters.*

5 *Adam's life totaled 930 years; then he died.*

6 *Seth was 105 years old when he fatherd Enosh.*

7 *Seth lived 807 years after the birth of Enosh, and he fathered sons and daughters.*

4. See J. Moffatt, *Epistle to the Hebrews,* ICC (Edinburgh: T. & T. Clark, 1924), pp. 163–64; and G. W. Buchanan, *To the Hebrews,* AB (Garden City, NY: Doubleday, 1972), p. 185. Some believe the antecedent is "sacrifice"; cf. C. Spicq, *L'Épître aux Hébreux,* 2 vols., Études bibliques (Paris: Gabalda, 1952–1953), 2:342.

1. An unsolvable problem in this chapter is the differences in numbers among the 3 ancient witnesses to the biblical text: MT, SP, and LXX. Below are the conflicting numbers; the first column for each source is the age at the birth of the first son, and the second column is the age at death.

8 *Seth's life totaled 912 years; then he died.*

9 *Enosh was 90 years old when he fathered Kenan.*

10 *Enosh lived 815 years after the birth of Kenan, and he fathered sons and daughters.*

11 *Enosh's life totaled 905 years; then he died.*

12 *Kenan was 70 years old when he fathered Mahalalel.*

13 *Kenan lived 840 years after the birth of Mahalalel, and he fathered sons and daughters.*

14 *Kenan's life totaled 910 years; then he died.*

15 *Mahalalel was 65 years old when he fathered Jered.*

16 *Mahalalel lived 830 years after the birth of Jered, and he fathered sons and daughters.*

17 *Mahalalel's life totaled 895 years; then he died.*

18 *Jered was 162 years old when he fathered Enoch.*

19 *Jered lived 800 years after the birth of Enoch, and he fathered sons and daughters.*

20 *Jered's life totaled 962 years; then he died.*

21 *Enoch was 65 years old when he fathered Methuselah.*

22 *Enoch walked with God. (He lived) 300 years after the birth of Methusaleh, and he fathered sons and daughters.*

23 *Enoch's life totaled 365 years.*

24 *Enoch walked with God, then was no more, for God took him.*

25 *Methusaleh was 187 years old when he fathered Lamech.*

	MT		SP		LXX	
Adam	130	930	130	930	230	930
Seth	105	912	105	912	205	912
Enosh	90	905	90	905	190	905
Kenan	70	910	70	910	170	910
Mahalalel	65	895	65	895	165	895
Jered	162	962	62	847	162	962
Enoch	65	365	65	365	165	365
Methusaleh	187	969	67	720	167	969
Lamech	182	777	53	653	188	753
Noah	500	950	500	950	500	950
(Age at flood)	100		100		100	
	1656		1307		2262	

Here then are 3 textual traditions about the time between Adam and the Flood: MT, 1656 years; SP, 1307 years; LXX, 2262 years. According to the MT Methuselah dies in the year of the Flood (130 + 105 + 90 + 70 + 65 + 162 + 65 + 969 = 1656).

26 *Methusaleh lived 782 years after the birth of Lamech, and he fathered sons and daughters.*
27 *Methusaleh's life totaled 969 years; then he died.*
28 *Lamech was 182 years old when he fathered a son.*
29 *He named him Noah, saying, "This one will bring us relief from the agonizing toil of our hands, from the very ground Yahweh has cursed."*
30 *Lamech lived 595 years after the birth of Noah, and he fathered sons and daughters.*
31 *Lamech's life totaled 777 years; then he died.*
32 *Noah was 500 years old when he fathered Shem, Ham, and Japheth.*

Most readers of Scripture do not normally consider the genealogies among its more exciting parts. Their virtual dismissal by most lay readers contrasts sharply with biblical scholars' obsession with them. For the latter, genealogy may be more fascinating than narrative, because of the historical curiosity that most biblical scholars bring to the text.

Of the opening eleven chapters of Genesis, two are given exclusively to genealogical concerns—chs. 5 and 10. (Two additional chapters in this unit combine narrative and genealogy, in that order—chs. 4 and 11.) Ch. 5 traces the lineage from Adam to Noah. Ch. 10 focuses on the three sons of Noah and their respective descendants, and where each settled. Both lists serve, as much as the narratives, as evidences of God's blessing upon these antediluvian figures and upon the eventual line that produces Abraham. Such blessing is manifested in chronological succession (ch. 5) and territorial expansion (ch. 10).

Throughout this opening section of Genesis narrative and genealogy alternate in the following way:

narrative: 1:1–4:16
genealogy: 4:17–5:32
narrative: 6:1–9:28
genealogy: 10:1–32
narrative: 11:1–9
genealogy: 11:10–32

This feature is by no means unique to Hebrew literature. The artistic combination of action and genealogy, say, in Homeric epic, should warn against the dismembering of the biblical text by tracing the narratives to one source and the genealogies to another.

The genealogies in Genesis take two different forms. One we may call linear or vertical. It traces an unbroken line of descendants from A to Z. Gen. 5:1–32 and 11:10ff. are two illustrations of this kind of genealogy. The first traces the line from Adam to Noah, and the second covers the generations from Shem to Terah. The other type of genealogy is segmented or horizontal. This form traces descent from one individual through several of his children. Examples are 10:1ff. (Noah's sons); 25:12ff. (Ishmael's sons); 36:1ff. (Esau's sons). The linear ones clearly carry more weight in Genesis, for they concentrate on the chosen line. It is around these two genealogies, rather than the other three, that the narrative traditions of Genesis are developed.[2]

Studies on the genealogy in ch. 5 have focused on two areas. First, what is the relationship of the genealogy in ch. 5 to that in 4:17–22? Second, what is the literary source behind ch. 5? One may observe some interesting parallels in these two genealogies:

4:17–22

1. Adam
2. Cain
3. Enoch
4. Irad
5. Mehujael
6. Methushael
7. Lamech

Jabal Jubal Tubal-cain Naamah

5:1–32

1. Adam
2. Seth
3. Enosh
4. Kenan
5. Mahalalel
6. Jared
7. Enoch
8. Methuselah
9. Lamech
10. Noah

Shem Ham Japheth

The most obvious parallel is that both are linear genealogies which suddenly shift to a segmented genealogy at the end, where both list three

2. See B. S. Childs, *Introduction to the Old Testament as Scripture,* p. 146.

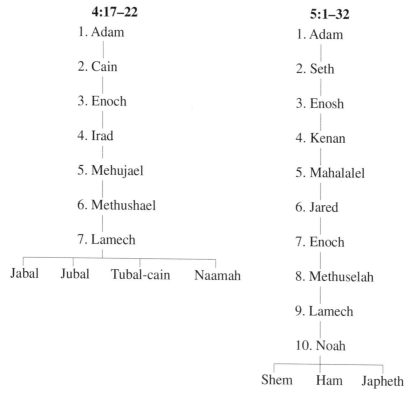

sons. Second, a few names in both are written the same. There is a Cainite Enoch (3) and a Sethite Enoch (7). There is a Cainite Lamech (7) and a Sethite Lamech (9). In addition, some names in both lists sound alike: Irad/Jared; Mehujael/Mahalalel; Methushael/Methuselah; Enoch/Enosh (some different consonants but the same vowel pattern).

A number of possibilities have been suggested to explain the similarity of names. The standard source approach is to take the second genealogy (ch. 5) as one produced by the postexilic Priestly writers (P). The similarities are due to the fact that the later composers had at their disposal the earlier Yahwistic genealogy (4:17–22). From this list they took their names and arbitrarily switched the order and in some cases the pronunciation. However, the differences in order and spelling seem to demonstrate the opposite. That is, if the author of ch. 5 is different from that of ch. 4, the differences are significant enough to say that P was unaware of J.

A second suggestion is that the writers of chs. 4 and 5 were dependent upon a single stock genealogy which may have circulated among the early tribal groups of Syria-Palestine. Both traditions secondarily and in their own way expanded this genealogy.[3]

A third suggestion, that of R. R. Wilson, appeals to sociological and anthropological data. He has suggested that one characteristic of genealogies is their fluidity; specifically, he notes that the form of a genealogy frequently changes when its function changes. The emphasis of J was the growth of sin. The emphasis of P was the transmission of the divine image. So then, these "contradictions" are not really contradictions at all. Each version is correct for the particular point it wishes to make.[4] But this explanation still does not provide the particulars on why Lamech is seventh in one list and ninth in another. How does the shifting of position underline this different function? Are such changes simply capricious?

Although it does not enjoy acceptance by critical scholars, the best explanation is the simplest one, that we are dealing here with two distinct lines. Ch. 4 traces the descendants of Cain and ch. 5 traces the descendants of Seth. It was not uncommon for two people to bear the same name at the same time. This approach, even if it is labeled as specious harmonization,

3. See J. M. Miller, "The Descendants of Cain: Notes on Genesis 4," *ZAW* 86 (1974) 164–74.

4. See R. R. Wilson, "The Old Testament Genealogies in Recent Research," *JBL* 94 (1975) 169–89; idem, *Genealogy and History in the Biblical World* (New Haven/London: Yale University, 1977), pp. 138–66; D. T. Bryan, "A Reevaluation of Gen 4 and 5 in the Light of Recent Studies in Genealogical Fluidity," *ZAW* 99 (1987) 180–88.

has certain advantages. First, it takes the text on its own terms and does not resort to hypothetical reconstruction. Second, it does not force the equation of names that are really incompatible. For instance, Jared and Irad, apart from the *r-d* sequence, are quite dissimilar in Hebrew (*yereḏ* and *ʿîraḏ,* respectively). Third, it removes imaginary problems such as the attempts to see in one person the conflicting image of a Cainite Lamech who is vengeful and a Sethite Lamech who is quite the opposite.

The sequence of the two genealogies is appropriate: the godly line follows the ungodly line. As a matter of fact, the more important line is so designated by back-to-back genealogies. First there is a brief one extending over three generations (Adam to Enosh), 4:25–26; and then a lengthier one extending over ten generations (Adam to Noah and his sons), 5:1–32. Inserted between these two Sethite lists is the information about the origin of confessional Yahwism (4:26b). This note, provocatively brief and coming where it does, highlights the significant contribution of this line to the world. Their bequeathal to history is not culture but theology.

The second issue related to the origins of ch. 5 is whether a case can be made for identifying some extrabiblical composition as the source from which the genealogy in ch. 5 was either borrowed or after which it was modeled. The most popular parallel is a composition known as the Sumerian King List.[5] The date of its compilation is debated,[6] but most likely it was composed during the reign of the Sumerian King Utuhegal (ca. 2000 B.C.). At this time two outstanding events in the history of Sumer took place: the end of the rule of Akkad over Sumer, and the rise of Ur III (2100–2000 B.C.). Perhaps it was these happy occasions that triggered the composition of the King List. Utuhegal, the king of Uruk, and the liberator of Sumer, may have compiled this list to "prove" that his country (Sumer) had always been united under one king, although the kings lived in different capitals. It presents an artificial unity, then, in the face of real dissension.[7]

5. The definitive edition of this King List is T. Jacobsen, *The Sumerian King List,* Assyriological Studies 11 (Chicago: Oriental Institute, 1939). See also *ANET,* p. 265.

6. See M. B. Rowton, "The Date of the Sumerian King List," *JNES* 19 (1960) 156–62.

7. This view of the raison d'être of the King List is not accepted by all. For example, Hallo fails to see such tendentiousness behind the work. He views it as a reflection of the tension between statism and imperialism. The King List "recognized the reality of different and even conflicting sovereignties among the separate city-states, while yet maintaining the ideal that, at any one time, one city and its king were recognized as first among equals" (W. W. Hallo and W. K. Simpson, *The Ancient Near East: A History* [New York: Harcourt, Brace, Jovanovich, 1971], p. 39).

The King List begins by stating that "kingship was lowered from heaven." Indeed, the native title for the King List is *nam-lugal,* "kingship." Then follows a list of eight kings, the cities over which they ruled, and the length of their reigns.

King	City	Length of Reign in Years
1. Alulim	Eridu	28,800
2. Alalgar	Eridu	36,000
3. Enmenluanna	Badtibira	43,200
4. Enmengalanna	Badtibira	28,800
5. Dumuzi	Badtibira	36,000
6. Ensipazianna	Larak	28,800
7. Enmenduranna	Sippar	21,000
8. Ubartutu	Shuruppak	18,600
8 kings[8]	5 cities	241,200 years

Then comes a reference to the Flood: "These are five cities, eight kings ruled them for 241,000 years. (Then) the Flood swept over (the earth)." This note about the deluge is followed by a list of thirty-nine postdiluvian kings. The length of reign for these postdiluvians is considerably shorter than their antediluvian counterparts. The longest reign here is that of Etana,[9] for 1560 years. Thus the structure of the Sumerian King List is:

(i) an introductory note about the origin of kingship
(ii) eight antediluvian kings who reign for 241,200 years
(iii) the Flood
(iv) thirty-nine postdiluvian kings who reign for 26,997 years.

Now, it is quite clear that there is a superficial parallel between the Sumerian King List and Gen. 5–11. This parallel consists in a list of pre-Flood individuals who lived amazingly long lives. Then the Flood brings civilization to a halt. Next there appears a line of post-Flood persons whose life spans are

8. Other editions of the King List have 10 instead of 8 kings. This tradition of 10 antediluvian kings is as ancient as Berossos, a Babylonian priest of the 3rd century B.C., who said that the Babylonians counted 10 generations from creation to the Flood. Some have used the variation between 8 and 10 kings as an antecedent for the variation between 7 generations in 4:17–22 and 10 generations in 5:1–32.

9. The first subdivision of the postdiluvian kings includes 23 kings. Etana is the only one who is known from a source outside the King List. Here he is listed as the thirteenth ruler, but these other sources list him as the first post-Flood ruler. See *ANET,* pp. 114ff., for the story of Etana. Hallo (*Ancient Near East,* p. 41 figure 7) attempts a reconstruction of the First (post-Flood) Dynasty of Kish.

considerably shorter. (In Gen. 11 the range is from 600 years for Shem to 148 years for Nahor.) The existence of such genealogical inscriptions as the Sumerian King List, plus others like it,[10] demonstrates that the Sumerians and Semitic tribes west of the Euphrates had evolved and elaborated genealogical traditions no later than the turn of the 3rd millennium B.C. Perhaps this evidence should caution one against attributing all, or most, biblical genealogies to a late period in OT history, specifically to the Priestly school.

Apart from structural parallels, Gen. 5 and the Sumerian King List are quite different. For one thing, the Sumerian King List addresses only the introduction of an institution—kingship. By contrast, Gen. 5 traces the descent of mankind from Adam, as a creation of God, to Noah and his sons.[11] However far one pushes back the origin of humanity, says Gen. 5, one never finds anything more than man. Man, even earliest man, never becomes a god. He is simply "earthling." The chasm between the infinte and the finite is never bridged.[12]

The farther one goes back in Sumerian history the more vague that line of demarcation becomes. Thus, the Sumerian King List has lines like these: "Mes-kiag-gasher, the son of the (sun) god Utu became high priest as well as king . . . the god Lugalbanda, a shepherd, ruled 1,200 years; the god Dumuzi . . . ruled 100 years; the divine Gilgamesh . . . ruled 126 years." Such notions of apotheosis are explicitly ruled out by the Genesis genealogies.

It will also be noted that the large numbers in Gen. 5 are dwarfed by those in the Sumerian King List. Methuselah's 969 years are relatively brief when laid alongside Enmenluanna's 43,200 years.[13] In addition, the Sumer-

10. See the Assyrian King List and the genealogy of the Hammurapi Dynasty. On the latter see J. J. Finkelstein, "The Genealogy of the Hammurapi Dynasty," *JCS* 20 (1966) 95–118, esp. p. 116.

11. See T. C. Hartmann, "Some Thoughts on the Sumerian King List and Genesis 5 and 11B," *JBL* 91 (1972) 28.

12. The Assyrian King List does have as its second king one called "Adamu." For bibliography on this genealogy compare A. Poebel, "The Assyrian King List from Khorsabad," *JNES* 1 (1942) 247–306, 460–92; 2 (1943) 56–90; I. J. Gelb, "Two Assyrian King Lists," *JNES* 13 (1954) 209–30. Finkelstein (*JCS* 20 [1966] 100) links Adamu with the name of a deity ^{d}Admun known in the Mari records, and the place name Admun. He notes that Adamu even occurs as the name of a woman in Old Babylonian texts from Chagar Bazar!

13. J. Walton ("The Antediluvian Section of the Sumerian King List and Genesis 5," *BA* 44 [1981] 207–8) suggests that the vast difference between the years in the two sources can be traced to the use of the decimal system by most Semites and the sexagesimal system by the Sumerians. According to Walton, a scribe read a notation as one number system when the document intended the other system.

ian King List gives the length of reign, but for Gen. 5 the years given designate the length of life. In view of the numerous differences between the two, perhaps it is best to designate the literary genre of the Sumerian inscription as king list and the literary genre of Gen. 5 as genealogy.[14]

This is not to say that Gen. 5 was produced in the midst of a literary vacuum. A. Malamat has shown that these early genealogies in Genesis stem from archetypes among West Semitic tribes from the Old Babylonian period where the ten-generation list is frequent.[15] Applying this observation to Gen. 5 leads us to believe that the names of Gen. 5 need not be understood sequentially. Thus the figures cannot be added to arrive at the age of mankind. Instead, what we have here are symmetrical genealogies: ten generations before the Flood (Gen. 5) and ten generations after the Flood (Gen. 11). So when Gen. 5 says that "*X* fathered *Y*" it may mean that "*X* fathered the line culminating in *Y*."[16]

1–2 The genealogy of Adam is introduced as the *document concerning Adam's descendants* (Heb. *sēp̄er tôlᵉḏōṯ 'āḏām,* lit., "book of the generations of Adam"). Our modern understanding of "book" (so AV, RSV) should not mislead us here. *sēp̄er* simply means something that is inscribed, irrespective of the external form it takes. For example, a tablet can be a *sēp̄er.*[17]

Hebrew *'āḏām* is used in two strikingly different ways in these two

14. G. F. Hasel ("The Genealogies of Gen. 5 and 11 and Their Alleged Babylonian Background," *AUSS* 16 [1978] 361–74) lists ten differences between the two. Cf. also Westermann, *Genesis,* 1:347–54, who minimizes the parallels between Gen. 5 and the Sumerian King List.

15. See A. Malamat, "King Lists of the Old Babylonian Period and Biblical Genealogies," *JAOS* 88 (1968) 163–73; idem, "Tribal Societies: Biblical Genealogies and African Lineage Systems," *Archives européennes de sociologie* 14 (1973) 126–36. Malamat's contention that the Amorites had genealogies of a standard four-part structure and a stereotypical depth of ten generations has been challenged by R. Wilson, "Old Testament Genealogies," *JBL* 94 (1975) 186–88.

16. The genealogy of Jesus in Matt. 1 is similarly symmetrical: 3 sections of 14 generations. Yet when Matt. 1:8 says that "Joram fathered Uzziah" we know that 3 generations are bypassed. The actual order is: Joram, Ahaziah, Joash, Amaziah, Uzziah. Thus "Joram fathered Uzziah" can only mean he fathered the line culminating in Uzziah. Three kings, 3 generations, and about 60 years stand between Joram and Uzziah. Note also that Matt. 1:11 calls Josiah the father of Jechoniah when in fact he was the grandfather of Jechoniah.

17. Perhaps the original meaning of the verb *sāp̄ar* is "to scrape," which would then include the scraping of a surface to make it smooth for writing. In Biblical Hebrew *sāp̄ar* means both "to count" and "to tell, relate." This double meaning is reflected in English, where a synonym for "retell" is "recount." Those who count money in a bank are called tellers.

verses. It is a proper name, as we saw throughout chs. 2–4, and it also refers here to "mankind," as we saw in ch. 1 and sporadically in chs. 2–3. These opening verses take us back into the milieu of 1:26–28. Now why does the narrative regress? Why another reference to the creation of the first human beings as the blessed and divine image bearers? To be sure, vv. 1–5 are different in structure from the following paragraphs. But it is not necessary to assume that originally vv. 1–5 conformed to the pattern throughout the rest of the chapter. We are unable to agree, therefore, with those who suggest that vv. 1b–2 are secondary.[18]

The originality of the verses can be defended on two grounds. First, their presence is necessary as a prolegomenon to the specifics that follow. Vv. 1b–2 are an introductory superscription that describes the cause of the effects detailed in the following verses. That Adam reproduces himself through Seth, and Seth through Enosh, etc., demonstrates that God's blessing has become effective. They are not only created by God but blessed by God. Such blessing is manifested in multiplication. It is appropriate that the creation of man be prefaced to Adam's descendants through Seth rather than through Cain.

Furthermore, the reference to Gen. 1 at the start of this chapter permits a contrast between a divine creative act and human creative acts. In a sense Adam and his posterity are doing what God did. He created and they are procreating. The excision of vv. 1b–2 would eliminate this contrast between divine and human activity.

3–5 These verses give us the structure that is used throughout the remainder of the chapter (with two exceptions). First comes the age of the father at the birth of his firstborn son (130 years), then the name of this son (Seth). The son's birth, and that of subsequent children, is described repeatedly with Heb. *wayyôleḏ,* the Hiphil of *yālaḏ*. (*wayyôleḏ* appears 23 times in this chapter, and only 17 times more in the OT, 8 of which are in ch. 11.) The third part of the structure is the mention of how many years the father lived after the birth of this son (800). Fourth is the reference to the fathering of other children, *sons and daughters.* Fifth, and last, is the recording of the father's age at his death (930).

This genealogy is concerned only with the firstborn son of each new generation and with the transmission of the divine image and likeness from generation to generation. There is no evidence that the events of ch. 3 have scarred this transmission. This does not mean that the author of ch. 5 is

18. See M. D. Johnson, *The Purpose of the Biblical Genealogies,* SNTSMS 8 (Cambridge: Cambridge University, 1969), p. 18.

unaware of the Fall, or that he considers the Fall unimportant, or that the Fall is not a part of his theological system. We need not isolate so-called P material from J material; quite the opposite. In spite of the quagmire of ch. 3, the genealogy of this chapter and the transmission of the divine image may be one way in which the writer is stressing his point about the operations of divine grace.

Further data in this chapter support the writer's emphasis on grace. We suggest that the longevity of these individuals is confirming evidence. The theological explanation of lives that span almost a millennium is that they are a reflection of God's blessing upon the Sethite ancestors of the human race.[19] It is well known that later books of the Bible, especially Deuteronomy, hold out before the obedient Israelites the promise of "growing old" (Deut. 4:25), "living long" (5:33; 11:9; 22:7), "length of days" (30:20), and "prolonging of days" (5:16; 6:2).

The fact that life spans diminish radically after the Flood may be the Bible's way of saying that history is regressing rather than advancing. Also, in the light of the widespread tradition among the ancients (the Sumerian King List, the OT, Hesiod's *Works and Days*) about heroic, distant ancestors who lived long lives, we need to ask whether the long lives of the Sethites reflect a common legendary theme, or whether they perpetuate what was once indeed the condition of the human race.[20] Of course, the pervasive existence of the motif of inordinately long life in the literature of the ancients does not in itself provide evidence for the historicity of these life spans in antiquity. And while a life of 900 years is more credible than a life of 43,000 years, it still defies rational explanation.

6–20 These verses continue the genealogical line and note the successive appearance of Seth, Enosh, Kenan, Mahalalel, and Jered. Three of these individuals (Kenan, Mahalalel, Jered) appear only here in the Bible (except for Jesus' genealogy in Luke 3:23–38). They are simply a link, like some of the individuals in the Cainite line. Like them, they are also incognito.

19. At the scientific level it has been suggested that before the Flood, while the vapor canopy was still in the heavens, deadly age-causing rays were filtered out from the atmosphere and as a result people were not subject to aging. See J. C. Whitcomb and H. M. Morris, *The Genesis Flood* (Philadelphia: Presbyterian & Reformed, 1963), pp. 399–405.

20. On the question of high numbers and historicity see K. A. Kitchen, *Ancient Orient and Old Testament* (Chicago: Inter-Varsity, 1966), pp. 39–41. The descending scale for life spans in the OT is roughly 1000–800 (Adam to Lamech); 600–200 (Noah to Abraham); 200–100 (Abraham to Joseph/Moses); 70 years (Ps. 90:10).

But however inconspicuous they may be in the biblical record, they still play a vital role in forwarding God's plan to produce an Abraham by whom the world will be blessed and a greater son of Abraham by whom the world again will be blessed.

21–24 The seventh person in this genealogy is *Enoch.* Biblical genealogists often placed in the seventh position individuals who are uniquely important.[21] Enoch is the one person of whom it is not said that he died. Instead, *God took him.* This may be one indication in this chapter that long life per se is not the most sacred and honorable blessing that can come from God. To be lifted aloft into God's immediate presence is perhaps more of an honor.[22] This is a privilege Enoch shares only with Elijah (2 K. 2:11), and so only "twice the gates of Sheol had not prevailed."[23]

We have here the intriguing situation of the father who does not die and the son who lives the longest of any human being. And we have the person in Gen. 5 living on earth the shortest and fathering the person who in Gen. 5 lives the longest on earth.

Enoch's life at his removal is 365 years, and it has often been noted that this corresponds in years to the number of days in a solar year.[24] The seventh king in the Sumerian King List—Enmenduranna—is associated with the city of Sippar, whose tutelary deity was Utu the sun-god. In the prologue of the Code of Hammurapi it is recorded that Shamash relaid the foundations of Sippar.[25] To commentators all these data have suggested that Enoch may have once been the pivotal figure around whom a sun-worship cult flourished. Further support of this theory is sought in Jewish apocalyptic literature, where two books are ascribed to him, the Ethiopic Book of Enoch (also called 1 Enoch, the one from which Jude quotes in vv. 14–15) and the Slavonic Book of Enoch (also called 2 Enoch). Both books deal with Enoch's journey through the universe in which he is granted a view of creation, judgment, the seven heavens, and various astronomical information. But surely anybody would agree that Gen. 5 has not the slightest trace of this

21. See J. M. Sasson, "A Genealogical 'Convention' in Biblical Chronography," *ZAW* 90 (1978) 175–76; idem, "Generation, Seventh," *IDBS,* pp. 354–56, who comments on Enoch as the seventh from Adam.

22. See L. Zachmann, "Beobachtungen zur Theologie in Gen. 5," *ZAW* 88 (1976) 272–74.

23. See Kidner, *Genesis,* p. 81.

24. See R. de Vaux, *Ancient Israel,* 2 vols., tr. J. McHugh (New York: McGraw-Hill, repr. 1965), 1:188. Here (v. 23) and in v. 31 MT reads sing. *way^{e}hî* instead of pl. *wayyihyû,* probably because of neighboring *way^{e}ḥî,* "and he lived."

25. See *ANET,* p. 164.

material. Rather than seeing the Genesis account of Enoch as one that is tremendously telescoped, we prefer to see the postbiblical Enoch traditions as embellishments that are more imaginary than anything.

Twice we are told (vv. 22, 24) that Enoch *walked with God (yiṯhallēḵ 'eṯ-hā'ᵉ lōhîm),*[26] a description applied also to Noah in 6:9. This expression may be compared to *hālaḵ* (or *yiṯhallēḵ) lip̄nê,* which indicates the service of a loyal servant, who goes before his master (sometimes human but mostly divine), paving the way, or who stands before his master ready to serve. Thus, Hezekiah walked before God (2 K. 20:3 par. Isa. 38:3), as did the patriarchs (Gen. 17:1; 24:40; 48:15). A bit more intimacy seems to be suggested by "walking with" as over against "walking before." "Walk with" captures an emphasis on communion and fellowship. In a number of passages, all addressed to a king or his dynasty, "to walk before God" strongly suggests obedience and subordination (1 K. 2:4; 3:6; 8:23, 25; 9:4), rather than worship and communion.

25–27 Methuselah's major notoriety is that he is history's oldest human being; as such he is the patron saint of geriatrics. His name means "man of the spear (or javelin)," although some have claimed to decipher the name of a god in his name—"man of Lah," Lah being an ancient Canaanite god of vigor.[27] M. Tsevat takes the name to mean "man of Shalah," possibly a Canaanite god of the infernal river.[28] The fact that the longest living human does not reach the age of 1000 years, which is a single "day" in God's life (Ps. 90:4), is another illustration of the Scripture's refusal to grant godlike status to its heroic mortals.

28–32 Lamech is the only father in this chapter who provides an explanation for his son's name: *He named him Noah* [Heb. *nōaḥ*], *saying, "This one will bring us relief* [*yᵉnaḥᵃmēnû*] *from the agonizing toil of our hands."* The problem here is that the explanation does not fit the name. If it had, we would expect the text to read "Noah . . . this one will give us rest [*yᵉnîḥēnû,* from *nûaḥ*]."[29] Nor does the name correspond to the explanation. If it had, we would expect the text to read: "he called his name Nahman[30] . . . this one will bring us relief [*yᵉnaḥᵃmēnû*]."

26. The various expansions of this phrase in the Targums are provided by M. L. Klein, "Converse Translation: A Targumic Technique," *Bib* 57 (1976) 519–20.

27. See A. Van Selms, "A forgotten god: Laḥ," in *Studia Biblica et Semitica,* Fest. T. C. Vriezen (Wageningen: Veenman, 1966), pp. 318–26.

28. M. Tsevat, "The Canaanite God Šälaḥ," *VT* 4 (1954) 41–49.

29. This is precisely what the LXX has done: *dianapaúsei hēmás,* "will give us rest." Accordingly, many have emended MT *nāḥam* to *nûaḥ*.

30. Hebrew proper names with *nāḥam* in them are attested. The best known is the king, *mᵉnaḥēm,* Menahem. Throughout this whole section of Genesis there is

The suggestion to emend MT and make it conform to the LXX is ruled out by the fact that nowhere else in the OT do we find a direct object after the causative form of *nûaḥ*. Instead, we would need a preposition following the verb.[31] Nor is it helpful to avoid the explanation completely and simply take Noah to mean "pleasant (or pleasing) person."[32]

Perhaps the *relief* that is found here, if any, is the renewed gift of the vine (9:20) and the introduction of viticulture, indicating a lifting of God's curse on the ground. Does Lamech already see the possibilities that his son will be a second Adam? Or should we understand Lamech's words not as an insight into the future but as a desperate call and hope for some kind of relief from the life of misery and servitude? In other words, is he speaking indicatively or subjunctively?

Cassuto interprets Lamech's words as a wish rather than a prophecy. But there is bitter irony here too, according to Cassuto. Comfort *(nḥm)* does come with Noah, but it is a different kind of comfort. What comes is the Lord's repenting desire *(nḥm)* to destroy humanity. Thus, Lamech's wish turns into a nightmare.[33]

A hint that *nûaḥ* and *nāḥam* are close in meaning to each other may be found in the parallelism of the two in Ezek. 5:13: "My anger will be spent. I will assuage [*waḥ^{a}niḥôṯî*] my fury against them, and get satisfaction [*w^{e}hinneḥām^{e}ṯî*]." This parallel lends some support to the proposition that Gen. 5:29 is not necessarily fanciful etymology.

The genealogy ends with the notation that Noah sired three children—Shem, Ham, and Japheth. The syntax of the sentence would allow for the birth of either three successive sons or triplets, but the first option makes better sense in the light of references to younger and older brothers elsewhere (e.g., 9:24; 10:21) when talking about Noah's family.

Here is a shift from what we have observed throughout this genealogy. Until now the concern has been only with the firstborn son. Now the concern is with three sons. We have to wait until 9:28–29 to read the

---

an extended paronomasia that could be called a leitmotif. Thus we have Noah *(nōaḥ)* shall bring relief (*y^{e}naḥ^{a}mēnû,* 5:29); the Lord was sorry (*wayyinnāḥem,* 6:6); but Noah found favor (*ḥēn,* 6:8); the ark came to rest (*wattānaḥ,* 8:4); "place to set her foot" (*mānōaḥ,* 8:9); "pleasing odor" (*nîḥōaḥ,* 8:21). See Cassuto, *Genesis,* 1:289; J. M. Sasson, "Wordplay in the Old Testament," *IDBS,* p. 970.

31. See Y. Zakovitch, "A Study of Precise and Partial Derivations in Biblical Etymology," *JSOT* 15 (1980) 39.

32. See F. Zimmermann, "Folk etymology of biblical names," in *Volume du Congrès: Genève, 1965,* VTSup 15 (Leiden: Brill, 1966), pp. 318–19.

33. See Cassuto, *Genesis,* 2:198; Zakovitch, JSOT 15 (1980) 40.

expected information about Noah after the birth of his sons. As R. Wilson has observed, "the effect of this division of Noah's biographical material is to present the flood story as an expansion of the biographical narrative and thus an expansion of the Sethite genealogy itself."[34]

THE NEW TESTAMENT APPROPRIATION

a. Gen. 5 and Matt. 1:1–17

The NT has two genealogies of Jesus. Matt. 1:1–17 includes forty-two generations, covering the time span between Jesus and Abraham. The genealogy in Luke 3:23–38 reckons Jesus as the seventy-seventh descendant of Adam. It is beyond the scope of this book to enter into a discussion of how these two lines relate to each other. It is our purpose only to show their (possible) use of the Genesis material.

In at least two ways Matt. 1:1–17 shows more affinity with Gen. 5 than does Luke 3:23–38. First, both Matt. 1 and Gen. 5 (LXX) start with the phrase *bíblos genéseōs,* and in both instances the title refers only to the genealogy and not to subsequent material. Second, Matthew starts with his genealogy of Jesus, then follows with the story of Jesus. Similarly, Gen. 5 begins with the genealogy of Noah, then follows with the story of Noah. In contrast, Luke tells us something about Jesus' life before giving us his genealogy, just as Exodus gives us biographical information about Moses before it gives us Moses' genealogy (Exod. 6:14–25).[1]

But these structural similarities must be placed beside a major difference between Gen. 5 and Matt. 1. The genealogy in Gen. 5 is a genealogy of Adam's descendants. The genealogy of Jesus is a genealogy of his ancestors. Jesus is not the subject, but the object, the one toward whom the action moves. "In Christian salvific history there can be no genealogy of Jesus' descendants because history has reached its goal in Jesus."[2]

b. Gen. 5:21–24 and Heb. 11:5, 6

Enoch is one of three pre-Abrahamic saints cited by Heb. 11 as exemplars of faith. The text of Heb. 11:5 is closer to the LXX than it is to the MT. The LXX of Gen. 5:24 reads, "And Enoch pleased God, and he was not found

34. R. Wilson, *Genealogy and History,* p. 161.

1. R. E. Brown, "Genealogy (Christ)," *IDBS,* p. 354.

2. R. E. Brown, *The Birth of the Messiah: A Commentary on the Infancy Narratives in Matthew and Luke* (Garden City, NY: Doubleday, 1977), p. 67.

because God translated him." The most obvious difference is that LXX's "and he was not found" replaces MT's ambiguous "and he was not." Not only does Heb. 11:5 cite the LXX of Gen. 5:24, it also augments it with "so that he should not see death." The addition of this phrase highlights the exaltation of Enoch into heaven, an understanding that was prominent in intertestamental Judaism (1 Enoch 12:3; 15:1; 2 Enoch 22:8; 71:14; Jub. 4:23; 10:17; 19:24–27; Josephus *Ant.* 1.3.4 [85]). Heb. 11:5 also adds the point that Enoch pleased God. (The verb for "please" is used in the NT only in Hebrews—see 11:5, 6; 12:28; 13:16.)

F. THE SONS OF GOD AND THE DAUGHTERS OF HUMANKIND: ILLICIT RELATIONSHIPS (6:1–4)

1 *When mankind began to become numerous over the surface of the ground, and daughters were being born to them,*
2 *the sons of God saw how attractive the daughters of humankind were. So they took as their wives any of them they chose.*
3 *Then Yahweh said, "My Spirit shall not remain in mankind forever inasmuch as he is but flesh. His days shall be one hundred and twenty years."*
4 *(The Nephilim were on the earth in those days—and later on too.) Whenever*[1] *the sons of God had intercourse with the daughters of humankind, they fathered children by them. These were the mighty men of old, men of reputation.*[2]

1 One of the functions of this verse is to link the genealogy of Adam (5:1–32) with the following event that is narrated in 6:2–4. Not only does it serve as an introduction to what follows, but it also summarizes the story about the rapid increase of Adam's progeny. Human beings were multiplying in the land. Thus it is something of a postscript, just as 2:1–3 summarizes

1. I understand the imperfect verb here, and in v. 1, to have frequentative force. This nuance is already advocated by the LXX *hōs án eiseporeúonto.* What is envisaged here is not one single event, but a scenario that is ongoing and habitual.

2. Lit., "men of name." This may be compared with the expression *'dm šm* that appears in column 3, line 13 of the Phoenician inscription of Azitawadda, which F. Rosenthal translates incorrectly as "a man who is (just) called a man," and then explains in a footnote, "an ordinary human being without titles of any sort" (*ANET,* p. 654 n. 6). The line is best rendered "if a man, who is a man of renown, shall expunge the name of Azitawadda." One may also compare the Old Akkadian name *a-wi-il šu-mi-im,* "man of name," which occurs at Mari (see S. Gevirtz, "West-Semitic curses and the problem of the origins of Hebrew Law," *VT* 11 [1961] 142 n. 4).

1:1–31 and 5:1–2 summarizes the Adam and Eve story. This connection is reinforced by the use of *ground* in 5:29 and 6:1.

Chapter 5 concentrated exclusively on the sons born to these antediluvians. 6:1 focuses on the daughters born to these men. Mankind is still fulfilling God's mandate to "multiply and fill the earth." But even those areas where God's blessing operates become a stage for the intrusion of evil.

2 Enter the problematic *sons of God* (Heb. *bᵉnê-hāʾĕ lōhîm*). Who are they? From whence do they come? They appear without fanfare or explanation. The narrator's assumption is that they are readily identifiable by his audience. But if his audience knew their identity, it has been lost to subsequent readers. Accordingly, our only recourse has been to raise some possibilities with the greatest strengths and the least weaknesses. The chief suggestions are as follows.

(1) The *sons of God* are angels. Many of the ancient versions so understood it, as witnessed by LXX *ángeloi toú theoú.* The major support for this interpretation is that elsewhere in the OT the expression "sons of God" does indeed refer to heavenly beings.[3] Examples come from both prose (Job 1:6; 2:1) and poetry (Job 38:7, where "sons of God" parallels "morning stars";[4] Ps. 29:1; 82:6; 89:7 [Eng. 6]; cf. also Dan. 3:25, "a son of the gods"). Heb. *bᵉnê-hāʾĕ lōhîm* is the same linguistically as Ugar. *bn il,* "the sons of El." In Canaanite mythology *bn il* are major gods who form part of the pantheon of which El is the head. By contrast, "the sons of God" in OT thought are angels who are members of the Lord's court and who expedite his bidding. They have no divine pedigree.

Some have simply dismissed this interpretation, labeling it "bizarre," while others deny its possibility on the grounds that the NT teaches that angels do not marry (Matt. 22:29–30; Mark 12:24–25; Luke 20:34–36).[5] The major

3. See G. Cooke, "The Sons of (the) God(s)," *ZAW* 76 (1964) 22–47.

4. This interesting parallelism may be compared with *UT,* 76:I:3–4, where *bn il* ("the sons of El") balances *pḫr kkbm* ("the assembly of the stars"), perhaps indicating that the "sons of God" in Job 38:7 are the stars. See W. F. Albright, *From the Stone Age to Christianity,* 2nd ed. (Garden City, NY: Doubleday, 1957), p. 296.

5. For the former, see L. Verduin, *Somewhat Less Than God: The Biblical View of Man* (Grand Rapids: Eerdmans, 1970), p. 24, who so dismisses it. For the latter, see H. Stigers, *Commentary on Genesis,* p. 97. W. A. van Gemeren ("The Sons of God in Genesis 6:1–4 [An Example of Evangelical Demythologization?]," *WTJ* 43 [1981] 320–48) calls for a positive reevaluation of the angel hypothesis, and suggests that conservative interpreters have avoided it not on exegetical grounds but only because they insist on a rational explanation of the event. Angels and women copulating is not "rational." Cf. too R. C. Newman, "The Ancient Exegesis of Genesis 6:2, 4," *GTJ* 5 (1984) 13–36.

contextual argument against this identification is that it has mankind being punished for the sins of angels. If the angels are the culpable ones, why is God's judgment not directed against them? Why do the innocent suffer for the sins of the guilty, and why do the guilty go unjudged? This is not a conclusive argument, for in the very next event recorded in Scripture, the Flood, we are told that the sin of *man* (6:5) results in the divine annihilation of not only man but *beast, creeping thing,* and *birds* (6:7). Later on, King David protests that God ought not to direct his wrath against the innocent people but against David himself for his sin in taking the census (2 Sam. 24:17). Must the populace bear the consequences of the sins of their monarch?

This interpretation assumes that the angels took corporeal form, which has support elsewhere in Scripture. For example, one need only recall the bold anthropomorphisms that are associated with the epiphany of the "angel of the Lord." On the darker side this idea extends into magic in which the incubus (or succubus) assumes a male (or female) body and has intercourse with the unsuspecting sexual partner.

Genesis 1–11 abounds with illustrations of human beings who were not content with being merely human. Accordingly they reached for divine status and attempted to overstep the boundaries that had been imposed on them. This story, with this approach, supplies another illustration of such transgression, albeit in the opposite direction. Here the divine or angelic world illegitimately impinges on the human world.[6]

(2) The sons of God are dynastic rulers, an early royal aristocracy.[7] The daughters of men, whom they took as wives, constituted the royal harems of these despots. The sin, then, is polygamy, along the lines of Lamech, who also "took wives" (4:19). A variation of this interpretation combines it with

6. See R. Maars, "The Sons of God (Genesis 6:1–4)," *RestQ* 23 (1980) 220–21.

7. See M. Kline, "Divine Kingship and Genesis 6:1–4," *WTJ* 24 (1962) 187–204; A. R. Millard, "A New Babylonian 'Genesis' Story," *TynBul* 18 (1967) 12, and nn. 27–29; cf. Westermann, *Genesis,* 1:363–83, esp. pp. 371–73. E. Kraeling ("The Significance and Origin of Gen. 6:1–4," *JNES* 6 [1947] 193–208) prefers to identify the "mighty men" of v. 4 as the biblical adaptation of the Babylonian tradition of the antediluvian kings, rather than as the "sons of God." For the "heroes" interpretation cf. also F. Dexinger, *Sturz der Göttersöhne oder Engel vor der Sintflut? Versuch eines Neuverständnisses von Gen 6:2–4 unter Berücksichtigung der religionsvergleichenden und exegesegeschichtlichen Methode* (Vienna: Herder, 1966), pp. 31–37. Dexinger makes the most extensive appeal to the Ugaritic material. Appropriate criticisms of Dexinger's handling of the Ugaritic sources are made by H. Haag, *"bēn," TDOT,* 2:158.

the first one, so that the sons of God are *both* divine beings *and* antediluvian rulers, much as Gilgamesh of Akkadian literature is both a historical figure (king of Uruk) and one about whom legendary features accrued (one-third human, two-thirds divine).[8]

Kline especially makes much of the fact that in the Keret epic from Ugarit King Keret is called *bn il.* This is a significant part of the titulary of the pagan ideology of divine kingship. Kline also appeals to verses in the OT where those who administer justice are called *'ĕlōhîm* (Exod. 21:6; 22:7, 8, 27 [Eng. 8, 9, 28]); and a son of David is called the son of God (2 Sam. 7:14 par. 1 Chr. 17:13; perhaps Ps. 82:6).

The major advantages of this view are that it removes Gen. 6:1–4 from any mythological or nonhistorical understanding; it allows the unit to serve as an appropriate introduction to the Flood story; and it attempts to be faithful to the immediately preceding context about Cainites and Sethites. The major weakness is that while both within the OT and in other ancient Near Eastern texts individual kings were called God's son, there is no evidence that groups of kings were so styled.

(3) The sons of God are the godly Sethites and the daughters of humankind are the ungodly Cainites.[9] The sin, then, is a forbidden union, a yoking of what God intended to keep apart, the intermarriage of believer with unbeliever. This approach is quite close to the previous one. But the objection aimed at the previous identification applies here too. Nowhere in the OT are Sethites identified as the sons of God. Again, this proposal forces on the word *'āḏām* in vv. 1 and 2 two different meanings. In v. 1 *'āḏām* would have to be "mankind" and in v. 2 *'āḏām* would be a specific group of men ("daughters of men," i.e., "daughters of Cainites").

In response we observe that while *sons of God* is indeed an enigmatic phrase, and appears here for the first time in the OT, notes about godliness abound in the context (4:26; 5:24, 29). Furthermore, the OT does not lack instances of a shift from a generic to a specific use of a word in one context.[10] Thus, *'āḏām* as "mankind" in v. 1 and as "Cainites" in v. 2 is not impossible.

8. See D. J. A. Clines, "The Significance of the 'Sons of God' Episode (Genesis 6:1–4) in the Context of the 'Primeval History' (Genesis 1–11)," *JSOT* 13 (1979) 34–35.

9. See J. Murray, *Principles of Conduct* (Grand Rapids: Eerdmans, 1957), pp. 243–49, for a reasoned defense of this position. It is the interpretation pursued by most Protestant conservative scholars.

10. Examples provided by C. F. Keil and F. Delitzsch, *Commentary on the Old Testament,* 10 vols., vol. 1: *The Pentateuch,* tr. J. Martin, 3 vols. repr. in 1 (Grand Rapids: Eerdmans, 1973), 1:130–31.

It is possible, however, to reverse this identification and see the daughters of men as Sethites and the sons of God as Cainites (really "Eveites").[11] For example, the birth of daughters occurs only among the Sethites of ch. 5. Again, the taking of wives for oneself (6:2) is paralleled by the Cainite Lamech (4:19). Could it be that here we have a replay of Gen. 3? As Eve the initiator led Adam astray, so the sons of God led astray the daughters of men.

Suffice it to say, it is impossible to be dogmatic about the identification of "sons of God" here. The best one can do is to consider the options. While it may not be comforting to the reader, perhaps it is best to say that the evidence is ambiguous and therefore defies clear-cut identifications and solutions.

We do know that the stimulus for the behavior of the sons of God was that the human daughters were *attractive.* Again, the description of the sons' activities is reminiscent of Eve's in the garden. She saw that the tree was "good" *(kî ṭôḇ),* and these sons saw that the daughters of men were "attractive" or "good" *(kî ṭōḇōṯ).*

The Bible has no shortage of stories in which human beauty is central to the context. See the stories concerning Abraham and Sarah (Gen. 12:11, 14), Isaac and Rebekah (Gen. 24:16), Jacob and Leah (Gen. 29:17), a prisoner of war who is an attractive woman (Deut. 21:11), Samson's sister-in-law (Judg. 15:2), David and Bathsheba (2 Sam. 11:2), Absalom's sister Tamar (2 Sam. 13:1), Absalom's daughter (2 Sam. 14:27), David's nurse (1 K. 1:3–4), Vashti (Esth. 1:11), Esther (Esth. 2:7), Job's daughters (Job 42:15), and of course the bride in Canticles.

The sons of God *took* wives. The Hebrew verb here, *lāqaḥ,* commonly describes marital transactions, including taking a wife for oneself (4:19; 11:29; 12:19; 20:2, 3; 25:1; 36:2, 6; Exod. 34:16) and taking a wife for another (Gen. 21:21; 24:4, 40, 48). One might also take somebody else's wife (2 Sam. 11:4). Most of the former instances involve polygamy or potential adultery but not rape. When indiscriminate rape is described some verb like "forced" (2 Sam. 13:14) is necessary. Furthermore, in the OT (Gen. 36:2; 2 Sam. 1:20, 24; Isa. 3:16) *bᵉnōṯ* ("daughters") followed by a gentilic or a place name normally designates those who are eligible for marriage, another indication that we are dealing here with marriage rather than rape.[12]

3 The order of the two remaining verses in this pericope is interest-

11. See L. Eslinger, "A Contextual Identification of the *bene ha'elohim* and *benoth ha'adam,*" *JSOT* 13 (1979) 65–73.

12. See G. Mendenhall, *Tenth Generation,* p. 111 n. 26.

ing. That is, the word about the divine displeasure comes between the cohabitation scene (v. 2) and the reference to the children produced by this union (v. 4). By placing the verse where it is, the author is making the point that this forbidden union itself is offensive to Yahweh, rather than the fact that such a union produced (hybrid) offspring.

God's decision is: *My spirit shall not remain in mankind forever.* The translation *remain* for Heb. *yāḏôn* is far from certain; it is based principally on LXX *katameínē* and Vulg. *permanebit.* But what is the source of the LXX rendering? It would seem to translate Heb. *yāḏûr* (from *dûr,* "to dwell") or *yālûn* (from *lûn,* "to lodge"). If the form in question is to be connected with the verb *dîn,* "to judge" (as in Symm. *krineí*)—"my spirit shall not judge"—one would expect *yāḏîn,* not *yāḏôn.*[13]

Unable to find an explanation within the Hebrew Bible of the verb in question, scholars have turned to related languages. J. Scharbert connects Heb. *yāḏôn* with Arab. *dun,* "to be humbled, humiliated, brought low"—"my spirit will not be humiliated in man forever."[14] The problem with this interpretation is that man's sins may anger and distress God, but not humble or humiliate him. Speiser identifies *yāḏôn* with the Akkadian root *dnn* and its nominal forms *dinānu, andunānu,* which mean "personal substitute, surrogate, scapegoat."[15] Thus 6:3 says "my spirit shall not answer for man forever." That is, the time is coming when human beings will have to shoulder the consequences of their behavior. However, as early as Gen. 3 human beings have been held accountable for their actions, and God was not one who shielded the guilty. Thus it is difficult to fit Speiser's suggestion into the larger context of Gen. 3–6, however linguistically attractive his proposal may be.

Another possibility is to associate *yāḏôn* with Akk. *danânu,* "to be strong, powerful, rule."[16] So understood, *yāḏôn* would be a stative Qal

13. One suspects that behind AV "to strive" is an association with the verb *dîn,* which has the meaning "to contend, dispute" only in Eccl. 6:10. Those who would translate "my spirit shall not rule in man forever" also appeal to the verb *dîn* in Zech. 3:7—"you shall rule [*tāḏîn*] my house."

14. J. Scharbert, "Traditions- und Redaktionsgeschichte von Gen. 6:1–4," *BZ* 11 (1967) 68 and also n. 9. This suggestion is reflected in JB "shall not be disgraced" (and in the French original *ne soit pas . . . humilié*). Incidentally, NEB "he for his part is mortal flesh" goes back to G. R. Driver's suggestion that the text be read as *beśārô gam hû' bāśār,* "(as for) his flesh, even it is flesh," in "Once Again Abbreviations," *Textus* 4 (1964) 89–90.

15. E. A. Speiser, "YDWN, Genesis 6:3," *JBL* 75 (1956) 126–29 (repr. in *Oriental and Biblical Studies,* ed. J. J. Finkelstein and M. Greenberg [Philadelphia: University of Pennsylvania, 1967], pp. 35–40). See also idem, *Genesis,* p. 44.

16. Von Rad, *Genesis,* p. 114.

imperfect form from the geminate root *dnn.* A verb with this meaning appears in several Ugaritic texts, and may be reflected in the Dannah of Josh. 15:49 ("stronghold, fortress"), an Israelite town in the vicinity of Debir.[17] But in what way is an imposition of life reduction for humanity a lessening of the strength of God's spirit in humanity? We follow the LXX and Vulg. at this point simply out of preference, but admit the inconclusiveness of this position. The verb *dānan* or *dûn* appears with the meaning "remain" in the Talmud and in Aramaic; Rabin argues for its presence in the Hebrew Bible in Gen. 30:6.[18]

We have already drawn attention to the echoes of Gen. 1–5 in this unit. Here is another one. The withdrawn Spirit of 6:3 calls to mind the hovering Spirit of 1:2. Where it hovers there is order, and chaos is restrained. Where it is withdrawn, chaos flourishes unchecked. (Strangely, *Spirit* is treated, correctly, as fem. in 1:2, but here it is the subject of a masc. verb. This is unusual, but Job 4:15 illustrates the same phenomenon.) The *forever* of this verse also evokes the "and live forever" of 3:22.

A second problem in this verse concerns the clause *inasmuch as* [*bešaggam*] *he is but flesh.* As it stands in the MT *bešaggam* is made up of three words: the preposition *be,* "in"; the relative *še,* "who, which"; and the adverb *gam,* "also." So it translates literally "in which also." Thus the verse says that the stimulus for God's retaliation is man's nature—he is flesh—rather than man's activity. It is what man is, rather than what man has done, that incites God not to permit his Spirit to remain in mankind forever.

A slight change in the MT, reading *bešaggām* for *bešaggam,* easily circumvents the awkwardness of the verse. Indeed, a number of ancient Hebrew manuscripts support this reading.[19] In revocalizing the word, what one now has is the preposition *be* and the infinitive construct form of the verb *šāgag* (or more likely *šāgâ*), "to move (in error), to stray." The verse would then say, "my spirit shall not remain in man forever; in their going astray he [i.e., man] is flesh." The problem with this interpretation is that *šāgag* is frequently used in the OT to describe wrongs that are perpetrated

17. See R. S. Hendel, "Of Demigods and the Deluge: Toward an Interpretation of Genesis 6:1–4," *JBL* 106 (1987) 15 n. 10.

18. C. Rabin, "Etymological Miscellanea," *Scripta Hierosolymitana* 8 (1961) 388–89.

19. The ms. evidence is accumulated by C. D. Ginsburg, *Introduction to the Massoretico-Critical Edition of the Hebrew Bible* (repr. New York: Ktav, 1966), p. 1021; for references see "Index of Principal Texts." Five of twenty-one mss. (those listed by Ginsburg on pp. 514, 712, 737, 942, 955) prefer the *ā* under the *g.* The remainder follow the MT with an *a.*

inadvertently, but of which the performer is conscious.[20] So, sins committed "inadvertently" are sins that result either from negligence or from ignorance. Certainly the sons of God act neither from negligence nor out of ignorance.

Sense can be extracted from the MT as it stands. First, we take the preposition *bᵉ* with causal force, "for, inasmuch," a nuance supported by LXX *diá tó eínai autoús.* Second, the proclitic relative *šᵉ* in the Pentateuch is not strange or inexplicable, although many scholars consider it so.[21] It appears thirty-two times in Canticles and sixty-eight times in Ecclesiastes (compared with the generally much more common *'ᵃšer,* which occurs 89 times in Ecclesiastes).[22]

These statistics do not permit us to say that this relative particle is late simply because it appears preponderantly in OT books that scholars consider late. On the contrary, its appearance in the early Song of Deborah (Judg. 5:7) testifies to its antiquity. Similarly, the personal name from Ugarit *šbʿl* (to be vocalized *šu-baʿal* or *šubaʿla*) may mean "the one of Baal," and thus give additional support for the early use of this particle.[23] Gen. 6:3, then, provides us with the only illustration of this relative in the Pentateuch.

The fact that God's judgment is directed at man would argue strongly for the fact that the culprits must be mortals. That being the case, this portion of the verse suggests that the ultimate root behind the sin of these sons of God was that they were *flesh.* Here is man at his weakest and most vulnerable. Man is many things—formed and animated by God, a divine image bearer, but he is also flesh. To be sure, the OT in general, and the opening chapters of Genesis in particular, do not teach that simply being flesh is sinful, as if the two were synonymous. After all, the man used this same word to describe his partner in 2:23, and together they became "one flesh" (2:25). But *bāśār* does seem to be a general term to describe the

20. The rich nuances in this word are creatively discussed by J. Milgrom, "The Cultic *Šᵉgāgā* and Its Influences in Psalms and Job," *JQR* 57 (1967) 115–25. See also D. Christensen, "Janus Parallelism in Genesis 6:3," *HS* 27 (1986) 20–24.

21. See G. Bergstrasser, "Das hebräische Präfix *š,*" *ZAW* 29 (1909) 40–56.

22. For Canticles see D. Broadribb, "Thoughts on the Song of Solomon," *Abr-Nahrain* 3 (1961/62) 11–36, esp. pp. 31–32, who identifies 7 functions of this relative particle in Canticles. The first of these is the meaning "because" in 1:6 and 4:2, a meaning that may apply to Gen. 6:3. For Ecclesiastes see M. J. Dahood, "Canaanite-Phoenician Influence in Qoheleth II," *CBQ* 33 (1952) 44–45.

23. See M. Dahood, "Hebrew Ugaritic Lexicography X," *Bib* 53 (1972) 401. Dahood also refers to *UT,* 1020:3–4, *ḥnny lpn mlk šink itn,* which he translates, "Plead for me before the king. I will give you what you don't have *(šink).*" Gordon, however, translates *šbʿl* not as "the one of Baal" but "man of Baal" (*UT,* p. 488).

limitation and fallibility of humankind. And it is this fallibility that makes possible any kind of trespass.[24]

The third problem in the verse is interpreting the force of *His days shall be one hundred and twenty years.* Is this an age limit, or is it a period of grace prior to the Flood (i.e., his [remaining] days shall be 120 years)? The first alternative faces the difficulty that most of the people in the rest of Genesis lived well beyond 120 years. It is possible to interpret the longer life spans of the patriarchs as a mitigation or suspension of the divine penalty, just as an earlier announced divine penalty ("on the day you eat of it you shall surely die") was not immediately implemented.

But the (imminent) withdrawal of the divine Spirit as a means of lowering the life span of humanity does not make a great deal of sense. Rather, it seems to presage some event that is about to occur. Accordingly, we prefer to see in this phrase a reference to a period of time that prefaces the Flood's beginning. It is parallel to Jon. 4:5, "Yet forty days, and Nineveh shall be overthrown." God's hand of judgment is put on hold.

4 In a parenthetical phrase we are told that *Nephilim* were present during this scenario. But in what capacity? Are they simply contemporaries? Or are the Nephilim the result, the fruit, of the union between the sons of God and the daughters of men? Or are the Nephilim the sons of God and therefore the perpetrators of the crime?[25] Had v. 4 preceded v. 3, the likelihood would have increased that we are to understand the Nephilim as the bastard offspring of this union. But the present order of the verses argues the contrary.[26]

The only other OT reference to the Nephilim is Num. 13:33, where they form part of the pre-Israelite population of Palestine. This passage indicates strongly that the Nephilim (here associated with the sons of Anak) were individuals of imposing stature beside whom the Hebrew spies appeared as grasshoppers. Probably for this reason the LXX (and see AV)

24. Interestingly, H. Wolff (*Anthropology of the Old Testament,* pp. 26–31) labels his discussion of flesh *(bāśār)* as "Man in his Infirmity." *BDB,* p. 142, cites Gen. 6:3 as an illustration of *bāśār* under its fifth meaning for the word—"man over against God as frail or erring." See also D. Lys, "L'arrière-plan et les connotations vétérotestamentaires de *sarx* et de *sōma* (étude préliminaire)," *VT* 36 (1986) 163–204, esp. p. 178. For Lys *bāśār* is what God is not, and what humankind is.

25. Few embrace the latter view. For a sympathetic treatment see L. Birney, "An Exegetical Study of Genesis 6:1–4," *JETS* 13 (1970) 43–52. Birney goes this direction only because he is tied down to the causal use of *'ašer,* when in fact a temporal use is much more likely. Support for Birney's interpretation is, however, as old as the Palestinian Targum, which translates v. 4 as "Shamhazzai and Uzziel fell from heaven and were on earth in those days."

26. See B. Childs, *Myth and Reality in the Old Testament,* p. 58.

translated Nephilim as "giants" *(hoi gígantes).* The use of the definite article with the word argues for a specific and well-known group of individuals. Perhaps we can see here a parallel between the unusual physical development of some people and the unusually long lives of others at this time.[27]

A literal translation of *Nephilim* is "fallen ones." The full implication of the passive adjectival formation *(qaṭīl)* can best be brought out by something like "those who were made to fall, those who were cast down."[28] Nephilim is not the passive plural participle of *nāpal* (which would be *n^e pûlîm*). The active form of the participle (*nōp^e lîm,* "the falling [fallen] ones") does occur in Deut. 22:4; Ps. 145:14; Ezek. 32:22–24. This form refers to those who fell down of their own accord, or who fell down in a natural manner and died.

The translation we have offered understands the Nephilim to be distinct from *the mighty men,* who alone are the offspring of the union between the sons of God and the daughters of men. Thus we have set off the first part of the verse in parentheses. Such explanatory, perhaps pedantic, asides may be compared with similar phenomena in Deut. 2:10–12; 2:20–23; 3:9; 3:11; 3:13b–14. Almost all modern versions of the Bible put these five passages from Deuteronomy in parentheses. Such "frame-breaks" supply extra information from the narrator (e.g., Deut. 2:10, "[The Emim formerly lived there. . .]"). The expression "as it is to this day" occurs frequently (Deut. 2:22; 3:11, 14), and that is the equivalent of Gen. 4:6—"and later on too."[29] It makes much better grammatical sense to take the antecedent of *hēmmâ* ("these") as the understood object of "they fathered children" rather than "Nephilim."[30]

The children produced by this union are called *the mighty men (haggibbōrîm).*[31] They are described further as being *of old* (*mēʿôlām,* the same word for "forever," *l^eʿōlām,* in v. 3), and *men of reputation,* that is, famous. What produced such fame, or infamy, we are not told.

27. See G. Aalders, *Genesis,* p. 156.

28. See R. S. Hendel, *JBL* 106 (1987) 22 n. 46. A parallel formation would be *'^asîrîm,* "imprisoned ones" (Gen. 39:22), alongside *'^asûrîm* (39:20).

29. R. Polzin (*Moses and the Deuteronomist* [New York: Seabury, 1980], pp. 30–31) notes that such frame-breaks are a frequent device by which an author may involve his readers more in his message.

30. See J. Morgenstern, "The Mythological Background of Psalm 82," *HUCA* 14 (1939) 84–86, 106–7.

31. *gibbōrîm* is normally a term for soldiers (2 Sam. 10:7; 16:6; 20:7; 23:8, 9, 16, 17, 22; 1 K. 1:10), most often associated with David. W. Wifall ("Gen. 6:1–4—A Royal Davidic Myth?" *BTB* 5 [1975] 294–301) suggests that Gen. 6:1–4 is a hybrid and reflects both pre-Israelite royal traditions and historical events from the David story. I believe the connection is more likely with the first of these two traditions than with the second.

The use of the name motif in Gen. 1–11 appears several times. It surfaces with a negative connotation in the Tower of Babel episode, where the builders wished "to make a name" for themselves (11:4). This self-aggrandizement contrasts with the promise of God that he, not Abraham, would make great the patriarch's name (Gen. 12:2; 2 Sam. 7:9). In other contexts to give someone a name means to engage in an act of intelligence (Gen. 2:20). Interestingly, the way Adam names his wife after they sin (3:20) is akin to the formula by which he named the animals, but different from the way he named her before they sinned (2:23).

By virtue of its placement, the incident in 6:1–4 is obviously intended as an introduction to the Flood story. Until this point the Scripture has discussed the sins of individuals: Adam, Eve, Cain, Lamech. Now for the first time the emphasis shifts to the sins of a group, "the sons of God," with the result that God's punishment is directed not against a man, but against mankind. This emphasis of the sins of a group is perpetuated in the Flood event.

THE NEW TESTAMENT APPROPRIATION

Gen. 6:1–4 and Jude 6; 2 Pet. 2:4

There is no doubt that intertestamental literature heavily favored the "angel" interpretation of Gen. 6:1–4. This is most clear in the book of 1 Enoch.[1] Do these two NT references to sinning, apostate angels support that view? At best the evidence from 2 Pet. 2:4 is mute, for here the allusion is to angels (note that in the Greek text *angélōn,* "angels," is anarthrous, i.e., "even angels") who sinned and thus were cast into hell. Peter does not elaborate on the nature of the angels' sin.

Jude 6 is another matter. He refers to angels who "left their proper habitation" and thus fell under divine judgment. V. 7 goes on to say, "as Sodom and Gomorrah and the cities around them, having in like manner with them [*toútois*] given themselves over to fornication and indulged in unnatural flesh." The crucial question is the identification of the antecedent of "them" *(toútois).* NIV circumvents the problem by simply ignoring "them": "In a similar way, Sodom and Gomorrah and the surrounding towns gave themselves up to sexual immorality."

If we identify the antecedent of *toútois* as Sodom and Gomorrah, we

1. See P. Hanson, "Rebellion in Heaven, Azazel, and Euhemeristic Heroes in 1 Enoch 6–11," *JBL* 96 (1977) 195–233; G. W. E. Nickelsburg, "Apocalyptic and Myth in 1 Enoch 6–11," *JBL* 96 (1977) 383–405.

need to read and punctuate as follows: "as Sodom and Gomorrah, and the surrounding cities in like manner with them, gave themselves. . . ." We know that *toútois* (masc.) cannot refer back to *póleis,* "cities" (fem.), unless we have here a case of gender confusion.

If we identify the antecedent of *toútois* as the angels of v. 6, then Jude must be seeing in Gen. 6:1–4 not marriage, but rape and fornication, and titanic lust, an interpretation favored by pseudepigraphical literature. See 1 Enoch 6–11 and Jub. 4–5, in which the sons of God are seen as rebels from heaven, and their fornication with earthly women, after whom they lusted, is their sin. It is quite obvious that Jude was very familiar with the book of 1 Enoch. Not only did he quote directly from it (Jude 14, 15 is from 1 Enoch 60:8), but he also used phrases that have parallels in 1 Enoch. For example, in the incident under discussion (the fallen angels), compare the following:

1 Enoch	**Jude**
[The angels] have abandoned the high heaven, the holy eternal place (12:4)	And the angels that did not keep their own position but left their proper dwelling (6a)
Bind Azaz'el hand and foot (and) throw him into the darkness (10:4)	have been kept by him in eternal chains in the nether gloom (6b)
that he may be sent into the fire on the great day of judgment (10:6).	until the judgment of the great day (6c).

G. THE GREAT FLOOD (6:5–9:29)

1. THE REASON FOR A FLOOD (6:5–10)

5 *When Yahweh saw how extensive was man's wickedness on the earth, and that every scheme in man's imagination was nothing but evil perpetually,*

6 *Yahweh regretted that he had made man on the earth, and there was pain in his heart.*

7 *Yahweh said: "I will wash from the earth the man whom I have created, both man and beast, creeping things and birds of the air, for I regret that I made them."*

8 *But Noah found favor*[1] *with Yahweh.*

1. There may be a pun in this verse. In Hebrew both "Noah" and "favor" are made up of the same two consonants, but in reversed order, *nḥ* and *ḥn,* respectively. See J. Sasson, "Word Play in Gen. 6:8–9," *CBQ* 37 (1975) 165. NEB "to win favor" (6:8) is challenged by A. N. Barnard, "Was Noah a Righteous Man?" *Theology* 74 (1971) 311–14.

9 *These are the descendants of Noah. Noah was a righteous person. Among his contemporaries he was blameless. With God Noah walked.*
10 *He fathered three sons: Shem, Ham, and Japheth.*

5 The God of the OT never acts arbitrarily; he does not run his world amorally, claims the author of this verse. Nobody will receive this divine judgment simply because he is human. God is moved to anger by man's deliberate violations of the code by which God wills his world to live. The only innocuous bystanders are the animals.

Here, first of all, is what God saw (v. 5), then how he felt (v. 6), then what he intends to do (v. 7). What God saw was both the extensiveness of sin and the intensiveness of sin. Geographically, the problem is an infested earth. Note that in 6:5–13, *the earth (hā'āreṣ)* is mentioned eight times. Thus the description has all the appearances of a universal condition rather than a local one. To be sure, *'ereṣ* is frequently rendered as "(local) land," "ground," and even "underworld." When *'ereṣ* refers to a particular piece of land, however, it is often followed by a prepositional phrase that further identifies the land (e.g., the land of the Canaanites, land of the east, land of the fathers), except in those places where mention is made theologically of the land promised to Israel. Furthermore, the reference in 7:3 to the animals of *kol-hā'āreṣ* argues for an understanding of *'ereṣ* elsewhere in the Flood narrative as "earth" in that almost all uses of *kol-hā'āreṣ* (outside Deuteronomy and Joshua-Samuel) are references to the earth (Gen. 1:26, 28; 11:1; Exod. 9:14, 16; 19:5). Yet, verses such as Gen. 13:9, 15 show that even in Genesis *kol-hā'āreṣ* refers to the whole land.

The situation is further aggravated because such depravity controls not only man's actions but also his thoughts *(māḥšeḇōṯ): every scheme in man's imagination was nothing but evil.* The mind, too, has been perverted, an emphasis made again in 8:21. *scheme,* Heb. *yēṣer* (or, "imagination, desire"), is a nominal form of the word used in 2:7, 19 to describe the "formation" of man and animal from the soil. There God was the potter, fashioning man. Now man himself has become the potter, fashioning his thoughts. What God forms is beautiful; what man forms is repulsive. *perpetually.* Finally, this verse informs the reader that this kind of malaise is a chronic condition, not just a spasmodic lapse.

It is important to observe that right at the beginning there is a clear-cut moral motivation behind sending the Flood. The Gilgamesh Epic (an Akkadian story about a flood), which does have clear parallels with Gen. 6–9, lacks such a parallel here. The closest it comes is: "when their heart led the great gods to produce the flood" (Tablet XI, line 14). That vague statement is left unamplified. Later in that same tablet (line 179) the god Ea speaks to Enlil (the one who sent the flood): "How could you, unreasoning, bring on the deluge?"

According to a related flood story, the Atrahasis Epic,[2] twelve hundred years after man's creation his noise and commotion has become so loud that Enlil starts to suffer from insomnia. Enlil sends a plague to eradicate boisterous humanity, only to have his plan thwarted. Next he tries drought and famine, which are also unsuccessful. Finally a flood is sent, which Atrahasis survives by building a boat. To call this noise moral turbulence or to understand the clamor of mankind as man's chronic depravity reads into the text far too much. The problem is simply that there are too many people, with the result that there is too much noise. There is a limit on Enlil's auditory capacities. It really should not surprise us that in a system of thought where the gods are not necessarily morally superior to human beings, and where the line between good and evil is blurred, there is no recording of the fact that man is to be drowned because he is a rebel and a sinner.

6 Viewing the debacle man has fomented, God is grieved, even to the point of experiencing *pain in his heart.* Note again here the echo of earlier language in Genesis. Previously Eve (3:16) and Adam (3:17) were the pain bearers. Now Yahweh himself feels that stab. Eve's and Adam's pain, however, is imposed due to their sin. Yahweh's is not. Rather, his pain finds its source in the depth of the regret he experiences over fallen humanity, and in the fact that he must judge such fallenness. It is easy, of course, to dismiss such allusions as anthropopathisms, and to feel that they can tell us nothing about the essential nature of God. But verses like this remind us that the God of the OT is not beyond the capability of feeling pain, chagrin, and remorse. To call him the Impassible Absolute is but part of the truth.

Yahweh regretted [*yinnāḥem*] that he had made man. This point is made again in v. 7b, "I regret [*'emḥeh*] that I made him." The AV translates *nḥm* as "repent." Here we are introduced to the idea of God repenting! As a matter of fact, the Niphal of the root *nḥm* (as here) occurs forty-eight times in the OT, and in thirty-four of these the subject (expressed or implied) is God.[3]

Interestingly, the LXX usually translates Heb. *nāḥam* with *metanoéō* or *metamélomai,* "to be sorry, repent, change one's mind," but here and in v. 7 it avoids either of those verbs. It reads "And God considered that he had

2. See W. G. Lambert and A. R. Millard, *Atra-ḫasīs: The Babylonian Story of the Flood* (Oxford: Clarendon, 1969).

3. These 38 passages are listed in J. B. Curtis, "On Job's Response to Yahweh," *JBL* 98 (1979) 499 n. 7.

made man" (v. 6) and "because I have become angry that I made them" (v. 7).[4] Here the LXX translators hesitated to have God repenting.

The Hebrew root in question *(nḥm)* is related to the noun *neḥāmâ,* "breath" (Ps. 119:50; Job 6:10), which describes the life-giving effect of God's word in a time of oppression. The Niphal and Hithpael stems have six basic meanings: (1) suffer emotional pain (Gen. 6:6); (2) be comforted (Gen. 37:35); (3) execute wrath (Isa. 1:24); (4) retract punishment (Jer. 18:7–8); (5) retract blessing (Jer. 18:9–10); (6) retract (a life of) sin (Jer. 8:5–6).[5]

It should be noted that only a few passages that speak of God's repentance refer to God repenting over something already done. The vast majority of the instances of Yahweh's *nḥm* have to do with his possible change of will concerning a future plan of action.[6] This is one significant difference between God's repentance and man's. Still, the fact that the OT affirms that God does repent, even over a fait accompli, forces us to make room in our theology for the concepts of both the unchangeability of God and his changeability.[7]

7 Yahweh's decision is to eliminate the source of the problem—man. The verb used to describe this intended action is appropriate. The root in question *(mḥh)* means "to erase by washing." Thus "to blot one's name out of a book" (Exod. 32:32–33) means to erase written words by washing off letters with water. In the trial of a woman suspected of adultery, the priest is "to write the curses in a book and then wash them off" (Num. 5:23). The psalmist prays that his enemies "be blotted" out of the book of the living (Ps. 69:29 [Eng. 28]). Exod. 17:14 also refers to God's blotting out Amalek.

In a positive sense the verb is used in the idiom, "the washing away of sins" (Isa. 43:25; 44:22; Jer. 18:23; Ps. 51:3, 11 [Eng. 2, 9]; Prov. 6:33). God not only erases sins, but he erases sinners—he judges them by drowning them.

4. Similarly, Exod. 32:12, "repent of the evil against your people," becomes "and be merciful concerning this evil." Exod. 32:14, "and Yahweh repented of the evil which he spoke to do to his people," becomes "and the Lord was propitiated concerning the evil he said he would do to his people."

5. See H. Van Dyke Parunak, "A Semantic Survey of NḤM," *Bib* 56 (1975) 512–32. It will be noticed that there is a polarity between several of these meanings; thus, *nḥm* means both "be pained" and "be relieved of pain." It means both "execute wrath" and "retract wrath." Such polarization appears in the verb *bāraḵ* (Piel), which means "to bless" and "to curse."

6. See Jörg Jeremias, *Die Reue Gottes: Aspekte alttestamentlicher Gottesvorstellung* (Neukirchen-Vluyn: Neukirchener, 1975).

7. On the "repentance of God" see L. J. Kuyper, "The Repentance of God," *RefR* 18 (1965) 3–16; idem, "The Suffering and the Repentance of God," *SJT* 22 (1969) 257–77.

both man and beast, creeping things and birds of the air. Again we note the wide impact of God's judgment. Not only humans but animals as well are mentioned as objects of divine wrath. Either the animals contributed to the depravity in the world, or else they are innocent victims. The form of judgment, a deluge, would of necessity kill all forms of life. It would be temerarious to suppose that this verse teaches a threefold division of the animal kingdom into beasts, insects, and fowl. The expression is to be understood as a hendiadys and means "all living creatures, human as well as animal."

8 Most translations of the Bible have Noah "finding" favor with Yahweh. A few (e.g., NEB) have Noah "winning" favor with Yahweh. There is a significant difference between the two. The former denotes no moral quality on the part of the person who is designated as having found favor. On these grounds Noah's election would be just that, and no causal relationship should be seen between Noah's finding favor (v. 8) and his character (v. 9).

The latter option, "winning favor," shows a nexus between the two verses, with the line of argumentation being effect to cause (i.e., substantiation) rather than cause to effect (i.e., causation). Of course, had the order of the two verses been switched, there would have been no doubt that Noah's righteousness and blamelessness were intended to supply a rationale for his election and escape from the Flood. If we translate Heb. *ḥēn* as "grace" instead of "favor," then further support for "finding" is available. Grace is found or received, not won.

The phrase "find favor in one's eyes" occurs a number of times in Genesis with a wealth of nuances that cannot be captured by one English equivalent. Thus, 18:3, "My lord, if I may *beg* of you this *favor*"; 19:19, "if you would but *indulge* your servant"; 32:5; 33:8, "in the hope of *gaining* your *favor*"; 39:7, "he took a fancy to."[8]

9–10 Here is the second instance in Genesis of the formula *These are the descendants of X* (cf. 2:4). The source critics, who assign such titles to P, suggest that there are here two introductions to the Flood story: 6:5–8 (J) and 6:9–11 (P). It seems more accurate to designate 6:5–8 as a preview to the whole story, the main emphasis of which is to let us see the major actor in this drama—Yahweh, with a quick look at a lesser light—Noah. In 6:9–11 the emphasis shifts to Noah and the earth as the major participants in the drama.

The previous verses first detailed the wickedness in the earth (vv. 5–7), then focused on Noah's exemption from divine judgment (v. 8). Vv. 9ff.

8. The translations are those of Speiser. Gen. 6:8 is the only place where he translates the idiom literally. See his *Genesis,* pp. LXVII and LXVIII.

reverse that order, targeting first Noah's exemplary character (v. 9), then describing a corrupted earth (vv. 11ff.).

Verses 9–10 picture Noah both as the first entry in a list of generations (the listing of his three sons) and as one who stands unique in his own generation. The allusion to Noah's character seems to interrupt the genealogical material. One might have expected the order to be v. 9a, 10, 9b, or v. 9b, 9a, 10. In sequence at least, the text gives preference to how Noah lived, rather than to how he reproduced himself.

Noah was a righteous person. Among his contemporaries he was blameless. With God Noah walked. These three sentences are only ten words in Hebrew. We remember too that Noah is the tenth generation from Adam according to the selective genealogy of Gen. 5:1–32. By using this sequence of ten words, perhaps the author is underscoring the fact that Noah formed the tenth generation from creation. In Hebrew, this section describing his behavior both begins and ends with his name.[9] The author must intend to put Noah in the spotlight, giving him as much attention as possible.

The word *blameless* means free from defect, as may be observed in the many passages describing the unblemished animal presented to God (Exod. 12:5; Lev. 1:3, 10; 3:1, 6; etc.). It is especially prominent in texts dealing with the cult and in Ezekiel. Of course, Noah was not "free from defect." He was *tāmîm,* but not sinless. Perhaps a word like "wholesome" or "sound" or "candid" would be appropriate when applying this word to people (see Gen. 17:1; Deut. 18:13; Ps. 15:2; 18:24 [Eng. 23] = 2 Sam. 22:24; Prov. 11:5; Job 12:4). Two of the more prominent Hebrew words for "sinner" are *ḥōṭē'* and *ḥaṭṭā'*. In form the only basic difference is that the medial consonant in the second one is doubled. But in meaning the difference is quite significant. The first word designates the person who sins only occasionally. By contrast, the second word refers to the habitual sinner. The word for *righteous person (ṣaddîq)* is interesting. With *ṣdq,* "righteous," the only possibility is the one we have here—*ṣaddîq,* that is, one who is habitually righteous. There is no *ṣōḏēq* (participle), for Scripture makes no room for the person who, with God's blessing, practices righteousness only occasionally. Of course, the righteous, the *ṣaddîq,* may turn from and repudiate his righteousness *(ṣeḏeq),* and thus die in and for his sin (Ezek. 3:20).

9. See J. Sasson, "Word Play in Gen. 6:8–9," *CBQ* 37 (1975) 165–66; idem, "Wordplay in the Old Testament," *IDBS,* p. 969. Sasson may be overdoing the puns here when he compares Enoch and Noah, both of whom walked with God, and notices that the consonants in Enoch's name—*ḥnk*—reappear in reverse order in the last three letters of v. 9—*knḥ*.

2. CORRUPTION AND VIOLENCE IN THE EARTH (6:11–12)

11 *Corrupted was the earth before God; the earth was full of lawlessness.*

12 *God viewed the earth, and indeed it was corrupt; for all flesh had corrupted its way on earth.*

11 The key term here is the verb *šāḥaṯ,* which appears first as a Niphal imperfect ("corrupted"—v. 11), then as a Niphal perfect ("it was corrupt"—v. 12), then as a Hiphil perfect ("had corrupted"—v. 12). We might note that v. 13b, read by all the modern versions as "behold, I will destroy them," is another form of this verb (Hiphil participle with suffix).

To capture this consistency of word choice we may render the above as "*gone to ruin* was the earth . . . indeed, it had *gone to ruin* . . . all flesh had *ruined* its way. . . . I will *ruin* them." The choice of the same word to describe both the earth's condition and the intended action of God must be deliberate. God's decision is to destroy what is virtually self-destroyed or self-destroying already. This verb is also used in Jer. 18:4 to describe the clay that was "spoiled" in the potter's hands. The spoiled clay he reworks. The spoiled earth is destroyed.

These two verses present the analysis of the narrator (v. 11) and of God (v. 12). Both are in agreement that the earth is polluted and in an irremediable situation. Note that God's analysis is prefaced by *God viewed . . . and indeed,* or "God saw, and behold. . . ." This construction appears a number of times in Genesis, and it frequently designates something that is not expected, something surprising (see 8:13; 18:2; 19:28; 22:13; 24:63; 26:8; 29:2; 31:2, 10; 33:1; 37:25; 40:6; 42:27; only in 1:31 is the element of surprise lacking). If this nuance applies here as well, then further support is found for the reason behind God's grief and pain. That is, the earth's contamination caught him by surprise.

In a sense vv. 11–12 are a condensation of the narratives extending from Gen. 3:1 to 6:4. This is most apparent in the report in v. 11 that the earth was full of lawlessness *(ḥāmās,* LXX *adikía).* Such lawlessness, which may lead to violence,[1] permeates both the Cain story (ch. 4) and the Lamech scenario (4:23–24).

1. Most commentators are satisfied with "lawlessness" or "violence" for *ḥāmās.* Only Cassuto (*Genesis,* 2:52–53) opposes this understanding, preferring "unrighteousness." For him, to consign *ḥāmās* to simply any deeds of outrage or violence is too restricting. He believes that the word describes anything that is not righteous. Certainly *ḥāmās* often does describe physical violence and brutality. In a few passages where *ḥāmās* is used, physical violence is not present (Gen. 16:5; 2 Sam.

The novel element in God's analysis, as distinct from that of the narrator, is that *all flesh* had gone awry. In some OT passages "all flesh" specifically indicates human beings (e.g., Jer. 25:31). But in view of the fact that elsewhere in the Flood story "all flesh" includes both animals and people (6:17, 19; 7:15, 16, 21; 8:17), it is most likely all-inclusive in 6:12.[2]

3. THE COMMAND TO BUILD THE ARK (6:13–22)

13 *Then God said to Noah, "I am resolved*[1] *to put an end to all flesh, for the earth is filled with lawlessness because of them. I am going to annihilate them from*[2] *the earth.*

14 *Make for yourself an ark of gopher wood; make the ark with compartments, and smear it inside and out with pitch.*

15 *This is how you shall make it: the length of the ark shall be 300 cubits, its width 50 cubits, and its height 30 cubits.*

16 *A roof you shall make for the ark. Unto a cubit upward you shall finish it. Put the entrance in the side of the ark, which you shall make with lower, second, and third decks.*

17 *For my part, I am about to bring the floodwaters on the earth to annihilate all flesh in which there is the breath of life from under the heavens; everything on earth shall expire.*

22:3; Prov. 16:29). Haag (*TDOT,* 4:482) defines *ḥāmās* as "cold-blooded and unscrupulous infringement of the personal rights of others, motivated by greed and hate and often making use of physical violence and brutality." Speiser (*Genesis,* p. 117) remarks that "*ḥāmās,* 'lawlessness, injustice' . . . is a strictly legal term, which trad[itional] 'violence' fails to show adequately."

2. Cf. Cassuto, *Genesis,* 2:54; D. Clines, "Noah's Flood: I: The Theology of the Flood Narrative," *Faith and Thought* 100 (1972–73) 133–34, 142 n. 34.

1. Heb. *bā'* may be either a perfect form or a participle; the two forms of this verb are written the same. Is this a past fact, or a scene that passes in front of God? "I am resolved" is lit. "it has come (or is coming) in front of me"; cf. Speiser (*Genesis,* p. 47), "I have decided," and Skinner (*Genesis,* p. 160), "it has entered into my purpose."

2. This phrase reads lit., "I am going to annihilate them, the earth." The LXX simply adds "and," and reads ". . . them and the earth." The SP replaces *'eṯ* with *min,* ". . . them from the earth." *BHS* assumes haplography and suggests reading *mašḥîṯām mē'ēṯ*. But none of these changes is necessary. The *-m* on the end of *mašḥîṯām* can be understood as an enclitic *mem* (see F. I. Andersen and D. N. Freedman, *Hosea,* AB [Garden City, NY: Doubleday, 1980], pp. 395–96); or *'eṯ* may have here separative force, "from." See M. J. Dahood, "Isaiah 53,8–12 and Massoretic Misconstructions," *Bib* 63 (1982) 566 n. 2. A good illustration of this separative thrust of *'eṯ* is found in Isa. 7:17, "since the day that Ephraim departed from [*min*] Judah, from [*'eṯ*] the King of Assyria."

18 *But I will establish my covenant with you; you shall enter the ark—you, your sons, your wife, and your sons' wives with you.*
19 *And from every living thing, from all flesh, two of each you shall take into the ark to stay alive with you. Male and female they shall be.*
20 *Of every kind of bird, cattle of every kind, every kind of creeping thing of the ground, two of each shall come to you to stay alive.*
21 *For your part, provide yourself with all the food that is to be eaten, and store it away for yourself and you will have food for yourself and for them."*
22 *This Noah did. Whatever God commanded he did.*

13 The Flood narrative has four divine speeches (6:13–21; 7:1–4; 8:15–17; 9:1–17; the last one has three subspeeches). Interestingly, nowhere does Noah speak. As a matter of fact, his first recorded words in Scripture are "cursed be Canaan" (9:25)! Noah is as silent in his ship-building project and throughout the ensuing storm as Abraham is at Moriah. This narrative has no hint of any dialogue. God speaks. Noah implements. But here, as in the Sodom and Gomorrah story (18:20–21), God gives inside information to a select person about his probable future course of action. Unlike Abraham, Noah offers no protestations.

14 *Make for yourself.* Here is the only imperative in the first divine speech. What follows through v. 22 is an amplification of this command. Noah is told how to build the ark (vv. 14–16) and what to do after the ark is built (vv. 19–21).

The Hebrew word for *ark (tēḇâ)* occurs only in the Flood narrative and in Exod. 2:3, 5, where it is the "basket" in which the infant Moses is placed by his mother. Thus two remarkable persons in Scripture are saved from drowning by being placed in an "ark."[3] The OT uses another word, *'^{a}rôn,* for the "ark of the covenant," although Mishnaic Hebrew also uses *tēḇâ* for this receptacle. The origin of Heb. *tēḇâ* is uncertain. Most scholars connect the word with Egyp. *dbꜣt,* "chest, box, coffin."[4] The Ebla texts seem to have a cognate term, *tiba/tiba,* found in various expressions: *tibā-hû',* "he is the ark"; *ti-ba-ti-íl-lí,* "arks of the gods"; *ía-ti-ba^{KI},* "Ya is the ark."[5]

The wood of which the ark is made is called *gopher wood,* probably

3. Behind English "ark" is Latin *arca,* which is from the verb *arcere,* "to enclose, keep off." "Ark," following the Latin origins of the word, designates a covered receptacle.

4. See, e.g., B. Waltke, *ISBE,* 1:291.

5. See M. J. Dahood, "Eblaite and Biblical Hebrew," *CBQ* 44 (1982) 7, 21–22.

a resinous type of wood, though we cannot be sure since the word appears only here in the OT. That Noah is commanded to build such a vessel suggests that he may be a shipwright. Cain's skills are in city building, and his descendants institute farming, music, and metallurgy. Are Noah's skills those of the navigational craftsman? It is more likely that his knowledge of ship building was minimal or nonexistent; hence God had to give him such detailed information about building the vessel. Moses had little experience in tabernacle construction when he received explicit instructions about how to put that place of worship together. But, unlike Noah, Moses had access to craftsmen whose skills in these areas made up for his ignorance (Exod. 31:1–11), individuals who had been divinely gifted for that construction project.

This ark is to be divided into *compartments (qinnîm).* Since everywhere else in the OT *qinnîm* refers to birds' "nests," some scholars have emended MT *qinnîm* to *qānîm,* "reeds."[6] Support for this emendation may be found in the fact that Moses' *tēḇâ* was made of papyrus *(gōme'),* and Atrahasis's boat was made of reeds.[7]

Linguistic support for retention of the MT is provided by Akk. *qinnu,* which means "family" as well as "nest," as does Mandean *qina* ("nest, brood, home, family, group"). Arab. *qunn* means "chicken-coop." Thus the emendation is not at all certain. The acceptance of the MT supports the concept that Noah's ark was not a reed boat, but a large, complicated, and seaworthy vessel.

After Noah builds the ark, he is to cover it with *pitch,* that is, caulking. This is the only place in the Hebrew Bible where the noun *kōp̱er* means "pitch."[8] The verb *smear (kāp̱ar)* is a Qal denominative from *kōp̱er;* thus the expression *smear . . . with pitch (kāp̱artā . . . bakkōp̱er)* is analogous to the expression "season with salt" (*bammelaḥ timlāḥ,* Lev. 2:13).

6. See Num. 24:21; Deut. 22:6; 32:11; Job 29:18; 39:27; Ps. 84:4 (Eng. 3); Isa. 10:14; 16:2; Obad. 4; Hab. 2:9. Cf. C. H. Gordon, *The Ancient Near East,* 3rd ed. (New York: Norton, 1965), p. 50 n. 37; idem, *Homer and Bible* (Ventnor, NJ: Ventnor, 1969), p. 14 n. 21; E. Ullendorff, *Is Biblical Hebrew a Language? Studies in Semitic Languages and Civilizations* (Wiesbaden: Harrassowitz, 1977), pp. 48ff. See also NEB "cover it with reeds."

7. See W. G. Lambert and A. R. Millard, *Atra-ḫasīs: The Babylonian Story of the Flood,* pp. 12, 126–27: *qá-ne-e gáb-bi lu bi-nu-us-sà,* "let its structure be [. . .] entirely of reeds."

8. See H. R. Cohen, *Biblical Hapax Legomena in the Light of Akkadian and Ugaritic,* SBLDS 37 (Missoula, MT: Scholars, 1978), pp. 33–34. Cohen connects Heb. *kōp̱er* with Akk. *kupru,* "bitumen."

15 Three circumstantial clauses give the dimensions of the ark. Translating the cubit measurement into feet, we have a vessel that is 440 feet long, 73 feet wide, 44 feet high, and yielding a displacement of about 43,000 tons. The point to be observed here is that the dimensions of Noah's vessel are completely logical, and what one would expect to find in a seagoing vessel. Compare these dimensions with those of Utnapishtim's boat (in Babylonian, *elippu*) in the Gilgamesh Epic, which is a perfect cube of 120 cubits. To be sure, Noah's ark does not compare in size with the *Queen Elizabeth II* or some other modern ocean liner, but it is considerably bigger than Columbus's *Nina, Pinta,* and *Santa Maria.* The size of Noah's ark possibly suggests that it was large enough and strong enough to weather the Flood, and that it contained enough space (an approximate total deck area of 95,700 sq. ft.) to accommodate all the animals.

16 Further directives are given for the ark's construction. These directives include information about the roof (or a skylight?), a side door for exit and entrance, and the three levels of the boat's interior. Nowhere does the Hebrew text refer to "decks" per se, only (lit.) "underneaths, seconds, thirds," but decks are no doubt intended. We may compare this construction with Utnapishtim's ship, which had seven decks and nine compartments on each level.

The only problematical part of this verse is the correct translation of the first word, *ṣōhar,* and the words that immediately follow it. *ṣōhar* appears only here in the OT. Both "roof" and "ceiling window" have been suggested for *ṣōhar.* Those who opt for "window" (cf. Vulg. *fenestra*) do so on the basis of the word's possible connection with *ṣāhorayim,* "noon, midday," thus an opening to let in the light of day. The *ṣōhar* would be the entrance place for the light, and the door on the side would be the entrance place for people and animals. Now, there is no doubt that Noah's ark was equipped with a window in its ceiling. Gen. 8:6 clearly refers to this window, but there the text uses the standard word for "window," *ḥallôn.* But why should 6:16 use such an unusual word if the same part is meant?

If we choose to render this word as "roof" we encounter the same problem.[9] Why would the writer use such a strange word for "roof" if he knew the more regular word, *gag̱?* Perhaps there is a reason why *gag̱* would be inappropriate to describe the ark's roof. Evidence from elsewhere in the OT would suggest that *gag̱* refers precisely to a flat roof. Thus Rahab hid the two Hebrew spies on *(ʿal)* the roof *(gag̱)* of her house (Josh. 2:6, 8). It was

9. See J. F. Armstrong, "A critical note on Genesis VI 16Aa," *VT* 10 (1960) 328–33.

while David was "walking on" the roof *(gag)* of his house that he saw Bathsheba bathing (2 Sam. 11:2). That a flat-roofed vessel would be less than ideal during a torrential downpour is obvious. We suggest that *ṣōhar* was used because it refers to a pitched or vaulted roof.

Still, we have the next phrase, *Upon a cubit upward you shall finish it* (lit., "and to a cubit you shall finish it upward"). The modern English translations differ remarkably in their rendering of these words.[10] One of the problems here is the identification of the antecedent for the pronominal suffix *-āh* in *tᵉkalennâ,* "you shall finish *it.*" If *it* refers back to *ṣōhar,* regardless of how one translates that word, then we would have to assume that *ṣōhar* is feminine, to agree with the feminine pronominal suffix *-āh.* A possible antecedent could be the ark *(tēḇâ),* which is feminine. This interpretation would indicate that the roof of the ark is to slope down on both sides, with a horizontal area one cubit wide between the two sloping sides.[11] Following our translation, however, the opening part of the verse refers to the elevation of the crease of the roof above the level of the walls' tops.

17 This verse, one of the few in this section that focuses on God's activity, is structured like v. 13. God's impending act is first preceded by the interjection *hinᵉnî,* and then the particular act is described with a participle, *mašḥîṯām* in v. 13, *mēḇî'* in v. 17. V. 13 was the general statement: God would annihilate all flesh from the earth. V. 17 tells how he will do that: with a flood *(mabbûl).* This word for *flood* occurs only in Gen. 6–9 and Ps. 29:10, "Yahweh sits enthroned over the flood," which shows that the *mabbûl* lies (figuratively) at the Lord's feet. Except for 9:11, 15, in the Flood story *mabbûl* occurs with the definite article, which may indicate that it was a well-known event. One wonders if the word *mayim* ("waters") that follows is not a gloss, since by itself *mabbûl* designates floodwaters (see *BHS*).

18 In contrast to what God will do with "all flesh," he will establish his covenant with Noah (and here the verbal form is not participial but a perfect form with *waw;* cf. 9:9, which has, interestingly, *hinᵉnî mēqîm*). This verse highlights not primarily God's establishment of a covenant, but rather the establishment of that covenant with Noah. He is the chosen recipient. This emphasis is brought out by the double use of *with you ('ittāḵ).* The second one sounds almost redundant: "you shall enter the ark—you, your sons, your wife, and your sons' wives *with you.*" This use of the resumptive

10. In addition to the versions cf. the translation of R. K. Harrison, "Genesis," *ISBE,* 2:438, "you shall make a peripheral window for the ark, and you shall take it to within a cubit of the top."

11. See Cassuto, *Genesis,* 2:65–66.

pronoun establishes Noah as the person of supreme significance in this paragraph.

This announcement of the covenant, even before the Flood commences, is interesting. It shows us that God's covenant with Noah in ch. 9 is no ad hoc arrangement, hatched in God's mind once the floodwaters had disappeared. Even before he unleashes his anger God announces his intention to save at least one human being. This sequence of grace and indignation has already appeared two times in Genesis. Before God banished Adam and Eve from the garden he clothed them. Before he exiled Cain he placed a mark on him to protect him. And here God announces his covenant even before he sends his flood.

19–21 God's concern for the survival of a remnant reaches into the animal world and the species represented in that world. A male and female representative of each of the animals will find salvation in the ark. God will repopulate his world not from nothing, but *from all flesh, two of each* (male and female).

The indication of v. 20 is that these animals will *come* to Noah. Noah does not have to find and trap the animals; apparently that is God's responsibility—he will guide them to the ark. Or at least some unexplained stimulus will move the animals in Noah's direction.

In our judgment most commentators have precipitately assumed a contradiction between the "one pair" (P) and "seven pairs" (J, 7:2–3) of animals which Noah was told to take into the ark. We will discuss the matter more thoroughly at 7:2–3, but for the moment we would suggest that these numbers are not mutually exclusive. One could consider 6:19–20 as a preliminary set of instructions which is expanded and specified in a subsequent set of directions (7:2–3). The reference to Noah's bringing aboard sufficient food to feed the passengers during the storm (v. 21) reminds one of Joseph's advice to the native Egyptians to gather up (*qāḇaṣ*) and store up *(ṣāḇar)* sufficient grain to help them withstand the coming seven-year famine (Gen. 41:35).

22 This is the only time the narrator speaks in this paragraph, except for the brief introduction of God in v. 13a. One can only wonder why this portion of the story provides the reader with details about (a) the wood from which the ark is to be built; (b) its division into rooms; (c) how it is to be caulked; (d) its dimensions; (e) its roof; (f) the list and number of those to go on board; and (g) a bountiful supply of vegetarian food, while omitting other details like (a) where Noah built the ark; (b) whether he built it by himself; and (c) how long the project took. The emphasis in Gen. 6:13–22 is on the divine disclosure of the ark's design and Noah's responsibilities; Noah's faithful expediting of those plans is succinctly noted. By contrast, in the tabernacle project, approximately the same amount of space is devoted to the revelation of the tabernacle's design (Exod. 25–31) as is the implementation of that revelation (Exod. 35–40). An equivalent to the refrain that appears repeatedly in Exod. 39–40, "as the Lord had commanded Moses," is not present in the terse notice of Gen. 6:22 (although see 7:5).

Nowhere in ch. 6 does God evaluate Noah's character. That is done by the narrator (vv. 8, 9, 22). The Lord's own statement will come in 7:1. The Hebrew of v. 22 underscores Noah's faithfulness by a chiasm: *wayyaʿaś nōaḥ . . . kēn ʿāśâ,* "and did Noah . . . thus he did."

4. THE COMMAND TO ENTER THE ARK (7:1–10)

1 *Then Yahweh said to Noah: "Go, you and all your household, into the ark, for I have chosen you, a righteous person in this generation.*

2 *Of every clean animal take for yourself seven pairs, a male and its mate; and of every unclean animal, a pair, a male and its mate.*

3 *Also of every bird of heaven, seven pairs, a male and a female, to keep alive their issue on the earth.*

4 *For in a week hence I will send rain upon the earth forty days and forty nights, thus washing away from the earth's surface every subsisting thing I have made."*

5 *Noah did just as Yahweh had commanded him.*

6 *Noah was six hundred years old when the floodwaters came upon the earth.*

7 *Then Noah went—and with him his sons, his wife, and his sons' wives—into the ark because of the waters of the flood.*

8 *Of clean animals, and those not clean, of birds, and of everything that creeps on the ground,*

9 *two and two, male and female, went with Noah into the ark, just as God had commanded Noah.*

10 *After a week the floodwaters came upon the earth.*

1 The observant reader will have noticed that the Flood story shifts back and forth in the way it refers to deity. Sometimes he is "God" (e.g., 6:9–22), and sometimes he is "Yahweh" (or "Lord"; e.g., 6:5–8; 7:1–10, except for v. 9; etc.). Those who perceive a doublet in Gen. 6–9 appeal to this phenomenon to support their case. In one of the Flood stories the writer uses the tetragrammaton (Yahweh) to refer to God (J). In the other Flood story the writer uses the more general *ʾᵉlōhîm* (God) to refer to God (P).

This interpretation of the two names for deity is open to serious challenge. There are other possibilities for explaining the name shifts than appealing to divergent sources that are behind the finished account. For example, Cassuto has noted that normally Gen. 6–9 uses the more general *ʾĕlōhîm* (since it is the world that is inundated), and that *YHWH* occurs only where there is a special reason for it.[1]

It is also evident that in those places where deity is thematic in a given paragraph *YHWH* is used. This explains why *YHWH* appears in 6:5–8, where the thematic participant is the Lord, but not in 6:9–22, where the thematic participants are Noah, the earth, and the ark. In 7:1–10 God (i.e., *YHWH*) and Noah are the major thematic participants.[2]

Unlike the previous paragraphs which registered the narrator's comments on Noah's integrity (6:8, 9, 22), here we find God addressing himself to Noah in direct discourse. This particular verse contrasts with 6:5 and 6:12, two other places where God "saw" something. There he saw wickedness and corruption on the earth, but here he sees one righteous person on the earth.

Translations that render the second half of the verse "for I have found that you are righteous" are wide of the mark. Such a translation would give the (false) impression that Noah's obedience in building the ark is the immediate reason for his salvation, and thus produce a works-righteousness emphasis. If the writer had wanted to make that point in 7:1, he would have used either the verb *māṣāʾ*, "to find," or *yāḏaʿ*, "to know," as in Gen. 22:12, and thus turn 7:1 into a recognition statement *(Erkenntnisaussage)*. He could have accomplished that same purpose by using this structure: *rāʾîṯî kî ṣaddîq ʾattâ lᵉpānay,* "I have seen that you are righteous before me" (verb plus *kî* plus direct object). But here we have a verb plus two direct objects: *I have seen you, a righteous person.*[3]

We rule out the possibility that this is a declarative statement ("I have seen that [or I declare that] you are a righteous person") on the grounds that there is no evidence that "see" plus pronominal direct object ("you") plus attribute ("righteous") can mean "declare/pronounce A to be B." Nor is it a causative statement ("I have seen you because you are righteous"), for the indirective accusative of cause is almost nonexistent in the Hebrew Bible.[4]

1. See Cassuto, *Genesis,* 2:35–36.

2. I have profited greatly from the stimulating essay of R. E. Longacre, "The Discourse Structure of the Flood Narrative," in SBLASP, 1976, pp. 235–62.

3. This is category "g" in W. M. Clark's examination of types of sentences with *rāʾâ* in "The righteousness of Noah," *VT* 21 (1971) 265ff. GKC, § 117h, notes that "*verba sentiendi* may take a second object, generally in the form of a participle or adjective and necessarily indeterminate, to define more exactly the action or state in which the object is perceived." See also Westermann, *Genesis,* 1:426–27.

4. Both GKC, § 118l, and Joüon, *Grammaire,* § 126k, cite only one illustration.

The only other alternative is that it is a prospective statement; and the verse may be compared with 1 Sam. 16:1, "Fill your horn with oil, and go: I will send you to Jesse the Bethlehemite, for I have chosen [or provided, *rā'îṯî,* as in Gen. 7:1] for myself a king among his sons." The point made by 7:1 is that the explanation for Noah's righteousness is not merit, but rather the purpose of Yahweh. God has chosen Noah as the suitable representative of the human race, the one by whom or through whom humanity might be preserved. Thus *ṣaddîq* has a functional nuance in 7:1.

2–3 This chapter presupposes Noah's completion of the ark. Now, just prior to entering the vessel, Noah is given a final and more detailed set of instructions. Earlier he had been told to take aboard a pair of every kind of living thing (6:19–20, *šᵉnayim,* a word that is dual in form). On this occasion he is told to take aboard seven pairs *(šiḇʿâ šiḇʿâ)* of all of the clean animals and one pair *(šᵉnayim)* of each of the unclean animals.

Just as the critical scholars appeal to the two names for deity to support two Flood accounts, so they find further support for their position in the fact that two different numbers of animals are cited here. One has Noah taking aboard one pair of animals, without reference to clean/unclean (P). The other tradition has Noah taking aboard seven pairs of the clean and one pair of the unclean (J).

The contradiction disappears, however, if we read *šᵉnayim* in 6:19–20 as a collective for "pairs"; one cannot form a plural of a word that is dual. Thus Gen. 6:19–20 is the general statement.[5] Noah is to bring aboard pairs of animals. Specifically the animal population is to consist of seven pairs of clean and one pair of unclean.

To be accurate, the text does not say that Noah is to take aboard clean and unclean animals. He is to bring with him animals that are clean and those that are "not clean." The chapter discreetly avoids using the word *ṭāmē',* "unclean." Still, it is interesting that Yahweh mandates the preservation of the animals that are not clean.

In later priestly legislation one must not eat unclean animals nor even touch their carcasses (Lev. 11:1–47). If one does, the violator himself becomes unclean, that is, unfit for participation in the communal worship of Yahweh. The entire OT places a prohibition on eating what is unclean (Deut. 4:3–20; Judg. 13:4, 7, 14; 1 Sam. 20:26; 2 Chr. 30:18–19; Ezek. 4:14). Yet these unclean animals are spared from drowning. They are as much an object

5. See K. A. Kitchen, *Ancient Orient and Old Testament* (Chicago: Inter-Varsity, 1966), p. 120 and n. 25; idem, *The Bible in Its World* (Downers Grove, IL: Inter-Varsity, 1978), p. 139 n. 23.

of Yahweh's compassion as is Noah himself. If nothing else, their inclusion in those who are delivered is partial confirmation of the fact that in the OT "sinful" is not normally a synonym for "unclean," especially in the cultic sections of the OT.

4 Noah is given a week's warning before the onset of the deluge. The expression *in a week* (*lᵉyāmîm ʿôḏ šiḇâ,* lit., "days yet seven") may be compared with 40:19, "in three days" *(bᵉʿôḏ šᵉlōšeṯ yāmîm).* The verse is made up of a circumstantial clause and a main clause. As we saw in 6:13, 17, the participle is used to describe imminent divine action. The main clause may be understood as stating either result ("thus washing away") or purpose ("in order to wash away").

The word for *send rain* here *(māṭar)* refers to a regular rainfall. It is not normally a torrential downpour. What makes this storm so potent is that it is to last forty days and nights. The word used later in v. 12 for "rain"—*gešem*—by itself does designate a heavy rain, as seen by the fact that *gešem* may be accompanied by words emphasizing that point (1 K. 18:41, 45; Ezek. 13:11, 13). There can be a mighty, rushing *gešem,* but not a mighty, rushing *māṭār.*

5 Again we have the sequence of commandment and execution (vv. 1–4 and 5), as we had in 6:14–21 (commandment) and 6:22 (execution). Presumably the writer could have supplied myriads of details about Noah's erection of the ark and the assembling of the animals, but he did not. Noah's rather long and complicated exploits are condensed into these words: he did it! Not a note about his expertise in construction and zoology. By condensing Noah's considerable achievements into an unbelievably skeletal statement, the author concentrates on one fact only, Noah's obedience to and successful completion of the divine mandate. The general statement made in v. 5 is particularized in the following verses, 6–9.

6–9 That Noah was six hundred years old when the Flood began[6] tells us that his sons, or at least one of them, would be one hundred years old (see 5:32). Apparently Noah fathered no additional children after the Flood, although he still had about one-third of his life left (9:28–29). In the post-Flood covenant Noah receives abundant promises from God, but more progeny is not among those promises.

The story continues to highlight Noah's activities. V. 6 is made up of two clauses, both of which are circumstantial to v. 7: "Noah, 600 years old, floodwaters are on the earth—(all this being so) Noah went." The focus is

6. Cf. the Sumerian King List: "In Shuruppak Ubar-Tutu became king and ruled 18,600 years. . . . (Then) the Flood swept over (the earth)" (*ANET,* p. 265).

clearly on Noah, as the singular verb and the use of the resumptive pronoun, *and with him,* indicate.

Verses 7–9 are essentially an elaboration of v. 5, which is really a hinge, summarizing and commenting on Noah's implicit actions mandated in vv. 1–4. Expressly, how did Noah do all that the Lord commanded him? Vv. 7–9 tell us how.

According to source analysis, 7:1–10 is from J. But what is to be done with the reference to *two and two . . . went with Noah into the ark, . . . just as God* [*'ĕlōhîm*] *had commanded Noah* (v. 9)? Does not this sound more like P? If one is bound to this theory, then one must suggest that the two stories of the Flood, juxtaposed up to this point, are now suddenly and unexpectedly spliced.[7] Or one must attribute the particular words in v. 8 that are at variance with J to a late redactor who sensed the forthcoming collision between J and P, and thus moved as neatly as possible to eliminate the discrepancies by artificial harmonization.[8]

We have already explained why we see no mutual exclusiveness between "a pair" and "seven pairs," and thus the *two and two* of v. 8 is anything but mechanical and arbitrary. But why in this section, which began with "Yahweh" (v. 1), and continued with "Yahweh" (v. 5), do we find the conclusion: *as God* [*'ĕlōhîm*] *had commanded Noah*? Can one explain the shift in the name for deity within the same unit, apart from recourse to sources and redactors? We would suggest that *God* is used in v. 9 because in this particular paragraph (vv. 6–10) God is a nonthematic participant. Noah is the thematic participant, as he leads the procession into the ark. This contrasts with the first paragraph in this unit (vv. 1–5), where God is the thematic participant, as indicated by the divine imperatives and indicatives. Thus there he is called "Yahweh."

10 The first paragraph in this unit (vv. 1–5) began with what God said Noah was to do and climaxed with the note that Noah did indeed implement the will of God. Also in this paragraph God told Noah what he himself was about to do—in seven days send rain. Vv. 6–9 represented Noah's fulfillment of the divine imperative of v. 1. V. 10 represents the fulfillment of the divine indicative (a promissory note) of v. 4. Noah does what God says. And God does what God says. He is as faithful to his own word as Noah is to God's word.

Note how the "seven days" motif surfaces again in the Flood narrative:

7. For example, Vawter, *On Genesis,* p. 122.
8. So Speiser, *Genesis,* p. 52.

7 days (flood begins 7 days after God sends Noah into the ark, 7:10)
40 days (rain on earth for this long, 7:12, 17)
150 days (waters prevail, 7:24; 8:3)
40 days (after 40 days Noah opens the ark's window, 8:6)
7 days (7 days later Noah dispatches, 8:10, 12)[9]

The Flood narrative abounds with illustrations by which the temporal structure of the plot is confirmed through the use of dates, which state when something happened or how long it lasted. See, for example, in succession 7:11; 8:4, 5, 13, 14, which cover the commencement of the Flood on the seventeenth day of the second month of Noah's 600th year (7:11) until its completion 365 days later on the twenty-seventh day of the second month of Noah's 601st year (8:14), with intervening years highlighted. In addition to dates, the above 7-40-150-40-7 arrangement illustrates the use of periods of time to enhance the plot structure in the Flood narrative.

5. THE START OF THE FLOOD (7:11–16)

11 *In the six hundredth year of Noah's life, in the second month, on the seventeenth day of the month—on that day—were split all springs of the great abyss, and the floodgates of the sky were opened.*
12 *Torrential rain fell on the earth forty days and forty nights.*[1]
13 *On that exact day, Noah—and Shem, Ham, and Japheth, Noah's wife, and the three*[2] *wives of Noah's sons with them—entered the ark,*
14 *they as well as every kind of beast, every kind of cattle, every kind of creature that creeps on earth, every kind of bird, and every winged thing.*

9. See S. Bar-Efrat, "Some observations on the analysis of structure in biblical narrative," *VT* 30 (1980) 168.

1. With its numerals, Biblical Hebrew, like Ugaritic, follows the rule that "3" to "10" usually go with nouns in the plural. But when the numeral is above 10, the following noun is often in the singular. Thus, 7:12 speaks of forty "day" and forty "night," just as 7:24 speaks of 150 "day." This is especially true of "day" when it follows a number above 10, both in Hebrew and Ugaritic, although Ugaritic (e.g., *UT,* 109:7) provides the anomalous *ḫmš ʿšr ymm,* "fifteen days." Cf. *UT,* p. 46, § 7.19.

2. Note the form of the numeral here, *š^{e}lōšeṯ,* with the suffixed *-t.* This form violates normal Hebrew usage by having the masc. form of the numeral before a fem. noun. In fact, in Biblical Hebrew a fem. form of the numeral is rare before fem. nouns (cf. Ezek. 7:2, "four corners"—*ʾarbaʿṯ kanpôṯ* [Ketib] and *ʾarbaʿ kanpôṯ* [Qere]). The integrity of *š^{e}lōšeṯ n^{e}šê* in Gen. 7:13 is supported by the expression "three sisters" *(š^{e}lōšeṯ ʾaḥyōṯêhem)* in Job 1:4. See C. H. Gordon, "The Authenticity of the Phoenician Text from Parahyba," *Or* 37 (1968) 80; idem, "The Canaanite Text from Brazil," *Or* 37 (1968) 430.

15 *They came to Noah inside the ark, pairs of all flesh in which there was the breath of life.*
16 *Those who entered, male and female of all flesh, came just as God had commanded Noah. Then Yahweh closed him inside.*

The source analysts assign this unit to P, except possibly for the reference to the forty-day downpour (v. 12, and 7:4 [J]), and certainly the phrase "then Yahweh closed him inside." These scholars fail to see any major advancement in the plot within this section. In fact, they see the verses only as a doublet of the preceding ones. Thus, twice we are told that Noah entered the ark (7:7, J; 7:13, P).

Such simplistic analysis overlooks one of the major features of epic composition—the deliberate use of resumption and summarization of an earlier part of the narrative.[3] This particular section of Genesis (7:6–16) swings back and forth between describing the Flood and the entry into the ark:

flood:	(v. 6)
entry into the ark:	(vv. 7–9)
flood:	(vv. 10-12)
entry into the ark:	(vv. 13–16)

11 The novel feature introduced in v. 11 is the information about two sources for the floodwaters: a vast tidal wave from the eruption of ocean waters and a massive downpour. Within this paragraph we find two causes for the Flood: water below and above; two kinds of occupants in the ark: human and animal; two names for deity: *ʾĕlōhîm* and *YHWH.*

There is no doubt that the two sources of water are intended to recall the "waters above and below" of 1:6–7. The Flood un-creates, and returns the earth to a pre-creation period when there was only "waters." The lower waters are sprung loose when the *springs of the great abyss* (*tᵉhôm rabbâ*) are split. This Hebrew expression occurs elsewhere in the OT only in poetry (Ps. 36:7 [Eng. 6]; 78:15 [*tᵉhōmôṯ rabbâ*]; Isa. 51:10; Amos 7:4). This, plus other factors noted below, may lend credence to the possibility that the compiler of Gen. 7 (and 8) had before him a poem which he had written as a narrative report, or that the compiler gives us his account of the Flood in a poem-like version.

The waters from above fall when *the floodgates of the sky* [*haššā-mayim*] *were opened.* Another possible indication of poetic influence is the

3. See B. W. Anderson, "From Analysis to Synthesis: The Interpretation of Genesis 1–11," *JBL* 97 (1978) 35.

use of chiastic structure in the two lines: verb (split), subject (fountains):: subject (floodgates), verb (opened). To this structural chiasm we may add the sonant chiasm produced by *nb* (in *nib̲q*^{e}*ʿû)* and *np* (in *nip̲tāḥû*), and by *rb* (in *rabbâ* and *ʾ*^{a}*rubbōṯ*).[4]

The action of the waters' release is described using Heb. *bāqaʿ* and *pāṯaḥ,* two verbs that occur again as a parallel pair in Job 32:19 and Num. 16:31b–32a. The former verb is especially provocative. The splitting of the *t*^{e}*hôm rabbâ* in 7:11 has been connected with the Babylonian creation story *Enuma elish,* in which Marduk creates the heavens above and the earth below by splitting in two the corpse of Tiamat.[5]

The verb *bāqaʿ* appears fifty-one times in the OT, with the meaning "to break into something," "to break out of something," or "to break something open," but not one of these passages has mythical overtones. Most frequently it is connected with water, either the dividing of the Reed Sea at the Exodus from Egypt (Exod. 14:16, 21; Neh. 9:11; Ps. 78:13; Isa. 63:12), or a cleaving action which produces water (10 times, as here in 7:11).

If this verb has mythic roots, it is odd that it is absent from a so-called mythical monster passage such as Isa. 51:9–10: "Was it not you who cut Rahab to pieces, who pierced that monster through? Was it not you who dried up the sea, the waters of the great deep?" We do find the verb in a similar text, Ps. 74:13ff.: "It was you who split open the sea [i.e., cosmic sea, not Reed Sea] by your power; you broke the heads of the monster in the waters. It was you who crushed the heads of Leviathan. . . . It was you who opened up [*bāqaʿ*] springs and streams." To be sure, the cleaving of water is here placed in a mythically oriented context. But there is no reference to the cleaving of a monster. Rather, the monster has been defeated, and thus the waters are sovereignly owned by, and are at the disposal of, Yahweh.[6]

4. See J. Kselman, "A Note on Gen. 7:11," *CBQ* 35 (1973) 493.

5. See, e.g., M. K. Wakeman, *God's Battle with the Monster* (Leiden: Brill, 1973), pp. 123–27. For her *bāqaʿ* means "to split open (a body)." She appeals especially to Ugar. *bqʿ*, which is used once when Anat cleaves Mot in a reenactment of harvest (*UT,* 49:ii:30–32—*tiḫd bn ilm mt bḥrb tbqʿnn),* and once when Danel rips open the livers of eagles looking for the remains of his son Aqhat (*UT,* 1 Aqht 109, 116, etc.—*ybqʿ kbdthm*).

6. Israel's historicizing of myth and appropriation of literary figures not native to her, esp. as it relates to the verb *bāqaʿ*, has been convincingly discussed by J. N. Oswalt, "The Myth of the Dragon and Old Testament Faith," *EvQ* 49 (1977) 163–72. He argues that the root meaning of *bāqaʿ* is not necessarily derived from the monster myth. At best, of the 51 uses of *bāqaʿ*, maybe six contain allusions to myth. And in those passages that use *bāqaʿ* in connection with God's victory over the monster (Isa. 51:9, 10; Ps. 74:12–17), there is no mention of Yamm ("the sea") being cleft.

Note that in Gen. 7:11 chaos is released by the splitting of *t^ehôm.* In *Enuma elish* the gods attempt to create some kind of order by bisecting Tiamat. In other words, the themes are reversed. Gen. 7:11 may be cited, then, as a confirming illustration of Yahweh's lordship over the waters. They are his to release (Ps. 74:15) or to control (Isa. 51:10).

12 Only one of the two sources of rain mentioned in the previous verse is picked up here, and that is the *torrential rain* from above. Such rain fell for *forty days and forty nights,* a much more reasonable figure for a flood of this proportion than the relatively brief seven days and seven nights found in both the Gilgamesh and Atrahasis epics.

It may only be a coincidence, but it is interesting to compare the forty days of the rainfall (7:12) and the one hundred and fifty days (7:24) that the waters prevailed (I shall present my case for including the fifty days as part of the one hundred and fifty days under my discussion of 7:24) with the length of time involved in an early prophetic act by Ezekiel. According to the LXX, he is told to lie on his right side for one hundred and fifty days (MT has three hundred and ninety days) as a sign of the length of Israel's punishment (Ezek. 4:4–5). Then he is to lie on his left side forty days as a sign of the length of Judah's punishment (Ezek. 4:6). Thus both in Gen. 7 and Ezek. 4 (LXX) we have a period of forty days and one hundred and fifty days as the time period for the sending of God's judgment.[7]

13 Every time Noah's family is mentioned, or listed, his sons are spoken of before his wife (6:18; 7:7, 13; 8:18). Also, they are named, but she is not. The emphasis is on the father and the father's married sons, perhaps underscoring the patriarchal orientation of the story. Men are named; women are unnamed. Noah's wife is like Job's wife. She is known only in reference to her husband. Noah's spouse plays no part at all in the narrative. She could not be more passive or marginal than the current story pictures her. Nor are the three daughters-in-law of Noah identified.

The three sons are living for a hundred years before the Flood, and yet no mention is made of any family they started. Noah fathers children only before the Flood. His sons father children only after the Flood is over. The post-Flood command to Noah and his sons "to be fruitful and multiply" (9:1) affects only the sons. This blessing of fertility, extended to Noah in the pre-Flood era, now becomes the privilege of his three sons in the post-Flood era.

14–15 The procession into the ark includes both human and animal

7. See M. Greenberg, *Ezekiel 1–20,* AB (Garden City, NY: Doubleday, 1983), p. 106.

passengers. The logistics of this procession are ignored, just as details about how Noah built the ark were passed over. Such lacunae do not indicate the deletion of folkloristic elements that would defy rational explanation, but rather the deliberate omission of details that are at best secondary in the account. The animals that join Noah and his family on board are further defined as those *in which there was the breath of life (rûaḥ ḥayyîm).* This exact phrase was used earlier (6:17) to refer to the object of God's wrath. Here it refers to those exempted from punishment. The phrase possibly recalls parallel references in the Creation account to aquatic life (1:7) and land animals (1:24) as *nep̄eš ḥayyâ.*

16 The most surprising element in this verse is the shift from *God* to *Yahweh* in the last half of the verse. We have seen that the documentary hypothesis assigns this last phrase, *Then Yahweh closed him inside,* to the J source because of the use of the tetragrammaton and because of the anthropomorphism which P would have eschewed.

But B. Anderson, himself convinced of this explanation, raises the crucial question: "How does this notice *function* in the received text?"[8] For him, *Yahweh* functions here as a final punctuation of the unit, and it anticipates what follows—God's "remembrance" (another anthropomorphism) of those inside the ark.

Cassuto suggests that God shut the door from the outside, and became, so to speak, an outside protector of the ark and of its vulnerable passengers—hence the use of *Yahweh* as the more appropriate name to describe God's act of door closing.[9] It is possible that neither sources nor theology is involved here. Perhaps *Yahweh* is used in this phrase for stylistic reasons. In 7:1–5 "Yahweh" and "Noah" are thematic. In 7:6–10 "Noah" and "the rain" are thematic. In 7:11–16a "Noah" and "the animals" are thematic. In 7:16b "Yahweh" is thematic. Thus 7:1–16 assumes the form of one long chiasmus:

Yahweh (7:1–5)
  Noah (7:6–10)
  Noah (7:11–16a)
Yahweh (7:16b)[10]

8. B. W. Anderson, *JBL* 97 (1978) 35. Italics his.
9. Cassuto, *Genesis,* 2:92.
10. See Longacre, SBLASP, 1976, p. 247.

6. THE CRESTING OF THE WATERS (7:17–24)

17 *The flood continued forty days on the earth. As the waters increased they carried the ark, so that it was raised above the earth.*
18 *The waters mounted and increased greatly upon the earth, and the ark floated on the waters' surface.*
19 *The waters mounted even more above the earth, and all the highest mountains everywhere were submerged.*
20 *At fifteen cubits higher the waters crested, resulting in the mountains being submerged.*
21 *And all flesh that moved on the earth expired—birds, cattle, beasts, all the creatures that swarmed on earth, and all mankind.*
22 *Everything which had the breath of life in its nostrils, everything which was on dry land, died.*
23 *He washed away every subsisting thing which was on the face of the earth: man and cattle, creeping things and birds of the air; they were washed away from the earth. Only Noah, and those with him in the ark, survived.*
24 *The waters maintained their crest over the earth one hundred and fifty days.*

Nothing at all is said in these verses about the passengers now safely locked inside the ark. The action here is totally outside the ark. The previous paragraph focused on those who moved from outside to inside the ark and thus survived. For this reason that paragraph named not only Noah but also his sons, and identified the animals who also embarked. In this last section only Noah is named. His fellow companions are simply "and those with him" (v. 23). Thus this last paragraph focuses on those who remained outside the ark and thus perished.

There is much here that is reminiscent of Gen. 3. Inside the ark parallels inside the garden; outside the ark parallels outside the garden. Inside there is salvation; outside there is not. Inside there is immunity from disaster; outside there is inevitable death. The ark is spared; the earth is doomed.

A closer look at the structure of the whole chapter reveals a reasonable logic and smoothness in its progression. It is anything but prosaic and jarring, as those who imagine a need to disentangle two stories or sources here might insist:

A. The divine command (vv. 1–4)
B. Execution of the divine command (vv. 5–9)
C. The Flood (vv. 10–12)
B′. Execution of the divine command repeated (vv. 13–16)
D. The cresting of the waters (vv. 17–20)

E. Universal death (vv. 22–23)
D′. The cresting of the waters (v. 24)

So, we find in vv. 5–24 the phenomenon of B:C:B′ and D:E:D′. The first part of the subunit is repeated in the third part of the subunit.[1] Such repetitions lend symmetry to the text and suggest that dissecting the whole will prove to be not only unproductive but actually misleading.

17 The first clause repeats the duration of the rain for a forty-day period, noted first in v. 12, except that v. 17 uses *mabbûl,* while v. 12 employs *gešem.* LXX adds "and forty nights," thus repeating the phrase for the downpour in v. 12. The effect of the Flood on the ark is noted in three brief sentences, each of which is in logical sequence, the second being the effect of the first and the cause of the third: "the waters increased"; "they carried the ark"; "it was raised above the earth."

18 Verses 18–24 mention the swelling and cresting of the waters two times each ("mounted," vv. 18, 19; "crested," vv. 20, 24); all four use some form of the verb *gāḇar,* and in a chiastic arrangement: v. 18, imperfect; v. 19, perfect; v. 20, perfect; v. 24, imperfect.[2]

In spite of the savagery of the storm, the ark neither sinks nor capsizes. Keep in mind also that Noah, unlike Utnapishtim and Atrahasis, does not have navigational personnel aboard with him, unless they be his wife, sons, or daughters-in-law. Nor is there any explicit reference to navigational apparatus on the ark, apart from the birds (who are like homing pigeons) and a ceiling window (i.e., navigation by the stars). Noah has obeyed explicitly. If Noah is to emerge alive from the ark, it will be because of the grace and protecting presence of Yahweh—divine mercy rather than human skill will be the determining factor.

19–20 Once again we note a chiasmus in the first two words of v. 19 and the first two words of v. 18. The order in v. 18 is verb plus subject *(wayyigḇ^{e}rû hammayim).* The order in v. 19 is subject plus verb *(w^{e}ham-*

1. Cogent observations on this chapter have been made by M. Kessler, "Rhetorical Criticism of Genesis 7," in *Rhetorical Criticism: Essays in Honor of James Muilenburg,* ed. J. J. Jackson and M. Kessler, PTMS 1 (Pittsburgh: Pickwick, 1974), pp. 1–17. Kessler concludes his article by saying, "There are no 'seams' in Gen 7; the garment is of one piece and if materials should be of different provenance, their joining has been executed with such artistry that they have been dissolved in the whole" (p. 17).

2. Gevirtz, *Patterns in the Early Poetry of Israel,* pp. 92–93, notes the use of the root *gāḇar* in ch. 7 for the increase of the waters, and the root *qālal* in ch. 8 for the recession of the waters. The same *gāḇar/qālal* parallelism is found in 2 Sam. 1:23; Jer. 46:6; Eccl. 9:11 ("strong/swift"). The use of two traditionally parallel terms at two extremes of a prose account suggested to Gevirtz the possibility of a poetic substratum underlying the Genesis narrative.

mayim gāḇerû). In fact, *gāḇerû* is the first perfect verb form in vv. 17ff., after seven successive imperfect forms. This sudden shift in verb form does not necessarily indicate a climax,[3] but it certainly suggests a change of focus on the writer's part away from the ark (vv. 17–18) to the effects of the Flood on the earth (vv. 19ff.).[4] Perhaps the dual reference in these two verses to the *submerging of the mountains,* which may sound clumsy to some, may be due to the fact that "the slackening of narrative pace by means of epic repetition in opposition can sustain tension at some high point in a story."[5]

21–22 As a single unit, these two verses begin and end with synonymous verbs (*wayyiḡwaʿ* and *mēṯû,* respectively). The point being made is the total loss of life brought about by the Flood. Nowhere does the text say "they drowned," although obviously it is death by drowning. I would suggest that the use of *mēṯû,* "they died," instead of *ṭāḇeʿû* or *šāṭep̄û,* "they drowned," reinforces the idea that the loss of life is a divine penalty (cf. "dying he shall die," 2:17), rather than death due to natural catastrophe.

In the preservation notice we were told first about the salvation of human beings and then that of the animals. In the death notice we are told first about the loss of animal life and then the loss of human life. The Hebrew of v. 21 takes eight words to describe the loss of animal life, but only two words to describe the demise of human life.

23 This verse summarizes the two previous ones, which form the main statement, much as v. 20 summarizes the main statement of v. 19. Here the repetition intensifies the contrast between *all flesh . . . expired* and *Only Noah . . . survived.* The contrast between the spared and the condemned is brought out even more in this verse by the use of two Niphals (*wayyimmāḥû,* "they were washed away," and *wayyiššā'er,* "he was left"). The use of two passive forms of the verb to describe the fate both of the ungodly and of the righteous Noah suggests strongly that it is Yahweh's action which controls eternal destiny. Noah does not survive this catastrophe by his own cunning or strength. He is saved because he is left behind, or left over (the literal rendering of *yiššā'er*) by Yahweh.

Note that the destruction notice of v. 21 moved from animal life to human life, but the opposite is the case in this verse. This order allows a contrast between the first half of the verse—human life that did not survive—and the last half of the verse—human life that did survive.

3. As argued by S. E. McEvenue, *The Narrative Style of the Priestly Writer,* AnBib 50 (Rome: Biblical Institute Press, 1971), p. 35.

4. See Kessler, in *Rhetorical Criticism,* p. 12.

5. See F. Andersen, *The Sentence in Biblical Hebrew,* p. 41.

Noah is saved because of Yahweh. And Noah's family is saved because of Noah. Everybody in this narrative owes his preservation to someone else. This is a concept appearing elsewhere in the OT, most immediately in the Sodom-Gomorrah story. There the family of Lot is preserved because of Lot.[6]

24 This verse "functions as a kind of ironic 'tranquil conclusion' " to the onset of the deluge.[7] Two times the expression *one hundred and fifty days* appears in the Flood narrative, here and in 8:3. As the translation above reflects, the phrase in 7:24 expresses the length of time the *waters maintained their crest over the earth.* In 8:3 the same expression conveys the beginning of the recession of the waters at the end of this period. Only then did a decline in the water's cresting commence.[8] The question arises whether one should consider the forty days and nights (7:4, 12, 17) as part of the one hundred and fifty days (40 days for the downpour, followed by 110 additional days of the water's cresting) or as distinct from and previous to the one hundred and fifty days (40 days for the downpour, followed by 150 days of the water's cresting; therefore downpour plus cresting equals 190 days). The data in 8:3–4 would support including the forty days within the one-hundred-and-fifty-day period, for there we are told that the ark rested upon one of the mountains of Ararat one hundred and fifty days after the Flood began:

Flood begins (1st of 40 days) on Noah's 600th year, 2nd month, 17th day (7:11)
Ark rests on mountain on Noah's 600th year, 7th month, 17th day (8:4) (i.e., 150 days later, possibly to be understood as 5 months of 30 days each).[9]

6. W. M. Clark ("The Flood and the Structure of the Pre-patriarchal History," *ZAW* 83 [1971] 195) draws instructive parallels between the Flood story and the Sodom story: (1) both concern non-Israelites; (2) both contain a complete destruction by a natural event of a cataclysmic nature; (3) there is an ultimate disgraceful outcome involving drunkenness and a breach of sexual mores; (4) both imply repopulation from a single hero; (5) the issue of righteousness is central to both; (6) both Noah (6:8) and Lot (19:19) "found favor in the eyes" of the deity or his representative; (7) the Heb. *mašḥîṯ* is found in both (6:13; 19:13) to indicate impending divine action.

7. Kessler, in *Rhetorical Criticism,* p. 13.

8. See Cassuto, *Genesis,* 2:44.

9. J. A. Emerton ("An examination of some attempts to defend the unity of the flood narrative in Genesis," *VT* 37 [1987] 402–4) addresses Cassuto's interpretation of "150 days" and finds it lacking. He argues that 150 days are the period between the beginning of the Flood and 8:2, when the rain stopped.

7. THE FLOODWATERS RECEDE (8:1–5)

1 *God remembered Noah, and all the beasts and cattle that were with him in the ark. God made a wind pass over the earth, and the waters began to recede.*
2 *The springs of the great abyss and the floodgates of the sky were sealed, and the rain from the sky was restrained.*
3 *The waters returned continually from off the earth; they began to withdraw at the end of a hundred and fifty days.*
4 *And the ark came to rest in the seventh month, on the seventeenth day of the month, on one of the mountains of Ararat.*
5 *And the waters continued to diminish until the tenth month, and in the tenth month, on the first day of the month, the tops of the mountains were spotted.*

1 The story now takes a dramatic turn. Indeed, a pivotal point is reached with the first clause of v. 1: *God remembered Noah.* The text does not say that God remembered Noah's righteousness and obedience. Had it gone that way, then 8:1 would have scored the point that Noah was spared principally because of his character, a character that merited deliverance. Nor does the text state that God recalled his earlier words to Noah about a forthcoming covenant (6:18). That would reduce the activity of God to simply a psychological flashback. By trimming the description of the divine remembrance as much as possible, the point is made that when all appears helpless God intervenes to prevent tragedy. For God to remember someone means that God extends mercy to someone by saving that person from death (8:1; 19:29) or from barrenness (30:22).

In this one clause, then, the subject and the verb are more crucial than the object. The significant thing is that *God remembered.* The closest immediate parallel to this clause is Gen. 19:29, "he (God) remembered Abraham." No less than seventy-three times in the OT is "remember" *(zāḵar)* used with God as the subject. Most often (18 times) it is followed by the preposition *l*e, "to," demonstrating that God's remembrance is interpreted more as "an action directed toward someone, rather than as a psychological experience of the subject."[1] Here we have the finite form of the verb followed by the sign of the accusative, *'eṯ* (see also 19:29; 30:22).

God's remembrance of Noah spurs him into sending a wind over the earth that starts the process of the drying out of the land. One need only recall

1. B. S. Childs, *Memory and Tradition in Israel,* SBT 37 (Naperville: Allenson, 1962), p. 31. Ch. 3, "God Remembers" (pp. 31–44), is relevant to Gen. 8:1. See also H. Eising, *"zākhar," TDOT,* 4:64–82, esp. pp. 69–72.

that Heb. *rûaḥ* translates as both "spirit" and "wind" in order to decipher here a blatant connection with 1:2. At creation, or just prior to creation, the divine *rûaḥ* hovers majestically, restraining the waters. Here the divine *rûaḥ* brings about the evaporation of the waters of judgment.

2 The last part of v. 1 dealt with cause (a wind) and an effect (waters receding). Added to this information is the fact that the two sources of water were sealed and thus unable any longer to spill water on the earth. Or one might also read v. 2 as chronologically prior to v. 1b. The cessation of the water from above and below (v. 2) makes possible the beginning of the waters' recession (v. 1b). Thus, the description is from result (v. 1b) to cause (v. 2). The two Niphals in this verse (*yissāḵrû,* "were sealed," and *yikkālē',* "was restrained"), signaling the end of the onslaught of waters, match the two Niphals used at the beginning of the inundation (7:11, *niḇqeʿû,* "were split," and *nipṯāḥû,* "were opened"). This fourfold use of a passive form of the verb says as strongly as possible that the Flood is not a freak of nature. Both its commencement and completion are divinely ordained and divinely controlled. Noah might well have said with Job (1:21), "The Lord gave and the Lord has taken away; blessed be the name of the Lord."

Note that the sun plays no role in the drying up of the waters, though in the pagan myths of castastrophe the sun plays a primary role in the flood's cessation. Note especially in the Sumerian Flood story, Ziusudra, after he left the ship, prostrated himself before Utu the sun-god, for it is the sun that has just come out and illuminated the earth and the sky.[2] Perhaps the lack of any reference to the sun indicates a deliberate dissociation in biblical thought between the Flood's end and a sun deity.

3 The waters do not vanish completely. Their mission now completed, they return to their original position, either above or below the earth. To make sense of the last part of the verse, one must attribute to the verb inceptive force (versus RSV "had abated"); that is, it describes the beginning of a process, not the conclusion of that process. V. 5, which refers to the continuation of the water's recession beyond the date of v. 3, shows that v. 3 cannot refer to the end of the process of the waters' diminishing.

4 The narrator informs us that it is on the seventeenth day of the seventh month that the ark's bottom scraped against some portion of terra firma. The date is very specific, but the location where the ark landed is vague. The Bible does not say that the ark landed on Mt. Ararat, but on *hārê 'ărāraṭ,* literally, "the mountains of Ararat." This expression may be under-

2. See *ANET,* p. 44.

stood as a distributive plural,[3] such as we find in 21:7, where "sons" *(bānîm)* refers only to one son, Isaac. Another way to analyze this expression is to say that the plural is used as an indefinite singular, "one [i.e., one of] the mountains of Ararat."[4]

Ararat is to be equated with ancient Urartu, the mountainous region of what is now Armenia (eastern Turkey). It was an area against which Assyrian kings in the 1st millennium B.C. carried out military campaigns (see 2 K. 19:37 par. Isa. 37:38). Attempts to identify which particular mountain the ark rested on are as old as the apocryphal book of Jubilees (5:28; 7:1), which specifies Mt. Lubar (?). The Aramaic and Syriac translations of 8:4 render "mountains of Ararat" with "Ture Kardu," that is, the mountains of Kurdistan (Jebel Judi) southeast of Lake Van.

The sections of the Sumerian Flood story and the Atrahasis Epic that have survived have no reference to where the ship landed. But the Gilgamesh Epic does have Utnaphishtim's boat landing on Mt. Nisir, about 9000 feet in elevation, and considerably to the south and east of Ararat.[5] In comparison to Mt. Nisir's height of 9000 feet Mt. Ararat is some 17,000 feet high.

There is wordplay in this verse. The verb *came to rest,* Heb. *tānaḥ,* is that from which the name Noah (Heb. *nōaḥ*) is derived. Thus one might say that the ark "noah-ed" on one of the mountains of Ararat.

5 Noah and his fellow passengers remain inside the ark for almost two and a half months before they can disembark, or at least before the peaks of surrounding mountains become visible. They are not yet out of danger. In one way Noah's experience at the top of one of the mountains of Ararat is no less frightening and undoing than is that of Moses at the top of Mt. Sinai. Both find themselves at the top of a mountain that is enveloped in either a rainstorm or an electrical storm. For Noah, as the waters go down his hopes go up.

I see no credible way of harmonizing the information of v. 5 with v. 4. V. 4 clearly states that the ark rested on one of the mountains of Ararat in the 17th day of the 7th month. Yet v. 5 states that no mountaintop was spotted until the first day of the 10th month. It sounds specious to suggest that what

3. See GKC, § 124o. Further illustrations of the plural of the noun as distributive, both in prose and poetry, are found in R. Gordis, "Job XL 29—an additional note," *VT* 14 (1964) 492–93.

4. M. Greenberg (*Ezekiel 1–20,* p. 68) cites Ezek. 3:6 as an illustration: "not to [one of] many peoples. . ." versus "not to many peoples" (RSV).

5. For the location of Mt. Nisir see E. A. Speiser, "Kurdistan in the Annals of Ashurnasirpal and Today," *AASOR* 8 (1926/27) 17–18; E. G. Kraeling, "Xisouthros, Deucalion, and the Flood Narrative," *JAOS* 67 (1947) 181.

v. 5 means by "the top of the mountains" is "the top of the [remaining and smaller] mountains."

8. THE EMERGENCE OF DRY LAND (8:6–14)

6 *At the end of forty days Noah opened the hatch of the ark which he had made,*

7 *and he released a raven;*[1] *it went to*[2] *and fro until the waters dried off from the earth.*

8 *Then he released a dove from him to see if the waters had diminished on the earth's surface.*

9 *But the dove did not discover a resting place for the sole of its foot, and it returned to him in the ark, for there was water all over the earth's surface. He stretched out his hand and caught it, and drew it inside the ark with him.*

10 *He waited one more week, and again he released the dove from the ark.*

11 *By*[3] *evening time the dove returned to him, and in its beak was a plucked olive leaf! Noah now knew that the waters had diminished on the earth.*

12 *He waited an additional week and released the dove; it returned no more to him.*

13 *In the six hundredth and first year, in the first month, the first of the month, the waters dried up from the earth. Noah removed the covering of the ark, and saw that indeed the surface of the ground had started to dry.*

14 *In the second month, on the twenty-seventh day of the month, the earth had dried.*

6 One gets a strong impression that Noah does not wish to leave the ark precipitately. He wants to make sure that all is safe before he disembarks. Thus it is not the side door that he opens (6:16), but a *hatch (ḥallôn),* presumably on the ark's roof or side. It is Noah's responsibility to ascertain whether the land is sufficiently dry so that he and the others may leave the

1. Throughout this section the MT has *hāʿōrēḇ* and *hayyônâ,* i.e., "raven" and "dove" are consistently written with the definite article, and yet the indefinite "a" is still warranted. For the replication of Heb. *ha-* by English indefinite "a," see GKC, §§ 126q, r.

2. This use of the infinitive absolute to follow the verb it intensifies *(wayyēṣēʾ yāṣôʾ)* is not frequent in Biblical Hebrew. See GKC, §§ 113r, s; and M. J. Dahood, "Hebrew-Ugaritic Lexicography viii," *Bib* 51 (1970) 394.

3. On the use of *lᵉ* to indicate motion in time and not point in time, i.e., "by" and not "at," cf. T. J. Meek, "Old Testament Notes," *JBL* 67 (1948) 236–38.

ark. But the actual moment of departure awaits God's command (8:15–17). The *forty days* can refer only to the period of time that Noah waited from the time the peaks of the mountains became visible (v. 5) until he sent out the birds. Perhaps Noah thought that such a period would give even more time for more of the submerged earth to reappear.

7–12 In order to determine how suitable the ground was for habitation, Noah sent out first a raven, and then a dove (the latter 3 times, vv. 8, 10, 12). *released.* Every time Noah sends forth one of these two birds the Hebrew uses the Piel of *šālaḥ* (e.g., v. 7, *wayyᵉšallaḥ*). This use contrasts with the Qal of *šālaḥ* used in v. 9 to refer to Noah's "stretching out" his hand to retrieve the dove. Now, at many places in the OT the Qal and Piel of this verb seem to be interchangeable. But sometimes the Qal means to send forth on a mission, with the expectation that those sent will return. Thus Moses (Num. 13:3) and Joshua (Josh. 2:1) "sent" (*šālaḥ,* Qal) the spies who will return with the needed information. The Piel of *šālaḥ* may mean to send away, to banish with no possibility of returning, as in Gen. 3:23: "Yahweh sent him forth [*wayyᵉšallᵉḥēhû*] from the garden of Eden." Applied to 7:7–12 the meaning would be that Noah does not send these birds forth on a trial run. He does not expect them to return to their nest in the ark.

It is interesting to note that Noah sends forth birds in order to determine the conditions on the earth. Up until this point Noah has received all his information from God. God informed him about the corruption in the earth. God told him to build an ark and what to take into that ark. God briefed him about the impending storm.

But God does not tell Noah when the ground is habitable again. Indeed, all revelation from God to Noah is halted once Noah is locked inside the ark—until the announcement in 8:15. He who had received direct revelation from God must now resort to ornithology (or augury) for further data. The Creator speaks to Noah, but so does the creature. Moses receives direct revelations from God, but it is his father-in-law who gives him the information about the best and most efficient way to administer juridical matters (Exod. 18). Joshua receives a direct promise from God that he will be given all the land (Josh. 1), yet he still sends spies to reconnoiter Jericho and then to report back to him (Josh. 2).

Earlier we noted that Noah takes no navigational equipment or sailors aboard as did his counterparts in the mythical flood stories of Mesopotamia. The reason for this omission is deliberate. It allows the biblical record to testify to the effect that if Noah is saved from drowning it will be only because of the grace of God. He has no professional crew with him who, when they put their skills together, will be able to weather this storm.

Still, there is an implicit reference to navigational equipment on the ark—the window (for reading the stars) and the birds (homing pigeons who help find directions). Thus Noah's releasing of the birds should be seen as a reflection of actual navigational practice, rather than as a bit of folkloristic coloring.[4]

It is well known that this part of the biblical Flood story has an interesting parallel in the Babylonian Epic of Gilgamesh. On the seventh day after Utnapishtim's boat landed on Mt. Nisir, he did the following:

> I sent forth and set free a dove.
> The dove went forth, but came back;
> Since no resting-place for it was visible, she turned round.
> Then I sent forth and set free a swallow.
> The swallow went forth, but came back;
> Since no resting-place for it was visible, she turned round.
> Then I sent forth and set free a raven.
> The raven went forth and, seeing that the waters had diminished,
> He eats, circles, caws, and turns not round.[5]

This quote is from the eleventh tablet of the Babylonian version of the epic, of which no copies earlier than 750 B.C. are known. The only other reference to birds is from the Babylonian priest Berossus, who wrote his account of the flood around 300 B.C. None of the earlier editions (e.g., the Sumerian Flood story from ca. 1800 B.C.) mentions birds. So then, "the only surviving testimony to the most telling parallel [between the OT and Mesopotamian Flood myths] happens to be later than the Biblical account."[6]

The scriptural account has Noah send out first a raven and then a dove. The Gilgamesh Epic reverses that order—first the dove and then the raven. The biblical sequence has more of the ring of truth about it. The raven is a carrion eater and did not return because it found food on the mountain peaks. The dove is a valley bird, and it was released in order to determine whether

4. "If the ancients sailed the seven seas before the age of literacy, they must have had a science and technology that gave them their capabilities. And if they lacked modern methods of science and instrumentation, they had other methods that enabled them to score their successes. A cage full of homing pigeons is not a bad method of direction finding. If it sounds quaint, it is only because we have devised methods more to our liking, but not necessarily better in all circumstances even today" (C. H. Gordon, *Before Columbus* [New York: Crown, 1971], p. 77).

5. *ANET,* pp. 94–95.

6. W. G. Lambert, "A New Look at the Babylonian Background of Genesis," *JTS* 16 (1965) 291–92.

the lower-lying areas were habitable. The progression from raven to dove makes more sense than that of dove to raven.

Noah is not heartless. He is concerned about the safety and well-being of others, even a female bird. Thus we read in v. 9 that he *stretched out his hand* to the returning dove and gave it the shelter of the ark. This is the second reference in Genesis to putting forth one's hand to take hold of something. Noah's hand is stretched forth to offer refuge to one of God's creatures. Earlier God had seen the possibility that man would "put forth his hand and take also of the tree of life" (3:22). This is not a giving hand. It is a grasping hand.

13–14 Both of these verses observe that the earth was dry. Is this needless repetition, or evidence of the presence of J and P? Perhaps there is another explanation.

Three comparisons may be made between these two verses. First, each uses a different verb for "to dry up." In v. 13 the verb is *ḥārab̲,* which means "to be free of moisture." In v. 14 it is *yāb̲aš,* which refers here to the complete absence of waters. This verb is related to the noun "dry land" *(yabbāšâ)* used in Gen. 1. Creation, destroyed in the Flood, is now resurfacing. The world of Gen. 1 that had recently been overturned is now righting itself. It is only logical that the action contained in *ḥārab̲* precedes that contained in *yāb̲aš.* To reverse them would be unusual.

Second, both verses begin with different datelines: v. 13—year 601, month one, day one (i.e., New Year's Day); v. 14—year 601, month two, day twenty-seven. If one compares this last date given in the Flood event with the first date given (7:11), an interesting point appears:

> flood begins (7:11): 17th day/2nd month/600th year of Noah
> flood has gone (8:14: 27th day/2nd month/601st year of Noah

The Flood "lasted twelve months and eleven days, the exact period required to equate the year of twelve lunar months, 354 days, with the solar year of 365 days."[7] The Flood lasted one solar year.

The third comparison to note in these two verses is the distinct

7. R. de Vaux, *Ancient Israel,* 1:188–89. This does not mean, for de Vaux, that a truly solar year ever prevailed in Israel. The reference throughout the Flood story to months by ordinal numbers ("first, second," etc.) would argue more for a lunar calendar. The inner coherence of the Flood dates has been established by E. Nielsen, *Oral Tradition,* SBT 1/11 (Chicago: Allenson, 1954), pp. 93ff. N. P. Lemche ("The Chronology in the Story of the Flood," *JSOT* 18 [1980] 52–62) sees only incoherence, and attributes the confusion to the redactor of J and P, with his penchant for advancing the dates of P.

perspective of each. V. 13 records the drying of the ground from Noah's observation—"he looked." V. 14 records the same result, but here it is an objective reporting statement. We have encountered the same dual reporting of the Flood's beginning: objective statement about earth's corruption (6:11), followed by God's personal observation of corruption in the earth (6:12). Whenever God and the narrator report or observe, or whenever Noah and the narrator report or observe, both parties are in agreement.

9. NOAH LEAVES THE ARK (8:15–22)

15 *Then God said to Noah:*

16 *"Go out of the ark, you and your wife and your sons and your sons' wives with you.*

17 *Every living thing that is with you—all flesh, be it bird, cattle, or any creeping thing of the earth—bring out*[1] *with you, and let them swarm on the earth, and breed and increase on the earth."*

18 *So Noah went out, his sons, his wife, and his sons' wives with him.*

19 *Every living thing, every creeping thing, every bird—everything that creeps on the earth—family by family they went out of the ark.*

20 *Then Noah built an altar to Yahweh, and choosing from every clean animal and every clean bird he offered up holocausts on the altar.*

21 *When Yahweh smelled the rest-inducing odor, Yahweh said to himself: "Never again will I devastate the ground because of man, however evil the imagination of man's heart from his youth. Never again will I ever strike down every living thing as I have done.*

22 *As long as earth endures,*
seedtime and harvest,
cold and heat,
summer and winter,
and day and night
shall not cease."

This final section of Gen. 8 finds God speaking twice, once to Noah (vv. 15–17) and once to himself (vv. 21–22). God had last spoken to Noah before Noah entered the ark. Now for the first time, and the only time, Noah hears the divine voice while he is inside the ark. And the directive he hears is to leave the ark.

1. The Qere *hayṣēʾ* alongside Ketib *hôṣēʾ* demonstrates that the root may have originally been *yṣʾ* rather than *wṣʾ*, which is often presumed on the basis of the Hiphil forms of this verb. See R. Gordis, *The Biblical Text in the Making: A Study of the Kethib-Qere,* rev. ed. (New York: Ktav, 1971), pp. 129–31. The Hebrew of the

15–19 Noah already knows that the earth is prepared for reoccupation, for the dove has not returned. Why not just leave the ark? Evidently, when Noah's future is at stake, he subordinates his own experiments, however noble and adroit, to a message from God.

Once again, in vv. 15–19, because Noah rather than Yahweh is the thematic participant, it is *God ('ĕlōhîm)* who speaks to Noah. And God speaks only to Noah, never to his family or to the entourage in the ark. Thus God will release Noah, and Noah will release the family and the animals.

Four times in these verses the verb *yāṣā'* occurs, and each time in a different form: (1) *ṣē',* Qal imperative, v. 16; (2) *hōṣē',* Hiphil imperative, v. 17; (3) *wayyēṣē',* Qal imperfect form with *waw* consecutive, v. 18; (4) *yāṣᵉ'û,* Qal perfect form, v. 19. By highlighting this particular verb, the author emphasizes the departure from the ark. Noah and his companions are not consigned to an ark existence. The ark is only a shelter, not a domicile.

Once again, as in 6:13–22 and 7:1–5, the sequence is a divine speech followed by the observation that Noah did what he was told to do. Quietly he implements the message from God. Noah has yet to speak, to utter a word to anyone. He is a doer more than he is a talker.

20 How now shall Noah orient himself to dry ground? After all, he has been floating on water for three hundred and sixty-five days. The first thing Noah does is to engage in worship: *Noah built an altar to Yahweh.* This is the first reference in the Bible to an altar. We should not conclude that Noah did not previously worship God (obviously, Noah could not have built an altar inside the ark), nor that altars had not been built before this time. The point here is that Noah's first act indicates his faith that God had brought him through the Flood.

It is appropriate that the offerings he presents to Yahweh are *holocausts* or "whole burnt offerings" *('ōlōṯ).* It is probable that this is the oldest and most frequent of all the OT sacrifices. A continual burnt offering *('ōlaṯ tāmîḏ)* was made twice daily, morning and evening (Exod. 29:38–42). Leviticus and Numbers mandate this offering after some kind of crisis, such as after childbirth (Lev. 12:6–8), after bodily discharges (15:14–15, 29–30), and after defilement during a Nazirite vow (Num. 6:10–11). The priestly legislation attaches an expiatory function to it (Lev. 1:4; 9:7; 14:20; cf. 1 Sam. 13:12; Job 1:5; 42:8). But whenever the whole burnt offering is presented,

---

Qere is not, in any case, a modification away from an abnormal form toward a more standard one. Rather, it reflects the maintenance of an unusual form alongside a more typical form. See J. Barr, "A New Look at *Kethibh-Qere,*" *OTS* 21 (1981) 34. See Ps. 5:9 (Eng. 8) for Ketib *hôšer* and Qere *hayšar.*

the motive is joyful, indicated by the fact that this holocaust is called a freewill offering (Lev. 22:17–25; Num. 15:1–11). It is anything but dour. In addition to expiation, this sacrifice serves at least two other functions. It is connected both with petition (1 Sam. 13:12) and with thanksgiving (Lev. 22:17–25; Num. 15:1–11). As such the whole burnt offering is "all-encompassing; it answers to all the emotional needs of the worshiper."[2]

Since *ʿōlâ,* the Hebrew word for "(whole) burnt offering," is related to *ʿālâ,* a verb meaning "to ascend," it is natural to perceive the smoke of Noah's offering ascending heavenward. Movement up and down has already been made in the Deluge story—rising sin, falling divine forbearance; rising waters, falling waters; rising smoke.

21 *Yahweh smelled the rest-inducing odor.* This aroma reaches God's nostrils. The OT does refer a few times to God's olfactory sense (Lev. 26:31; 1 Sam. 26:19; Amos 5:21; perhaps Ezek. 20:41); such references are to be understood as anthropomorphisms, akin to references to God seeing, hearing, stretching out his hand, etc. Here he smells a *rēaḥ hannîḥōaḥ*. This expression is very close to the "pleasing aroma" phrase *(rēaḥ nîḥōaḥ)* that occurs so often in connection with sacrifices in Leviticus (17 times) and Numbers (18 times). The second word—*nîḥōaḥ,* a Polel infinitive of the verb *nûaḥ*—provides another acoustical connection with Noah (Heb. *nōaḥ*), the rest-giving one, hence our translation, *rest-inducing odor.*

P. A. H. de Boer has suggested that Heb. *rēaḥ* refers not to an odor inhaled but an odor given off, and the related verb *rîaḥ* or *rûaḥ* may (like English "smell") mean not perceive an odor but give off an odor. So, if God says "I will not smell your solemn assemblies" (Amos 5:21; lit., "I will not smell in," *yrḥ b*), what he means is that he will withhold his sweet savor. If we apply this interpretation to Gen. 8:21, the verse would then read, "And Yahweh spread a smell of peace (or security)."[3] This argument would be more convincing if here *yāraḥ* was followed by the preposition *bᵉ,* as in Amos 5:21, instead of the sign of the direct object *(ʾeṯ).*

This verse does not mention the motif of God's craving for food. The lack of this theme is striking when one compares the biblical story with the Gilgamesh Epic and the Atrahasis Epic. In both the Mesopotamian stories the survivor also offers a food sacrifice to the gods, who swarm around it

2. J. Milgrom, "Sacrifice and Offering, OT," *IDBS,* p. 769.

3. P. A. H. de Boer, "*wmrḥwq yryḥ mlḥmh*—Job 39:25," in *Words and Meanings: Essays Presented to David Winton Thomas,* ed. P. R. Ackroyd and B. Lindars (Cambridge: Cambridge University, 1968), pp. 29–38, esp. pp. 33ff.; idem, "An Aspect of Sacrifice," in *Studies in the Religion of Ancient Israel,* VTSup 23 (Leiden: Brill, 1972), pp. 27–47, esp. pp. 46–47.

"like flies," for they have gone without food for seven days and seven nights, the Flood's duration.

Noah's sacrifice moves Yahweh to make a dramatic announcement, albeit *to himself* (*'el-libbô,* lit., "to his heart"). This soliloquy should not be interpreted as a non sequitur; quite the opposite. The first and second halves of this verse have a cause-and-effect relationship. Observing Noah's actions and smelling the aroma of his offering, Yahweh binds himself to a negative course of action for the future. But this pronouncement is not made to Noah. Instead, we find another instance of divine self-deliberation. Had Noah been the recipient of this information, the story would have opened the door to the possibility that what is involved here is not genuine propitiation but magic, that is, the deity can be manipulated by human actions.

The latter half of the verse has generated much controversy. If we translate the conjunction *kî* as "for, because," instead of "however, even though," then we are faced with a conundrum. God will never again destroy the earth because of man, because from the start man's heart is evil. But according to 6:5, this is precisely the reason God sends the Flood in the first place. Here is the paradox: God inundates the earth because of man's sinfulness, and subsequently promises never again to destroy the earth because of man's sinfulness.

Some commentators take this position. In more blunt terms, their interpretation is that God is frustrated because the Flood has not really worked. It has destroyed the human race, but it has not changed human nature. Post-Flood man is also a reprobate. In retrospect God sees that he has acted unwisely and too simplistically. But happily he admits his mistake and is willing to learn from it.[4]

It is possible to retain the causal nuance of *kî* and observe here not a contradiction but a vivid demonstration of God's grace. In spite of a justifiable motivation for continued judgment, God chooses not to exercise that option. No longer will man be treated as under a curse. The power of the divine curse of 3:17 is significantly cancelled.[5] Yet there is no evidence that

4. See D. L. Petersen, "The Yahwist on the Flood," *VT* 26 (1976) 438–46. "The Yahwist . . . thought it [the Flood story] to be a divinely ineffectual ploy. The flood had solved nothing" (p. 446). This explains for Petersen why the P and J Flood stories were spliced, unlike the P and J Creation stories, which were juxtaposed. The J Flood story, by itself, is lifeless and radical in its criticism of God. P tries to camouflage some of J's blatant blasphemies.

5. The seminal essay here is R. Rendtorff, "Genesis 8,21 und die Urgeschichte des Jahwisten," *KD* 7 (1961) 69–78. He translates 8:21 as "I will no longer designate the earth as accursed [as I have done before] on account of mankind because

phenomena associated with the curse in 3:17, such as pain in childbearing, or hard work on unyielding soil, come to an abrupt end in post-Flood days.

The weakest point in this approach is that it demands that *l*^{e}*qallēl* be translated not as "to curse" but "to view as accursed, to designate as accursed." H. C. Brichto is of the opinion that *qālal* in the Piel hardly ever means "to imprecate." Specifically, here the verb refers to a known nonoral action, and it means "to abuse, to treat harshly."[6] It would make no sense to have God saying, "I will no longer designate the earth as abused."

Brichto's observations about *qālal* can be coupled with the fact that *kî* often has concessive force in Biblical Hebrew: "although, even though." The rule we follow is that *kî* be given its more usual causal force unless greater sense can be extracted by taking the conjunction as a concessive or an emphatic, as is the case here.[7] Thus this verse functions as a ringing testimony to the mercy of God, who henceforth will not give man his just deserts. The punishable will not be punished.

22 On the contrary, there will be a return to regularity and predictability in the world of nature.[8] Seedtime/harvest, cold/heat, summer/winter, and day/night are the four couplets testifying to the resurrection of predictability in the world. However irregular the human heart may be (8:21b), there will be a regularity in God's world and its cycles.

It is interesting that the Bible here introduces the promise of seasonal

---

the imagination of man's heart is evil from his youth, and I will never again destroy every living thing as I have done" (p. 69). See also W. M. Clark, "The Flood and the Structure of the Pre-patriarchal History," *ZAW* 83 (1971) 206–8, for an endorsement of Rendtorff's position. In objecting to Rendtorff, Petersen (*VT* 26 [1976] 441–44) seems to make too much of the different placement of *ʿôḏ* (after or before the infinitive). The difference is not syntactical but literary. *ʿôḏ* forms a chiasm with the infinitives. The parallelism of *l*^{e}*qallēl* and *l*^{e}*hakkôṯ* is reproduced in Exod. 21:15, 17; Lev. 24:15, 17; Neh. 13:25.

6. See H. C. Brichto, *The Problem of "Curse" in the Hebrew Bible,* pp. 119–20.

7. Cf. NIV; W. Woller, "Zur Übersetzung von *kî* in Gen. 8,21 and 9,6," *ZAW* 99 (1982) 637–38. T. C. Vriezen labels the *kî* in Gen. 8:21 an emphatic concessive and translates *wie sehr auch,* "however much, as much as" ("Einige Notizen zur Übersetzung des Bindeswort *kî,*" in *Von Ugarit nach Qumram,* BZAW 77, Fest. Otto Eissfeldt, ed. J. Hempel and L. Rost [Berlin: Töpelmann, 1958], pp. 266ff.). A. Schoors ("The Particle *kî,*" *OTS* 21 [1981] 273) remains unconvinced about Vriezen's handling of Gen. 8:21 and is content to retain a causal nuance.

8. See W. Brueggemann, "Kingship and Chaos (A Study in Tenth Century Theology)," *CBQ* 33 (1971) 320. Brueggemann's observations about the emergence in this verse of *shalom* out of chaos are on target, but his connection of this verse with the memory of the Absalom rebellion (p. 331) is strained.

cycles after the Flood. But note how it denies the dynamics of the fertility cult by stressing that man's actions for good or evil have no impact on the patterns of the season.[9] The biblical mind has no room for the concept of sympathetic magic wherein the desired result is first mimed. Regularity in nature is a given, a promise of God. Thus Yahweh has spoken negatively (v. 21) and positively (v. 22). Both what he will not do and what he will do stem from unmerited grace.

10. GOD'S COVENANT WITH NOAH (9:1–17)

1 *God blessed Noah and his sons, saying to them: "Be abundantly fruitful*[1] *and fill the earth.*

2 *Dread fear of you shall come upon every living thing on the earth, upon all the birds of the air, on everything that creeps on the ground, on all the fish of the sea; into your power they have been given.*

3 *Every creeping thing that is alive shall be yours to eat, as I did for you with all the plants.*

4 *Surely flesh together with*[2] *its lifeblood you shall not eat.*

5 *Surely of your lifeblood I will demand an account, from every living thing I will demand it, and from man in relation to his fellow man I will demand an account of a man's life.*

6 *He who sheds a man's blood*
by man shall his blood be shed,[3]
for in the image of God
he made man.

7 *As for you, be abundantly fruitful,*
teem on the earth and multiply[4] *on it."*

8 *God said to Noah, and to his sons with him:*

9. See E. Fisher, "Gilgamesh and Genesis: The Flood Story in Context," *CBQ* 32 (1970) 401.

1. I take *p^{e}rû ûr^{e}ḇû* as hendiadys, as also with *ûmôra'^{a}ḵem w^{e}ḥitt^{e}ḵem* in v. 2.

2. The *b^e* here is a *beth comitatus.* See GKC, § 119n.

3. The clear chiasmus in this phrase is noted by A. R. Ceresko, "The Chiastic Word Pattern in Hebrew," *CBQ* 38 (1976) 305.

4. On the basis of LXX most commentators emend MT *ûr^{e}ḇû* to *ûr^{e}ḏû,* "and subdue (it)." However, the discovery of the word sequence ABCB as a feature of Hebrew poetic diction argues for the retention of MT, and provides us with this sequence of verbs: *p^{e}rû* (A) . . . *r^{e}ḇû* (B) . . . *širṣû* (C) . . . *r^{e}ḇû* (B). See B. Porten and V. Rappaport, "Poetic Structure in Genesis IX 7," *VT* 21 (1971) 363–69; J. S. Kselman, "The Recovery of Poetic Fragments from the Pentateuchal Priestly Source," *JBL* 97 (1978) 167.

9 *"For my part, I am about to establish my covenant with you, and with your descendants after you,*
10 *and with every living creature that was with you: birds, cattle, and every living thing of the earth with you, all that went out of the ark—indeed, every living thing on earth.*
11 *I will establish my covenant with you, that never*[5] *again shall all flesh be cut off by the waters of a flood; there shall not be another flood to annihilate the earth."*
12 *God said, "This is the sign of the covenant which I am instituting between me and you, and every living being with you, for all succeeding ages.*
13 *My bow I have placed in the cloud, and it shall function as a sign of the covenant between me and the earth.*
14 *When I bring a cloud over the earth, and the bow appears in the cloud,*
15 *I will remember my covenant which is between me and you and every living being, so that waters shall not again become a flood to annihilate all flesh.*
16 *When the bow appears in the cloud I will look at it in order to remember the everlasting covenant between God and every living being—every mortal on the earth."*
17 *God said to Noah, "This is the sign of the covenant I have established between me and every mortal on the earth."*

This last section of the Flood story comprises four speeches by God, three of which are addressed to Noah and his sons (vv. 1–7, 8–11, 12–16)—never is Noah's wife or his daughters-in-law included—and one of which is addressed only to Noah (v. 17). In our judgment it is a misreading of vv. 1–17 to interpret it as a second conclusion to the Flood story (P), parallel to that of 8:20–22 (J). We would suggest that 8:20–22 is the announcement of God's post-Deluge covenant in incipient form. Then 9:1–17 would be seen as an amplification and specification of this anticipatory note.[6]

The first speech in this section is an *inclusio.* It begins and ends with

5. In 8:21 the adverb *ʿôḏ* was arranged chiastically with two infinitives. Here it appears chiastically with two subjects of sentences: *kol-bāśār ʿôḏ* and *ʿôḏ mabbûl,* "never again shall all flesh . . . another flood."

6. R. Longacre ("The Discourse Structure of the Flood Narrative," in SBLASP, 1976, pp. 255–58) provides cogent explanations for the use of Yahweh in 8:20–22 and *ʾĕlōhîm* in 9:1–17. In 8:20–22 deity is the thematic participant, and as such he is referred to as Yahweh. In 9:1–7 the addressees (in the 2nd person pl.) are thematic, while God is a secondary thematic participant. In 9:8–11 the covenant itself is thematic and the partners to the covenant, God and man, are more incidental. In 9:12–17 it is the covenant sign that is thematic.

essentially the same imperatives: be fruitful, multiply, fill, teem (vv. 1, 7). The use of this kind of language and emphasis serves at least two purposes. First, such an exhortation transports the reader back to the world of Gen. 1, much as the mention of dry land in 8:13–14 recalled the Creation story of Scripture's first chapter. Noah is a second Adam. What God told Adam he now tells Noah.

A second point is underscored by the biblical emphasis on the command to repopulate the earth after the Flood. In the Gilgamesh Epic, Enlil is appeased quite easily and briefly after the Flood is over and gone. Utnapishtim and his wife are made immortal, and they are to dwell in a faraway place, at the mouth of the rivers, segregated from the gods.

But in the Atrahasis Epic, Enlil is appeased only by a bargain involving Nintu, the Lady of Birth, and Enki. This is the substance of that arrangement:

> In addition let there be a third category among the peoples,
> (Let there be) among the peoples women who bear and women
> who do not bear.
> Let there be among the peoples the *Pašittu*-demon
> To snatch the baby from the lap of her who bore it.
> Establish *Ugbabtu*-women, *Entu*-women, and *Igiṣitu*-women,
> And let them be taboo and so stop childbirth.[7]

Thus the Atrahasis Epic concludes on a note exactly the opposite of the biblical story. It says that overpopulation is the earth's primary problem, hence the need for population control, which can be accomplished either by nature or by the gods. "Viewed in this light, Gen. 9:1ff looks like a conscious rejection of the Atrahasis Epic."[8]

2–3 This chapter is establishing elements of both continuity and discontinuity with the emphases of Gen. 1. The continuity between the two has been stressed in 9:1. These next two verses, however, demonstrate that Gen. 9 is not simply a replay of Gen. 1. The opening chapter of Genesis was quite explicit that in the beginning man and the animals were vegetarian. Man's authority over the animals did not include exploitation or using those animals for food. Here, the exercise of man's authority provides terrifying consequences for the animal world. Not all the pre-Flood relationships will

7. Translation from Lambert and Millard, *Atra-ḫasīs,* p. 103.

8. W. L. Moran, "Atrahasis: The Babylonian Story of the Flood," *Bib* 52 (1971) 61; A. D. Kilmer, "The Mesopotamian Concept of Overpopulation and Its Solution as Reflected in the Mythology," *Or* 41 (1972) 160–77, esp. pp. 171–73 and 174–75, where she connects the Atrahasis Epic with Noah.

be restored. At least a few situations will be different, and man's relationship to the animal world is one of them. Human exploitation of animal life is here set within the context of a post-Flood, deteriorated situation. It is radically different from the ideal of Gen. 1.

4 The pattern in this verse and the preceding one is the same as that of 2:16–17: a generous permission ("every tree of the garden," "every creeping thing") followed by a single prohibition ("of the tree of the knowledge of good and evil you shall not eat," "flesh together with its lifeblood you shall not eat"). This verse is the first of many in the Bible that prohibit the consumption of blood (see Lev. 3:17; 7:26–27; 17:10–14;[9] Deut. 12:15–16, 20–24; Acts 15:29). This law has no parallel in the ancient Near East, though this prohibition and that concerning murder are the only specific OT prohibitions addressed to humanity rather than to Israel alone. Eating blood and taking life are Noachian commandments, not Sinaitic ones. Here, and elsewhere in the OT, blood is equated with life, and that is why its consumption or shedding is forbidden. The fact that Israel's neighbors possessed no parallel law indicates that the prohibition "cannot be a vestige of primitive taboo, but the result of a deliberate, reasoned enactment."[10]

The Hebrew language has two ways of stating a prohibition: *lōʾ* with the indicative and *ʾal* with the jussive. The first is much stronger than the second. It is used to express a categorical prohibition, one that is permanently binding.[11] It is this form that is used here, and, for example, in the Decalogue.

5 This verse deals with the second post-Flood prohibition—the taking of another's life. This includes people killing people and animals killing people. Perhaps we are surprised to read in this verse that even animals are accountable for their crimes![12] We will see shortly that the animals are

9. It is not accidental that every ban on eating blood in Leviticus appears in a section where the peace offering is under discussion. This is the one sacrifice where the offerer himself is allowed to eat part of the animal that is presented, and thus the rationale for the prohibition at this particular point.

10. J. Milgrom, "Blood," *EncJud,* 4:1115.

11. See J. Bright, "The Apodictic Prohibition: Some Observations," *JBL* 92 (1973) 185–204.

12. See Exod. 21:28, 32, and S. Paul, *Studies in the Book of the Covenant in the Light of Cuneiform and Biblical Law,* VTSup 18 (Leiden: Brill, 1970), p. 79. On p. 79 n. 5 Paul refers to an unpublished study by J. J. Finkelstein to the effect that execution by stoning (as in Exod. 21:28 for the goring ox) is often a punishment for the offense of insurrection, but not for homicide. The ox's goring a human being to death is an insurrection against the established order since man was created to lord it over animals, not vice versa.

included in the covenant God makes with Noah (v. 9). Punishment for spilling the lifeblood of another is exacted by God.

6 The theme of the taking of human life continues in this verse, with some special emphases. Murder is placed in the orbit of sacral law. To kill another human being is to destroy one who is a bearer of the divine image.[13] Thus man's divine creation should be a deterrent to criminal behavior. There is no evidence here that sin has effaced the divine image. It is still resident in post-Flood, post-paradise man.

The controversy in the verse is the identification of who is to carry out the sanctions for murder—God or another human being. On the one hand, most of the modern versions read, "by man [*bā'ādām*] shall his blood be shed."[14] As such, this verse has become the scriptural locus classicus for capital punishment. It is the *lex talionis* in operation. The penalty must be commensurate with the crime. A life taken demands the taking of another life.

On the other hand, some suggest that *bā'ādām* does not mean "by man" but "(in exchange) for that man."[15] In other words, this verse does not at all delegate authority to man to institute capital punishment. The implication of "for that man his blood shall be shed" is that God will administer the punishment. The weakness in this interpretation is that it ascribes to the preposition *b*e an unusual meaning when one of the standard uses of *b*e makes sense in the verse. Also, if v. 6 is ascribing responsibility to God for meting out punishment, then the verse is essentially a tautology of v. 5. We prefer to see vv. 5 and 6 together, with both prohibiting the taking of human life. The penalty for shedding blood may be exacted either by God (v. 5) or by man (v. 6).

13. V. 6a refers to "man" twice. The first "man" is the murdered victim. The second "man" is the executioner of the criminal. V. 6b has a third reference to "man," presumably to the victim, but it could equally refer to the executioner. See C. C. Carmichael, "A Time for War and a Time for Peace," *JSS* 25 (1974) 63. Does "image of God" function as a deterrent to murder, or does it legitimate the authority of the executioner to deal out justice?

14. Many scholars support the agential or instrumental use of *b*e in 9:6. See M. Greenberg, "The Biblical Conception of Asylum," *JBL* 78 (1959) 128; H. McKeating, "The Development of the Law on Homicide in Ancient Israel," *VT* 25 (1975) 65. McKeating is puzzled as to why the violation of a sacral law is left to man.

15. NEB, "for that man his blood shall be shed." Cf. B. S. Jackson, "Reflections on Biblical Criminal Law," *JJS* 24 (1973) 24–25. This rendering is buttressed by LXX *antí toú haímatos autoú*. See also D. Daube, *Studies in Biblical Law* (Cambridge: Cambridge University, 1974), pp. 129–30, 149 n. 17. A. Phillips ("Another Look at Murder," *JJS* 28 [1977] 122) refuses to side with either explanation. He maintains that the only purpose of Gen. 9:6 is to show that a murderer must die, and that for murder excommunication may not serve as a substitute for execution.

7 By repeating two of the imperatives of v. 1, v. 7 brings this unit to completion. The verse contrasts vividly with v. 6. Noah and his sons are to be life producers, not life takers.

8–9 In vv. 1–7 God had spoken to Noah about Noah and his offspring, their privileges and prohibitions. Now God talks about himself to Noah and his sons. Exhortation is replaced by testimony. The positive-negative emphases of the first paragraph continue into this section, though the subject is different. What man must not do parallels what God will do (establish a covenant) and will not do (never again send a universal flood). Here are the boundaries within which both mankind and deity will operate.

God's resolve is to *establish* a covenant with Noah. The word *establish* (here, and in a different form in vv. 11, 17) translates the Hiphil of *qûm* and means literally "to make stand, to erect." God "erects" a covenant with Noah. Thus the verb may indicate that God here institutes a new relationship. However, a number of times in the OT the Hiphil of *qûm* refers not to a new situation, but to the implementation of a previous word, or promise, or action. In these instances the verb does not mean "to institute" but "to fulfil, carry out, keep" (Num. 23:19; Deut. 8:18; 9:5; 1 Sam. 1:23; 3:12; 1 K. 2:4; Jer. 29:10; 33:14; 34:18). Perhaps then 9:8ff. is to be seen as the fulfillment of the promise first made to Noah in 6:18.

10 The animals that had been housed in the ark are also recipients of this unilateral covenant. God not only holds animals responsible for crimes of brutality, but also enters into promissory arrangements with them. Animals have an honorable role in the biblical economy. They are part of the eschatological period (Isa. 9:5–8 [Eng. 6–9]), and are even capable of repentance (Jon. 3:7–8). In the tenth plague visited on the Egyptian gods, judgment is directed against firstborn sons and the firstborn of cattle (Exod. 11:5). That the covenant is extended to animals is certain proof that the validity of this covenant is not dependent upon acceptance by the recipient of the covenant promise. Animals do not accept a covenant.

11 The thrust of this covenant is that the Flood is unique. The possibility of future judgment is not eliminated, but that judgment will not be manifested as a flood. As if to reinforce the one-time sending of the Flood, God twice in this verse vetoes the chance of a second flood: *lōʾ . . . ʿôḏ mimmê hammabbûl weloʾ . . . ʿôḏ mabbûl.*

12–13 God's promise about no more floods would have been sufficient for Noah and his posterity. But to that promise he appends a covenant, and to that covenant he attaches a sign—a bow in the sky. Two other passages in the Torah refer to something as a *sign of the covenant:* in Gen. 17:11 it is circumcision, and in Exod. 31:16–17 it is the Sabbath. The selection of these three under the rubric "sign" can hardly be fortuitous. "The Sabbath, the rainbow, and circumcision are, in fact, the three great covenants established by God at the three critical stages of the history of mankind: the creation . . . the reestablishment of mankind after the flood . . . and the birth of the Hebrew nation."[16]

The Hebrew language uses *qešeṯ* for both the rainbow and the bow as a weapon. A common motif in ancient Near Eastern iconography is that of a bow-wielding deity. It is a symbol of his prowess. With this lethal weapon he eliminates his foes. The OT itself describes Yahweh as a warrior (Exod. 15:3) who vanquishes his opponents with a bow and a quiver full of arrows (Hab. 3:9). So too do God's representatives fight off their assailants with the bow (Gen. 49:23–24).

But here, in what is nothing less than a radical reinterpretation of divine power, the bow ceases to function as a symbol of combat and is now a symbol of peace and well-being. Its placement in the clouds points to the cessation of God's hostilities against mankind.[17]

Some commentators have suggested that the *bow* retains here its symbolic significance as a weapon of conquest. One has to assume, if this is the case, either that this chapter has vestiges of an old myth in which Yahweh has vanquished his old nemesis Yamm (the Ugaritic sea-god, here called "flood," Heb. *mabbûl*) with the bow, or that this chapter pictures the sea as an independent power which is temporarily let loose by God but, having fulfilled its purpose, is immobilized and forced to reassume its position of subjugation to Yahweh. It is now prostrate beneath his bow.[18] It seems, however, that to equate the promise of nonreturning floodwaters with the concept of a subordinate, lifeless sea is reading quite a bit into the narrative. Nor is it persuasive to take the "I will look at it" of v. 16 and modify it to "he [i.e., the Flood] will look at it," as this theory would suggest.

Finally, we may observe that evidence from ancient Near Eastern literature supports the identification of the bow and arrows as masculine

16. M. Weinfeld, *"b^{e}rîth," TDOT,* 2:264.

17. See G. Mendenhall, *Tenth Generation,* p. 57 n. 8; M. Weinfeld, *Deuteronomy and the Deuteronomic School* (Oxford: Oxford University, 1972), pp. 205–6.

18. The first of these explanations is advanced by P. A. H. de Boer, "Quelques remarques sur l'Arc dans la Nuée (Genèse 9,8–17)," in *Questions disputées d'Ancien Testament,* Bibliotheca Ephemeridum Theologicarum Lovaniensium 33, ed. C. Brekelmans (Louvain: Université de Louvain, 1974), pp. 105–14. The second explanation is forwarded by C. J. L. Kloos, "The Flood on Speaking Terms with God," *ZAW* 94 (1982) 639–42.

symbols and the quiver as a feminine symbol.[19] At best the OT has a few possibilities for this nuance, Job 29:19–20 and Gen. 49:24 being the most likely, but the interpretations of these verses are far from clear. The most transparent use is in the apocryphal Sirach (26:12), where arrow and quiver represent the phallus and vulva. Applied to Gen. 9:6, the bow would be a sign of divine glory and potency.[20] God's flood is gone but his majesty and power have not evaporated.

The reference to *earth* near the end of the verse should be understood as metonymy for all creatures of the earth—man and all animals. *between me and the earth* parallels "Between me and you, and every living being with you" of vv. 12, 15, and "between God and every living being" of v. 16, and "between me and every mortal on the earth" of v. 17. God always refers to himself first and then to the recipients of the promised covenant. And he refers to himself normally in the first person (vv. 12, 13, 15, 17), and once in the third person (v. 16).

14 There can be no bow unless there is a storm. Not only does God place the bow in the sky, but he brings the cloud out of which the rainbow emerges. We need to ask whether the cloud that precedes the bow is simply descriptive of overcast skies on a stormy day, or whether it points to a theophany in the form of a storm cloud, such as one finds in Exod. 19.[21] The clouds which envelop the presence of the Aweful One release the beauty of the curved bow. Whenever the bow appears, it serves as a reminder that despite the fact that the world deserves judgment, God will show restraint and mercy.

15–16 It is surprising, perhaps, to read that the sign is for God's benefit, not for man's. When he sees it, he will remember the promise he made to Noah. Does God need to remind himself in this way? Is he capable of a lapse of memory? Commentators who accept the JEDP theory of the Pentateuch have frequently segmented P's account of creation and the Flood from J's by appealing to J's more crass anthropomorphisms from which P is supposed to be relatively free. But what are we to make of this most conspicuous anthropomorphism right in the middle of a pericope that all source critics attribute to P?

19. See H. A. Hoffner, Jr., "Symbols for Masculinity and Femininity: Their Use in Ancient Near Eastern Sympathetic Magic Rituals," *JBL* 85 (1966) 326–34; D. R. Hillers, "The Bow of Aqhat: The Meaning of a Mythological Theme," in *Orient and Occident: Essays Presented to Cyrus H. Gordon on the Occasion of His Sixty-fifth Birthday,* ed. H. A. Hoffner, Jr., AOAT 22 (Kevelaer: Butzon und Bercker; Neukirchen-Vluyn: Neukirchener, 1973), pp. 71–80.

20. See M. H. Pope, "Rainbow," *IDBS,* pp. 725–26.

21. See G. Mendenhall, *Tenth Generation,* p. 57 n. 58.

The language here appears again in connection with the Passover observance in Egypt. The people are told to splash blood over the sides and tops of the door frames. Although the blood is called a sign for the people (Exod. 12:13), it is splashed on the door frames so that God may also "see" it, and when he sees it he will pass over the house. God is certainly in no need of external evidence about the identity of the occupants of each house. In fact, the Israelites are living by themselves in Goshen. Who else could be there? Still, the blood, like the bow in Gen. 9, is a sign which God observes, and upon seeing it he is moved to a certain course of action.

The point is made, as unequivocally as possible, that God's promises are entirely believable. His words are totally trustworthy. He backs up his word with an act to eliminate even the possibility of forgetfulness. One need not worry that God is capable of stooping to prevarication. He stands by his word.

17 In vv. 8–17 God makes three speeches. The content of the first (vv. 8–11) is the announcement of the covenant. The second speech (vv. 12–16) focuses on the sign of the covenant. The last, and briefest, speech (v. 17) recapitulates the second speech. The concluding emphasis is not on the covenant but on the sign of the covenant. This emphasis is caught in the rhyming of the first two words of the speech, *zō'ṯ 'ôṯ, This is the sign.*

Three times in vv. 8–17 forms of the verb *qûm* are used in connection with the covenant or the sign of the covenant. The progression is interesting: participial form (v. 9); *waw* plus perfect verb (v. 11); perfect verb (v. 17). The development is from what God is on the verge of doing (v. 9), to what he will do (v. 11), to what he has done (v. 17).

In conclusion, we note again the two subunits within vv. 1–17: what man must and must not do (vv. 1–7); what God will do (vv. 8–17). Had this sequence been reversed and vv. 1–7 followed vv. 8–17, the obligations placed on man could only have been read as covenantal stipulations. Thus the Noachian covenant's main characteristic would have been bilaterality. This is precisely the sequence in, for example, Exod. 19 (what God has done) and Exod. 20ff. (what the people must do). The present order preserves the emphasis on the unilaterality of the post-Flood situation. No "you shall" follows "I will."

11. NOAH'S NAKEDNESS (9:18–29)

18 *Noah's sons who went out of the ark were Shem, Ham, and Japheth. Ham was the father of Canaan.*

19 *These three were the sons of Noah and from these the whole earth branched out.*

20 *Now Noah, the farmer, was the first*[1] *to plant a vineyard,*

21 *and drinking the wine, he became drunk, and exposed himself in the middle of his tent.*

22 *Ham, the father of Canaan, saw the nakedness of his father, and told his brothers outside.*

23 *Shem and Japheth, however, took*[2] *the garment and placed it on the shoulders of the two of them, and they went backward and covered the nakedness of their father, but their faces were turned, so that their father's nakedness they did not see.*

24 *After Noah had slept off the effects of the wine he learned what his youngest son had done to him.*

25 *He said, "Cursed be Canaan! An abject servant may he be to his brothers!"*

26 *He said, "Blessed be Yahweh, Shem's God; Canaan shall be his servant.*

27 *May God enlarge Japheth, and let him occupy Shem's tents. Let Canaan be his servant."*

28 *Noah lived after the flood three hundred and fifty years.*

29 *All the days of Noah were nine hundred and fifty years, then he died.*

18–19 The Flood story is bracketed by references to Noah and his three sons (6:9–10; 9:18–19).[3] Two additional pieces of information are given in the second reference. The first is a reference to a post-Flood third generation. *Ham was the father of Canaan.* This reference anticipates 10:6, which tells that Canaan was the youngest and fourth son of Ham: Cush, Egypt, Put, Canaan. Although no specific references have been made to it, the notation here about Canaan is an evidence that the divine imperative of 9:1 is already at work: "Be abundantly fruitful and fill the earth," as is the promise of the covenant with Noah, his sons, and their descendants. Here is one of those descendants.

The second novel piece of information is that Noah's three sons

1. RSV "Noah was the first tiller of the soil" is misleading, for Cain (4:2) was the first tiller of the soil. The Hiphil of *ḥālal* often denotes the first occurrence, doing something for the first time. Thus it is not accurate to translate, "Noah began to plant a vineyard." Cf. H. C. Brichto, *Problem of "Curse" in the Hebrew Bible,* p. 110 n. 68; P. P. Saydon, "The inceptive imperfect in Hebrew and the verb 'to begin,'" *Bib* 35 (1954) 47.

2. For the use of a sing. verb before a pl. subject cf. Gen. 11:29 and 21:32; also GKC, § 146f.

3. See G. J. Wenham, "The Coherence of the Flood Narrative," *VT* 28 (1978) 336–48, esp. the palistrophe that appears on p. 338.

represent the progenitors of the human race. The emphasis of common ancestry was first sounded in Gen. 1 and 2. That theme is reechoed here. Yet the narration about the peopling of the earth is postponed until after the interlude about Noah, his drunkenness, and his sons. Ch. 10 could just as easily have followed 9:19. The diffusion and multiplication of the "Canaanites" (10:15–20) or of the larger "Hamites" (10:6–20) take place in spite of Ham's dubious behavior and the curse that is placed on Canaan.

20–21 That Noah even was able to plant a vineyard that produced lush growth is testimony to the lifting of the curse on the ground (8:21). Noah is not pictured as eking out a miserable, hand-to-mouth existence as he works among thorns and thistles. Of course, in order for the vineyard to grow, there had to be rain. But the rain has been a life-producing one, not like the earlier life-taking one.

Perhaps in the process of his viticulture, Noah imbibes too much and becomes intoxicated. The vintner becomes the inebriated. Commentators are prone to point out here an alleged contradiction, a different Noah in 9:18–29 from the Noah of 6:5–9:17. The obedient, righteous Noah now finds himself drunk and naked. But is this really a different Noah?

Genesis does not stop to moralize on Noah's behavior. It is neither condemned nor approved. To be sure, wine was not forbidden in Israel. It was used to cheer the heart (Judg. 9:13; Ps. 104:15), and as a sedative (Prov. 31:6). The Nazirite vow of abstention from wine would be meaningless if Israel as a nation already abstained. Nevertheless, the Bible does not hesitate to condemn winebibbing (Prov. 23:29–35), and even equates it with harlotry (Hos. 4:10–11, 18), which numbs the longing for God. The two incidents in Genesis describing drunkenness (here and 19:31ff.) become the occasion for sins of debauchery.

We know from the literature of Ugarit that the Ugaritians pictured their supreme god El as one who was not only loving, all powerful, and wise, but also one who was not infrequently drunk. For example, one text describes a divine banquet:

> El sits in his *mrzḥ*-shrine
> [El] drinks [wi]ne to satiety
>   Liquor, to drunkenness.
> El goes to his house
>   Proceeds to his court
> Ṭkmn and Šnm carry him.[4]

4. Translation of C. H. Gordon, "El, Father of Šnm," *JNES* 35 (1976) 261. Gordon also points out that according to the Aqhat legend a model son is expected, among other forms of service, to carry his father when the latter is too drunk to walk

The composers of this piece saw no inherent problems with the idea that their supreme god could, on occasion, get so completely drunk that he needed two junior gods to walk him back to his throne room. Given the emphasis on fertility in this kind of religion, one can only surmise that both cultic prostitution and cultic intoxication played a central role, and both of these elements the OT abhors and prohibits.

We are not told why Noah was naked at this time. The stem of *gālâ* used here is the Hithpael, which is found again only in Prov. 18:2 (the fool "uncovers his heart," i.e., displays his folly).[5] Has Noah shed his clothes to prepare for coitus with his wife? Is wine an aphrodisiac? Was wine thought not only to stimulate sexual desire but also to increase one's power of fertility?[6] For the connection of drunkenness and nakedness elsewhere in the Bible, see Hab. 2:16 and especially Lam. 4:21b. Maybe the biblical writer is simply saying that too much wine reduces a normally rational being to a buffoon.

22 Ham was in the wrong place at the wrong time. His sin was apparently that he *saw the nakedness of his father.* The suggestions to explain this expression and the nature of the sin are several. Is it some kind of euphemism for castration, a popular explanation found in the midrashim, or perhaps sodomy? The problem with this kind of interpretation is that it forces a nuance of abuse on to the verb "had done" in v. 24.

F. W. Basset suggests that the sin here is incest.[7] In Lev. 18:6–19; 20:11, 17–21; Ezek. 16:36–37, "to uncover [*gālâ* in the Piel] the nakedness of *X*" means to commit fornication, to engage in heterosexual (never homosexual) intercourse with a relative. Thus, Lev. 18:7, "you shall not uncover the nakedness of your father," prohibits cohabitation with one's mother. In Lev. 20:17 "uncover" is relaced by "see": "if a man takes his sister . . . and sees her nakedness and she sees his nakedness . . . ," suggesting the interchangeability of "uncovering" and "seeing." To do the first is to do the second.

Applied to Gen. 9:21, this suggestion would mean that while Noah

---

by himself: "One who holds my hand in drunkenness carries me when I am sated with wine." A similar emphasis appears in Isa. 51:17–18, where the sons get under the arms of their father, who has drunk the cup of God's wrath.

5. See H. J. Zobel, *"gālāh," TDOT,* 2:479–80.

6. See H. H. Cohen, *The Drunkenness of Noah,* Judaic Studies 4 (Tuscaloosa, AL: University of Alabama, 1974). Cohen's study makes astute observations here and there, but it is mostly an exercise in imagination rather than in exegesis.

7. See F. W. Basset, "Noah's nakedness and the curse of Canaan. A case of incest?" *VT* 21 (1971) 232–37.

was inebriated and unawares, his son Ham slept with his mother, and Canaan was the offspring of this incestuous relationship. This interpretation would explain why Noah curses Canaan after he sleeps off his hangover. The major problem with this interpretation is that it is almost impossible to square it with the biblical story.[8] For example, when Shem and Japheth "covered their father's nakedness" (v. 23), does this mean simply that they abstained from sexual relationship with their mother? Basset himself is forced to admit that v. 23 is awkward, and that it comes from the hand of a later redactor who failed to understand the subtleties of the event.

We are on much safer ground in limiting Ham's transgression simply to observing the exposure of the genitalia and failing to cover his naked father. Otherwise, the other two brothers' act of covering their father's nakedness becomes incomprehensible. We deliberately entitled this section "The Nakedness of Noah" rather than "The Drunkenness of Noah." Noah's drunkenness is only circumstantial to his nakedness. It is Noah's nudity, not his inebriated state, which Ham saw, and then passed on to his brothers. His sin would have been equally reprehensible had his father been sober.

23 Shem and Japheth are as commendable as Ham is obnoxious. They are restrained and respectful enough to cover their nude father.[9] Unlike Ham, they do not talk; they only act. Shem and Japheth are of "too pure eyes to behold iniquity" (Hab. 1:13).[10]

24 After he regained sobriety, Noah *learned what his youngest son had done to him.* How he found out we do not know. It is unwarranted to press the verb *had done* (Heb. *ʿāśâ*) to mean some physical act or abuse; *ʿāśâ* is simply the common word for "do, make." Perhaps it refers to Ham's talking to his brothers. May not Noah have been more provoked by his son's mouth than by his son's hand? Not only is Ham not honoring his father (and mother; Exod. 20:12), but he is fomenting a situation of fraternal strife not unlike that of Cain and Abel.

25 Two interpretative problems present themselves in the first line

8. See G. Rice, "The Curse That Never Was," *JRT* 29 (1972) 5–27, esp. pp. 11–13.

9. Cf. the seraphim, who with two of their wings "covered their feet" (Isa. 6:2); cf. also Ruth, who "uncovered the feet" of Boaz (Ruth 3:7). Since "feet" is probably a euphemism for the genitalia in such passages, then the seraphim are as modest as Ruth is seductive. Like the seraphim, Ham and Japheth are coverers.

10. What the two brothers did not do is underscored by the sudden shift in verb form. Vv. 20–23 have used in succession 11 imperfect forms with *waw,* but at the end of v. 23 a perfect form occurs—"but their father's nakedness they did not see [*rāʾû*]."

of the poem: the force of the word *Cursed,* and the enigma of Noah's curse on his grandson Canaan, rather than on the son Ham, who is the actual villain.

Cursed [*'ārûr*] *be Canaan* are Noah's first words in Scripture. He built a ship, gathered a crew, weathered a storm, offered a sacrifice, and lived righteously, but the text never mentions any words that he spoke. A more taciturn man would be difficult to find. Now he finally speaks, though some will doubt whether this is the most auspicious way to enter the world conversationally.

The OT does have examples of human beings uttering curses (Josh. 6:26; 9:23; Jer. 20:14, 15–17). When a person curses, are we to understand that curse as a precative, an optative (a wish?), or is it an immediately effective decree? Is Noah praying and wishing that Canaan will be cursed, or is Canaan cursed because Noah has pronounced the anathema? Does *'ārûr* *kᵉnā'an* (a nominal sentence) mean "Cursed be Canaan" or "Cursed is Canaan"? Now, there is no doubt that "cursed," when spoken by God, is declarative and not precative (Gen. 3:14, 17–19; 4:11). But does *'ārûr* have one nuance in the divine mouth and another nuance in the human mouth? Here the optative thrust seems preferable, for *'ārûr,* a passive participle, is followed by four jussives (*wîhî,* vv. 26–27; *yapṯᵉ,* v. 27, and probably *yiškōn,* v. 27).[11] That Noah appeals to God in v. 27 also lifts the words of Noah out of the area of potent magic and into the realm of request.[12]

The second problem concerns the curse being placed on Canaan, instead of on his father Ham, as one would expect. A number of proposals have been advanced. (1) Did the text originally read "Ham" (so LXX), and only later was "Canaan" read in the light of what happened to the Canaanites in Palestine under Joshua and David? (2) Were there originally two versions of the story, one in which Noah's sons are Shem, Ham, Japheth and another in which they are Shem, Canaan, and Japheth, that a redactor has artificially blended? (3) Was Canaan indeed the perpetrator of the crime or an accessory to the crime? (4) Is this an illustration of the principle of *lex talion* justice? The youngest son of Noah is responsible for the curse that is placed on his own youngest son.

In addition to these standard explanations, found from the times of the rabbinical and early Christian commentators to the present, we may add

11. Perhaps *yihyeh* (v. 25) may also be a jussive of a final *-h* verb. See Cassuto, *Genesis,* 2:157. This is the morphology of a final *-h* verb in pause, or immediately before a pause.

12. For the precative understanding of "curse" in 9:25, cf. F. I. Andersen, *The Sentence in Biblical Hebrew,* pp. 54, 112; S. H. Blank, "The Curse, the Blasphemy, the Spell, the Oath," *HUCA* 23 (1950-51) 75–78.

more exotic suggestions. One of these is that Canaan was written because of its associations with the root *knʿ*, "humble," an appropriate name for a person who is about to be placed in submission to his brothers.[13] Ham, meaning something like "hot," would not be suitable.

A perusal of these attempts to unravel a mystery makes clear that we do not know why the son bears the consequences of the father's improprieties. Primeval history has informed us that all flesh will suffer because of the sin of man. That same history tells us that man must bear the consequences of the illicit behavior of the "sons of God." Thus we are already catching glimpses of the fact that God visits the iniquities of the fathers unto the third and fourth (and second!) generation. Canaan's father has eaten sour grapes and therefore Canaan's teeth are set on edge. Later, however, verses like Jer. 31:29 and Ezek. 18:2 rebut the idea of vicarious or deferred punishment. Perhaps Jeremiah and Ezekiel do so in order to stress to their audience (especially to Ezekiel's audience, who are in captivity) that they are being punished because of their own sins, not those of their parents, and therefore they may repent and return to their Lord since their fate is not an inherited one.

26 Noah's "Cursed" is matched by a "Blessed," but unexpectedly it is not Shem who is blessed but *Yahweh, Shem's God.* The curse is directed not against Ham but against Canaan, and the blessing is directed not toward Shem but toward his Lord.[14] The blessing directed to Yahweh matches the curse directed at Canaan. Ham has done nothing and is cursed. Yahweh has done nothing and is blessed. In addition, by directing the blessing to Yahweh instead of to Shem, the narrator subordinates the human actors to the divine actor. It is Yahweh, rather than Shem, who is praised.

27 Noah next addresses a word of blessing to Japheth. His prayer, *May God enlarge Japheth,* is a pun in Hebrew: *yap̄teʾĕlōhîm leyep̄eṯ.*[15]

Whom does *Japheth* represent? In Gen. 10:2–4 and 1 Chr. 1:5–7 Japheth has seven sons and seven grandsons, and he appears as the ancestor of sundry peoples to the west and north of Israel in the Anatolian and Aegean

13. See A. Guillaume, "Paronomasia in the Old Testament," *JSS* 9 (1964) 283.

14. If Shem himself were the immediate object of the blessing, one would expect the Piel imperative, *bārēḵ,* instead of *bārûḵ,* the Qal passive participle (i.e., "bless, Oh Yahweh, Shem"). See J. Scharbert, *"brk," TDOT,* 2:284ff.

15. Note that the play on words, *ʾĕlōhê šēm,* "Shem's God," and *beʾoholê-šēm,* "(in) Shem's tents," forms a chiasm with another play on words, *yap̄te,* "(God) will enlarge," and *leyep̄eṯ,* "for Japheth." See A. R. Ceresko, "The Chiastic Word Pattern in Hebrew," *CBQ* 38 (1976) 309.

areas. They are people largely, but not exclusively, of Indo-European stock. As a generalization we may say that the Japhethites are the Gentiles. Some scholars draw the circle a bit more tightly and identify the sons of Japheth with the Sea Peoples, specifically the thalassocratic Philistines. Japheth has been connected with Greek Iapetos, a Titan and son of Uranos, and the father of mankind among the Philistines.[16]

The second sentence in this verse reads smoothly enough: *let him occupy* [lit., dwell in] *Shem's tents.* The question here is the identification of *him.* Is God or Japheth to dwell in the tents of Shem?

Influenced no doubt by the postbiblical Heb. *šᵉḵînâ,* "Shekinah," most ancient Hebrew sources posit God as the subject. Thus Targ. Onqelos reads, "and he shall make his Shekinah to dwell in the tabernacles of Shem." The book of Jubilees adopts the same position: "and God shall dwell."[17]

Few modern commentators take this approach. W. Kaiser, Jr., gives the most substantive defense of "God" as the subject.[18] Kaiser's main syntactical argument is that the subject of the previous clause ("May God enlarge Japheth") is presumed to continue into the next clause, where the subject is unexpressed ("and let him occupy Shem's tents"). That sounds plausible, but we observe that Kaiser does not apply this rule to a later verse in Genesis where again the phenomenon appears of one clause with a subject followed by another clause with an unexpressed subject (15:6): "Abraham believed in Yahweh and he [Abraham? God?] reckoned it to him [God? Abraham?] as righteousness." By Kaiser's rule "he" would have to be Abraham and "him" would have to be the Lord. Thus the rule Kaiser follows in his translation of 9:27 he rejects in his translation of 15:6.

The passage makes most sense when Japheth is seen as the subject of "occupy." Not only will Japheth's territory and influence be enlarged, but he will experience a peaceful cohabitation with Shem.[19]

16. See A. van Selms, "Judge Shamgar," *VT* 14 (1964) 308; D. Neiman, "The Date and Circumstances of the Cursing of Canaan," in *Biblical Motifs: Origins and Transformations,* ed. A. Altmann (Cambridge: Harvard University, 1966), pp. 113–34, esp. pp. 125ff.; idem, "Canaan, Curse of," *EncJud,* 5:97–98.

17. For further postbiblical references see T.B. *Yoma* 10a: "Even though God enlarges Japheth, the Shekinah rests upon the tents of Shem." That the deity dwells in a tent is biblically authenticated by the tabernacle. Cf. also *UT,* 128:III:18–19: *tity ilm lahlhm dr il lmšknthm,* "the gods go to their tent, the assembly of El to their dwellings."

18. W. Kaiser, Jr., *Toward an Old Testament Theology* (Grand Rapids: Zondervan, 1978), pp. 37–39, 81–82.

19. For *šāḵan bᵉʾohᵒlê,* "occupy (dwell in) the tents of," as a symbol of peace, see J. P. Brown, "Peace symbolism in ancient military vocabulary," *VT* 21 (1971)

Canaan is to be a *servant,* a slave, to Japheth. Rather than seeing this oracle as an etiology of Israel's rise to power (the conclusion most often reached when form-critical questions are raised), we prefer to read it as a prophetic, futuristic view of relationships between Israel (and the Sea Peoples) and the Canaanites. In effect it outlines future history, when Israel conquered Canaan and the Sea Peoples were carving out their own niche in Canaanite-held lands.[20]

28–29 Concluding biographical information about Noah is herewith provided. He lives three hundred and fifty years after the Flood, but we know of only two events during that long time: the sacrifice at the altar, and the imbroglio inside his tent. His total life falls short of a millennium by only fifty years. Two-thirds of his life is pre-Flood and one-third of his life is post-Flood. By postponing this biographical material from 5:32, where it might plausibly have come, until 9:28–29, the narrator has succeeded in presenting the Flood story as an expansion of both the biographical narrative and of the Sethite genealogy itself.[21]

THE NEW TESTAMENT APPROPRIATION

Gen. 6:5–9:17 and 1 Pet. 3:20–21; 2 Pet. 2:5

The two epistles of Peter differ significantly in their use of the Flood story, and of Noah in particular. In 2 Pet. 2:5 Noah is coupled with Lot as illustrations of two righteous individuals who were spared by God. Both are contrasted with their contemporaries, who received a devastating divine judgment. Noah's family is obliquely referred to as "seven other persons." Both of these incidents serve notice on the false teachers that they too now know what is in store for them. If Noah's generation did not escape, how shall they?

The same incident is mentioned in 1 Pet. 3:20–21, but here Peter is primarily interested in using the Flood story typologically. What happened to Noah and his family in the Flood is a type of what happens to believers when they are baptized. The text reads (RSV): "in the days of Noah, during

---

20–23. Only in Ps. 78:55 and 1 Chr. 5:10 does *šāḵan beʾohŏlê* mean not fraternization but enforced dispossession.

20. See D. Neiman, "The Date and Circumstances of the Cursing of Canaan," in *Biblical Motifs,* p. 127; A. P. Ross, "The Curse of Canaan," *BSac* 137 (1980) 232–33.

21. See R. R. Wilson, *Genealogy and History in the Biblical World,* p. 161.

the building of the ark, in which a few, that is, eight persons, were saved through water. Baptism, which corresponds to this, now saves you."

The boldest innovation here appears to be Peter's assertion that Noah and his family were saved *through* (Gk. *dia*) water. Genesis would seem to suggest that they were saved *from* water. Now, Gk. *dia* can convey several meanings, the two most likely here being instrumental and local. If the former, has Peter changed Genesis' emphasis on the waters as a medium of destruction into the waters as a medium of salvation? Sensing this oddity, E. Best comments that "strictly Noah was saved from water but the baptismal reference which follows *has forced our writer into the strange statement* 'through water' in relation to Noah."[1] Peter then is attributing a double quality to the waters, and is suggesting that the same waters that decimate the unbeliever deliver the believer. In baptism one is saved by water, and therefore Peter was saved in the same way (arguing from antitype back to type).

If we understand the phrase *di' hýdatos* not as instrumental, "by means of water," but as local, "through water," then Noah was saved by going through the water and stepping into the ark, as Gen. 7:11–13 suggests. He got soaked, but he did not drown. Furthermore, the particle *hó,* "which," at the start of v. 21 would then refer not just to the water as its antecedent, but to the entry into the ark and the passage through the waters inside the ark. It is not the Flood that is a type of baptism, but rather it is the passing through death into salvation that is the type.[2] This explanation obviates the need to justify Peter's twisting the Flood story—he is doing nothing of the sort.

1. E. Best, *1 Peter,* NCBC (repr. Grand Rapids: Eerdmans, 1982), p. 147 (italics mine). Similarly, A. R. C. Leaney, *The Letters of Peter and Jude* (Cambridge: Cambridge University, 1967), p. 53: "The water of baptism, passing through which brings spiritual *safety,* unexpectedly compared to the water of the great Flood which provided an ordeal through which the eight had to pass, and which was the death of the unworthy. . . . The water of the Flood destroyed while that of baptism saves."

2. See D. Cook, "I Peter iii:20: An Unnecessary Problem," *JTS* 31 (1980) 72–78. Also Charles Bigg, *The Epistles of St. Peter and St. Jude,* ICC (Edinburgh: T. & T. Clark, 1901), p. 164, "The water expresses not the instrument through which we receive the grace, but rather the evil life we leave behind." B. Reicke (*The Epistles of James, Peter, and Jude,* AB [Garden City, NY: Doubleday, 1964], p. 113) says it is of "minor importance whether the expression 'through water' is to be understood as having local or instrumental meaning. The emphasis is placed on Noah's salvation from a godless environment." In other words, for Reicke, "through water" is almost an incidental expression, simply detailing the means by which Noah found deliverance from his pagan environment.

Gen. 6:5–9:17 and Matt. 24:37–39; Luke 17:26–27

Both Matthew and Luke use the "days of Noah" as analogous to the days that shall precede the Lord's coming. In those days before the Flood people were "eating and drinking, marrying and giving in marriage, until the day when Noah entered the ark." We agree with those commentators who see these words as a description of normal, day-to-day activities. The Gospel writers are not indicting the behavior of Noah's contemporaries, as is evident from the verbs used in Luke 17:28: "they ate, they drank, they bought, they sold, they planted, they built." These are not per se sinful activities.[3]

According to Matthew and Luke, then, Jesus is focusing not on immorality or licentiousness but on a total preoccupation with everyday affairs. The people of both Noah's day and his day are so engrossed in the routines of another day, the routines of another year, that eschatological awareness and openness are missing.[4]

Gen. 6:5–9:17 and Heb. 11:7

Noah is the first real link between the definition of faith given in 11:1 and the list of the faithful that follows. Part of faith's definition is that it is "the conviction of things not seen." Noah was warned by God concerning events "as yet unseen." God spoke and Noah believed, and his beliefs produced appropriate reactions. The author of Hebrews does not call Noah righteous, although he is the first individual so styled in the Bible (Gen. 6:9) and the author of Hebrews has already called Abel righteous (Heb. 11:4). Instead, Noah is described as "an heir of the righteousness which comes by faith." Noah's faith entitled him to and brought him into possession of righteousness.

3. See Q. Quesnell, "Made Themselves Eunuchs for the Kingdom of Heaven (Mt. 19,12)," *CBQ* 39 (1968) 345 n. 14; I. H. Marshall, *The Gospel of Luke,* NIGTC (Grand Rapids: Eerdmans, 1978), p. 663. J. Fitzmyer (*The Gospel According to Luke, X-XXIV,* AB [Garden City, NY: Doubleday, 1985], p. 1167) remarks: "Verses 26–32, in comparing the arrival of the day(s) of the Son of Man with the days of Noah and Lot, warn against the insouciance and indifference of 'this generation.' . . . In the days of Noah and Lot people pursued their earthly existence with nonchalance; this is to be counteracted with vigilant expectation."

4. See D. R. Catchpole, "The Son of Man's Search for Faith," *NovT* 19 (1977) 85. D. L. Balch ("Backgrounds of I Cor. vii: Sayings of the Lord in Q," *NTS* 18 [1972] 355) is one of the few writers to see in Jesus' words, as recorded in Matt. 24:38, a negative attitude toward marriage. Noah abstained from sexual intercourse after he entered the ark (according to Philo, who credits Noah with "his conquest of his lower passions").

The antecedent of "by this" *(di' hḗs)* can only be faith and not building the ark. It was his faith that condemned the world, and it was by faith that he became an heir of righteousness. Thus Gk. *di' hḗs* governs both clauses that follow it. The antecedent of "by this" might well be the building of the ark in reference to the first phrase ("by this he condemned the world"), but not for the second phrase ("by this he became an heir of the righteousness which comes by faith").[5]

H. THE TABLE OF NATIONS (10:1–32)

1. THE JAPHETHITES (10:1–5)

1 *These are the lines of Noah's sons, Shem, Ham, and Japheth, to whom were born sons after the flood.*

2 *Japheth's sons: Gomer, Magog, Madai, Javan, Tubal, Meshech, and Tiras.*

3 *Gomer's sons: Ashkenaz, Riphath, and Torgarmah.*

4 *Javan's sons: Elishah, Tarshish, Kittim, and Dodanim.*

5 *And from these sprang the islands of the nations, in their own territory, each with its own language, by their clan within the nations.*

This chapter is given over exclusively to a segmented genealogy of the descendants of Noah's three sons. The three sons are little more than links. Their contributions to the biblical drama are, apart from fathering, minimal. They never speak in Scripture (Ham's speech is referred to but not recorded in 9:22). They all perform their duties like automatons.

In some ways this genealogy may be read as a fulfillment of the divine blessing given to Noah and his sons. The three sons are now multiplying and populating the earth (9:1). Their prolificness is made possible by God's blessing rather than Noah's blessing. The divine blessing is given to all three sons. The father's blessing bypasses Ham. But in this world-population chart

5. J. Moffatt, *A Critical and Exegetical Commentary on the Epistle to the Hebrews,* ICC (Edinburgh: T. & T. Clark, 1924), p. 168. Also, S. J. Kistemaker, *Exposition of the Epistle to the Hebrews* (Grand Rapids: Baker, 1984), pp. 318–19; H. W. Attridge, *The Epistle to the Hebrews,* Hermeneia (Philadelphia: Fortress, 1989), p. 319 n. 180. B. F. Westcott (*The Epistle to the Hebrews* [Grand Rapids: Eerdmans, repr. 1965], pp. 356–57) is one of the few commentators to argue for "ark" as the antecedent of "by this." Perhaps also G. W. Buchanan, *To The Hebrews,* AB (Garden City, NY: Doubleday, 1972), p. 187, but he does not make his position clear on the matter.

not only does Ham reproduce, but Ham's son Canaan, who was cursed by Noah, is the second most productive father, with eleven names to his credit. Only Joktan produces more.

Scholars who accept the JEDP sources are fond of using this genealogy as another illustration of a composite. Their breakdown is: P, vv. 1–7, 20, 22–23, 31–32; J, vv. 8–19, 21, 24–30. Thus they assign about two-thirds of the chapter to J (20 verses) and one-third to P (12 verses). In this scheme, summarizing statements (vv. 5, 20, 31, 32) are assigned to P, and any parts bordering on narrative (vv. 8–19, 24–30) are assigned to J. Yet the chapter, read as a whole, does not appear disjointed. Indeed, the entire genealogy provides an example of chiastic summary that streamlines the parts into a whole: (1) Noah's sons are listed in the opening verse in this order: Shem, Ham, Japheth; yet in the paragraphs that follow this order is reversed: Japheth (vv. 2–5), Ham (vv. 6–20), Shem (vv. 21–31); (2) each paragraph begins with the name of the patriarch (vv. 2, 6, 21), and ends with a formulaic reference to the families, languages, lands, and nations evolving from that patriarch (vv. 5, 20, 31); (3) the last verse of the chapter (v. 32) forms an *inclusio* with the chapter's first verse.[1]

1 The *tôl^e^ḏôṯ* passages scattered throughout Genesis use a variety of formulae to refer to descendants. To describe the descendants of Adam (ch. 5) the text uses consistently the Hiphil of *yālaḏ* in imperfect form. The Qal of *yālaḏ* may be used if the mother is the subject of the verb (4:17, 20, 22, 25). Unlike Gen. 5, which uses the Hiphil of *yālaḏ* (imperfect) when speaking of "fathering," ch. 10 uses consistently the Qal of *yālaḏ* (imperfect: vv. 8, 13, 15, 24, 26), except for v. 1, which provides the only use of the Niphal of *yālaḏ* in the chapter. Elsewhere in the chapter the formula is simply: "the sons of" (vv. 2, 3, 5, 6, 7, 20, 22, 31). Each instance of "fathered" falls within the section of the chapter attributed to J, and "the sons of" is to be found in the P sections of the chapter.[2]

2 In v. 2 we begin with the sons of Japheth. The remainder of the

1. See H. Van Dyke Parunak, "Oral Typesetting: Some Clues of Biblical Structure," *Bib* 62 (1981) 163.

2. See J. Simons, "The 'Table of Nations' (Gen. x): its general structure and meaning," *OTS* 10 (1954) 171–73, who suspects the secondary character of the *yālaḏ* formula. Note that the line of Japheth uses only the formula "the sons of." But the lines of Ham and Shem use both "the sons of" and "fathered." The phrase "the sons of" points to the ancestor. By contrast, *yālaḏ,* "fathered," points to the descendants. The first focuses on the beginning; the second focuses on continuing results. Thus the past and the present are bridged. See A. P. Ross, "The Table of Nations in Genesis 10—Its Structure," *BSac* 137 (1980) 346–47.

chapter is a sophisticated exercise in world cartography. Gen. 11:1 summarizes the findings of Gen. 10 in two Hebrew words: *kol-hā'āreṣ,* literally, "all the earth." This reference to the whole (known) world is what we would call the ecumene, that is, a group of peoples that are so interlocked by give-and-take that they constitute one world civilization. All writers on Gen. 10 continue to be perplexed by some of the peoples who are united in this chapter (e.g., Nimrod from Cush, or a Hamitic Canaan rather than a Shemitic Canaan), but such links testify to the ecumenic nature of civilization's beginnings. Internationalism precedes nationalism and provincialism.

Japheth is credited with seven sons of whom the first is *Gomer* (spelled the same as Hosea's wife). Gomer as a nation is mentioned in Ezek. 38:6, and may be identified with the Akk. *Gi-mir-ra-a* (the Cimmerians). They are a migratory people who made their first historical appearance in eastern Asia at the end of the 8th century B.C. For *Magog* the most reasonable identification put forward, in view of the coupling of Gog and Magog in Ezek. 38–39, is Gyges king of Lydia. In Ezekiel Magog and Gog are distinctly belligerent.

Madai is the word used by the OT to designate the Medes, a people who inhabited the territory between the upper Tigris River and the Caspian Sea (2 K. 17:6; 18:11; Isa. 13:17; 21:2). They were formidable opponents for the Assyrians in the 9th and 8th centuries B.C. Subsequently (late 6th century B.C.) they became partners with the Persians. *Javan* is to be connected with the Hellenic tribal name Ionia, which refers to the western coast of Asia Minor and the Aegean area. Later on (by the Hellenistic period) Javan refers to all Greece. Javanites are merchants trading with the Phoenicians of Tyre (Ezek. 27:13) and with Philistines (Joel 4:6 [Eng. 3:6]).

Tubal may be connected with the Tabali, who were located in eastern Anatolia. Approximately the same territory covers the descendants of *Meshech,* the Mushki of the upper Euphrates River. *Tiras* is to be linked with the Turasha of Egyptian texts, that is, the Tyrrhennians, or later, the Etruscans of Italy.

3 Japheth has seven sons (v. 2), and seven grandsons (vv. 3–4). *Ashkenaz* represents a people and a country on the upper Euphrates in Armenia. The same name occurs in a passage calling on the kingdoms of Ararat and Minni to rise up against Babylon (Jer. 51:27). Again the land of Armenia is pinpointed. Scholars have connected Ashkenaz with the Ashkuza (or Ashguza/Ishguza) who fought the Assyrians in the reign of Esarhaddon (680–669 B.C.) as allies of the Minni.

Riphath is an enigma. In the light of his brothers that are identifiable, he is probably Anatolian. In 1 Chr. 1:6 "Diphath" occurs, but manuscript evidence fully supports an initial *R* rather than *D* here. *Togarmah* exports horses to Tyre (Ezek. 27:14) and is in Gog's army (Ezek. 38:6). Is he to be connected with Tegarama of Hittite texts and Til-garimmu of Assyrian texts? This area is also located near the upper Euphrates in Asia Minor (formerly Togarmah was thought to be in Armenia).

4 *Elishah* is Alashiya, the cuneiform name for the island of Cyprus (see, e.g., Ugar. *'ṯy*). In the OT *Tarshish* is identified as a distant port from which silver, iron, tin, lead, ivory, monkeys, and peacocks were exported (1 K. 10:22; Jer. 10:9; Ezek. 27:12). In this table of nations Tarshish could be a Mediterranean port since he is said to be a son of Javan (Greece). Wherever Tarshish is, it was Jonah's destination in the west (Jon. 1:3). Yet 1 K. 10:22 refers to Solomon's fleet of Tarshish (i.e., larger seagoing vessels) whose home port was Ezion-geber, pointing to a route along the Red Sea and the Indian Ocean (cf. 2 Chr. 9:21 and 1 K. 22:49, the latter being a reference to Jehoshaphat's ships of Tarshish sailing for Ophir from Ezion-geber). Tarshish, then, may be reached either by the Mediterranean or by the Indian Ocean, and in either case it is a place reachable only by ship.

Most scholars have identified Tarshish with Tartessus, a mining village in southwestern Spain. The name is connected with Akk. *rašāšu,* "to be smelted," which suggests that Tarshish means "refinery."[3] C. H. Gordon has taken the position that Tarshish was located on the shores of the Atlantic, and could even be Mexico.[4] In a more general way Tarshish may refer to the open sea, to any far-off lands that are reached by oceangoing ships. Furthermore, maintains Gordon, Heb. *taršîš* is not a *taqṭîl* form of *ršš,* as maintained by Albright, but is a *qaṭlîl* formation of the denominative root *trš,* which comes from *tîrôš,* "wine," and means "wine-red, wine-dark."[5]

Kittim is to be equated with Kition, a Phoenician city on the southeast coast of the island of Cyprus near the present city of Larnaka. Kition was a prominent Phoenician base on Cyprus as early as the 9th century B.C. In the Bible Kittim may refer to a land (Isa. 23:1) and to islands (Ezek. 27:6). Jeremiah (2:10) uses the coasts of Kittim as a western geographical pole when

3. Following the lead of W. F. Albright, "New Light on the Early History of Phoenician Colonization," *BASOR* 83 (1941) 14–22, esp. pp. 21–22.

4. C. H. Gordon, "Tarshish," *IDB,* 4:517–18; idem, *Before Columbus* (New York: Crown, 1971), pp. 113–15, 136–37.

5. C. H. Gordon, "The Wine-Dark Sea," *JNES* 37 (1978) 51–52. Heb. *taršîš* is close to Gk. *thálassēs,* "sea," suggesting that throughout the Bible Tarshish is to be understood as the general expression for "sea." See S. B. Hoenig, "Tarshish," *JQR* 9 (1979) 181–82.

he assails the sins of his fellow Judeans. The prophecies of Balaam (see Num. 24:24) demonstrate that Kittim is a land associated with ships.

On the basis of the LXX and 1 Chr. 1:7, many commentators have emended *Dodanim* to *Rodanim,*[6] perhaps a reference to the island of Rhodes, one of the largest islands of the Aegean, lying off the southwest coast of Turkey. The MT of Gen. 10:4 can be retained only by the suggestion that both Rodanim and Dodanim came from an original *dananim,* Gk. *danaoi,* a people of the Peloponnesus during the Mycenean period.

5 That the names given throughout ch. 10 are not exhaustive is borne out by this verse, which refers to *the islands of the nations,* unidentifiable but perhaps transoceanic areas. Each of these nations has its own territory, its own language, and its own social structure ("clan"). It is difficult to say precisely what is the meaning of *mišpāḥâ* in Gen. 10, but elsewhere it appears as a synonym of *'elep̱,* "clan," that is, the largest unit within the tribe (cf. Judg. 6:15 with 1 Sam. 9:21).[7]

Speiser has observed that *gôy,* "nation," is consistently used in this chapter, but *'am,* "people," never is.[8] The difference is that *'am* is a term denoting close family connections, consanguineous relationships. *gôy* is less personal, and refers to large conglomerates held together from without rather than from within. This distinction suggests an explanation of why *gôy* is used regularly in Gen. 10 and *'am* never appears. Never does the OT speak of the *gôy* of Yahweh, for example, but the *'am* of Yahweh is standard.

It is clear that the descendants of Japheth are primarily, if not exclusively, ethnic groups that represent maritime nations, peoples who practiced the profession of seafaring and whose interchange was largely by sea. In the expression *from these sprang the islands of the nations,* "these" may refer only to the preceding sons of Javan (v. 4), or more likely to all the sons of Japheth.[9] However, not all maritime nations in Gen. 10 are confined to the sons of Japheth. For example, the thalassocratic Philistines are absent from this grouping. This is due, no doubt, to geographical factors. All the nations or peoples enumerated in vv. 1–5 are located either north,

6. B. M. Newman, Jr. ("Some Hints on Solving Textual Problems," *BT* 33 [1982] 432) appeals to Gen. 10:4 and Josh. 9:4, where a *d* was mistakenly written for an *r.*

7. Josh. 7:14 lists the following units according to decreasing size: tribe *(šeḇeṭ),* clan *(mišpāḥâ),* household *(bayiṯ),* individual *(geḇer).*

8. E. A. Speiser, " 'People' and 'Nation' of Israel," *JBL* 79 (1960) 157–63, esp. p. 159.

9. See B. Obed, "The Table of Nations (Genesis 10)—A Socio-cultural Approach," *ZAW* 98 (1986) 29.

northeast, or northwest of Israel, unlike the contiguous and more southerly Philistines.

2. THE HAMITES (10:6–20)

6 *Ham's sons: Cush, Mizraim, Put, and Canaan.*

7 *Cush's sons: Seba, Havilah, Sabtah, Raamah, Sabteca. Raamah's sons: Sheba and Dedan.*

8 *Cush fathered Nimrod. He was the first*[1] *to be mighty in the land.*

9 *He was the hero of the chase by Yahweh's grace,*[2] *hence it was said: "Like Nimrod, a hero of the chase by Yahweh's grace."*

10 *The major parts of his kingdom were: Babylon, Erech, Accad, and Calneh in the land of Shinar.*

11 *From that land emerged Asshur. He built Nineveh, Rehoboth-Ir, Calah,*

12 *Resen, between Nineveh and Calah, the latter being the outstanding city.*

13 *Mizraim fathered Ludim, Anamim, Hehabim, Naphtuhim,*

14 *Pathrusim, Caphtorim, and Casluhim from whom the Philistines emerged.*

15 *Canaan fathered Sidon, his firstborn, and Heth,*

16 *the Jebusites, the Amorites, the Girgashites,*

17 *the Hivites, the Arkites, the Sinites,*

18 *the Arvadites, the Zemarites, and the Hamathites. Afterward the Canaanites' clans branched out*

19 *so that the border of the Canaanites reached from Sidon all the way*[3] *to Gerar, near Gaza, all the way to Sodom, Gomorrah, Admah, and Zeboiim near Lasha.*

20 *These are Ham's sons, by their clans, languages, territories, and nations.*

1. See P. P. Saydon, "The inceptive imperfect in Hebrew and the verb *hēḥēl,*" *Bib* 35 (1954) 47. That Nimrod was "the first to be mighty" means he was the first to do heroic deeds.

2. *lip̄nê,* lit., "to the face of," usually has spatial force ("in front of") or temporal force ("before"). Here the translation must connote the approving attitude of the involved party, hence "by the grace of." See Speiser's comment on 6:11 in *Genesis,* p. 51.

3. *bō'aḵâ* is the infinitive construct of *bô',* "to go," with the 2nd person pronominal suffix, lit., "your coming." Since an indefinite personal subject (Eng. "one," French *on,* German *man*) can be expressed by the 2nd masc. sing. form of the verb, the sense of this expression is "as one comes." See GKC, § 144h, for further examples.

6 Ham's sons are four. *Cush* represents the area of northeast Africa. The Greek appellation for it is Nubia. The LXX uses two forms for Cush: *chous* when it refers to the sons of Ham, and *aithiopia* in other instances. It is questionable whether one is dealing here with a homonymous Cush: an Ethiopian Cush (v. 6), a North Arabian Cush (v. 7), and a Kassite Cush (v. 8), to be discussed below.

Mizraim is the regular Hebrew word for Egypt. It is dual in form *(-aim)* because of the division of Egypt into two parts, Upper and Lower. *Put* is the only son of Ham who is not provided with a further genealogy in this chapter. Jer. 46:9 mentions "men of Cush and Put who handle the shield." Ezekiel also places Put with Ethiopia, Lud, Arabia, and Cub (Libya?) as nations doomed to fall by the sword (Ezek. 30:5). Ezek. 38:5 places Put alongside Persia and Cush. Thus an African location appears probable. Except for Ezek. 38:5 the LXX translates Put in the prophetic passages as "Libyans."

The appearance of *Canaan* as a Hamite is surprising, but the genealogy herewith provided reflects the story of Gen. 9:20–27 in which Noah cursed Ham's son Canaan. But are not the Canaanites as Semitic as the Hebrews? Is this an artificial arrangement by which the Hebrews showed their disdain for the Canaanites? Or is the connection between Canaan and Africa/Egypt to be understood only in terms of geographical proximity? Or do we have another evidence here of the worldwide ecumene in operation? Possibly Canaan is linked with the likes of Egypt and Babylon in this unit (and all under the rubric of Hamites) because like them Canaan was, from the Bible's perspective, a sedentary population, dwelling in cities "which are great and walled up to heaven" (Deut. 1:28). Thus the reason for listing Canaan as Hamitic is not personal or geographical but sociocultural. Note that two nouns occur in this unit, but in neither the preceding nor following ones do *mamleḵâ* ("kingdom," v. 10) and *ʿîr* ("city," v. 12).

7 Some of Cush's sons are identifiable and some are not. As a whole these are nations on the shores of the Red Sea and the southern district of Arabia. The identification of *Seba* is uncertain. *Havilah* too defies exact placement. It is one of two names in this entire genealogy that appears twice (the other is Sheba, vv. 7, 27). This Havilah is a descendant of Ham through Cush, and the other Havilah is a descendant of Shem through Joktan (v. 29). Havilah was a region rich in gold (2:11). It was the territory in which Ishmael and his descendants lived ("from Havilah to Shur, which is opposite Egypt," 25:18). The Amalekites living "from Havilah to Shur" were vanquished by Saul (1 Sam. 15:7). All this evidence points to some location in Arabia.

Sabtah and *Sabteca* may be the only two names in vv. 6–7 that are not names of Arabian peoples. M. C. Astour has suggested that Sabtah is the equivalent of Sabaka (ca. 712–700 B.C.), a ruler of Ethiopia when that nation emerged as a major power in the eastern Mediterranean to conquer Egypt (the 25th Dynasty). Sabaka died and was succeeded by his brother Sabataka (i.e., Sabteca), who reigned from 700 to 689/88 B.C., and whose brother Tirhakah (or Tirhaqah) is mentioned in 1 K. 19:9 and Isa. 37:9.[4]

Raamah is probably an African/Arabian tribe. A South Arabian Minean inscription mentions this city as one near Maʿin in southwest Arabia. *Sheba* is in the southwest corner of Arabia, and is perhaps modern Yemen. In Gen. 25:3 and 1 Chr. 1:32 Sheba is coupled with Dedan as a descendant of Abraham. Sheba was famous as a trading center, especially from the time of Solomon on (1 K. 10:1ff.; 2 Chr. 9:1ff.; Isa. 60:6; Jer. 2:20). *Dedan* is another Arabian tribe. Its territory lay in northern Arabia bordering on Edom (Jer. 49:8; Ezek. 25:13). Its merchants traded with Tyre (Ezek. 27:5).

8 *Nimrod* receives more comment than anyone else in ch. 10. Two basic questions arise about him: who is he, and what is the etymology of his name? At least three suggestions have been made for Nimrod's identification. (1) Nimrod is to be equated with Ninurta, a Babylonian war-god and god of the hunt, also called "the Arrow, the mighty hero," whose cult was widespread in Mesopotamia in the late 2nd millennium B.C.[5] (2) Nimrod is to be connected with the Assyrian King Tukulti-Ninurta I (who bears the divine name Ninurta), who reigned in the last half of the 13th century B.C. (ca. 1246–1206 B.C.).[6] He was the first Assyrian king to rule over both Babylon and Assyria. He accomplished this task by defeating Babylon and taking its defeated king (Kashtiliash IV) into Assyrian captivity together with the statue of Marduk, Babylon's god. In addition, he engaged in massive building programs, which, together with his military operations, forced him to tax his people highly (in the manner of Solomon) to keep his empire afloat. His death marked an eclipse in Assyrian power. The linking of Nimrod (son of Cush) with the Assyrian Tukulti-Ninurta I, would assume that "Cush" here is to be

4. M. C. Astour, "Sabtah and Sabteca: Ethiopian Pharaoh Names in Genesis 10," *JBL* 84 (1965) 422–25.

5. See, e.g., KB, p. 619 (and its 1983 ed., 3:663). Albright, however, ruled out this equation unless we assume drastic corruption of the Hebrew form of the name. See his portion of the article "The Babylonian Matter in the Predeuteronomic Primeval History (JE) in Gen 1–11," *JBL* 58 (1939) 99, coauthored with S. Mowinckel.

6. For this identification see E. A. Speiser, "In Search of Nimrod," *Eretz-Israel* 5 (1958) 32–36 (Hebrew); repr. in *Oriental and Biblical Studies,* ed. J. J. Finkelstein and M. Greenberg (Philadelphia: University of Pennsylvania, 1967), pp. 41–52.

read as "Cassites." (3) To preserve the Cushite origins of Nimrod some have connected Nimrod with the Egyptian Pharaoh Amenhotep III (ca. 1416–1379 B.C.) of the 18th Dynasty.[7] The Amarna Letters refer to him as Nimmuri.[8] He claims to have extended his rule as far away from Egypt as the Euphrates. In Egypt he is remembered for the enormous temples he built at Luxor and Karnak, and his own palace and mortuary temple. During his reign a set of five commemorative scarabs was issued dealing with the events of Amenhotep's life. One of them records a wild cattle hunt, on which one hundred and two lions were captured.[9] Not without reason do historians call him "the Magnificent."

That Gen. 10 has Cush, a Hamite, as a father of Nimrod is unexpected—unexpected, that is, if Nimrod is a ruler of Assyria! It is possible that Nimrod is African or Egyptian, but Mic. 5:5 (Eng. 6), with its "land of Nimrod" as a synonymous variant of Assyria, establishes Nimrod as a territory to the east of Palestine. But again, we may have here another illustration of the worldwide ecumene. One need only think of what Mesopotamia and Egypt have in common (e.g., architecture and the rebus system of writing). The Egyptian language and the Semitic languages have enough similarities that one may properly speak of "Egypto-Semitic" linguistic phenomena.

The etymology of Nimrod is also uncertain. Most writers have connected it with the Hebrew verb *māraḏ,* "to rebel." In the Haggadah (T.B. *Hag.* 13a; *Pes.* 94b) Nimrod is pictured as the prototype of rebellion, the builder of the Tower of Babel, and as the one who led the people in rebellion against God. Dahood has noted that at both Ebla and Ugarit some proper names combine an animal and a deity. He notes particularly Ugar. *ni-mi-ri-ya* (which he translates "panther of Yah"), which leads him to suggest that Nimrod means "panther of Hadd" (i.e., Baal), analogous to *nqmd* ("victory of Hadd").[10]

7. See von Rad, *Genesis,* p. 146. Years ago the Assyriologist A. Poebel ("The Assyrian King List from Khorsabad," *JNES* 1 [1942] 256) suggested that Nimrod is a corruption of *MAR.TU,* the name of the Amorites in Sumerian inscriptions. The *MAR.TU* that took possession of parts of Babylon and Assyria came there as nomads.

8. See, e.g., the seven letters of Tushratta to Amenophis III which begin "To Nimmuria, king of Egypt" *(a-na* ^{I}*ni-ib-mu-a-ri-a šàr* $^{m\hat{a}tu}$*mi-iṣ-ri-i),* in J. A. Knudtzon, *Die El-Amarna Tafeln* (Aalen: Otto Zeller Verlagsbuchhandlung, 1964), 2:131–54, 179–88.

9. A. Gardiner, *Egypt of the Pharaohs* (Oxford: Clarendon, 1961), p. 206.

10. M. J. Dahood, "Ebla, Ugarit, and the Old Testament," *TD* 27 (1979) 129; idem, "Ebla, Ugarit, and the Bible," in G. Pettinato, *The Archives of Ebla: An Empire Inscribed in Clay* (Garden City, NY: Doubleday, 1981), p. 277.

9 So well known was Nimrod that an aphorism came to be associated with his name.[11] That Nimrod is styled as *the hero of the chase* points both to the martial prowess of this individual against other nations and to the hunting of wild game. This power, however, is a gift of God's grace. The Persian king Cyrus is not the only pagan king whom Yahweh guided, even though the king knew not Yahweh.

10 Four (or three?) cities are connected with Nimrod. Three of them are well known: *Babylon,* the ancient capital city of Mesopotamia, situated on a branch of the Euphrates, southwest of Baghdad; *Erech* (ancient Uruk, modern Warka), an important Sumerian city (esp. 4th–3rd millennium B.C.), located about 160 miles southeast of Baghdad; *Accad* (also spelled Akkad or Agade), the capital city of the dynasty of Sargon of Akkad, situated on the Euphrates in northern Babylonia, though its site has never been discovered.

The city about which there is uncertainty is *Calneh.* Amos 6:2 mentions a city by this name, along with Carchemish, Hamath, and Arpad, as cities conquered by the Assyrians, and hence pointing to northern Syria. It is difficult, however, to identify this northern Calneh with the one in Gen. 10, which is specifically designated as being *in the land of Shinar,* that is, Sumer, which is in the south, unless the northern Calneh (Amos 6:2) is to be seen as a commercial colony named after the mother city in the south (Gen. 10:10).[12] Furthermore, the extant cuneiform literature has no references to a southern (i.e., Babylonian) Calneh.

Accordingly, many versions of the Bible read "all of them" instead of "Calneh" (e.g., RSV, NJPS). This reading is obtained by emending MT *w*^{e}*ḵalnēh* to *w*^{e}*ḵullānāh,* "and all of them."[13] J. A. Thompson cited ancient Samaritan evidence that supports this suggestion.[14]

11–12 *Asshur* can refer to both the nation of Assyria and a city in

11. For the use of the Niphal with impersonal meaning to report a byword, or something that is habitually said, particularly in comments on names, cf. Gen. 22:14. Also, C. R. Fontaine, *Traditional Sayings in the Old Testament* (Sheffield: Almond, 1982), p. 238.

12. So C. H. Gordon, "Calneh," *IDB,* 1:490.

13. This emendation received its scholarly impetus from W. F. Albright, "The End of 'Calneh in Shinar'," *JNES* 3 (1944) 254–55. Cf. E. Lipiński, "Nimrod et Assur," *RB* 73 (1966) 77–93, esp. pp. 83–84. Poebel (*JNES* 1 [1942] 256 n. 17) managed to dispose of the problematical Calneh by simply suggesting the insertion of a *waw* between the *n* and *h* in *kalnēh,* hence *ûḵōl nāwê,* "and every pasture ground."

14. J. A. Thompson, "Samaritan Evidence for 'All of Them in the Land of Shinar'," *JBL* 90 (1971) 99–102. Westermann (*Genesis,* 1:517) suggests that such an alteration is "hazardous, because there is no such formation with *kl* anywhere else in Genesis 10. A combination such as 'all of them in the land . . .' occurs nowhere else."

Assyria which for a time was the capital of the empire. Here he is the ancestor of the Assyrians. *Calah* was also one of the Assyrian capital cities, and is located where the Tigris and Upper Zab rivers meet. *He built Nineveh.* The subject of *he built* is ambiguous; it could be either Nimrod or Asshur. *Nineveh* was located on the east side of the Tigris, directly across the river from modern Mosul. Interestingly, *Calah,* not Nineveh, is described as *the outstanding city.* In Jonah (1:2; 3:3; 4:11) the same phrase is applied to Nineveh. Perhaps this accolade is given to Calah in Gen. 10 because it was the capital of Assyria before Nineveh was.

Rehoboth-Ir is not identifiable. Heb. *r^e^ḥōḇōṯ* means "open space" and *ʿîr* means "city." Comparison may be made with Assyrian *rêbīt ali,* "open spaces in a city, unbuilt area," and specifically with *rêbīt Ninua,* "unbuilt areas of Nineveh." Is the reference here to peripheral sections of the city of Nineveh rather than to a separate city?[15] *Rehoboth* may be taken as an adjective in the plural construct bound to a noun in the (collective) singular, to express a superlative. The meaning of *Rehoboth-Ir* is then "the widest city," in reference to Nineveh.[16] But such an interpretation requires the deletion of the *w^e^ʾeṯ* before the place name. *Resen* is situated between the identifiable Nineveh and Calah, but in spite of this precise datum we do not know its location. Possibly it was part of the sprawling urban complex around Nineveh.

13–14 All names in these two verses end in *-im,* which indicates the ethnic character of the names. *Ludim* is associated with peoples of Asia Minor in Isa. 66:19 and with African peoples (Cush, Put) in Jer. 46:9 and Ezek. 30:5. This association suggests identifying the Ludim with the Lydians. The *Anamim* are unknown, except for a possible identification with a people of Cyrene, the *A-na-mi,* mentioned in a cuneiform text from the time of the Assyrian king Sargon II (8th century B.C.).[17] The *Lehabim* are perhaps the Libyans, though this identification is uncertain. The *Naphtuhim* are unknown, but the Hebrew word *(naptuḥîm)* looks like a Hebraization of Egyp. *n3 ptḥ,* "the Ptahites," that is, the people of Memphis (i.e., middle) Egypt.

Patrusim is a Hebrew equivalent of Egyp. *p3 t3 rśy,* and refers to the inhabitants of Pathros, or Upper (i.e., southern) Egypt. *Casluhim* is a mystery, and may be the one bona fide gloss in this chapter. However, since the verse makes reference to southern Egypt (Patrusim) and to middle Egypt (Naphtuhim), Casluhim may therefore be plausibly understood as being part of

15. T. Jacobson, "Rehoboth-Ir," *IDB,* 4:31.

16. J. M. Sasson, *"Rehōvōt ʿir,"* *RB* 90 (1983) 94–96.

17. See W. F. Albright, "A Colony of Cretan Mercenaries on the Coast of the Negeb," *JPOS* 1 (1920/21) 191.

northern Egypt, the Delta region, thus rounding out all major areas of Egypt. It is not necessary to change the order of Casluhim and Caphtor, and thus depart from the MT, as do Speiser (p. 68) and Westermann (1:497). Indeed, Amos 9:7 states that the Philistines came from Caphtor. Possibly Casluhim and Caphtorim were used interchangeably.[18] Or more likely, together Amos 9:7 and Gen. 10:14 support the likelihood that the Philistines came to Egypt by way of Crete.[19] *Caphtorim* must be connected either with Crete or with some other island in the Aegean Sea.

15 As we said earlier, *Canaan* is the second most productive ancestor in the Table of Nations. His firstborn is *Sidon,* a well-known Phoenician city on the Mediterranean coast, some twenty-eight miles south of Beirut. Throughout the 2nd millennium it was the leader of Phoenician cities. Not until the 11th century B.C. did it yield its hegemony to Tyre, twenty-five miles to the south. *Heth* is connected with the Hittites, who ruled over much of western Asia from Anatolia, with the zenith of their rule around 1450–1200 B.C. But they settled in Asia Minor as early as 2000 B.C. The Hittites are thus clearly grouped with the Canaanites and Phoenicians of Palestine and Syria.

16 The *Jebusites* appear among the pre-Israelite inhabitants of Palestine (Gen. 15:21; Exod. 3:8, 17; 13:5; etc.). At some point they inhabited Jerusalem until it was captured by David (2 Sam. 5:6–8). Interestingly, *Amorites* are classified as Hamites (for geographical reasons?).[20] Geographically the name designates the territory northwest of Babylonia. They are mentioned ("Amurru") as early as the 3rd millennium B.C. by Sargon of Akkad. Mari on the Euphrates was one of their capitals. Hebrew ancestry is connected with these peoples: "your father was an Amorite" (Ezek. 16:3, 45). The Amorites settled in Palestine in the 2nd millennium B.C. Mamre, of Abraham's day, is an Amorite (Gen. 14:3), and Shechem is called an Amorite city (Gen. 48:22). *Girgashites* are another component in the pre-Israelite population of Palestine. The name appears in the OT only in such lists (Gen. 15:21; Deut. 7:1; Josh. 3:10; 24:11). The Girgashites may be connected with NT Gadarenes/Gerasenes/Gergesenes (Matt. 8:28; Mark 5:1; Luke 8:26, 37), the inhabitants of a place where Jesus exorcised some demons out of a man (or two men, according to Matthew) into a herd of swine.

18. See D. I. Block, "Table of Nations," *ISBE,* 4:711.

19. See G. A. Rendsburg, "Gen 10:13–14: An Authentic Hebrew Tradition Concerning the Origin of the Philistines," *JNWSL* 13 (1987) 89–96.

20. See J. Van Seters, "The Terms 'Amorite' and 'Hittite'," *VT* 22 (1972) 64–81, who views the use of these two terms in Genesis as rhetorical and ideological rather than historical.

17 *Hivites* may be an alternative spelling for Horites, who in turn may be related to the Hurrians, an important people in the upper Mesopotamian region in the 2nd millennium B.C.[21] Mitanni is the kingdom of the Hurrians, and it is located in Subartu, a geographical name designating Mesopotamia north of Akkad. They entered (from Armenia?) Mesopotamia in the 22nd century B.C. and Palestine in the 17th century B.C.

Arkites and *Sinites* appear only here and in 1 Chr. 1:15–16. The Arkites may be connected with the place name Arqat/Irqata in the Amarna Letters (62:13, ^{al}*ir-qat*^{ki}; 140:10, ^{māt}*ir-qa-ta*), a town in Phoenician territory, approximately 11 miles north of modern Tripoli, Lebanon. The current name of the site is Tell ʿArqah.[22] The Sintes are another northern Canaanite people, and their home of origin may be identified with the northern Phoenician city-state of Siyan(n)u. They were seldom self-governing, being controlled in turn by Ugarit, the Hittites, and the Assyrians.[23]

18 The *Arvadites* are the inhabitants of Arvad, a city in Phoenicia, and are associated with Tyre (Ezek. 27:8, 11). Arvad is about ninety-five miles north of Beirut. Like Tyre, it was an island city, situated about two miles off the coast. The *Zemarites* are unknown, but a city south of Arvad is reflected in Akk. *ṣimirra* and Amarna *ṣumur.* The *Hamathites* are the inhabitants of the city of Hamath, which is approximately one hundred and thirty miles north of Damascus and inland on the Orontes River. It was administered in succession by Egyptians, Hittites, and Assyrians. The "entrance to Hamath" (Num. 13:21; 1 K. 8:65; etc.) is the northern boundary of Canaan and Israel in the OT.[24]

19 The boundaries of Canaan stretch from Sidon in the north to Gerar in the south, and over to various cities in the southern end of the Dead Sea area, all of which are near the mysterious *Lasha.* We note that only the two individuals who sired the most offspring are provided with a sketch of their geographical horizons: Canaan (10:19) and the Joktanites (10:30).

20 The concluding note about the Hamites is much like that of the Japhethites, except that the sequence "lands . . . languages . . . clans" for the Japhethites is reversed here ("clans . . . languages . . . lands"), and in the parallel colophon for the Shemites too (v. 31). Thus the progression of terms

21. See R. North, "Hivites," *Bib* 54 (1973) 43–62. North notes (p. 62) that Hurrians and Hittites of the Bible are in one sense not identical, but in another sense they are. He suggests the plausibility of migration and intermarriage to account for this ambiguity.

22. See W. S. LaSor, "Arkite," *ISBE,* 1:294.

23. See J. M. Wiebe, "Sinite," *ISBE,* 4:529.

24. See H. F. Vos, "Hamath," *ISBE,* 2:602–3.

for the Japhethite colophon is (1) geographical; (2) linguistic; (3) ethnopolitical. In the colophon for the Hamites (and Shemites) the progression is (1) ethnopolitical; (2) linguistic; (3) geographical. I am not able to discern any special significance of this chiastic *(abc:cba)* arrangement.

3. THE SHEMITES (10:21–32)

21 *And to Shem also, the ancestor of all of Eber's sons and Japheth's older brother, sons were born.*

22 *Shem's sons: Elam, Asshur, Arpachshad, Lud, and Aram.*

23 *Aram's sons: Uz, Hul, Gether, and Mash.*

24 *Arpachshad fathered Shelah, and Shelah fathered Eber.*

25 *Two sons were born to Eber: The name of the first was Peleg, because in his time the earth was divided; his brother's name was Joktan.*

26 *Joktan fathered Almodad, Sheleph, Hazarmaveth, Jerah,*

27 *Hadoram, Uzal, Diklah,*

28 *Obal, Abimael, Sheba,*

29 *Ophir, Havilah, and Jobab. All these are Joktan's sons.*

30 *Their settlements stretched from Mesha all the way to Sephar, the eastern hill country.*

31 *These are Shem's sons by their clans, their languages, their lands, their nations.*

32 *These are the clans of Noah's sons, according to their origins, by their nations. From these branched out nations throughout the earth after the flood.*

21 The Shemites are the last in this table because they are the most crucial, the line from which Abraham will emerge. Thus, their placement is for climactic effect. Also, within the line of Shemites, Eber seems to be significant, for he is three generations removed from Shem, and yet his name appears in the introductory formula. So, it is not just Shemites that are pivotal, but the Eberites in particular.

A word has apparently fallen out of the text. The beginning of the verse reads, "And to Shem was born also. . . ." I have supplied *sons* in my translation for sense. Shem is further cited as *Japheth's older brother.* This brief notation serves to remind the reader of Shem's firstborn status, in spite of the final position of the Shemite line in this Table of Nations. He is not last because he is youngest. Ham is said to be the youngest of Noah's sons (9:24), although he is always mentioned second among the three (5:32; 6:10; 7:13; 9:18; 10:1; 1 Chr. 1:4).

22 *Elam* is the most eastern country named in this chapter. It lay to the east and northeast of the Euphrates and of Mesopotamia. The Elamites are mentioned as early as the time of Sargon of Akkad. That the language of the Elamites was patently not Semitic would indicate that the listing of Elam under Shem is because of geographical proximity. Along with other cities, *Asshur* served as the capital of Assyria (northern Mesopotamia). Its territory was along the upper Tigris River.

Arpachshad has defied both identification and etymology. Do the last three letters in Hebrew, *-kšd,* have anything to do with the Kasdim, that is, the Chaldeans? Josephus (*Ant.* 1.6.4) says that from Arpachshad the Chaldeans were called "Arphaxadaeans." A more likely connection is with the Arrapḫu of cuneiform inscriptions, perhaps to be identified with Kirkuk. The apocryphal book of Judith begins (1:1) by referring to an Arphaxad who was ruling over the Medes from Ecbatana. Yet, no king of Persia or of the Medes is known by this name. For *Lud* refer back to our comments on Ludim in v. 13. *Aram* is the ancestor of the Arameans (Syrians). Their territory, in the OT, covers the area from beyond the Jordan and northeast of Palestine into the Tigris-Euphrates Valley.

23 *Uz* is to be placed somewhere in northwest Mesopotamia (cf. 22:21 and Josephus *Ant.* 1.6.4), rather than near Edom (as might be suggested by passages like Gen. 36:28; Jer. 25:20–21; and Lam. 4:21, which clearly point to an Uz near Edom in the Arabian desert). *Hul, Gether,* and *Mash* are probably Aramean cities. If Mash is the same as Akk. *Māšu,* then it refers to Lebanon. It is also possible that Mash may be identified with a mountain, perhaps the Mt. Masius of classical writers (Strabo *Geog.* 11.14.2) on the northern boundary of Mesopotamia.

24 *Shelah* is thus far unidentified. Later in the OT (Gen. 46:12; Num. 26:20; 1 Chr. 2:3) Shelah is enumerated among the clans of Judah. One of the Shelah families, according to 1 Chr. 4:21–23, ruled in Moab.

Eber is the ancestor of the Hebrews. The discovery of the proper name *Ebrum* at Ebla (he was king of Ebla ca. 2300 B.C.) shows that Eber was a bona fide Semitic name in existence as early as the second half of the 3rd millennium B.C. This is not, of course, to equate Gen. 10's Eber with the Ebla Ebrum.[1]

25 Eber's two sons are *Peleg* and *Joktan.* Additional information is provided about Peleg: *in his time the earth was divided.* Here obviously is

1. See G. Pettinato, "The Royal Archives of Tell-Mardikh-Ebla," *BA* 39 (1976) 47: "Ebrum, whose resemblance to Eber, the eponymous ancestor of the Hebrews (Gen. 10:21) is striking."

but a torso of a much more extensive tradition. Does this comment mean that the Semitic groups were divided into two branches, Pelegites and Joktanites? Or, in the light of the fact that Akk. *palgu* means "canal" or "district," does this information point to a culture hero to whom was attributed the construction of irrigation canals?[2] Or, more likely, does this datum presage the Tower of Babel story in which men were driven away, divided from each other, and forced to settle elsewhere?

26–29 Joktan's sons number thirteen. Joktan means "the younger son." The names of his sons point to Arabian groups.[3] *Almodad,* if read as in the LXX "Elmodad," means "God is a friend." He is an ancestor of one of the South Arabian peoples, possibly the tribe of Al-Murad (exchange of *r* for *d*). *Sheleph* is the same as the Arabian Salaf or Salif, and occurs in Sabean inscriptions as the name of a Yemenite district. *Hazarmaveth* is the ancestor of a people settled in the Wadi Hadramaut in South Arabia, and whose capital was at Shabwa. *Jerah* might be related to a people close to Hazarmaveth. *Hadoram* might be located in Yemen. According to Arabic tradition, *Uzal* (or Auzal) was the original name of Sanaa, the capital of Yemen, but an earlier name for Sanaa was Tafidh. Uzal could be a town in the neighborhood of Medina, named Azalla, a city invaded by Ashurbanipal of Assyria in his campaign in Arabia. *Diklah,* because of its meaning "date-palm grove," may have been an oasis rich in palms. *Obal* is ancestor of another Arabian group that cannot be positively identified. There is an Ubal located between Hadeida and Sanaa, the capital of Yemen. *Abimael* is unidentifiable. *Sheba* may refer to the Sabeans, a Semitic people who dwelt in the southwest corner of the Arabian Peninsula. However, Sheba's appearance here may also indicate northern or northeastern peoples, especially since Gen. 25:3 lists Sheba as a descendant of Jokshan, the son of Abraham by Keturah, making Israel and Sheba closely related. *Ophir* was a region noted for its production of fine gold (1 Chr. 29:4; 2 Chr. 8:18; Job

2. Manetho, the Egyptian historian, wrote concerning a Pharaoh of the 2nd Dynasty: "Boêthos (reigned) for thirty-eight years. In his reign a chasm opened at Bubastis. Many perished." See J. M. Sasson, "A Genealogic 'Convention' in Biblical Chronography?" *ZAW* 90 (1978) 176 n. 14.

3. "Abimael" may be compared with Abiel, "my father is El," in 1 Sam. 9:1. The *"-ma-"* in Abimael may be taken as the enclitic particle interposed between subject and predicate: "my father indeed is El." See M. J. Dahood, "Eblaite and Biblical Hebrew," *CBQ* 44 (1982) 15. "Jobab" is comparable to names like Joab, "Yo [an abbreviation for Yahweh] is father," and Joel, "Yo is El." The meaning of Jobab would be, "Yo is the gate." See M. J. Dahood, "The God Ya at Ebla?" *JBL* 100 (1981) 607.

22:24; 28:16; Ps. 45:10 [Eng. 9]). Solomon's ships sailed from there with precious cargo (1 K. 9:28), a feat later attempted by Jehoshaphat (1 K. 22:49 [Eng. 48]). Ophir has variously been located in India, Arabia, and Africa. Context suggests a location somewhere in the Arabian Peninsula, but no site can be argued for persuasively. *Havilah* has already been mentioned in 2:11–12, but that Havilah need not be equated with this Havilah. The Ishmaelites are located in the territory from Havilah to Shur (25:18). The most widely accepted location for Havilah is on the west coast of Arabia, north of Yemen. *Jobab* may be connected with the town of Juhaibab, which is located in the vicinity of Mecca.

30 Their territory stretches from *Mesha,* in the northern part of Arabia, to *Sephar* (?). The latter may be an actual place, but unidentifiable, or simply a general term meaning "border country."

31 The colophon concludes this subsection of Noahites, as do vv. 5, 20. None of these verses is exactly the same; either the sequence of nouns or the prepositions that are prefixed to these nouns differ. Vv. 20 and 31 are the closest to each other. Here is the respective sequence with the preposition which is prefixed to each:

v. 5: lands *(b);* language *(l);* clans *(l);* nations *(b)*
v. 20: clans *(l);* language *(l);* lands *(b);* nations *(b)*
v. 31: clans *(l);* language *(l);* lands *(b);* nations *(l)*

32 The Table of Nations is brought to an end with this verse, which summarizes the entire list of entries. Geographically the list has gone as far east as Persia (Elam), as far south as Ethiopia (Cush) and the Arabian peninsula, as far north as Anatolia (Gomer, Madai), and as far west as Crete (Kittim, Caphtorim) and Libya. It is not without interest that such a table of nations is unique to OT literature. Neither the hieroglyphic nor the cuneiform worlds produced a parallel document. The theological value of the Table is that it affirms Israel as part of one world governed by one God. In this world he has chosen Israel to be his own, and to carry the knowledge of him throughout that world. Yet, Gen. 10 emphasizes Israel's commonality with the other nations more than it does its uniqueness. What the chapter affirms is that all of humanity, in spite of geographical and linguistic differences, share a common origin. And in this common origin is to be found humanity's nobility and inherent value. One wonders if Gen. 10 was not in the thinking of Paul when he asserts that God has "made from one every nation of men to live on all the face of the earth, having determined allotted periods and the boundaries of their habitation" (Acts 17:26).

The positioning of Gen. 10 is interesting. Should it not follow Gen. 11, where a story is told explaining why humanity was dispersed? In other words, we have here the unusual order of effect (ch. 10) before cause (ch. 11), or result preceding explanation.

Of the possible explanations for this striking reversal of expected sequence, the least fruitful approach would be to see here only another instance of a doublet. This scheme attributes ch. 10 (most of it) to P, whose reasons for the dispersal of mankind are in a context of peace and blessing. 11:1–9 is then traced to J, and here we are provided with a totally different explanation for humanity's dispersal: they are scattered over the face of the earth both because of their own pride and disobedience and because of God's judgment. But even if this explanation is valid, it still leaves unexplained the significance of the sequence. Why did the redactors place P's account of the dispersal ahead of J's rather than vice versa?

A more promising explanation for such dischronologization focuses on the themes of grace and judgment in Gen. 1–11. If Gen. 10 had followed 11:1–9, then obviously the Table of Nations could be interpreted only negatively. The Noahites, filled to the brim with ego, were forcibly scattered throughout the earth. The significance of its present position, however, is that the Table fills out and fulfills the divine promise and imperative in 9:1, "be abundantly fruitful."[4] Thus the dispersal of humanity throughout the world reflects both God's blessing (ch. 10) and his displeasure (ch. 11), just as the dispersal of one person earlier—Cain—pointed to both God's wrath and God's mercy.

An alternative suggestion for the juxtaposition might begin, perhaps, with Gunkel's observation that, as he saw it, the Flood story (chs. 6–9) and the Tower story (11:1–9) form a composite narrative in which two similar but originally different tales converged.[5] The point of similarity in each is that some monstrous behavior by mankind provoked the deity to make drastic reprisals.

By placing the Tower of Babel incident just prior to the patriarchal stories, the biblical writer is suggesting, in the first place, that post-Flood humanity is as iniquitous as pre-Flood humanity. Rather than sending something as devastating as a flood to annihilate mankind, however, God now places his hope in a covenant with Abraham as a powerful solution to

4. See D. J. A. Clines, "Themes in Genesis 1–11," *CBQ* 38 (1976) 494.

5. H. Gunkel, *Genesis,* 3rd ed. (Göttingen: Vandenhoeck, 1910; repr. 1964), pp. 92–97.

humanity's sinfulness. Thus problem (ch. 11) and solution (ch. 12) are brought into immediate juxtaposition, and the forcefulness of this structural move would have been lost had ch. 10 intervened between the two.[6]

THE NEW TESTAMENT APPROPRIATION

Gen. 10 and Luke 10:1

Luke is the only Gospel writer to mention a special sending out of seventy (-two) disciples by Jesus (Luke 10:1). The number of disciples is uncertain; the manuscript evidence is divided between reading "seventy" and "seventy-two."[1] The MT numbers seventy nations, but the LXX has seventy-two nations (is Luke following LXX?).

The significance of the number has been traced to the number of the Sanhedrin or to the number of elders in Israel (Exod. 24:1), but the most likely explanation is that Jesus is here reflecting Gen. 10 with its listing of the seventy nations of the then known world. Taken in this way, the number signifies that Jesus is sending his representatives into all the known nations of their day. The world he created he must also redeem.

6. See J. Sasson, "The 'Tower of Babel' As a Clue to the Redactional Structuring of the Primeval History [Gen. 1–11:9]," in *The Bible World: Essays in Honor of Cyrus H. Gordon,* ed. by G. Rendsburg, et al. (New York: Ktav, 1980), pp. 218–19. Sasson also notes this structural correspondence:

a Sin of Cain (Gen. 4)	a′ Sin of Ham (Gen. 9:18–27)
b Genealogy (Gen. 4:17–5:32)	b′ Genealogy (Gen. 10)
c Sin of the sons of God (Gen. 6:1–4)	c′ Sin of the tower builders (Gen. 11:1–9)

1. See B. Metzger, "Seventy or Seventy-Two Disciples?" *NTS* 5 (1958/59) 299–306; I. H. Marshall, *The Gospel of Luke,* NIGTC (Grand Rapids: Eerdmans, 1978), pp. 414–15. RSV, AV, NEB mg., JB mg. read "70." NEB, JB, NIV, RSV mg. read "72." "70" is read by Sinaiticus, Alexandrinus, Ephraemi Rescriptus, Peshitta, and others. "72" is read by the Bodmer Papyrus xiv, xv ($\mathfrak{p}^{75}$), Vaticanus, Bezae Cantabrigiensis, and others. Marshall notes (p. 415), "The combination of Alexandrian, Western and Syriac evidence in favour of 72 is the stronger." Further, the less frequent use of 72 in the Bible argues for its authenticity here.

I. SHINARITES AND SHEMITES (11:1–32)

1. TOWER BUILDERS AT BABEL (11:1–9)

1 *The entire land had one language and one speech.*[1]

2 *As they migrated from the east, they chanced upon a plain in the land of Shinar, and settled there.*

3 *They said to one another, "Come, let us mold*[2] *bricks and harden them with fire." They had brick for stone and bitumen for mortar.*

4 *They said, "Come, let us build for ourselves a city, and a tower, with its peak in the heavens, and thus make a reputation for ourselves; otherwise, we shall be dispersed all over the world."*

5 *Yahweh came down*[3] *to inspect the city and the tower that the men had built.*

6 *Yahweh said: "If they, being one people with one language for all of them, and this is but the start of their doings, henceforth*[4] *nothing which they presume to do will be impossible for them.*

7 *Come, let us go down and confuse their language so that each will not understand the language of his neighbor."*

8 *Thus Yahweh dispersed them from there over all the land, and they stopped*[5] *building the city.*

9 *Accordingly it was called*[6] *Babel, because there Yahweh confused the language of the entire world, and from there Yahweh dispersed them over all the land.*

1. The Heb. *d^{e}ḇārîm '^{a}ḥāḏîm* provides us with one of the five instances in the OT of the masc. pl. of the numeral "one" (see Gen. 27:44; 29:20; Ezek. 37:17; Dan. 11:20).

2. On the Canaanite parallelism of *lbn lbnt,* "to make bricks," and *bny,* "to build," as in Gen. 11:3–4, cf. M. J. Dahood, in *Ras Shamra Parallels,* ed. L. R. Fisher, AnOr 49 (Rome: Biblical Institute Press, 1972), 1:II:325 (p. 246).

3. In an Ugaritic text (*UT,* Krt 77–78) the king is commanded by El, the chief god: *šrd bʿl bdbḥk,* "make Baal come down by your sacrifice."

4. See H. A. Brongers, "Bemerkungen zum Gebrauch des adverbialen *w^{e}ʿattāh* im alten Testament," *VT* 15 (1965) 282; he renders the Hebrew with *hinfort.*

5. D. W. Thomas ("Some Observations on the Hebrew Root *ḥdl,*" *Volume du Congrès: Strasbourg, 1956,* VTSup 4 [Leiden: Brill, 1957], pp. 8–16) suggests, on the basis of both Arabic cognates and Targ.'s frequent rendering of *ḥāḏal* by the Hithpael of *mny,* that the best meaning of *ḥāḏal* is "to hold oneself back, refrain from." Thomas limits the translation "cease" to only 8 OT passages, and Gen. 11:8 is not one of them.

6. For the expression of the indefinite personal subject by the 3rd masc. sing. verb form, see GKC, § 144d.

It is a distinguishing feature of these opening chapters of Genesis to bracket narrative blocks by genealogical citations. There are three instances of this structure:

(1) (a) 5:32 genealogy (Noah's sons)
(b) 6:1–8 narrative (the sons of God)
(a′) 6:9–10 genealogy (Noah's sons)

(2) (a) 6:9–10 genealogy (Noah's sons)
(b) 6:11–9:17 narrative (the Flood)
(a′) 9:18–19 genealogy (Noah's sons)

(3) (a) 10:21–31 genealogy (Shemites)
(b) 11:1–9 narrative (Tower of Babel)
(a′) 11:10–32 genealogy (Shemites)

(This literary artistry provides another reason for the order of chs. 10 and 11.)

1 This chapter opens with the assertion that the *entire world had one language and one speech.* How are we to square this information with Gen. 10, which tells us, not once but three times, that mankind already possessed multiple languages (vv. 5, 20, 31, "their languages")? We have suggested an answer to this question in our discussion of ch. 10—we are dealing here with a case of deliberate dischronologization.

One can make sense of the biblical material in another way, however. Students of ancient and modern languages are well acquainted with the phenomenon of a lingua franca, a medium of communication among representatives of different speech groups. At various times in antiquity, Sumerian, Babylonian, Aramaic, and Greek each served in this capacity. In our own day the English language is taking on more and more the flavor of an international language. Thus Gen. 10 and 11 would make linguistic sense in their current sequence. In addition to the local languages *(lᵉšōnôṯ)* of each nation (ch. 10), there existed "one language" (*śāpâ 'eḥāṯ,* ch. 11) which made communication possible throughout the world (ch. 10).[7]

7. C. H. Gordon has led the way in this interpretation. See *Before Columbus: Links Between the Old World and Ancient America* (New York: Crown, 1971), pp. 107, 165–66; idem, "The Ebla Tablets and the World of the Bible," *HS* 22 (1981) 39–47; idem, "Ebla and Genesis 11," in *A Spectrum of Thought,* Fest. Dennis F. Kinlaw, ed. Michael L. Peterson (Wilmore, KY: Francis Asbury, 1982), pp. 125–34. Gordon's latest word on the issue is found in his article "Ebla as background for the Old Testament," *Congress Volume: Jerusalem, 1986,* VTSup 40 (Leiden: Brill, 1988), p. 295: "When we read in Gen. XI 1 that all the Earth had one language *(śāpâ 'eḥāt)* after the Flood, the meaning is that while the component ethnic elements of the International Order had their speech for family and ethnic communication, there was

The phrase *one speech* is not just a repetition of *one language*. The two phrases are related but not interchangeable. This age possessed a common language ("one language") with a conventional vocabulary ("one speech").[8] The Tower narrative has a symmetry: it begins and ends with a reference to a universal language *(śāp̱â),* once flourishing but now destroyed (vv. 1, 9).

2 Similarly, the emphasis in this verse on permanent settlement *(yāšaḇ)* is balanced by the "dispersed" (*pûṣ* of v. 8). What the tower builders wanted—a tower and a name—they lost or never obtained. What they wanted to avoid—a nonsedentary life-style—was imposed on them. Interestingly, this whole chapter begins and ends (vv. 2, 31) with attention on a group of people who moved from place *x* to place *y* and settled in the latter place. In fact, both verses use the same form of the verb *yāšaḇ: wayyēšeḇû* (translated "settled" in this commentary). But there is quite a difference between the tower settlers and the Terahite settlers. With the first group, and their insistence on their selfishly conceived project, God is most displeased; but to the second group God promises great blessing.

The text supplies no subject for the three third person plural verbs in this verse—*they migrated, chanced upon, settled.* The same goes for the third and first person plural verbs of vv. 3–4. While the *kol-hā'āreṣ* of v. 1 might possibly extend into vv. 2ff. as the subject of the verb (though notice the sing. *wayehî* with which v. 1 begins), it is more likely that "the men" of v. 5 *(benê hā'āḏām)* provides the subject for these verbs. But the general expression "the men" prohibits one from identifying these wanderers with any precision.

Shinar is the place of settlement. Shinar undoubtedly represents the land of Mesopotamia, a territory that was first called Sumer, then Sumer and Akkad, and then Babylonia. Why "Sumer" should appear as "Shinar" is not clear.[9]

---

an international lingua franca that made communication possible so that great projects like the Tower of Babel could be constructed. God broke up the arrogant Order in Babylonia (Šinʿar < Šumer) by confounding the lingua franca. International projects require mutual understanding. . . . Gen. XI reflects the break-up of the old Order as following the end of Babylonian as the lingua franca." Cf. also M. Rottenberg, "The Words *'eḥāḏ* and *'aḥaṯ* as Pronouns of Identity," *Leš* 46 (1981/82) 141–42 (Hebrew). For an explicit identification of this one language as Sumerian, and the possible linkage of the scattering motif to the eclipse of the Ur III period, see D. S. DeWitt, "The Historical Background of Genesis 11:1–9: Babel or Ur?" *JETS* 22 (1979) 15–26.

8. See C. H. Gordon, "Hebrew 'ḤDYM = ILTÊNÛTU Pair," in *Sepher Segal,* ed. J. M. Grintz and J. Liver (Jerusalem: Israel Society for Biblical Research, 1965), pp. 5–9. See also *UT,* p. 43, § 7.8.

9. One suggestion is that Heb. *šinʿar* is taken from Sumerian, and represents *šingi-uri,* a variant form of the better-known *Kengi-Uri,* "Sumer and Akkad," which the Sumerians used to express the idea of Babylonia as a whole. See A. Poebel, "The

Events in Gen. 1–11 have consistently been identified with *the east.* The garden of Eden is in the east (2:8). The cherubim are posted on the east side of the garden to prohibit entrance to the garden (3:24). Cain's home-away-from-home is in Nod, east of Eden (4:16). Shem's descendants, appropriately, occupy the hill country of the east (10:30). And here, an unidentified group march to Shinar from the east.

3–4 These verses present the human deeds, which are to be contrasted with the divine deeds (vv. 6–9). In both cases a speech of intention precedes the implementation of the content of their speech. Just as the human speech is set off by the interjection *hāḇâ,* followed by the cohortative ("Come, let us mold bricks"; "Come, let us build"), so a feature of the divine speech is also the use of *hāḇâ,* followed by the cohortative ("Come, let us go down").[10] Both speeches are also conversational: "They said to one another"; "Come, let us go down."

3 This verse demonstrates three arresting features. One is the use of a cognate accusative. The expression we have translated *let us mold bricks* reads literally "let us brick bricks" *(nilbᵉnâ lᵉḇēnîm).* Another is the use of homonymy. Thus "bitumen for mortar" reads in Hebrew *ḥēmār . . . lāḥōmer.* The third is the chiastic structure of part of the verse: *wattᵉhî lāhem hallᵉḇēnâ lᵉʾāḇen wᵉhaḥēmar hāyâ lāhem lāḥōmer,* literally, "and was for them brick for stone, and bitumen was for them for mortar" (verb, indirect object, subject, prepositional phrase::subject, verb, indirect object, prepositional phrase).

4 The human project includes building a city and a tower that is the equivalent of a modern skyscraper.[11] This is the second reference to city

---

Name of Elam in Sumerian, Akkadian, and Hebrew," *AJSL* 48 (1931/32) 26. The consensus among scholars now is that there is no clear Sumerian or Akkadian equivalent for Heb. *šinʿār.* See W. S. LaSor, "Shinar," *ISBE,* 4:481; R. Zadok, "The Origin of the name Shinar," *ZA* 74 (1984) 240–44.

10. The use of *hāḇâ* followed by the cohortative appears again in the OT only in Exod. 1:10.

11. It cannot be gainsaid that the inspiration for this story is the Mesopotamian ziqqurat (or ziggurat), a temple tower (from Akk. *zaqāru,* "to raise up, elevate"). Toward the end of the last century, the discovery of Esagila, the great temple of Marduk in Babylon, suggested this particular edifice as the source behind the biblical narrative. The ziqqurat of this temple was called *E-temen-an-ki,* "house of the foundations of heaven and earth." Rising three hundred feet above ground, with two sanctuaries in it, it was believed to have been built by the gods. This background makes the assertion of 11:5 very interesting: it was built by earthlings. See further E. A. Speiser, "Word Plays on the Creation Epic's Version of the Founding of Babylon," in *Oriental and Biblical Studies,* ed. J. J. Finkelstein and M. Greenberg (Philadelphia: University of Pennsylvania, 1967), pp. 53–61.

building, the first being 4:17. The word for *tower* is *migdāl,* which is related to the word "great" *(gāḏôl),* thus suggesting the Olympian nature of the building project. *migdāl* normally refers to a fortified tower or acropolis (Judg. 8:9, 17; 9:46–52; Ps. 48:13 [Eng. 12]; 61:4 [Eng. 3]; Ezek. 26:9). In Isaiah especially *migdāl* is a symbol of strength and pride (Isa. 2:15; 30:25; 33:18), and thus what it represents is abhorred by God (Isa. 25:2–3). The impression created is that these builders are megalomaniacs.

This impression is strengthened by the fact that the aspiration is to build a tower *with its peak in the heavens.* Had the writer wanted to say simply that the plan was to build a high tower he had at his disposal a number of words that would easily have conveyed that idea. Yet it is clear from other OT passages that the expression "with its peak in the heavens" is figurative language to describe edifices of impressive and monumental proportions. Thus the returning spies reported to Moses that the cities of the Canaanites "are great and fortified up to heaven" (Deut. 1:28). Even God describes the cities Israel is to dispossess as "cities great and fortified up to heaven" (Deut. 9:1). The oracle of Jeremiah against Babylon includes a passage strikingly similar to that in Gen. 11—"Though Babylon should mount up to heaven, and though she should fortify her strong height, yet destroyers would come from me upon her, says the Lord" (Jer. 51:53).

The text does not say expressly how the erection of such an edifice would guarantee that they would make a name for themselves. If we take "name" to signify *reputation,* as our translation reflects, then the connection would be that the completion of such a titanic building would bring a certain fame and immortality to its builders.[12]

The builders also thought that the existence of such a fortified city would be the guarantee of their security. With such a fortress they would be less vulnerable. A plain (v. 2) offers the least amount of protection in time of crisis. Thus settled in, the builders would no longer be scattered over the face of the earth. This hoped-for result flies directly in the face of the divine commandment to multiply and fill the earth.

12. There may be a play on words here through the use of alliteration; note the *š-m* in *šēm,* "name," *šāmayim,* "heaven," and even the adverb *šām,* "there," in vv. 1, 7, 9. Westermann (*Genesis,* 1:548) quotes from an article by P. J. Calderone, "Dynastic Oracle and Suzerainty Treaty. 2 Samuel 7, 8–16," *Logos* 1 (1966) 1–80: "with [the verb] *ʿśh* it [*šem*] is confined to the king (2 Sam 7:9; 8:13), to Yahweh working wonders in Egypt (Jer 32:20; Isa 63:12, 14; Dan 9:15; Neh 9:10 . . . and to the builders of the tower of Babel (Gen 11:4) who in some way are rebelling against God and trying to be like Him" (p. 45). Note the comparison made in Sir. 40:19, "children and the building of a city make a man's reputation; better than either, the discovery of wisdom."

5 It is difficult to miss the irony in this verse. The builders' intention is to erect a tower whose top will be "in the heavens," that is, among the gods. But even though they build the tower, it is so far from the heavens that God must *come down* to see it.[13]

Verse 5 functions structurally as a bridge joining vv. 1–4 and vv. 6–9. It is in effect the midpoint of the story, as the emphasis shifts from the human act to the divine act. Kikawada has suggested that 11:1–9 is told as three episodes. Episode one (vv. 1–4) consists of two paragraphs (vv. 1–2, 3–4), the first of which is indirect discourse, and the second of which is direct discourse. Episode three (vv. 6–9) also consists of two paragraphs (vv. 6–7, 8–9), except that here the first paragraph is predominantly direct discourse, while the second one is indirect discourse. Sandwiched between these two episodes is the second episode, and it is confined to this one verse. Thus it is a thin wedge between two larger halves.[14]

In this verse the builders are styled as *b^e^nê hā'ādām* (lit., "sons of Adam," or "sons of the man"), which we have translated simply *the men.* Earlier they had been referred to individually as *'îš* (lit., "man," v. 3). The shift here to a term beginning with *b-* allows for alliteration with the verb *bānû.* Also, the shift reduces these pretentious human beings to their real size. They are but mere earthlings.

6 We suggested in our exposition of v. 5 that it is ironical that God must come down to bring into focus, so to speak, what was supposed to be a building invading celestial heights. But v. 6 indicates that we need not press that irony too far. God does not scoff at the building and consider it much ado about nothing. There is no suggestion that he views it as a joke. He does not laugh at them or ridicule them. Rather, he takes the scheme quite seriously. In fact, if something is not done to abort the project, the consequences can be far-reaching. It is God's judgment that any other scheme the human mind could entertain would pale into insignificance by comparison with this enterprise. His concern is also that such a hubris-motivated scheme will become a precedent and stimulation for other schemes.

Two verbs in the latter part of this verse call for special attention, if for no other reason than that they are uncommon words. The first is *bāṣar,*

13. See Cassuto, *Genesis,* 2:224.

14. See I. M. Kikawada, "The Shape of Genesis 11:1–9," in *Rhetorical Criticism: Essays in Honor of James Muilenburg,* ed. J. J. Jackson and M. Kessler, PTMS 1 (Pittsburgh: Pickwick, 1974), pp. 18–32. Kikawada suggests (p. 27) that "the basic shape of this story is that of an hourglass. Episodes 1 and 3 form the two glass bulbs which are connected by the narrow passage, Ep 2."

rendered above as *be impossible,* and the second is *zāmam, they presume.* The former is in the Niphal *(yibbāṣēr),* which occurs elsewhere only in Job 42:2. Both times the verb is followed by the preposition *min* plus pronominal suffix *(mēhem, mimm*ᵉ*ḵā).* The second word, *zāmam,* has as its basic meaning "consider, purpose, devise." The verb does not occur in Job 42:2, but the related noun *m*ᵉ*zimmâ* ("purpose, discretion, device") does. These are the only two verses in the OT in which both *bṣr* and *zmm* occur. Both verses make a similar point, but from different directions. Job states, "I know that . . . no purpose [*m*ᵉ*zimmâ*] of thine can be thwarted [*bāṣar*]." Nothing or nobody can restrain or thwart the workings of God. In Gen. 11:6 Yahweh states that nothing will be able to restrain or thwart the workings of man unless this initial building project, a threat to the divine will and rule, is halted. As in Gen. 3, mankind is trying to overstep his limits, and in fact does so, only to pay a price for that self-exaltation. This proposed or potential action must be thwarted, here as it was in Gen. 3.[15]

7 To that end God comes down not to inspect the scenario, as in v. 5, but to thwart it. His method is perhaps surprising: he will *confuse their language.*[16] Why not simply topple the tower? Because that would solve the problem only temporarily. Towers are replaceable. Even if the people did not build another tower, they could choose another equally presumptuous project. The solution must go deeper than that. It is not the tower that must be done away with, but what makes possible the building of that tower—an international language that provides communication among linguistic groups. If this ability to communicate is removed, it is unlikely that the individuals will continue with their work.

We also note that here there may be a "sound-chiasmus."[17] The order of the consonants in Heb. *nāḇ*ᵉ*lâ,* "let us confuse" (i.e., *n-b-l*), is the reverse of the consonants in *l*ᵉ*ḇēnîm,* "bricks" (v. 3) (i.e., *l-b-n*). Does the reversal of

15. H. L. Ginsberg ("Babel, Tower of," *EncJud,* 4:25–26) translates v. 6, "If this is what, as one people with one language common to all, they have been able to do as a beginning, nothing they propose to do will be beyond their reach." He connects this note of divine anxiety with that sounded in Gen. 3:22. Just as the Lord set up a barrier of enmity between human beings and the snake to eliminate the danger of further baleful results from cooperation between humanity and snake, here he eliminates the threat of disastrous consequences from the cooperation of men with each other by erecting among them barriers of language and distance.

16. The verb for "confuse" *(bālal)* seems to be a technical term in cookery meaning to mix or mingle different elements in preparing some dish (Lev. 2:5; 7:10; 9:4; 14:10, 21, and many other times in Leviticus and Numbers).

17. See J. P. Fokkelman, *Narrative Art in Genesis* (Assen: Van Gorcum, 1975), p. 15.

sounds suggest a reversal by God of the human machinations? Will he unbrick what they brick? Will the wrecking crew undo what the building crew has accomplished?

8 The text does not refer explicitly to Yahweh's confusing the language. We have a statement of intention (v. 7) and a statement of accomplished fact (v. 9), in which the name is followed by the supplied etymology. One could move directly from v. 7 to v. 9: "and let us confuse their language .... Babel, because there Yahweh confused their language."

But between the word of intention and the word of accomplishment is the note about the builders being scattered. This note is not superfluous. Not content to confuse their language, Yahweh must disperse them too. The sin of these tower builders is undoubtedly the sin of pride and pretentious humanism.[18] This tower is vastly different from Jacob's ladder (28:12), the top of which also reached to heaven. In the former the initiative is with man. In the latter the initiative is with God. And, of course, Jacob's ladder reaching to heaven *(weᵉrōʾšô maggîaʿ haššāmāyᵉmâ)* is but a dream, whereas this city with a tower whose peak is in the heavens *(weᵉrōʾšô ḇaššāmayim)* is a reality, an enterprise undertaken by mankind.

The fact that God scatters the builders suggests that more than egoism is involved. Here we see the divine will agitated not only by earthlings who would essay to become deity, but also by a resistant humanity that "prefers the settled security of homogeneity and centralization."[19] The story is an example of "man's futile attempt to gain security apart from God through city-building."[20] Whereas earlier verses in the narrative mentioned both the city and the tower (vv. 4, 5), the conclusion to v. 8 focuses only on the halting of the building of the city. This indicates that it was the building of the city, and not the tower per se, that provoked the divine displeasure.

18. Looked at in this way, the sin at Babel is exactly the same as the first sin in the garden. The divine will and word is abandoned. One's own desire becomes most important, and doing my will takes precedence over doing God's will. Eve and the tower builders think alike. Cf. D. E. Gowan, *When Man Becomes God: Humanism and Hybris in the Old Testament,* PTMS 6 (Pittsburgh: Pickwick, 1975), pp. 25–29, who views 11:1–9 as a "subdued form" of a hubris passage.

19. See B. W. Anderson, "Babel: Unity and Diversity in God's Creation," *CurTM* 5 (1978) 69–81. Note that the scattering motif appears in various modulations throughout Gen. 9–11. In addition to its triple use in 11:4, 8, 9, it appears earlier—in a positive context—in 9:19 and 10:18.

20. F. S. Frick, *The City in Ancient Israel,* SBLDS 36 (Missoula, MT: Scholars, 1977), p. 208. P. D. Miller ("Eridu, Dunnu and Babel: A Study in Comparative Mythology," *Hebrew Annual Review* 9 [1985] 242) suggests the story should more properly be captioned "The City of Babel," not "The Tower of Babel."

9 We indicated above, in our discussion of v. 5, one of the ironic elements in the narrative. Here is another. The people wanted to make a name *(šēm)* for themselves, and, indeed, they did, but it is a name of shame. The city, once destined for greatness, now has its builders dispersed. The author connects Yahweh's confusing of the language *(bālal)* with his name for Babylon, *Babel (bāḇēl).* It is not clear whether the name Babel is given to this city by Yahweh, by the narrator, or by somebody else. Hence the verb must be understood with an indefinite subject—*it was called.*[21] It is most unlikely that the author intended his audience to understand the verb *bālal* to provide a literal etymology for his name for Babylon, *bāḇēl,* for one cannot explain the origin of the place name *bāḇēl* in the verb *bālal.* Hence this must be a popular, nonliteral etymology.

The oldest attested extrabiblical name for Babylon is *ká-dingir-ki* (usually written *ká-dingir-ra),* "gate of god."[22] This name is reflected in later Babylonian *bab-ili(m),* "gate of god(s)," a name that may itself be a popular etymology for the name of the city. In any case, there is a clear difference between the explanation of Babylon in cuneiform languages and Gen. 11:9, which connects the name with the verb *bālal,* "to confuse."

To this point in the episode (vv. 1–8) it is not stated how, or even that, Yahweh confused the language. V. 7 describes God's intention to do this; however, the following verses refer only to Yahweh's dispersal of the culprits over all the world. Thus, the reference to Yahweh's having confused the language in the etymological statement of v. 9 is descriptive of an act that is only implied in vv. 1–8.

Linguists still debate whether all languages are descended from a single original language (an *Ursprache*), that is, the theory of monogenesis, or whether languages emerged independently among several groups of early peoples, that is, the theory of polygenesis. Of course, our best control of linguistic change is by comparing written records (which only go back to ca. 3000 B.C.) of languages over long periods of times. A survey of such material will demonstrate how, as the result of a linguistic change over a long period, a group of distinct, though historically related, languages came into being. Such changes are slight but progressively cumulative. Eventually such minute changes take the form of dialectical differentiation, and eventually result in the emergence of distinct languages.

It is true that linguists speak of an original unitary language, such as

21. See B. O. Long, *The Problem of Etiological Narrative in the Old Testament,* BZAW 108 (Berlin: Töpelmann, 1968), pp. 23–25.

22. See D. J. Wiseman, "Babylon," *ISBE,* 1:385.

Proto-Germanic or Indo-European, from which subfamilies of language are constituted, but even if such a language actually existed, none of these unitary languages is necessarily the original language of humanity. All that the existence of such alleged proto-languages does is to help one reconstruct the prehistory of attested and living languages.

It is unlikely that Gen. 11:1–9 can contribute much, if anything, to the origin of languages. I have already suggested that the diversification of languages is a slow process, not something catastrophic as Gen. 11 might indicate. I have stated above my reasons for not interpreting the movement from v. 1 to v. 9 as that from a monoglot world to a polyglot world. Such an interpretation, common among commentators, leads to the conclusion that Gen. 11 provides a most incredible and naive explanation of language diversification. If, however, the narrative refers to the dissolution of a Babylonian lingua franca, or something like that, the need to see Gen. 11:1–9 as a highly imaginative explanation of language diffusion becomes unnecessary.[23]

This scenario has taken place in the land of Shinar. Here both the tower and the city are constructed. We recall from ch. 10 that the land of

23. A breakup of language in Sumer at some point is suggested by S. N. Kramer in "The Babel of Tongues: A Sumerian Version," *JAOS* 88 (1968) 108–11:

> Once upon a time there was no snake, there was no scorpion,
> There was no hyena, there was no lion,
> There was no wild(?) dog, no wolf,
> There was no fear, no terror;
> Man had no rival.
>
> In those days the lands Shubar and Hamazi,
> Harmony-tongued(?) Sumer, the great land of the decrees of princeship,
> Uri, the land having all that is appropriate,
> The land Martu, resting in security,
> The whole universe, the people in unison
> To Enlil in one tongue. . . .
> The Ada the Lord, Ada the prince, Ada the king,
> Enki, Ada the Lord, Ada the prince, Ada the king,
> Ada the Lord, Ada the prince, Ada the king,
> Enki, the Lord of abundance (whose) commands are trustworthy
> The Lord of wisdom who understands the land,
> The leader of the gods
> Endowed with wisdom the Lord of Eridu,
> Changed the speech in their mouths,
> And [brought?] contention into it,
> Into the speech of man that (until then) had been one.

Shinar is connected to Nimrod (10:9–10). Gen. 10 also informs us that Nimrod is the grandson of Ham (10:6–8). Thus in the two post-Flood scenes involving sin and disgrace (9:20ff. and 11:1–9), Ham is involved directly or indirectly. The Hamites of Shinar are indeed aping their ancestor.

2. GENEALOGY OF SHEMITES (11:10–32)

10 *These are the descendants of Shem. When Shem was one hundred years old he fathered Arpachshad, two years after the flood.*

11 *Shem lived five hundred years after he fathered Arpachshad. He fathered sons and daughters.*

12 *When Arpachshad was thirty-five years old he fathered Shelah.*

13 *Arpachshad lived four hundred and three years after he fathered Shelah. He fathered sons and daughters.*

14 *When Shelah was thirty years old he fathered Eber.*

15 *Shelah lived four hundred and three years after he fathered Eber. He fathered sons and daughters.*

16 *When Eber was thirty-four years old he fathered Peleg.*

17 *Eber lived four hundred and thirty years after he fathered Peleg. He fathered sons and daughters.*

18 *When Peleg was thirty years old he fathered Reu.*

19 *Peleg lived two hundred and nine years after he fathered Reu. He fathered sons and daughters.*

20 *When Reu was thirty-two years old he fathered Serug.*

21 *Reu lived two hundred and seven years after he fathered Serug. He fathered sons and daughters.*

22 *When Serug was thirty years old he fathered Nahor.*

23 *Serug lived two hundred years after he fathered Nahor. He fathered sons and daughters.*

24 *When Nahor was twenty-nine years old he fathered Terah.*

25 *Nahor lived one hundred and nineteen years after he fathered Terah. He fathered sons and daughters.*

26 *When Terah was seventy years old he fathered Abram, Nahor, and Haran.*

27 *These are the descendants of Terah. Terah fathered Abram, Nahor, and Haran; and Haran fathered Lot.*

28 *Haran died in the lifetime of Terah his father, in the land of his birth, in Ur of the Chaldeans.*

29 *Abram and Nahor took wives; the name of Abram's wife was Sarai, and the name of Nahor's wife was Milcah, the daughter of Haran, the father of Milcah and Iscah.*

30 *Sarai was barren; she had no child.*[1]

31 *Terah took Abram his son, his grandson Lot, son of Haran, and Sarai his daughter-in-law, the wife of Abram his son, and he went*[2] *with them from Ur of the Chaldeans to go to the land of Canaan. Upon reaching Haran they settled there.*

32 *The lifetime of Terah was two hundred and five years; then Terah died in Haran.*

10–26 The genealogy of Shem in 11:10ff. is very close to the genealogy of Shem in 10:21–31.

10:21–31

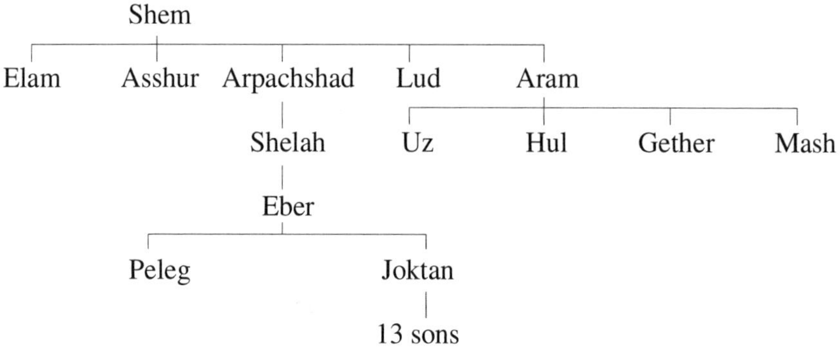

11:10ff.

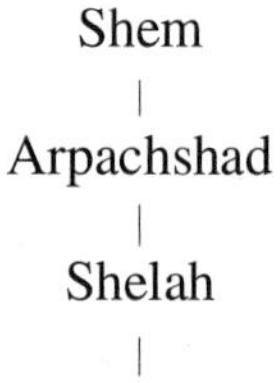

1. The form *wālāḏ* is unusual, and many scholars emend the text to eliminate the abnormal morphology. But the form may be understood as the conjunction *w^{e}-* plus the infinitive absolute of *yālaḏ* (*w^{e}yālōḏ* contracting and reducing to *wālāḏ*). See F. I. Andersen, "Biconsonantal Byforms of Weak Hebrew Verbs," *ZAW* 82 (1970) 274. Or, in the light of Eblaite *walad,* "child," Heb. *wālāḏ* might be a survival from a period when Hebrew, or a dialect of Hebrew, preserved initial *w*. See M. J. Dahood, "Ebla, Ugarit, and the Bible," in G. Pettinato, *Archives of Ebla,* p. 278. Cf. Westermann, *Genesis,* 2:139, who notes that the same form occurs in 2 Sam. 6:23 (Ketib) in a similar context (Michal is barren) and thus should be retained.

2. MT reads "they went with them."

Eber
|
Peleg
|
Reu
|
Serug
|
Nahor
|
Terah

Abram — Nahor — Haran
Haran | Lot

The differences are twofold. First, the genealogy in 11:10ff. is concerned only with firstborn sons. Second, this genealogy is deeper than 10:21–31. It doubles the number of generations covered, from five to ten. As a result, a number of novel names turn up in 11:10ff.: Reu, Serug, Nahor, Terah, and Abram. Three of these names—Serug, Nahor, and Terah—all turn out to have counterparts in northern Mesopotamian place names, as evidenced by the nineteenth-century B.C. cuneiform texts from Mari (Sarug, Nahur, and Turahi).

In structure the genealogy in 11:10ff. is much like that in ch. 5, a linear genealogy, which ends as a segmented genealogy:

Noah

Shem — Ham — Japheth

Terah

Abram — Nahor — Haran

Special emphasis is given in this list (and the one in Gen. 5) to certain names simply by the order in which they come. Thus from Adam to Eber (the ancestor of the Hebrews) is fourteen generations. Standing at the midway point between these two is the illustrious and saintly Enoch. From Eber to Abram is also seven generations. Similarly, Abram is tenth from Shem, and twentieth from the creation of Adam. If one follows the LXX (as does Luke

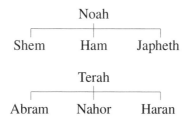

3:36), then Kenan is to be inserted between Arpachshad and Shelah. This would make Abram twenty-first from Adam. Thus, three crucial figures in these genealogies (Enoch, Eber, and Abram) come at points divisible by seven or ten.[3]

As in the genealogy of ch. 5, the ancient souces (MT, LXX, SP) disagree about the age at which *X* fathered *Y* and how long *X* lived after he fathered *Y*. These three versions agree among themselves only in the information they provide about Shem. He was one hundred when he fathered Arpachshad, and he lived five hundred years after that. From there on the ancient versions disagree. Thus, Arpachshad was thirty-five years old (MT) or one hundred and thirty-five years old (LXX, SP) when he fathered Shelah. After this he lived for four hundred and three years (MT), three hundred and three years (SP), or four hundred and thirty years (LXX).[4]

27–32 The focus in these verses is on Terah and his three sons and their wives. Terah fathers Abram, Nahor, and Haran. Abram is married to Sarai, and Nahor is married to Milcah, who was his niece,[5] and whose sister is Iscah. Both Milcah and Iscah have a genealogy; they are daughters of Haran. For some unknown reason Sarai is the one woman here without genealogy.[6]

For reasons unexplained, Terah leaves *Ur of the Chaldeans* with Abram, Sarai, and Lot (but not Nahor and Milcah), moves to Haran, and settles there. This one piece of information (v. 31) provides a structural explanation for the genealogy of Shem (11:10–32) being placed after the

3. See J. Sasson, "A Genealogical 'Convention' in Biblical Chronography?" *ZAW* 90 (1978) 176.

4. The debate about reconciling these numbers, or arguing for the priority of one system over the others, goes on. The consensus is that the MT is the primary system. A recent study suggests that the differences between the MT and LXX in Gen. 5 and 11 can be explained as "rational" alterations of a primary MT system to a later LXX system; see G. Larsson, "The Chronology of the Pentateuch: A Comparison of the MT and LXX," *JBL* 102 (1983) 401–9. See also R. W. Klein, "Archaic Chronologies and the Textual History of the OT," *HTR* 67 (1974) 255–63.

5. For the marriage of an uncle to the daughter of a deceased brother, see the Nuzi documents entitled *ṭuppi mārtūti u kallatūti,* "document of daughter—and daughter-in-lawship." See Speiser, *Genesis,* p. 78.

6. Why is Sarai's paternity conspicuously absent? C. H. Gordon suggests that Sarai has no patronymic because she is of divine parentage ("Yahweh visited Sarah . . . and Sarah conceived," Gen. 21:1–2) in the original patriarchal narratives. See his *Homer and Bible,* pp. 41–42. One suspects, however, that Milcah (and Iscah) are provided with a patronymic only because of the unusual circumstances surrounding Milcah's marriage to her uncle.

Tower of Babel story (11:1–9). Both stories involve the movement of a group of people from one place to another, with the result that the group "settled" in this second place. Both groups are traveling in a generally east-west direction. The first migration will end in frustration and dispersal. The second migration provides the antecedents, or the incipient stages, of the divine blessing on and divine election of Abram.

Some of the names of the Terahites provide an insight into the kind of religious world from which Abraham emerged. Although some scholars argued that *Terah* occurred as a divine name in the Canaanite texts from Ras Shamra, most now agree that there is no evidence of a god *trḫ* at Ugarit.[7] Yet the possible connection of *Terah* (Heb. *teraḥ*) with the word *yārēaḥ,* "moon," and *yeraḥ,* "lunar month," if substantiated, would suggest that Abram's family and ancestors were worshipers of the moon. One suggestion is that Terah means "Têr is (the divine) brother (or protector, Heb. *'aḥ*)," *têr* being a dialectal variant of *šhr,* a South Arabic term for the moon.[8] *Sarai* (Sarah) is the equivalent of *šarratu,* "queen," an Akkadian translation of a Sumerian name for Ningal, the female partner of the moon-god Sin. *Milcah* is the same name as the goddess Malkatu, the daughter of Sin. *Laban* (Heb. *lāḇān*) means "white," and *leḇānâ,* "the white one," is a poetic term for the full moon. In addition, both Ur and Haran were thriving centers of moon worship; thus it is probable that the theological milieu in which Abram lived for a good bit of his life was one in which the cult focused its adoration on moon worship.

Scholars debate the precise identification of *Ur of the Chaldeans* from which Abram moved. The excavations of Sir Leonard Woolley at Ur in the 1920s and 1930 have led many to assume that the Ur from which Abram departed is the Sumerian Ur, that is, the great city in Lower Mesopotamia located on the Euphrates. Woolley excavated sections of private houses at Ur from the Isin-Larsa period (20th–19th centuries B.C.) and from the Old Babylonian period (19th–16th centuries B.C.), which he felt lent even more credibility to Ur as Abram's birthplace.

Other scholars have challenged this identification and suggested that Abram's Ur is to be located in Upper Mesopotamia.[9] Before Sumerian Ur

7. See W. F. Albright, "Was the Patriarch Terah a Canaanite Moon-God?" *BASOR* 71 (1938) 35–40; C. H. Gordon, "*TRḪ, ṬN,* and *NKR* in the Ras Shamra Tablets," *JBL* 57 (1938) 407–10. See P. K. McCarter, "Terah," *ISBE* 4:792–93.

8. See A. F. Key, "Traces of the Worship of the Moon God Sin Among the Early Israelites," *JBL* 84 (1965) 21.

9. That this "northern" interpretation has worked its way into the commentaries is evidenced by positive remarks by Speiser, *Genesis,* p. 80; and Stigers, *Commentary on Genesis,* pp. 133–34.

came to light, writers were already equating Abraham's Ur with Urfa (now called Edessa), which is about twenty miles northwest of Haran. A more recent proposal is to identify the Ur of Gen. 11 with a town called Ura in Hittite territory.[10]

The evidences in favor of the northern location are: (1) A journey from Sumerian Ur to Canaan via Haran, as Gen. 11 indicates was done, would have been possible from southern Ur to Canaan, via the Fertile Crescent,[11] but an incredibly long journey for one family to take. A trip from a site in northern Mesopotamia is more plausible. (2) In the hundreds of references to Ur in cuneiform texts, not once is it called "Ur of the Chaldeans." (3) Sumerian Ur could never have been called "Ur of the Chaldeans." The Chaldeans were an ethnic group related to the Arameans. They did not penetrate southern Mesopotamia until the end of the 2nd millennium B.C. Note that they do not appear in any of the venerated genealogies of Genesis. Not until Gen. 22:22 are they linked with their ancestor Chesed.[12] (4) Some OT references put Abram's birthplace in Upper Mesopotamia (Gen. 24:4, 7). Abram's servant is to go to Aram-Naharaim, where Laban lived—and this territory is described as Abram's land of birth—to fetch a bride for Isaac. (5) An Ebla tablet refers to "Ur in Haran."[13] (6) The expression "Ur of the Chaldeans" appears four times in the OT: Gen. 11:28, 31; 15:7; Neh. 9:7. In each instance the LXX translates "Ur" by *chṓra,* "land, field, region." This

10. See C. H. Gordon, "Abraham and the Merchants of Ura," *JNES* 17 (1958) 28–31; idem, "Abraham of Ur," in *Hebrew and Semitic Studies Presented to G. R. Driver,* ed. D. W. Thomas and W. D. McHardy (Oxford: Clarendon, 1963), pp. 77–84.

11. N. K. Gottwald (*The Hebrew Bible: A Socio-Literary Introduction* [Philadelphia: Fortress, 1985], p. 39) defines the Fertile Crescent as follows: "If one traces a line from the mouth of the Tigris-Euphrates rivers on the Persian Gulf northward along the course of the rivers, curving west to the Mediterranean Sea and then southward through Syria and Palestine as far as the Nile Delta of Egypt, this line will appear as an arc, half-moon, or crescent. The swath of land demarcated by this arc includes the largest concentrations of population, the most fertile agricultural areas, the most frequently travelled routes, the territories most fought over by armies, and the great majority of powerful states in the ancient Near East. This so-called Fertile Crescent designates the crucial zone of economic and political development in the ancient Near East. It embraces and connects the two great river valleys at either end along a route of easy access that avoids the hazards of desert and high mountain transport."

12. Akk. *kaldu* becomes Heb. *kaśdîm* (cf. Gk. *chaldoi*) as a result of a phonetic shift in which *l* becomes a sibilant (here *ś*) when followed by a dental *(d).*

13. See C. H. Gordon, "Where Is Abraham's Ur?" *BAR* 3/2 (1977) 20–21, 52.

translation does not indicate that the LXX was ignorant of a site called Ur. Rather, the correctness of the LXX is borne out by a number of places in the Hebrew text where *'wr* (i.e., *'ûr,* "field," should be read for MT *'ôr,* "light") is parallel with *'ereṣ,* "earth."[14] While, in itself, this does not support a northern site for Ur, it shows that the LXX reflects a tradition connecting Abraham not with the "Ur" of the Chaldeans but with "the land" of the Chaldeans, a designation that obviously covers a much broader territory than the southern Ur. (7) Some of Abram's relatives bear names that may be connected with sites in northern Mesopotamia. Thus, there is probably a connection between Terah and Til (ša) Turaḫi, "ruin of the ibex[?]," a town located in the basin of the Balikh River in Upper Mesopotamia, near Haran. In the same approximate vicinity were the towns of Tell Naḫiru/Naḫuru (to be connected with Nahor?) and Sarugi (to be connected with Serug?).

Most scholars still maintain the identification of Ur with the Lower Mesopotamian site,[15] and they offer the following counterarguments: (1) A migration by herdsmen with livestock would go around the desert rather than across it directly. (2) The Ura mentioned in the Ugaritic texts, as well as in Hittite texts from Boghazköy, is a seaport town on the Cilician coast, and therefore is not likely to be the biblical Ur of the Chaldeans.[16] (3) A migration of Abram from southern Mesopotamia accords with historical facts, specifically with the presence of Amorites who entered Babylonia from the end of the 3rd millennium B.C. onward, who reached Ur, and who are usually connected to the patriarchs.[17] In our opinion, however, none of these arguments is decisive, and the balance of evidence favors a northern Ur.

14. References cited by M. J. Dahood, *Psalms,* 1:223. So understood, "Chaldeans" in Gen. 11:28, 31 would refer not to the Chaldeans who were to become the ruling class of the Neo-Babylonian empire, but to the Indo-Aryan Haldai, who are connected with ancient Armenia.

15. The standard study is H. W. F. Saggs, "Ur of the Chaldees," *Iraq* 22 (1960) 200–209. Also see the shorter studies of D. J. Wiseman, *The New Bible Dictionary* (Grand Rapids: Eerdmans, 1962), pp. 1304–5; W. S. LaSor, "Ur," *ISBE,* 4:954–55.

16. See A. F. Rainey, "Business Agents at Ugarit," *IEJ* 13 (1963) 319.

17. See R. de Vaux, *The Early History of Israel,* tr. D. Smith (Philadelphia: Westminster, 1978), pp. 190–91.

THE NEW TESTAMENT APPROPRIATION

Gen. 11:1–9 and Luke 14:28–30

The NT has many references to building operations and procedures, but the only one involving the building of a tower *(pýrgos)* which subsequently was abandoned is Luke 14:28–30. On the one hand, it may well be that Jesus is teaching through this parable the necessity of counting the cost before commencing a life of discipleship with him. On the other hand, many other references in the NT would challenge that interpretation, for in these contexts Jesus placed the emphasis on faith rather than on calculation. Peter did not make a calculation before he left his boat on the Sea of Galilee.

This story (Luke 14:29–30) emphasizes that the unfinished tower draws a crowd of curious onlookers who turn into those who mock and jeer. In the Genesis event the erection of the tower starts out as a project, part of whose aim is to mock God.[1] But the roles are reversed, and God turns in derision upon the people and confuses their language. Here the spectators become the deriders.

Not only does God confuse their language but he also scatters them. It is difficult to establish an antecedent for the words of Mary in the Magnificat: "he has scattered the proud in the imagination of their hearts" (Luke 1:51), but the Tower of Babel story would fit nicely. Note that the verb in Luke 1:51 for "scatter" is *diaskorpízō,* which serves in the LXX as a translation for the Hiphil of *pûṣ* (the verb in Gen. 11:9) in Neh. 1:8; Jer. 9:16; Ezek. 11:16; 12:15; 22:15, etc.[2] Note, however, that *diaskorpízō* is not used in Gen. 11:1–9. The verb used there is *diaspeírō* (vv. 4 [*pûṣ* in the Qal], 8, 9 [*pûṣ* in the Hiphil]).

Gen. 11:26–32 and Acts 7:4

The chronology of Gen. 11:26–32 is as follows. Terah is seventy years old when Abram is born (Gen. 11:26). Since Terah dies in Haran at the age of

1. This point is especially vivid in the postbiblical haggadic midrash on the story. Here we are told that 600,000 men worked on the tower and attempted to place at the tower's peak an idol with a sword in its hand. See L. Ginzberg, *Legends of the Jews,* 7 vols. (Philadelphia: Jewish Publication Society, 1909–1938), 1:179–80; 5:201–4.

2. J. D. M. Derrett, "Nisi dominus aedificaverit domum: Towers and Wars (Lk XIV 28-32)," *NovT* 19 (1977) 252 n. 42. Hatch and Redpath list 10 references where *diaskorpízō* translates the Hiphil of *pûṣ* (*A Concordance to the Septuagint* [Grand Rapids: Baker, repr. 1983], 1:310).

205 years (11:32), Abram would be 135 years old at his father's death. Yet 12:4 informs us that Abram left Haran at the age of seventy-five to enter Canaan.

If no other text were considered, this sequence would present no problem, for one would understand Abram to have left Haran sixty-five years before his father died. But this explanation contradicts Acts 7:4, which says that Abram left Haran for Canaan only after the death of his father. Is Stephen following the chronology of Gen. 11–12, or is he not?

Three suggestions have been made to deal with Stephen's understanding of early events in the life of the patriarch. One explanation appeals to the SP, which has Terah dying not at 205 (as in MT and LXX) but at 145.[3] This, we are told, is the source that Stephen was using, and thus the inconsistencies disappear. Terah was seventy when Abram was born. Seventy-five years later Terah died, and Abram left Haran for Canaan. This fact is then presented, with others, as evidence that Stephen's speech in Acts 7 is Samaritan in its interpretation of OT history.[4]

A second suggestion is a variation of the above. Rather than limiting Stephen's source to the SP, we are told that at this time a plurality of textual families or traditions existed, and the SP is but a representative of an expanded and reworked Palestinian text that differed from MT and LXX. Certainly Philo, who also gave Terah's age at death as 145, did not rely on the SP, for he would not use a sectarian Torah.[5]

A third approach harmonizes the Genesis data and Acts 7:4 without appealing to a text other than MT or LXX. The basic tenet of this approach is that 11:26 does not say that Terah was seventy years old when he fathered Abram. Rather, it says that Terah was seventy years old when he began to beget. Perhaps Abram is mentioned first because he is the most important of the three. Thus Terah was 130 years old, near the end of his life, when Abram was born.[6]

3. In fact, only the MT has Terah dying at 205. According to the LXX the years of Terah were 205 *in Haran*!

4. See A. Spiro, Appendix V, "Stephen's Samaritan Background," in J. Munck, rev. by W. F. Albright and C. S. Mann, *The Acts of the Apostles,* AB (Garden City, NY: Doubleday, 1967), pp. 285–300; C. H. H. Scobie, "Development of Samaritan Christianity," *NTS* 19 (1973) 390–414, esp. p. 393; idem, "The Use of Source Material in the Speeches of Acts III and VII," *NTS* 25 (1979) 399–421. Incidentally, the tradition about Terah's death at 145 is not unique to SP. It is also found in Philo, *Migration of Abraham,* 177.

5. See E. Richard, "Acts 7: An Investigation of the Samaritan Evidence," *CBQ* 39 (1977) 190–208, esp. p. 197; R. Punmer, "The Samaritan Pentateuch and the New Testament," *NTS* 22 (1976) 441–43.

6. W. H. Mare, "Acts 7: Jewish or Samaritan in Character?" *WTJ* 34 (1971)

Lest one dismiss this last approach as artificial and rationalistic harmonization, observe that the immediately preceding chapters of Genesis provide a parallel to sons being listed in an order unrelated to their age. Gen. 5:32 lists the three sons of Noah in this sequence: (1) Shem, (2) Ham, (3) Japheth. But this cannot be the order of their birth, for 9:24 identifies Ham as the youngest son of Noah. Thus, the birth order is more likely Shem, Japheth, Ham.

F. F. Bruce suggests that relegating Abram's birth to near the end of Terah's lifetime is an "improbable expedient."[7] Bruce himself follows the number for Terah's age at death as 145, not 205. This does not mean, for Bruce, that this is evidence of Samaritan influence on Stephen's speech. Rather, Stephen can say that Abram left Haran after Terah died (and not sixty years before his father died, as Gen. 11:26, 32; 12:4 would suggest) because he was using a Greek version which agreed with the Samaritan reading of Gen. 11:32.

1–21, esp. pp. 18–19. A possible flaw with this solution is that it posits Abram himself being born well after his father is 100 years old, while he himself registers surprise that a son may be born to him when he is a centenarian—"shall a child be born to a man who is a hundred years old?" (Gen. 17:17).

7. F. F. Bruce, *The Book of Acts,* NICNT, rev. ed. (Grand Rapids: Eerdmans, 1988), p. 134 n. 21.

II. THE ABRAHAM CYCLE, PART I (12:1–17:27)

A. THE EMERGENCE OF ABRAM (12:1–20)

1. THE CALL OF ABRAM (12:1–9)

1 *Yahweh said to Abram: "Go forth*[1] *from your country, from your homeland,*[2] *and from your father's house to a land which I will show you.*

2 *I will make of you a great nation,*
and I will bless you;
I will make your name famous,
and be[3] *a blessing;*

1. T. Muraoka ("On the So-called *DATIVUS ETHICUS* in Hebrew," *JTS* 29 [1978] 495–98) rejects the construction *l^{e}ḵā* (after the imperative) as an ethical dative. Instead, he sees the construction of verbs of motion followed by the preposition *l^{e}* with pronominal suffix as centripetal in force. "Basically it serves to convey the impression on the part of the speaker or author that the subject establishes his own identity, recovering or finding his own place by determinedly dissociating himself from his familiar surrounding" (p. 497).

2. The expression *mē'arṣ^{e}ḵā ûmimmôlaḏt^{e}ḵā* may be taken as a hendiadys (native land). But it should be compared with the slightly different *ûmē'ereṣ môlaḏtî* (24:7) and *'ereṣ môlaḏteḵā* (31:13). This slight distinction suggests that here a graded sequence of three terms was intended, from the less personal to the more personal. See A. Berlin, "Shared Rhetorical Features in Biblical and Sumerian Literature," *JANES* 10 (1978) 38 n. 14.

3. I see no reason for not retaining MT *wehyēh,* an imperatival form of *hāyâ* found in 17:1; Exod. 24:12; 34:2; Judg. 17:10; 18:19. The emendation to *w^{e}hāyâ,* "it [your name] will be a blessing," on the basis of SP, is unnecessary. The same may be said about D. N. Freedman's suggestion that underlying the MT is the form *wa'ah$^{\breve{e}}$yēhû,* the Hiphil 1st sing. with the 3rd masc. sing. suffix, "I will cause it to become a blessing" ("Notes on Genesis," *ZAW* 64 [1952] 193). 17:1 provides an excellent parallel to 12:2: "walk [imperative] . . . and be [imperative] perfect."

3 *I will bless those blessing you, but the one who abuses you*[4] *I will utterly ban; and by you all the earth's clans shall be blessed."*
4 *Abram went as Yahweh commanded him, and Lot went with him. Abram was seventy-five years old when he departed from Haran.*
5 *Abram took his wife Sarai, his nephew Lot, and all the possessions they had accumulated, and the persons they had acquired in Haran. They set out for the land of Canaan and arrived in the land of Canaan.*
6 *Abram journeyed in the land as far as Shechem, by the terebinth of Moreh. (The Canaanites were then in the land.)*
7 *Yahweh appeared to Abram and said: "To your descendants I will give this land." He built there an altar to Yahweh who had appeared to him.*[5]
8 *From there he moved on to the hill country east of Bethel, pitching his tent, with Bethel to the east and Ai to the west. And he built there an altar to Yahweh and invoked Yahweh by name.*
9 *Abram then traveled by stages*[6] *to the Negeb.*

1 Yahweh's first and last words to Abram (12:1; 22:1) begin with an imperative ("Go . . . . Take . . ."). Both times the imperative is followed by a triple object: "Go forth from (1) your country, (2) your homeland, (3) your father's house"; "Take (1) your son, (2) your only son whom you love, (3) Isaac." The objects in 12:1 are arranged in a sequence of less intimate to more intimate. Each succeeding phrase narrows the base as far as Abram is concerned. In both chs. 12 and 22 God's directive to Abram falls short of supplying explicit directions; Abram is simply pointed in the right direction.

Westermann translates, "so that you will be a blessing." He justifies this rendering by appealing to GKC, § 110i: the imperative with *waw copulative* "frequently expresses also a consequence which is to be expected with certainty" (*Genesis,* 2:144). Westermann does not so render the imperative of *hāyâ* with *waw copulative* in Gen. 17:1 ("live always in my presence and be perfect," p. 253), possibly because there it follows an imperative, and not a cohortative, as here.

4. The second participle is sing., *ûm^{e}qallelkā,* but LXX and Vulg. read as a pl., for sake of consistency with the preceding pl. participle *(m^{e}ḇār^{e}ḵeḵâ).* See A. Berlin, *The Dynamics of Biblical Parallelism* (Bloomington: Indiana University Press, 1985), pp. 49, 50. She suggests that the ancient versions were not sensitive to this type of parallelism, or could not render it idiomatically into the language of their translations. On the translation of v. 3b see H. C. Brichto, *The Problem of "Curse" in the Hebrew Bible,* p. 157 n. 92. V. 3ab provides a clear instance of chiasm: 1st person verb, participle, participle, 1st person verb.

5. For the participle with pluperfect force cf. 35:1.

6. Heb. *wayyissaʿ . . . hālôḵ w^{e}nāsôaʿ,* a finite verb followed by two infinitives absolute. Such a construction, with *hālôḵ,* expresses an action extending over a long period; see GKC, § 113u.

About the terminal point of that pilgrimage he is unclear. Here he is told to go to a land "which I will show you." In ch. 22 he is told to take Isaac to a mountain "of which I shall tell you."

The covenant is not mentioned at this point; that will come in ch. 15. Both the command of God (v. 1) and the promises of God (vv. 2–3) antedate the implementation of the covenant. Moreover, Abram's faith is also in operation prior to his commitment to be Yahweh's servant. The only thing made clear to Abram is that where he is now (Haran) is not where he is to remain. Haran is not to become a domicile for him any more than the ark was to become such for Noah. Interestingly, the promise to give the land to Abram (v. 7) follows the promise to show the land to Abram (v. 1), and "show" becomes "give" only when Abram makes his move.

There is no problem with calling the Haran area Abram's *country* and the territory in which he is located *your father's house.* But in what sense is Haran his *homeland?* Heb. *môleḏeṯ* (from *yālaḏ*) can mean "birthplace," and if that is the case here, then we would have further support for Abram coming from Upper Mesopotamia. In some OT passages (esp. Gen. 43:7; 48:6; Esth. 8:6) this word is translated as "descendants, offspring, kindred," perhaps suggesting that Haran was the place where his family and descendants lived. And yet it would be strange to refer to Haran as the land where Abram's family settled before he had even one descendant, though such a reference might simply be proleptic.

2 Exclusive of the command in v. 1, the blessing of God to Abram contains seven clauses (vv. 2–3). The OT, understandably, has a penchant for grouping literary material in heptads.[7]

Of the first four clauses, located in v. 2, the first three are phrased as imperfects and the fourth is an imperative. In some ways the first clause is the most surprising—God will make of Abram *a great nation.* This expression is intriguing, for the Hebrew word for *nation* is *gôy,* a word used frequently in the OT to describe the gentile nations in the world, as we noted in 10:5, 20, 31, 32. God does not here promise to make of Abram a great people *(ʿam).* Israel will be a *gôy* among the *gôyîm.* Abram is already an *ʿam* simply because he has his nephew Lot. The use of the word *gôy* in this context adds the special elements of "the status and stability of nationhood in a land

7. See R. Gordis, "The Heptad as an Element of Biblical and Rabbinic Style," *JBL* 62 (1943) 19. The midrash (Bereshit Rabbah 39:11) makes this point by drawing attention to "the three promises of greatness and the four blessings." Note Paul's heptadic statement of the unity of the faith: one body, one spirit, one hope, one Lord, one faith, one baptism, one God (Eph. 4:4–6).

designated for that purpose."[8] Whereas *ʿam* refers to people or nations in terms of centripetal unity and cohesiveness, *gôy* is linked with government and territory. Abram's descendants will be those who grow into the status of a nation.[9] This same thrust is observable in 18:18; 25:23; 35:11; 46:3.

No particular content is read into the second phrase: *I will bless you.* To receive a promise of becoming a great nation would itself be a blessing, especially in view of Sarah's barrenness (11:30). A great nation, at least to get started, needs both an ancestor and an ancestress.

Not only will Abram's loins be fertile but his *name* will be *famous.* This is doubtless another deliberate contrast with the Tower of Babel incident. One of the aspirations of those builders was "to make a name for ourselves." As we saw, they did get an ironic name for their city: Babel. The builders' aggressiveness is matched by Abram's passiveness. If his name is ever to become great it will not be because of any self-initiated effort. The great name will be a gift, not an achievement.

Abram is not the only recipient in the Bible of this particular promise. God would later say to David, "I will make your name great" (2 Sam. 7:9); and Ps. 72:17, a prayer for the king, mentions among its requests for the king: "may his name endure forever." This is clearly royal language, and Abram is to be viewed as a regal figure. Genesis makes this point quite plain in at least two instances. First, Abram is promised that "kings" will come from him (17:6), and Sarah too is identified as the mother of "kings" (17:16). Second, in 23:6 Abraham is referred to as a "prince" by the Hittites from whom he is attempting to purchase a plot of ground on which to bury Sarah. The LXX, interestingly, translates the Hebrew word for "prince" *(nāśîʾ)* with *basileús,* "king." It is fitting, then, that royal terminology first appears in connection with Abram long before the emergence of the monarchy in Israel. The language of Samuel and the Psalms is to be seen as an adaptation of this

8. See E. A. Speiser, " 'People' and 'Nation' of Israel," *JBL* 79 (1960) 162–63.

9. See A. Cody, "When is the chosen people called a *gôy*?" *VT* 14 (1964) 1–6. Cody answers his own question with seven categories: (1) in a hypothetical generalization that is semantically applicable to all nations; (2) when Israel is emerging into nationhood status; (3) when Israel is to take possession of a land; (4) on the lips of foreigners; (5) in words of rejection by God; (6) parallel with *ʿam;* (7) parallel with some word expressing rule or sovereignty. The only other occurrence of this root in Semitic languages is the Akk. *gaʿum/gawum,* which has been found only in texts from Mari. Earlier translations of this word favored "territory," but this has been abandoned by the major lexicons of Akkadian, which now prefer "group, troop of workers" (*CAD,* 5:59) or "people" (W. von Soden, *Akkadisches Handwörterbuch,* 1:284).

earlier idiom. This royal language does not mean that the Abram cycle was reduced to writing only after the establishment of kingship in Israel, with the latter serving as a model for the former.

Verse 2 concludes with an imperative, *and be a blessing*. We have already noted some of the problems surrounding the verbal form in this phrase,[10] and we have stated our distaste for emending it to a perfect verb form (as in SP, JB, and NEB), or casually reading it as a second person verb, "and you shall be a blessing" (as in LXX, RSV, and NIV).[11]

The larger syntax of vv. 1–2 suggests that another route must be followed. Hebrew grammar provides numerous instances of an imperative (with *waw- copulative*) depending on an earlier imperative. Here the first imperative states the exhortation, and the second imperative touches on the results which are brought about by the implementation of the first imperative.[12] Applied to Gen. 12:1–2, this construction means that the first imperative, *go,* is related as effect to cause to this second imperative, *be.* Abram cannot be a blessing if he stays in Haran. But if he leaves, then a blessing he will be.

If we are correct in seeing here seven phrases in God's initial speech to Abram, then this one is the middle one, and perhaps for that reason a more crucial statement, or at least a pivotal one. The blessings of God are not all to be turned in on Abram. A great nation, blessed, a great name—yes. But Abram must be more than a recipient. He is both a receptacle for the divine blessing and a transmitter of that blessing.

3 Furthermore, God states that his relationship to others will be determined by the relationship of these others to Abram. Abram can expect to encounter both those who will bless him and those who will curse him.[13] One need not go beyond ch. 12 to see an immediate fulfillment of this promise. Pharaoh cursed Abram by taking the patriarch's wife, albeit in ignorance about her married status. As a result diseases and plagues fell on Pharaoh and his household.

10. See n. 3 above.

11. The Hebrew Bible does have instances of an imperative functioning as though it were an imperfect or a jussive. GKC, § 110i, notes that the imperative after a cohortative may express consequence, e.g., in Gen. 45:18 and Exod. 3:10. Thus this fourth phrase, though imperatival in form, would be saying "so that [i.e., purpose] (or, with the result that [i.e., result]) you will be a blessing."

12. For examples of this construction cf. Gen. 17:1; 1 K. 22:6; 2 K. 5:13; Isa. 36:16. See W. Yarchin, "Imperative and Promise in Genesis 12:1–3," *StBTh* 10 (1980) 167–68.

13. The use of the pl. participle for "those blessing you" and the use of the sing. participle for "the one who abuses you" does not necessarily mean that there will be more of the first than of the second.

The grand finale in this catalogue of blessings and promises is: (so that) *by you all the earth's clans shall be blessed.* Again, the syntax of this passage helps isolate this climactic phrase. This unit began with an imperative, continued with a number of first singular imperfects (punctuated with an imperative that has imperfective force), and now climaxes with a perfect *(nib̲rᵉk̲û).*[14] V. 2 had already said that Abram would be a blessing. But to whom? For whom? Now we have our answer: *all the earth's clans* (or peoples, families), like those mentioned in Gen. 10. Here is Yahweh's programmatic statement. Sinister nations and peoples of the earth, such as we read about in chs. 3–11, are to be blessed through Abram.

Scholars have debated a great deal whether the verb here should be translated *shall be blessed* or "shall bless themselves." Is the verb passive or reflexive? The stem used here is the Niphal, which is primarily reflexive but often passive. The problem is compounded by comparing 12:3 with 18:18; 22:18; 26:4; and 28:14, all of which deal with the nations being blessed or blessing themselves in Abram (and in his seed). Three of these passages use the Niphal (12:3; 18:18; 28:14); the remaining two (22:18; 26:4) use the Hithpael, the thrust of which is reflexive or reciprocal. Because the Hithpael does not connote a passive sense (except in rare instances), and because the Niphal may express both the passive and the reflexive, most modern versions of the Bible opt for "shall bless themselves."

This is not a point of esoteric grammar. Speiser is right when he says of these two translations: "the distinction may be slight on the surface, yet it is of great consequence theologically."[15] If the verb in question has passive force, then 12:3 clearly articulates the final goal in a divine plan for universal salvation, and Abram is the divinely chosen instrument in the implementation of that plan.

B. Albrektson has written at length in support of the reflexive interpretation.[16] This is not surprising, for one of the basic theses of his book is that *Heilsgeschichte* was not a distinctive element in Hebrew historiography.

14. On the syntax of 12:1–3 cf. H. Wolff and W. Brueggemann, *The Vitality of Old Testament Traditions* (Atlanta: John Knox, 1974), p. 47. P. D. Miller, Jr. ("Syntax and theology in Genesis xii 3a," *VT* 34 [1984] 472–75) notes that *'ā'ōr,* "I will utterly ban," breaks the string of cohortative verbs with the prefixed *waw.* For Miller this means that *'ā'ō r* does not indicate purpose. The curse of God is not the purpose of the divine command. Miller thus translates: "—and should there be one who regards you with contempt I will curse him."

15. Speiser, *Genesis,* p. 86.

16. B. Albrektson, *History and the Gods,* ConBOT 1 (Lund: Gleerup, 1967), p. 79.

He failed to see, after examining several Hebrew words for "plan," that the OT consistently developed the concept of a divine plan for history. Accordingly, he interpreted the three Niphals of *bārak̲* in the light of the two Hithpaels of *bārak̲*, and suggested that Gen. 12:3 pointed only to a statement of the blessing on Abram.

Some have sought further support for the reflexive interpretation in Ps. 72:17b. Referring to the king, the verse says, "all nations will bless themselves [or be blessed—Hithpael] through him, and they will call him blessed [Piel of *'āšar*]." For example, M. Weinfeld translates these words: "all nations will bless themselves through him, and all the nations will deem him happy," and concludes that the parallelism of the Hithpael of *bārak̲* with the Piel of *'āšar* demonstrates that *bārak̲* here is reflexive and not passive.[17]

But Ps. 72:17b may be support for a passive interpretation of *bārak̲* in Gen. 12:3. If *bārak̲* in Ps. 72:17 has reflexive meaning, why do both LXX and Vulg. translate it with passive verb forms? Dahood's translation reflects this passive force: "Let his progeny be blessed through him, by him all nations made happy."[18] One passive verb form is balanced by another.

We also would call into question the axiom that the Hithpael does not carry passive force. A case can be made for a number of scriptural passages where the Hithpael is best rendered as a passive.[19] If that is the case, perhaps we need to read the Hithpaels of *bārak̲* in Genesis in the light of the Niphals of *bārak̲*, rather than vice versa.

Finally, we may ask what is the meaning of "bless oneself"? How is that done? One may bless God, or bless another, but how does one bless oneself? The Hithpael in these passages does not make sense when translated reflexively. It must be stretched to mean something like "pray to be blessed." In view of all these factors, it is best to retain the passive force of 12:3, and to see in this last of seven phrases, with its emphatic perfect, the culmination of this initial promise of God to the patriarch.

Genesis supplies several illustrations of the fulfillment of this prom-

17. M. Weinfeld, "The Old Testament—the discipline and its goals," *Congress Volume: Vienna, 1980,* VTSup 32 (Leiden: Brill, 1981), p. 426 n. 8.

18. Dahood, *Psalms,* 2:179. Dahood understands consonantal *y'šrhw* not as a Piel (as in MT *yeʾaššerûhû*), but as a Pual *(yeʾuššerûhû),* to balance the first passive, *yitbārek̲û.*

19. See W. C. Kaiser, Jr., *Toward an Old Testament Theology* (Grand Rapids: Zondervan, 1978), p. 13. Kaiser refers to a study by an earlier scholar, O. T. Allis, "The Blessing of Abraham," *PTR* 25 (1927) 263–98, who lists 18 OT references where the Hithpael may have a passive meaning. To that list I would add Prov. 31:30; Eccl. 8:10; and Ps. 72:17.

ise. Thus, Laban of Aram-Naharaim can say to Jacob that "Yahweh has blessed me because of you" (30:27). Of the Egyptian Potiphar we read that "Yahweh blessed the household of the Egyptian because of Joseph" (39:5). Not only was the household of Jacob saved from starvation by the presence of Joseph in Egypt, but so was the country of Egypt itself. In that sense they were blessed. Instead of famine there was plenty for all to eat, even in the lean years.

4–5 From time to time the narrator pinpoints specific years in the life of a patriarch. An event is related to a specific age of Abram (12:4; 16:16; 17:1, 24; 21:5; 25:7), of Isaac (25:20, 26; 35:28), of Joseph (37:2; 41:46; 50:22), of Jacob (47:9). In Abram's case the specific years represent a crisis or pivotal point in his life: departure from Haran, birth of Ishmael, circumcision and covenant, birth of Isaac, death.

No commentary is provided, but it is clear that Abram is presented to the reader as a paragon of faith and obedience. God speaks and the narrator speaks, but Abram is silent. He leaves Haran "not knowing where he is going." Only the departure and arrival of Abram's odyssey are highlighted. This journey from Haran to Canaan parallels Abram's last journey from Beer-sheba to Moriah (22:2), except that it is in the opposite direction. On his first journey his traveling companions are Lot, his wife, and several servants. On the last journey his companions are Isaac and two servants.

We note here two references to Lot's accompanying Abram (v. 4 and v. 5). This repetition may sound clumsy to some; thus source critics remove the awkwardness by assigning vv. 4b–5 to P, with everything else traced to J, primarily on the basis that chronological notations are the work of the priestly tradents. Perhaps the double notation about Lot is not due to multiple sources, but rather is the author's way of dropping hints about the forthcoming dispute and debacle involving Lot.

Chapter 11 informed us that when Terah left Ur for Canaan he took with him his son Abram, his barren daughter-in-law Sarai, and his grandson Lot. With his son Haran deceased and with Nahor left behind in Ur with his wife, only Abram remains as the channel through which Terah's family may be perpetuated. But Sarai is barren. Terah's only grandchildren, besides Lot, are daughters (Milcah and Iscah). That leaves only Lot to perpetuate his grandfather's family. V. 4 adds to that possibility with its note that "Abram went . . . and Lot went with him." That Lot went with Abram may be termed, as far as plot is concerned, "the teasing motif of the presumed heir."[20]

6 The first site at which Abram stops is *Shechem,* located in the pass

20. See L. Silberman, "Listening to the Text," *JBL* 102 (1983) 19.

between Mounts Ebal and Gerizim. The exact spot at which he stayed is called *the terebinth* (or oak) *of Moreh.* This phrase may be translated as "the terebinth of the teacher." The same expression, in the plural, occurs in Deut. 11:30, and again it is identified with Mounts Ebal and Gerizim west of the Jordan. Gen. 35:4 refers to "the terebinth at Shechem," a place where Jacob buried the foreign gods belonging to members of his household. Joshua set up a large stone at this tree (Josh. 24:26). This tree was to be the place where Abimelech sought his own coronation (Judg. 9:6). Judg. 9:37 refers to this tree as "the terebinth of the diviners." Other trees are also mentioned in connection with the patriarchs in Gen. 13:18; 14:13; 18:1; 21:33; 35:8.

Nowhere does Genesis say that the patriarchs engaged in religious rites at these trees. Later biblical condemnation of worshiping Yahweh "on high mountains, on hills, under any spreading tree" (Deut. 12:2; 1 K. 14:23; Jer. 2:20; Hos. 4:13; etc.) is a repudiation of Canaanite practices rather than of patriarchal practices.[21]

7 Yahweh's first revelation to Abram was through an audition, "Yahweh said to Abram." Here the mode of revelation shifts to a theophany, *Yahweh appeared to Abram.* The shift is not incidental. "A theophany is a way of augmenting an audition to heighten its dramatic force, and reinforce the claim that a divine intervention has occurred."[22]

The promise of God that comes in this theophany is the promise of land to Abram's *descendants.*[23] This promise clearly eliminates Lot as the presumptive heir. The heir will be Abram's own seed. Just as clearly, this promise is not directed at Abram himself but at his progeny. The promise of God cannot be implemented in Abram's lifetime. Promise of land to Abram's descendants (12:7) precedes the promise of land to Abram himself (13:17).

Abram the pilgrim becomes Abram the builder. But he is intent on

21. In Targ. Onqelos "terebinth" is replaced by "plain, valley" in 12:6, as well as in 13:18; 14:13; 18:1; 35:8. This is comparable to the Vulg. rendering of "the terebinth of Moreh" by *convallis illustris* in 12:6. The Targ. plays down the possibility that the patriarchs engaged in cultic rites akin to those of the Canaanites.

22. See D. Patrick, *The Rendering of God in the Old Testament,* p. 92.

23. See S. Loewenstamm, "The Divine Grants of Land to the Patriarchs," *JAOS* 91 (1971) 509–10. In the land promises given in Genesis, the indirect object after *nāṯan* takes four forms: (1) "I will give it to your seed" (12:7; 15:8; 24:7); (2) "I will give it to you" (13:7); (3) "to you I will give it and to your seed" (13:15); (4) "I will give it to you and to your seed" (26:3). R. Rendtorff tries to arrange these phrases in a historical sequence: the promise was originally to Abram, then "seed" was added, then "seed" replaced the patriarch (Rendtorff, "The 'Yahwist' as Theologian? The Dilemma of Pentateuchal Criticism," *JSOT* 3 [1977] 8).

building neither a tower nor a city. His project is an *altar.* This is an activity in which the patriarchs often engaged (12:8; 13:18; 22:9; 26:25; 33:20; 35:7). We are never told, however, that the patriarchs offered sacrifices on any of them, except for 22:9. In two of these references (12:8; 26:25) building an altar is associated with invoking God's name.

8 From Shechem Abram moves on to Bethel, where he erects another altar. *pitching his tent* contrasts with *he built . . . an altar.* The tents are dismantled, but the altars are left standing. For a second time in this chapter we read that Abram built an altar to Yahweh. The additional element here is Abram's invoking Yahweh by name (lit., "he called upon the name of Yahweh"). Thus, worship for the patriarchs, at least on some occasions, is composed both of action (altar building) and of word (invocation of deity).[24] When this latter phrase is used in the primeval (4:26) or patriarchal traditions (12:8; 13:4; 21:33; 26:25), it is simply a technical term for worship. There is no indication that it is some kind of petition that elicits a response from God. By contrast, when "call upon the name of Yahweh" appears outside the Pentateuch, it is used either in a context where an answer from deity is to be expected (1 K. 18:24; 2 K. 5:11; Ps. 116:4; Isa. 64:6 [Eng. 7]; Lam. 3:55; Joel 3:5 [Eng. 2:32]; Zech. 13:9), or it is used doxologically (Ps. 80:19 [Eng. 18]; 105:1; 116:13, 17; Isa. 12:4; Zeph. 3:9). Those who do not know Yahweh cannot, of course, call upon his name (Ps. 79:6; Jer. 10:25).[25]

This verse observes that Abram did not settle in Bethel but in between Bethel and Ai. The patriarchs did not dwell in Canaanite cities but pitched their camps on the outskirts. Heb. *nāweh* ("pasturage, abode") is not used in the patriarchal narratives, but in extrapentateuchal passages it refers to the "habitations of Jacob" (Jer. 10:25; Lam. 2:2; Ps. 79:7).[26] *nāweh* may be related to Akk. *nāwum,* which in the Mari texts means an encampment on the edge of urban centers.

9 Abram's last stop is in *the Negeb,* the desert area in the southern sections of Palestine. It has often been noted that the trip of Abram (Shechem to Bethel to Negeb) is parallel to that of Jacob, and most importantly to the direction followed by the Israelites in their conquest of Canaan. Does this mean that the journeys of Abram and Jacob function as a sign unto their

24. C. Westermann, *Genesis,* 2:156.

25. See H. A. Brongers, "Die Wendung *bᵉšem jhwh* im Alten Testament," *ZAW* 77 (1965) 12–14; A. S. van der Woude, *"šēm," THAT,* 2:952.

26. See A. Malamat, "Mari and the Bible: Some Patterns of Tribal Organization and Institutions," *JAOS* 82 (1962) 146. For other references to the patriarchs dwelling near cities cf. 13:18; 33:18; 35:27.

children's children that the conquest had, as it were, already taken place symbolically in the time of the patriarchs?[27]

2. ABRAM IN EGYPT WITH SARAI (12:10–20)

10 *There was a famine in the land; so Abram went down to Egypt to sojourn there, for the famine in the land was severe.*
11 *As he drew near to Egypt, he said to Sarai his wife: "Look, I know what an attractive woman you are.*
12 *When the Egyptians spot you they will say: 'She is his wife'; they will kill me but you they will spare.*[1]
13 *Please say, therefore, that you are my sister, so that it may go well with me on account of you and my life be spared because of you."*
14 *When Abram came to Egypt the Egyptians saw how very attractive the woman was.*
15 *And when Pharaoh's courtiers spotted her, they praised her to Pharaoh, and the woman was taken into Pharaoh's palace.*
16 *It went well for Abram on her account, and he received sheep, cattle, he-asses, male and female servants, she-asses, and camels.*
17 *But Yahweh afflicted Pharaoh and his palace with severe plagues because of Sarai, Abram's wife.*
18 *Then Pharaoh summoned Abram and said: "How could you have done this to me? Why did you not inform me that she was your wife?*
19 *Why did you say, 'She is my sister,' so that I took her for my wife? Now here is your wife. Take her and be gone!"*
20 *Then Pharaoh put men in charge of him. They sent him away along with his wife and all that he had.*

10 Unlike the first section in this chapter, which began with an imperative, this one begins with an indicative. In 12:1, for the first time since ch. 2, a narrative began with the initiative of Yahweh. This second narrative of ch. 12 reverts to the pattern of the initiative from one other than Yahweh. A devastating famine sends Abram with Sarai (but no mention of Lot!) scurrying to Egypt. The text neither supports nor rebukes Abram for this temporary journey away from Canaan. The first unit in this chapter had Abram living among the Canaanites (v. 6). In this section he is living with the Egyptians. How he responds in both situations as an alien moving into the territory of an indigenous group is strikingly different.

27. See U. Cassuto, *The Documentary Hypothesis and the Composition of the Pentateuch,* tr. I. Abrahams (Jerusalem: Magnes, 1961), p. 81.

1. Note how the objects are arranged in chiasmus.

A patriarch's descent to Egypt because of famine in his own land surfaces as a pivotal event again in the journey of Jacob's family to Egypt. Egyptian texts substantiate the possibility of such an itinerary in the 2nd millennium B.C. The famous painting in the tomb of Khnum-hotep III at Beni Hasan, about 150 miles north of Cairo, from the time of Sesostris II (1897–1878 B.C.), shows the arrival of thirty-seven Asiatics, men, women, and children, in Egypt.[2] The story of the Egyptian courtier Sinuhe is also relevant.[3] From Libya, where he was on an expedition for the Pharaoh, Sinuhe traveled across Egypt and up into Canaan but eventually returned to Egypt. Sinuhe's odyssey is exactly the opposite of Abram's: from Egypt to Canaan, back to Egypt. A later Egyptian text from the reign of Merneptah (1224–1214 B.C.) notes that the Egyptians had "finished letting the Bedouin tribes of Edom [the Shasu] pass the Fortress [of] Mer-ne-Ptah . . . to the pools of Per-Atum . . . to keep them alive and to keep their cattle alive";[4] this is approximately Abram's itinerary in Gen. 12:10–20.

11 Abram is correct about two things. One is that he is married to an extremely attractive woman, despite the fact that she is at least sixty-five years old, that is, about mid-life (see 23:1). Ironically, when Abram tries at a later point in his life to perpetrate the same ruse (20:1ff.), he makes no remarks about his wife's beauty! In this second situation she is eighty-nine (see 17:1). Is her pulchritude waning?

12 Abram is also correct in his role as a prognosticator. As a stranger in a foreign land he will be especially vulnerable, and so will his spouse. We are not told the source of Abram's knowledge about the Egyptians and their reputed reputation for wife abduction. On what is he basing his prediction? The Canaanites had not tried to take his wife in the pre-famine days in Canaan. Abram's fear of the Egyptians may show that the law of hospitality, so central to biblical thought, was absent in other cultures, at least in Abram's mind. The stranger, rather than being an alien to be welcomed and protected, is one of whom advantage may be taken. Wherever Abram goes, he finds himself in a potentially hazardous situation. The famine threatens his life, and the sojourn to Egypt also threatens his life. A simple change in scenery circumvented the first threat. The next verse will inform us of his strategy for circumventing the second threat.

Of course, in requesting Sarai to be duplicitous about her true identity,

2. The text is translated in *ANET,* p. 229, and the painting is reproduced in *ANEP,* no. 3.

3. The story of Sinuhe is found in *ANET,* pp. 18–22.

4. See *ANET,* p. 259.

Abram mentions only that she will not be killed, *but you they will spare.* He does not raise the possibility with her that one of the Egyptians will take her as wife. Maybe that possibility never entered his mind, if for no other reason than that his concern is with his own fate, not Sarai's.

13 In an attempt to neutralize a potentially hazardous situation, Abram requests that Sarai deceive their hosts. But he thereby aggravates the situation, as the story will subsequently make clear. Sarai is instructed to tell any man who confronts her that she is Abram's *sister.* This is a half-truth, as 20:12 indicates (although "daughter of my father" could mean adopted daughter).

Scholars debate the proper understanding of Abram's plan. Why does he think he may come out of this nightmare alive if he can only convince his hosts that the woman traveling with him is his sister? E. A. Speiser suggested that the Nuzi texts provided an answer or a source behind this strange practice.[5] A marriage practice among the upper Hurrian classes, and one without counterpart in any other Near Eastern society, allowed a wife to be adopted by her husband as his sister; moreover, a woman given in marriage by her brother (as with Rebekah to Isaac by Laban) would legally become her husband's sister. Since Abram spent part of his life at Haran (a major Hurrian city), Speiser assumed that it was while he was living in Haran that Abram was exposed to this custom.

Three Nuzi texts (HSS v:80, 69, 25) provided fuel for Speiser's interpretation. In the first Akkulenni gives his sister Beltakkadummi to Hurazzi in marriage. In the second Hurazzi adopts Beltakkadummi as his sister, and in return the brother receives forty shekels of silver as the price for sister adoption. In the third we are told that Beltakkadummi was married to Hurazzi by her own free will.

Many scholars have remained unconvinced by Speiser's handling of the Hurrian material.[6] Their objections pursue the following routes:

5. E. A. Speiser, "The Wife-Sister Motif in the Patriarchal Narratives," in *Biblical and Other Studies,* ed. A. Altmann (Cambridge: Harvard University, 1963), pp. 15–28; repr. in *Oriental and Biblical Studies,* pp. 62–82. See also Speiser, *Genesis,* pp. xl–xli, 91–94.

6. Among them, J. Van Seters, *Abraham in History and Tradition* (New Haven and London: Yale University, 1975), pp. 71–78; C. J. M. Weir, "The Alleged Hurrian Wife-Sister Motif in Genesis," *TGUOS* 22 (1967–70) 14–25; D. Freedman, "A New Approach to the Nuzi Sistership Contract," *JANES* 2 (1970) 77–85; T. L. Thompson, *Historicity of the Patriarchal Narratives,* pp. 234–47; S. Greengus, "Sisterhood Adoption at Nuzi and the 'Wife-Sister' in Genesis," *HUCA* 46 (1975) 5–31; M. J. Selman, "The Social Environment of the Patriarchs," *TynBul* 27 (1976) 119–21.

(1) Speiser arranges the three Nuzi texts in a sequence that is artificial. Who is to say that chronologically no. 69 (the woman is taken as a sister, *ana aḫati*) follows no. 80 (the woman is taken as wife, *ana aššati*)? It could just as easily be the reverse, with sisterhood preceding wifehood. (2) It is incorrect to say that such marriages reflected the characteristics of the top levels of Hurrian society. In fact, in four of the thirteen instances of sister adoption *(aḫatûtû),* the adopted sister was originally a manumitted slave girl. (3) There is serious doubt that such adoptions were used as a means of creating a patriarchal bond between a man and his exogamous wife.

If one eliminates the Nuzi material from consideration, there is little to set in its place. One explanation that has attracted less support than even the Hurrian parallels is that Abram was temporarily divorcing his wife.[7] The basis for this interpretation is Islamic law, in which the clauses "you are no longer my wife: you are as a sister to me" are a divorce declaration.

Perhaps one need not appeal to extrabiblical literature to explain Abram's ploy. The answer may be found in the Uriah-Bathsheba-David debacle (2 Sam. 11). David would not have had to eliminate Uriah had Uriah been Bathsheba's brother, any more than the Egyptians would have had to execute Abram so they could have his sister. Siblings are tolerable, spouses are not, when the female is highly desirable to another male.

14–15 Abram's worst suspicions, if we may use that word, are realized. Throughout these events Sarai has remained quiet. What does she think of her husband's scheme? Does she condone it and does she willingly cooperate? Or is her opinion irrelevant? I interpret her silence as agreement to cooperate in the ruse. Now Sarai is taken from Abram and *taken into Pharaoh's palace.* This is doubtless a case of actual adultery between Pharaoh and Sarai, rather that potential adultery such as we find in 20:3–4.[8] Later in the narrative Pharaoh says, "I took her for my wife" (v. 19). Thus, to exacerbate the situation, Sarai is not only asked to engage in deception, but in the process she becomes vulnerable and is eventually forced into cohabiting with one other than her husband.

Here Abram's plan has completely backfired. Surely he had not counted on losing Sarai in the process. Again we are denied information that tells us about Abram's response here. Did he willingly let his wife go, or did

7. See L. Rost, "Fragen zum Scheidungsgerecht in Gen. 12,10–20," in *Gottes Wort und Gottes Land,* Fest. H. W. Hertzberg, ed. H. G. Reventlow (Göttingen: Vandenhoeck & Ruprecht, 1965), pp. 186–92.

8. See R. Polzin, " 'The Ancestress of Israel' in Danger," *Semeia* 3 (1975) 83, 87.

he offer strenuous protest? We may compare Abram's separation from his wife (ch. 12) with his separation from his nephew Lot (ch. 14). In the latter case he was anything but passive. He immediately mustered all the men at his disposal and pursued the armies that had taken Lot.

Why did Abram find himself in such an unpredictable situation anyway? Why did he feel constrained to resort to deception? How different is the Abram of 12:10–20 from the trusting, obedient Abram of 12:1–9! Could it be that he acts, however despicably, in order to keep alive the promises of God that he had recently received? It is impossible for God to make of Abram a great nation if Abram is dead before he fathers one child. How can God give Canaan to Abram's seed if he has no seed? To prevent such a possibility, Abram must do all he can to stay alive. He is giving Yahweh a little assistance in a potentially embarrassing situation! Here is the first threat to the realization of God's promises: a dead Abram, dead either through starvation or through execution.

16 In compensation for the loss of his "sister," Abram is given a retinue of animals and servants. Abram leaves Egypt a wealthy man, but unlike many other OT individuals whose material prosperity is directly tied to God's blessing, Abram has come upon his wealth through a means other than divine blessing. This is quite an exchange. Abram relinquishes his wife and gains animals and servants. Everything that comes to Abram comes because of Sarai. In one chapter Proverbs can make a case for the fact that "the blessing of the Lord makes rich" (10:22), and show its contempt for "treasures gained by wickedness" (10:2). While Proverbs attributes all poverty to laziness, which is a sin, it does not attribute all wealth to virtue.

Most of the commentary on this verse has focused on the mention of camels as among those animals that Pharaoh gave to Abram. If one accepts that (to the best of our knowledge) camels were not domesticated until much later in the 2nd millennium B.C., then we have here a clear anachronism. W. F. Albright has led the argument most forcibily in this direction.[9] He observes

9. See, e.g., *From the Stone Age to Christianity,* 2nd ed. (Garden City, NY: Doubleday, 1957), pp. 164–65; idem, *The Biblical Period from Abraham to Ezra* (New York: Harper & Row, 1963), p. 7; idem, *Yahweh and the Gods of Canaan* (repr. Winona Lake, IN: Eisenbrauns, 1978), pp. 62, 156. C. H. Gordon (*The Pennsylvania Tradition of Semitics* [Atlanta: Scholars, 1986], p. 53) remarks, "he [viz., Albright] abominated camels and adored donkeys. This had a subconscious effect on his pronouncements and publications concerning the patriarchal age. He 'got rid' of the camels by turning their very mention in the patriarchal narratives into anachronisms. His love of the donkey impelled him to stress the role of the Fathers as donkey caravaneers."

the absence of references to camels in the Mari texts, the Amarna Letters, and the Ugaritic texts, all of which have much to say about nomadic peoples. In contrast to ch. 12, ch. 13, where Abram and Lot part company, makes no mention of camels, though flocks or herds are mentioned (13:5). Note, however, that in other events in Abram's life camels are mentioned, especially in the story of the search for Isaac's bride-to-be (Gen. 24), which has sixteen references to camels.

Others are not so skeptical about the reliability of the references to camels in Gen. 12.[10] For example, a text from Alalakh (18th century B.C.) appears to refer to a domesticated camel.[11]

17 Not only has Sarai been silent so far—so has Yahweh. He has also been inactive. Now it is time in the narrative to switch from "a history under the control of Abraham's plan . . . to a history under the control of Yahweh's plan."[12] A series of plagues is unleashed on Pharaoh, much as they were later on a different Pharaoh who also tried to keep incarcerated what was not his (Exod. 7–12).

Sarai is the pivotal figure here. Abram prospers because of her. Pharaoh suffers because of her. She is a catalyst for good and for evil. It is true that Pharaoh acted in ignorance, but he is nonetheless culpable. The sin of ignorance takes two forms in the OT. Such a sin may be committed through negligence (the sinner knows that what he did is wrong, but he did not do it on purpose) or through ignorance (the sinner does not know that what he did was wrong). Clearly, Pharaoh's sin was the latter type. And yet the OT does not exonerate the sinner on the basis of either negligence or ignorance. For such a person expiation, accompanied by confession, is required. Of course, the sacrificial system is there for the sons and daughters of Israel, not for Egyptian pharaohs. And yet even one who is not a child of Abraham and stands outside the covenant family is held accountable for crimes perpetrated

10. See J. P. Free, "Abraham's Camels," *JNES* 3 (1944) 187–93; K. A. Kitchen, *Ancient Orient and Old Testament* (Chicago: Inter-Varsity, 1966), pp. 79–80.

11. See D. J. Wiseman, "Ration Lists from Alalakh VII," *JCS* 13 (1959) 29, where text 269:59 reads 1 *SA.GAL ANŠE.GAM.MAL,* "one (measure of) fodder—camel." In a following article, "Remarks on the Ration Lists from Alalakh VII," A. Goetze remarks (p. 37), "This early occurrence of camels, missing in CAD, to be fed and, therefore domesticated, is worthy of special note." W. G. Lambert ("The Domesticated Camel in the Second Millennium—Evidence from Alalakh and Ugarit," *BASOR* 160 [1960] 42–43) objects to the interpretation of Wiseman and Goetze, and suggests that the ideogram in question means "stag," not "camel."

12. D. L. Petersen, "A Thrice-Told Tale: Genre, Theme, and Motif," *BR* 18 (1973) 37.

unwittingly, and must consequently be subjected to the appropriate punishment. And in this particular case the crime is committed against a member of Abram's family.

18–19 Pharaoh now assumes the double role of judge and of one of the contending parties (for others in this double role, see 20:10; 26:9; 44:14–34; Exod. 1:18–19; 1 Sam. 22:6–16; 24:8–22; 1 K. 2:42–45). He rebukes Abram for his irresponsible behavior, and then orders him to leave the country and to take his wife with him. Pharaoh's two "why" questions, in which he shares his indignation with Abram, are but one illustration of many in the OT in which several "why" questions occur in sequence, always with *lāmmâ* rather than *maddua'* (cf. Laban to Jacob, 31:27, 30; Egyptians to Joseph, 47:15, 19; Moses to God, Exod. 5:22; Num. 11:11).[13] It is not uncommon, especially in prophetic literature, for God to assume the role of both plaintiff and judge (cf., e.g., Isa. 1).

We should give this Egyptian king some credit. Upon learning of his embarrassing mistake (but note that the text nowhere suggests that the Pharaoh interpreted the plagues as punishment), he immediately returns Sarai to her husband. Furthermore, the king's three questions addressed to Abram reveal that the pagan king indeed knows that adultery is a moral evil. In fact, Pharaoh exemplifies a higher degree of moral sensitivity than does the patriarch.[14] The Egyptian emerges rather saintly, but Abram, the one in whom the Egyptians and other nations are to be blessed, appears rather sinister. This Egyptian monarch does not operate by the principle of the divine right of kings. Unlike Jezebel (1 K. 21), he will not kill to get what he wants. But there is more here than just polite restraint. If he experienced plagues for taking Abram's wife, what would happen to him if he were to take Abram's life? As Westermann has correctly said, "The reason Abram emerges unpunished is solely that the Pharaoh has experienced the power behind him."[15]

20 Pharaoh does not ask for the return of the animals and servants he gave to Abram. Abram, Sarai, and their retinue are escorted out of the country. We have no idea how long Abram remained in Egypt,[16] but however long, it was an experience he surely wanted to forget. That Pharaoh *put men in charge of him* is a further expression of his concern that nothing happen

13. See J. Barr, " 'Why?' in Biblical Hebrew," *JTS* 36 (1985) 29–30.

14. See P. D. Miscall, "Literary Unity in Old Testament Narrative," *Semeia* 15 (1979) 32.

15. Westermann, *Genesis,* 2:166.

16. See B. Z. Wacholder, "How Long Did Abram Stay in Egypt?" *HUCA* 35 (1964) 43–56.

to Abram and his entourage to arouse further the wrath of Abram's deity against Egypt.

They sent him away. Abram's expulsion from Egypt is expressed by the Piel of *šālaḥ*. This form was used earlier when God "sent forth" Adam and Eve from the garden (3:23). It appears in later texts that describe Pharaoh's release of the Israelites from his tight hold (Exod. 6:1; 11:1; 12:33).

The movement famine-sojourn-captivity-return anticipates other portions of Scripture. This same sequence is certainly reflected in the experiences of Moses and the Exodus. And it comes quite close to events in the exilic period, where geographically the action has shifted to Babylon. In all of these events the infidelity of the people is subordinated to the faithfulness of Yahweh.[17] This early experience of Abram thus anticipates the destiny of Abram's descendants at two pivotal points in their history.

Yet, there are some obvious differences between Abram's Egyptian experiences and those of Moses and Israel. Unlike the Egyptians in Exodus, the Egyptians in Gen. 12:10–20 are not oppressors. Pharaoh is not cruel to Abram. Israel survives Egypt because of the intervening activities of God on its behalf, and because of his earlier promises to the fathers (Exod. 2:23–25). Abram survives Egypt primarily because of Pharaoh's reluctance to punish him beyond expulsion. Throughout Gen. 12–50 Egypt is a symbol of safety and provision for the patriarchs and their families. If anything, Egypt is the oppressed in Genesis. Note that it is Sarai who "dealt harshly" with her Egyptian maidservant, forcing her "to flee" (16:6). Later she urges her husband to "cast out" this Egyptian.[18]

THE NEW TESTAMENT APPROPRIATION

Gen. 12:1, 4 and Heb. 11:8; Acts 7:3

The only passage in the NT to emphasize the element of uncertainty in the commencement of Abraham's faith pilgrimage is Heb. 11:8. Indeed, Heb. 11:8 offers the most definite assertion of this uncertainty (more so even than Genesis) with the addition of the phrase "even though he did not know where he was going." Nowhere in his epistles does Paul employ Abraham's departure from Ur or Haran as a striking illustration of the life of faith. Instead,

17. See R. L. Pratt, Jr., "Pictures, Windows, and Mirrors in Old Testament Exegesis," *WTJ* 45 (1983) 156–67, esp. 160–67.

18. See P. D. Miscall, *The Workings of Old Testament Narrative* (Philadelphia: Fortress; Chico, CA: Scholars, 1983), pp. 42–45.

Paul focuses on Abraham's ability to believe God for a child in spite of the age of both himself and his wife.

Hebrews 11:8 makes it clear that Abraham was called to leave his home. The writer uses the present participle *kaloúmenos,* which is perhaps his way of emphasizing Abraham's immediate response to God. The command is "to go out." Attridge notes that up until now the dominant image of movement in Hebrews has been that of "entry," especially into rest, or the heavenly sanctuary (3:11, 18, 19; 4:1–6, 10–11; 6:19–20; 9:12, 24–25).[1]

Gen. 12:3 and Gal. 3:8

In order to cement his case about faith apart from works, Paul cross-examines the Galatian witnesses with a battery of questions, the answers to which are self-evident. God's Spirit works when faith is functioning (Gal. 3:5).

To further his case Paul offers in vv. 6–18 a list of Scripture citations (Deut. 27:26; Hab. 2:4; Lev. 18:5; Deut. 21:23) in which Abraham is presented as a historical example, an *exemplum.*[2] In the midst of this illustration Paul appeals to Abraham as the father of the Gentiles. The promise of Gen. 12:3 is then referred to as "the gospel in advance." Here Paul clearly takes the Genesis passage with passive, rather than with reflexive, force. To buttress scripturally God's justifying the Gentiles by faith, Paul employs *tá éthnē,* and not LXX *hai phylaí* (Heb. *mišpāḥôṯ*), when he quotes Gen. 12:3. Because *tá éthnē* (the nations) are to be blessed in Abraham, Christ's invitation to his disciples was to make disciples of *pánta tá éthnē* (Matt. 28:19). Thus a scriptural basis for the missionary outreach of the church is found in Gen. 12:3.

Gen. 12:7 (and 13:15; 24:7) and Gal. 3:16

The larger context for Gal. 3:16 is the relation of the promise of God to the law of God. This particular verse focuses on the characteristics of the covenant concept in biblical thought. First, its antiquity is established—it was given to Abraham. Second, its character is delineated—it consists of promises (perhaps plural because the one promise was often repeated). Third, this covenant was not limited to Abraham but extended to his seed. Fourth, if one strictly interprets *seed,* it is a reference to one person, the Christ. In essence all Abraham's descendants are summed up in one person.

1. H. W. Attridge, *Hebrews,* Hermeneia (Philadelphia: Fortress, 1989), p. 322.

2. See H. D. Betz, "The Literary Composition and Function of Paul's Letter to the Galatians," *NTS* 21 (1975) 371.

Paul certainly knew that *spérma* may have a collective sense even in the singular. A plural of *spérma* to designate "descendants" would have been unnecessary. But for Paul the true fulfillment of the singular is only in Christ, even if he reaches that conclusion *via* a generic singular. It is well known that the traditional Jewish interpretation of "seed" encompasses a plurality of descendants, and is so used by Paul himself on occasion (e.g., Rom. 4:18). But the OT also supplies instances where "seed" can refer only to a single individual (e.g., Gen. 4:25; 21:12, 13; 1 Sam. 1:11; 2 Sam. 7:12–15). "Paul is speaking from the standpoint of fulfilled prophecy in the conviction that the 'issue' of the original promise can, in the event, refer only to Christ."[3]

B. THE SEPARATION OF LOT AND ABRAM (13:1–18)

1 *Abram went up from Egypt, he, his wife, his possessions, and Lot, to the Negeb.*

2 *Now Abram was very wealthy in livestock, silver, and gold.*

3 *From the Negeb he traveled by stages toward Bethel to the place between Bethel and Ai, where his tent had formerly stood,*

4 *to the site of the altar which he had built previously, and there he invoked Yahweh by name.*

5 *Lot, who accompanied Abram, also had sheep, cattle, and tents,*

6 *so that the land could not support*[1] *them dwelling together, for their possessions were so abundant that they could not dwell together.*

7 *There was a dispute between the herdsmen of Abram's livestock and the herdsmen of Lot's livestock. The Canaanites and Perizzites were then occupying the land.*

8 *So Abram said to Lot: "Let there be no strife between me and you, or*[2] *between my herdsmen and your herdsmen, for we are kinsmen.*

9 *Is not the whole land available to you? Separate from me. If you wish the left, I will take the right. If you wish the right, I will take the left."*

3. R. Y. K. Fung, *Galatians,* NICNT (Grand Rapids: Eerdmans, 1988), p. 156; cf. F. F. Bruce, *Epistle to the Galatians,* NIGTC (Grand Rapids: Eerdmans, 1982), pp. 171–73; H. D. Betz, *Galatians,* Hermeneia (Philadelphia: Fortress, 1979), pp. 156–57.

1. Note the disagreement between the subject "earth" (Heb. *'ereṣ,* fem.) and the verb "support" (Heb. *nāśā',* 3rd sing. masc.); see M. G. Slonim, "Masculine Predicates with Feminine Subjects in the Hebrew Bible," *JBL* 63 (1944) 299. SP makes the subject and verb consistent with its *nāśe'â.*

2. D. W. Baker ("Further Examples of the *waw explicativum,*" *VT* 30 [1980] 132) reads "let there not be any dispute between me and you, *that is,* between my herdsmen and your herdsmen."

10 *Lot looked about and saw how well watered was the whole Jordan plain—this was before Yahweh destroyed Sodom and Gomorrah—much like Yahweh's garden*[3] *or like Egypt, as far as Zoar.*
11 *Accordingly, Lot chose for himself the whole Jordan plain and set out eastward. Thus they separated from each other.*
12 *Abram dwelt in the land of Canaan while Lot dwelt in the cities of the plain. He acquired grazing rights as far as*[4] *Sodom.*
13 *The men of Sodom were very*[5] *evil, sinners against Yahweh.*
14 *Yahweh said to Abram after Lot had left: "Look about, please, and from where you are look northward, southward, eastward, and westward;*
15 *for all the land you see I will give to you and to your descendants forever.*
16 *I will make your descendants as the dust of the ground; if a person could count the dust of the ground, then your descendants also could be counted.*
17 *Get up, walk throughout the land, through its length and breadth, for to you I will give it."*
18 *Abram thus acquired grazing rights and eventually settled by the terebinths of Mamre which are by Hebron. There he built an altar to Yahweh.*

1 Abram's return to Canaan is recorded with as little commentary as possible, and the chapter is unaware of any famine in the land, still in process or recently ended. His journey from Egypt up to Canaan is a silent one, as was to be his later journey from Beer-sheba up to Moriah (22:1). What does one talk about, how do spouses communicate, after recent events like these? In early references to both Sarai and Lot, sometimes Lot is mentioned first (11:31), and sometimes Sarai is mentioned first (12:5). In 12:10–20, only Sarai is referred to. The order in 12:20 was Abram, Sarai, Abram's possessions. In this opening verse of ch. 13 even Abram's possessions are listed before Lot.

3. It may be that "Yahweh" is used here to express the superlative, in which case one would read "an exquisite garden." See P. A. H. de Boer, "Y-H-W-H as epithet expressing the superlative," *VT* 24 (1974) 233–35.

4. H. L. Ginsberg ("A Preposition of Interest to Historical Geographers," *BASOR* 122 [1951] 12–14) shows that the preposition *ʿaḏ* may also mean "near, at." Cf. Gen. 10:19; 12:6; 25:18; 38:1; Judg. 4:11.

5. Because of the odd placement of *m^eʾōḏ* at the end of the sentence, just after the tetragrammaton, Dahood emends MT *m^eʾōḏ* to *māʾēḏ,* and reads it as a title of Yahweh: "now the men of Sodom were wicked and sinful before Yahweh the Grand" ("Northwest Semitic Notes on Genesis," *Bib* 55 [1974] 78).

2 The patriarch's ill-gotten wealth is again mentioned, as if to reinforce the point that in acquiring his wealth he lost the respect of his wife and any sense of self-respect and dignity. A fortune has been amassed, but an opportunity for trust has been missed. Among Abram's plenteous resources his livestock is listed before his silver and gold. As we will see later in this narrative, problems emerge between Abram and Lot over livestock, not over precious metals.

3–4 Retracing his steps, Abram returns to the site on which he had built his altar, and once there he engages in an act of worship. Is he glad to put Egypt behind him? Does the place of worship also become the place of contrition? If it is, the text is silent about any remorse or repentance on Abram's part. But at least Abram has left behind the unknown and the threatening, and is now back in the familiar, but more importantly in the place where he had earlier built an altar and called on the name of his God. Not once while he was in Egypt did Abram either erect monuments to or invoke his deity.

5 Lot had obviously accompanied Abram and Sarai to Egypt. The phrase *who accompanied Abram* should not be read as an artificial attempt to harmonize ch. 13 (the presence of Lot) with ch. 12:10ff. (the absence of Lot). Lot is not mentioned in 12:10ff. because he is peripheral to the story's themes, which focus on Abram, Sarai, and Pharaoh. Both uncle and nephew share one possession in abundance: livestock. Each has one unique possession in abundance: Abram has silver and gold; Lot has tents. Abram too lived in a tent (12:8), but this verse focuses only on Lot's possession of several or many tents. Abram's wealth was greater than that of Lot. V. 2 says that Abram was "very wealthy" (*kāḇēḏ me'ôḏ; kāḇēḏ* was the word also used in 12:10 to describe the "severe" famine in the land), while it says of Lot only that he "also had [*weḡam . . . hāyâ*] sheep, cattle, and tents." The text does not specify the source of Lot's possessions.

6 They encounter an impasse. How will two comparatively wealthy individuals share the same land? Domestic conundrums of unbelievable complexity are never far from Abram. The tension now shifts from husband and wife to uncle and nephew. Confined to a relatively small parcel of land, the two men must separate. Not only were these possessions illegitimately obtained, but their continued presence among Abram and Lot will shortly drive a wedge between them. The situation is potentially explosive.

7 Crowding leads to disputation and in-house bickering. The respective employees of Lot and Abram engage in verbal sparring, with each claiming legitimate sovereignty over the parcel of land in question. Such quarreling is referred to as a *dispute (rîḇ)* in v. 7, and *strife (merîḇâ)* in v. 8.

Because of the frequent occurrence of the root *rîḇ* in the prophets, and elsewhere, many commentators have seized on the idea that implicit in this word is the concept of a lawsuit.[6] When the text says that God has a "controversy" *(rîḇ)* with his people, it thereby indicates that he is introducing a lawsuit against them.

In strict legal terms, the word *lawsuit* can only be properly used when the two disputing parties are unable to resolve their differences through either peaceful or violent means. As a result they turn to a third party to act as adjudicator. This is not the procedure pursued in Gen. 13, for Abram and Lot are able to solve their quarrel without resort to a mediating party. Hence, the situation does not involve a lawsuit of any kind.[7]

But if a lawsuit is not involved, strife is involved, and it is a strife that is not followed by reconciliation.[8] The irony is that Abram and Lot seem to be able to share the land with the *Canaanites and Perizzites,* for these peoples were also *occupying* or "dwelling" *(yōšēḇ)* in the land, but there is not enough room for Abram and Lot "to dwell" *(lāšeḇeṯ)* adjacently.

8–9 Abram capitalizes on the chance to defuse the debate and settle it amicably.[9] The Abram now resettled in Canaan contrasts sharply with the Abram in Egypt. He who earlier fomented strife now moves to nip strife in the bud. The manipulation that Abram formerly manifested now gives way to magnanimity. Lot, unlike Sarai, is given a free hand. One wonders if Abram's return to the altar and meeting with God (v. 4) had anything to do with this change of disposition.

The father's attitude here is evidently passed on to his son, for it later controls his son's response in a similar situation. The servants of Isaac dug wells, only to have them claimed by the herdsmen of Abimelech at Gerar.

6. For example, B. Gemser, "The *rîb-* or Controversy-pattern in Hebrew mentality," in *Wisdom in Israel and in the Ancient Near East,* Fest. H. H. Rowley, ed. M. Noth and D. Winton Thomas, VTSup 3 (Leiden: Brill, 1955), pp. 128–33; J. Limburg, "The Root *ryb* and the Prophetic Lawsuit Speeches," *JBL* 88 (1969) 291–304; G. E. Wright, "The Lawsuit of God: A Form-Critical Study of Deuteronomy 32," in *Israel's Prophetic Heritage,* Fest. J. Muilenburg, ed. B. W. Anderson and W. Harrelson (New York: Harper & Row, 1962), pp. 26–67.

7. See M. De Roche, "Yahweh's *rîb* Against Israel: A Reassessment of the So-Called 'Prophetic Lawsuit' in the Preexilic Prophets," *JBL* 102 (1983) 567.

8. See G. W. Coats, "Strife and Reconciliation: Themes of a Biblical Theology in the Book of Genesis," *HBT* 2 (1980) 26.

9. The clause "Let there be no strife between me and you" may be understood as a *Streitverhinderungsformel,* to be used to settle a quarrel outside of court. See G. W. Ramsey, "Speech-Forms in Hebrew Law and Prophetic Oracles," *JBL* 96 (1977) 50.

The latter quarreled (*yārîḇû,* from *rîḇ*) with Isaac's crew (26:21). Rather than press his rights, Isaac relinquished the wells to Abimelech and built wells on other pasturage (26:22). Both Abram and Isaac have learned the truth of Zech. 4:6, that success comes "not by might nor by power." The particulars are different, but Joseph too will discover that the rise to power is by way of exile and prison.

In refusing to exercise the prerogatives of the *paterfamilias,* Abram essentially releases any part of the promised land to Lot. In so doing, he is prepared to sacrifice what has been promised to him, as he will later willingly offer Isaac who had been promised to him.[10] Lot is given the first choice of any part of the land. He may choose anything on *the left* or *the right,* and Abram will take the other part. If directions are determined from the perspective of one facing east, then *the left* would be land to the north, and *the right* would be land to the south. Westermann does not see the nobility in Abram's proposal that all other commentators have seen. He suggests that Abram is motivated more by prudence than he is by magnanimity. Abram will make that decision which will bring the greatest amount of well-being and security to the group which he heads, and thus he must circumvent any approach that will foment violence and threaten that well-being.[11]

10–11 The lush Jordan plain catches Lot's eye. Here is another instance in Genesis of a person seeing something *(rā'â kî),* and on the basis of that seeing they followed with what they deemed appropriate action. Thus, Eve saw that the tree was good *(wattēre' . . . kî ṭôḇ)* and she then took from its fruit (*wattiqqaḥ,* 3:6). *rā'â kî* in that instance would be a covetous look. Also, the sons of God saw that the daughters of men were beautiful *(wayyir'û ḇenê-hā'ĕlōhîm . . . kî ṭōḇōṯ)* and they took them as wives (*wayyiqḥû,* 6:2). I have argued above that this was not a lustful look, but rather a passionate look (in the good sense of the word "passionate"). Again, God saw that the earth was replete with evil *(wayyar' . . . kî rabbî rā'aṯ hā'āḏām bā'āreṣ)* and his subsequent resolve, based on that observation, was to destroy it (*'emḥeh 'eṯ-hā'āḏām,* 6:5, 7). Thus, *rā'â kî,* so far in Genesis, may mean "to look at something covetously," "to look at something romantically," or "to make an observation." I suggest the latter of the three fits best in the *rā'â kî* of this verse. Lot saw or observed how well watered was the plain of Jordan, and accordingly chose this territory *(wayyar' . . . wayyiḇḥar).*

10. The sacrificing of the land (ch. 13) and of Isaac (ch. 22) have been imaginatively connected by W. Vogel, "Abraham et l'offrande de la terre (Gn. 13)," *SR* 4 (1974–75) 51–57.

11. Westermann, *Genesis,* 2:176.

Two similes are employed to make vivid the richness of the land chosen by Lot. The first compares the land to be occupied by Lot to *Yahweh's garden,* that is, Eden. Paradise regained! The second compares Lot's newly gained land to *Egypt, as far as Zoar,* presumably a reference to the fertile Delta area. This second comparison is interesting in the light of Deut. 11:10–12, "The land you are entering is not like the land of Egypt from which you have come." The exact location of Zoar is not known, but a site south or southeast of the Dead Sea is most likely. The Mishnah (*Yebam.* 16.7) calls Zoar "the City of Palms," and Ptolemy (*Onom.* 231, 261) claimed that Zoar was widely famous for its balsam and date palms.

It is clear from v. 12 that the territory chosen by Lot lies outside the borders of Canaan. In choosing such a place for his grazing grounds, Lot effectively removes himself from any possible consideration as the one who shall inherit the land promised to his uncle. Ancient Near Eastern legal corpora do provide instances of adoption of an heir in case of childlessness (see Gen. 15:2). But Lot's choice to dwell outside Canaan eliminates him as Abram's heir.[12] The promise that the "seed" of Abram would inherit the land (12:7) had made clear already that Lot could not be Abram's beneficiary. Lot's own actions simply confirm and consolidate the divine promise of 12:7.

It is not necessary to view Lot's choice as based on avarice. There is no indication that he is covetous. He makes the natural and logical decision. Given the alternatives, he opts for a section of land that holds much potential for his grazing flocks. He can hardly be blamed for that choice. That this lush land will one day be the target of divine wrath is a fact Lot could hardly have known.

12 The author emphasizes Abram and Lot in this sentence by placing both proper names before the verb: "Abram—he dwelt . . . Lot—he dwelt. . . ." *His grazing rights extended as far as Sodom.* Heb. *ye'ĕhal* is usually translated "he pitched his tent" (AV, NIV; cf. JB, NEB, Speiser, Westermann), but this translation leads to an awkward tautology: "he dwelt . . . and he pitched his tent," unless we understand here a move from general ("he dwelt") to more specific ("he pitched his tent") terminology. *'āhal,* a denominative verb from *'ōhel,* "tent," occurs again only in v. 18. In the

12. See L. R. Helyer, "The Separation of Abram and Lot: Its Significance in the Patriarchal Narratives," *JSOT* 26 (1983) 77–88. G. Coats ("Lot: A Foil in the Abraham Saga," in *Understanding the Word: Essays in Honor of Bernhard W. Anderson,* ed. James T. Butler et al., JSOTSup 37 [Sheffield: JSOT, 1985], p. 117) makes the further remark: "To separate from Abram is to separate from the Lord's blessing, indeed, to invite the Lord's curse."

context of searching for land for livestock to graze, it is best rendered as "acquire grazing rights."[13]

13 This verse provides a commentary on the moral status of the Sodomites. They are wicked sinners. Lot was not aware of it, and probably would not have chosen the territory had he known. The preceding verse placed Sodom outside Canaan, beyond its southernmost border. Yet these Sodomites, not living in the promised land, are culpable as *sinners against Yahweh.* Apparently God's jurisdiction and sovereignty are not confined to his land. His authority does not stop at the border. He judges an Egyptian Pharaoh for his sins, showing the extension of his power into foreign soil. So too the residents of Sodom may be tagged as "sinners against Yahweh." Certain passages in the OT (Gen. 35:2ff.; Judg. 11:24; 1 Sam. 26:19; 2 K. 5:7) appear, at first reading, to restrict Yahweh's domain to his land and the doings of his own people. And yet the OT repeatedly affirms that God's dominion and power are universal. These two concepts are not necessarily in conflict. "While YHWH governs and manifests his activity everywhere—in Sodom, Shinar, Egypt, Nineveh and Tarshish—the area of his sanctity is restricted to the boundaries of the land of Israel."[14]

14 For the first time in this section Yahweh speaks to Abram. The sudden change in the narrative's direction is evidenced even by the unusual word order. It is subject plus verb (in the perfect) instead of verb (in the imperfect) followed by subject. Lot's departure leaves Abram alone. Sarai is not mentioned in this scene for the same reason that Lot was not mentioned in the previous incident in Egypt—she has no role in the action being described. Yahweh asks Abram to look as far as possible in all four directions. Many translators ignore the small Hebrew particle *nā'* in the divine speech, but it is reflected in our translation as *please,* which is its normal English equivalent. It occurs many times in the OT, some sixty times in Genesis alone. But only four times in the entire OT does God use the word in addressing a human being: here; 15:5; 22:2; Exod. 11:2. In each of these four passages God asks somebody to do something that transcends human comprehension: have faith that a son will be born to one of advanced age (15:5); sacrifice an only son (22:2); ask former Egyptian masters for parting gifts (Exod. 11:2). In this passage Yahweh asks Abram to exercise faith that the land, as far as Abram's eye can see in any direction, will one day be his.[15]

13. See C. Rabin, "Etymological Miscellanea," *Scripta Hierosolymitana* 8 (1961) 384–86.

14. Y. Kaufmann, *The Religion of Israel,* tr. and abridged by M. Greenberg (Chicago: University of Chicago, 1960), p. 128.

15. See Y. T. Radday, "The Spoils of Egypt," *ASTI* 12 (1983) 136–37.

15–17 These three verses, especially v. 15, are a variation of 12:7. Two new features are added, however. First, not only are Abram's descendants to receive the land, but so will he himself *(I will give to you and to your descendants).* Second, Abram is told, through a hyperbole, that his descendants will be a multitude *(as the dust of the ground).* The expansiveness of the divine promise regarding descendants is mandatory in the light of the expansiveness of the divine promise regarding the acquisition of land *(all the land you see).*

To that end Abram walks throughout the land,[16] claiming it proleptically as God-promised territory. In viewing the land Abram is like Moses, who also viewed the land that God would give to Abram's offspring (Deut. 34:1–4). But in walking throughout the land Abram anticipates the later promise to Joshua: "I will give you every place where you set your foot" (Josh. 1:3).

What started as a situation of discontent, quarreling, and friction has now turned into one of divine promise and blessing. Thus this chapter contrasts with ch. 12. There the promise and blessing (12:1–9) preceded the friction (12:10–20). Here the friction (13:1–13) precedes the promise and blessing (13:14–18).

18 Abram settles with his flocks in the Negeb area, and establishes his base at Mamre near Hebron.[17] Appropriately, Abram, for a second time (see 12:7), builds an altar. *Mamre,* if connected with modern Ramet el-Khalil, is situated about one and two-thirds miles north of Hebron. All references to Mamre are in Genesis. Gen. 14:13ff. claims that it was named after an Amorite, Mamre, who, together with his brothers Aner and Eshcol, joined Abram in the pursuit and defeat of Chedorlaomer and his allies. It is the place from which Abraham interceded for the sparing of Sodom and Gomorrah

16. Y. Muffs says in connection with texts concerning property transfer: "It is quite possible that the transfer of ownership was effectively established only after the new owner had asserted his ownership in an act, creative or destructive, such as walking into the property . . . breaking a branch, or by settling and building the property" (*Studies in the Aramaic Legal Papyri from Elephantine* [Leiden: Brill, 1969], p. 24 n. 2).

17. We have already seen (12:6) Abram's tendency to locate in an area where there are trees. Here again he settles near the terebinths of Mamre (see also 14:13). M. B. Rowton notes that in the 2nd millennium B.C. *ḫapiru* bands were particularly active in areas having considerable woodland ("The Topological Factor in the Ḫabiru Problem," in *Studies in Honor of Benno Landsberger on his Seventy-Fifth Birthday,* ed. H. G. Güterbock and T. Jacobsen, Assyriological Studies 16 [Chicago: University of Chicago, 1965], pp. 375–87). For a discussion of whether this has any bearing on the phrase "Abram the Hebrew" in 14:13, see the commentary below.

(18:1ff.). The cave in the field of Machpelah, which he later purchased for use as a family tomb, was located east of Mamre (23:17ff.). In Josephus's day an oak or terebinth tree in Mamre was said to have been there from the day of creation (*J.W.* 4.9.7; *Ant.* 1.10.4). The terebinth tree *('ēlâ, 'ēlôn)* along with the oak *('allôn)* is among the best shade trees in Palestine (see Hos. 4:13). It grows, on an average, to 20–25 feet, and has a thick trunk and heavy branches.

THE NEW TESTAMENT APPROPRIATION

Gen. 13:3–5, 12 and Heb. 11:9

The writer of Hebrews adds to Abraham's "by faith he obeyed . . . and went out" (v. 8) the second element that by faith Abraham "sojourned in the land of promise." The verb for "sojourned" *(parṓkēsen)* often has connotations of temporary dwelling as opposed to *katoikeín,* which may imply a more permanent residence, although both verbs are used side-by-side in this verse ("he sojourned . . . living [in tents]"). *Parṓkēsen* means literally "he dwelt beside," as if Abraham were not one of the nation's citizens. For *katoikeín* to describe living in tents cf. Gen. 13:3–5; 18:1–2; 26:25. Actually, according to Gen. 13, Abraham lived in tents with Lot. Heb. 11:9 must have in mind that the three patriarchs, at different times, all lived in tents as strangers in the land. Isaac and Jacob are "fellow heirs" *(synklēronómōn)* of the promises of God, a term used elsewhere in the NT for Christians (Rom. 8:7; Eph. 3:6; 1 Pet. 3:7).

C. MILITANT ABRAM AND THE KINGS (14:1–24)

1. FOUR KINGS AGAINST FIVE (14:1–12)

1 *When*[1] *Amraphel king of Shinar, Arioch king of Ellasar, Chedorlaomer king of Elam, and Tidal king of Goiim*
2 *declared war, against Bera king of Sodom, Birsha king of Gomorrah,*

1. Speiser (*Genesis,* p. 101) provides a lengthy footnote about the syntax of v. 1 and its relationship to v. 2. The two verses read lit., "(1) in the days of Amraphel . . . king of Goim, (2) they declared war. . . ." Since there is no explicit subject for "they declared war," one would expect a resumptive pronoun *(hēm)* (as in Esth. 1:1—*wayhî bîmê 'aḥašwērôš hû' 'aḥašwērôš hammōlēḵ*), to show that in the days of these kings, these kings declared war. Speiser suggests that Heb. *bîmê* does not represent the construct form "in the day(s) of," but is a rendition of the cognate

Shinab king of Admah, Shemeber king of Zeboiim, and the king of Bela (that is,[2] *Zoar),*
3 *these formed a coalition in the Valley of Siddim (that is, the Salt Sea).*
4 *For twelve years they were subject to Chedorlaomer, but in the thirteenth year*[3] *they rebelled.*
5 *In the fourteenth year Chedorlaomer and the kings allied with him came and defeated the Rephaim in Ashteroth-karnaim, the Zuzim in Ham, the Emim in Shaveh-kiriathaim,*
6 *the Horites in the hill country of Seir,*[4] *near El-paran, which is close to the wilderness.*
7 *Then they swung back to En-mishpat (that is, Kadesh), and took over all the territory of the Amalekites, and also of the Amorites who dwelt in Hazazon-tamar.*
8 *The king of Sodom, the king of Gomorrah, the king of Admah, the king of Zeboiim, and the king of Bela (that is, Zoar) went forth and did battle with them in the Valley of Siddim:*
9 *Chedorlaomer king of Elam, Tidal king of Goiim, Amraphel king of Shinar, and Arioch king of Ellasar—four kings against five.*
10 *The Valley of Siddim was full of bitumen pits; as the king of Sodom and of Gomorrah fled, they hid out*[5] *in them while the rest fled to the hills.*
11 *They seized all the horses*[6] *of Sodom and Gomorrah and all their food, then vanished.*

Akkadian conjunction *e/inūma/i,* "when." Andersen (*Sentence in Biblical Hebrew,* p. 41) suggests that vv. 1–3 serve as a kind of title for the whole narrative.

2. The gloss here uses *hî',* but the older form—*hiw'*—is used in vv. 7, 8, a witness to the antiquity of the chapter. Does this mean that the glosses in Gen. 14 may be dated to the transitionary period in which *hî'* was gradually replacing *hiw'* for the 3rd fem. sing. pronoun? See G. Rendsburg, "Late Biblical Hebrew and the Date of 'P'," *JANES* 10 (1980) 79–80.

3. D. N. Freedman ("Notes on Genesis," *ZAW* 64 [1952] 193–94) reads "twelve years they served . . . and thirteen years they rebelled." "Twelve . . . thirteen" is thus an instance of the numerical ladder, so common in Semitic languages. In this Freedman is seconded by M. J. Dahood, *Ugaritic-Hebrew Philology,* BibOr 17 (Rome: Pontifical Biblical Institute, 1965), p. 13. The suggestion has much to commend it, and the Hebrew certainly allows this reading, but it is unlikely that overlord kings would tolerate a rebellion stretched over thirteen years by their vassals.

4. The MT reads *b*^{e}*har*^{e}*rām śēʿîr,* lit., "in their hills, Seir." The construction is easily cleared up if the final *-m* on *b*^{e}*har*^{e}*rām* is understood as an enclitic *mem.* See W. L. Moran, "The Putative Root *ʿtm* in Is 9,18," *CBQ* 12 (1950) 154; H. Hummel, "Enclitic *mem* in Early Northwest Semitic, Especially Hebrew," *JBL* 76 (1957) 92.

5. Heb. *wayyipp*^{e}*lû,* lit., "they fell," but see the commentary below.

6. Heb. *r*^{e}*ḵuš* means "possession, property." But in vv. 11, 16, 21, the LXX

12 *They captured Lot, Abram's nephew, together with his belongings;*[7]
he had been living in Sodom.

The key chapters in Genesis for the institution of the covenant with Abraham are chs. 15–17. But standing on both sides of this crucial pericope are events involving Lot in unpleasant situations. He separates from Abram (ch. 13); he is separated from Sodom (ch. 14); he is spared while Sodom is incinerated, but while intoxicated he fathers two sons by his two daughters (chs. 18–19). Thus a high moment of revelational significance and inspiration is bracketed by narratives detailing less than exemplary behavior by a relative.

This chapter is unique in the Abraham cycle. Source critics hesitate to assign it to any of the preliterary strata of the Pentateuch, preferring instead to view it as an independent tradition. Accordingly, attempts to date the writing of the tradition vary dramatically. Those who view the chapter as reflecting an actual historical event in the life of Abram, with or without secondary accretions, tend to date the episode rather early in the 2nd millennium B.C., around the 19th–17th centuries B.C.[8] But, of course, this says nothing about when the tradition was reduced to writing.

Those who see the chapter as essentially fictional, and who maintain that the episode contributes nothing to our understanding of the historical Abraham, correspondingly date the chapter's composition quite late, anywhere from the time of the "Deuteronomic school" to the end of the 4th century B.C.[9] A mediating position suggests that the story began as a popular

---

translates *r^{e}ḵuš* with *tḗn híppon,* "horse(s), chariotry," apparently reading Heb. *reḵeš,* "horse, steed." We prefer the LXX here, for in other places in this chapter where *r^{e}ḵûš* appears (vv. 12, 16), the LXX uses *aposkeuḗn,* "property," one of its regular terms for *r^{e}ḵûš.* See C. H. Gordon, *The Common Background of Greek and Hebrew Civilizations* (New York: Norton, 1965), p. 140 n. 2.

7. The word order of the MT is strange—"they captured Lot, together with his belongings, Abram's nephew." The phrase "Abram's nephew" should not, however, be read as an awkward insertion. Instead, it is an afterthought, a return to an earlier part of the sentence; for analogies cf. Num. 13:23; 1 Sam. 18:4; 2 Sam. 13:36–37. See M. H. Gottstein, "Afterthought and the Syntax of Relative Clauses in Biblical Hebrew," *JBL* 68 (1949) 36.

8. See W. F. Albright, "A Third Revision of the Early Chronology of Western Asia," *BASOR* 88 (1942) 33–36; idem, "Abraham and the Caravan Trade," *BASOR* 163 (1961) 49–54. Albright's earlier studies on the subject include "A Revision of Early Hebrew Chronology," *JPOS* 1 (1920) 68–79; and "The Historical Background of Genesis XIV," *Journal for the Society of Oriental Research* 10 (1926) 231–69; see also K. A. Kitchen, *Ancient Orient and Old Testament,* pp. 43–47.

9. For the former, see M. C. Astour, "Political and Cosmic Symbolism in Genesis 14 and Its Babylonian Sources," in *Biblical Motifs: Origins and Transfor-*

oral tradition about Abraham and evolved through five succeeding editorial stages, the references to Lot reflecting the latest of these steps.[10] We shall argue below for the accuracy of the narrative and suggest reasons for the plausibility of an early date for composition.

Perhaps what makes this event so unique is that it is the only one in the Abraham cycle in which the patriarch engages in military activity. This pastoralist-shepherd-nomad-merchant man suddenly takes on the role of warrior and successfully snatches Lot out of the hands of four titanic kings (none of whom can be certainly identified) who have just put down a revolt by five vassal kings. In this process a tenth king appears (Melchizedek), who thus far had not been part of the story at all.

This chapter is distinctive in other ways. For example, it is the only one in chs. 12–22 in which the divine voice does not speak to somebody. It is also the only chapter in chs. 12–22 from which the promise theme is absent, but surely the narrative, in the absence of the formulae, provides convincing documentation of the promises functioning. Two specific promises are vividly illustrated: (1) the divine presence (Abram's own life is in jeopardy, but he is spared), and (2) "those who curse you I will curse" (Lot is captured, and as a result his captors are humiliated by a band of Abram's men; thus these easterners lose face and Lot).

1 A major source of tension in this chapter's interpretation has been our inability to identify, unequivocally, the four kings from the east who invaded the territory south of the Dead Sea. Suggestions have been made for Amraphel, Arioch, Chedorlaomer, and Tidal, but even these suggestions have compounded the problem, for the names presented do not constitute four contemporary kings.

Chedorlaomer king of Elam is leader of the coalition. We know of no Elamite king by this name, even though the personal name is composed of two authentic Elamite elements. Albright earlier connected Chedorlaomer with Kudur-Lagamar, an Elamite king (?) of the 17th century B.C.,[11] but a list which identified some forty kings of Elam who reigned between 2100 and 1100 B.C. had no Kudur-Lagamar! Abandoning that equation, Albright later connected Chedorlaomer with Kudur-Nankhundi (Kudur-Naẖuti) of Elam, who is to be dated about 1625–1610 B.C.[12] This Elamite king was famous for

---

mations, ed. A. Altmann (Cambridge: Harvard University, 1966), pp. 65–112. For the latter, see J. Van Seters, *Abraham in History and Tradition,* pp. 296–308.

10. See J. A. Emerton, "The Riddle of Genesis XIV," *VT* 21 (1971) 403–39, esp. p. 438.

11. Albright, *JPOS* 1 (1920) 71–72.

12. Albright, *BASOR* 88 (1942) 33–34.

his crushing military expedition against the cities of Akkad. Indeed, he was a crusading monarch.

Amraphel is a complete mystery. Earlier attempts to identify him with Hammurapi are now generally abandoned, primarily because the first and last consonants in the names differ. K. Jaritz has pointed out that an Amorite chieftain was named Amudpiel, meaning "enduring is the command of El," and this would be close to Amraphel, if we assume an *r* for *d* shift (these letters are quite similar in Hebrew).[13] Because Gen. 11:2 and Zech. 5:11 associate *Shinar* with the land of Babylon, we can identify where Amraphel was king, but he himself remains unknown.

The personal name *Arioch* is well documented and may be compared with the name *Ar-ri-wu-uk* (fifth son of Zimri-Lim) in the Mari archives (18th century B.C.) and with *Ar-ri-uk-ki* in the Nuzi texts (15th century B.C.).[14] There is another Arioch in the Bible, but he appears much later as the captain of Nebuchadrezzar's guard (Dan. 2:14, 15, 24, 25), and may be equivalent to Iranian Āryā-va(h)u-ka, "the good Iranian."[15] Earlier scholars identified Arioch's kingdom of *Ellasar* with the Babylonian town of Larsa, but phonetically that is impossible. Modern suggestions for identification include Alsi/Alsiya in northern Mesopotamia at the source of the Tigris, and Ilansura between Carchemish and Haran.[16]

Tidal is a name borne by four Hittite kings (= Tudhalia) between the 18th and 13th centuries B.C. The connection between Heb. *tiḏʿāl* and Hittite *Tudḫalia* is evidenced by the Ugaritic spelling of the Hittite royal name as *tdǵl*. That Tidal is named as king of *Goiim* (lit., "nations") is perplexing. The term is deliberately vague, and is reminiscent of the phrase *Umman-Manda* (lit., "much people"), which was used later in cuneiform texts to describe the hordes of the northern and warlike Cimmerians and Scythians.

Four kings, then—an Elamite, an Amorite, a Hurrian, and a Hittite—joined forces and together waged war against five cities south of the Dead Sea. The identity of these kings remains unknown, as does information about a military alliance involving these four world powers.[17]

13. K. Jaritz, "Wer ist Amraphel in Genesis 14?" *ZAW* 70 (1958) 255–56.

14. Cf. M. Noth, "Arioch-Arriwuk," *VT* 1 (1951) 136–40, who opposes any connection of Arioch with the similar name in cuneiform documents.

15. See R. Zadok, "On five Iranian names in the Old Testament," *VT* 26 (1976) 246. The Indo-Iranian background of "Arioch" is applied to Gen. 14:1 too by P. Grelot, "Ariok," *VT* 25 (1975) 711–19.

16. See Albright, *JPOS* 1 (1920) 74–75.

17. Kitchen (*Ancient Orient and Old Testament,* p. 45) notes that "the system of power-alliances . . . is typical in Mesopotamian politics within the period *c.*

2 The five petty kings, placed on the defensive, are Bera of Sodom, Birsha of Gomorrah, Shinab of Admah, Shemeber of Zeboiim, and *X* of Bela. No small stir was created when a claim was made that one text from Ebla (an economic text listing commercial transactions between Ebla and other cities) listed these five cities of the plain, and in the same order as they appear in Gen. 14: *si-da-mu, è-ma-ra, ad-ma, si-ba-i-um,* and *be-la.*[18] Subsequent readings have, however, eliminated the third and fourth names in this sequence, and the names in fact do not occur on the same tablet.[19] Even the equation of *si-da-mu* with Sodom and *è-ma-ra* with Gomorrah is uncertain. Only time and further publication will tell whether the Ebla tablets furnish a spectacular bit of historical confirmation.

The names of the kings of the Dead Sea area pentapolis are interesting, if not obscure. *Bera* is apparently related to the verb *rāʿaʿ,* "be evil," and means "in evil." *Birsha* may be related to the verb *rāšaʿ,* "be wicked," and means "in wickedness." The third king is *Shinab* of Admah. It may be of some significance that the first two names of these petty kings begin with the second letter of the alphabet, and the last two named kings begin with the penultimate letter of the alphabet, suggesting perhaps that the names are pseudonyms. *Shinab* may translate as "Sin [the moon-god] is (my) father." The fourth king *Shemeber* would also translate quite well as "Shem is powerful" or "powerful name."

The name of the fifth king is lacking unless "Bela king of Zoar" be read instead of MT "king of Bela, that is, Zoar." The five instances in this chapter (vv. 2, 3, 7, 8, 17) in which onomastic entries had to be updated by later glosses strongly suggest the antiquity of the document. The earlier name of places had to be supplied with the current name in order to make the reference intelligible to the reader. Elsewhere in the OT *Zoar* is located in the Jordan valley (Deut. 32:3) and near Moab (Isa. 15:5; Jer. 48:34).

2000-1750 BC, but *not* before or after this general period when different political patterns prevailed"; see also idem, *The Bible in Its World* (Downers Grove, IL: Inter-Varsity, 1978), pp. 72-73. R. de Vaux is one of the few scholars who earlier argued in favor of the historical authenticity of the event ("Les Patriarches hébreux et les découvertes modernes," *RB* 55 [1948] 321–47, and esp. pp. 327–36). Subsequently he withdrew this positive vote and took the position that the story cannot be regarded as historically useful, primarily on the basis that he considers it impossible for these five cities south of the Dead Sea to have been at one time the vassals of Elam in the 2nd millennium B.C. See also his *Early History of Israel,* tr. D. Smith (Philadelphia: Westminster, 1978), pp. 216–20.

18. See D. N. Freedman, "The Real Story of the Ebla Tablets, Ebla and the Cities of the Plain," *BA* 41 (1978) 143–64.

19. See, e.g., R. Biggs, "The Ebla Tablets," *BA* 43 (1980) 82.

3–4 The relationship of the five vassal kings to Elam is described through the successive use of the verbs *ʿāḇaḏ* and *māraḏ*. Both verbs are used frequently in the OT to describe political relationships between nations. The first one means "to be subject to" a sovereign. The second one means to "refuse allegiance to, rise up against" a sovereign.[20] By natural extension both verbs were also used to describe Israel's relationship to God (*ʿāḇāḏ:* Exod. 3:12; 4:23; 7:16, 26, etc.; *māraḏ:* Num. 14:9; Josh. 22:16, 18, 29, etc.).

5–7 The geographical exactness given to the description of the route followed by the invaders (Ashteroth-karnaim, Ham, Shaveh-kiriathaim, Seir/El-paran, En-mishpat, Hazazon-tamar) is striking.[21] Equally striking is that the place names which are identifiable are all to be found along the central mountain range of Transjordan, which, according to Deut. 1–3, is the route followed in the opposite direction by the Israelites after they left Sinai for Palestine. This route is the "king's highway" (Num. 20:17), which was the one that caravans and military expeditions followed between Syria in the north and the Dead Sea in the south.[22]

The names of other peoples whom the Elamites and their allies subdued—Rephaim, Zuzim, Emim, Horites, Amalekites, Amorites—would indicate that the uprising of the five southern kinglets was but one part of a massive effort to resist continued Mesopotamian control in Transjordan. The invading kings repress such attempted revolts in grandiose and unmitigated style. Nobody can stand before them, even though the defeated *Rephaim, Zuzim,* and *Emim* are themselves imposing threats, people of giant stature (Deut. 2:10–12, 20–23).[23] This makes Abram's ability to rout these potentates all the more impressive.

8–9 How will these minor kings stand up against the eastern four when forces much more powerful than they have already capitulated? It is to

20. See M. Greenberg, *Ezekiel 1–20,* AB (Garden City, NY: Doubleday, 1983), p. 63.

21. On Ashteroth-karnaim and Ham see K. A. Kitchen, "Theban Topographical Lists, Old and New," *Or* 34 (1965) 3. On El-paran see N. Avigad, "The Jotham Seal from Elath," *BASOR* 163 (1961) 21 n. 11.

22. Cuneiform texts supply information about diplomatic and commercial traveling practices between locations in Mesopotamia and in Syria-Palestine during the 18th century B.C. For example, note the diplomatic mission from Larsa in southern Mesopotamia to Emar in Syria in the time of Zimri-Lim that took 87 days going and 107 days returning. See references in W. W. Hallo, "The Road to Emar," *JCS* 18 (1964) 57–88.

23. May "Rephaim" be connected with the god in Ugaritic literature *rp'u,* who is the patron of an elite military-aristocratic group called *rp'um*? See, in support of this, C. L'Heureux, "The Ugaritic and Hebrew Rephaim," *HTR* 67 (1974) 265–74.

the credit (or foolishness?) of these five kings that they take the offensive against their suzerain. They will take the battle to the invaders.

The OT has at least two other instances in which five kings joined a coalition. In Josh. 10:5 the five Amorite kings of Jerusalem, Hebron, Jarmuth, Lachish, and Eglon joined forces against Gibeon. Similarly, Josh. 13:3 speaks of five Philistine rulers (from Gaza, Ashdod, Ashkelon, Gath, and Ekron) whose effective leadership had stalled Israelite penetration into their territory. Also, in Josh. 10 the five confederate kings are mentioned by name only once (v. 3). In Gen. 14, as well, the allied defenders of the pentapolis are named only once (v. 2), whereas the attackers are named twice (vv. 1, 9).

10 *they hid* (Heb. *wayyippᵉlû,* lit., "they fell"). Some commentators (e.g., Westermann) have registered surprise that the story would have the kings of Sodom and Gomorrah falling (so AV, RSV, NIV, etc.) into the bitumen pits (and as a result perishing), only to have the king of Sodom reappear later in v. 17. But this apparent problem disappears once it is remembered that *nāp̄al* may also refer to a voluntary lowering of oneself. For example, Gen. 24:64 refers to Rebekah who "lowered herself [lit., "fell"!] from her camel." Also, verses like Gen. 25:18 and 1 Sam. 29:3 show that the verb may also mean "to settle, dwell, camp," or even "flee to," as in Jer. 38:19.[24]

11–12 In the process of putting down the revolt, the conquerors helped themselves to booty from their victims. This booty includes food and prisoners, one of whom is Abram's nephew Lot. This incident has a number of parallels with earlier incidents in Abram's life. In ch. 12 Sarai was taken *(lāqaḥ)* from Abram (12:15). In this chapter Lot is *captured* (*lāqaḥ,* a verb that again has the nuance of "capture" in Job 40:24). In both cases the one taken had no say in controlling her or his own destiny. Each is an innocent bystander caught in the cross fire between two parties. And both Sarai and Lot are abducted while staying outside the land of promise (in Egypt and Sodom, respectively). Meanwhile, Abram appears in a quite different light in ch. 14 than in ch. 12. In this second event he is much more winsome and noble.

24. See M. Delcor, "Quelques cas de survivances du vocabulaire nomade en hébru biblique," *VT* 25 (1975) 314–15. The same semantic range is found in Akk. *maqātu,* "to fall" and "to flee," "to take refuge."

2. THE RECAPTURE OF LOT (14:13–16)

13 *An escapee came and informed Abram the Hebrew (he was living by the terebinths of Mamre the Amorite, a kinsman of Eshkol, and of Aner—they were allies with Abram).*

14 *Upon hearing that his relative had been abducted, he mustered his retainers, household servants, three hundred and eighteen, and took off in pursuit as far as Dan.*

15 *He and his men deployed against them at night and defeated them. He pursued them as far as Hobah, which is north of Damascus.*

16 *He retrieved all the horses, and also Lot his relative. His possessions he returned, together with the women and the people.*

13 Abram is informed, through an unidentified source (like the unidentified Amalekite of 2 Sam. 1), that Lot has been captured. The narrator unexpectedly refers to Abram here as *the Hebrew,* and this is the only time he is so designated. Why in this one instance is this particular title applied to him? Elsewhere he interacts with peoples living outside the land of Palestine (e.g., chs. 12 and 20), and yet this designation is not used in those contexts.

The similarity between *Hebrew* and *Habiru* (also spelled *Ḫapiru* or *ʿApiru*) has led some scholars to connect these two peoples.[1] The Habiru appear in Near Eastern texts from the 20th to the 11th centuries B.C. They were a settled people rather than a nomadic or desert population, and comprised heterogeneous racial elements. They had great mobility, and consequently they were regarded as outsiders wherever they settled. They were often fugitives, uprooted and propertyless. In times of disorganization they played a large part as auxiliary soldiers in petty wars between rulers and towns. With the establishment of a relatively stable society at the end of the 2nd millennium B.C., they sank into insignificance and eventually disappeared. On account of their militaristic exploits, commentators have raised the question whether it is accidental that in the one place where Abram engages in military activity he is styled as a "Hebrew" (Habiru?).

More and more scholars are rejecting an equation of "Hebrew" and "Habiru" on both historical and philological grounds (the development of *ḫapir* or *ʿapir* to *ʿibr* is without parallel, and the variation between *p* and *b* is

1. For a specific connection see W. F. Albright, "Abram the Hebrew: A New Archaeological Interpretation," *BASOR* 163 (1961) 36–54, esp. pp. 52–54. For basic studies on the Habiru see M. Greenberg, *The Ḫab/pirû,* AOS 39 (New Haven: American Oriental Society, 1955); M. G. Kline, "The ḪA-BI-RU—Kin or Foe of Israel?" *WTJ* 19 (1956–57) 1–24, 170–84; 20 (1957) 47–70; M. C. Astour, "Habiru," *IDBS,* pp. 382–85; B. J. Beitzel, "Habiru," *ISBE,* 2:586–90.

unlikely in the light of Ugaritic evidence to the effect that *ʿapiru* was the Northwest Semitic original).[2] To connect *ʿapir* and *ʿibr* calls for a most unlikely dual transformation that is both consonantal ($p \rightarrow b$) and vocalic ($a \rightarrow i$).

What, then, shall we do with the term *Hebrew* here and elsewhere in the OT? It occurs thirty-three times in the OT. With the exception of Gen. 14:13 and Jon. 1:9, these references fall into three groups: (1) the time of Joseph and Moses while the Israelites are in Egypt; (2) Saul's wars against the Philistines; (3) the laws dealing with the emancipation of the "Hebrew" slave (Exod. 21:2–6; Deut. 15:12–18; Jer. 34:9, 14). This term is frequently used by a non-Israelite when speaking to or about an Israelite (an Egyptian speaking, 5 times: Gen. 39:14, 17; 41:12; Exod. 1:16; 2:6; a Philistine speaking, 5 times: 1 Sam. 4:6, 9; 13:19; 14:11; 29:3). Conversely, eight times the term is used by an editor (or by an Israelite himself) to distinguish an Israelite from a foreigner (Gen. 40:15; 43:32; Exod. 1:15; 2:11, 13; 1 Sam. 13:3, 7 [?]; 14:21).[3] Clearly, then, the word *Hebrew* is used primarily as an ethnic term in the OT.

There seems to be no good reason to depart from this understanding of *Hebrew* in Gen. 14:13. Accordingly, Heb. *ʿiḇrî* is the gentilic of *ʿēḇer,* and here it distinguishes Abram from other residents already living in Canaan.[4] He is a descendant of Eber of the line of Shem.

14 Abram holds no grudges against Lot, nor does the uncle dismiss his nephew as avaricious and compulsive, and therefore not worth the necessary effort to free him from his captors. The patriarch's instinctive response is to help the one in need. In quick fashion Abram mobilizes what forces he has and takes off toward the north in pursuit of Lot.

mustered is an unusual translation for Heb. *wayyāreq,* "he emptied, poured out." The LXX *(ērίthmēsen)* read the Hebrew consonants as *wayyip̱qōḏ,* "he visited," or "he mustered," and the SP read *wayyāḏeq,* "he called up."[5] As it stands, the MT allows the translation *mustered* solely on

2. See, e.g., Astour, *IDBS,* p. 384; Beitzel, *ISBE,* 2:589.

3. See R. de Vaux, *The Early History of Israel,* pp. 209–16; M. Weippert, *The Settlement of the Israelite Tribes in Palestine,* SBT 2/21 (Naperville: Allenson, 1971), pp. 84–98; P. K. McCarter, Jr., *I Samuel,* AB (Garden City, NY: Doubleday, 1980), pp. 240–41.

4. The view that *ʿiḇrî* in Gen. 14:13 is an appellative is as ancient as LXX, which has *perátē,* "the one from across" (cf. Josh. 24:3), based on the Hebrew verb *ʿāḇar,* "to pass, cross." Only here and in Jon. 1:9 *(Doúlos kyríou)* does the LXX render *ʿiḇrî* with something other than *Hebraios.*

5. BDB, p. 938, and *BHS* follow SP.

the basis of a possible equation with *rîq* in Ps. 2:1—"Why do the nations forgather, and the peoples number their troops [*rîq*]?"[6]

retainers, household servants. In addition to the verb, the two nouns following it also present some problems. This is the only place *ḥanîḵîm (retainers)* appears in the Hebrew Bible, but its cognate is attested in cuneiform documents. It is probably of Egyptian origin *(ḥnk.w),* specifically from the early period of Egyptian history.[7]

This *hapax legomenon* is further explained by the phrase *household servants (yelîḏê ḇêṯô).* Here *yālîḏ* does not refer to physical descent; rather, it designates membership in a group by a means other than birth. Here in particular the term is applied to a slave or servant whose major function is to provide military assistance.[8] They are not shepherds who grabbed a spear or a sling and headed north for some 125 miles. They are individuals capable of making a successful attack against imposing odds.

The report that Abram drafted *three hundred and eighteen* troops lends historicity and specificity to the narrative. The precision here is difficult to miss. But is there any significance in this number? The rabbis frequently observed that the name of Abram's servant who is mentioned in the next chapter of Genesis—Eliezer—has a numerical equivalent of 318 (*aleph:* 1; *lamed:* 30; *yod:* 10; *ʿayin:* 70; *zayin:* 7; *resh:* 200 = 318).[9] Some early Christian traditions also attempted to perceive a hidden meaning in the

6. Dahood's translation, *Psalms,* 1:6–8. Dahood also appeals to the expression *'anāšîm rêqîm* in Judg. 9:4 and 11:3 and translates it as "enlisted men" rather than the more usual "worthless fellows." For some inexplicable reason, R. Boling (*Judges,* AB [Garden City, NY: Doubleday, 1975], p. 165) translates the phrase as "idle mercenaries" in 9:4, but only as "mercenaries" in 11:3 (p. 196).

7. See W. F. Albright, "A Prince of Taanach in the Fifteenth Century," *BASOR* 94 (1944) 12–27. Letter no. 6 from Amenophis to Rewašša reads in part: *ša-ni-tam la-a-mi i-na ma-an-ṣa-ar-ti i-ba-aš-š(u) ḫa-na-ku-u-ka,* "further, in the garrison there are none of thy retainers [*ḫa-na-ku-u-ka*]." See also T. O. Lambdin, "Egyptian Loan Words in the Old Testament," *JAOS* 73 (153) 150.

8. See F. Willesen, "The *Yaliḏ* in Hebrew Society," *ST* 12 (1958) 192–210; C. E. L'Heureux, "The *yelîdê hārāpā'*—A Cultic Association of Warriors," *BASOR* 221 (1976) 83–85. Willesen suggests that the *yālîḏ* was a slave "dedicated to the deity who was head of the social unit into which he was admitted by consecration" (p. 210). For L'Heureux the *yālîḏ* was a member of a military group into which one was admitted by "adoption, initiation, or consecration" (p. 84).

9. See J. Sasson, "Wordplay in the OT," *IDBS,* p. 968; G. Scholem, "Gematria," in *EncJud,* 7:369–74; L. Ginzberg, *The Legends of the Jews* (Philadelphia: Jewish Publication Society, 1925), 5:224 n. 93; for a Christian appropriation of "318" see N. J. McEleney, "153 Great Fishes (John 21,11)—Gematriacal Atbash," *Bib* 58 (1977) 414.

number 318. Thus the Epistle of Barnabas 9:8 (see also Clement *Stromateis* 6.11) understood the Hebrew phrase "eighteen and three hundred" by writing it in Greek, representing the 18 as *IH* (the first two letters of the name Jesus in Greek) and the 300 as *T* (i.e., a cross).[10] Josephus (*J.W.* 5.9.4) goes well beyond the Genesis text when he writes that Abraham had 318 officers at his beck and call, each in command of a "boundless army."[11]

A more recent suggestion is that the figure has symbolic rather than historical value. S. Gevirtz has proposed that the origin of 318 is to be found in an application of prime numbers (i.e., one that is divisible only by itself) between 7 and 7^2. All of the prime numbers here would be: 7, 11, 13, 17, 19, 23, 29, 31, 37, 41, 43, 47 (= 318).[12]

15–16 The narrator does not provide any details on how Abram and his men managed to attack so successfully, except for the fact that it was a nocturnal campaign. The whole event has definite parallels with Gideon and his three hundred men and their nocturnal blitz against the Midianites (Judg. 7). Part of God's earlier promise to Abram had been, "those who curse you I shall curse." We have seen that promise fulfilled with Pharaoh, who mistreated Abram when he took the patriarch's wife. Plagues fell on him and his household. Are the four mighty kings now being cursed by God (they are defeated by a group of Abram's servants) because they mistreated Abram when they made Lot a prisoner of war?

3. ABRAM MEETS TWO KINGS (14:17–24)

17 *The king of Sodom went out to greet him after he returned from defeating Chedorlaomer and the kings who accompanied him in the Valley of Shaveh (that is, the King's Valley).*

18 *Melchizedek king of Salem brought out bread and wine; he was a priest of God Most High.*

10. See S. J. Lieberman, "A Mesopotamian Background for the So-Called *Aggadic* 'Measures' of Biblical Hermeneutics?," *HUCA* 58 (1987) 168.

11. See L. Feldman, "Abraham the General in Josephus," in *Nourished with Peace: Studies in Hellenistic Judaism in Memory of Samuel Sandmel,* ed. F. E. Greenspahn, E. Hilgert, and B. L. Mack (Chico, CA: Scholars, 1984), pp. 43–49.

12. S. Gevirtz, "Abram's 318," *IEJ* 19 (1969) 110–13. This explanation presupposes a prominence for the number 7 in the narrative. Gevirtz notes (p. 113 n. 18) (1) that from the appearance of Abram in v. 13 to the end of the chapter his name occurs 7 times; (2) that each of the two blessings pronounced by Melchizedek in vv. 19 and 20 contains 7 words each; (3) that Abram with his confederates—Aner, Eshkol, Mamre, Lot, Melchizedek, and the king of Sodom constitute a postwar council of 7.

19 *He blessed him, saying, "Blessed be Abram by God Most High, the creator of heaven and earth;*
20 *and blessed be God Most High who has delivered your adversaries into your hand." He gave him a tenth of everything.*
21 *The king of Sodom said to Abram: "Give me the people; the horses keep for yourself."*
22 *But Abram said to the king of Sodom: "I hereby swear*[1] *by uplifted hand to Yahweh, God Most High, creator of heaven and earth,*
23 *that neither a string nor a sandal lace would I take, from anything that is yours, lest you say, 'I have enriched Abram.'*
24 *I will accept nothing except that which my troops have consumed and the portion that belongs to the men who accompanied me—Aner, Eshkol, Mamre. Let them take their portion."*

17 The *king of Sodom* heads the welcome-home party for the victorious Abram, and the meeting takes place at *the King's Valley,* also called *the Valley of Shaveh* ("Valley of the Ruler").[2] This particular site appears in the OT again only in 2 Sam. 18:18. It was situated at the confluence of the Kidron Valley and the Valley of Hinnom, south of the city of David.[3] The choice of such a place for the extension of greetings shows the exhilaration of the king of Sodom, who has traveled northward, eager to meet triumphant Abram. The site also prepares us geographically for the sudden appearance of Melchizedek king of Salem.

18 While the king of Sodom and Abram celebrate in the environs of Jerusalem, they are joined by the local chieftain *Melchizedek king of Salem,* who wished also to toast the victor.[4] The *bread and wine* presumably

1. In Biblical Hebrew verbs in the 1st person perfect often have a present perfect aspect and therefore need to be translated "I hereby. . . ." This is why I render *hᵃrîmōṯî* as "I hereby swear" rather than "I have sworn." See S. R. Driver, *A Treatise on the Use of the Tenses in Hebrew and Some Other Syntactical Questions,* 3rd ed. (Oxford: Clarendon, 1892), § 10.

2. See A. A. Wieder, "Ugaritic-Hebrew Lexicographical Notes," *JBL* 84 (1965) 160–62, for this explanation.

3. See P. K. McCarter, Jr., *II Samuel,* AB (Garden City, NY: Doubleday, 1984), p. 408.

4. Most scholars believe that vv. 18–20 are secondary to the narrative. This suspicion is based on two factors: (1) there is a literary continuity between v. 17 and v. 21 which vv. 18–20 interrupt; (2) the sudden appearance of Melchizedek, who has nowhere functioned in the narrative up to this point. A thorough attempt to dissect Gen. 14 may be found in W. Schatz, *Genesis 14: Eine Untersuchung* (Bern: Herbert Lang, 1972), esp. pp. 263–89, where he states his belief that Gen. 14 is composed of three separate traditions: the war of the eastern kings, Abram meeting with Sodom's

represented physical provisions for the exhausted warriors. From here on the focus is on Abram. He is the only one honored, not his 318 troops who joined him in the foray against the Elamite-led coalition. As one would expect, it is the general, not the private, who gets the kudos.

Melchizedek may translate as "my king is just (or legitimate)," or "my king is Ṣedeq." Proper names in the Bible are either descriptive or theophoric (a divine name constitutes part of the name). Without much success many writers have taken Melchizedek as a theophoric name, but which part is theophoric: *mlk* or *ṣdq*? Does the name mean "Malk is just" or "Tsedeq is my king"?[5] This king's proper name is close to another name in the OT—Adonizedek (Josh. 10:1–3), "my master is just." It is better to take Melchizedek as a descriptive name, primarily because other OT names with the first element *malkî-* (e.g., Malchiel, "El is my king" [Gen. 46:17]; Malchiah, "Yahweh is my king" [Jer. 38:6]) are read unanimously as names with *mlk* as an epithet rather than a theophoric element. A better case can be made for reading the second element *-zedeq* as the name of a god Ṣedeq, but the possibility of reading it as an adjective is heightened by other OT names such as Jozadak, "Yo [Yahweh] is upright" (Ezra 3:2); Jehozadak, "Yahweh is upright" (Hag. 1:1).

Melchizedek is connected with the city of *Salem,* traditionally identified as Jerusalem. Ps. 76:3 (Eng. 2) explicitly connects Salem with Jerusalem (Zion). But how can we connect Salem *(šālēm)* with Jerusalem *(yᵉrûšālayim)?* For it was not customary among the Hebrews to shorten a compound name by dropping the first element. Hypocorism (i.e., abbreviation) is done most often by apocopation (i.e., omission of the last sound or syllable of a word) or by the omission of sounds from a name's interior.[6] The connection between the two names may be clarified by the fact that

---

king, and Abram's relation with Melchizedek. Few, if any, studies have attempted to integrate exegetically the Melchizedek episode with the larger narrative.

5. For the former, see M. Noth, *Die israelitischen Personennamen im Rahmen der gemeinsemitischen Namengebung* (Stuttgart: Kohlhammer, 1928), p. 161 n. 4; for the latter, see R. A. Rosenberg, "The God Ṣedeq," *HUCA* 36 (1965) 163.

6. See R. H. Smith, "Abram and Melchizedek (Gen. 14:18–20)," *ZAW* 77 (1965) 141. Smith's own proposal is to read *šālēm* as an adjective ("whole, perfect") rather than as a noun: "Melchizedek, a covenanted king." He notes the use of *šālēm* to allude to a covenant relationship inside and outside the OT (e.g., Gen. 34:21, and the use of the root *šlmm* in Ugaritic texts to indicate covenanting). I find this suggestion more appealing than Albright's attempt to emend the passage from *meleḵ šālēm* to *meleḵ šᵉlômô,* "a king allied to him" (W. F. Albright, "Abram the Hebrew: A New Archaeological Interpretation," *BASOR* 163 [1961] 52). Albright's suggestion is actually foreign to biblical diction.

the first element of "Jerusalem" *(y^e^rû-)* is the word for "city" in Sumerian *(uru),* as is evidenced by the Sumero-Akkadian name for Jerusalem, *uru-salim.* This indicates that a Sumerian name was given to Jerusalem long before David appeared, possibly when Jerusalem was an outlying trading post of the Sumerians.[7] The Genesis Apocryphon (1QapGen 22:13) clearly connects Salem and Jerusalem with its reading, "he came to Salem, that is, Jerusalem," but of course this is a reflection of first-century A.D. tradition.

In addition to fulfilling the role of king, Melchizedek is also *a priest of God Most High (ʾēl ʿelyôn).* This dual capacity aligns Melchizedek with Abram, who performs some priestly functions (altar builder and circumciser) and is considered a king (Gen. 23:6, LXX). It is difficult to say that the El Elyon of Gen. 14:18 is a Canaanite deity simply on the basis that "El Elyon, creator of heaven and earth" corresponds to no actual deity in the Canaanite pantheon.[8] This pantheon has a god El whose grandson is Elyon. If we are dealing with a Canaanite god in Gen. 14, then what we have is a fusion of two originally separate deities, or the possibility that Elyon is an alternate name for El.[9] One would expect a Canaanite king to bless in the name of one of his own gods. However, v. 22 explicitly identifies Yahweh with El Elyon.[10] Only one other OT text refers to the full name *ʾēl ʿelyôn,* Ps. 78:35: "they remembered that God [*ʾĕlôhîm*] was their rock, the Most High God [*ʾēl ʿelyôn*] their redeemer." In many places *ʿelyôn* occurs by itself (Num. 24:16; Deut. 32:8; Isa. 14:14; Lam. 3:35, 38; Dan. 7:18, 22, 25 [twice], 27, plus 21 times in the Psalter). *ʿelyôn* is used in parallelism with *ʾēl* (Num. 24:16; Ps. 73:11), with Yahweh (2 Sam. 22:14 par. Ps. 18:14 [Eng. 13]), with *ʾĕlōhîm* (Ps. 46:5 [Eng. 4]; 50:14), with *šadday* (Ps. 91:1). Ps. 57:3 (Eng. 2) and 78:56 speak of "God Most High" *(ʾĕlōhîm ʿelyôn),* while Ps. 7:18 (Eng. 17) refers to "Yahweh, the Most High."

19 Melchizedek's treatment of Abram contrasts vividly to the east-

7. See C. H. Gordon, "Ebla and Genesis 11," in *A Spectrum of Thought,* Fest. Dennis F. Kinlaw, ed. Michael L. Peterson (Wilmore, KY: Francis Asbury, 1982), p. 131. Also, the Ebla texts speak of a Palestinian "Salem" as being in existence in the 3rd millennium B.C. See G. Pettinato, "The Royal Archives of Tell Mardikh-Ebla," *BA* 39 (1976) 46.

8. See G. Levi Della Vida, "El ʿElyon in Genesis XIV 18–20," *JBL* 63 (1944) 9.

9. See F. M. Cross, "Yahweh and the God of the Patriarchs," *HTR* 55 (1962) 241.

10. Note that Abram does not call on the name of El Elyon, nor engage in a religious act such as altar building, as he and Jacob do in other places where "El" is present (21:33, *ʾēl ʿôlām;* 33:20, *ʾēl ʾĕlōhê yiśrāʾēl;* 31:13; 35:7, *ʾēl bêṯ-ʾēl*).

ern kings' treatment of him. The latter "cursed" Abram. The former *blessed* Abram, and here we find, in one sense, the beginning of the actualization of God's promises to Abram: "those who bless you I will bless." The benediction reflects an attitude of gratitude to Abram for his bold stroke against the eastern horde.

El Elyon is further described here as *the creator* [*qōnēh*] *of heaven and earth.* Scholars have debated extensively whether the correct translation of *qōnēh* is "creator" or "possessor" (cf. Jerome's *possessorem*). The problem is complicated further by those who insist that this section of Gen. 14 presents a Canaanite picture of El, for in the Ras Shamra texts all allusions to El's creativity are in terms of generation and paternity. Theogony is connected with El, but not cosmogony.[11] It is Phoenician texts, particularly the inscription from Karatepe (in Cilicia), dating to the 9th or 8th century B.C., which connect El with creation. Near the end of his inscription Azitawaddu invokes a series of gods to protect his citadel; one of the gods is *'l qn 'rṣ,* "El, the creator of the earth."[12]

Of the eighty-three times that *qānâ* occurs in the OT, the more frequent nuance is "to acquire" and therefore "to own, possess."[13] But in some passages the translation "create" is a legitimate possibility, such as Gen. 4:1; Exod. 15:16; Deut. 32:6 (where it is parallel to *kûn* and *ʿāśâ*); Ps. 78:54 (perhaps); Ps. 139:13 especially (here parallel to *sāḵaḵ,* "to shelter," thus a verse speaking of both creation and providence); Prov. 8:22.[14]

Other Semitic languages provide firm support for the translation of *qānâ* as "create." We refer especially to two passages from the Ugaritic texts:

11. See M. Pope, *El in the Ugaritic Texts,* VTSup 2 (Leiden: Brill, 1955), pp. 49–64; R. Rendtorff, "El, Baʿal, und Yahwe. Erwägungen zum Verhältnis von kanaanäischer und israelitischer Religion," *ZAW* 78 (1966) 277–92.

12. See R. T. O'Callaghan, "The Great Phoenician Portal Inscription from Karatepe," *Or* 18 (1949) 203–5. The same expression *('l qn 'rṣ)* is found in a Neo-Punic inscription from Leptis Magna in Phoenician North Africa. See G. Levi Della Vida, "El Elyon in Genesis XIV 18–20," *JBL* 63 (1944) 4–6.

13. Normally LXX translates *qānâ* with *ktásthai,* but 3 times (Gen. 14:19, 22; Prov. 8:22) it uses *ktízein.* The significance of this is not clear.

14. B. Vawter ("Prov. 8:22: Wisdom and Creation," *JBL* 97 [1980] 205–16) concludes that there are no indubitable examples of *qānâ* meaning "create" in the OT, and, as a result, he finds none of these verses I have cited as ones that provide convincing evidence to the opposite. However, I believe he has strained the interpretation of some of these texts, esp. Ps. 139:13, to avoid "create." For a subsequent statement by Vawter see his "Yahweh: Lord of the Heavens and the Earth," *CBQ* 48 (1986) 461–67. Cf. R. Boling, *Joshua,* AB (Garden City, NY: Doubleday, 1982), p. 15 n. 16.

UT, 2 Aqht VI:41: *tṣḥq ʿnt wblb tqny,* "Anat laughed and in her heart she contrived";[15] and *UT,* 76:III:5–7:

wyʿny ʾalʾiyn[bʿl]
lm kqnyn ʿlm [ ]
kdrd(r) dyknn [ ]
Then ʾAlʾiyn [Baʿl] responded: [ ]
. . . that our creator is eternal, [ ]
that unto all generati(ons) is he who fashioned us [ ].[16]

Most telling here is the parallel of *qnyn* to *dyknn,* "he who created/fashioned us" (the same parallel as in Deut. 32:6); thus *qnyn* must mean "our creator, progenitor."

The late ninth-century B.C. Aramaic inscription of Kilamuwa provides another instance of *qny* meaning "create": "Statue which Kilamuwa, son of Haya, fashioned [*smr z qn klmw br ḥy*] for Rakib-ʾEl. May Rakib-ʾEl grant him length of life."[17] The fashioning of a statue may be compared to Yahweh's fashioning of man (Exod. 15:16; Deut. 32:16; Ps. 139:13) or his fashioning of the earth and the heavens (Gen. 14:19, 22).

20 Melchizedek has the proper perspective. He knows the real source of Abram's victories, and that is God. Thus, doxologies flow not only outward but upward. *delivered* is a verb *(miggēn)* from the same root as "shield" *(māgēn)* at the beginning of the next chapter (15:1). Thus this root links the two chapters together.

Words subsequently give way to action: *He gave him a tenth of everything.* Who gave whom a tenth? Did Abram present the tithe to Melchizedek, or did Melchizedek give the tithe to Abram?[18] Versions that have

15. See W. F. Albright, "A Vow to Asherah in the Keret Epic," *BASOR* 94 (1944) 34 n. 21; H. L. Ginsberg translates, "Anat laughs, while in her heart she forges a plot," in "The North-Canaanite Myth of Anat and Aqhat," *BASOR* 98 (1945) 22 n. 68.

16. Translation of H. L. Ginsberg, "Baʿl and ʿAnat," *Or* 7 (1938) 9. An attempt to retain the idea of creation, but along the lines of the parenthood of the creator, is suggested by W. A. Irwin, "Where Shall Wisdom Be Found?" *JBL* 80 (1961) 138. For Irwin this is further evidence of the mythological substratum in Genesis particularly. A god and goddess copulate and become the parents of the heavens and the earth.

17. See P. Swiggers, "The Aramaic Inscription of Kilamuwa," *Or* 51 (1982) 249–53.

18. R. H. Smith (*ZAW* 77 [1965] 134) argues for Melchizedek as the subject, and then proceeds to suggest—imaginatively—that the tithe was an attempt by Melchizedek to bribe the aggressor (Abram) to leave the city!

"Abram" as the subject of the verb (e.g., LXX, followed by NEB) have artificially supplied the proper noun. Heb. 7:6 clearly identifies Abram as the subject. Cf. also the Genesis Apocryphon (1QapGen 22:17): "he gave him a tithe of all the flocks of the king of Elam and his confederates."[19] W. Schatz notes that, "Though Melchizedek is the grammatical subject, logically Abraham must have paid tithes to the priest-king."[20]

Nevertheless, the traditional interpretation still seems preferable: Abram presents a gift to Melchizedek. But this *tithe* is not a tax paid by Abram as part of his obligation to his king, that is, a tithe of the spoils which he obtained as the result of fighting for his king.[21] Rather, we suggest this incident reflects the postbellum distribution of booty, in which the spoils are distributed equally between those who personally fought (Abram and his men), and those who for one reason or another did not actively engage in the fighting.[22] Num. 31:17—"divide the booty into two parts, between the warriors who went out to battle, and all the congregation"—provides an illustration of such a procedure.

1 Samuel 30 also provides instructive inner biblical parallels to Gen. 14. David's two wives—Ahinoam and Abigail—are abducted by the Amalekites. With the help of four hundred men he rescues both them and all the spoils that had been taken. Later David insists that the spoils be divided equally among both combatants and noncombatants.

21–24 The king of Sodom does not want more than his share, and he desires Abram to have no less than what is due him. To that end he asks for the people, but is willing to leave the property with Abram. This request provokes a negative response from Abram. He does not wish to enrich himself from his expedition. (Earlier he had done quite well in Egypt and only too eagerly accepted Pharaoh's lavish gifts.) In public he takes an oath that he will personally accept nothing. He requests only that the king of Sodom be responsible for the rations of his soldiers (v. 24).

Speiser correctly observed that the phrase *miḥûṭ weʿaḏ śerôḵ-naʿal,* translated above as *neither a string nor a sandal lace,* is based on Near Eastern formulae, especially Aram. *min ḥam weʿad ḥuṭ,* "be it blade of straw or piece of string," and older Akk. *lu ḫāmu lu ḫuṣābu,* "be it blade of straw

19. See J. A. Fitzmyer, *The Genesis Apocryphon of Qumran Cave I,* 2nd ed., BibOr 18A (Rome: Biblical Institute Press, 1971), pp. 72–73, 177–78.

20. W. Schatz, *Genesis 14,* p. 72.

21. As argued by L. R. Fisher, *JBL* 81 (1962) 268–69.

22. See Y. Muffs, "Abraham the Noble Warrior: Patriarchal Politics and Laws of War in Ancient Israel," *JJS* 33 (1982) 92–94.

or splinter of wood."[23] The Aramaic term is used in the division of marriage property after a divorce, while the Akkadian expression is found in a discussion of the liquidation of partnership holdings. But these circumstances are considerably removed from those in Gen. 14, which concern the division of booty.

We now have a text from Ugarit remarkably close to Gen. 14 in some ways. Niqmaddu, king of Ugarit, has been plundered by his enemies. His suzerain, the Hittite king Suppiluliuma, comes to his rescue and drives the invaders away. In response Niqmaddu attempts to give Suppiluliuma a gift as a sign of his appreciation. The text is damaged at this point, but may be restored to read as follows: "Suppiluliuma, the Great King, saw the loyalty of Niqmaddu, and as far as what belongs to Ugarit. . . . Suppiluliuma, the Great King, will not touch anything, be it straw or splinter [*(ḫama u)ḫuṣābu*]."[24] Abram appears to follow similar royal etiquette in refusing anything from the king of Sodom in return for his accomplishments.

THE NEW TESTAMENT APPROPRIATION

Gen. 14:18–20 and Heb. 5:6–10; 6:20–7:28

Melchizedek is first introduced in Heb. 5:6, "you are a priest forever, after the order of Melchizedek" (a quote from Ps. 110:4). A second reference to him comes a few verses later in v. 10, where Christ is "designated by God a high priest after the order of Melchizedek." But Melchizedek is not picked up again until the last verse of ch. 6, and on throughout ch. 7.

Chapter 7 explores thoroughly analogies between Christ and Melchizedek. The larger context is the author's presentation of the superiority of Christ's priesthood over the Levitical priesthood. In this argument three basic points from Genesis are scored in order to establish Christ's superiority: (1) Like Melchizedek, Jesus lacked a genealogy. Melchizedek is "without father, without mother, without genealogy." This is essentially an elaboration on the silence of Genesis. As such, Melchizedek is unrelated and unaccounted for. He, as an august, numinous figure, comes from nowhere, blesses, and then utterly disappears.[1] As an extension of this point, the author of Hebrews

23. Speiser, *Genesis,* p. 105.

24. See RS 17.340 = *PRU,* 4:48–52. Cf. Y. Muffs, "Abraham the Noble Warrior," *JJS* 33 (1982) 83–88, and esp. p. 86 for text and translation.

1. See C. S. Lewis, *Reflections on the Psalms* (New York: Harcourt, Brace and World Inc., 1958), pp. 122–23.

states that both Melchizedek and Christ possess the power of an indestructible life (v. 16), and therefore are priests forever (v. 24). Neither has received his priestly office from a predecessor, nor can either transfer that office to a successor. (2) Melchizedek blessed Abram, and "the inferior is blessed by the superior" (v. 7). (3) After Melchizedek blessed Abram, Abram paid Melchizedek a tithe of everything (vv. 4–6). Thus Levi actually paid tithes to Melchizedek, for Levi was still in the loins of his ancestor (Abram) when Melchizedek met Abram (v. 10).[2]

It seems obvious that Heb. 7 is addressing itself not only to a controversial topic, but also to a people who held the figure of Melchizedek in high respect, at least prior to their conversion to Christianity. Perhaps the believers were tempted to embrace him in their search for something foundational.[3]

Conflicting opinions about Melchizedek are to be found in two scrolls from Qumran. In one—the Genesis Apocryphon (1QapGen)—he appears in much the same light as in Hebrews. But in the second scroll—the Melchizedek scroll from cave 11 (11QMelch)—the picture is quite different.[4] In the second text Melchizedek appears as an eschatological and soteriological figure who passes judgment, in the time of the tenth or last Jubilee, on Belial and his cohorts. This judgment takes place in heaven, and there follows

2. For the isolation of these three emphases see J. A. Fitzmyer, " 'Now This Melchizedek . . .' (Heb. 7,1)," *CBQ* 25 (1963) 314–20.

3. See R. Longenecker, "The Melchizedek Argument of Hebrews: A Study in the Development and Circumstantial Expression of New Testament Thought," in *Unity and Diversity in New Testament Theology,* Fest. George E. Ladd, ed. R. A. Guelich (Grand Rapids: Eerdmans, 1978), pp. 173, 174, 176–77.

4. For translation and (one) interpretation of 11QMelch cf. A. S. van der Woude, "Melchizedek als himmlische Erlösergestalt in den neugefundenen eschatologischen Midraschim aus Qumran—Höhle XI," *OTS* 14 (1965) 354–73; M. de Jonge and A. S. van der Woude, "11Q Melchizedek and the NT," *NTS* 12 (1966) 301–32. Note also J. A. Fitzmyer, "Further Light On Melchizedek From Qumran Cave 11," *JBL* 86 (1967) 25–41. Fitzmyer admits that the presentation of Melchizedek in the Qumran Cave 11 text may not have influenced directly the presentation of Melchizedek in Heb. 7, but he does suggest that the text's exaltation of Melchizedek and its emphasis upon him as a heavenly liberator "makes it understandable how the author of the epistle to the Hebrews could argue for the superiority of Christ the high priest over the levitical priesthood by appeal to such a figure" (p. 41). Y. Yadin ("A Note on Melchizedek and Qumran," *IEJ* 15 [1965] 152–54) adds philological comments to this text, and suggests that the dual emphasis in the Qumran texts on Melchizedek as the Messianic priest (Genesis Apocryphon) and Messianic King (11QMelch) made him an appropriate figure for the writer of Hebrews to use to present Jesus' unique position.

immediately the day of slaughter on which Melchizedek is both judge and executor of his decree (see Isa. 61:1–2). Then the atonement of the faithful children of God will occur, for this is "the acceptable year of Melchizedek."[5]

In presenting his case for the priesthood of Christ, the writer to the Hebrews must first answer the question: How can a priest come out of the tribe of Judah? Second, he must address the issue of how Jesus, the Judean priest, is superior to the eschatological savior of Qumran messianology. In so doing he moves beyond functional statements of Christ's priesthood (esp. 2 Cor. 5:18–21) to ontological and metaphysical ones, and in the process does not compare Jesus to Melchizedek, but Melchizedek to Jesus (v. 4). Such a procedure is comparable to Paul's statement that Adam is a "type" of Christ (Rom. 5:4). Thus O. Michel is correct when he says that "Melchizedek has no independent significance to salvation; he is simply a divine intimation of the Son of God."[6]

The appropriation of the Melchizedek figure by the author of Hebrews, and especially those traditions embedded in Gen. 14 and Ps. 110, makes a twofold contribution to the argument of the epistle. First, it substantiates that the Levitical priesthood, now to be replaced by Christ's priesthood, had already been preceded by that of Melchizedek, and hence had only a relative importance, a kind of built-in obsolescence. Second, the model of Melchizedek furnishes the relatively new Christian movement with the guarantee of antiquity, something that is indispensable for obtaining credibility in its confrontation with non-Christians.[7]

5. The parallels between Heb. 11 and 11QMelch may be reduced to a minimum, or even dismissed altogether (F. L. Horton, Jr., *The Melchizedek Tradition: A Critical Examination of the Sources to the Fifth Century* A.D. *and in the Epistle to the Hebrews,* SNTSMS 30 [Cambridge: Cambridge University, 1976], esp. his concluding fifth chapter). I too would give prominence to the distinction between the two sources. F. F. Bruce notes that for the author of Hebrews "Melchizedek is a human being, albeit a very great one, and one would not gather from his exposition that the people for whom it was intended thought Melchizedek to be anything else" (F. F. Bruce, "Recent Contributions to the Understanding of Hebrews," *ExpTim* 80 [1968/69] 263). A statement in support of parallels between Heb. 7 and 11QMelch may be found in A. S. van der Woude, "Melchizedek," *IDBS,* pp. 585–86.

6. O. Michel, *TDNT,* 4:570.

7. See C. Gianotto, *Melchísedek e la sua tipologia: Tradizioni gindaiche, christiane e gnostiche* (sec. II a. C.—sec. III d. C.) Supplementi alla Rivista Biblica 12 (Brescia: Paideia, 1984), esp. pp. 121–44, which discuss the role of Melchizedek in Heb. 7.

D. THE COVENANT WITH ABRAM (15:1–21)

1. THE COVENANT PROMISES (15:1–6)

1 *Later Yahweh's word came to Abram in a vision:*
"Fear not, Abram!
I am a benefactor for you;
your reward shall be exceedingly great."

2 *But Abram queried: "O Lord Yahweh, what purpose will your gifts serve if I die*[1] *childless, and have as my heir the son of Meshek (that is, Damascus), Eliezer?"*

3 *Abram continued, "But look! To me you have given no offspring and accordingly a member of my household will succeed me."*

4 *Back came Yahweh's word to him: "That one shall not succeed you; none but your own flesh and blood*[2] *shall succeed you."*

5 *He took him outside and said: "Look up at the heavens and number the stars, if you are able to number them. Just so," he added, "shall be your offspring."*

6 *He put his faith in Yahweh, and for that reason he credited it*[3] *to him as righteousness.*

1 The divine voice, muted since 13:17, now speaks again in a negative imperative: *Fear not!* God speaks this word of assurance again to Isaac in 26:24 and to Jacob in 46:3, and both times these patriarchs find themselves in potentially dangerous situations. But Abram does not have his back to the wall here. Indeed, he has just emerged unscathed from a situation fraught with danger (ch. 14). Where he might have given into fear he did not. Now Yahweh speaks to the fearless one and says, "Fear not!"

This formula occurs frequently in the OT on the lips of a prophetic

1. Lit., "What will you give me, and I am going [*hôlēḵ*] childless?" For *hālaḵ* with the connotations of death cf. Gen. 25:32. See also BDB, p. 234 (§ II.1); F. Andersen and D. N. Freedman, *Hosea,* AB (Garden City, NY: Doubleday, 1980), p. 427 (discussion of Hos. 6:4).

2. Heb. *'ăšer yēṣē' mimmēʿeyḵā,* lit., "what comes out from your innards."

3. The fem. suffix on the verb "refers in a general sense to the verbal idea contained in a preceding sentence (corresponding to our *it*)" (GKC, § 135p). In effect, the verbal suffix appended to *ḥāšaḇ* transforms the perfect clause into an object clause: "Yahweh credited the fact that Abram believed Yahweh to him as righteousness." Incidentally, the economic background of Heb. *ḥāšaḇ* ("credit") and *ḥešbôn* ("reckoning, account," found only in Eccl. 7:25, 29; 9:10) is established by an Ugaritic text which begins: *ṯt mat ksp ḥṯbn ybnn,* "600 shekels of silver is the account [*ḥṯbn*] (owed by) YBNN." See *PRU,* 2:127, 1–2.

spokesman when he encourages a group, or an individual, not to be intimidated by an enemy who is shortly to be encountered (Num. 21:34; Deut. 1:21; 3:2; 7:18; 20:1; 31:8; Josh. 8:1; 10:8; 11:6; Isa. 7:4; 10:24). Of whom need Abram be afraid? The juxtaposition of ch. 14 and ch. 15 suggests that it is not nearly as fearful to meet an antagonist on the battlefield as it is to encounter the deity in a *vision.* Abram may confront Chedorlaomer and live, but can he confront Yahweh and live?

It may well be that Yahweh's *Fear not* is prompted by more than a need to alleviate the fear of the sudden appearance of deity. It may also serve to encourage and provide comfort to a man who is childless. As such, the words *Fear not* function in a way similar to the "fear not" words addressed in the NT to Zechariah, the eventual father of John the Baptist (Luke 1:12, 13). In both passages a childless father is comforted with a reassuring "fear not," and is informed that, although both he and his wife are currently without children at their advanced age, they will have a son.[4]

Yahweh's method of communicating with Abram was through a vision *(maḥ^a^zeh),* or literally "in the vision" *(bammaḥ^a^zeh),* a word that occurs only three more times in the OT (Num. 24:4, 16; Ezek. 13:7). But related words which also mean "vision," such as *ḥāzôn* (35 times), *ḥāzûṯ* (5 times), and *ḥizzāyôn* (9 times), appear frequently. What is transmitted from God to a mortal in such visions is not a visual image but a word from God. This is what distinguishes a vision from a dream. Accordingly, the emphasis in vv. 1–6 is that Abram had a vision of Yahweh in which the following action and dialogue took place. Normally such a vision would take place at night (see Gen. 15:5; 1 Sam. 3:1–3; 2 Sam. 7:4, 17; Job 4:13; 20:8; 33:15; Mic. 3:6). That God's word was revealed most frequently to the prophets through a vision may suggest that in Gen. 15:1 Abram is represented as a prophet, a designation specifically attached to him in 20:7. What follows in the vision is an oracle of assurance. This experience may be compared with three similar experiences in the life of Paul (Acts 18:9ff.; 23:11; 27:23ff.). Like Gen. 15:1ff., they are all nocturnal auditions, and Paul is urged to "fear not."

The divine imperative is followed by a word of divine self-disclosure. Two clauses in apposition state the same fact twice. The first states a fact from the speaker's point of view: *I am a benefactor for you.* The second states the same point, but from the addressee's point of view: *your reward shall be exceedingly great.*[5]

4. See E. W. Conrad, "The Annunciation of Birth and the Birth of the Messiah," *CBQ* 47 (1985) 656–63, esp. pp. 661–62.

5. See F. Andersen, *The Sentence in Biblical Hebrew,* p. 44. Cf. the phrase

Most translations have rendered "shield" for MT *māḡēn* (e.g., AV, RSV, NIV). On the heels of Yahweh's words to Abram that he "fear not," the promise that he will be the patriarch's shield would be appropriate. Thus we have a metaphorical term signifying divine protection (see Deut. 33:29; Ps. 3:4 [Eng. 3]; 18:3 [Eng. 2]; 28:7; etc.).

Some scholars have suggested slight emendations, however. For example, M. Kessler suggested emending MT *māḡēn* to a participle, *mōḡēn* (cf. *miggēn* in 14:20), thus providing this translation: "I am about to deliver to you a very great reward." This rendering would explain Abram's retort: "what will you give [*titten*] me?"[6]

A second emendation calls for reading *māḡān,* "benefactor, suzerain."[7] This suggestion has the advantage of making more sense of the following line: "your reward [*śeḵārеḵā,* MT] shall be exceedingly great," or "who will reward you [*śōḵēreḵā*] greatly." It is a benefactor, rather than a shield, who provides a reward. Abram has already had one benefactor from whom his "reward" was substantial (Pharaoh, ch. 12). He refused the donation of a second potential benefactor (king of Sodom, ch. 14). But this benefactor he will pursue. One passage in the OT, Ps. 127:3, lists "the fruit of the womb" as a "reward" *(śāḵār)* for a man. This might suggest that the reward Yahweh has prepared for Abram is a son.

2–3 For the first time there is dialogue between God and Abram. Heretofore there has been only monologue (12:1ff., 7; 13:14ff.). Abram listened and acted, but he offered no verbal response. He has spoken to Sarai, to Lot, to the king of Sodom; but now he speaks to God, in the form of a challenging question.

His concern is not that he has no male progeny (he does not query, why am I childless?), but the possibility that he may never have any progeny.

---

in an Akkadian oracle of Ishtar to King Esarhaddon: "Esarhaddon . . . my mercy is your shield" (*ANET,* p. 450). The "fear not" passages in Genesis (15:1; 21:17; 26:24; 46:3) are distinguished from the "fear not" passages in the Prophets and Deuteronomic writings by the presence in the former of the promise formulated with verbs in the 1st sing. (clearly in 21:17; 26:24; 46:3). Gen. 15:1 is no exception to this if *harbēh* be understood as infinitive absolute with the subject *'ānōḵî.* Thus the recipients of the oracles assume a more passive role. It is Yahweh's future activity that is stressed. See E. W. Conrad, "The 'Fear not' oracles in Second Isaiah," *VT* 34 (1984) 143–45.

6. See M. Kessler, "The 'Shield' of Abraham," *VT* 14 (1964) 494–97.

7. See M. J. Dahood, "Hebrew-Ugaritic Lexicography iv," *Bib* 47 (1966) 414; idem, "Northwest Semitic Notes on Genesis," *Bib* 55 (1974) 78. Dahood has further suggested that 12 of the 19 occurrences of *mgn* in the Psalms be translated "suzerain" rather than "shield"; cf. the response of W. H. Shea, "David's Lament," *BASOR* 221 (1976) 142 n. 5.

What useful purpose would be served by a reward that could not be transmitted? God's self-revelation to Abram, his word of encouragement and promise to Abram, do not silence or settle the patriarch's concern. It is not necessarily a fact that Abraham interprets Yahweh's promise of a reward as a promise of a child. That may or may not be read into Abram's lament in v. 2. No gift, whatever its nature, would be adequate compensation for Abram dying without a son. Nor would it really be useful or meaningful.

Rather than waiting for Yahweh to respond, Abram attempts to answer his own question: Will Eliezer his servant and steward be his heir? Will Abram have to concoct an ad hoc solution because of a divine oversight? Yahweh has delivered his enemies into his hand, but is he able to deliver a son into Abram's household? In essence the concern voiced by Abram in v. 2 is not essentially advanced by his concern voiced in v. 3. In both verses Abram is perplexed as to why God has not given him a child. All that is different is a change in vocabulary when Abram addresses his lament to God. In v. 2 he laments that he is "childless" *(ʿarîrî)* and in v. 3 that God has not given him any offspring *(lî lōʾ nāṯattâ zāraʿ),* with "to me" placed at the beginning of the clause for emphasis.

Scholars have noted that Abram's suggestion reflects an adoption procedure known from the Nuzi texts. A childless couple adopts a son, sometimes a slave, to serve them in their lifetime and bury and mourn them when they die. In return for this service they designate the adopted son as the heir presumptive. Should a natural son be born to the couple after such action, this son becomes the chief heir, demoting the adopted son to the penultimate position.[8]

Although Gen. 15:2–3 says nothing about adoption per se, it does declare that servants such as Eliezer could inherit property, as Prov. 17:2 attests.[9] Abram is concerned that he be able to leave such an inheritance to a person he trusted. He does not wish to leave behind him a situation fraught with legal complications.

Our discussion of vv. 2–3 would be incomplete without a mention of some of the textual and translation problems involved in *ûḇen-mešeq bêṯî hûʾ dammeśeq ʾĕlîʿezer,* translated above as: *and have as my heir the son of Meshek (that is, Damascus), Eliezer?* This is a notorious crux that

8. See E. A. Speiser, "Notes to Recently Published Nuzi Texts," *JAOS* 55 (1935) 435–36, who pinpoints the use of the word *ewuru* for designated heirs rather than direct heirs, viz., adopted sons; see also C. H. Gordon, "Biblical Customs and the Nuzu Tablets," *BA* 3 (1940) 2–3.

9. See J. Van Seters, *Abraham in History and Tradition,* pp. 85–87.

continues to baffle the best of Hebraists. Here are some of the proposed solutions.

H. L. Ginsberg suggests four changes in the text: (1) eliminate *mešeq* as a ghost word which is a variant of *dammeśeq;* (2) emend *dammeśeq* to *yîrāšennû,* "he will possess it"; (3) transpose *ʾĕlîʿezer* from the end to the beginning of the sentence: "and only my steward Eliezer is to possess it"; (4) possibly emend *ʾĕlîʿezer* to *ʾên zeraʿ:* "if I am to pass away childless and only my steward is to possess it."[10]

G. R. Driver wants to eliminate the word *mešeq* as incomprehensible and transpose the last two words, *ʾĕlîʿezer* and *dammeśeq,* to produce a personal name in the construct state: "and the heir of my house is Eliezer of Damascus."[11] Thus these first two solutions, befuddled by the presence of the noxious *mešeq,* simply excise it!

M. J. Dahood appeals to Ugar. *mšq,* "punch bowl, goblet" (from *šqy,* "to drink") to understand Heb. *mešeq:* "if I pass away childless and he who pours libations on my grave [*ben mešeq bēṯî*] is Eliezer of Damascus."[12] He thus connects the phrase with funeral procedures and suggests the unusual rendering of *bêṯ* as "grave." Not only is this a strange translation of *bêṯ,* but the suggestion that the statement is concerned with burial customs is alien to the chapter.

O. Eissfeldt retained the equation of Ugar. *mšq* with Heb. *mešeq* and offered this translation: "the possessor of the goblet of my house is Eliezer," for the goblet represents the essence and the life of the house. *hûʾ dammeśeq* is ignored as an intrusive gloss.[13]

C. H. Gordon has suggested that *ben-mešeq* is good Hebrew of which the Aramaic equivalent is *dammeśeq.* This Aramaic term he explains as a common noun designating a servant. He observed that one of the ancient cuneiform names for Damascus is *ša-iméri-šu,* "he of his donkeys," that is, a donkey-boy, a servant. Yet *mešeq* resembles no known word for "donkey." Gordon suggested that when "Damascus" was translated and transliterated into Akkadian there was no problem reproducing Aram. *d-* as *šu-,* the proclitic relative pronoun. However, the Assyrians made a slight error in reading

10. See H. L. Ginsberg, "Abram's 'Damascene' Steward," *BASOR* 200 (1970) 31–32.

11. See G. R. Driver, "Reflections on Recent Articles," *JBL* 73 (1954) 127. In support of his second point Driver notes the Peshitta's *ʾelîʿāzār darmûsqāyā.*

12. See M. J. Dahood, *Ugaritic-Hebrew Philology,* p. 65.

13. See O. Eissfeldt, "The alphabetical cuneiform texts from Ras Shamra published in 'Le Palais Royal D'Ugarit,' Vol. II, 1957," *JSS* 5 (1960) 48–49.

ḥamar, "wine," as though it were *ḥamār,* "donkey." *mešeq* should be connected with *maškeh,* "butler," making Eliezer Abram's wine-serving butler.[14]

F. Pomponio appeals to the texts from Ebla. In a bilingual text the Semitic root *mu-ša-qu-um* is given as the equivalent of Sum. *igi-du*$_8$, "a gift," and *igi-ḫe-du*$_8$, "a future gift." Could then *ben-mešeq* be understood as "heir"?[15]

W. F. Albright has explained the name of the capital city of the land of Damascus as *Dhî-miśqi* or *Dhî-maśqi,* with the variant *Dhat-maśqi,* whence Heb. *dammeśeq.* Thus *mešeq* is taken as an older name of Damascus than *dammeśeq.* Eliezer was called "son of Damascus" following common usage in Ugaritic and Akkadian, where "son of" was used of a native of a given town.[16] The addition of *dammeśeq* would be an evident gloss to explain to a later generation that *mešeq* is *dammeśeq.*[17]

Albright's case is confirmed, in my judgment, by an Aramaic inscription in which one of the kings of Aram, Benhadad (Bir-hadad), calls himself "the Damascene": *br hdd br ʿzr mśqyʾ,* "Bir-Hadad, son of ʿEzer, the Damascene." Aram. *mśqyʾ* may be compared with Heb. *ben-mešeq.*[18]

4 My translation *Back came* is an attempt to capture the adversative nature of *hinnēh,* the first word of the verse. God assures Abram that Eliezer will be no surrogate heir. That role shall be played by Abram's own *flesh and blood* or issue. Again Yahweh speaks to Abram proleptically by the promise of a future son. This promise, however wonderful, will be severely challenged by a seemingly insuperable hurdle—Sarai's inability to conceive (ch. 16). The promise of God to Abram finds a reverberation in the divine promise to David: "I will raise up your offspring after you, who shall come forth from your body" (1 Sam. 7:12). Both verses use the same verb and noun to express the emergence of the issue of one's own body (*kî-ʾim ʾašer yēṣēʾ mimmēʿeyḵā,* Gen. 15:4; *ʾeṯ-zarʿaḵā . . . ʾašer yēṣēʾ mimmēʿeyḵā,* 2 Sam. 7:12). The language of 2 Sam. 7:12 is ambiguous enough to allow one to read this promise of offspring either collectively or singularly. The subsequent verse (v. 13),

14. See C. H. Gordon, "Damascus in Assyrian Sources," *IEJ* 2 (1952) 174–75.

15. See F. Pomponio, "*Mešeq* di Gen 15,2 e un termine amministrativo di Ebla," *BeO* 25 (1983) 107–9.

16. See W. F. Albright, "Abram the Hebrew: A New Archaeological Interpretation," *BASOR* 163 (1961) 47.

17. See M. F. Unger, "Some Comments on the Text of Genesis 15:2, 3," *JBL* 72 (1953) 49–50.

18. See F. M. Cross, "The Stele Dedicated to Melcarth by Ben-hadad," *BASOR* 205 (1972) 40.

however, makes it clear that an individual is intended. The same ambiguity is present in Gen. 15:4. However, the next verse makes it clear that what God means by his promise is both the next generation and a series of generations thereafter.

5 We now discover that the word of Yahweh came to Abram while the patriarch was inside his home, for Yahweh *took him outside.* Also, this vision is received at night,[19] for Abram is told to look heavenward and count the stars. The emphasis here now shifts from "your own flesh and blood" (v. 4) to the many descendants (v. 5). This theme of mass numbers of offspring appears frequently in Genesis with comparisons to the stars (here, 22:17; 26:4), sand at the seashore (22:17; 32:12), and the dust of the earth (13:16; 28:14).

This promise does mean that Israel was destined to become the most populous nation of the Mediterranean world. The emphasis here on multiplication of numbers needs to be set alongside a verse like Deut. 7:7, "It was not because you were more in number than any other people that Yahweh set his love upon you . . . for you were the fewest of all peoples." A zeal for numbers is to be matched by a zeal for holiness and righteousness.

6 In response to these promises, Abram *put his faith in Yahweh.* This is the first time that this word—the Hiphil of *'āman*—appears in the Bible, and it will be used only two more times in Genesis (42:20; 45:26). Of course, this is not the first time that Abram has put his trust in Yahweh's word (see 12:1ff.). The action of faith preceded the vocabulary of faith. That is, by virtue of his earlier obedient response to a word from God, Abram was putting his faith in Yahweh (see, e.g., 12:1ff.).

Hebraists wonder why the verb for *put faith* or "believe" is in the Hiphil stem (which generally has a causative force), and why the verb is sometimes followed by the preposition *b^e* (23 times) and other times by the preposition *l^e* (14 times). On this second issue one may say that in some instances the choice of the following preposition is inconsequential; note especially the parallelism of Ps. 106:12, 24: "They believed [*he'ĕ mîn b^e*] his words" (v. 12); "they did not believe [*he'ĕ mîn l^e*] his word" (v. 24). However, note that there are more instances where the verb followed by *b^e* is used in a positive sense.[20] Almost all the examples with *l^e* are negative ones, as in the above example from Ps. 106:24 (except Exod. 4:8b; Prov. 14:15 is technically

19. For nocturnal revelations in Genesis see also 15:17; 26:24; 28:11–13; 31:11–13 (?); 46:2.

20. See Exod. 14:31; 19:9; Num. 14:11; 20:12; Deut. 1:32; 28:66; 1 Sam. 27:12; 2 K. 17:14; Jer. 12:6; Jon. 3:5; etc.

positive, but it describes the gullible person who believes anything and everything).[21]

The first issue, the use of the Hiphil stem for "believe, have faith," has been explained in various ways. The standard nuance attached to the Hiphil, that is, a causative, "to make firm," is certainly ruled out for Gen. 15:6. Some commentators (e.g., Speiser) have suggested a declarative-estimative function: "he declared him (or considered him) firm, steadfast." This shifts the emphasis from the subject of the action to the object of the action, and so in 15:6 it is Yahweh who is highlighted, not Abram. This suggestion is ruled out grammatically by the fact that verbs used declaratively are followed by a direct object. *he*^{ʾĕ} *min,* on the contrary, is followed by a preposition or is used absolutely (Ps. 116:10, "I have remained faithful").

Close to the latter suggestion is the idea that we have here a delocutive use of the Hiphil.[22] Gen. 15:6 would be read something like: "He declared, 'Amen' in Yahweh."[23] Thus Abram gives not just a mental response, but a verbal, confessional statement, to which Yahweh responds in v. 6b. Grammatically there is not the same need for a direct object after a delocutive verb as there is after a declarative one.

The traditional explanation has been to assign to the Hiphil of this verb an internal-transitive function, that is, "the entering into a certain condition and, further, the being in the same."[24] Abram "became steadfast (or firm) in Yahweh." This nuance differs from the previous two in that it emphasizes the certainty and the sureness of the believer, rather than the certainty of the object or statement in which faith was placed. What prompted Abram's faith was certainly the promise of the Lord, and that is the incentive to faith. But this is a theological observation, not a linguistic one.[25]

21. See Gen. 45:26; Exod. 4:1, 8a; Deut. 9:23; 1 K. 10:7; 2 Chr. 9:6; Isa. 43:10; 53:1; Jer. 40:14; Ps. 106:24.

22. See D. R. Hillers, "Delocutive Verbs in Biblical Hebrew," *JBL* 86 (1967) 320–24; R. J. Williams, *Hebrew Syntax: An Outline,* 2nd ed. (Toronto: University of Toronto, 1976), p. 28 (§ 148). Examples: "to be just, right" (Qal); "to pronounce in the right, justify" (Hiphil); "to be wrong" (Qal); "to pronounce in the wrong, condemn" (Hiphil); "to be happy" (Qal); "to pronounce happy" (Hiphil). Williams also sees a delocutive use of the Piel (ibid., § 145).

23. See M. G. Kline, "Abram's Amen," *WTJ* 31 (1968) 1–11.

24. So GKC, § 53e; see also J. Barr, *The Semantics of Biblical Language* (Oxford: Oxford University, 1961), pp. 176–87; A. Jepsen, "*ʾāman,*" *TDOT,* 1:298–309.

25. It is not necessary to emend *w*^{e}*he*^{ʾĕ} *min* to *w*^{e}*haʾ*^{a}*mēn* (infinitive absolute) to get rid of *w*^{e} plus the perfect, as suggested by J. Huesman, "The Infinitive Absolute and the Waw + Perfect Problem," *Bib* 37 (1956) 413. It is adequate to understand

The second part of this verse records Yahweh's response to Abram's exercise of faith: *he credited it to him as righteousness.* But even here there is a degree of ambiguity. Who credited whom? Of course, one may say that the NT settles the issue, for Paul expressly identifies the subject as God and the indirect object as Abram (Rom. 4:3). If we follow normal Hebrew syntax, in which the subject of the first clause is presumed to continue into the next clause if the subject is unexpressed, then the verse's meaning is changed. (This is the same problem we encountered in 9:27, "May God enlarge Japheth, and may he [?] dwell in Shem's tents.") In 15:6 is the subject of *wayyaḥšeḇehā* God or Abram? Abram is the subject of the first clause. Does he, therefore, continue as the logical subject of the second clause?

The Hebrew of the verse certainly permits this interpretation, especially when one recalls that *ṣeḏāqâ* means both "righteousness" (a theological meaning) and "justice" (a juridical meaning). The whole verse could then be translated: "Abram put his faith in Yahweh, and he [Abram] considered it [the promise of seed(s)] justice."[26] Nevertheless, as we have noted above, the traditional interpretation makes the most sense in the wider biblical context and is grammatically justifiable.

The verb *ḥāšaḇ* has two basic meanings throughout the OT. One is "count, value, calculate." The second is "plan, think out, conceive, invent." The first encompasses the bringing together of numbers and quantities and values with an eye to weighing or evaluating or calculating. The second encompasses the bringing together of ideas and plans for some intended project. In addition, the OT provides instances of *ḥāšaḇ* with an impersonal accusative object and a dative of the person involved, who is introduced by the preposition *le*, "to"; the meaning of this construction is "to reckon or credit something (as something) to someone's account." This idiom appears in both active and passive constructions. This is what one finds in Gen. 15:6: (1) the verb *ḥāšaḇ* ("he credited or reckoned"); (2) double impersonal accusative object, *-hā* ("it") and *ṣeḏāqâ* ("righteousness"); and

---

wehe'ĕmin as a preterit plus *waw* (copulative) form. See O. Loretz, "The *Perfectum Copulativum* in 2 Sm 7,9–11," *CBQ* 23 (1961) 294–96. Most of the verbs in 15:1–5 are *waw* (consecutive) plus imperfect forms. Suddenly in 15:6a we are confronted with a *waw* (*copulative*) plus perfect form. Then 15:6b shifts back to a *waw* plus imperfect. I suggest that both changes in tense in v. 6 express the consequence of the immediately preceding section.

26. See M. Oeming, "Ist Genesis 15:6 ein Beleg für die Anrechnung des Glaubens zur Gerechtigkeit?" *ZAW* 95 (1983) 182–97, and a response to Oeming by Bo Johnson, "Who reckoned righteousness to whom?" *SEÅ* 51 (1986) 108–15.

(3) dative of the person involved, who is introduced with the preposition *l*e ("to him"). Thus our translation, *he credited* (or reckoned, imputed) *it to him as righteousness.* A second instance of this construction appears in 2 Sam. 19:20 (Eng. 19). Shimei, the Benjamite secessionist who had led a revolt against David, now comes before a restored David and pleads for mercy. His plea to the king is "let my lord not reckon [*'al-yaḥašāḇ*] to me [*lî*][27] [my] wrongdoing [*'āwōn*]." Again, we have the verb *ḥāšaḇ,* followed by the dative of the person involved, introduced with the preposition *l*e*,* and then the impersonal accusative object. This illustration is very close to Ps. 32:2, "blessed is the man whom Yahweh does not impute [*lō' yaḥšōḇ*] to him [*lô*] iniquity [*'āwōn*]."

For the idiom with the passive voice of the verb, see Lev. 7:18, which deals with illegally eating the flesh of the peace offering on the third day. For such a violation the offering will not be accepted by the priest *(lō' yērāṣeh),* nor will it be credited to the offerer by the priest *(lō' yēḥāšēḇ lô).* See also Lev. 17:4, which is concerned with the person who does not bring his sacrifice and offer it to Yahweh before the tabernacle. The result of such omission is that "blood guilt [*dām*] shall be imputed [*yēḥāšēḇ*] to that man [*lā'îš hahû'*]." Cf. Num. 18:27, "your heave offering shall be reckoned to you [*w*e*neḥšaḇ lāḵem*] as grain from the threshing floor," and Prov. 27:14, which deals with the loudmouthed individual who "blesses" his friend very early in the morning. What happens to his blessing is that "as a curse [*q*e*lālâ*] it will be reckoned to him [*tēḥāšeḇ lô*]."

Von Rad has appealed to the two passages in Leviticus (7:18; 17:4) and the one in Numbers (18:27) to suggest that the origin of "he credited it to him for righteousness" in Gen. 15:6 is to be found in the Israelite cultus. Such priestly passages illustrate a declaratory act performed by the priest, using declaratory formulae, to state the cultic acceptance of the individual's sacrifice, albeit Gen. 15:6 spiritualizes such a process.[28] It is quite valid to assert that *ḥāšaḇ* was used in the OT in cultic acts; however, the same may not be said for *ṣ*e*ḏāqâ,* at least when sacrifices are presented. Following Seybold, we suggest that *ḥāšaḇ* in Gen. 15:6 is used to demonstrate Yahweh's

27. The LXX omits the preposition and pronominal suffix. It reads "let not my Lord think of wrongdoing" *('l yḥšb 'dny 'wn).* So read, 2 Sam. 19:20 would not be an illustration of the idiom I am detailing.

28. G. von Rad, "Faith Reckoned as Righteousness," in *The Problem of the Hexateuch and Other Essays,* tr. E. W. Trueman Dicken (New York: McGraw-Hill, 1966), pp. 125–30. See also idem, *Old Testament Theology,* tr. D. M. G. Stalker (New York: Harper & Row, 1962), 1:379–80.

reckoning of Abram's act of faith as the deciding factor in his relationship with Abram.[29] *ḥāšaḇ* "defines Yahweh's momentary reaction theologically as an act of conscious judgment."[30]

2. THE COVENANT CEREMONIES (15:7–21)

7 *He then said to him: "I am Yahweh who brought*[1] *you from Ur of the Chaldeans to give you this land as a possession."*

8 *"O Lord Yahweh," he responded, "how am I to know that I will possess it?"*

9 *He answered him: "Bring me a three-year-old heifer, a three-year-old she-goat, a three-year-old ram, a turtledove, and a young pigeon."*

10 *He brought him all these, and split them down the middle, placing one half opposite the other; the birds, however, he did not split.*

11 *Whenever birds of prey swooped down on the carcasses Abram put them to flight.*[2]

29. K. Seybold, *"ḥāšaḇ," TDOT,* 5:243–44. Note the perceptive comment by B. Childs (*Old Testament Theology in a Canonical Context* [Philadelphia: Fortress, 1985], pp. 219–20: "To understand this narrative [viz., Gen. 15:1–6] it is necessary to recall that righteousness is not an ideal, absolute norm, but a right relationship. One is righteous who does justice to the claims which a covenantal relationship entails. In Gen. 15 Abraham's faith is declared to have established Abraham as righteous in God's sight. His righteousness is not the result of any accomplishment. . . . Rather, it is stated programmatically that belief in God's promises alone has established Abraham's right relation to God. He has made the proper response through faith."

30. Seybold, *TDOT,* 5:244.

1. Lit., "I am Yahweh who I brought you from Ur of the Chaldeans." Hebrew syntax demands that whenever the subject of the main clause is in the 1st or 2nd person, the corresponding subject in the subordinate, relative clause must also be in the 1st or 2nd person. The relative particle *'ᵃšer* does not function as a subject of a clause. See GKC, § 138.

2. This is the reading of the MT, *wayyaššēḇ 'ōṯām,* a Hiphil of *nāšaḇ,* a verb occurring only here and in Ps. 147:18; Isa. 40:7. The LXX apparently misread the words as *wayyēšeḇ 'ittām,* hence *kaí synekáthisen autoís,* "and he sat down with them"; but this reading makes little sense. See J. Barr, "Vocalization and the Analysis of Hebrew among the Ancient Translators," in *Hebräische Wortforschung,* Fest. Walter Baumgartner, VTSup 16 (Leiden: Brill, 1967), pp. 3–4; G. R. Driver, "Notes and Studies," *JTS* 47 (1946) 167. Aquila grasped the sense of the Hebrew with his *apesobēsen,* "he scared away." See also E. Tov, *The Text-Critical Use of the Septuagint in Biblical Research* (Jerusalem: Simor, 1981), p. 169.

12 *As the sun was setting a deep sleep fell on*[3] *Abram, and lo, a deep, frightening darkness engulfed*[4] *him.*

13 *He said to Abram: "Know for certain that your descendants shall be strangers in a land not theirs. They shall be enslaved and oppressed for four hundred years.*

14 *But the nation which enslaves them I will judge. Subsequently they will depart with abundant provision.*

15 *As for you, you will go peacefully to your forefathers and be buried at a ripe advanced age.*

16 *They shall return here, but only in the fourth generation, for only then will the iniquity*[5] *of the Amorites*[6] *have run its course."*

17 *When the sun had set and it was dark a smoking fire pot*[7] *and a flaming torch passed*[8] *between these sections.*

18 *That very day Yahweh made a binding promise*[9] *with*[10] *Abram saying:*

3. *nāp̄al ʿal* is used of the sudden onset of overpowering forces, often bad (Exod. 15:16; Ps. 105:38; Isa. 47:11; Dan. 10:7), but also neutral or supernatural (here; 1 Sam. 11:7; 26:12; Job 4:12–13; Ezek. 8:1; 11:5).

4. Lit., "fell on him"; again, *nāp̄al ʿal.*

5. Heb. *ʿāwōn* means not only "sin," but what one must bear when he has sinned. Cain protests in Gen. 4:13 that his *ʿāwōn* is too great for him to bear. Verses like Gen. 15:16 and Exod. 20:5 show that *ʿāwōn* describes a condition that may become progressively worse.

6. J. Van Seters ("The terms 'Amorite' and 'Hittite' in the Old Testament," *VT* 22 [1972] 74) calls this a pejorative use of "Amorite," reflecting the ideological and rhetorical usage of the term in Deuteronomic literature.

7. Heb. *tannûr* may refer to a fixed or portable earthenware stove, used esp. for baking bread (cf. Lev. 2:4; 7:9; 26:26), or to an incinerator (Mal. 3:19 [Eng. 4:1]).

8. Although the sentence has two subjects the verb is singular.

9. Heb. *kāraṯ bᵉrîṯ,* lit., "cut a covenant." This expression is not unique to the OT. One may compare the phrase "cut a contract" *(batâqu/nâkasu beriti)* from cuneiform sources; see W. F. Albright, "The Hebrew Expression for 'Making a Covenant' in Pre-Israelite Documents," *BASOR* 121 (1951) 21–22. Cf. Gk. *hórkia támnein* and Lat. *foedus icere* (see J. Fitzmyer, "The Aramaic Inscriptions of Sefire I and II," *JAOS* 81 [1961] 190).

10. Hebrew allows four different prepositions after "cut a covenant" when the covenant is between human beings: (1) *lᵉ,* when the subject of the verb is the superior party, conferring a treaty as a favor or imposing it (Josh. 9:6, 11, 15, 16; 24:25; 1 Sam. 11:1, 2; 1 K. 20:34; Job 31:1), or a conqueror's relationship to a conquered people (Exod. 23:32; 34:12, 15; Deut. 7:2), or making the lesser party swear itself to loyalty to the higher power (2 Sam. 5:3; 2 K. 11:4; 1 Chr. 11:3). Also to be included here are instances where a devotee makes a covenant with *(kāraṯ bᵉrîṯ lᵉ)* one's God (Jer. 34:18; 2 Chr. 29:10); (2) *'eṯ,* when the contracting parties have more or less equal bargaining powers (2 Sam. 3:12, 13, 21, although Jer. 34:8 and Ezek. 17:13 show otherwise); (3) *ʿim,* when the subject of the verb is the suppliant (Gen. 26:28; 1 Sam. 22:8; Hos. 12:2 [Eng. 1]); (4) *ʿal,* only one time, Ps. 83:6 (Eng.

"To your descendants I give this land, from the river of Egypt to the great river, the river Euphrates,

19 *(the land of) the Kenites, the Kenizzites, the Kadmonites,*

20 *the Hittites, the Perizzites, the Rephaim,*

21 *the Amorites, the Canaanites, the Girgashites, the Jebusites."*

7 Both revelations of God to Abram in this vision (vv. 1–6, 7–21) commence with an identification statement by the giver of the vision: "I am your benefactor"; "I am Yahweh who brought you from Ur of the Chaldeans." The difference between the two is that the first formula focuses on the future, what Yahweh intends to do with Abram. The second at least begins by focusing on the past—what Yahweh has recently done on behalf of Abram. In this vein it is impossible to miss the similarities between 15:7a and Exod. 20:2: "I am Yahweh your God, who brought you out of the land of Egypt, out of the house of bondage"; then comes the Decalogue. This kind of identification formula legitimates the credentials of the one introducing himself, and speaks particularly of the availability and resources of the vision speaker to the vision receiver. In addition to Exod. 20:2, note verses like Exod. 6:6 and especially Lev. 25:38, which also use the Hiphil of *yāṣā'* to describe God's deliverance of Israel from Egypt. Unlike the experiences of Israel in Egypt, however, there is no explicit biblical tradition that Abram was in any peril in Ur from which he needed liberation.[11]

8 This verse also parallels the first section of this chapter. Abram's earlier "What purpose will your gifts serve?" is now matched by *how am I to know that I will possess it?* On neither occasion does God castigate Abram for raising an honest question or for pressing him for further, explicit details. It is not a question of doubt that Abram raises. Rather it is a question in which he presses God for further empirical evidence about the promise of v. 1b. For

5), God's enemies in concert against God. But when God is one of the parties, any of the first three prepositions may be used, for he transcends all limitations. Thus with God/Yahweh as subject, *kārat̲ b^{e}rît̲ l^{e}* is used 8 times (Judg. 2:2; 2 Chr. 21:7; Ps. 89:4 [Eng. 3]; Isa. 55:3; 61:8; Jer. 32:40; Ezek. 34:25; 37:26); *kārat̲ b^{e}rît 'et̲* is used 6 times (Exod. 34:27; Deut. 5:3; 28:69 [Eng. 29:1]; 29:13 [Eng. 14]; 31:16; 2 K. 17:15, 35, 38; 1 Chr. 16:16; Ps. 105:9; Jer. 11:10; 31:31, 32, 33; 34:13; Zech. 11:10); *kārat̲ b^{e}rît̲ 'im* is used 10 times (Exod. 24:8; Deut. 4:23; 5:2; 9:9; 29:11 [Eng. 12]; 29:24 [Eng. 25]; 1 K. 8:21; 2 Chr. 6:11; Neh. 9:8; Hos. 2:20 [Eng. 18]).

11. M. Fishbane (*Biblical Interpretation in Ancient Israel* [Oxford: Clarendon, 1985], p. 376) suggests that the Hiphil of *yāṣā'* was used in Gen. 15:7 as part of the stock of traditional terms used to convey the Exodus, thus permitting the establishment of a typological nexus between the patriarch and later Israel.

the use of *bammâ* in similar contexts where further supporting data is desired, see Exod. 33:16; Mal. 1:2, 6, 7; 2:17; 3:7–8.

9–11 The patriarch is instructed to bring to Yahweh three animals: *a three-year-old heifer, she-goat, and ram;* plus two birds: *a turtledove and a young pigeon.* The animals are cut in half with the sections arranged across from each other in parallel rows. The birds are slaughtered, but not split in two. Fiery symbols will soon pass between these rows (v. 17), and the covenant with Abram will have been inaugurated (v. 18). This is an unusual custom, and the only clear parallel to it in the OT is Jer. 34:18, 19: "the men who transgressed my covenant . . . I will make like the calf which they cut in two and then passed between its parts—the princes of Judah, the princes of Jerusalem, the eunuchs, the priests, and all the people of the land who passed between the parts of the calf." Jeremiah's prophecy is prompted by the actions of King Zedekiah, who had "cut a covenant" with the Jerusalemites in order to set free all male and female Hebrew slaves, but after which his people turned around and took their slaves right back.[12] While Jer. 34:18, 19 provides the only indubitable OT parallel to Gen. 15, a similar covenant understanding may be behind the ritual summonses described in Judg. 19:11–20:48; 1 Sam. 11:1–10; and possibly Amos 5:17b.[13]

The biblical world offers widespread evidence that animals were slaughtered in treaty contraction ceremonies.[14] Some of these texts—but not all of them—suggest that the two parties to the treaty walked between the rows of freshly killed animal flesh, and in so doing placed a curse upon themselves if either party should prove disloyal to the terms of the treaty: May they too be torn apart if they are responsible in any way for violating the arrangement.[15]

The most frequently cited text to support the thesis that the procedures taken by Abram function as a dramatized curse is a seventeenth-century B.C. treaty from Alalakh between Yarimlim and Abban. Abban has just given the

12. On this Jeremiah text see P. Miller, Jr., "Sin and Judgment in Jeremiah 34:17–19," *JBL* 103 (1984) 611–13.

13. On Amos 5:17b, and its relationship with Jer. 34 and Gen. 15, see M. J. Hauan, "The Background and Meaning of Amos 5:17b," *HTR* 79 (1986) 337–48.

14. For an extensive bibliography on discussion of ancient treaties dealing with the dissection of animals see E. Lipiński, "Notes on the Mešaʿ Inscription," *Or* 40 (1971) 337 n. 50.

15. This idea of self-imprecation is reflected in the prospective witness who swears under oath: "I promise to tell the truth, the whole truth, and nothing but the truth, so help me God." If I prevaricate on the witness stand, then I will have to contend with God.

city of Alalakh to Yarimlim, the vassal ruler, and to cement that transaction the text says: "Abban placed himself under oath to Iarimlim and had cut the neck of a sheep (saying): '(Let me so die) if I take back that which I gave thee!' "[16]

Not only does this text provide an illustration of an animal slaughter as a dramatized curse, but it provides the further analogy with Gen. 15 in that it is the superior party who places himself under sanctions. This is one of the main reasons why commentators have been hesitant to accept Gen. 15:7ff. as a *Drohritus* (threatening ritual), for in this interpretation it is God who leaves himself open to dismemberment should he become a covenant violator. In the parallel from Jer. 34:18, the vassal passed between the parts, not the suzerain.

The forcefulness of this parallel has been blunted by other translations of the same lines, for example, the more literal: "Abba-AN is under oath to Yarimlim and also he cut the neck of a lamb. (He swore): I shall never take back what I gave thee."[17] This translation suggests that animal slaughter is a genuine part of treaty ratification but does not constitute an acted-out curse.

Another second-millennium B.C. analogy often placed alongside Gen. 15 is the treaty and covenant ritual from the Mari texts. One text reads: "I went to Ašlakka and they brought me a young dog and a she-goat in order to conclude a covenant [lit., "kill a donkey foal"] between the Ḫaneans and the land of Idamaraṣ. But, in deference to my lord, I did not permit (the use of) the young dog and the she-goat, but (instead) had a donkey foal, the young of a she-ass, killed, and thus established a reconciliation between the Ḫaneans and the land of Idamaraṣ."[18]

Of interest here is the use of the phrase *ḫayaram qaṭālum,* "to kill a donkey foal," to denote the concluding of a covenant. The comparisons of this text with Gen. 15 are obvious: the custom of slaughtering animals in covenant ritual. But there is no indication that the slaughtering procedure constituted a symbolic curse on one of the contracting parties. The slaughtering simply ratifies the covenant.

Only one second-millennium B.C. text refers to the custom of dividing

16. Translation of D. Wiseman, "Abban and Alalah," *JCS* 12 (1958) 129. Wiseman is seconded by M. Weinfeld, "The Covenant of Grant in the Old Testament and in the Ancient Near East," *JAOS* 90 (1970) 196; idem, "The Loyalty Oath in the Ancient Near East," *UF* 8 (1976) 400–401.

17. Translation of D. J. McCarthy, *Treaty and Covenant,* AnBib 21 (Rome: Pontifical Biblical Institute, 1963), p. 185.

18. Translation of M. Held, "Philological Notes on the Mari Covenant Rituals," *BASOR* 200 (1970) 33.

a sacrificial animal in half and the covenanting parties passing between the pieces: "If the troops have been beaten by the enemy they perform a ritual 'behind' the river, as follows: they 'cut through' a man, a goat, a puppy, and a little pig; they place half on this side and half on that side, and in front of them they make a gate of . . . wood and stretch a . . . over it, and in front of the gate they light fires on this side and on that, and the troops walk right through, and when they come to the river they sprinkle water over them."[19]

Another text from the same period reads: "And in front of the gate they shall place one half on this side, and they place one half on that side."[20] Neither of these texts involves treaty ratification or symbolic curse. What is involved is the attempt to regroup troops, via ritual purification, after a setback on the battlefield.

Two references from later texts (1st millennium B.C.) do involve both the slaughtering of sacrificial animals and the symbolic curse in a treaty context. In the Aramaic inscription Sefire I.A, lines 39–41 (ca. 750 B.C.), involving a treaty between Bir-Ga'yah (or Barga'yah) king of KTK and Matî'el (or Matti'el) king of Arpad, part of the ceremony pointing to possible violation by Matî'el reads: "[Just as] this calf is cut in two, so may Matî'el be cut in two, and may his nobles be cut in two! [And just as] a [ha]r[lot is stripped naked], so may the wives of Matî'el be stripped naked."[21]

The second reference comes from the curses of the vassal treaty of Esarhaddon, a seventh-century B.C. king of Assyria: "Just as male and female kids and male and female lambs are slit open and their entrails fall down upon their feet, so may the entrails of your sons and daughters roll down over your feet."[22]

One observes immediately that these two texts are much closer to Jer. 34:18 than they are to Gen. 15. For in both, as in Jer. 34:18, animal slaughter and symbolic curse are clearly present. The absence of these emphases in Gen. 15 has moved many commentators to the position that Gen. 15 is not concerned with God placing himself under any kind of potential curse at all.

19. Translation of O. Gurney, *The Hittites* (Baltimore: Penguin, 1954), p. 151.

20. Translation of A. Goetze, *The Hittite Ritual of Tunnawi* (New Haven: American Oriental Society, 1938), p. 90.

21. Translation of J. A. Fitzmyer, *The Aramaic Inscriptions of Sefîre,* BibOr 19 (Rome: Pontifical Biblical Institute, 1967), pp. 14–15, 56–57. Cf. F. Rosenthal's translation in *ANET,* p. 660.

22. Translation of D. J. Wiseman, "The Vassal Treaties of Esarhaddon," *Iraq* 20 (1958) 69–72. Cf. also the translation of E. Reiner, *ANET,* p. 539 (§ 70, lines 551ff.).

Instead, what one finds here is that the slaying and arrangement of the animals is simply a sacrificial practice by means of which a covenant is ratified.[23]

To be sure, the sacrificial procedures carried out in Gen. 15 do not exactly parallel those in the Sinaitic legislation. No blood is shed, nothing is burnt, there are no altars.[24] Nevertheless, there are some possible parallels. For example, is there any connection between Abram's splitting the animals into halves, and Moses, at the ratification of the Sinai covenant, splashing half the blood on the altar and the other half on the people (Exod. 24:6, 8)? One would not expect to find exact analogies to Gen. 15, for by its very nature it was never intended to be repeated. Those interpreters who downplay the sacrificial elements in the story indeed see Jer. 34:18 as an excellent parallel to Gen. 15, and they understand the force of the ritual to be God's way of making a solemn oath to Abram, much as elsewhere God swears by himself (Gen. 22:6; 26:3; etc.).[25]

This ritual concludes with the interesting notice that *Whenever birds of prey* [who fly only in the daytime] *swooped down on the carcasses, Abram put them to flight.* Elsewhere in the OT *birds of prey* (who are unclean, Lev. 11:13–19; Deut. 14:12–18) represent foreign nations (Ezek. 17:3, 7; Zech. 5:9), most likely Egypt. If a case can be made that the slain animals, all appropriate as sacrificial victims, represent the nation of Israel, then here in a sense Abram is protecting his descendants from the attacks of outsiders.[26] This note parallels Abram's behavior in the preceding chapter. There he

23. See D. L. Petersen, "Covenant Ritual: A Traditio-Historical Perspective," *BR* 22 (1977) 7–18; G. F. Hasel, "The Meaning of the Animal Rite in Gen. 15," *JSOT* 19 (1981) 61–78, esp. pp. 68–70. Hasel states (p. 70), "The killing and sectioning of the animals by Abram is a sacrificial *preparatio* for the subsequent divine *ratificatio* of the covenant by Yahweh who in passing between the pieces irrevocably pledges the fulfillment of his covenant promise to the patriarch." G. J. Wenham ("The Symbolism of the Animal Rite in Genesis 15: A Response to G. F. Hasel, *JSOT* 19 [1981] 61–78," *JSOT* 22 [1982] 134–37) agrees with Hasel that the rite is not a divine self-imprecation. He states (p. 136), "It is not a dramatised curse that would come into play should the covenant be broken, but a solemn and visual reaffirmation of the covenant that is essentially a promise."

24. B. Levine (*In the Presence of the Lord* [Leiden: Brill, 1974], p. 37 n. 93) states: "In the description of covenants in the Bible where some amount of detail is provided it is most often the case that no sacrificial activity is recorded. This allows for the conclusion that sacrifice was not essential to the process of covenant enactment itself." He then cites 9 examples, of which Gen. 15 is one, but the only one involving deity and man.

25. See J. Van Seters, *Abraham in History and Tradition,* pp. 100–103, 249–78.

26. See G. J. Wenham, *JSOT* 22 (1982) 135.

successfully fought against outsiders and rescued Lot. He is the protector in both contexts.

12 The phrase *As the sun was setting* appears problematic, for in v. 5 the stars are shining, so it must already be night. But this chronological problem disapppears when we recall that v. 11 has mentioned birds of prey, who hunt their victims during the day, thus implying that Abram's vision has moved into its second day.[27]

This is the one time that Abram experiences fear in the presence of God. Adam in the presence of God was fearful (3:10), as was Jacob (28:17), Moses (Exod. 3:6), and the Israelites (Exod. 20:18); with the first three individuals the fear is spawned by the memory of unholy behavior and comes upon them while they are conscious. The dread of God engulfs Abram only when he is in an unconscious state, for a *deep sleep*[28] has overtaken him. Cf. Jacob, who is afraid after he awakes, and Abram, who experiences fear just after he falls asleep. No illicit action by Abram has prompted this dread, as in the case of Adam and Jacob. The dread or terror is brought on simply by the presence of God. The Hebrew word for "terror" *('êmâ),* which we have translated *frightening,* reflects a human emotion that is inspired most often by Yahweh's presence (Exod. 15:16, where it is parallel to *paḥaḏ;* 23:27; Deut. 32:25; Ps. 88:16 [Eng. 15]; Job 9:34; 13:21). Such terror is destructive (Exod. 23:27; Deut. 32:25; Ps. 88:16), immobilizing (Exod. 15:16), intimidating and coercive (Job 9:34; cf. 33:7), or unnerving (Job 13:21). None of these nuances, however, is found in the use of *'êmâ* in Gen. 15:12. In fact, we would know of no terror that seized Abram in this narrative, had v. 12 not stated it so.

13 Suddenly Yahweh clarifies his promise to Abram. He had begun by promising the land to Abram (v. 7), but now it becomes clear to Abram that only his descendants will possess the land and only after a hiatus of *four*

27. See the discussion of chronology in G. Vos, *Biblical Theology,* p. 71.

28. The Hebrew term *tardēmâ* means an abnormally deep sleep or lethargy (Gen. 2:21; 1 Sam. 26:12; cf. the verb *rāḏam* in Judg. 4:21; Ps. 76:7 (Eng. 6); Prov. 10:5; Jon. 1:5; Dan. 8:18; 10:9). It may also refer to a mental state of apathy (Prov. 19:15) or obduracy (Isa. 29:10). Job 4:13 and 33:15 are the closest in meaning to Gen. 15:12. Both passages speak of receiving nocturnal visions when a heavy sleep has fallen upon one. J. Hartley (*Book of Job,* NICOT [Grand Rapids: Eerdmans, 1988], p. 112) suggests that in such instances *tardēmâ* refers not to a deep natural sleep but to a "stupor that God causes to fall on a person, blocking out all other perceptions, in order that the person may be completely receptive to the divine word." See also J. Lindblom, "Theophanies in Holy Places in Hebrew Religion," *HUCA* 32 (1961) 91–106, esp. p. 94.

hundred years. For four centuries they will be abused and victimized as aliens. Lot became an alien, forced to live under another (ch. 14), and Abram's descendants will encounter the same fate, but for a much longer period.

strangers or sojourners are those who live or move outside their own territory, and Abram himself employs this term when among the Hittites (23:4) or the Egyptians (12:10). It describes a visitor or guest spending the night in the house of another (19:9). To make certain that Abram knows that God is speaking in certainties and not possibilities when talking about exile, the MT has the finite form of the verb preceded by the infinitive absolute: *Know for certain.* The *know* here picks up the "how am I to know" of v. 8.

The *four hundred years* of exile mentioned here (which Stephen quotes in Acts 7:6) seems not to match the four hundred and thirty years of exile mentioned in Exod. 12:40–41 (which Paul quotes in Gal. 3:17). We take it that the *four hundred years* refers to both the period of sojourning and the eventual enslavement. The best way to reconcile these different numbers is to see that "the 400 years is a round figure in prospect, while the 430 years is more precise in retrospect."[29]

Interestingly, the time before the Israelites possess the land is clearly delineated. But the land in which they will sojourn, the land that is not theirs, is not identified. Does Abram assume that that land is Egypt? In the light of his own earlier sojourn to Egypt, one assumes that in his thinking that is the only real possibility.

14 The persecuting nation remains unknown, but its fate is clear: God *will judge* them, as he judged Pharaoh for taking Abram's wife. But again, the nature of this judgment is not revealed.

One wonders if the sentence *they will depart with abundant provision* did not remind Abram of the day when he too left an alien land with enormous provision (Gen. 12), though he had gained it at great cost. *r*ᵉ*ḵuš* is what the descendants of Abram will bring out of the alien land after the period of their servitude is over, and *r*ᵉ*ḵuš* is what Abram brought back with him after he fought against the kings and won Lot's freedom (14:16, 21).

29. K. A. Kitchen, *Ancient Orient and Old Testament,* p. 53. But R. de Vaux (*Early History of Israel,* pp. 317–20) argues that neither a sojourn of 430 or 400 years in compatible with the rest of the biblical data. He is misled in this conclusion by his approach to the genealogies and by his refusal to understand them as selective lists. Similarly S. Kreuzer ("430 Jahre, 400 Jahre oder 4 Generationen. Zu den Zeitangaben über den Ägyptenaufenthalt der 'Israeliten'," *ZAW* 98 [1986] 199–210) sees no historical basis in such numbers, and attributes them to a typological understanding of antiquity by later tradents who also had to confront the reality of exile.

15 Abram will be spared a turbulent future. To go to one's grave *peacefully* means to come to the end of one's life with a sense of contentment and fulfillment. Here are back-to-back prophecies: one of Abram's descendants' future, and one of his own future.

Advanced age alone is not what makes this prediction so intriguing. Rather, it is that the advanced age is qualified as *ripe (ṭôḇâ).* Jacob illustrates that the elder years of one's life can be those of misery (42:38; 44:29, 31). For the expression *śēḇâ ṭôḇâ* see Gen. 25:8 (Abraham); Judg. 8:32 (Gideon); 1 Chr. 29:28 (David).

16 The ultimate destiny of Abram's descendants is not in doubt. Four *generations* of sojourning and enslavement will end and they will return to the land. Our understanding of *dôr* is based on the following statement by Albright: "The early Hebrews . . . dated long periods by lifetimes, not by generations (which replaced the count by lifetimes about the tenth century B.C. at latest). Heb. *dôr* (for older *dahru>dâru,* properly 'lap in a race, cycle of time') means 'lifetime' in Gen. 15:16; the 400 years of 15:13 is simply the translation of the archaic terminology into classical Hebrew."[30]

Only when *the iniquity of the Amorites* (i.e., the pre-Israelite inhabitants of Palestine) has run its full measure will the Israelites enter Palestine to claim it and possess it. Only when the iniquity of the Amorites has reached the point of no return will they forfeit the land. This last half of the verse articulates the idea that the fixing of times is conditioned not on necessity but on morality.[31] This commentary on the immorality of the indigenous population of Canaan also establishes Joshua's invasion as an act of justice rather than of aggression.[32]

17 The *smoking fire pot* and the *flaming torch* remind one of the smoke and fire that surrounded the summit of Mt. Sinai.[33] Fire in the Bible

30. W. F. Albright, "Abram the Hebrew: A New Archaeological Interpretation," *BASOR* 163 (1961) 50–51.

31. See Y. Kaufmann, *The Religion of Israel,* tr. and ed. M. Greenberg (New York: Schocken, repr. 1972), p. 73.

32. See D. Kidner, *Genesis,* p. 125.

33. Noting the connections between Gen. 15 and Exod. 19, J. Van Seters suggests that in the exilic period there was a conscious confessional shift from Yahweh as God of the Exodus to Yahweh as the God of the patriarchs. This suggestion reflects Van Seters's penchant for dating just about everything Abrahamic to the Exile. See his "Confessional reformulation in the Exilic period," *VT* 22 (1972) 448–59, esp. 454–56. Why may we not follow the canonical order and say there was a (natural) confessional shift from Yahweh as God of the patriarchs to Yahweh as God of the Exodus? The God who manifested himself in fiery form to Abram later manifests himself in fiery form to Abram's seed.

is often a symbol of the presence of God. (We have already drawn attention to the close parallel in form between 15:7 and Exod. 20:2.)

That only something representing deity passes between the rows of flesh shows that this covenant is unilateral. If it were bilateral, we would have expected something representing Abram as well to pass through, as we saw in the Hittite text discussed above on vv. 9–11.

Of special significance here is the idea of Yahweh, represented by fiery symbols, passing between *(ʿāḇar bēn)* the rows of animal flesh. Here *ʿāḇar* is clearly a theophanic term. As such, the verb may be compared with two other important OT passages, Exod. 33–34 and Josh. 3–4. The first of these deals with the renewal of the covenant after the sin with the golden calf, and the second with the start and completion of Israel's crossing the Jordan. The three references have the following items in common:

(1) a proclamation of Yahweh's name: Gen. 15:7; Exod. 34:5, 6; Josh. 3:9
(2) something is "cut": Gen. 15:18, a covenant; Exod. 34:4, tablets; Josh. 3:16, the waters of the Jordan
(3) Yahweh's appearance expressed through *ʿāḇar:* Gen. 15:17; Exod. 33:32; Josh. 3:11
(4) a justification for the theophany: Gen. 15:8, to confirm to Abram that he will possess the land; Exod. 33:16; to demonstrate that Moses and his people have found Yahweh's favor; Josh. 3:10, to convince the Israelites that there is among them a living God. (Note how each of these theophanies supplies knowledge for one who does not have that knowledge yet: "how am I to know?" [Gen. 15:8]; "for how shall it be known?" [Exod. 33:16]; "you shall know" [Josh. 3:10].)
(5) a list of nations Yahweh is to expel (in the form of a promise): Gen. 15:18–21; Exod. 34:11; Josh. 3:10–11
(6) each is in the context of a covenant, or covenant renewal.[34]

We may deduce, then, that these three passages provide support for positing a covenant ritual ceremony which involved a theophany that was expressed by the verb *ʿāḇar.* It is not necessary to read into Gen. 15:17 any sanctions or self-curse to which Yahweh exposes himself. Rather, it is a confirmation of Yahweh's promise of land to Abram's descendants.

18–21 Animals are cut and now a covenant *(binding promise)* is cut. V. 18 provides the only instance of the word "covenant" in the chapter. Etymologically the Hebrew word for covenant, *b*ᵉ*rîṯ,* is associated with Akk.

34. The working out of these parallels I owe to M. J. Hauan, *HTR* 79 (1986) 343–46.

birītu, "clasp, fetter." This etymology suggests that covenant, in the biblical sense, is not an agreement between two parties, but something that is imposed, an obligation.[35] Nothing, however, in this chapter is imposed on Abram. He is free of any obligations. The only imposition or obligation that Yahweh lays upon anybody is upon himself, and that is the obligation to implement his promise of descendants, and especially of land, to Abram and to his descendants. For this reason Westermann has suggested, correctly, that *b^erîṯ* not be translated here as "covenant" but with something that captures the broader nuances of *b^erîṯ*. He offered, "On that day Yahweh gave Abraham the solemn assurance. . . ."[36] Three elements in Yahweh's covenant with Abram—unconditionality, an oath taken by deity, and gift—find their clearest parallel in the later covenant with David (2 Sam. 7). The major difference between the two is that the first is a promise of land (for all descendants) and the second is a promise of dynasty (for one family).[37]

God obliges himself to give to Abram's descendants the land of ten nations, all of which fall within the land of Canaan proper. The *river of Egypt* (see Num. 34:5; Josh. 15:4, which use *naḥal* instead of *nāhār*) is not the Nile but the modern Wadi el-Arish, the dividing line between Palestine and Egypt. The geographical extremes of the promise obviously extend beyond Canaan, witnessed especially by the phrase *to the great river, the river Euphrates.* In fact, only during the apogee of David's reign, many hundreds of years later, was this promise actualized. But even then the empire was maintained only for a generation. By Solomon's time cracks appeared in the empire, and portions of the empire rebelled and reclaimed their own land for themselves.

THE NEW TESTAMENT APPROPRIATION

Gen. 15:6 and Rom. 4:3, 9, 22; Gal. 3:6

Paul's references to Abraham's faith in Gal. 3 and Rom. 4 are so close in spirit that the discussion of one will cover the other. In both instances the use of

35. See M. Weinfeld, *"b^erîṯ," TDOT,* 2:253–79.

36. C. Westermann, *Genesis,* 2:229.

37. R. Clements (*Abraham and David: Genesis XV and Its Meaning for Israelite Tradition,* SBT 2/5 [Naperville, IL: Allenson, 1967]) explores richly the transmission of the Abrahamic covenant in the development of Israelite tradition. I am not prepared to maintain, as does Clements, that the covenant with Abraham and the covenant at Sinai go in absolutely diverse directions.

the Abraham precedent follows one, or several, rhetorical questions. Because Paul pursues the Abraham analogy more fully in Rom. 4 than in Gal. 3, we shall concentrate our analysis on the Roman epistle.

Before examining Rom. 4:1ff., we must first observe how it flows naturally out of the preceding paragraphs, that is, 3:21–31. The general theme in 3:21–31 is the righteousness of God, which is now set over against the wrath of God (1:18–3:20). Punitive righteousness gives way to redemptive righteousness. In 3:22–26 Paul underscores the element of universality in relationship to the righteousness of God. The universal condition for a saving experience of this righteousness is faith (v. 22). There is a universal condition because there is a universal problem—all have sinned, Jew and Gentile (v. 23). Paul then emphasizes the mode by which this righteousness occurs, and that involves justification and grace (v. 24). Finally, the means by which all this takes place is Christ, who provides redemption and expiation (vv. 24–25). Then in 3:27–28 Paul takes one of these universal elements and particularizes on it, and the element he lifts out for special attention is faith. Faith, says Paul, excludes boasting, and is antithetical to the works of the law. In 3:29–30 he returns again to the universality of this condition. But here the rationale offered is monotheism (v. 30). That is, God has to be consistent in dealing with the same problem.

Chapter 4 functions as a test case of Paul's thesis elaborated in 3:21–31. Is this the way God has always saved people and always will save people? Paul now uses the Jewish Scriptures to prove that this justification by faith is universal and that the Jew has no special privilege with regard to salvation because of the law. Abraham is his example. Had Abraham been justified by works then he would have had a right to boast (see 3:27)—before God and man.

Then he provides scriptural support for his thesis by quoting Gen. 15:6. (Paul quotes the LXX, as evidenced by its passive "it was reckoned to him" over against MT's active "he reckoned it to him.") This verse contains both a negative argument—it says nothing about works—and a positive argument—Abram believed God. If the text had said "Abraham believed in God and this earned him righteousness," then the verse would be saying that faith itself was the work that provided the basis for justification. By using the term *reckoned* the text shows that justification is a matter of grace, not wages. Works, boasting, and wages are indivisible. So are faith, no boasting, and grace.

In 4:6–8 Paul appeals to the David episode to show that the

Abraham episode is not unique, to appeal to another outstanding person in Israel's history, and to use the religious experience of one whose life was post-Sinaitic, thus balancing the pre-Sinaitic Abraham. God did not reckon man's good works (Abraham) or man's sinful works (David). The essence of what justification means in Paul's mind involves ultimately not reckoning sin against one, but rather counting one's faith as rightness before God.[1]

Gen. 15:6 and Jas. 2:20–24

Martin Luther was not the only biblical student to see a tension between the thought of Paul and James. Says Martin Dibelius, "Whoever comes to James after a look at Paul (Rom. 4) must completely forget Paul's interpretation."[2] Paul could not agree more, so goes the argument, with James's statement that faith without works is dead. Where Paul would sharply dissent is in James's contention, via a rhetorical question, that Abraham was justified by works (*ouk ex érgōn edikaiṓthē,* v. 21).

It is our contention that James and Paul are not at loggerheads over their teachings on justification. Following the study of J. G. Lodge,[3] we suggest that the very literary structure of Jas. 2:20–24 leads to the conclusion that the passage is concerned with how to understand faith, how it acts, how it is perfected, and how it is not apart from works. Note, for example, how James emphasizes the true relationship between faith and works by arranging the two terms chiastically at the very center of the larger unit—v. 22: faith . . . works . . . works . . . faith (not all translations

1. In the formulation of my thoughts on Rom. 4 I have been helped by all the major commentators on Romans, plus the following studies: E. Käsemann, "God's Righteousness in Paul," in *New Testament Questions of Today,* tr. W. J. Montague (Philadelphia: Fortress, 1969), pp. 168–82; idem, "The Faith of Abraham in Romans 4," in *Perspectives on Paul,* tr. Margaret Kohl (Philadelphia: Fortress, 1971), pp. 79–101; J. Ziesler, *The Meaning of Righteousness in Paul: A Linguistic and Theological Enquiry* (Cambridge: Cambridge University, 1972); and the review of this book by N. M. Watson in *NTS* 20 (1974) 217–28, esp. 226–27; O. P. Robertson, "Genesis 15:6: New Covenant Expositions of an Old Covenant Text," *WTJ* 42 (1980) 259–89; unpublished lecture notes on Romans by Professor Robert Traina of Asbury Theological Seminary, Wilmore, KY.

2. M. Dibelius, *A Commentary on the Epistle of James,* rev. H. Greeven, tr. Michael A. Williams, Hermeneia (Philadelphia: Fortress, 1976), p. 164.

3. J. G. Lodge, "James and Paul at Cross-Purposes? James 2,22," *Bib* 62 (1981) 195–213.

reflect this chiasmus of the Greek; e.g., AV and NEB do, but RSV, NIV, JB, NAB do not).

Also note the chiasmus of v. 22b, "his faith was perfected" *(hē pístis eteleiṓthē)*—noun, passive verb—and v. 23a, "and the Scripture was fulfilled" *(kaí eplērṓthē hē graphḗ)*—passive verb, noun. This chiasmus puts the focus of Gen. 15:6 on faith, not on a dual fulfillment of Scripture by Abraham's faith on the one hand and his works on the other.

When James says that Abraham was "justified by works" (v. 21), he is surely using the verb with demonstrative force, and so it takes on this meaning: "Abraham was shown to be just by works." The biblical writer is not defining the way to justification but rather the sequence or evidence of justification. Abraham's trust in God's promises produced a resulting trust in the commands of God. He believed to the point of living his beliefs, even if that involved the offering of Isaac.

Interestingly, just as Paul in Rom. 4 followed his reference to Abraham with a reference to David as a bit of confirming evidence, so here James follows his reference to Abraham with one to Rahab. Abraham the patriarch and Rahab the prostitute! The patriarch of Israel and the harlot of the streets are juxtaposed as two illustrations of works, not as a merit for salvation but as a mark of salvation. The extremes of both legalism and fideism are thus circumvented.

E. HAGAR AND ISHMAEL (16:1–16)

1. STRIFE IN THE FAMILY (16:1–6)

1 *Sarai, Abram's wife, had borne him no children. But she had an Egyptian maidservant whose name was Hagar.*[1]

2 *Sarai said to Abram: "Look,*[2] *Yahweh has restrained me from bearing*

1. The lexicons do not offer an interpretation of the name Hagar, but M. Görg ("Hagar, die Ägypterin," *BN* 33 [1986] 17–20) suggests that the name is part of an Egyptian title which means "royal concubine." For the same name on a Hebrew seal impression at Jericho ("belonging to Hagar, [daughter of] Uriah"), which is dated to the late 4th or 3rd century B.C., see P. C. Hammond, "A Note on a Seal Impression from Tell Es-Sulṭân," *BASOR* 147 (1957) 37–39.

2. For *hinnēh* followed by *-nā'* cf. 12:11; 18:27, 31; 19:2, 8, 19, 20. BDB, p. 609, suggests that this construction conveys "craving a favorable consideration of the fact pointed to by *hinnēh,* and of the request found upon it."

children. Have intercourse with[3] *my maidservant. Perhaps by her I shall reproduce."*[4] *Abram heeded her suggestion.*[5]

3 *Sarai, Abram's wife, took Hagar the Egyptian, her maidservant, ten years after Abram had lived in the land of Canaan, and gave her to Abram her husband as his concubine.*[6]

4 *He had intercourse with Hagar and she conceived. When she learned*[7] *that she had conceived, her mistress lost status*[8] *in her estimation.*[9]

3. Lit., "go into." Cf. Gen. 6:4; 30:3; 38:8, 9; 39:14; Deut. 22:13; 2 Sam. 12:24; 16:21; 20:3; Prov. 6:29; Ezek. 23:44 (3 times), all of which are followed by the preposition *'el.* For *bô' ʿal* see Gen. 19:31; Deut. 25:5. There seems to be no apparent difference between the two, for both *bô' 'el* (Gen. 38:8, 9) and *bô' ʿal* (Deut. 25:5) are used to describe the brother-in-law's responsibility to his deceased brother and widowed sister-in-law. (Cant. 5:1, "I come to [*bô' le*] my garden, my sister, my bride," might also be an instance of *bô'* for having sexual relations with a woman.) In some instances the expression describes licit sex (Gen. 16:2; 30:3; 38:8, 9; Deut. 22:31; 25:5; 2 Sam. 12:24 [for Bathsheba is now his wife and not just his lover with whom David earlier "laid," *šāḵaḇ,* 11:4]; 20:3). On a few occasions it refers to illicit sex (Gen. 39:14; 2 Sam. 16:21 [a usurpation of the royal harem]; Prov. 6:29; Ezek. 23:44). Gen. 6:4 is ambiguous. To be sure, the relationship of the partners is condemned by God, but at least the sons of God engage in sexual activity with their "wives." In some instances references to the birth of children follow *bô' 'el/ʿal* (Gen. 6:4; 16:2; 19:31; 30:3; 38:8, 9; Deut. 25:5; 2 Sam. 12:24).

4. Lit., "I shall be built." For the Niphal of this root meaning "to have children" see Gen. 30:3, and possibly Job 22:23. Also, note the similarity of sound between "son" *(bēn)* and this verb *(bānâ),* suggesting perhaps the presence of a pun. In fact, *bānâ* may be a denominative verb from *bēn* (Dahood, *Psalms,* 2:184).

5. Lit., "listened to the voice of Sarai." The same expression was used back in Gen. 3:17 to refer to the man who listened to the voice of his wife. Cf. also Exod. 4:9, God's suggestion to Moses that his people in Egypt may not listen to his voice, i.e., heed him.

6. Speiser (*Genesis,* p. 117) notes that Heb. *'iššâ,* like Akk. *aššatum,* may signify either "wife" or "concubine." The usual Hebrew word for "concubine" *(pîlegeš)* is never used to describe Hagar, except indirectly in 25:6. Other women in Abraham's life are specifically designated as "concubines" (see 22:24). See also Gen. 30:4. I note, however, that neither *CAD* nor von Soden in his *Akkadisches Handwörterbuch* in their respective entries on *aššatu* give an illustration of *aššatu* = "concubine." In fact, *CAD,* under the *aššatu* entry (vol. 1/2:463, § c, end of col. 1; p. 464, § m), cites texts in which *šugitu* ("concubine") and *esirtu* ("concubine") appear, and they are not intended as synonyms for *aššatu.*

7. Lit., "and she saw" *(wattēre'),* here in the sense of "become aware of."

8. V. 4b can hardly be translated "she looked with contempt on her mistress" (so RSV). Such an active display of contempt would require the Piel form of this verb, with its factitive effect. It is the loss of face which Sarai felt that impelled her to complain to Abram in v. 5 as she does. Cf. NJV "her mistress was lowered in her esteem." See J. Weingreen, "The case of the blasphemer, Lev. xxiv 10ff.," *VT* 22 (1972) 119–20; idem, *From Bible to Mishna* (Manchester: Manchester University, New York: Holmes & Meier, 1976), p. 90.

9. Lit., "in her eyes."

5 *Sarai then said to Abram: "The violence done to me*[10] *is because of*[11] *you. I myself gave my maidservant to your embrace, and when she learned that she had conceived I lost status in her estimation. May Yahweh decide between you and me!"*
6 *Abram answered Sarai: "Your maidservant*[12] *is in your power.*[13] *Do with her as you please." Sarai abused her so that she fled from her.*

1 The preceding chapter of Genesis had several references to God's promise to Abram that he would have both a descendant (v. 4) and descendants (vv. 5, 13, 18). The problem with that possibility ever becoming reality is Sarai's inability to conceive (see 11:30). In some ways the issue is the same as that in 12:10ff. What good are the promises of God if Sarai is dead (12:10ff.), or if her womb is dead? How is the problem of nonfunctioning reproductive organs to be overcome? For at least ten years (16:3) Abram and Sarai have been childless. The brief mention of the presence of an Egyptian maidservant, Hagar (for which see 12:16), opens a window to the following narrative.

Note in these six verses that whenever the narrator simply states a fact about Sarai he adds that she was *Abram's wife* (vv. 1, 3). When, however, she precedes direct discourse she is referred to simply as "Sarai" (vv. 2, 5, 6).

2 No reason is given for why Sarai is barren, other than that Yahweh has *restrained* or prevented her from conceiving. The same verb *(ʿāṣar)* is used in 20:18 again to describe the prevention of women conceiving. It is clear in Gen. 20 that the closing of the wombs of the Philistine women is due to Abimelech's taking of Sarah; that is, barrenness is a sign of divine displeasure or divine punishment. Gen. 16:2 makes no such statement (nor is it so stated as an explanation of Hannah's barrenness, 1 Sam. 1:5). Rather,

10. *ḥms* as a verb may take a direct object (Lam. 2:6), and hence it can form an objective genitive (here; Judg. 9:24; Obad. 10; Hab. 2:17).

11. For *ʿal* as "because of" cf. *UT,* 49:V:11–12: *ʿlk bʿlm pht qlt,* "because of you, Baal, I have seen abasement." See also M. J. Dahood, "Eblaite, Ugaritic, and Hebrew Lexical Notes," *UF* 11 (1979) 145. See also LXX *adikoúmai ék soú,* "I am injured through you." Cf. C. F. Whitley, "Ps. 99:8," *ZAW* 85 (1973) 228–29 for other OT examples, of which Ps. 99:8b is one.

12. In this chapter Hagar is identified consistently as a *šip̄ḥâ* (vv. 1, 2, 3, 5, 6, 8), but in ch. 21 she is called an *ʾāmâ* (vv. 10 [twice], 12, 13). The first is a maid who serves the mistress *(g^{e}ḇereṯ)* of the house. The second is a slave woman, standing in the service of her master or mistress, and hence is the more oppressive term. See A. Jepsen, "Ama^h und Schiphcha^h," *VT* 8 (1958) 293–97; and H. W. Wolff, "Masters and Slaves. On Overcoming Class Struggle in the Old Testament," *Interp* 27 (1973) 266.

13. Lit., "your hand." See BDB, p. 390.

Sarai's words reflect an OT perspective that Yahweh is the ultimate source behind all of life's experiences, from the exhilarating to the annoying and depressing. And in most cases moral analysis is not required.

To mitigate the problem Sarai suggests that her husband cohabit with Hagar, a suggestion which Abram took to heart. Note, however, that Sarai never addresses or talks of Hagar by name, but only by label or role, *my maidservant* (see also v. 5; even Abram avoids her name, v. 6). Other ancient texts have provided parallels to what the modern reader of Scripture might consider blatant immorality:

1. Hammurapi's Code, § 146: "When a seignior [i.e., a free man] married a hierodule [priestess] and she gave a female slave to her husband and she has then borne children, if later that female slave has claimed equality with her mistress because she bore children, her mistress may not sell her; she may mark her with the slave-mark and count her among the slaves."[14]
2. A Nuzi text: "If Gilimninu (the bride) will not bear children, Gilimninu shall take a woman of N/Lullu land (whence the choicest slaves were obtained) as a wife for Shennima (the bridegroom)."[15]
3. An Old Assyrian marriage contract: "Laqipum took (in marriage) Ḫatala, the daughter of Enišrû. In the country Laqipum shall not take (in marriage) another (woman), (but) in the city (of Ashshur) he may take (in marriage) a priestess. If within two years she has not procured offspring for him, only she may buy a maid-servant and even later on, after she procures somehow an infant for him, she may sell her wherever she pleases."[16]
4. A Neo-Assyrian text: (41) "If Ṣubetu does not conceive (and) (42) does not give birth, she may take a maidservant (and) (43) as a substitute in her position she may place (her). (44) She [Ṣubetu] will (thereby) bring sons into being (and) the sons will be her [Ṣubetu's] sons. (45) If she loves (the maidservant) she may keep (her). (46) If she hates her she may sell her."[17]

14. Translation of T. Meek, *ANET,* p. 172.

15. Translation of C. H. Gordon, "Biblical Customs and the Nuzu Tablets," *BA* 3 (1940) 3. See also Speiser, *Genesis,* pp. 120–21; idem, "New Kirkuk Documents Relating to Family Laws," *AASOR* 10 (1930) 31–32.

16. Translation of J. Lewy, "Old Assyrian Institutions," *HUCA* 27 (1956) 9–10.

17. Translation of A. K. Grayson and J. Van Seters, "The Childless Wife in Assyria and the Stories of Genesis," *Or* 44 (1975) 485–86. See also J. Van Seters, "The Problem of Childlessness in Near Eastern Law and the Patriarchs of Israel," *JBL* 87 (1968) 401–8; idem, *Abraham in History and Tradition,* pp. 68–71. It is unlikely

The first three of these texts date to the 2nd millennium B.C., and the last from the 1st millennium B.C. All four demonstrate a marriage practice spread over two millennia in which an infertile wife procures a surrogate wife, a maidservant. These four texts (plus Gen. 16) do differ from each other in minor ways, and it is to Van Seters's credit that he reminds us that it is not adequate to refer only to selective archeological data (i.e., second-millennium B.C. literature) when attempting to date the patriarchal period. It is impossible, simply on the basis of archeology, to date Gen. 16 to either the 2nd or the 1st millennium. We are dealing here with marriage customs which by their very nature are conservative and long-lived.

It would appear that Sarai's options are limited. Either she may choose to remain barren for the remainder of her life, or until Yahweh changes her circumstances. Or, assuming that her condition is a permanent one, she may present Hagar to Abram who will bear children on her behalf. It is difficult to determine whether this is an obligation or a privilege for Sarai. Both the biblical text in Gen. 16 and the extrabiblical texts cited above are ambiguous enough to support either conclusion. But given the emphasis on the indispensability of (male) progeny to perpetuate the family line, I am inclined to think that Sarai's action was obligatory, and that no ignominy was attached to such a procedure.

There are a number of references in the OT to men having one or more concubines. Excluding the patriarchs in Genesis, there are seven individuals of whom the OT says they had concubine(s). In order they are (1) Caleb (1 Chr. 2:46, 48); (2) Gideon (Judg. 8:31); (3) a Levite (Judg. 19–20); (4) Saul (2 Sam. 3:7; 21:11); (5) David (2 Sam. 5:13; 15:16; 16:21, 22; 19:6 [Eng. 5]; 20:3; 1 Chr. 3:9); (6) Solomon (1 K. 11:3); (7) Rehoboam (2 Chr. 11:21). And in all but the Levite of Judg. 19–20, there are references to a wife or wives of the man involved. Four of these seven are kings, suggesting that, during the monarchic period at least, concubinage was a royal institution. Some of these seven had children by their concubines (Gideon, Saul, David, Rehoboam), but concubines were charged as well with household chores (2 Sam. 15:16; 16:21; 20:3).

In every one of the above references the Hebrew word for concubine is *pîlegeš*. In fact several verses distinguish clearly between "wives" and

---

that Sarai is hoping to use the adoption of Hagar's children as a remedy for her own infertility, as argued by S. Kardimon, "Adoption as a Remedy for Infertility in the Period of the Patriarchs," *JSS* 3 (1958) 123–26. Kardimon takes "by her I shall reproduce/be built up" as expressive of Sarai's wish that upon seeing the children of another her own womb will again be restored to fertility.

"concubines" (see 2 Sam. 5:13 [which, interestingly, lists concubines before wives], 19:6; 1 K. 11:3; 2 Chr. 11:21). That is, *pileg̱eš* and *'iššâ* are distinct terms, and one never represents the other. Note, for example, that in Judg. 19–20 *pileg̱eš* is used 11 times, but *'iššâ* is never used. However, matters are somewhat different in Genesis. Here we find three instances where a man's partner is styled as both a *pileg̱eš* and an *'iššâ*. Thus 1 Chr. 1:32 calls Keturah Abraham's *pileg̱eš,* while Gen. 25:1 calls her Abraham's *'iššâ*. Gen. 16:3 calls Hagar Abraham's *'iššâ,* while 25:6 calls her (and Keturah) Abraham's *pileg̱eš*. Gen. 35:22 calls Bilhah Jacob's *pileg̱eš,* while 30:4 and 37:2 call her Jacob's *'iššâ*. (I note that in Judg. 19:3 and 20:4 the Levite is the concubine's "husband/man" [*'îš*].) Unlike the rest of the OT, where women are either wives or concubines, in Genesis we have three instances (Hagar, Keturah, and Bilhah) of a concubine-wife. This may well indicate that the concubines of Abraham and Jacob were not *pilagšîm* in the later sense, but that no term was available for that type of concubinage; thus *pileg̱eš* and *'iššâ* were used as synonyms to describe these women in the patriarchal narratives.[18]

3 Just as Abram gave Sarai to Pharaoh, now Sarai gives Hagar to Abram. Abram the donor becomes Abram the receiver, and Sarai the pawn becomes Sarai the initiator. Hagar has no choice in the matter. She is "taken," then "given," that is, she is essentially an instrument.[19] This all transpires after the couple have lived in Canaan for a decade.

The account provides another illustration of how a child of God, with his or her back to the wall, feels pressed to take the initiative in order to bring God's promises to pass. Sarai must through some means, any means, have progeny. This story also reflects the replacing of marriage's primary purpose of companionship (Gen. 2:18) by that of reproduction, with all the resulting negative effects.

4–5 Hagar, ironically, has no problem at all in becoming pregnant.

18. C. Rabin ("The Origin of the Hebrew Word *Pileg̱eš,*" *JJS* 25 [1974] 362) remarks: "The terminological difficulty was solved . . . by using the two terms together; but while today we would place them next to each other, possibly with a connecting hyphen, this was not possible in a language using descriptive opposition to such a large extent as Biblical Hebrew. By alternating the terms within the easily apprehended framework of a story, a similar impression of 'in-betweenness' was created."

19. See P. Trible, *Texts of Terror,* OBT 13 (Philadelphia: Fortress, 1984), p. 11. Also, C. Gordon, "Hagar: A Throw-Away Character Among the Matriarchs?" SBLASP, 1985 (Atlanta: Scholars, 1985), pp. 271–77, and esp. p. 273. "Her [viz., Hagar's] role is one of passivity, disenfranchisement, vulnerability . . . she has virtually no means of retaliation or redress if wronged . . . there seems to be no assumption that she has rights or legitimate claims that can be violated."

She is taken or brought to Abram. He has intercourse with her, with no emotional reactions described beforehand or after. But she turns against the very one who solicited her help and becomes pompous toward her (at least Sarai perceives it that way). In actuality Hagar is taking pride in her pregnancy. I would not doubt that Hagar's judgment about Sarai in v. 4b is the same as is found in the law stated above from the Code of Hammurapi, "if later that female slave has claimed equality with her mistress." This is quite different, however, from saying something like, "if later that female slave shows contempt toward her mistress," or some other insulting expression. Sarai is now a non-child-producing *'iššâ,* and Hagar is a child-producing *'iššâ.* And that is what annoys Sarai and not any barbs that Hagar is throwing at her. Sarai is understandably irked at the conflict this new situation has introduced into her household.[20] Her original intention in making the proposition to Abram was that Hagar would conceive. She did not anticipate the tension that would ensue. By comparison, there seems to be no tension present between concubine and wife when Bilhah and Zilpah become surrogate mothers for Rachel and Leah. Possibly this is so because they are, so to speak, already members of the family, given to the two sisters by their father, whereas Hagar is an Egyptian alien.

Sternberg has pointed out that Hagar's evaluation of Sarai has received the same formulation from the narrator (v. 4) as from Sarai (v. 5). He suggests that such repetition legitimates the concern of the party with a grievance. He says, "the reader infers from the equivalence in language an equivalence in vision where the character's involvement might otherwise cast doubt on her objectivity."[21] But perhaps Sternberg is reading too much of a denigrating nuance into Sarai's words. In any case, Sarai sees her rights as wife and mistress threatened, and the humiliation that accompanies that.[22]

6 If Hagar shows some pride, and if Sarai shows a false blame, Abram demonstrates a false neutrality.[23] He too, like Sarai, does not refer to Hagar by name but only by label. For Abram, Hagar is either *your maidser-*

20. See C. Westermann, *Genesis,* 2:240, "The narrator is not describing a gross violation of law or custom by Hagar, but a conflict which was almost unavoidable."

21. M. Sternberg, *The Poetics of Biblical Narrative* (Bloomington: Indiana University, 1987), pp. 389–90, and p. 402 (where the quote is found).

22. This is what Sarai must mean by use of the word *ḥ^a^māsî,* "the violence done to me." This is the one OT instance where *ḥāmās* is done by a woman. Haag (*TDOT,* 4:482) suggests that *ḥāmās* in this verse refers to "humiliation through impudent self-aggrandizement."

23. See Kidner, *Genesis,* p. 126.

vant or *her.* If v. 5 casts Abram in the role of defendant, v. 6a casts Abram in the role of judge.[24] And if Abram will not offer her legal protection, then Yahweh will *(may Yahweh decide between you and me).* Abram's judgment on the matter is, at best, lame and passive.

Sarai's abuse of Hagar (*ʿānâ* III), which forces Hagar to flee *(bāraḥ),* finds a parallel in the exodus of Israel from Egypt. There, the Egyptians' oppression of the Hebrews (*ʿānâ,* Gen. 15:13; Exod. 1:11, 12) moved the latter, by God's power, to flee (*bāraḥ,* Exod. 14:5). But in Gen. 16 the roles of oppressor and oppressed are just the opposite from Exodus. Here it is a matriarch of Israel oppressing an Egyptian.

The whole event and its unusual character are reflected in the OT's wisdom literature: "Under three things the earth trembles, under four it cannot bear up: . . . and a maid [*šip̱ḥâ*] when she succeeds her mistress [*g^{e}ḇirtāh*]" (Prov. 30:21–23).[25] These are the two terms used in Gen. 16 to describe the relationship of Sarai and Hagar to each other.

2. THE BIRTH OF ISHMAEL (16:7–16)

7 *The angel of Yahweh found her by a water spring in the wilderness, the spring on the road to Shur.*

8 *He said: "Hagar, maidservant of Sarai, from where have you come and where are you going?" She replied: "From my mistress Sarai I am fleeing."*

9 *The angel of Yahweh said: "Return to your mistress and accept ill-treatment at her hand."*

10 *"For," the angel of Yahweh said to her, "I will make your descendants so numerous that they cannot be counted because of size."*

11 *The angel of Yahweh also said to her:*
"You are with child and shall bear[1] *a son;*

24. For the structure of 16:5–6, cf. C. Mabee, "Jacob and Laban. The structure of judicial proceedings (Genesis XXXI 25–42)," *VT* 30 (1980) 206.

25. For the connection with Proverbs see R. B. Y. Scott, *Proverbs, Ecclesiastes,* AB (Garden City, NY: Doubleday, 1965), p. 182. On the rift between Sarai and Hagar as a commentary on the lack of compassion between two women, mistress and maid, see A. Brenner, "Female social behavior: two descriptive patterns within the 'birth of the hero' paradigm," *VT* 36 (1986) 257–73, esp. pp. 260–61, 272–73.

1. MT *w^{e}yōlaḏt^{e}* is problematic, for it seems to be a mix of the fem. participle *(yōleḏeṯ)* and the 2nd fem. sing. perfect *(yālaḏt^{e});* see *BHS.* But according to GKC, §§ 80f, 94f, the MT form here reflects an original form of the participle. In two OT birth narratives a unique form of the participle of *yālaḏ* is used in the birth announcement to the women. Here in Gen. 16:11 the woman (Hagar) is

You shall name him Ishmael,
For Yahweh has been attentive to your humiliation.[2]
12 *As for him, he shall be a wild ass of the*
steppe land,[3]
his hand against every man
and every man's hand against him.
In defiance of[4] *his kin shall he camp."*

13 *She called the name of Yahweh who spoke with her "You are a God of seeing"; for she reasoned, "Have I here really seen the back of him who sees me?"*

14 *That is why the well was called Beer-lahai-roi. It is between Kadesh and Bered.*

15 *Hagar bore Abram a son, and Abram named the son Hagar bore him Ishmael.*

16 *Abram was eighty-six years old when Hagar bore Ishmael for Abram.*

7 This narrative is similar in some details to the story of Elijah (1 K. 19). Both Hagar and Elisha flee in order to escape abuse or potential abuse. Left alone in the wilderness, each is accosted by *the angel of Yahweh.*[5] Both are instructed to return whence they came.

---

already pregnant, while in Judg. 13:5, 7 the woman (Samson's mother) is about to become pregnant. (One cannot decide, therefore, on grammatical grounds whether the virgin/young maiden of Isa. 7:14 [also a participial construction, *w^e yōleḏeṯ*] is pregnant or about to become so.)

2. *'onyēḵ,* the word we have translated "your humiliation," always refers to barrenness when used by or with reference to a woman (see Gen. 29:32; 1 Sam. 1:11). Westermann (*Genesis,* 2:234, 246) translates "your cry" (cf. JB "cries of distress").

3. I prefer to take *'āḏām* here to mean "steppe" and not "man." Instances of *'āḏām* meaning "steppe" are provided by M. J. Dahood, *Proverbs and Northwest Semitic Philology* (Rome: Pontifical Biblical Institute, 1963), pp. 57–58; idem, "Hebrew-Ugaritic Lexicography I," *Bib* 44 (1963) 292; idem, *Psalms,* 3:40; M. Pope, *Job,* AB, 3rd ed. (Garden City, NY: Doubleday, 1973), p. 86.

4. Lit., "and upon the face of" *(w^e'al-p^enê).* BDB, p. 818, discusses this idiom in 16:12 under II.7.a. (d), "of localities, 'in front of,' mostly (but not always) = 'east of.' . . . Gen. 16:12 . . . with collateral idea of defiance." Westermann, *Genesis, 12–26* translates "in confrontation with." B. Margalit (*The Ugaritic Poem of AQHT,* BZAW 182 [Berlin/New York: de Gruyter, 1989], p. 295) suggests emending *'eḥāyw* ("his kin") into *'āḥû* ("meadow")—". . . and upon the face of every meadow he doth camp." This suggestion would make more attractive the reading of *'āḏām* as "steppe land" in the first part of the verse.

5. For "the angel of Yahweh (the Lord)" cf. G. Vos, *Biblical Theology,* pp. 72–76; W. Eichrodt, *Theology of the Old Testament,* OTL, 2 vols., tr. J. A. Baker (Philadelphia: Westminister, 1961–1967), 2:23–29; R. Ficker, *"mal'āḵ," THAT*

It has sometimes been suggested, especially by earlier commentators (e.g., Gunkel),[6] that the sudden introduction of *the angel of Yahweh* (or "the angel of Elohim") into the biblical narrative serves as a mitigation of the direct (and primitive) theophany of the deity. This suggestion hardly seems valid, if for no other reason than that the introduction of the angel in the narratives is too spasmodic and leaves other bold anthropomorphisms untouched. It is better to say that the angel is the accompaniment of the deity's anthropomorphic appearance, rather than being a dilution of it.[7]

The phrase "angel of Yahweh" appears 58 times in the OT and "angel of God" 11 times. Most interesting are stories in Genesis, Exodus, Numbers, and Judges which both equate the angel with deity and dissociate it from deity. Thus, (1) in Gen. 16:7, 9 the angel of Yahweh speaks to Hagar, but in v. 11 this angel of the Lord says, "Yahweh has been attentive to your humiliation." Thereupon in v. 13 Hagar "gave a name to Yahweh who spoke to her." (2) In 21:17 God heard the voice of Ishmael, but it was the angel of God who called to Hagar from heaven. (3) In 22:11 the angel of Yahweh calls to Abraham from heaven to prevent him from killing Isaac, and then goes on to say, "now I know that you fear God . . . since you have not withheld your son from me" (v. 12). Later in the narrative the angel of the Lord says, "by myself I have sworn, says the Lord" (v. 15). (4) Jacob narrates a dream in which he says, "the angel of God said to me in a dream . . . I am the God of Bethel" (31:11, 13). (5) In Exod. 3:2 the angel of Yahweh appeared to Moses in or as a flame of fire, and subsequently "God called to him out of the bush" (v. 4). (6) In the Balaam story (Num. 22–24) it is the anger of God that flares (Num. 22:22), but the angel of Yahweh who stands in the way of the donkey. In vv. 28 and 31,

---

1:904–8; R. North, "Separated Spiritual Substances in the Old Testament," *CBQ* 29 (1967) 419–49, esp. pp. 432–49. The translation "*the* angel of Yahweh" is to be favored over "*an* angel of Yahweh," for a noun in construct with a proper name is thereby determined (see GKC, § 127a, although exceptions to this rule are frequent—§ 127e). Furthermore, the Hebrew language has a perfectly good way of expressing the second, as in "*a* psalm of David" *(mizmōr lᵉḏāwîḏ).* In *Mytharion: The Comparison of Tales from the Old Testament and the Ancient Near East,* AOAT 32 (Neukirchen-Vluyn: Neukirchener, 1978), D. Irvin compared the "messenger stories" of Gen. 16; 18–19; 21:8–21; 22; and 28:10–12 to other stories from the ancient Near East. Her study concludes that there is no concept of angels in the earlier period of the OT, even as early as the conventional dating of J and E!

6. See M.-J. Lagrange, "L'ange de Iahvé," *RB* 12 (1903) 217.

7. See J. Barr, "Theophany and anthropormorphism in the Old Testament," in *Congress Volume: Oxford, 1959,* VTSup 7 (Leiden: Brill, 1960), pp. 31–38. Barr reminds us (p. 34) that the OT does not say that God is invisible, but rather that it is fatal for a human being to see him.

Yahweh, and not the angel, opened the donkey's mouth and Balaam's eyes. (7) In the Gideon story one reads "and the angel of the Lord appeared to him" (Judg. 6:12), and a little later, "and Yahweh turned to him and said" (6:14). In v. 22 Gideon equates the two. (8) Ten times the angel of Yahweh appears in the Samson annunciation narrative (and the angel of God two times, 13:6, 9) to announce the birth of a son. Toward the end of the narrative Manoah exclaims, "we shall surely die, for we have seen God" (v. 22).

It is clear from the above that the angel of Yahweh is a visible manifestation (either in human form or in fiery form) of Yahweh that is essentially indistinguishable from Yahweh himself. The angel of Yahweh is more a representation of God than a representative of God. In the words of R. North, "*mal'āk* means representation, as a 'presence' or manner of rendering oneself present, rather than the specific form of this representative which is messenger."[8]

Hagar is confronted by Yahweh's angel at *a spring on the road to Shur.* Other biblical references (Gen. 20:1; 25:18; Exod. 15:22; 1 Sam. 15:7; 27:8) suggest that *Shur* is located at the southern boundary of Canaan (from the Canaanite viewpoint); and "the way to Shur" is the road entering the land from Kadesh-barnea (parallel to "the way of the land of the Philistines" for the northern route). Unless Abram and Sarai were residing far down in the Negeb, Hagar has traveled no small distance before she is stopped. Earlier Abram had fled Canaan to survive a famine. Now one of his employees flees Canaan to survive a miffed mistress.

Deity as the subject of *māṣā'* is infrequent in the OT. When God is the subject of *māṣā',* and the following object is impersonal, the reference is normally to God's discovery of evil or sin in somebody (Gen. 44:16; Ps. 10:15; 17:3; Jer. 2:34; 23:11). But when God is the subject of *māṣā',* and the following object is personal, *māṣā'* "carries a technical meaning going well beyond connotations of the English verb: it includes elements of encounter and of divine election."[9] See, for example, Deut. 32:10; Hos. 9:10 (and possibly 12:5 [Eng. 4]), all referring to the divine finding of Israel, and Ps. 89:21 (Eng. 20), the divine finding of David. And the nuance is to find by search, rather than find by stumbling upon one or something.[10]

8. R. North, *CBQ* 29 (1967) 448. Westermann (*Genesis,* 2:244) adds, "God is present not in the messenger, but in the message."

9. S. E. McEvenue, "A Comparison of Narrative Styles in the Hagar Stories," *Semeia* 3 (1975) 69. P. Trible (*Texts of Terror,* p. 14), on the contrary, does not see that nuance in *māṣā'* in 16:7. Rather, it holds "uncertain meaning." Will the finding counter or confirm Sarai's affliction of Hagar?

10. See BDB, p. 593.

8 In the light of the fact that v. 13 clearly connects the angel with Yahweh, it is interesting that the angel should solicit information about Hagar's origin and destiny.[11] The question parallels again the divine question to Elijah: "What are you doing here, Elijah?" (1 K. 19:9). Interestingly, Hagar answers only the angel's first question. She knows her recent history, but not her future. The fact that she does not respond to "and where are you going?" suggests that Hagar is wandering aimlessly in the wilderness, or trying to avoid telling the angel that Egypt, her home, is her destination.

This request for information is thrown into even bolder relief by the fact that before Hagar speaks, the angel knows her name, her position, and the identity of her mistress. The impression given by all this is that the whole episode is under Yahweh's control and vigilance.

9 The runaway Hagar may be compared with the runaway Christian slave Onesimus, whom Paul was prepared to send back to his owner Philemon (Phlm. 12). The angel's directive to Hagar is to return to Sarai and *accept ill-treatment at her hand.* This verb is the Hithpael of *ʿānâ (hiṯʿannî).* The Hithpael stem of *ʿānâ* appears only 6 times in the OT. The source of affliction may be either men (1 K. 2:26 [twice]) or God (Ps. 107:17). Two passages speak of "humbling oneself" before God (Ezra 8:21; Dan. 10:12). But the prepositional phrase following the verb in Ezra 8:21 and Dan. 10:12 is *lip̄nê ʾĕlōhênû/ʾĕlōheyḵā,* "before the face of our/your God." Hagar is told to place herself "under her hand" *(taḥaṯ yāḏeyhā). taḥaṯ yaḏ* almost always conveys the idea of authority or control (Gen. 41:35; Judg. 3:30; Ps. 106:42; Isa. 3:6). Earlier Abram had said to Sarai about Hagar, "your maidservant is in your hand" (v. 6). Now Hagar is to be under her hand.

In so directing her, possibly the angel is sending Hagar back to a certain death. In the words of P. Trible, it is a "divine word of terror to an abused, yet courageous, woman."[12] The angel does not attempt to anticipate, or delineate for Hagar, what Sarai's response will be other than what is generally conveyed by the verb the angel employs. Knowing now that the situation may be even more tense than before, Hagar offers no resistance or rebuttal. She is a lady of faith and obedience.

10 The divine command is followed by a divine promise. Hagar's descendants too will be innumerable. This promise is dramatic, for the angel announces to Hagar that she will have many offspring even before she has

11. For *ʾê-mizzeh* meaning "whence" cf. Judg. 13:6; 1 Sam. 25:11; 30:13; 2 Sam. 1:3, 13; Job 2:2. For questions addressed by a supernatural being to a mortal see Gen. 3:9, 11, 13; 4:9a, 10a; 18:9.

12. P. Trible, *Texts of Terror,* p. 16.

one child![13] There are many instances in the patriarchal stories where the man is promised a child(ren)/descendants (Abraham in Gen. 12:2; 13:13–16; 15:5; 17:8; 18:14; 22:17; Isaac in 26:4; Jacob in 28:3, 4), but Hagar is the only woman in Genesis who is honored with such a revelation. This sets her apart from the matriarchs of Israel. Ishmael will be but a beginning. This emphasis on looking beyond the imminent to the future is paralleled by Moses' instruction to the Israelites about Passover observance. Even before the people celebrated the first Passover Moses is talking to them about future Passovers (Exod. 12:24–27). The promise of God guarantees a future beyond the present.

11 For the third time in this section (also vv. 9, 10) a verse begins with the brief phrase: *The angel of Yahweh said to her.* Perhaps this repetition reinforces the fact that Hagar too is the recipient of a divine revelation. She is not hallucinating under the duress of a nightmare or the hot midday sun of the wilderness. The word of the Lord can come to Hagar in the wilderness as it did to Moses (Exod. 3:1), to Elijah (1 K. 19:4), and to John the Baptist (Luke 3:2). At no time does Hagar respond.

Hagar already knows she is pregnant. Her flaunting that pregnancy before barren Sarai is the cause of her downfall. The novel information given to her now is that she is carrying a male, and that this child is to be named *Ishmael.* That name is then defined: *Yahweh has been attentive to your humiliation.*

Scholars have long been puzzled by the fact that the theophoric part of Ishmael's name—*'ēl*—is replaced in the etymology of that name with Yahweh. Would not consistency demand that either the name be "Ishmaiah," or that the etymology read: "God (El) has been attentive to your humiliation"—even in the Yahwist's account?

Dahood has responded to this question by producing the following translation: "For Yahweh has heard you, El has answered you." But to arrive at this translation Dahood has to (1) read MT *kî šāmaʿ* as *kî yišmāʿ;* (2) read the preposition *'el* as the divine name *'ēl;* (3) emend MT *ʿonyēḵ,* "your humiliation," to *ʿanāyāḵā,* "he has answered you."[14] O. Loretz makes an equally strained attempt to explain Gen. 16:11. He does not resort, as does

13. The parallels in the biblical annunciations of birth—both Testaments—are conveniently charted in R. Brown, *The Birth of the Messiah* (Garden City, NY: Doubleday, 1977), p. 156; C. Westermann, *Genesis,* 2:245–46; E. W. Conrad, "The Annunciation of Birth and the Birth of the Messiah," *CBQ* 47 (1985) 656–63.

14. M. J. Dahood, "The Name *Yišmāʿ'ēl* in Genesis 16,11," *Bib* 49 (1968) 87–88; idem, "Nomen-Omen in Gen 16,11," *Bib* 61 (1980) 89.

Dahood, to Northwest Semitic philology, repointing, and redivision. Instead, he suggests that in the *Ur-form* of the text it was El who spoke to Hagar in the wilderness. A redactor subsequently inserted "the angel of Yahweh" to rid the story of unwholesome Canaanite ideas (the god El). After this change the etymology was provided as a kind of insignificant correction to the text.[15]

Both Dahood's appeal to Ugaritic philology and Loretz's attempt to unravel the story form critically seem unnecessary. The OT provides at least one good instance of an *X* plus El name being explained with a phrase using the tetragrammaton: 1 Sam. 1:20—"She called his name Samuel [*šᵉmû'ēl*], for she said, 'I have asked him of Yahweh.'"[16]

12 The announcement by the angel proceeds to delineate the destiny of Hagar's child. Ishmael is to be *a wild ass of the steppe land.* This designation is derogatory and derisive. Here we have the metaphorical use of animals, a frequent device in the OT. The *wild ass* is the onager, whose habitat is in waste places (Job 39:5–8; Isa. 32:14; Jer. 14:6; Hos. 8:9), suggesting a desert, nomadic life-style for Ishmael and his descendants.[17] Jer. 2:24 compares Israel's zealous pursuit after baals to a wild ass in heat. Once she has picked up the scent of the male's urine, she becomes frantic for the male; nothing stops her in her lustful pursuit of the male.[18]

Hagar is also told that her child will be involved with belligerent forces and neighbors. This is the thrust of the idiom *his hand against every man and every man's hand against him.*[19] Ishmael will both give and receive some crushing blows. For this reason the first part of the last line of the announcement—*wᵉʿal-pᵉnê*—should not be translated "before," or "east

15. O. Loretz, "Repointing und Redivision in Gen 16," *UF* 8 (1976) 452–53.

16. On the problems in ascertaining the meaning of the name "Samuel," both its original meaning (His-name-is-'El) and its interpretation in 1 Sam. 1 (He-who-is-from-God), see P. K. McCarter, Jr., *I Samuel,* AB (Garden City, NY: Doubleday, 1980), p. 62. I cite "Samuel" merely as an example of an *"-'ēl"* name which is connected in the narrative's explanation with the tetragrammaton.

17. "We should not take it for granted that in Israel the ass was proverbial for stupidity, as in our culture. . . . The general impression [conveyed by *pere'*] is that of a figure forlorn and friendless" (F. I. Andersen and D. N. Freedman, *Hosea,* AB [Garden City, NY: Doubleday, 1980], p. 505).

18. See W. Holladay, *Jeremiah: Spokesman out of Time* (Philadelphia: United Church, 1974), p. 41; idem, *Jeremiah,* Hermeneia (Philadelphia: Fortress, 1986), 1:100–101; G. R. Fontaine, *Traditional Sayings in the Old Testament* (Sheffield: Almond, 1982), pp. 238–39.

19. Cf. Ruth 1:13, "the hand of Yahweh has gone forth against me [Naomi]." Cf. also the use of "hand" in the sense of power in Gen. 16:6 (Hagar is in Sarai's "hand").

of," or "in the vicinity of,"[20] but as "in defiance of, against" (for parallels see Exod. 20:3 [perhaps!]; Deut. 21:16; Isa. 65:3).

Because Hagar's words in v. 13 address the fact that she has seen God, rather than the announcement she has just heard, some have moved to isolate vv. 11–12 from the original story and see the announcement as a secondary, literary tradition.[21] However, the presence of this part of the narrative is necessary to do justice to v. 9. The explicit revelation to Hagar that she is bearing a child with a manifest destiny means that even her return to Sarai (v. 9) cannot be for nought. Hagar need not fear that Sarai will abuse her to the extent that she might lose the child she is carrying.

13 Hagar revels not in the child she is about to deliver, but in the fact that she has been privy to a divine revelation. She is fascinated more by the origin of the revelation than by the content of the revelation. Her attitude here is remarkably different from that in the beginning of the chapter. No longer is she gloating over her procreating abilities or her role as progenitress. The text does not state that she "called upon the name [*qārāʾ bᵉšēm*] of Yahweh," an expression we saw in 4:26 and 12:8 (and 19 more times in the OT). Rather it states, *she called the name* [or named] *Yahweh who spoke with her (wattiqrāʾ šēm-yhwh haddōḇēr ʾēlêyhā).* Hagar actually confers on deity a name. No other character in the OT, male or female, does that. It is not unusual for mortals to give names to family members, to animals, to sacred sites, but never to one's God, with the exception of Hagar. Her name for God is "a God of seeing" *(ʾēl rᵒʾî).*" It is not certain whether *rᵒʾî* should be read as an objective genitve ("a God who may be seen") or a subjective genitive ("a God who sees"). While both the LXX *(ho theós ho epidṓn me)* and Vulg. *(tu deus qui vidisti me)* read the MT not as *rᵒʾî* but as *rōʾî* (Qal participle with suffix), which is the MT form in the latter half of the verse, there are no inherent problems with MT *rᵒʾî.*[22]

Have I really seen the back of him who sees me? The Heb. *hᵃḡam hᵃlōm rāʾîṯî ʾaḥᵃrê rōʾî* has long been a source of bewilderment to Hebraists. A literal

20. See J. F. Drinkard, Jr., "ʿAL PĚNÊ as 'East of,' " *JBL* 98 (1979) 285–86.

21. See R. Neff, "The Annunciation in the Birth Narrative of Ishmael," *BR* 17 (1972) 51–60; idem, "Saga," in *Saga, Legend, Tale, Novella, Fable,* ed. G. W. Coats, JSOTSup 35 (Sheffield: JSOT, 1985), p. 26.

22. SP reads *ʾel rāʾâ,* "a God who has seen." The effect created by reading *rōʾî* as a participle, most clearly supported by LXX, is that it throws the focus of v. 13 onto Yahweh's seeing Hagar, rather than onto Hagar's seeing Yahweh. See K. Koenen, "Wer sieht wen? Zur Textgeschichte von Genesis xvi 13," *VT* 38 (1988) 468–74. Koenen translates the verse (p. 472): "You are the God who has seen me. Truly here have I seen [in the sense of "met"] the one who sees/delivers me."

translation produces the following (senseless) words: "Have I also here (or hither) seen after the one who sees me?" Numerous suggestions have been offered in order to clarify the sentence. The RSV "Have I really seen God and remained alive after seeing him?" involves at least two major textual emendations: *h^{a}lōm,* "here," is read as *'ĕlōhîm,* "God"; and *wā'eḥî,* "and I have remained alive," is inserted before the preposition *'aḥ^{a}rê.* This suggestion was first made by Wellhausen in the late 1800s and is still widely accepted.[23] But the cavalier emending of and addition to the text without any supporting evidence from the ancient versions limits the value of this suggestion.

H. Seebass proposes a less drastic emendation. He reads *l^{e}ḥayyîm* for *h^{a}lōm* and then translates: "Was it not for life that I here saw him who has chosen me?"[24] But this suggestion also involves arbitrary emendation plus the attribution of the unusual meaning "choose" to *rā'â.*

One can make sense of the passage without resorting to textual emendation. For example, T. Booij takes the thrust of *rā'îṯî* to be "I have searched for," but sees it not as expressing a fact that has happened but a fact which could not happen. He translates, "Would I have gone here indeed searching for him that watches me?" or "Would I have gone here indeed looking for him that looks after me?"[25] It seems unlikely, however, that Hagar would have asked herself this question in this context.

If the Heb. *'aḥ^{a}rê* is taken as a noun meaning "back" (as in 2 Sam. 2:23, "the hinder end of his spear"),[26] then the sentence reads: "Have I really seen the back of him who sees me?"[27] This idea of seeing the back of someone parallels in Exodus Moses who saw God's back (*w^{e}rā'îṯā 'eṯ-'^{a}ḥōrāy,* Exod. 33:23).[28]

23. J. Wellhausen, *Prolegomena to the History of Ancient Israel,* tr. Black and Menzies (Edinburgh: A. and C. Black, 1905), p. 323 n. 1. Wellhausen's translation was: "Have I seen God, and am I kept in life after my seeing?" See also *BHS,* NEB, NAB, and KB^3, p. 1080. Cf. also M. Tsevat, "Hagar and the Birth of Ishmael," in *The Meaning of the Book of Job and Other Biblical Studies* (New York: Ktav, 1980), p. 63 n. 21; C. Westermann, *Genesis,* 2:247–48.

24. H. Seebass, "Zum Text von Gen. xvi 13b," *VT* 21 (1971) 254–56.

25. T. Booij, "Hagar's words in Genesis xvi 13b," *VT* 30 (1980) 1–7.

26. See BDB, p. 30.

27. See J. Lindblom, "Theophanies in Holy Places in Hebrew Religion," *HUCA* 32 (1961) 102 n. 21; H. C. White, "The Initiation Legend of Ishmael," *ZAW* 87 (1975) 285 n. 60. White does not actually translate *'aḥ^{a}rê* by "back," as does Lindblom, but by "the effects of an appearance of God," and then adds, "*'aḥărê* in Gen 16:13 refers to the effects of God's presence, or what God leaves behind him after he has departed."

28. It is not necessary to suggest that the text originally read "Have I really seen the face of him who sees me?" as argued by A. Schoors, "A *tiqqun sopherim* in

If one is not content to assign substantive value to *'aḥ*^{a}*rê* (admittedly very infrequent), and insists it can only be a preposition, then we also may recall that this preposition, indeed normally translated "after," may also mean "with, beside, next to, upon." Thus *rā'â 'aḥ*^{a}*rê* may mean "to look upon": "Have I really looked upon the one who sees me?"[29]

14 Yahweh was the first one in this chapter to confer a special name on someone (v. 11), and then he himself provided the explanation of that name. Here it is Hagar who confers the special name: *Beer-lahai-roi,* which means "the well belonging to the Living One who has seen me."[30]

Note the difference between Hagar's exclamation in v. 13 that she has seen (something of) God, and the name given to commemorate the place where this theophany happened. This name focuses on the fact that God showed himself to her. She does not call it "the well belonging to the Living One whom I have seen." Hagar is the object, not the subject. In effect, then, *Beer-lahai-roi* focuses on the graciousness of the God who manifested himself to a pregnant woman in the wilderness, rather than on any special status accorded to Hagar.

The well is located somewhere *between Kadesh and Bered.* Kadesh (or Kadesh-barnea) is located in northeast Sinai on the southern border of the Wilderness of Zin. This is the only reference to Bered in the OT.

15–16 In these verses Hagar's name appears three times and Abram's name four times. But Sarai is conspicuously absent! Although Hagar

---

Genesis xvi 13b?" *VT* 32 (1982) 494–95. But is there any pun intended by the fact that Ishmael is to dwell "in defiance of" (*'al-p*^{e}*nê,* lit., "upon [or against] the face of") his kin, while his mother sees the back *('aḥ*^{a}*rê)* of God?

29. See R. B. Y. Scott, "Secondary Meanings of *'aḥar,* After, Behind," *JTS* 50 (1949) 178–79; F. I. Andersen and D. N. Freedman, *Hosea,* AB (Garden City, NY: Doubleday, 1980), p. 407.

30. S. Gevirtz notes that *ḥay* may also denote "clan, family, kindred group"; thus he takes the name to mean "the well belonging to the clan of R," and then connects *rō'î* with the personal name Haro'eh in 1 Chr. 2:52 (S. Gevirtz, "Of Patriarchs and Puns," *HUCA* 46 [1975] 42 n. 34). According to B. O. Long, *The Problem of Etiological Narrative in the Old Testament,* BZAW 108 (Berlin: Töpelmann, 1968), pp. 5–9, the etymology in v. 11 conforms to what he calls Form I: a main clause, usually with some form of *qārā',* followed by a *kî* clause which contains the etymological explanation and a key word which is assonant with the name given. By contrast, v. 14 provides an illustration of Form II: "therefore one calls its name so and so." This form is (1) always introduced by *'al-kēn;* (2) the act of naming is not narrated. Rather, there is a logical inference from speech, reported event, or descriptive report. (3) The subject of the verb *qārā'* is always indefinite and best translated by an English passive; and (4) this form is used almost exclusively for place name etymologies.

had earlier been told that she was to name the child, it is actually Abram who names the boy *Ishmael.* That Ishmael was born in Abram's house and named by Abram himself indicates that he is to be fully reckoned as Abram's son.

The OT has instances of the mother naming the child (Gen. 4:1, 25; 29:32, 33, 34, 35; 30:18, 20, 24; Judg. 13:24; 1 Sam. 1:20; Isa. 7:14), of the father naming the child (Gen. 16:15; 17:19; 21:3; Exod. 2:22; 2 Sam. 12:24; Isa. 8:3), of both parents naming the child (Gen. 4:25; 5:3), of each parent giving a different name to the child (Gen. 35:18). It is Leah who names the children borne to Jacob by her maidservant Zilpah (30:11, 13), and it is Rachel who names the children borne to Jacob by her maidservant Bilhah (30:6–7). But Sarai does not name the child Hagar bears to Abram. The implication of this is that Sarai's original intention ("perhaps by her I shall reproduce") will not be realized. Hagar is denied the privilege of naming the son she has carried to birth, and Sarai is denied the son she apparently cannot herself conceive. Clearly Hagar bore Abram (not Abram and Sarai) a son (v. 15a). Abram named the son Hagar bore for him (not them) Ishmael (v. 15b). Hagar bore Ishmael for Abram (not for the childless couple) (v. 16).

THE NEW TESTAMENT APPROPRIATION

Paul's treatment of Hagar, Ishmael, Sarah, and Isaac in Gal. 4 will be discussed following the commentary on Gen. 21.

F. THE REAFFIRMATION OF THE COVENANT (17:1–27)

1. A NAME CHANGE FOR ABRAM (17:1–8)

1 *When Abram was ninety-nine years of age Yahweh appeared to Abram and said to him: "I am El Shaddai; walk in front of me and be blameless;*

2 *so that I may establish*[1] *my covenant between me and you, and will make you exceedingly numerous."*

3 *Abram fell on his face as God spoke with him:*

4 *"For my part, my covenant with you is: you are to become the father of a host of nations.*

1. Lit., "give [*nāṯan*] a covenant"; see Gen. 9:12 and Num. 25:12 for the same combination. The expression is not unique to biblical tradition, for one finds Akk. *riksā nadānu* and Gk. *hórkon didonai.* See M. Weinfeld, *"b*ᵉ*rîth," TDOT,* 2:260.

5 *No longer will you be named Abram; but your name will be Abraham, for a father of a host of nations I am making you.*
6 *I will cause you to be exceedingly fertile, and I will make of you nations; kings will issue from you.*
7 *I will maintain my covenant between me and you, and your descendants to follow, throughout the ages, as an eternal covenant to be God to you and to your descendants to follow.*
8 *I will give to you and to your descendants to follow the land of your sojourning, the entire land of Canaan, as a permanent possession. I shall be for them God."*

The critics unanimously accept Gen. 17 as P's account of the covenant with Abraham, a later version to be placed besides J's earlier account (ch. 15). For, so goes the argument, here one finds "God" rather than "Yahweh"; here one finds the issue of circumcision, surely a priestly concern; and here one finds verbal parallels with other priestly material such as the P version of the Flood story.

The traditional view argues that ch. 17 represents a reconfirmation of God's covenant promises and oath to Abraham. Since at least eleven years had elapsed from the first announcement of a covenant, since Sarai was still sterile, and since the patriarch's household was rife with rancor and deep strife, one might wonder if the covenant promises still hold true. Or have these promises been amended to adopt to novel conditions?

From the perspective of overall structure, the chapter is concerned with speech (vv. 1–21) and action (vv. 22–27).[2] There are no less than five speeches of God to Abraham: I, vv. 1–2; II, vv. 3–8; III, vv. 9–14; IV, vv. 15–16; V, vv. 19–21. Abraham speaks only twice, once to himself (v. 17), and once briefly to God (v. 18). In three of these speeches (nos. II, IV, V), the focus is on God's commitment to bless. In the remaining two (nos. I, III), the focus is on God's expectations of Abraham. The major speech by God to Abraham about Abraham's need to take appropriate action (vv. 9–14) is ringed by speeches of God's promises to Abraham (vv. 3–8 and 15–21), showing that the demands of God must be interpreted within the context of the promises of God.

2. Through the application of stylistic criticism S. McEvenue has argued lucidly for the unity of this chapter (*The Narrative Style of the Priestly Writer,* AnBib 50 [Rome: Biblical Institute, 1971], pp. 145–78). In this conclusion he is followed by J. Van Seters, *Abraham in History and Tradition,* pp. 279–93. From a different approach (using the model of the covenant treaty) S. R. Kulling reaches the same conclusion (*Zur Datierung der "Genesis-P-Stücke" namentlich des Kapitels Genesis XVII* [Kampen: Kok, 1964]).

1 Thirteen silent years pass between two verses of Scripture: 16:16 (Abram, 86 years old) and 17:1 (Abram, 99 years old). The narrative in ch. 16 stopped with the birth of Ishmael. Those tense years of Hagar and Ishmael under the same roof as Sarai have been omitted.

The verse indicates that Yahweh *appeared* to Abram *(wayyērā',* the Niphal of *rā'â*). The same stem of this verb was used back in 12:7 to describe Yahweh's revelation to Abram. For subsequent texts in Genesis that also use the passive/reflexive of *rā'â* and refer to God as the agent of revelation, see 18:1; 26:2, 24 (Isaac); 35:9 (Jacob). *rā'â* is one of three prominent verbs used throughout the OT to describe a person's encounter with God in revelatory situations, the other two being *gālâ* (mostly in the Niphal with God as subject) and *yāḏaʿ* (again, mostly in the Niphal). In Exod. 6:3 God says to Moses, "I appeared [*wā'ērā'*, Niphal of *rā'â*] to Abraham . . . as God Almighty, but by my name Yahweh I did not make myself known to them [*nôḏaʿtî,* Niphal of *yāḏaʿ*]." Thus Abraham's encounter with God is covered by the verb *rā'â,* while Moses' encounter with God in this particular revelation of Yahweh's name is covered by *yāḏaʿ*.

Some scholars have made too much of the distinctions in these verses. Thus, Rendtorff says, "There can be no doubt that, bearing in mind the very precise language patterns of the Priestly Document, this [viz., *râ'â,* then *yāḏaʿ*] was done quite deliberately. The visible appearance of Yahweh is assigned to a provisional stage; with Moses a new phenomenon emerges: Yahweh allows himself to be perceived as he himself is."[3] For Rendtorff, then, there is in the OT a development of the conception of revelation from a primitive to a more sophisticated level of understanding, the patriarchal version as reflected in Gen. 17:1 being the most primitive, that is, deity shows himself to a mortal.

Two options present themselves as to why the author of Exod. 3:6 used *rā'â,* then *yāḏaʿ*. One, the author is carefully, systematically choosing his verbs to delineate a progression in how deity revealed himself to mortals, from the crude to the more refined. A second option, and the one I find attractive, is that the use of *rā'â* and *yāḏaʿ* is to be "attributed to a customary stylistic idiom rather than to a calculated word choice by the author of the Priestly Document which was triggered by theological considerations. . . . If the term *nodaʿ* is 'apposed' to *nir'ah* and not 'opposed' to it, . . . then perhaps the divine name should not be regarded as a substitute . . . but rather as an additional designation of God which comes to be considered as the divine

3. R. Rendtorff, "Die Offenbarungsvorstellungen im Alten Israel," in *Offenbarung als Geschichte,* ed. W. Pannenberg, R. Rendtorff, and U. Wilckens (Göttingen: Vandenhoeck & Ruprecht, 1963), p. 25.

name *par excellence* after the revelation at the burning bush."[4] Such an interpretation has the advantage of seeing the overlap in meaning and use of *rā'â* and *yāḏa'*, rather than forcing upon them differences they do not have.

This is not the first time Abraham has received a divine imperative. Compare earlier "leave" (12:1); "lift up your eyes" (13:14); "fear not" (15:1); "look heavenward" (15:5); "bring me" (15:9). This particular one, however—*walk in front of me and be blameless*—has more of an ethical charge behind it. Although the emphasis is on the unilaterality of God's covenant with Abraham, any covenant relationship, if it is to be healthy, needs accountability by both partners.

The expression *walk in front of* (and its parallel "stand in front of") is well chosen. This phrase usually expresses the service or devotion of a faithful servant to his king, be the latter human (1 K. 1:2; 10:8; Jer. 52:12) or divine (prediluvians: Gen. 5:22, 24; 6:9; the patriarchs: here; 24:40; 48:15; priests and Levites: Deut. 10:8; 18:7; Judg. 20:28; Ezek. 44:15).[5] The related expression, "to walk after," normally connotes the passive allegiance of the vassal or the vassal's repudiation of his vows through "going after" other gods (Deut. 11:28; 28:14; Judg. 2:19; 1 K. 11:10; 21:26; Jer. 7:9, though all with Qal, not Hithpael).

blameless was first applied to Noah (6:9). The difference between 6:9 and 17:1 is that for Noah blamelessness is an accomplished fact (as in 2 Sam. 22:24 par. Ps. 18:24 [Eng. 23]), while for Abraham it is a goal. The LXX translates Noah's *tāmîm* with *téleios* ("complete, perfect") but Abram's *tāmîm* with *ámemptos* ("blameless, faultless"), a word used in the NT to describe the parents of John the Baptist (Luke 6:1), Paul before he became a Christian (Phil. 3:6), and Paul's prayer for the establishment of the Thessalonian believers' hearts "unblamable" in holiness (1 Thess. 3:13). This Hebrew word—*tāmîm*—is used frequently in the sections of the OT dealing with ritual procedure. It is imperative that the animal brought for sacrifice be one that is "unblemished" (Exod. 12:5; Lev. 3:1, 6; 4:3, 23; etc.). Thus *tāmîm* may describe either a life-style or a physical condition. The use of the phrase *beṯāmîm ûḇe'ĕmeṯ* (lit., "in completeness and in truth," possibly a hendiadys for "in complete honesty") in a covenant context in Josh. 24:14, and only again in Judg. 9:16, 19, suggests that *tāmîm* may also carry the idea of transparent or candid.[6]

4. S. Talmon, "Revelation in Biblical Times," *HS* 26 (1985) 59.

5. For related terms in cuneiform documents cf. M. Weinfeld, "The Counsel of the 'Elders' to Rehoboam and Its Implications," *MAARAV* 3 (1982) 42 n. 76.

6. Dahood (*Psalms,* 1:102) translates Ps. 18:24 (Eng. 23) as "I have always

The one who gives this directive to Abram is *El Shaddai.* This divine name appears forty-eight times in the OT, most often in Job (31 times, but without the accompanying "El"). On the basis of the LXX translation of this term in Job (always *pantokrátōr*) and the most frequent Vulg. translation *(omnipotens),* many modern versions render *El Shaddai* as "God Almighty." There have been several attempts to ascertain the etymology of *Shaddai.* An ancient suggestion sees in *šadday* the relative particle *šᵉ* and the adjective *day,* "sufficient," thus, "he who is sufficient." This is reflected in Aquila and Symm. *(hikanós).*

A second suggestion links Shaddai with the verb *šāḏaḏ,* "to destroy, overpower"; thus "he who destroys, overpowers." This etymology is surely the source of LXX *pantokrátōr.* It is also suggested by the wordplay in Isa. 13:6, "the day of the Lord is near; as destruction from Shaddai [*šōḏ miššad-day*] it will come."

Some proposals have geographical features. One connects *šadday* with *śāḏeh,* "El of the plain (or the fields, the steppe)."[7] Another connects it with a Semitic root *ṯdw/y,* whose original meaning was "breast" but which later evolved into "mountain."[8] Thus El Shaddai is "El of the mountain" or "the mountain one." A third, more recent attempt links El Shaddai with *bêl sadê,* the most common title given to the god Amurru in early Babylonian texts.[9] For *bêl sadê* the most accurate meaning is "Lord of the steppe," and

---

been candid [*tāmîm*] with him" (RSV "blameless before him") and Ps. 18:26 (Eng. 25) as "with the candid [*tāmîm*] you are candid [*tāmam*]" (RSV "with the blameless man thou dost show thyself blameless").

7. See M. Weippert, "Erwägungen zur Etymologie des Gottesnames 'El Šaddaj," *ZDMG* 111 (1961) 42–62; but to do so, Weippert has to label *šadday* as a loanword equivalent to *śāḏeh,* and bypass the phonetic difference in the initial consonant—*š* rather than *ś*.

8. See W. F. Albright, "The Names Shaddai and Abram," *JBL* 54 (1935) 180–87; F. M. Cross, "Yahweh and the God of the Patriarchs," *HTR* 55 (1962) 244ff.; idem, *Canaanite Myth and Hebrew Epic,* pp. 52–60. On the concept of a mountain as the meeting place of the gods, and hence a place of veneration, see R. J. Clifford, *The Cosmic Mountain in Canaan and the Old Testament* (Cambridge, MA: Harvard University, 1972), although Clifford does not discuss the name El Shaddai. N. Walker's attempt to link "Shaddai" with a Sumerian word for "omniscient" is not persuasive ("A New Interpretation of the Divine Name 'Shaddai'," *ZAW* 72 [1960] 64–66). Nor is the suggestion of E. C. B. MacLaurin, "Shaddai," *Abr-Nahrain* 3 (1961–62) 99–118, to link Shaddai with a root *dd,* "he who gives power."

9. See L. R. Bailey, "Israelite 'El Sadday and Amorite Bel Sadê," *JBL* 87 (1968) 434–38; J. Ouellette, "More on 'El Sadday and Bel Sadê," *JBL* 88 (1969) 470–71.

if the connection with Heb. *šadday* is sustained, then El Shaddai is "El of the steppe."[10]

The same name occurs in other patriarchal stories, always in connection with Jacob. Either he himself uses it (43:14; 48:3; 49:25), or he is addressed by El Shaddai (35:11) or by one who invokes the name El Shaddai on him (28:3). In five of the six places in Genesis where El Shaddai is used, the name is followed by the promise of posterity. The one exception is 43:14. And three times (28:3; 48:3; 49:25) the activity of El Shaddai is described with the verb *bāraḵ,* "bless."

2 The structure in 17:1–2 is the same as 12:1–2, imperative(s) followed by imperfects (with *waw* consecutive), and the imperfects express intention.[11] God's intention to bless Abraham and make him into a great nation is predicated upon his obedience to the divine word to leave Ur. Similarly, God's command for Abram to walk blamelessly is but a means to an end. If Abram so conducts himself, God will multiply him abundantly. With this kind of person God will *establish* his covenant. This verse introduces one of the key words in the chapter—"covenant." Whereas it occurred but once in ch. 15 (v. 18), in ch. 17 it occurs thirteen times (vv. 2, 4, 7 [twice], 9, 10, 11, 13 [twice], 14, 19 [twice], 21). The first four and the last three of these thirteen appear in God's promissory speeches to Abram. The middle six (vv. 9, 10, 11, 13 [twice], 14) occur in God's speech about circumcision.

3 It is not the theophany per se that brings Abraham to a position of prostration. If it were, v. 3 would have to follow immediately after v. 1a. It is a combination of the theophany and the divine word of directive and promise that follows that produces awe in Abraham. Both the visual and the audible affect him.

Abraham's reaction here contrasts with his earlier reaction when he received covenantal promises. There his response was a complaint (15:2–3). Here it is obeisance. Abram is mellowing; he is maturing. There is also a change in the sequence concerning the promise of children to Abraham in chs. 15 and 17. In the earlier chapter the promise of a specific son (15:4) precedes the promise of numerous progeny (15:5). Here the promise of numerous progeny (17:2, 4) precedes the promise of a specific son (17:16).

4–5 To signify this promise of many descendants, Abram's name is changed to *Abraham,* which is connected with *father of a host of nations* in both v. 4 and v. 5. This is not the first place in Genesis where a name's

10. See R. de Vaux, *Early History of Israel,* p. 277 and n. 54.
11. See McEvenue, *Narrative Style of the Priestly Writer,* p. 162.

significance is explained. But it is the first time that an individual's name is changed.

The meaning of *Abram* is either "he is exalted (as to his) father," that is, noble by birth, if one takes the *'aḇ* element as an adverbial accusative, or else "the father is exalted." But *Abraham* does not literally mean "father of nations" (which would be *'aḇ hamôn,* "Abhamon"). To be sure, *'aḇrāhām* is similar phonemically to *'aḇ hamôn,* witnessed to by the repetition of *'aḇ* and *ham* in both the name and the explanation.[12] Other Semitic languages provide instances in which *-h-* is inserted either in a weak root or in a long syllable. Ugaritic is particularly rich with plurals formed by the insertion of an *h: bt, bht,* "house(s)"; *'mt, 'mht,* "maidservant(s)"; *'m, 'mht,* "mother(s)."[13]

The shift in Abraham's name is indicated even further by the chiastic structure in vv. 4b–5: *wehāyîṯā le'aḇ hamôn gōyim* balances with *'aḇ-hamôn gōyim neṯattîḵā.* For the second time in this chapter we encounter the verb *nāṯan,* "to give." God *establishes* (or gives) a covenant (v. 2) and he names Abram anew (v. 5). He is the giver. The verb appears twice more in this section: v. 6, "make of you nations" (or "establish you as nations"), and v. 8, "give to you . . . the land of Canaan."

One significance of the patriarch's new name is that it universalizes Abraham's experience with God. This point contrasts with the later emphasis in the chapter on circumcision, which particularizes Abraham's relationship with God. His circumcision identifies him as the father of Israelites. His new name identifies him as the father of the faithful, regardless of what particular ethnic group they represent. He is to be the father of many *gōyim,* not many *yehûḏîm.*[14]

6 The added note that Abraham will *be fertile (pārâ)* recalls the earlier use of this verb with the fish and fowl at creation (1:22), with Adam and Eve (1:28), and with Noah (9:1, 7); and the later use of the verb with Ishmael (17:20) and with Jacob (28:3; 35:11; 48:4). 47:27 records the actualization of that promise to Abraham and Jacob. Of course, Abraham has not been exceedingly fertile up to this point. The *'aḇ* (father) part of his destiny is not yet fulfilled, except for Ishmael.

Three times the pronominal suffix *-kā* ("you") is used in this verse—

12. See A. Strus, *Nomen-Omen: La stylistique sonore des noms propres dans le Pentateuque,* AnBib 80 (Rome: Biblical Institute, 1978), p. 83.

13. An example from Phoenician is *dlt, dlht,* "door(s)."

14. We have already discussed the significance of *gôy* in our commentary on 12:2, where we saw that *gôy* designated a people who are politically organized, as opposed to *'am,* which refers to a people extending from a family.

once in each of the three clauses—pointing all the more to Abraham—"I will cause you . . . make of you nations . . . from you." He is indeed the one God has chosen.

Abraham is further informed that part of his issue will be *kings*—not just *gôyim,* but *melāḵîm.* For similar promises of royal prosperity cf. v. 16; 35:11. He who earlier had not hesitated to challenge the powerful *melāḵîm* of the east (ch. 14) is now himself to become the founder of the royal line.[15]

7 The Hebrew for *maintain* is the Hiphil stem of the verb *qûm,* "to raise, erect, establish."[16] The Hiphil of this verb allows a range of meanings from "establish" to "fulfill." This covenant with Abraham is something God initiates, something he maintains, and something he brings to fulfillment.

No less than three times in this chapter (vv. 7, 13, 19) we are told that God's covenant with Abraham was an *eternal* one, and one time (v. 8) that Canaan was to be the *permanent possession* of Abraham's descendants. W. Kaiser well points out that "the word *ʿôlām* must add something more to the noun it went with, for in the case of covenant there was already a strong idea of perpetuity."[17]

It may be no accident that the word *eternal* is present in ch. 17 but absent in ch. 15. Is it not interesting that in the chapter where at least four covenant stipulations are placed before Abraham—walk before me; be blameless; keep my covenant; circumcise yourselves—the covenant should be thrice described as an *eternal* one? This repetition of *eternal* emphasizes that God's covenant with Abraham has not suddenly shifted away from the unilateral emphasis of ch. 15 to a bilateral pact here in ch. 17. To be sure,

15. Matt. 1 traces the genealogy of Jesus, King of the Jews, back through David to Abraham, the first Hebrew and the founder of the royal line. I note that in Gen. 23:6 the LXX calls Abraham a *basileús,* a king. It is to be expected that a king will produce a dynasty of kings. Matthew may be suggesting that Joseph, the "father" of Jesus, descended not only from David the *basileús,* but also from Abraham, who was not only the first ancestor of the Jews, but also their first *basileús.* See the letter of C. H. Gordon in *BAR* 4/3 (1978) 47.

16. For *hēqîm berîṯ* cf. Gen. 6:18; 9:9, 11; 17:7, 10, 19; Exod. 6:4; Lev. 26:9; Deut. 8:18; 2 K. 23:3 (with the king as subject); Jer. 34:18 (with covenant transgressors as subject).

17. W. C. Kaiser, Jr., *Toward an Old Testament Theology,* p. 90. It is significant that the word *berîṯ* never appears in the OT in plural form. Because the covenant with Israel is eternal it cannot be replaced without compromising the integrity of God's promises. The one exception to this is the "new covenant" spoken of by Jeremiah in 31:31–34, the only time the phrase "new covenant" appears in the OT. And even in the Jeremiah prophecy, the similarities to the old covenant are greater than the differences between the two.

God has expectations concerning Abraham's behavior, but these do not become grounds for the establishment and authentication of God's covenant with Abraham. Rather, the covenant remains a personal commitment by God in which he binds himself to this open-ended promise to Abraham.[18]

8 This is not the first time that Abraham has been promised a specific piece of land; see 12:7 ("to your descendants") and 15:18 ("to your descendants"). What is unique here is the placement of this promise in relationship to the ones just uttered.[19] The covenant promises in this chapter are basically found within vv. 4–6. V. 7 is a commitment by God to the implementation of these promises, a kind of summarization in the form of an oath. Then comes the promise of land (v. 8). Perhaps the isolation of this promise is to suggest that the promise of territory is made to future generations rather than to Abraham. Note that the end of this particular promise, *I shall be for them God,* focuses on Abraham's progeny, not on himself.

One scholar at least has suggested that Abraham was a merchant prince, a *tamkaru,* rather than a wandering, bedouin-like nomad.[20] Abraham's wandering was not nomadism in the traditional sense, but rather was an occupational feature befitting such a merchant. Our knowledge of these ancient merchants is helped by a text from Ugarit written by Hattusili III (ca. 1280–1252 B.C.), king of the Hittites, to Niqmepa, king of Ugarit. Niqmepa has written to Hattusili III complaining about the illegal activities of merchants from Ura in his area. The tablet records Hattusili's response, which is to impose several restrictions on the activities of these roving merchants. For example,

18. Source critics observe that *ʿôlām* is a favorite word of the Priestly tradition whenever covenant is under discussion. This emphasis of P is then interpreted as a challenge by the Priestly tradent against the Deuteronomist, who opts for the possibility of the breaking of the covenant made at Sinai. M. Weinfeld ("The Covenant of Grant in the Old Testament and in the Ancient Near East," *JAOS* 90 [1970] 199) notes that the formulations of conveyance in perpetuity in Gen. 17 are identical with the legal formulae of conveyance of property in the ancient Near East. As one example, Weinfeld quotes an Akkadian text from Ugarit (see *PRU,* 3:160, 16.132:27–38): *u ittadinšu ana* ^{m}*Adalšeni [u] ana mārēšu adi dārīti,* "and gives it to Adalsheni and his sons forever." Weinfeld also cites similar formulae in texts from Susa, Alalakh, and Elephantine (see nn. 146, 147, 149), as well as Assyrian and Babylonian texts (see nn. 150–52).

19. The reference to Canaan as a "permanent possession" for Abraham and his offspring occurs again only in 48:4b, though 13:15 is quite similar: "this land for ever."

20. See C. H. Gordon, "Abraham and the Merchants of Ura," *JNES* 17 (1958) 28–31; idem, "Abraham of Ur," in *Hebrew and Semitic Studies Presented to Godfrey Rolles Driver,* ed. D. W. Thomas and W. D. McHardy (Oxford: Clarendon, 1963), pp. 77–84.

the merchants could work at Ugarit only during the summer (lit., "the harvest"). When winter came they had to leave and return to their own country.

The second restriction is the one that interests us here. These merchants were not allowed to purchase Ugaritic real estate.[21] Now if the case for Abraham's mercantilism can be sustained—and the position is not without its detractors[22]—these promises of the land of Canaan to Abraham (and his descendants), who comes to Canaan as an outsider, take on added significance.[23] By law, Abraham was not to assume proprietary rights over foreign real estate, and any land he did acquire (see Gen. 23) had to be expedited through legal process.

Of course, Abraham is never informed that he will receive the land from the Canaanites. It is not their land to transmit. The donor of the land is none other than Yahweh.

2. THE SIGN OF THE COVENANT (17:9–14)

9 *Further, God said to Abraham: "For your part, my covenant you must keep, you, and your descendants after you throughout the ages.*

10 *This is my covenant between myself and you, and your descendants after you, which you must keep:*[1] *every male shall be circumcised by you.*[2]

11 *You shall circumcise*[3] *the flesh of your foreskin, and that shall be the mark of the covenant between me and you.*

21. *ù bîtâti*ḫá *eqlâti*meš *i-na kaspi*meš*-šu-nu la-a i-ṣa-ba-[t]u4,* "nor shall they get real estate with their silver."

22. E.g., R. de Vaux, *Early History of Israel,* tr. David Smith (Philadelphia: Westminster, 1978), pp. 228–29; K. A. Kitchen, *Ancient Orient and Old Testament* (Chicago: Inter-Varsity, 1966), p. 49 n. 71.

23. This point applies especially to those places where Abraham alone is designated as the one to receive the land, or the one who already received the land (28:4), in distinction from those other references, such as Gen. 17:8, where Abram's descendants are pinpointed as the recipients of land.

1. The verbal form of "keep" is here 2nd pl. *(tišm*e*rû),* unlike the "keep" of the preceding verse, which is 2nd sing. *(tišmōr).* LXX *diatērḗseis,* however, reflects the latter. See E. Tov, *Text-Critical Use of the Septuagint,* p. 221.

2. We take *lāḵem* not to mean "among you" but "by you," understanding the *l* as the *lamedh* of agency. See R. Althann, "*mwl,* 'circumcise' with the *lamedh* of Agency," *Bib* 28 (1981) 239–40. Cf. also v. 12.

3. The form *n*e*maltem,* if a Niphal of *mûl,* "circumcise," is strange. We would expect *n*e*mōlôṯem,* or *n*e*mulōṯem.* As it stands it looks like an abbreviated Niphal of *mālal* IV, "circumcise," a rare by-form of *mûl (n*e*mallōṯem).* See BDB, p. 557b; GKC, § 67dd; Skinner, *Genesis,* p. 294. M. Greenberg (*Ezekiel,* p. 249) compares this form

12 *Let each male when he is eight days old be circumcised by you, throughout the ages, even a houseborn slave or one bought with money from any foreigner who is not of your seed.*
13 *Indeed, the houseborn slave*[4] *and the one bought for money must be circumcised, so that my covenant might be in your flesh*[5] *as an eternal covenant.*
14 *An uncircumcised male, the flesh of whose foreskin has not been circumcised, let that one be cut off from his kinsmen; my covenant he has nullified."*

We have noted above the shift in this section from second singular to second plural and back: v. 9—singular; vv. 10–12—plural (except for "your descendants [seed] after you" in v. 10 and "your seed" in v. 12b); v. 13a—singular; v. 13b—plural. Most of this section is cast in the plural, and the reason for this should be plain. The prescriptions covered in these verses are to become legally incumbent upon all generations. God is speaking to those who are not yet born. It is going much too far to claim that these verses are in disarray, and that an earlier stratum (vv. 9–12a) of a more general nature has been swelled by a subsequent stratum of more explicit directives (vv. 12b–13a).[6]

9 *For your part.* The emphatic pronoun *'attâ* puts the spotlight on Abraham.[7] After a series of "I will's" by God, Abraham becomes the subject of a verb, instead of an object. However subsidiary one makes the human commitment to the divine obligation, it still remains a vital part of this covenant relationship.[8] But Abraham is not yet told explicitly all that his part involves. Thus v. 9 is a general commandment which is specified in v. 10.

---

with *yinnāzēr* in Ezek. 14:7, "he falls away." He notes that "*nzr* is backformed from *nazoru,* as though its *n* were radical (cf. *nmltm* Gen. 17:11 backformed from *nmwl* 'be circumcised' from *mwl*), and is inflected (like it) in nif'al!"

4. On the basis of SP, and against MT and LXX, N. Lohfink ("Textkritisches zu Gn 17,5.13.16.17," *Bib* 48 [1967] 439–42) emends sing. *yelîḏ* to pl. *yelîḏê.* This shift then gives the symmetrical structure of *yelîḏ* (sing., v. 12), *yelîḏê* (pl., v. 13), *yelîḏê* (pl., v. 23), *yelîḏ* (sing., v. 27).

5. Here and elsewhere *bāśār,* "flesh," may be a euphemism for penis. See also Lev. 15:2, 3, 7; Ezek. 16:26; 23:20; and N. P. Bratsiotis, *"bāśār," TDOT,* 2:319.

6. As is claimed, e.g., by P. Weimar, "Gen 17 und die priesterschriftliche Abrahamgeschichte," *ZAW* 100 (1988) 22–60, esp. pp. 28–31.

7. Here emphatic *'attâ,* "as for you," needs to be seen in the light of emphatic *'anî,* "as for me," in v. 4.

8. For instances of *šāmar* (with a human subject) followed by *berîṯ,* cf. Exod. 19:5; Ps. 78:10; 103:18.

10 Specifically, Abraham and all his male descendants are to be circumcised. Not only is the covenant with Abraham an eternal one, but the law concerning circumcision is an eternal law. Neither of them is confined to Abraham's time.

It is appropriate then that an eternal law is accompanied by a sign that is permanent. We know that circumcision was practiced long before the Israelites, or even their patriarchal ancestors, came on the scene. Many of Israel's contemporaries practiced it (see Jer. 9:24–25 [Eng. 25–26], which mentions Egypt, Edom, Ammon, and Moab as practitioners of circumcision), as is evidenced by the fact that the Philistines alone in the OT are designated as the "uncircumcised ones" (Judg. 15:18; 1 Sam. 17:26, 36). Nor does circumcision appear to have been practiced in Babylonia or Assyria. Further, an ivory found at Megiddo dating to the 14th or 13th century B.C. shows Canaanite prisoners who are circumcised.[9] The earliest evidence we have for circumcision is a number of bronze statuettes found at Tell el-Judeideh in northern Syria, dating to about 2800 B.C.[10]

But what was the purpose of this rite? Stories such as Gen. 34:14–16 indicate that circumcision signified entrance into marriage and into the communal life of the clan by an outsider. Josh. 5:2–9 also provides evidence for circumcision at puberty or adulthood, but this is an unusual circumstance, describing as it does the circumcision of "children" (v. 7) born during the wilderness wanderings.[11] Gen. 17 nowhere suggests that circumcision was an essential prerequisite for marriage into the tribe. Here the reason is not social but religious.[12]

The mark of the covenant is confined to the male descendant; the female has no corresponding mark. This lack may be attributed either to the

9. *ANEP,* no. 332. Zipporah, the Midianite wife of Moses, is aware of the practice too (Exod. 4:24–26).

10. See J. M. Sasson, "Circumcision in the Ancient Near East," *JBL* 85 (1966) 473–76.

11. For an understanding of circumcision in antiquity as an initiatory rite associated with puberty and marking the passage from childhood to manhood, see B. Bettelheim, *Symbolic Wounds, Puberty Rites and the Envious Male* (Glencoe, IL: Free Press, 1954).

12. For general surveys on the practice and meaning of circumcision see R. de Vaux, *Ancient Israel,* 1:46–48; *EncJud,* 5:567–76; J. P. Hyatt, *IDB,* 1:629–31; T. Lewis and C. E. Armerding, *ISBE,* 1:700–702. See also J. Morgenstern, "The 'Bloody Husband'(?) (Exod. 4:24–26) Once Again," *HUCA* 34 (1963) 35–70; idem, *Rites of Birth, Marriage, Death and Kindred Occasions among the Semites* (Cincinnati: Hebrew Union College/Quadrangle Books, 1966); S. B. Hoenig, "Circumcision: The Covenant of Abraham," *JQR* 53 (1962/63) 322–34.

heavily patriarchal structure of OT society, or to the OT teaching about the "one flesh" principle in marriage. If two have become one there is need for a mark only on one.[13]

11 Circumcision is called both "my covenant" (v. 10) and a *mark* (or sign, *'ôṯ*) *of the covenant* (v. 11). The designation of circumcision itself as a covenant is a synecdoche for covenantal obligation: "this is [the aspect of] my covenant you must keep."

Circumcision is designated as a sign of the covenant, but a sign for whom? The one who is circumcised (and his family)? God? The outsider? This is the fourth passage in Genesis that mentions a sign (Heb. *'ôṯ*). In 1:14 the luminaries serve as signs to identify the seasons. In 4:15 the sign on Cain identifies him to the outsider as one under divine protection. He belongs to that category. Along with these two identity signs we have the mnemonic sign of the rainbow (9:8–17, "when I see it, I will remember"), put in the heavens by God to remind him of his promise to Noah not to destroy the world by a deluge again.

Circumcision does not identify Israelites *qua* Israelites to non-Israelites, for many non-Israelites already practiced the same rite. And the later verses of this chapter record the circumcision of Ishmael, who is not part of the covenant that is to be perpetuated by Isaac! Also, how would one identify an Israelite via circumcision when clothing concealed it?

May the act of circumcision be a sign for the benefit of the one circumcised? Every time he looks at his body he is reminded that he is part of Yahweh's covenant. Thus interpreted, circumcision is a mnemonic sign, reminding God's people of who they are (as in Exod. 13:9, 16; 31:12–17; Num. 15:37–40; Deut. 6:8; 11:18; Josh. 4:6–7), from what they have been delivered, and by whom they have been delivered.

It is equally possible that circumcision is a sign to God, as was the rainbow in ch. 9. God will see the circumcised penis of the Israelite before and during sexual congress, and will then "remember" his promise to Abraham and to all his descendants to make them very fertile.[14]

One factor that militates against the idea of circumcision as a sign for the one circumcised and favors the idea of circumcision as a sign for God is

13. Alice L. Laffey (*An Introduction to the Old Testament: A Feminist Perspective* [Philadelphia: Fortress, 1988], pp. 62–64) notes that the further directive in Scripture (e.g., Deut. 10:16; 30:6) about the circumcision of the heart transfers a physical act possible only for males, to a symbolic act, possible for all human beings.

14. See M. Fox, "The Sign of the Covenant: Circumcision in the Light of the Priestly *'ôt* Etiologies," *RB* 81 (1974) 595–96.

the lack of an explanation for the sign. In other instances where a sign is given to the Israelites, the function or purpose of that sign is also given.

We may note the following: (1) The Feast of Unleavened Bread (Exod. 13:3–10) is to be "a *sign* of your hand and as a memorial between your eyes *that* the law of the Lord may be in your mouth" (13:9). (2) The consecration of the firstborn (13:1–16) is to be "a *mark* on your hand or frontlets between your eyes, *for* by a strong hand the Lord brought us out of Egypt" (13:16). (3) The Sabbath (31:12–17) is "a *sign* between me and you throughout your generations, *that* you may know that I, Yahweh, sanctify you" (31:12; also v. 17). (4) The bronze censers for the altar (17:1–5 [Eng. 16:36–40]) are "to be a *reminder* to the people of Israel . . . *so that* no one who is not a priest . . . should draw near to burn incense before Yahweh" (17:5 [Eng. 16:40]). (5) Aaron's rod is to be "a *sign* . . . *so that* you make an end of their murmurings against me" (16:25 [Eng. 17:10]). (6) The placing of the phylacteries between one's eyes and on the doorposts of the house is to remind God's people of his word (Deut. 6:8; 11:18). (7) The monument of stones (Josh. 4:1ff.) is to be a "a *sign* among you," reminding both the present and succeeding generations of the redemptive acts of God ("*so that* all the people of the earth may know that the hand of Yahweh is mighty"; Josh. 4:24).

In two passages the sign *('ôṯ)* is for God. The rainbow is for his benefit, and it serves to remind him of his earlier promise to Noah never again to drown the earth (Gen. 9:12–17). The blood on the doorposts at Passover (Exod. 12:7–13) is a sign for God to observe. When he sees it he is to "pass over" that house. This example is all the more remarkable when it is recalled that the Israelites already are living apart from the Egyptians, confined to the land of Goshen. The occupants of these houses can only be Hebrews. Clearly the sign of the blood does not identify the occupants of the house as Hebrews, when Yahweh passes over, but rather is an evidence to Yahweh of their compliance with his directive about the blood on the doorposts.

How, then, may one account for the absence of a clause explaining the purpose of this sign of circumcision? God sees the rainbow with the result that he remembers. He sees the blood with the result that he passes over the house. One might suggest that the delicacy of the circumstances mandated this omission in Gen. 17. It is unlikely that the OT would have inserted "And when I see you copulating I will remember my promise to make Abraham fertile"!

The major problem with this interpretation is that it is unable to explain why the *kareth* ("cut off") penalty is invoked (v. 14) for failure to circumcise. If the sign is for God, why is the ultimatum for man? We take the position that circumcision is a means by which Abraham and his seed ratify

God's lordship over them. It is their identity sign as God's covenant people.[15] As such, circumcision is not a cognition sign, one for God's benefit, but rather a confirmation sign, one bearing witness to Abraham's belief that God would fulfill his promises with respect to progeny. Accordingly, Abraham's circumcision is as much an amen to Yahweh as was his affirmation in 15:6.

12 The information given to Abraham thus far about the institution of circumcision includes who is to be circumcised, where one is to be circumcised, and why one is to be circumcised. Added to that package of data is information when circumcision is to take place: *when he is eight days old.*[16] Gen. 34:12 may represent a vestige of a period when circumcision was a puberty rite, or a marriage rite, but here it is an infant rite. A social rite has been transformed into a religious rite. Circumcision has nothing to do with age or marital status, but is connected with the covenant. The Hebrews alone focused on the intimate relationship between a covenant from God and circumcision as a mark of that covenant.

Furthermore, the juxtaposition of covenant and circumcision suggests that there is no necessary, automatic, or direct connection between circumcision and fertility. It is the covenant, and not circumcision per se, that makes fertility possible. Accordingly, circumcision does not have any kind of mythic or magical significance.[17]

13 This verse—at least the first half—repeats the data of v. 12b, that is, that circumcision is to extend even beyond the family circle. It is to be done even for the *houseborn slave* or for *one bought with money from any foreigner.* Perhaps this extension accounts for the repetition of this particular piece of instruction. To circumcise a son is expected, but to circumcise a slave is to expand the range of the recipients of the covenant.[18] God's covenant,

15. See M. Kline, *By Oath Consigned: A Reinterpretation of the Covenant Signs of Circumcision and Baptism* (Grand Rapids: Eerdmans, 1968), p. 87. Kline suggests, further, that circumcision was symbolic of the oath-curse: excision from Yahweh's covenant. He states (pp. 47–48) that the immediate function of circumcision in covenant administration is to serve as an "oath-rite and, as such, a pledge of consecration and a symbol of malediction."

16. The Talmud (*Menaḥ.* 43b) observes that once when David looked at himself naked in the bath chamber, he was upset because he did not see God's commandments being fulfilled in his life until he was circumcised. Whereupon, he composed Ps. 12, which includes in its title "On The Eighth," i.e., the day of circumcision. See also the title of Ps. 6. But "On The Eighth" is likely a musical term, as reflected in Vulg. *pro octava.*

17. See M. Fox, *RB* 81 (1974) 596.

18. C. Westermann, *Genesis,* 2:266, "The extension of the prescription to circumcise the household can only mean that for P the whole household is a cultic unity, and that the circle of worshippers of Yahweh is expanded by the slaves beyond the members of the Israelite people."

however, is directed to no elitist class of society. Nor is it directed to sons, but rather to households. The firstborn son is no more in the covenant tradition than the slave. Hierarchialism gives way to egalitarianism.

14 To dispel the notion that circumcision is optional, or something to be done only when convenient, Abraham is further instructed that failure to be circumcised is a violation of sacral law. The consequences for omission are that the uncircumcised is *cut off from his kinsmen.* This expression undoubtedly involves a wordplay on *cut.* He that is not himself cut (i.e., circumcised) will be cut off (i.e., ostracized). Here is the choice: be cut or be cut off.

He is to be cut off, for in this sin of omission he has broken God's covenant.[19] But can an eight-day-old boy be cut off from his people for not being circumcised? Does accountability come only later in life (as in Exod. 4:24–26), or is the onus on the parent or owner rather than on the one to be circumcised?

In the OT the penalty *be cut off* is normally applied to acts of commission—doing what one is not supposed to do, such as eating blood (Lev. 7:27; 17:10, 14), eating sacrificial fat (7:25), eating the peace offering while unclean (7:20), eating what is unclean (7:21).[20] Only in a few cases is it applied to acts of omission—not doing what one is supposed to do. In fact, circumcision is only one of two performative commands, the neglect of which bring the *kareth* penalty. (The other is the failure to be cleansed from corpse contamination, Num. 19:11–22.)

19. Although the usual subordinating conjunction is absent, the final clause of the verse stands in causal relationship to the previous clause simply by apposition; see F. Andersen, *The Sentence in Biblical Hebrew,* p. 58.

20. The uses of "be cut off" have been studied by D. J. Wold, "The *Kareth* Penalty in P: Rationale and Cases," in SBLASP, 1979, 1:1–45. He studies them under the categories of: (A) Violations against sacred time: (1) failure to observe Passover at its proper time (Num. 9:13); (2) eating leaven on Passover and the Feast of Unleavened Bread (Exod. 12:15, 19); (3) working on the Sabbath (Exod. 31:14); (4) working or eating on the Day of Atonement (Lev. 23:29, 30); (B) Violations against sacred substance: (1) eating blood (Lev. 7:27; 17:10, 14); (2) eating sacrificial suet (Lev. 7:25); (3) compounding or misusing the oil of installation (Exod. 30:33); (4) duplicating or misusing the sanctuary incense (Exod. 30:38); (5) eating of the well-being sacrifices on the third day (Lev. 7:18; 19:8); (6) eating the sacred offerings while ritually impure, either the layman (Lev. 7:20) or the priest (Lev. 22:3); (7) unauthorized contact with sacred property (Num. 4:18 [RSV "be destroyed"]); (C) Failure to perform purification rituals: (1) neglect of circumcision (Gen. 17:14); (2) failure to be cleansed from corpse contamination (Num. 19:13, 20); (D) Illicit worship: (1) slaughtering outside the sacred precinct (Lev. 17:4); (2) sacrificing outside the sacred precinct (Lev. 17:9); (3) worshiping Molech (Lev. 20:2–5); (4) consulting the dead (Lev. 20:6); (5) idolatry (Ezek. 14:8); (E) Illicit sexual relations (Lev. 18:29); (F) Blasphemy (Num. 15:30–31).

Biblical scholars have advanced two different interpretations of the phrase *be cut off,* as a penalty for various kinds of infractions. One suggestion is that to "be cut off" means to be excommunicated from the community.[21] The other suggestion is that "be cut off" means execution, occasionally a human execution of a divinely ordained death penalty (Josh. 8:21 [RSV "wiped out"], 1 Sam. 28:9; 1 K. 11:16; Ps. 101:8), but normally one carried out by God,[22] that is, premature death. I am inclined to support this second interpretation. Excommunication may have been a preliminary act, but not a part of *kārēṯ* itself (contra Morgenstern). It is to be noted that the phrase in question is used at times in conjunction with other phrases where extirpation is clearly intended. Cf. its use near *mēṯû,* "they die" (Lev. 22:9); *môṯ yûmāṯ,* "shall be put to death" (Exod. 31:14; Lev. 20:2–5); *'āḇad,* "destroy" (Lev. 23:30); *šāmaḏ,* "destroy" (Ezek. 14:9).[23]

The failure to circumcise is a breach of covenant. It is the omission of this ritual act that nullifies the covenant, rather than the failure to walk obediently and blamelessly before Yahweh (v. 1). Such a covenant breach is described in the last phrase of v. 14 by *pārar* (in the Hiphil) *berîṯ.* This is the most frequently used phrase for covenant violation by mankind in the

21. For this interpretation, see J. Morgenstern, "The Book of the Covenant, Part III—The Ḥuqqim," *HUCA* 8–9 (1931/32) 1–150, esp. pp. 33–58. He states (p. 53) that the expression "was really excommunication, cutting off in the most literal sense, from association with the religious community, and perhaps also exile, until such time as the Deity would, in accordance with his purpose and way, inflict the appointed punishment of premature death upon the sinner." See also W. Zimmerli, "Die Eigenart der prophetischen Rede des Ezechiel," *ZAW* 66 (1954) 1–26, esp. pp. 14–19; A. Phillips, *Ancient Israel's Criminal Law* (Oxford: Blackwell, 1970), pp. 28–32, who perceives a development in *kāraṯ* from execution (the preexilic position) to excommunication (the postexilic position).

22. Cf. M. Tsevat, "Studies in the Book of Samuel," *HUCA* 32 (1961) 191–216, esp. pp. 195–201; M. Weinfeld, *Deuteronomy and the Deuteronomic School* (Oxford: Clarendon, 1972), pp. 241–43; M. Greenberg, *Ezekiel,* 1:250; D. J. Wold, SBLASP, 1979, 1:1–45: "Nothing has been found in the biblical cases to suggest that *kareth* was perceived as anything but a divine curse of extinction visited upon the sinner and his seed" (p. 24); W. Horbury, "Extirpation and excommunication," *VT* 35 (1985) 13–38, esp. pp. 16–18, 31–34. The phrase was also understood as premature death in talmudic times (see I. M. Ta-Shma, "Karet," *EncJud,* 10: 788–89, for references).

23. Horbury (*VT* 35 [1985] 34) puts the matter thusly: "Did *kārēt,* then, after the Exile, straightforwardly refer to excommunication. . . ? It is hard to accept that the meaning of *krt* was thus transformed, in view of the usages just noted, the continuance of covenantal thought which they illustrate, and the vigour of the associated recognition that apostasy deserves death."

OT.[24] Alongside these frequent references to mankind breaking or nullifying God's covenant, we may place a few references where the subject of the verb is Yahweh, and he, unlike mankind, is not a covenant breaker (Lev. 26:44; Judg. 2:1; Jer. 14:21; but cf. Zech. 11:10, the one reference to God's nullifying a covenant expressed by *pārar*).

3. SARAH AND ISAAC (17:15–22)

15 *God further said to Abraham: "As for your wife Sarai, do not call her Sarai. Rather,*[1] *Sarah shall be her name.*

16 *I will bless her; what is more, I will give you a son by her, thus blessing her.*[2] *She will give rise to nations; rulers of peoples shall stem*[3] *from her."*

17 *Abraham prostrated himself, and he laughed as he said to himself, "Can a child be born*[4] *to a centenarian?*[5] *Or can Sarah give birth at ninety?*[6]

24. Lev. 26:15; Deut. 31:16, 20; 1 K. 15:19; Isa. 24:5; 33:8; Jer. 11:10; 31:32; 33:20, 21; Ezek. 16:49; 17:15, 16, 19; 44:7.

1. For the meaning of *kî* as "rather" only after a negative cf. Gen. 24:3–4; Exod. 16:8; Deut. 21:12; 1 Sam. 6:3; Isa. 10:7; Ps. 44:8 (Eng. 7); 118:17; and R. Gordis, "Quotations as a Literary Usage in Biblical, Oriental and Rabbinic Literature," *HUCA* 22 (1949) 191 n. 66; also F. Andersen, *The Sentence in Biblical Hebrew,* p. 183 ("Antithetical *kî*").

2. Instead of MT *ûḇēraḵtîhā,* "and I will bless her," some ancient versions (LXX, Vulg., Syriac) read *ûḇēraḵtîw,* "and I will bless him," referring the promise to Isaac and not to Sarah. And to be consistent, LXX, Vulg., and Syriac read the next word as *wᵉhāyâ,* "he will," for MT "she will," and *mimmennû,* "from him," for MT "from her." We prefer the MT if only because Sarah is central to this part of the unit. Isaac will come later. The repetition of "I will bless her . . . thus blessing her" sounds awkward and repetitious.

3. Lit., "be" *(yihyû).* Westermann (*Genesis,* 2:253) reads "come forth from." Speiser (*Genesis,* p. 123) translates "shall issue from."

4. N. Lohfink ("Textkritisches zu Gen 17,5.13.16.17," *Bib* 48 [1967] 439–42) prefers SP *'ôlîḏ* (Hiphil, 1st sing. imperfect) to MT *yiwwālēḏ* (Niphal, 3rd sing. imperfect): "will I, even though one hundred years old, beget?" In addition to relying on SP, Lohfink also must take the *lᵉ* in *hallᵉḇen* as the emphatic *lamedh,* "even though." A. Berlin (*The Dynamics of Biblical Parallelism* [Bloomington: Indiana University, 1985], p. 37) cites this verse, and others, as an illustration of morphologic parallelism in which morphologic pairs from the same word class appear in contrasting conjugations: "can a child be born [Niphal of *yālaḏ*] . . . can Sarah give birth [Qal of *yālaḏ*]?"

5. "One hundred years old" is normally expressed by *mᵉ'aṯ šānâ* (Gen. 5:3, 6, 18, 25, 28; 11:10; 21:5; etc.). Here the form is *mᵉ'â šānâ.*

6. Admittedly, the interrogatives *ha-* . . . *wᵉ'im* . . . *hᵃ-* in *hallᵉḇen* . . . *wᵉ'im śārâ hᵃḇaṯ tiš'îm šānâ* are strange. GKC, § 150g, notes that disjunctive questions are, as

18 *Then Abraham said to God: "Surely*[7] *Ishmael lives before you."*
19 *God replied: "Yes, but*[8] *Sarah your wife is to bear you a son, and you shall name him Isaac. I will maintain my covenant with him and with his descendants as an everlasting covenant.*
20 *As for Ishmael, I have heard you. Indeed I will bless him, make him fruitful, and exceedingly numerous. He will father twelve chieftains, and I will make a great nation of him.*
21 *But my covenant I shall establish with Isaac, whom Sarah shall bear to you by this time next year."*
22 *When he finished speaking with him God disappeared from Abraham's sight.*

15 The first two (of five) speeches by God to Abraham in this chapter (vv. 1–2, 3–8) deal with the promise of much progeny. The last two speeches (vv. 15–17, 19–21) deal with the promise of one particular son, Isaac. But before the son enters the picture due regard must be given to the matriarch. At the same time as Abram's name is changed to Abraham, Sarai is changed to *Sarah.* But unlike the name change for the husband, the change to *Sarah* is not explained. Nor is Sarai's new name disclosed to Sarai, as Abram's new name was disclosed to Abram.

Most likely *Sarah* ("princess") is a dialectical variant of Sarai, with the latter name being comparable to feminine names found in the Ugaritic texts, such as *Pdry* (Pidrai), *Ṭly* (Tallai), and *'Arṣy* (Arsai), Baal's three daughters. The ending *-ay* (or *-ai*) is like the ending *-aya,* found in a group of feminine Amorite names.[9]

---

a rule, introduced by h^{a}—*'im,* or by h^{a}—w^{e}*'im.* Here for one time the h^{a} is repeated after w^{e}*'im.* Or is the h^{a} on h^{a}*ḇaṯ* the definite article (hence we should read *habbāṯ,* "the daughter of ninety years"), in which case this is a rare example of a definite article on a word in construct (S. McEvenue, *Narrative Style,* p. 172 n. 45)? Or should we delete *h* on *hbt* as a dittography from the preceding *śrh?* See J. S. Kselman, "The Recovery of Poetic Fragments from the Pentateuchal Priestly Source," *JBL* 97 (1978) 168.

7. In most instances Heb. *lû* expresses a wish or a desire, so that Gen. 17:18 comes out in most translations as "may Ishmael live in your sight!" Here, however, *lû* may have the value of "surely." Abraham already has legitimate issue through Hagar, he thinks. See C. F. Whitley, "Some Remarks on *lû* and *lō',*" *ZAW* 89 (1975) 203.

8. The particle *'*^{a}*ḇāl* has both adversative and affirming nuances. Here and in 1 K. 1:43 the function of *'āḇāl* is to provide a negative response to a statement just made. See N. Kilwing, "*'āḇāl* 'ja, gewiss'—'nein, vielmehr'?" *BN* 11 (1980) 23–28.

9. For the Ugaritic names, see *UT,* p. 62, § 8.54. For the Amorite names, see H. B. Huffmon, *Amorite Personal Names in the Mari Texts* (Baltimore: Johns Hopkins University, 1965), p. 135.

16 This verse is the complement to v. 6. In the earlier verse Abraham was the recipient of the promise of nations and kings. Now Sarah is cast in the role as progenitress of nations and kings. She will share that honor with her husband. But Abraham knows about that promise before she does. According to 18:9ff. it appears that Abraham kept this information to himself. Sarah finds the announcement a bit amusing, not because she hears the story from Abraham, but because she overhears Yahweh talking with her husband. The following verse (v. 17) explains his reticence to share the news with Sarah.

17 One wonders whether Abraham's act of prostration here is exactly the same as that described earlier in v. 3. To be sure, both acts of falling follow a word from God that sounds like a sheer impossibility: "I will make you exceedingly numerous"; "rulers of peoples shall stem from her." In v. 3 Abraham's falling to the ground ends there. He is quiet until God speaks another word. But here he engages in musing (v. 17b), before addressing a further point to God (v. 18).

Perhaps v. 17 means that Abraham fell over laughing about God's most recent proposition.[10] Abraham is no expert on gynecology, but he knows that he and his wife are well beyond the parenting years. Much like Moses later on, Abraham believes that his circumstances limit the promises of God. God is ignoring some fundamental problems that in effect make his promises stillborn. So thinks Abraham. That Abraham had already fathered a child as recently as fourteen years ago (16:16) seems not to affect his thinking.

This is the first of three times that the appearance of Isaac is connected with someone laughing. Abraham laughs (here), and Sarah laughs (18:12; 21:6). Nowhere is there any indication that Abraham is rebuked for such a response, but Sarah is taken to task for her laughter (18:13–15).

18 In ch. 15 Abram was prepared to suggest that his servant Eliezer serve as a surrogate for a son and be his heir. Now he is advancing Ishmael as his heir apparent.[11] Twice, then, Abraham's philosophy has been pragmatic. Abraham is apparently more open to the acceptance of Ishmael than is Sarah. Possibly discretion forbade Abraham from mentioning this suggestion to Sarah. She will have nothing to do with either Ishmael or Hagar.

10. Speiser (*Genesis,* p. 125) tones down *yiṣḥaq,* "he laughed," to "he smiled" and notes "that the concept of Abraham in a derisive attitude toward God would be decidedly out of keeping with P's character." This may explain, if Speiser is correct, the absence of any rebuke to Abraham.

11. See Westermann, *Genesis,* 2:268: "Abraham's prayer for Ishmael is the expression of fatherly acquiescence in the one son given him by the secondary wife."

Abraham is more magnanimous and conciliatory. At the same time, one may compare Abraham's response to this promise vis-à-vis Sarah (to put it mildly, he is skeptical), with his response to the promise of a son back in 15:6. Here, there is no "and Abraham believed [*he'ĕmin*] in God."

19 Now the text shifts to a prophetic oracle. Sarah herself shall conceive, Abraham's doubts notwithstanding. Not only is the gender of the child specified—no mention is made of the possibility that Sarah's child might be a daughter—but the name is also given—*Isaac.* Thus even before the wife conceives, the name and the sex of the child are revealed (v. 19a), as is the fact that this child will have offspring (v. 19b). Even before Isaac is conceived God is talking to Abraham about Isaac's children!

Isaac means "he laughs." Assuming that Jacob is likely an abbreviation of *yaʿaqōḇ-'ēl* ("may El protect"), scholars suggest that, by analogy, *yiṣḥāq* is a diminutive form of a name composed of a verb in the imperfect followed by the subject of the verb which is either a divine name or the name of a relative—*yiṣḥāq-'ēl,* "may God laugh, may God be favorable, God laughs," or *yiṣḥāq-'āḇ,* "the father laughs, may the father laugh." *yiṣḥāq-'ēl* would then be comparable to his brother *yišmāʿē'l.*[12] But why would *yišmāʿē'l* (Ishmael) be written out in full, and *yiṣḥāq'ēl* (Isaacel) be abbreviated to *yiṣḥāq* (Isaac)? In any case, God as the subject of "laugh" in a positive sense does not occur in the OT. When he laughs, such laughter is never a sign of his favor. It is a sign of his scorn and mocking. See Ps. 2:4; 37:13; 59:9 (Eng. 8); Hab. 1:10 (all from the dialectal variant *śāḥaq* rather than from *ṣāḥaq*).[13]

20–21 God now returns to address the observation Abraham made about Ishmael back in v. 18. God promises Ishmael (1) blessing, (2) many descendants, (3) twelve princes (see 25:12–18), and (4) nationhood. But there is no covenant here, as there is to be with Isaac (v. 21, which essentially

12. In names formed with the imperfect tense the predicate-subject type is more prevalent in the earlier periods of biblical history (Moses-Judges) than the subject-predicate type. This second type appears basically in the later monarchical and postexilic periods. See H. L. Ginsberg, "Names," *EncJud,* 12:803. Amorite personal names have abundant parallels to this type of name, but Canaanite-Phoenician examples of this type are relatively rare.

13. The Ugaritic texts, however, do supply instances of El smiling or laughing in a beneficent sense. In one text Asherah, the chief consort of El, makes a journey to El's abode and persuades him to authorize the construction of a palace for Baal. Apparently El has not seen her in a long time, for "he cracks a smile and laughs" (*yprq lṣb wyṣḥq,* text II AB iv–v:28 [*UT,* 51:iv:28]); translation of C. H. Gordon, *Ugarit and Minoan Crete* (New York: Norton, 1966), p. 67; see also M. H. Pope, *El in the Ugaritic Texts,* VTSup 2 (Leiden: Brill, 1955), p. 36.

reinforces v. 19b). It is significant that in this chapter God does not "make" *(kāraṯ)* a covenant, but he maintains or establishes it (Hiphil of *qûm*). The first expression refers to the maintenance of a covenant already in operation (v. 19). The second refers to the making of a new covenant (v. 21).

The listing of the promises to Ishmael demonstrates that he is not rejected by God as the covenant heir because he is a sinner. He has not disqualified himself in any way and thus forfeited any privilege. The promises of God, while not totally sidestepping human conduct, are basically unconditional. Divine sovereignty dictates the selection of one son over the other, quite apart from personal life-styles.

We note that God's promises to Isaac are made to him before he is born. God's promises to Ishmael are made after he is born. Still, the word here to Abraham about Ishmael represents a considerable advance over the first word to Hagar about Ishmael (16:11–12).

22 This last promise of intention by God closes the door on further dialogue and debate. The meeting is adjourned and the theophany is officially ended. The divine presence *disappeared* (*yaʿal,* lit., "went up"), as in 35:13 and Ezek. 11:23. The phrase *ʿālâ mēʿal* describes the departure of one person from another (2 Sam. 23:9 [without the preposition]; 1 K. 15:19; 2 K. 12:19 [Eng. 18]; Jer. 21:2). The verb may also be used, as it is here, with God as subject.[14] When God is the subject of *ʿālâ mēʿal,* however, what we have is a term that marks the end of theophanies. The closest analogies to Gen. 17:22 are Gen. 35:13 and Ezek. 11:24 ("the vision I had seen lifted up from me," i.e., disappeared from my sight). Abraham's encounter with God on this occasion began with "Yahweh appeared to him." It concludes with "God disappeared from Abraham's sight." What Abraham saw of God he now ceases to see.

4. THE CIRCUMCISION OF ABRAHAM AND ISHMAEL (17:23–27)

23 *Then Abraham took Ishmael his son, and houseborn slaves, and those bought with money—every male in Abraham's household—and he circumcised the flesh of their foreskins on that very day God had told him.*

24 *Abraham was ninety-nine years old when he was circumcised in the flesh of his foreskin.*

14. Cf. the ascending of God to his throne in Zion (Ps. 47:6 [Eng. 5]) and to his throne on Sinai (Ps. 68:19 [Eng. 18]). See also Ezek. 11:23 for the ascension of the glory or majesty of God over Jerusalem.

25 *Ishmael his son was thirteen years old when he was circumcised in the flesh of his foreskin.*
26 *On that very day Abraham, together with his son Ishmael, was circumcised;*
27 *all his retainers, houseborn slaves, those bought with money from foreigners, were circumcised along with him.*

23–27 These verses narrate Abraham's execution of the instructions God had given him earlier. He, Ishmael, and every male connected in any way with his household are all circumcised. Biblical faith is never simply a cerebral exercise. What is said and thought is also done.[1] From this point on there is no turning back. Abraham will forever be unable to undo the circumcision himself. The mark of identity is ineradicable.

Abraham shares this moment with every male in his extended family. It is not a private, individualistic experience. Already God's covenant is with groups.

Interestingly, Ishmael is deliberately designated as one who would not receive the covenant, as would Isaac, yet here Ishmael receives the covenant sign of circumcision. He too is to walk as one of Yahweh's children. The extension of circumcision to domestic servants shows that not even a patriarch has a monopoly on divine grace, not only the patriarch is to live obediently. Grace cuts across all social categories.

That Ishmael is circumcised by Abraham would be a strong argument against the interpretation that circumcision took on a new importance and significance in Jewish life during the period of the Exile, that is, it became a mark of religious uniqueness, as opposed to earlier periods when circumcision was viewed by (both Israel and her neighbors) as more of a prenuptial rite or rite of passage into the community. Weinfeld asks correctly: "Who would be interested in the time of the exile, when circumcision became the badge of Jewish distinctiveness, to share this very symbol of devotion with the Ishmaelites?"[2] It is more likely, given the distribution of circumcision among the ethnic groups belonging to the family of the Hebrews, that the circumcision of Ishmael reinforces the concept, made in Gen. 17, that Abraham is to be the father of many nations.

1. See Brueggemann, *Genesis,* p. 155.

2. M. Weinfeld, "The Covenant of Grant in the Old Testament and in the Ancient Near East," *JAOS* 90 (1970) 203. See also M. Haran, "The Religion of the Patriarchs," *ASTI* 4 (1965) 42–43.

THE NEW TESTAMENT APPROPRIATION

The NT provides us with examples of individuals who were circumcised, following the regulations of Jewish law. This list includes Jesus (Luke 2:21), John the Baptist (Luke 1:59–60), Paul (Phil. 3:5), and Timothy.[1] At the same time it provides us with a view of circumcision's questionable value. For example, Paul would say that the "truly circumcised" are those "who worship God in spirit, and glory in Christ Jesus, and put no confidence in the flesh" (Phil. 3:3). The apostle also argues for a "spiritual" circumcision, one made without hands (Col. 2:11–13). See also Rom. 2:28, 29.[2]

On at least two occasions (1 Cor. 7:19; Gal. 5:6) Paul says that neither circumcision nor uncircumcision is ultimately decisive. Neither the presence of the symbol nor the absence of the symbol confers sacrosanctity.

One suspects that Paul's misgivings about circumcision are not aimed at the OT institution itself. After all, circumcision was not Abraham's idea. It was God who established the procedure and it was God who told Abraham to circumcise himself and other males in his household. It seems likely that in Paul's day certain Jewish groups had made circumcision an end in itself, the sine qua non of genuine religion. It was against such distortions that the Jerusalem Council took swift action (see Acts 15:6ff.), removing circumcision as requirement to membership in the church. The heat generated by this controversy is reflected in numerous passages in Galatians (5:2, 6; and esp. 6:12–15, where circumcision, or its absence, is clearly subordinated to a new creation).

The value in circumcision is that it was, on Abraham's part, a sign or seal of the righteousness God has already given him (Rom. 4:9–12).[3] To that end both those who believe without being circumcised (because of the presence of spiritual circumcision, v. 11), as well as those who are circumcised both physically and spiritually (v. 12), may claim him as father.

If we take the position that the NT spiritualizes, or internalizes, what in the OT was quite physical and external, then we must also say that the OT itself has already initiated this shift. One does not have to wait until the NT to encounter the concepts of heart circumcision (Lev. 26:41; Deut. 10:16; 30:6; Jer. 4:4; Ezek. 44:7, 9, "uncircumcised in heart and flesh") and ear

1. On Paul's circumcision of Timothy, see C. Bryan, "A Further Look at Acts 16:1–3," *JBL* 107 (1988) 292–94.

2. For illustrations of the figurative use of circumcision at Qumran as well see 1QS 5.4–5, 26; 1QpHab 11.13.

3. On the interpretation of Rom. 4:12 see J. Sweetnam, "The Curious Crux at Romans 4,12," *Bib* 61 (1980) 110–15.

circumcision (Jer. 6:10).[4] As one would expect, these OT verses occur always in a parenetic context. This is something the people being addressed need to do.

For obvious reasons Christian readers of the OT have often equated, functionally, circumcision with infant baptism.[5] Nowhere, however, does the NT make this equation, and the only place where circumcision and baptism appear together is Col. 2:8–12. It is clear in this passage that the author is suggesting that baptism is a kind of Christian circumcision. But lest his readers equate circumcision with baptism, he immediately draws a distinction between the two by saying that the circumcision of which he speaks is one "made without hands" *(acheiropoiḗtos).* This Greek word occurs elsewhere in the NT to refer to something that God himself has made or will make, and never something a human being has done. Thus, Jesus' detractors charged him with threatening to destroy the temple "made with hands," then build another "not made with hands" (Mark 14:58). Again, Paul spells out for the believers that they can anticipate in the life to come "a building from God, a house not made with hands, eternal in the heavens" (2 Cor. 5:1). To further emphasize that God is the one responsible for the Christians' change from an old life to a new one, the writer employs passive verbs to describe the believers' condition: "you were circumcised"; "you were buried"; "you were raised." That the writer of Col. 2:11–12 draws a comparison or contrast between circumcision and baptism is uncontestable. This observation,

4. "It was not the removal of the loose foreskin that covered the extremity of the male organ that was significant, but the removal of the hard excrescence of the heart" (J. A. Thompson, *The Book of Jeremiah,* NICOT [Grand Rapids: Eerdmans, 1980], p. 215).

5. Those who advocate the position that infant baptism is a NT doctrine that perpetuates the OT's teaching of infant circumcision include: O. Cullmann, *Baptism in the New Testament,* SBT 1/1, tr. J. K. S. Reid (London: SCM, 1950); J. Jeremias, *Infant Baptism in the First Four Centuries,* tr. D. Cairns, Library of History and Doctrine (Philadelphia: Westminster, 1960); idem, *The Origins of Infant Baptism; A further study in reply to Kurt Aland,* tr. D. M. Barton (Naperville: Allenson, 1963); M. G. Kline, *By Oath Consigned. A Reinterpretation of the Covenant Signs of Circumcision and Baptism* (Grand Rapids: Eerdmans, 1968). Those who believe a doctrine of infant baptism cannot be deduced from the OT's emphases on infant circumcision would include: G. R. Beasley-Murray, *Baptism in the New Testament* (Grand Rapids: Eerdmans, repr. 1977); K. Aland, *Did the Early Church Baptize Infants?,* tr. G. R. Beasley-Murray (Philadelphia: Westminster, 1963); P. Jewett, *Infant Baptism and the Covenant of Grace* (Grand Rapids: Eerdmans, 1978). See also the debate between G. Bromiley and G. R. Beasley-Murray on infant baptism in *CT* 9 (1964) 7–14.

however, does not help us to decide whether the NT advocated the practice of infant baptism on the analogy of infant circumcision.[6]

It would appear that the concept of circumcision being replaced or supplanted by baptism was not an issue that emerged among the apostles at the Jerusalem conference (Acts 15), where circumcision was discussed. The absence of a simple statement in Acts 15 to the effect that now baptism replaces circumcision, thereby rendering circumcision unnecessary, may suggest that the early church did not envision baptism's role as that of a supplanter for circumcision.

6. E. Lohse, *A Commentary on the Epistle to the Colossians and to Philemon,* tr. W. R. Poehlmann and R. J. Karris, Hermeneia (Philadelphia: Fortress, 1971), pp. 101–6, esp. p. 102 n. 64.

INDEXES

SUBJECTS

AUTHORS

SCRIPTURE REFERENCES

OLD TESTAMENT

Genesis

17:13b 468
17:14 463, 471, 473-75
17:15 476
17:15-16 459
17:15-17 476
17:15-22 475-76
17:16 205, 372, 463, 465, 468, 477
17:17 368, 459, 468, 477
17:17b 477
17:18 459, 476, 477-78
17:19 458, 463, 465, 478, 479
17:19-21 459, 476
17:19a 478
17:19b 478, 479
17:20 464
17:20-21 478-79
17:21 463, 478, 479
17:22 479
17:22-27 459
17:23 468
17:23-27 71, 479-80
18–19 398, 450
18 32, 234
18:1 192, 377, 460
18:1-2 396
18:1-6 418
18:1ff. 396
18:2 278
18:3 276
18:9 193, 452
18:9ff. 477
18:12 161, 477
18:13 44, 231
18:13-15 477
18:14 453
18:15 44
18:18 40, 372, 374
18:20-21 280
18:23-33 71
18:24 162
18:26 162
18:27 158, 441
18:31 441
19–21 284
19 32, 44, 436
19:2 441
19:5 220
19:8 435, 441
19:9 435
19:13 298
19:19 276, 298, 441
19:20 441
19:21 227
19:28 278
19:29 299
19:31 442
19:31ff. 321
19:32 198
19:33-34 121
19:34 198
20 15, 17, 47, 404, 443
20:1 451
20:1-17 23
20:1ff. 47, 380
20:2 265
20:3 265
20:3-4 382
20:7 173, 418
20:9 227
20:10 385
20:12 381
20:18 44, 443
20:19 382
21 15, 458
21:1 70
21:1-2 362
21:1-34 62
21:3 458
21:5 236, 376, 475
21:6 477
21:7 301
21:8-21 450
21:9-14 62
21:10 443
21:12 199, 388, 443
21:13 198, 388, 443
21:15 154
21:17 419, 450
21:19 65
21:21 265
21:22 141
21:30 65
21:32 320
21:33 65, 68, 69, 377, 378, 410
21:48 265
22 41, 370, 371, 392, 450
22:1 43, 370, 389
22:1-14 41
22:1-19 18, 31, 32
22:2 376, 394
22:3 187
22:6 433
22:9 378
22:11 41, 450
22:12 286, 450
22:13 71, 74, 278
22:14 41, 42, 339
22:15-18 41, 42, 43
22:17 423, 453
22:17-18 199
22:18 40, 374
22:21 344
22:22 364
22:23 7
22:24 442
23 467
23:1 380
23:1-20 17
23:4 435
23:6 112, 372, 410, 465
23:10 162
23:17ff. 396
24 384
24:1-67 62
24:3-4 475
24:4 265, 364
24:7 40, 364, 369, 377, 387-88
24:16 265
24:40 258, 265, 461
24:45-49 166
24:50 165
24:63 278
24:64 403
25:1 265, 446
25:3 337, 345
25:4b 7
25:6 442, 446
25:7 376
25:8 436
25:12 3, 9, 150
25:12-18 478
25:12ff. 249
25:13-19a 8, 9
25:16 7
25:18 169, 336, 346, 389, 403, 451
25:19 150
25:19a 2, 3
25:19a–36:1 9
25:19b–36:1 8
25:20 376
25:21 47, 48, 71
25:23 372
25:26 48, 376

INTERTESTAMENTAL BOOKS

HEBREW WORDS

tîrôš 333
t^{e}ḵalennâ 283
tāmîḏ 307
tāmîm 277, 461-62
timlāḥ 281
tāmam 463
timšōl 201
  timšol-bô 225, 228
tānaḥ 301
tannûr 428
tannîn 129-30
tannînim 129, 130
tāp̱ar 191
taṣmîaḥ 195
tardēmâ 434
teraḥ 363
trš 333
taršîš 333
t^{e}šûqâ 201, 227
t^{e}šûqāṯô 201
t^{e}šûqāṯēḵ 201
tišmōr 467
tišm^{e}rû 467
tišʿîm 475